W9-AZS-655

THE CAMBRIDGE COMPANION TO
AMERICAN JUDAISM

This volume provides readers with a comprehensive introduction to the most important and interesting historical and contemporary facets of Judaism in America.

Written by twenty-six leading scholars from the fields of religious studies, American history and literature, philosophy, art history, sociology, and musicology, *The Cambridge Companion to American Judaism* adopts an inclusive perspective on Jewish religious experience. Three initial chapters cover the development of Judaism in America from 1654, when Sephardic Jews first landed in New Amsterdam, until today. Subsequent chapters go beyond a presentation of the basic material and include cutting-edge scholarship and original ideas while remaining accessible at an introductory level.

While influenced by Christian patterns of religious life, American Jews have understood the idea of religious identification quite differently from American Christians. Thus, a secondary goal of this volume is to help both its Jewish and non-Jewish readers better understand the more abstract meaning of religion in a Jewish context.

The Cambridge Companion to American Judaism will be of interest not only to scholars but also to all readers interested in social and intellectual trends in the modern world.

DANA EVAN KAPLAN is Visiting Research Scholar at the Sue and Leonard Miller Center for Contemporary Jewish Studies and the Cuban and Cuban-American Institute at the University of Miami. He is also rabbi of Congregation B'nai Israel in Albany, Georgia. His previous books include *American Reform Judaism: An Introduction* (2003), *Platforms and Prayerbooks: Theological and Liturgical Perspectives on Reform Judaism* (2002), and *Contemporary Debates in American Reform Judaism: Conflicting Visions* (2001).

THE CAMBRIDGE COMPANION TO

AMERICAN JUDAISM

Edited by Dana Evan Kaplan

CAMBRIDGE
UNIVERSITY PRESS

CAMBRIDGE UNIVERSITY PRESS
Cambridge, New York, Melbourne, Madrid, Cape Town, Singapore, São Paulo, Delhi

Cambridge University Press
32 Avenue of the Americas, New York, NY 10013-2473, USA

www.cambridge.org
Information on this title: www.cambridge.org/9780521822046

First published 2005

A catalog record for this publication is available from the British Library

Library of Congress Cataloging in Publication data

The Cambridge companion to American Judaism / edited by Dana Evan Kaplan.
    p.   cm. – (Cambridge companions to religion)
Includes bibliographical references and index.
ISBN 0-521-82204-1 (casebound) – ISBN 0-521-52951-4 (pbk.)
1. Judaism – United States.   I. Kaplan, Dana Evan.   II. Title.   III. Series.
BM205.C35   2005
296′.0973 – dc22   2004024336

ISBN 978-0-521-82204-6 hardback
ISBN 978-0-521-52951-8 paperback

Transferred to digital printing 2009

Contents

List of Contributors

Yaakov Ariel is Associate Professor of Religious Studies at the University of North Carolina at Chapel Hill. He has several written books and articles on the Jewish–Christian relationship in America.

Isa Aron is Professor of Jewish Education at the Rhea Hirsch School of Education, Hebrew Union College–Jewish Institute of Religion, Los Angeles. She was the founding director of the Experiment in Congregational Education, a project of the Rhea Hirsch School of Education, now in its twelfth year. She is the senior editor of *A Congregation of Learners* and the author of *Becoming a Congregation of Learners* (2000) and *The Self-Renewing Congregation* (2000).

Matthew Baigell is Professor Emeritus of Art History at Rutgers University. He has written many books and articles on American art, Jewish American art, and Soviet and post-Soviet East European art.

Murray Baumgarten is Director of Jewish Studies at the University of California, Santa Cruz, where he holds the Neufeld-Levin Chair in Holocaust Studies with Peter Kenez; he is Professor of English and Comparative Literature. He also edits *Judaism: A Quarterly Journal of Jewish Life & Thought*, published by the American Jewish Congress.

David Biale is Emanuel Ringelblum Professor of Jewish History at the University of California, Davis. He is the author, most recently, of *Eros and the Jews* (1997) and the editor of *Cultures of the Jews: A New History* (2002).

Carmel U. Chiswick is Professor of Economics at the University of Illinois at Chicago. She is a development economist and a labor economist and serves on the Technical Advisory Committee to the National Jewish Population Study. Her recent work focuses on the economics of religion, especially as it applies to the American Jewish family, to religious observance, and to Jewish communal institutions.

Eli Faber is Professor of History at John Jay College of Criminal Justice and at the University Graduate Center, both of which are part of The City University of New York. He is the editor of *American Jewish History*, the journal of The American Jewish Historical Society. He is the author of *A Time for Planting: The First Migration, 1654–1820*, which is Volume I of the five-volume work, *The Jewish*

People in America; he is also the author of *Jews, Slaves, and the Slave Trade: Setting the Record Straight*.

Sylvia Barack Fishman is Associate Professor of Contemporary Jewish Life in the Near Eastern and Judaic Studies Department; she is also Codirector of the Hadassah-Brandeis Institute, both at Brandeis University. She is the author of *Double Or Nothing? Jewish Families and Mixed Marriage* (2004), *Jewish Life and American Culture* (2000), *Follow My Footprints: Changing Images of Women in American Jewish Fiction* (1992), and *A Breath of Life: Feminism in the American Jewish Community* (1992).

Lloyd P. Gartner is Professor Emeritus of Jewish History at Tel Aviv University. His most recent book is *History of the Jews in Modern Times* (2000).

Nathan Glazer is Professor of Education and Sociology Emeritus at Harvard University. He was one of the original editorial staff of *Commentary* magazine, and for many years he was editor of the public policy quarterly, *The Public Interest*. He is the author of *American Judaism*, published by the University of Chicago Press in 1957, with revised editions in 1972 and 1989 and still in print. Among his other books is *Beyond the Melting Pot* (with Daniel P. Moynihan), *Affirmative Discrimination, Ethnic Dilemmas, The Limits of Social Policy*, and most recently *We Are All Multiculturalists Now*.

Lawrence Grossman is a coeditor of the *American Jewish Year Book* and Associate Director of Research at the American Jewish Committee. Beginning in 1988, his annual articles on "Jewish Communal Affairs" for the *Year Book* have traced the development of Judaism in contemporary America.

Dana Evan Kaplan is Visiting Research Scholar at the Sue and Leonard Miller Center for Contemporary Jewish Studies and the Cuban and Cuban-American Institute at the University of Miami. He is also rabbi of Congregation B'nai Israel in Albany, Georgia. His previous books include *American Reform Judaism: An Introduction* (2003), *Platforms and Prayerbooks: Theological and Liturgical Perspectives on Reform Judaism* (2002), and *Contemporary Debates in American Reform Judaism: Conflicting Visions* (2001).

Debra Renee Kaufman is Director of Jewish Studies, a Matthews Distinguished Professor, and Professor of Sociology at Northeastern University. Her more recent books include *Rachel's Daughters: Newly Orthodox Jewish Women* (1991) and a special edited edition of *Contemporary Jewry, Women and the Holocaust* (1996), as well as other publications on post-Holocaust Jewish identity politics. She is currently researching intergenerational ties among adult Jewish daughters and their mothers.

Mark Kligman is Associate Professor of Jewish Musicology at Hebrew Union College–Jewish Institute of Religion in New York, where he teaches in the School of Sacred Music. He specializes in the liturgical traditions of Middle Eastern Jewish communities. He has published several articles on the liturgy of Syrian Jews. His work also extends to historical trends in the liturgical and contemporary music of Ashkenazic and Sephardic traditions.

Sara S. Lee is Director of the Rhea Hirsch School of Education and a Professor of Education. She has edited *Touching the Future: Mentoring and the Jewish Professional* with Michael Zeldin; *A Congregation of Learners* with Isa Aron and Seymour Rossel; "Religious Traditions in Conversation" with Mary Boys, in *Religious Education* (1996); and *Communities of Learning: A Vision for the Jewish Future* (1997).

The late **Charles S. Liebman** was Professor Emeritus of Political Science at Bar Ilan University. He published many books and articles on American Jewish life as well as on religion and politics in Israel. Dr. Liebman was the recipient of the Israel Prize in Political Science.

Rela Mintz Geffen is President of Baltimore Hebrew University. Previously, she was Professor of Sociology and Dean for Academic Affairs at Gratz College. She is a graduate of Columbia University (B.S. and M.A.), the Jewish Theological Seminary (B.R.E.), and the University of Florida (Ph.D). Her major research interests are in the area of sociology of religion, particularly the American Jewish community. Dr. Geffen has written more than forty scholarly articles and edited or coedited three books, including *Celebration and Renewal: Rites of Passage in Judaism* (1993) and *The Conservative Movement in Judaism* (2000), coauthored with the late Daniel J. Elazar. She has served as president of the Association for the Social Scientific Study of Jewry and as vice president of the Association for Jewish Studies.

Alan Mittleman is Professor of Modern Jewish Thought at the Jewish Theological Seminary and the director of the Louis Finkelstein Institute. He is the author of three books, most recently *The Scepter Shall Not Depart from Judah: Perspectives on the Persistence of the Political in Judaism* (2000). He has edited three books on Judaism and politics, most recently *Religion as a Public Good: Jews and Other Americans on Religion in the Public Square* (2003).

Bruce Phillips is Professor of Sociology and Jewish Communal Service at Hebrew Union College–Jewish Institute of Religion, Los Angeles. He is one of the leading sociologists studying American Jewry. He has been a leader in Jewish social research for more than twenty years, conducting local demographic studies in Los Angeles, Phoenix, Denver, Milwaukee, Houston, Las Vegas, Chicago, Seattle, and San Francisco. His study, "Re-Examining Intermarriage," published by the Wilstein Institute for Jewish Policy Studies, is considered an essential reference on this subject. He served on the National Technical Advisory Committee of the 1990 and 2000 National Jewish Population Studies.

Lynn Rapaport is Associate Professor of Sociology and Department Chair at Pomona College. She is the author of *Jews in Germany after the Holocaust: Memory, Identity, and Jewish–German Relations* (1997), which won the 1998 Best Book Award in the Sociology of Religion from the American Sociological Association. She is currently working on a project on how the Holocaust is portrayed in popular culture.

Steven T. Rosenthal is Associate Professor of History at the University of Hartford. He is the author of numerous articles and two books, including *Irreconcilable Differences: The Waning of the American Jewish Love Affair with Israel* (2001).

Jonathan D. Sarna is Joseph H. and Belle R. Braun Professor of American Jewish History at Brandeis University, and he chairs the Academic Board of the Jacob Rader Marcus Center of the American Jewish Archives. He has authored or edited more than twenty books on American Jewish history and life, including his most recent work, *American Jewish History: A History* (2004). He is also the chief historian of the National Museum of American Jewish History and of the 350th commemoration of Jewish life in America, 1654–2004.

Byron L. Sherwin is Distinguished Service Professor of Jewish Philosophy and Mysticism at Chicago's Spertus Institute of Jewish Studies. A protégé of Abraham J. Heschel, he is the author of twenty-three books and more than 150 articles and monographs.

Chaim I. Waxman is Professor of Sociology and Jewish Studies at Rutgers University, the State University of New Jersey, and he specializes in the sociology of religion in general and the sociology of Jews and Judaism in particular. His books include *The Stigma of Poverty* (1977, 1983), *America's Jews in Transition* (1983), *American Aliya* (1989), and *Jewish Baby Boomers* (2001). He is coauthor of the *Historical Dictionary of Zionism* (2000), and he has edited and coedited more than a half-dozen books, including, with Roberta Rosenberg Farber, *Jews in America: A Contemporary Reader* (1999) and, with Uzi Rebhun, *Jews in Israel: Contemporary Social and Cultural Patterns* (2003).

Jonathan Woocher is President and Chief Executive Officer of JESNA, North America's organization for Jewish education advocacy and excellence. Previously, he was Associate Professor in the Benjamin S. Hornstein Program in Jewish Communal Service at Brandeis University. He is the author of the book *Sacred Survival: The Civil Religion of American Jews* (1986), and he has written extensively on a wide range of Jewish communal and educational issues.

Michael Zeldin is Professor of Jewish Education, Hebrew Union College–Jewish Institute of Religion, Los Angeles. His specialties are day school education, educational change, and mentoring in the Jewish professions. He was the national chair of the Network for Research in Jewish Education and project director of Day Schools for the 21st Century (JDS-21), the Rhea Hirsch School of Education's pilot project in day school education. He is director of DeLet@HUC- Day School Leadership Through Teaching, a national initiative to prepare teachers for Jewish day schools. He is also the Senior Editor of the *Journal of Jewish Education*.

Chronology

1636   Roger Williams founds Rhode Island, the first colony to endorse freedom of religion.

1654   Twenty-three Jews sail to New Amsterdam from Brazil on the *St. Catherine*, creating the first Jewish presence in what would become the United States.

1656   Abraham de Lucena, Salvador Dandrada, and Joseph Jacob Cohen petition Governor Peter Stuyvesant of New Amsterdam for the right "to be permitted to purchase a burying place for their nation."

1678   Jews purchase a plot of land for a cemetery in Rhode Island.

1697   Four Jews settle and are given citizenship in South Carolina.

1730   Jews complete and dedicate a synagogue in Lower Manhattan.

1740   Congregation Mikveh Israel in Philadelphia dedicates land for a cemetery.

1761   The first English prayerbook for High Holy Day services is printed in New York.

1789   Gershom Mendes Seixas, Minister of New York's Sephardic congregation Shearith Israel, is invited to George Washington's inauguration.

1823   Solomon Henry Jackson publishes *The Jew*, the first Jewish monthly in the United States.

1824   Jews in Charleston, South Carolina, establish the Society of Reformed Israelites, the first Reform congregation in the United States.

1825   Mordecai Manuel Noah tries to found Ararat, a Jewish homeland near Buffalo, New York.

1838   Rebecca Gratz establishes a Sunday School in Philadelphia.

1843   B'nai B'rith, a Jewish fraternal organization, is established.

1845   Isaac Leeser publishes a translation of the *Pentateuch* into English.

1859   The Board of Delegates of American Israelites, the first national organization of Jewish congregations, is formed.

1860 Morris Jacob Raphall of New York opens a session of the House of Representatives with prayer.

1867 Maimonides College, the first rabbinical school in America, is founded in Philadelphia but folds shortly thereafter.

1875 Isaac Mayer Wise founds the Hebrew Union College in Cincinnati.

1885 A group of Reform rabbis meeting in Pittsburgh writes a statement of principles encapsulating the basic beliefs of Reform Judaism.

1886 The Jewish Theological Seminary is founded in New York.

1889 The Central Conference of American Rabbis is founded.

1892 The American Jewish Historical Society is founded.

1893 The National Council of Jewish Women is founded in Chicago.

1893 Rabbis are invited to participate in the World Parliament of Religions in Chicago.

1898 The Union of Orthodox Jewish Congregations is established in New York with Henry Pereira Mendes as its first president.

1902 Agudath ha-Rabbanim, the Union of Orthodox Rabbis, is established to represent the more traditional Orthodox rabbis.

1902 Solomon Schechter comes to the Jewish Theological Seminary in New York from Cambridge University in England.

1904 The first Jewish museum in the United States is founded in the library of the Jewish Theological Seminary of America.

1906 The American Jewish Committee is founded.

1912 Henrietta Szold founds Hadassah, the Zionist women's organization, in New York.

1913 Shortly after the trial of Leo Frank, the Anti-Defamation League of B'nai B'rith is founded.

1913 The first Hebrew College is founded in Boston.

1917 The National Jewish Welfare Board is founded.

1918 The American Jewish Congress is founded.

1922 Mordecai M. Kaplan founds the Society for the Advancement of Judaism in New York.

1927 Al Jolson stars in the *Jazz Singer*, the first film with sound.

1928 The National Council of Christians and Jews is established.

1928 Yeshiva College, the first liberal arts college under Jewish auspices, is established in New York.

1930 Modern Hebrew is introduced into the public high school curriculum by the New York City Board of Education.

1930 Salo Wittmayer Baron is named to the Miller Chair of Jewish History, Literature, and Institutions at Columbia University, the first chair in Jewish studies to be established at a secular university in the United States.

1933 Adolf Hitler becomes chancellor of Germany.

1934 Hank Greenberg refuses to play for the Detroit Tigers on Yom Kippur.

1934 Mordecai M. Kaplan publishes *Judaism as a Civilization*.

1937 Moses Feinstein immigrates from Luban, White Russia, to the Lower East Side of Manhattan.

1937 The Central Conference of American Rabbis passes the Columbus Platform.

1938 Roman Catholic priest Charles E. Coughlin uses the media to attack Jews and Judaism.

1939 The *S.S. St. Louis*, carrying 907 Jewish refugees from Germany, is turned back by Cuba and the United States.

1940 Lubavitch Rebbe Joseph Isaac Schneersohn emigrates from Warsaw, Poland, to Crown Heights, Brooklyn.

1941 Agudath Israel moves its international headquarters from London to New York.

1942 Stephen S. Wise confirms the mass murder of European Jews after receiving the Riegner report.

1942 Nazi leaders meet at the Wannsee Conference to decide on the "Final Solution."

1945 *Commentary* magazine founded.

1945 The Union of Orthodox Rabbis of the United States and Canada issues a herem against Mordecai Kaplan for the editing of his Sabbath Prayer Book. The *New York Times* reports that the prayerbook was actually burned during the herem ceremony at the Hotel McAlpin in New York.

1947 Jacob Rader Marcus founds the American Jewish Archives on the campus of the Hebrew Union College in Cincinnati.

1948 The *Publications of the American Jewish Historical Society* is transformed from an annual to a quarterly publication. Its name is later changed to *The American Jewish Historical Quarterly* and then *American Jewish History*.

1949 Chaim Weizmann is elected Israel's first president.

1950 Paula Ackerman, widow of William Ackerman, begins serving Temple Beth Israel of Meridian, Mississippi, as its unofficial rabbi.

1950 Joseph I. Schneersohn passes away. His son-in-law, Menachem Mendel Schneerson, becomes the seventh Rebbe, assuming the leadership of the worldwide Chabad-Lubavitch movement.

1954   Stern College for Women, the first degree-granting college of liberal arts and sciences for women under Jewish auspices, is established in New York.

1956   Hank Greenberg of the Detroit Tigers is inducted into the Baseball Hall of Fame.

1958   Leon Uris writes *Exodus*, which becomes a runaway best seller.

1965   Abraham Joshua Heschel marches with Martin Luther King, Jr., for civil rights in Selma, Alabama.

1966   Elie Weisel publishes the *Jews of Silence* on the Jews of the Soviet Union.

1967   Israel conquers the West bank and Gaza Strip in the Six Day War.

1968   Havurat Shalom, a Jewish renewal community, is founded in Somerville, Massachusetts. It declares itself devoted to egalitarian prayer and learning. The community serves as a model for a Jewish counterculture Havurah.

1969   The Association for Jewish Studies, a learned society and professional organization that seeks to promote Judaic studies on the university level, is founded in Boston.

1972   Sally J. Priesand is ordained a rabbi by Hebrew Union College.

1972   Gerson D. Cohen succeeds Louis Finkelstein as chancellor of the Jewish Theological Seminary.

1973   *The Jewish Catalog* is published, helping counterculture Jews to become personally involved in the many aspects of Jewish ritual life.

1976   The Central Conference of American Rabbis passes the Centennial Perspective in San Francisco.

1983   The Reform movement accepts patrilineal descent as well as matrilineal descent as determining the Jewish status of offspring born to intermarried couples.

1985   The Jewish Theological Seminary votes to admit women to the rabbinical school.

1985   President Ronald Reagan visits the German military cemetery at Bitburg, which contains the graves of forty-seven members of the Waffen S.S.

1985   Joseph Soloveitchik ordains the 2,000th Orthodox rabbi at the Rabbi Isaac Elchanan Theological Seminary of Yeshiva University.

1986   Ismar Schorsch becomes chancellor of the Jewish Theological Seminary.

1986   Elie Wiesel is awarded the Nobel Peace Prize.

1988   The leadership council of Conservative Judaism issues an official statement of belief entitled "Emet Ve-Emunah: Statement of Principles of Conservative Judaism."

1994   The seventh Lubavitcher Rebbe Menachem Mendel Schneerson dies and is buried in Queens, New York. No successor is appointed, and many of his followers continue to believe that he is the messiah.

1999   The Central Conference of American Rabbis passes a new Pittsburgh Platform. The "Statement of Principles for Reform Judaism" calls for greater observance of mitzvot.

2001   David Ellenson becomes president of the Hebrew Union College–Jewish Institute of Religion.

2003   Richard Joel replaces Norman Lamm as president of Yeshiva University.

2004   The American Jewish community celebrates 350 years of American Jewish life.

Glossary

Agudath ha-rabbanim: Union of Orthodox rabbis.

Ark: The sacred space where the Torah scrolls are kept, usually at the front of the sanctuary. The Hebrew term is *Aron hakodesh.*

Ashkenazi: This was the term use to describe those Jews who settled in Central Europe in the middle ages. The word *Ashkenaz,* which came to mean "Germany" in medieval Hebrew, appears in Genesis 10:3.

Bagel: Round bread product with a hole in the middle that became known as a traditional American Jewish food item.

Bar mitzvah: Coming-of-age ceremony for boys at age thirteen at which the young men are called up to read from the Torah.

Bat mitzvah: Coming-of-age ceremony for girls at age twelve or thirteen. The ceremony itself varies, depending on the denomination, but it usually includes the reading of the Torah.

Ben or *shalom zachor:* The ceremony held on a Friday night after the birth of a baby boy.

Bimah: The pulpit or raised platform in the synagogue.

Brit: The covenant between God and Israel.

Brit Bat: The covenant of a daughter ceremony.

Brit Goral: The covenant of fate.

Brit Milah: The covenant of circumcision, which is performed on all Jewish males at eight days of age.

Challah: Braided loaf that is baked in preparation for the Sabbath and holy days.

Chanukkah: See Hanukkah.

Charoset: A mixture of apples, nuts, and wine that is eaten during the Passover Seder as part of the evening ritual.

Chutzpah: A Yiddish word meaning "having a lot of nerve."

Dvar Torah: A brief comment on the weekly Torah portion, which is replacing formal sermons in many synagogues.

Daven: The act of praying, usually referring to traditional prayer.

Derashot: Collections of sermons.

Edelkeit: Traditional virtue of scholarly refinement.

Emet Ve-Emunah: The most recent statement of principles issued by the Conservative movement.

Etrog: A citron that is one of the four species waved on Sukkot.

Etz Hayim: Recent Torah commentary commissioned by the Conservative movement.

Galut: Exile.

Gefilte fish: Chopped up white fish and pike baked in loaves or balls. A traditional Eastern European Jewish food.

Gemara: Extensive legal debates on the contents of the Mishnah, brief rabbinic legal statements. The Mishnah and the Gemara together form the Talmud.

Gemillut hasadim: Social welfare.

Gemillut hesed: Acts of kindness.

Gelt: Money.

Grogger: A noisemaker used on Purim when the name of Haman is read from the Scroll of Esther.

Goy, goyim: Gentile, Gentiles.

Haftorah: A reading chanted from one of the books of the prophets, following the Torah reading in traditional synagogues.

Haggadah: The liturgy for the Passover Seder.

Halakha: Jewish Law.

Hamantaschen: A triangular-shaped pastry stuffed with apricot, prune, or poppy seed filling, baked in the shape of Haman's hat.

Hametz: Food that is prohibited during Passover, which includes all bread products.

Hanukkah: Eight-day festival of lights celebrating the victory of the Maccabees over the Hellenizers in the second century BCE.

Haskamot or *askamot:* Earlier bylaws in keeping with Sephardic tradition.

Hassid: A type of Ultra-Orthodox Jew who follows a Rebbe.

Havdalah: A short ritual with multiwicked candle, wine, and spices that marks the end of the Sabbath and the beginning of the working week.

Hazan: The cantor who chants and sings Hebrew prayers during services in the synagogue.

Huppah: The canopy held over the bride and groom at Jewish weddings.

Kabbalah: Jewish mysticism.

Kaddish: Mourner's prayer for the dead.

Knish: Dough-filled baked good.

Kashrut: The Jewish dietary laws.

Kavanah: Having intent; concentrating on a religious thought or act.

Kedushah: Holiness or sanctity.

Kehillot or *kehillah:* Community.

Ketubah: A Jewish marriage contract.

Kibud: Honor.

Kiddush: The prayer chanted over wine to consecrate the Sabbath and holidays.

Kiddushin: The halachic aspect of the Jewish marriage ceremony.

Kippah: A head covering worn by men (and now some women) to show respect for God during worship. Also called a Yarmulke or skullcap.

Kittel: White robe worn by a groom, and traditionally by men in the synagogue on Yom Kippur.

Kollel: Yeshiva for married men.

Kol Nidre: The prayer annulling all vows that opens the Yom Kippur evening service.

Kosher: Ritually "fit," usually used to refer to food.

Latkes: Fried potato pancakes that are eaten on Hanukkah to remember the miracle of the oil that burned for eight days instead of one in the Temple in Jerusalem.

Lox: Smoked salmon.

Lulav: The palm branch that is waved on Sukkot with myrtle twigs (hadasim) and willow branches (Aravot).

Manischewitz: Name brand of the most popular Kosher wine used for ritual occasions.

Mashgiach: The supervisor over Kosher food production.

Matzah: Unleavened bread eaten during Passover.

Matzah ball: Chopped matzah mixed with eggs and oil to make a round dumpling, often eaten in chicken soup.

Mechitzah: The physical divider between the men's and women's sections in Orthodox synagogues.

Menorah: Candelabra that is lit incrementally one candle per night during Hannukah to represent the one cruse of oil left in the Temple.

Mezuzah: Scroll with a decorative casing placed on the doorpost of Jewish homes.

Midrash: Scriptural interpretation and teaching.

Minyan: A quorum of ten adult Jewish males (and now females in all non-Orthodox streams) required for public worship.

Mishnah: A compilation of brief rabbinic legal statements edited by Rabbi Judah the Prince around the year 200 CE.

Mitzvah: A commandment (in religious terms) or a good deed (in popular terminology).

Mohel: A ritual circumciser.

Oy vay: Oh my!

Payos: Side curls worn by Hassidic Jews.

Pidyon haben: Redemption of the firstborn son from sacred service on the thirtieth day after birth.

Rav ha-kollel: Chief rabbi.

Rebbe: Charismatic Hassidic rabbi.

Rebbetzin: A rabbi's wife.

Rosh Hashanah: The Jewish New Year, which is observed by Jews around the world by attending synagogue services and undergoing a process of repentance and forgiveness.

Seder: The ritual meal conducted on the first (and in traditional homes on the second) night of Passover.

Sephardi: Jews who descended from the Spanish exile of 1492 and Portugal.

Seudah shel mitzvah: Special added benedictions to the grace after meals.

Shaggitz: A derogatory Yiddish term for a male non-Jew.

Shacharit: The morning prayer service.

Shehitah: The ritual of slaughtering a kosher animal for the purpose of eating.

Shema: The central prayer of Judaism encapsulating the religious concept of ethical monotheism. The text, which begins with the words "Hear oh Israel, the Lord is our God, the Lord is one," is taken from Deuteronomy 6:4–9.

Sheva brachot: The seven benedictions traditionally recited at a Jewish wedding ceremony.

Shiksa: A derogatory Yiddish term for a female non-Jew.

Shochet: A ritual slaughterer.

Shofar: A ram's horn that is blown 100 times as part of the Rosh Hashanah liturgy, and at the conclusion of Yom Kippur.

Shtetl: Yiddish for predominantly Jewish village in Eastern Europe's Pole of Settleret; sometimes extended metaphorically to Jewish neighborhood.

Shul: A Yiddish term for a synagogue, almost always used to refer to a traditional congregation.

Shulhan Arukh: An authoritative code of Jewish law.

Siddur: The Jewish Prayer book.

Tahara: The process of preparing and purifying the deceased for burial.

Taharat ha-mishpakhah: The laws governing sexual relations between husbands and wives.

Tallit: A rectangular, fringed prayer shawl.

Talmud: The oral law that consists of the Mishnah and the Gemara. It is a vast compilation of legal discussions divided into six orders and 63 tractates.

Teshuvah: Repentance.

Torah: The first five books of the Hebrew Bible.

Treif: Unkosher food.

Torah min ha-shamayim: Torah from Heaven.

Trop: The musical system for chanting Torah.

Tzedakah: Charity.

Verklempt: Overcome with emotion.

Yarmulke: Skullcap for men and, in the liberal movements, for women too. The yarmulke traditionally indicated humility before God. Also called kippah.

Yahrzeit: The annual observance commemorating the anniversary of the death of a family member.

Yom Kippur: The Day of Atonement.

List of Abbreviations

ADL	Anti-Defamation League
AIPAC	American Israeli Public Affairs Committee
AJC	American Jewish Committee
AJCongress	American Jewish Congress
AJS	Association for Jewish Studies
CCAR	Central Conference of American Rabbis
CJF	Council of Jewish Federations and Welfare Funds
CLAL	National Jewish Center for Learning and Leadership
HIAS	Hebrew Immigrant Aid Society
HUC	Hebrew Union College
HUC-JIR	Hebrew Union College–Jewish Institute of Religion
JCC	Jewish Community Center
JDL	Jewish Defense League
JOFA	Jewish Orthodox Feminist Alliance
JTS	Jewish Theological Seminary
JWB	Jewish Welfare Board
NCCJ	National Council of Christians and Jews
NJPS	National Jewish Population Survey
OU	Union of Orthodox Jewish Congregations of America
RA	Rabbinical Assembly
RCA	Rabbinical Council of America
UAHC	Union of American Hebrew Congregations
UJA	United Jewish Appeal
UOR	Union of Orthodox Rabbis
URJ	Union for Reform Judaism
WCC	World Council of Churches
WPR	World Parliament of Religions
WZO	World Zionist Organization
YKUF	Yiddisher Kultur Farband
YU	Yeshiva University

Introduction

DANA EVAN KAPLAN

The *Cambridge Companion to American Judaism* is a comprehensive survey that attempts to cover Judaism as a religion in the United States rather than Jewishness as an ethnicity in this country.[1] The title of this volume thus requires a word of explanation. In popular usage today, *Judaism* usually implies a broad sociological approach to the subject of Jewish life and culture, while the term *Jewish religion* suggests a more specific concern with beliefs and practices that are somehow associated with a supernatural reality. Although this collection uses the more general term in its title, its focus is on American Jewish religious phenomena. It is, however, an appropriate title, I believe, because the volume's essays describe a quite inclusive Jewish religious experience in America. This includes aspects that frequently have been neglected or ignored or are understood as outside the purview of religion by a largely Christian America, which sometimes draws different and more impenetrable boundaries between the sacred and the secular. Understanding the subject in such broad terms, one can see that Jewish religion in America means much more than just religious ritual or belief. Contributors also discuss the sociology, psychology, theology, and history of American Judaism. A number of essays concentrate on the culture of American Judaism, including musical, artistic, and literary expressions.

Perhaps, though, any division between what is and isn't religious in a Jewish context is perpetually negotiable, and this problem of placing barriers gestures to the elusiveness of Jewish identity in general. Nathan Glazer writes in this volume that to characterize present-day "Jewishness" is not an easy task. It is not easy because of the myriad, heterogeneous ways that Jews in America understand their relationship with their religion. Even within the denominational categories of Conservative, Reform, Reconstructionist, and Orthodox, there is great diversity among individuals. Speaking in quite general terms, one can say that most American Jews understand Jewish tradition as cosmopolitan and universalistic. They see Judaism as pragmatic rather than ideological, utilitarian rather than theological, and rational rather than mystical. Many in this group see their practice of Judaism as an all-encompassing pursuit, determining not only religious ritual but also ethical behavior. Another sizable group sees the specifics of Judaism as playing a crucial but more limited role in their lives, believing that their commitment to universal ethical causes derives from their core Judaic values – even if they do not frequently articulate these values in a synagogue or temple. These Jews see liberalism as applied Judaism, identifying Judaism with liberal social causes. However, in recent years, even among this group there has been a pronounced move toward greater ritualism as well. The essays in this collection attempt to analyze various aspects of this *American Judaism*, a term that – as we shall see – does offer some tentative unity to a religious people with tremendous diversity.

There are a variety of perspectives in the American Jewish community that are reflected in attitudes toward specific questions dealing with personal and communal Jewish identity today, such as patrilineal descent, Outreach, the role of the non-Jew in the synagogue, rabbinic officiation at mixed-marriage ceremonies, the ordainment of women, and gay and lesbian participation in the synagogue. All of these issues are being heatedly debated within and across the different denominations (also referred to as movements, streams, or even wings). In addition to these strictly "religious issues," there are also debates on social and political issues that affect American society as a whole. It is not possible to say that American Judaism has a particular position on abortion, capital punishment, euthanasia, or homosexual rights. Many of the denominations have taken official stands on some of these issues, but in most cases there are minorities even within those streams who believe that their religion holds a different view.

The most passionately debated question is whether Judaism can survive in an open American society that has, since the 1950s, become increasingly tolerant toward Jews. Since the 1990 National Jewish Population Survey (NJPS) found that American Jews were intermarrying at a rate of 52 percent, there has been a frantic debate in the American Jewish community: Is Judaism in danger of disappearing in the United States? Some of the optimistic contributors to this volume support the transformation argument: Contemporary American Judaism is not vanishing but is rather transforming itself. These individuals believe that it is essential to look at what is happening in a more sophisticated way and not restrict one's perspective to outdated criteria. Many American Jews are creating new ways of "doing Jewish," blending their own traditions with non-Jewish family rituals favored by spouses or embracing a syncretic creation of American culture and Judaism. Because of all of these changes, one must look in new places to find new approaches.

The pessimists feel that the majority of American Jews have lost all interest in Judaism, and many others have only nominal links. These individuals believe that their future as a people is threatened and only a "return to tradition" can reverse the radical decline. These pessimists argue that low levels of synagogue affiliation, high rates of intermarriage, low levels of Jewish literacy, and weak commitments to ritual observance are undermining Jewish continuity.

Another debate centers on the future makeup of the American Jewish community. Some contributors accept the polarization argument that there will be two completely separate Jewish communities in the near future – the Orthodox and the non-Orthodox. The two groups have less in common and have less contact with one another than ever before. They disagree not only on how Judaism should be practiced but also on the very definition of who is a Jew. Without some consensus on such a basic question, the pessimists believe that American Judaism will split into two separate sects. The optimists hope that some common ground can still be found.

CONTENTS OF THE VOLUME

So that we can better understand and contextualize these questions and issues that occupy the American Jewish community, this book is divided into two sections.

Part I provides three historical overviews of American Judaism. Eli Faber deals with the period from 1654, when the first Jews arrived in New Amsterdam, up to 1880, when the mass immigration from Eastern Europe was about to begin. Faber reports that some colonial Jews posed for portraits without head coverings, violated the Sabbath laws, and even ate pork, particularly when they were traveling. A small percentage even married out of the faith. Others were highly observant and followed Jewish law scrupulously. The main difference between then and now was that all five synagogues founded before the Revolution followed Orthodox Sephardic custom. However, American Judaism changed dramatically in the years during and immediately after the Civil War. Faber writes that "the impulse to change Judaism in America surged between 1860 and 1870." Reforms were introduced, including mixed seating, the elimination of the head covering for men, and the use of an organ. New prayer books were edited that eliminated certain theological concepts that were now found objectionable.

Lloyd P. Gartner describes the "reshaping" of American Judaism from the late nineteenth century until after World War II. The large-scale Eastern European immigration completely changed American Judaism. Hundreds of small Orthodox synagogues were created in mostly urban neighborhoods. Many people attended Orthodox synagogues because that was what they were comfortable with, but they refused to follow the Halacha strictly, despite the many sermons preached by Orthodox rabbis. Gartner reports that the immigrant congregations reached their peak during the World War I period and then began to decline slowly. New, larger, and more affluent congregations were established. English replaced Yiddish, and American ways replaced European Jewish customs and practices.

In the postwar period, large numbers left the urban neighborhoods for the suburbs. As I describe in my chapter, a Jewish civil religion developed that stressed loyalty to both the United States and to the Jewish people. Levels of anti-Semitism declined, and Jews became fully integrated into American society. They felt a great deal of pressure to express their Jewishness religiously rather than ethnically, and hundreds of suburban synagogues were soon built. The Conservative movement became the largest American Jewish denomination, and the Orthodox denomination continued to decline. However, this pattern began to reverse in the 1970s. Orthodoxy began a remarkable revival, spurred on by the missionizing done by the Baal Teshuva movement among other Jews. Lubavitch (also called Chabad) sent emissaries to hundreds of Jewish communities around the country and the world. Among the non-Orthodox, the Reform movement grew, which was due in large measure to the joining of many intermarried couples.

Part II, the bulk of the volume, deals with essential topics in contemporary American Judaism. This Themes and Concepts section is subdivided into Religious Culture and Institutional Practice, Identity and Community, Living in America, and Jewish Art in America. It has essays on religious belief and behavior, structures and institutions, and patterns and stages. Considerable attention is devoted to the Jewish civil religion, Judaism and democracy, and the essence of American Judaism, as protean as it may be. Other writers focus on gender roles, life-cycle rituals, interfaith dialogue, and religious economics. Particularly innovative are the essays that focus on American Judaism broadly conceived. Mark Kligman explains the role that music plays in American Judaism and Matthew Baigell describes the visual arts. Murray Baumgarten talks about "American Midrash," by which he means the new American Jewish literature that focuses on Judaic story lines.

The final essay by Bruce Phillips is a separate subsection entitled "Present and Future Tense: American Judaism in the Twenty-First Century." The volume then concludes with an afterword written by Jonathan Sarna.

There are certain ideas and concepts that are essential for understanding the essays. Let us begin with the two defining events of twentieth-century Jewish history.

THE TWO DEFINING EVENTS OF
THE TWENTIETH CENTURY

Since the end of World War II, there have been enormous changes in American Judaism. The essays in the second part of this collection attempt to describe the what, where, when, and how of this transformation. For a whole generation that came of age after 1945, the Holocaust and the creation of the State of Israel were the two defining events. Even today, studies show that most American Jews believe memorializing the Holocaust is one of the most important obligations that they have as Jews. In one survey mentioned by Lynn Rapaport, the respondents felt that remembering the Holocaust was more important than celebrating the Jewish holidays or participating in synagogue services. All Jews realize that the Nazis would have murdered them, regardless of denominational affiliation or level of piety. All Jews are therefore part of what Joseph Soloveitchik calls the *B'rit Goral*, the covenant of fate.[2]

What kind of religion can lean so heavily on a terrible tragedy for inspiration? Many years ago, the famous Jewish historian Salo Baron spoke of the lachrymose conception of Jewish history. Baron felt it was harmful then, and were he to be alive today, he without a doubt would continue to rail against a dark vision of Jewish life preoccupied with destruction and death. Fortunately, the American Jewish obsession with the Holocaust has had a positive parallel – enthusiastic identification with the State of Israel. Philosopher Emil Fackenheim has written that there should be a 614th commandment – not to "give Hitler posthumous victories."[3] Anything that contributed to the weakening of Judaism or the Jewish people fell into this category, so it was important to do everything possible to strengthen what was left. The most obvious response was to support the State of Israel, which was created just three years after the end of the Holocaust. The American Jewish community also raised large sums of money to help endangered or embattled Jewish communities throughout the world. "Jewish survival," the perpetuation of Jewish identity through the generations, assumed paramount importance for its own sake.

The Six Day War of 1967 was a radically transforming event for most American Jews and certainly for American Jewry as a group. American Jews felt a sense of responsibility for and commitment to the State of Israel that awakened their Jewish inner selves. Arthur Hertzberg remembers how "the immediate reaction of American Jewry to the crisis [preceding Israel's miraculous defeat of the Arab armies] was far more intense and widespread than anyone could have foreseen. Many Jews would never have believed that the grave danger to Israel would dominate their thoughts and emotions to the exclusion of all else."⁴ Yet, as Steven T. Rosenthal explains, "the relationship of Zionism and Israel to American Jews has long been notable for its ironies and contradictions." As Rosenthal bluntly puts it, "the vast majority of American Jews have remained astonishingly ignorant of the object of their devotion." He explains this by arguing that the American Jewish devotion to Israel has been "circumscribed by American priorities and needs."

In recent years, the American Jewish community has shifted some of its attention away from the State of Israel and toward its own concerns at home. Many American Jews are interested in the personalistic aspects of the Jewish spiritual message, while others are focusing on how to combat assimilation and fuel an American Jewish renaissance. A series of events over the past twenty years has contributed to this change. The Israeli invasion of Lebanon, the Jonathan Pollard spy case, the Palestinian Intifada, the "Who is a Jew?" controversy, and the recent outbreak of Palestinian–Israeli violence have all been contributing factors. In short, many persons in the American Jewish community have come to realize that support for Israel cannot be a substitute for a substantive Judaism. Rosenthal explains how "there has been a belated recognition that a half-century of obsession with Israel has prevented the laying of the spiritual, cultural, and intellectual bases for future generations."

RELIGIOUS PLURALISM

The United States has a unique history that has influenced how American Judaism has developed. This history is very different from that of Europe and has prompted a number of Jewish writers to stress that "America is different!" The United States was, for the Jews, a post-emancipation society from its beginning, whereas in Europe, Jews were legally restricted in many ways until the French Revolution and even after. The United States was a brand new nation that was composed of people with diverse backgrounds. The new nation was inherently pluralistic, and even when many hoped that immigrants would jump into the "melting pot," there was always a strong tradition of cultural pluralism.

The first article in the Bill of Rights states that "Congress shall make no law respecting an establishment of religion or prohibiting the free exercise thereof." The Founders of the United States believed in the free exercise of religion and the non-establishment of a state religion, which has allowed for the growth of a rich religious pluralism. Because there was no establishment religion that would benefit from state support and funds, churches and other religious organizations needed to hustle to attract and keep congregants. The separation of church and state meant that this idea of pluralism was actually a legal obligation.[5] Jews therefore had greater opportunities in the United States than in almost any other society and were accepted to a far greater degree.

When Alexis de Tocqueville visited the United States in the 1820s, he was surprised to find that, despite a lack of state support, religion was thriving in tremendously diverse forms of expression. At first, tolerated religious differences stopped at the different Protestant denominations. After World War II, it expanded to include Catholics and Jews. Since the Immigration Act of 1965 eliminated quotas linking immigration to national origins, Muslims, Buddhists, Hindus, Sikhs, Jains, Zoroastrians, and people with all sorts of other religious affiliations have settled in this country and begun creating American forms of their respective religious traditions.

SPIRITUALITY AS A MATTER OF PERSONAL CHOICE

Today most Americans regard religion as a matter of personal choice rather than an inherited obligation. Many Americans are looking for existential meaning. They hope to create a spark of spiritual holiness by participating in various religious experiences. This participation will, they hope, enrich their lives by uplifting their souls. An emerging, privatized Judaism stresses how one feels, in contrast to the Jewish law that stresses what one does. The accumulated religious wisdom of the ancient Sages or even belief in traditional notions of God in order to search for spiritual fulfillment is no longer necessary. The majority of American Jews want to create an American Judaism that would be distinctly American and, at the same time, distinctly Jewish. They want the synagogue to meet them where they are rather than accepting that a divinely revealed religion has certain truths that have to be believed and observed.

But how far could they go? Charles Liebman writes in this volume that, at one time, it was easy to say that American Judaism had an essence. Judaism in the United States "contained a set of norms, values, and beliefs, many of which, all would agree, refer to God and to the relationship between the Jewish people and God. These norms, values, and beliefs existed independently of how individual Jews behaved or what individual Jews believed." However, there is no longer any Judaic "essence" if individual religious autonomy allows each Jew to interpret his or her own Judaism. American Jews are then free to mold their Judaism to fit their personal needs, privatizing a religion that has always stressed the collective. This privatization frees individual congregations and even entire religious denominations from the need to legitimize the religious innovations that they introduce by appealing to historical precedent. Unmoored from history, Judaism begins to reflect more readily contemporary individual needs.

Because of the voluntaristic nature of Jewish life in the United States, levels of observance could be puzzling to someone expecting religious consistency. Some practices attract a large enthusiastic following, while others are observed mainly by the most devout or, more precisely, the most observant. For example, the three pilgrimage festivals are all important Jewish holidays, but Passover is widely observed whereas Sukkot and Shavuot are not. Why? Many Jews are interested in observances that reflect their "affection for Jewish family, food, and festivals."[6] In a much more privatized religious environment, many Jews gravitate toward the more familial holidays. That explains why the Passover Seder is attended annually by so many American Jews and why large numbers light Hanukkah candles, while eating latkes (potato pancakes) with applesauce.

One aspect of Judaism that most American Jews do observe is life-cycle events. Rela Mintz Geffen writes that "every religion, ancient and modern, has special rites of passage tied to both biological and sociological events that typify life." In the United States, American Judaism has developed distinctive life-cycle rituals. Ceremonies now recognize men and women in nontraditional as well as traditional families. Geffen argues that life-cycle commemorations are the most democratic Judaic rituals because all men and women are entitled to celebrate their births, marriages, and deaths. Many people reinterpret traditional ideas to fit their understanding of what a life-cycle event means to them in a modern (or postmodern) context.

Throughout the book, the reader will find interesting innovations that have been adapted for the American reality. For example, Chaim I. Waxman explains how the Jewish Renewal Movement has reinterpreted traditional views of certain religious concepts. Specifically, the leaders in this movement argue that American Jews should practice "eco-kosher," which would expand the categories of what is kosher and non-kosher to include new criteria. According to this way of thinking, modern conceptions of kashrut have to take environmental, social, and financial factors into account, as well as the traditional considerations. In this context, it may be more important to think about where the paper used to produce a newspaper comes from, or where a bank invests its money. This is not what the Sages at least explicitly understood by the term *kosher*, but it may be important to expand what is covered by this term in order to keep Judaism relative and contemporary and to better establish its engagement with the larger world.

Some Jews seek to combine Jewish institutional affiliation with spiritual elements from Eastern practices, including Buddhism, Hinduism, Taoism, and Sufism. Many are interested in combining practices from outside of their religion with some that are from traditional Jewish practice. Some are willing to experiment with different types of religious ceremonies, rituals, and practices ranging from Kabbalistic meditation to Hebrew tattooing. This syncretistic approach is appealing to many Americans. For most American Jews, it is acceptable to blend some degree of foreign spiritual elements with Judaism. The one exception is Christianity, which is perceived to be incompatible with any form of Jewishness. Jews for Jesus and other Messianic Jewish groups are thus seen as antithetical to Judaism and are completely rejected by the majority of Jews.

THE TENSION BETWEEN ETHNICITY AND RELIGION

Despite a diminution in the ethnic component in Judaism in recent years, the Jewish religion remains tethered to the Jewish people. A generation ago, sociologist Marshall Sklare wrote that American Judaism was an "ethnic church" in which virtually everyone in the ethnic group followed a single religion and all of the believers in the religion had the same ethnic background. Today, the situation is radically different. Substantial numbers of non-Jews have converted to Judaism, including Asian Americans, African Americans, and Latinos. Even larger numbers have married Jews and may participate with them in home rituals and even synagogue observances. Some have become so active that they are regarded as practicing Jews, despite the fact that they never formally converted.

This is one of many reasons that privatized Judaism is becoming dominant over ethnic identity. Ethnic Judaism stresses community solidarity. For years, the United Jewish Appeal (UJA) raised money using the slogan "We Are One." American Jews were urged to give money and volunteer time for an impersonal, ideologically motivated cause. Privatized Judaism, in contrast, emphasizes a journey of discovery and a search for individual meaning and spiritual fulfillment. It is interpersonal rather than collective and stresses sincerity and authenticity rather than ideology and group achievement. Privatized Judaism is relatively non-judgmental and nonobligating, whereas ethnic Judaism makes demands and requires loyalty.[7]

Nevertheless, even adherents to some form of a more personalized Judaism see themselves as part of the Jewish people and therefore part of the same symbolic family. "Historical familism" is the ability and willingness to see oneself as part of an extended family.[8] A family is usually that group into which a person is born and is composed of one's blood relatives. In this context, the term is broadened to include the entire Jewish people. The Jewish people have endured a common experience through 4,000 years of history and are seen as sharing a common fate. While all Jews share this feeling, American Jews interpret what familism means differently from that of Israeli Jews and most Jews throughout the world.

American Jews mediate tribal loyalties with a strong streak of universalism. While they publicly affirm that they have a strong connection with other Jews in the United States and throughout the world, most American Jews stress that their religious heritage leads them to a universalized commitment to fight against all manifestations of evil. It is acceptable to affirm particularity, but it has to be balanced with an equal or greater degree of concern for the universal. For many Israelis, no such balancing act is required. Indeed, the political environment encourages just the opposite. This dynamic has obvious implications for the manifestation of religious belief in general and for the American Jewish receptiveness to pluralistic expressions of religious identity.

THE CENTRALITY OF SUBURBAN SYNAGOGUE LIFE

The American synagogue affords greater opportunities for religious participation than any other Jewish voluntary institution in the United States.[9] Whereas most congregations were once located in urban settings, the vast majority have followed the mass exodus to the suburbs. Nathan Glazer writes that "for better or worse, Jewishness in the United States is now centered in the large suburban synagogue. The alternative and competitive forms that once existed have virtually disappeared." Suburban Jews have come to depend on the synagogue for much of the inspiration that the family unit once provided. While Judaism has popularly been regarded as a religion based on home practice, the synagogue attempts to fill the void left by steadily declining levels of home-based ritual observance.

This attempt has been more successful in some cases than in others. Some congregations grew larger and became known as vibrant and lively places, while others developed reputations as "bar mitzvah factories." People looking for a painless life-cycle event were attracted, but those searching for something more spiritually meaningful were disenchanted. A whole generation grew up seeing their suburban parents' Judaism as vapid and pointless. The children were sent to Hebrew schools that ironically failed to teach Hebrew, and most learned very little about the Jewish religion. One such child, now an adult, remembers that "I walked away from Judaism – even ran sometimes, disliking the Hebrew school I attended three times a week after public school." He believes that the "ordeal of Hebrew school left me not only with a distaste for Judaism, but also with a strong lack of interest in religion."[10]

Now, many of the younger Baby Boomers and Generation Xers are finding their way back to the synagogue. Some are spiritually hungry; others are just looking for a place to park the children. Either way, they join congregations in large numbers on the suburban frontier. However, it is not so easy to become religiously involved. Meaningful religious life requires knowledge and learning takes time, something that many young families lack. Most of the parents also lack basic religious skills. The vast majority of American Jews do not know how to read prayer book Hebrew, and this makes it difficult for them to participate in an active manner in synagogue ritual. This frustrates them and their egalitarian religious expectations. Rabbis reach out to as many different types of people as possible and encourage them to find ways of connecting to the congregation, and, through the synagogue, with God. Given the barriers of language, though, it is a difficult challenge.

Many of those who choose to engage with their Jewish religious traditions do so in the context of a temple or synagogue, yet less than half of American Jews are members of a congregation at any one time. While this suggests widespread secularism, a fact commented on by many of the scholars in this volume, it is also a function of the economic realities of American religious life. To put it bluntly, belonging to a synagogue costs a lot of money. Since many join so that their children can attend Sunday school and be bar or bat mitzvah, it is one of the many expenses associated with raising children. Once the relevant life-cycle occasions have been celebrated, many families decide that synagogue membership is a luxury that they no longer need and cannot afford.

This utilitarian approach to religion is not new. Carmel U. Chiswick argues that investment in Jewish religious skills was a costly diversion for most immigrants. Religious observances took up a lot of time, and, in the United States, time was money. Although American Jews spent less time on the formalities of Judaism, they were not deliberately rejecting the Jewish religion. They found an American solution to an American problem, practicing whatever was pragmatic and time efficient. This partially explains the seemingly haphazard nature of American Jewish religious life.

DENOMINATIONALISM

The *Cambridge Companion to American Judaism* deliberately avoids breaking down American Judaism into its denominational components. Without underestimating the differences between the streams, the scholars writing in this collection look at the totality of American Judaism rather than at its constituent parts. In this way the book is quite different than most of the previous works on the subject, which divided American Judaism by denominations, covering the history, theology, and sociology of Reform, Conservative, Orthodox, and Reconstructionist Jews and Judaism.[11]

It is my belief that focusing primarily on the denominations can obstruct rather than clarify the nature of contemporary American Jewish identity. Denomination identity is defined in large measure by theological statements and prayer book publications. One of my earlier books on Reform Jewish theology was entitled *Platforms and Prayer Books*, an indication that the Reform movement has expressed its belief system in great measure through the production of a series of statements of principle and prayer books. The same could be said for most of the American Jewish denominations. With the partial exception of the Orthodox, all of the streams have been busy producing statements of what they believe in and editing prayer books for use in their congregations. Many are gender sensitive or even gender neutral and include transliterations for those unable to read the Hebrew text. Some include extensive teaching tools and commentaries, while others emphasize simplicity in order to put the worshiper at ease. These efforts must be initiated and supported by religious movements because, with rare exceptions, they are far too grandiose to be undertaken by individual congregations. Partially as a consequence, historians have tended to study American Judaism through this denominational prism.

Throughout the twentieth century, American Judaism has maintained a denominational structure. Denominational leaders believed in different theologies and wanted to express their religious commitments in different ways. They also had different social origins and represented different classes and community orientations. The Reform, Conservative, Orthodox, and Reconstructionist movements all built rabbinical schools, congregational organizations, and various other institutions. Everything concerning Judaism was seen through the perspective of this denominationalism. Each of the major religious movements claimed to be the wave of the future.

This is no longer the case. Lawrence Grossman explains that the larger synagogue movements no longer claim to be synonymous with American Judaism. Both the Conservative and the Reform movements have changed from inclusive, encompassing sounding names to ones that more accurately reflect their actual mandate. The leaders of these movements understand that they can no longer claim to represent the entirety of American Judaism and so maintaining organizational names that appear to make that claim is misleading and counterproductive. Rather, it is the Orthodox who proudly claim to represent the only true Judaism. Orthodox polemicists argue that only "Torah-true" Judaism will survive because it is the only authentic form of the Jewish religion. The other denominations appear to be far less confident.

The proportion of American Jews who self-identify as denominational has declined and the labels of Reform, Conservative, and Orthodox are becoming less useful. Social psychologists explain that while it is helpful to describe synagogues and rabbis in denominational terms, these categories fall short in characterizing the full variety of Jewish individuals and the nature of their connections to Jewishness and Judaism. Carmel U. Chiswick ends her essay on the economics of American Judaism by suggesting that the American Jewish denominations have facilitated an adaptation process. This allows many to engage with Judaism while participating in an economic environment that was seemingly incompatible with traditional Judaism. She hints that the religious movements may not "survive the test of time in their current forms," but argues that "they have surely laid the foundation for the Jewish community of the future to engage meaningfully in an ancient religion."

INCREASING POLARIZATION

The United States is the only country in the world where the non-Orthodox dominate. Elsewhere, most Jews belong to Orthodox synagogues, although they do not necessarily observe Jewish practices in a halachic manner. Some governments, including that of the State of Israel, fund Orthodox synagogues exclusively, which means that alternative movements are put at an extreme disadvantage. The already widely held perception that Orthodox Judaism is the only authentic stream is reinforced by government recognition. Jews in most of the world look to Israel for religious direction, but in the United States this is true only of the Orthodox community. In contrast, the non-Orthodox feel an obligation to help Israel develop a more pluralistic religious orientation.

Orthodox Judaism has historically been the only type of Judaism that the Israeli population has been exposed to from the Ottoman period, through the British mandate, and since the establishment of the state in 1948. Orthodoxy is linked directly to the state through a number of important institutions, including the chief rabbinate, the rabbinical courts, the state religious educational system, and the local religious councils. In addition, an Israeli civil religion has emerged that accepts Orthodoxy as an integral part of the identity of the state. This means that even most secular Israelis accept Orthodox Jews and Orthodox Judaism as being the only legitimate representatives of the Jewish religion.

In contrast, the American Jewish community is religiously pluralistic. One has the choice of joining an Orthodox, Conservative, Reform, Reconstructionist, Secular Humanist, Jewish Renewal, Havurah Judaism, or any one of a number of other congregations belonging to numerous streams or denominations. If one prefers, there are nondenominational and independent congregations as well. The American Jewish religious landscape includes many divergent religious belief systems as well as a wide range of ritual practices. This has allowed for tremendous innovation, something that many more liberal Jews have applauded and the most Orthodox have condemned.

The gap between the Orthodox and the non-Orthodox is widening. Orthodox Judaism holds that all of the commandments of the Torah must be practiced in their entirety. The Reform fundamentally disagrees, arguing that only those commandments that are spiritually meaningful should be observed today. Conservative theology sees Halacha as binding but evolving. Since the Torah is divinely given, most Orthodox do not believe that there is any possibility for deliberate adaptation or reinterpretation of traditional practices to fit new social realities. In truth, such processes are occurring even in the most Orthodox circles, but they take place unconsciously over a long period of time. In contrast, the American liberal movements have consciously set out to reinterpret traditional religious concepts and have made deliberate changes in how the Jewish religion is practiced.

The Orthodox and the non-Orthodox Jews have such different conceptions of what the Jewish religion should be that observers have suggested that "a Jewish culture war" is inevitable.[12] Both sides view the other in unappreciative terms. The late Rabbi Aaron Soloveitchik, an important Talmudic scholar from Chicago, compared the idea of Orthodox participation with non-Orthodox organizations to the sin of the Golden Calf because it would "mislead ignorant Jewish masses to worship the idol of Reform and Reconstructionist Judaism."[13] Rabbi Alexander Schindler, the late president of the Union of American Hebrew Congregations (UAHC), spoke openly of his view of Jewish fundamentalism: "Where Orthodoxy alone prevails – stale repression, fossilized tradition, and ethical corruption hold sway."[14] If the rhetoric has cooled somewhat, it is only because the denominational leaders no longer see any viable hope for meaningful dialogue.

There is a fundamental difference in how the Orthodox and the non-Orthodox determine who is a "member of the tribe." Most Orthodox Jews believe that a Jew is someone born of a Jewish mother or who has converted to Judaism under Orthodox supervision. They feel strongly that allowing for alternative definitions of Jewish identity will harm Judaism and destroy the unity of the Jewish people. Because of this concern, they have tried repeatedly to lobby the Israeli government to accept their definition of who is a Jew, generating a series of coalition crises and frantic Israel–Diaspora negotiations. Many Conservative Jews likewise believe that a Jew must either be born of a Jewish mother or convert through a halachic process. Most religiously liberal Jews accept patrilineal as well matrilineal descent and are willing to consider a host of other innovations. As the reader will see, a number of the essays refer to these issues of identity, gender, and corporality. In particular, Rela Mintz Geffen and Sylvia Barack Fishman discuss the impact of changing societal gender roles on American Judaism. David Biale writes about how the Jewish body is portrayed in American Jewish culture, tracing changes that encouraged theorists to pioneer new theological constructions of what God, Torah, and Israel can mean. More liberal religious thinkers see these innovative approaches as theological breakthroughs; the fervently Orthodox see these same ideas as heresies.

THE PAUCITY OF THEOLOGICAL DISCOURSE

Jewish leaders argue over how the Jewish community can best ensure its future. Prominent rabbis have tried to point the way back to Judaism, arguing that religion alone can provide the justification necessary to perpetuate Jewishness once ethnic memory fades.[15] Various types of conversion campaigns have been proposed, although none have attracted large numbers of "unchurched gentiles."[16] Those who look at where the money is being spent debate how Outreach can best complement Inreach. Many American Jews are losing interest in their tradition. Should they be allowed to drift off, or should the Jewish community try to entice them back? What would bring them back? Would the money best be spent on those who remain committed to Judaism and to the Jewish community?

The future of American Judaism depends on the ability to fashion and market a compelling religious vision. Although most American Jews are not terribly concerned with abstract religious beliefs, it is crucial for the future of Jewish life in the United States. In my book on American Reform Judaism, I argue that the Reform movement needs at this time to develop a coherent theology. In his afterward to the volume, Union for Reform Judaism (URJ, formerly UAHC) President Eric H. Yoffie disagreed with the need for an immediate formulation and articulation of such a theology: "We need to immerse ourselves in Jewish *doing*, guided always by our liberal principles, and if we do so, appropriate theological formulation will be developed afterwards."[17] This debate tells us a lot about the current state of American Judaism. American Jews resist discoursing about God because they are activists and pragmatists rather than ideologues or theologians. They tend to be more concerned with doing things than thinking about them, so they want a religion of action rather than of doctrine. Nevertheless, there have been numerous Jewish religious thinkers of importance since World War II. Many worked within one of the seminaries associated with a particular movement, but those who have really made an enduring contribution were able to transcend their denominational affiliation.

Thinkers such as Abraham Joshua Heschel, Mordecai M. Kaplan, and Joseph B. Soloveitchik have taught the American Jews who will lead the community into the future, and a new generation of teachers is now inspiring the Jewish leaders of tomorrow. Without serious theological reflection, American synagogues will become generic community centers. American Jewishness will become just a residual ethnic identity that people will mention casually in conversation before they move on. Byron L. Sherwin suggests in this volume that "the greatest challenge to American Jewish theologians in the near future may not be the 'isms' of the past, nor the secularism of the present, but the American trend toward custom-made individualized forms of religion." Theology cannot be understood in isolation from what is happening in the society.

IMPROVING THE QUALITY OF JEWISH EDUCATION

The Jewish community has long recognized that while there is no single panacea for concerns about increasing assimilation, Jewish education is a vital component in ensuring "Jewish survival." Studies consistently show that the more Jewish education a child receives, the more likely he or she is to practice Judaism, support its goals and institutions, and raise a Jewish family. Day school education in particular has a proven record of success. Despite this, Jewish communal leaders have historically placed a low priority on Jewish education. There were certainly legitimate reasons why their attention was focused elsewhere. Individual Jewish immigrants had to worry about making a living. Jewish communal leaders were busy fighting anti-Semitism, fending off missionaries, urging intervention in the Nazi Holocaust, organizing assistance on behalf of oppressed Jewish communities throughout the world, and lobbying for support for the State of Israel. They were too preoccupied to worry about the relatively trivial issue of the quality of American Jewish education. However, in recent years a consensus developed that, without more effective Jewish education, the community would lose many of its own children.

Judaism requires all Jews to study throughout their entire lives. This is based on a fundamental difference between Jewish and secular education. As Isa Aron and her coauthors explain, secular education focuses on mastering a particular subject matter. In contrast, Jewish education sees study as a mitzvah. That means that study is a religious obligation in its own right, regardless of what is achieved. The morning prayers include a number of Biblical and Talmudic texts, which are quickly studied as a part of the traditional Shacharit (morning) service. American Jewish communities are now reenvisioning Jewish education in line with this theological principal. Rather than providing Sunday schools where parents can drop their children off on the way to the grocery store or the gym, synagogues and Jewish community centers are designing challenging educational programs for the entire family. While it seems obvious, American Jews are only now beginning to realize that they need to educate the younger generation if they are to perpetuate Judaism as a religion. Increasingly sophisticated study programs have been initiated, sometimes merging formal and informal approaches.

Jewish education is being taken increasingly seriously and will be the primary focus of Jewish institutional efforts in the coming years. There will be an emphasis on lifelong learning, rather than restricting education to those of school age. Informal educational experiences will continue to be as, or more, important than formal educational programs. Computer and digital technologies will enrich the Jewish religious experience in ways that we cannot even imagine yet. Committed Jews will continue to strive to build a vibrant and fulfilling Judaism. They will use the newest of ideas, including new approaches and new expertise, to more effectively study Judaism and live spiritual Jewish lives.

THE FUTURE

What will Judaism be like in the United States in 50 to 100 years? No one can know for sure, but there are certain trends that give us some likely hints. Polarization will continue. Those who remain affiliated will move to the extremes. In the late twenty-first century, there may be two Judaisms in the United States. They will represent contrasting viewpoints and have little contact with each other. Many of those raised Conservative will join Reform, whereas many Orthodox Jews will become more fervently Orthodox. Substantial numbers of intermarried couples will join more liberal synagogues, although Bruce Phillips reports in his essay that the majority will not.

The bulk of the Orthodox will continue to take conservative social and political positions and will increasingly form alliances with the Christian right on political and social issues such as school vouchers, pornography, gay marriage, and abortion. Many Jews who were raised Conservative or Reform will either no longer identify with their current denominations or will see those denominational affiliations as representing minor differences. They will be increasingly willing to innovate religiously and will continually redefine who a Jew is and what Judaism means.

Non-Orthodox American Jews, already very acculturated, will become even more assimilated. Intermarriage rates, already perceived to be over the 50 percent mark, may increase further. Many non-Orthodox synagogue members will have at least one non-Jewish parent. Most "half-Jews" will not identify as Jewish, yet many Americans will turn to Judaism as an authentic source for their spiritual yearnings. Many will want to celebrate life-cycle events in the traditional manner, and others will blend foreign practices with some form of Judaism.

Using the most recent data from the NJPS 2000, Phillips has come to some startling conclusions. He states that "perhaps the most important phenomenon emerging in the twenty-first century is the declining number of Jews whose religion is Judaism." Fully 40 percent of Jewish adults in the survey did not identify Judaism as their religion. Phillips expects that this process will continue and that therefore the number of Americans practicing Judaism will decline. The impact on those who continue to believe in and practice Judaism will be enormous. Family structure is also an important factor in determining the nature of American Judaism in the twenty-first century. There will be large numbers of singles and divorcees, as well as increasing numbers of openly gay and lesbian Jews, both singles and couples. There is even a transgendered individual now studying for the Reform rabbinate.

One of the most interesting findings is the unconventional use of Jewish rituals. Many of the people performing these ceremonies identify themselves ethnically as Jews but claim not to be practicing Judaism as a religion. Others may have no direct Jewish connection and are influenced by the pervasiveness of Jewish references in American popular culture. Television and film are filled with scenes of brises (circumcisions), Jewish weddings and funerals, and sometimes even bizarre Jewish home scenes (such as that on *Friends* in which Ross dresses up as an Armadillo to explain Hanukkah to his son, Ben). Characters freely discuss their ambivalent relationships with Judaism and struggle to reconcile their ancestral religion with their American lifestyle.

It is possible that Judaism is losing the battle to maintain a distinct religious denomination while at the same time becoming increasingly influential in the culture at large. Universalized Judaism is ubiquitous while particularistic Judaism is under siege. Nevertheless, current trends do not guarantee a definite future. While the Jewish religion faces severe challenges in pluralistic America, there may be some interesting surprises in store for those of us following its development in the New World.

Notes

1. I thank Andrew Beck of Cambridge University Press for his enthusiastic encouragement and Julie Angulo for her dedicated assistance in the preparation of this manuscript. Thank you to Rela Mintz Geffen and Lawrence Grossman for their comments on this introduction and to Murray Baumgarten for his suggestion on the division of Part II, to Matthew Baigell for his advise on the cover art and to Ken Karpinski for his technical assistance. On behalf of all of the contributors, I also thank the four anonymous readers for their many helpful suggestions.

2. Joseph Soloveitchik, *Divrei Hagut Veha'arakhah* (Jerusalem: World Zionist Organization, 1981), 32–48.

3. Emil Fackenheim, *God's Presence in History: Jewish Affirmations and Philosophical Reflections* (New York: New York University Press, 1970).

4. Arthur Hertzberg, "Israel and American Jewry," *Commentary* 44, 2 (August 1967), 69–73.

5. Jerome A. Chanes, "'America is Different!': Reform Judaism and American Pluralism," in *Platforms and Prayer Books, Theological and Liturgical Perspectives on Reform Judaism*, ed. Dana Evan Kaplan (Lanham: Rowman & Littlefield, 2002), 42–43.

6. Steven Cohen, *Content or Continuity? Alternative Bases for Commitment* (New York: American Jewish Committee, 1991), 4.

7. Bernard Susser and Charles S. Liebman, *Choosing Survival, Strategies for a Jewish Future* (New York and Oxford: Oxford University Press, 1999), 69.

8. Charles S. Liebman and Steven M. Cohen, *Two Worlds of Judaism: The Israeli and American Experiences* (New Haven and London: Yale University Press, 1990).

9. Jack Wertheimer, *Introduction from Jews in the Center: Conservative Synagogues and Their Members*, ed. Jack Wertheimer (New Brunswick and London: Rutgers University Press, 2000), 1.

10. Stephen Miller, "Confessions of a Rootless Cosmopolitan Jew," in *The Chosen People in an Almost Chosen Nation: Jews and Judaism in America*, ed. Richard John Neuhaus (Grand Rapids: William B. Eerdmans, 2002), 131–32.

11. See, for example, Marc Lee Raphael, *Profiles in American Judaism: The Reform, Conservative, Orthodox, and Reconstructionist Traditions in Historical Perspective* (San Francisco: Harper & Row, 1984); Gilbert S. Rosenthal, *Contemporary Judaism, Patterns of Social Survival* (New York: Human Sciences Press, 1986); Jack Wertheimer, *A People Divided: Judaism in Contemporary America* (New York: Basic Books, 1993).

12. Jack Wertheimer, *A People Divided: Judaism in Contemporary America* (New York: Basic Books, 1993), 170.

13. Lawrence Grossman, "Jewish Communal Affairs," *American Jewish Yearbook* 91 (1991), 200.

14. Alexander Schindler, "Remarks by the President of the UAHC," *CCAR Yearbook* 92 (1982), 63.

15. David J. Wolpe, *Why Be Jewish?* (New York: Henry Holt, 1995); Daniel Gordis, *God Was Not in the Fire: The Search for a Spiritual Judaism* (New York: Scribner, 1995).

16. Dana Evan Kaplan, "Opening the Gates of the Jewish Community: A Consideration of Recent Proposals for 'Proactive Conversion,'" *Conservative Judaism* 52, 4, (Summer 2000), 32–46.

17. Eric H. Yoffie, "Afterword," in *American Reform Judaism: An Introduction* (New Brunswick: Rutgers University Press, 2003), 259–62.

Part I

Historical overviews

1 Preservation and Innovation: Judaism in America, 1654–1880

ELI FABER

Judaism in America dates to 1654, when twenty-three Jewish refugees from Brazil arrived at the small Dutch settlement of New Amsterdam on Manhattan Island. Two Jewish individuals are known to have been present in the Dutch colony shortly before the newcomers arrived, but it is to the advent of the twenty-three, in flight from the Portuguese recapture of north-eastern Brazil after more than twenty years of Dutch rule there, that a Jewish presence in North America is usually traced. Few of the group that arrived in 1654 remained in New Amsterdam for any lengthy period, but during their stay they acquired land for a cemetery in 1656, thereby creating the first Jewish religious institution in North America.[1]

Of the twenty-three refugees who arrived from Brazil, the two who were already present on Manhattan Island, and a few others who appeared in New Amsterdam during the 1650s and early 1660s, only Asser Levy is known with certainty to have remained permanently. A well-known historical figure because of his challenge to Governor Peter Stuyvesant's attempts to severely restrict the civic rights of the Jews in New Amsterdam (New York after the British seized it in 1664), Levy continued to live there until his death in 1682, serving as a bridge between the refugees who came in 1654 and later Jewish arrivals. By the time of his death, a sufficient number of Jews had settled in New York so that it is possible to date a truly permanent Jewish presence in the colony, and by extension to all the English colonies on the mainland of North America, to the decade of the 1680s. Indeed, the growing Jewish presence in New York necessitated the acquisition of additional land for a cemetery in 1682.[2]

However, their numbers were too few to permit the creation of a communal structure and the construction of a synagogue. Worship took place in private homes until the late 1720s, when the Jews who resided in New York at last felt sufficiently well established to organize themselves as a community and to undertake construction of a synagogue, the first in mainland North America. Construction began in 1728, and worship in it commenced in 1730.[3] Subsequently, the community added an adjoining building where it conducted its business, built a ritual bath, purchased a house for the synagogue's caretaker, and engaged a teacher.[4]

This pattern – the arrival of a small number of settlers; the acquisition of land for a cemetery; worship in private quarters; and, finally, construction of a synagogue – proved typical in the four additional locations where Jews settled in colonial America, for Jewish law required interment in a cemetery in which only Jews were buried, but it permitted worship in any kind of location. Jews settled in Newport, Rhode Island, as early as 1658 and purchased land for a cemetery in 1677, but they could not undertake construction of a synagogue until 1759, dedicating it for use in 1763.[5] In Philadelphia, emigrants from the Jewish community in New York arrived in the latter part of the 1730s and bought property for a cemetery in 1738, and their successors undertook to organize a community during the 1760s. They worshiped, however, in a house located in Cherry Alley until the premises became inadequate because of the large influx of Jews from other parts of the country in the wake of wartime hostilities. Faced by overcrowding in the Cherry Alley house, Philadelphia's artificially (and temporarily) enlarged Jewish population built and dedicated their first synagogue structure in 1782.[6] In the southern colonies, Jews settled in Savannah in 1733 and in Charleston by 1750, although Jews had been present there intermittently since the 1690s. A petition by Savannah's few Jews to the legislature in 1773 for permission to enlarge their cemetery attests to its existence well before the community there could construct a synagogue for the first time in 1820.[7] In Charleston's case, a cemetery existed for certain by 1764, but there was no synagogue until 1794.[8]

Jewish worship in colonial America, whether at the early stage of a community's development in private quarters or later in a synagogue structure, adhered to the Sephardic rite. Furthermore, the architecture of the synagogues was in the Sephardic tradition.[9] The Sephardim, one of the two subdivisions of the Jewish people, traced their ancestry to the Jewish inhabitants of Spain and Portugal who had either been expelled from those two nations by monarchical decree in the late sixteenth century or who had remained there because they or their forbears had converted to Catholicism while still, in many cases, adhering secretly to Judaism. Most of the twenty-three refugees from Brazil who arrived in New Amsterdam in 1654 and most of the Jewish settlers who resided in New York by the 1680s were Sephardim, and the form of worship and ritual observance they established in their new home accordingly reflected their history and who they were.

Ashkenazim, members of the other great subdivision of the Jewish people who traced their origins to central and eastern Europe, were also present in 1654 as well as during the 1680s, although in smaller numbers in both instances than those who were Sephardic in origin. However, the balance shifted thereafter, and by 1720 Ashkenazim comprised the majority of colonial America's Jews; they maintained their lead for the remainder of the eighteenth century.[10] Nevertheless, the synagogue rite remained Sephardic, for, according to an important principle of traditional Jewish religious law, the custom established in a locality becomes the law in that locality, so long as it conforms with the governing norms of religious law. Although the Ashkenazic majority in the mainland English colonies may well have maintained Ashkenazic practices within the confines of their homes – and we do not have historical sources that would elucidate this point – in the public realm of the synagogue they accepted and abided by the Sephardic rite.

In fact, Ashkenazim and Sephardim in colonial North America achieved a level of cooperation rarely attained by the two groups when they encountered each other elsewhere, whether in Europe, in England's and Holland's colonies in the Caribbean, or in the Dutch colony of Suriname in South America. In all those locations, Ashkenazim and Sephardim regarded each other with well-established, disdainful views, refusing, in the social realm, to intermarry or to enter into business partnerships, and, in the religious realm, to worship together in the same synagogue – or to lie together in the same cemetery. Such hostilities did surface in North America in the colony of Georgia during the mid-1730s, but only briefly, dissipating when the bulk of the Jewish population left Georgia by the early 1740s. Then too, the traditional animosity that Sephardim had toward marriage with Ashkenazim manifested itself in New York around 1740, but thereafter the two groups in the mainland colonies intermarried at a higher rate than anywhere else in the New World. Above all, they did not establish separate synagogues or cemeteries, as was almost always the case elsewhere.[11]

Within the synagogues, the Ashkenazic majority not only accepted the Sephardic system of worship but also shared in governance. In the case of the synagogue in New York – the one among the early American synagogues for which extensive records for the period prior to the American Revolution exist – the Ashkenazim actually predominated as officeholders. Of the forty-six individuals who served between 1728 and 1760 as parnas (the term for synagogue president in the Sephardic system) and as assistants to the parnasim, sixteen (35 percent) were Ashkenazim and fifteen (33 percent) were Sephardim. The remaining fifteen included at least nine individuals who were probably Ashkenazim; adding them to the number of those who definitely were Ashkenazim yields a total of 54 percent of the officeholders as Ashkenazic in origin.[12]

In addition to administering the synagogue and overseeing the affairs of the entire Jewish community, the parnasim and assistants also undertook to enforce adherence to the requirements of traditional Jewish religious law and practice. In this aspect of their responsibilities they could not count upon guidance by a haham (the term for rabbi in the Sephardic tradition), for the Jewish communities in mainland North America had no rabbis throughout the lengthy colonial era, nor for many years thereafter. In contrast to the communities in the English colonies of Barbados and Jamaica, which employed hahamim as early as the 1680s, neither the Jewish communities in the mainland British colonies nor in the United States after 1776 had a rabbi until 1840. In the absence of trained rabbinical leadership, the colonial parnasim and assistants could turn for rulings on religious questions to the Sephardic community in London, the parent body of Sephardic congregations throughout the contemporary English-speaking world. However, for all intents and purposes the colonial congregations were largely on their own. Judaism in colonial America was almost entirely defined and maintained by laymen.[13]

Operating on their own, unguided by rabbinical authority, the community's officers endeavored to maintain compliance with traditional normative Judaism – there was, as yet, no other option than what would later be called Orthodoxy – through a variety of disciplinary methods. The mildest was admonition, but if that failed, harsher penalties could be imposed: the denial of Torah honors, that is, being called up to the Torah when it was read in the synagogue on Sabbaths, festivals, or on Mondays and Thursdays; expulsion from membership; and denial of burial in the community's cemetery. The community's leaders could also impose the herem, or excommunication, a powerful disciplinary procedure because it required members of the community to shun the excommunicate not only in the synagogue but outside as well; there could be no social or commercial contact with a person in herem. In practice, the New York congregation imposed excommunication only once, in that instance not because of violations of religious law but because of outrageous behavior on the part of the individual so punished. However, once placed in herem, a person could make amends and be restored to full contact with the community, as occurred subsequently in the case of the individual who had been excommunicated by the New York community.[14]

To guarantee conformity with the laws of kashrut (the laws and procedures governing the ritual purity of food), the community monopolized the slaughter of meat according to religious law. Butchering meat could not be left to free enterprise. Instead, the parnasim and assistants, sometimes in consultation with the entire membership, designated who could serve as shochet (slaughterer), paid him a salary, and devised a seal that, affixed to the meat, certified it had been slaughtered according to law. Through its officers, the congregation spent a great deal of time supervising and, if necessary, disciplining the slaughterer in order to guarantee the kashrut of its meat supply. When necessary, the parnasim and assistants advertised for a shochet in the other communities of the wider Atlantic trading world.[15]

Reliance on the other Jewish communities in the larger Atlantic world for religious purposes extended beyond the ritual slaughterer. Colonial America's Jews were part of a network of coreligionists that extended to England's and Holland's Caribbean possessions, to Suriname in South America, to London and Amsterdam, and to each other in New York, Rhode Island, Pennsylvania, South Carolina, and Georgia. In large measure, this network was maintained because of the careers in commerce that many of them pursued – or aspired to pursue. The Jewish inhabitants of England, Holland, and their respective colonies were hardly unique in this respect; Quaker and Huguenot merchants also maintained trading connections that spanned the Atlantic.

For the population of Jews of colonial America, the far-flung, overseas network to which they belonged supported not only their commercial ventures but also their efforts to maintain the practice of Judaism. In addition to advertising in other localities for a ritual slaughterer, the colonial mainland community also looked abroad for teachers and, perhaps most important of all, for a hazan, the reader who led services in the synagogue and chanted from the Torah. Although a professional hazan is not a requirement in Judaism – any adult male may lead a service of at least ten men over the age of thirteen and read from the Torah scroll – the colonial congregations advertised around the Atlantic when necessary for such a functionary. To be sure, the Jewish community in Charleston recruited Isaac Da Costa as hazan from within their congregation, a position in which he served for much of the period between 1750 and 1775. In New York, in contrast, the congregation hired a hazan from abroad when necessary, until Gershom Mendes Seixas, the first hazan born in North America, assumed the position in 1768, serving until his death in 1816. Adhering to the usual pattern, the Newport community secured the services of Judah Touro from the West Indies in 1759. Touro continued as hazan in Newport until 1779, when he relocated to New York and remained there, behind British lines, until the end of the Revolution.[16]

The larger Atlantic world also supplied Torah scrolls as well as funds to build synagogues. New York's congregation, for example, received contributions from Jews in Boston, London, Jamaica, and Barbados, and a large sum from the Jewish community in Curaçao when it undertook construction of its synagogue in 1728. Approximately thirty years later, New York assisted Newport with a Torah scroll and with funds to build its synagogue. Newport also received Torah scrolls from London and Amsterdam, as well as contributions for its synagogue building from the Jewish communities of Curaçao, London, Jamaica, and Suriname. Philadelphia's small Jewish population received a Torah from New York in 1761.[17]

However, the most significant of the Atlantic world's contributions to the perpetuation of Judaism among Jewish English colonists were their transatlantic marriages. Marriage within the faith (or to a convert who has become Jewish according to the principles of Jewish law) is a fundamental tenet of the Jewish religion, but the pool of potential partners in colonial America was minute. Because the number of Jews in mainland North America remained low throughout the eighteenth century, the search for a spouse necessarily encompassed the length and breadth of the Atlantic Jewish world.[18] Marriages between individuals in the five English colonies on the mainland were the rule, as were marriages with parties in Jamaica and Barbados, Curaçao, and London. Nuclear families paid the price of dispersal, but they also thereby guaranteed the continuity of Judaism in the New World.[19]

But what kind of Judaism? The only model of Judaism that existed as a reference point was what we, at present, would readily identify as Orthodoxy, but to what degree did colonial American Jews observe the strictures of Orthodox law and tradition in their personal lives and within their homes? On this the evidence is mixed. It indicates that many did adhere to traditional religious law and practice, while others deviated.

Abigail Franks of New York, to take one example of the tenacity of the religious tradition, clearly observed the laws governing the festivals, for, in one of her letters in 1739, she noted she had encountered difficulty writing because of the holiday of Sukkot (Festival of Booths). In another, she enjoined her son in London to maintain the laws of kashrut and to pray each morning. Then too, shortly after the American Revolution, Matthew Josephson of Philadelphia decried failures by women to bathe ritually after menstruation, and he pushed the community to construct a ritual bathhouse that complied with religious law. At Lancaster, in what was then the interior of Pennsylvania, Joseph Simon maintained a ritual slaughterer at his expense and conducted services in his home, complete with a pair of Torah scrolls and an ark in which to house them. Newport Jews who fled to Massachusetts during the American Revolution impressed the local inhabitants with their scrupulous observance of Sabbath rituals, for they closed their shops on Friday evenings and kept them shut on Saturdays (and did not reopen them until Monday morning out of regard for Sunday observances among their new neighbors). Finally in this vein, Uriah Hendricks of New York looked askance on a person who proposed to marry his aunt, for the man in question did not observe the Sabbath laws and ate food that was not kosher.[20]

In contrast, the presence of the suitor who had "no Regard to Religion," as Uriah Hendricks described him, provides evidence to the contrary in the matter of religious observance. Indeed, in 1757 the officers of New York's congregation dramatically threatened to expel from membership all who repeatedly disregarded the laws of Sabbath and the dietary rules. They had learned of offenders who were involved in activities "such as Trading on the Sabbath, Eating of forbidden Meats & other Heinous Crimes," and they brandished not only the weapon of expulsion but also exclusion from the cemetery. Further attesting to the diminution of traditional religious practices, colonial American Jews did not cover their heads. In the portraits that have come down to us, men do not wear traditional head covering and women do not appear to have cropped their hair upon marriage and worn wigs thereafter. Non-Jewish observers reported that Jews ate pork. According to one observer in the late 1740s, this development was especially noticeable among the young, although not limited to them, and occurred particularly when they traveled. In 1761 and 1765, New York's hazan published English translations of the prayer book for use in the synagogue, complete with directions for following the service. As he explained, many worshipers were otherwise incapable of participating. Finally, a marriage contract drawn up in 1779 hints at the degree to which, in the absence of trained and qualified rabbinical leadership, familiarity with religious law foundered. In the contract between Solomon Myers-Cohen and Belle Simon, the bride's father signed the document as a witness, an action at odds with halacha (Jewish religious law), which precludes a relative from serving as a witness.[21]

Perhaps most revealing of all, a small percentage of the Jewish population in colonial America married non-Jews. While the numbers were small in comparison with rates of intermarriage in later eras of American Jewish history, particularly in the last quarter of the twentieth century, here, clearly, was an indication that adherence to Judaism in early America could not be taken for granted.[22]

None of these departures from traditional Judaism can be attributed to a nascent reform movement in colonial America. To be sure, in a remarkable (but brief) passage she penned in 1739, Abigail Franks of New York praised the author of a book whose reliance on reason proved to her that he could not have been Jewish, and she decried what she regarded as religious superstition and useless ritual:

I Must Own I cant help Condemning the Many Supersti[ti]ons wee are Clog'd with & heartly wish a Calvin or Luther would rise amongst Us I Answer for my Self, I would be the first of there followers for I don't think religeon Consist in Idle Cerimonies & works of Supperoregations

Wich if they Send people to heaven wee & the papist have the Greatest title too[.][23]

However, the unique nature of Abigail Franks's view of Judaism – unique in that it is the only such statement known for the colonial period – precludes taking it as evidence of any coherent, much less organized, desire among American Jews to modify the tenets of Jewish law and observance. Franks herself, as noted previously, enjoined her son in London to adhere to morning prayer and to eat only kosher food; and she fell into a state of depression and evidently also experienced a deep sense of shame when her daughter secretly married a non-Jewish man.[24] The development of a less rigorous form of Judaism in America was to occur in a later era, after 1850, although signs of a desire to alter religious principles and practices already manifested themselves during the 1790s and again in the mid-1820s.

In the midst of the American Revolution, the five small Jewish commu-nities in the newly established United States of America found them-selves thoroughly disrupted, with many of their members choosing exile behind American lines rather than remain in areas under British control. A great many made their way from New York, Charleston, and Savannah to Philadelphia, which, until the war ended, served as a national gathering place for the new nation's small Jewish population. The effect upon the Jews of Philadelphia was to give a sharp boost to their earlier attempts to estab-lish a viable community and to construct a synagogue building. The enlarged wartime congregation adopted regulations and dedicated Philadelphia's first synagogue in 1782. Following the termination of hostilities, the same new vigor also characterized the congregations in New York and the two southern cities as their respective members made their ways from Philadelphia back to their places of origin. The Savannah community, meager in size prior to the Revolution, organized itself and adopted a system of government, although it did not construct a synagogue until 1820. In Charleston's case, however, a synagogue, the community's first, was built in 1794. A new community also took root in Richmond, Virginia. Only in the case of Newport, Rhode Island, did one of early American Jewry's congregations falter and then fail. Newport never recovered from the effects of the Revolution. From its earlier position as one of colonial America's most important seaports, the town sank into insignificance as a commercial center. The Jewish community shared in the decline, and by the early 1820s no Jews remained there. In the interim, yet another new community began to emerge, this one in Baltimore.

Everywhere, the congregations demonstrated their postwar energy by adopting new regulations and new governing instruments. Mirroring concurrent ideological and political developments in the wider young Republic, the Philadelphians referred to their charter and to a later revision as a constitution, as did the New Yorkers in 1790, when they adopted a new governance document and in addition drew up what they called a members' bill of rights. The new nation's Jewish communities also took pains to affirm their commitment to the Sephardic rite. The New York congregation, for example, wrote that, "The establishment of this congregation, having always been *keminhag Sephardim* ['according to the Sephardic ritual'], is hereby confirmed and declared to be the constitution of the same. . . . " Similarly, Savannah's new regulations proclaimed that "the mode of worship be according to the Pourtuguese minhauge. . . . "[25]

The congregations also asserted they had every intention to underwrite adherence to traditional Jewish law and religious practices, spelling out penalties for those who refused to comply. Accordingly, the New York congregation adopted a regulation in 1790 specifying that an individual who ate nonkosher food, violated the Sabbath, or similarly transgressed on a festival day could not receive religious honors in the synagogue or serve in office. In the following year, the Savannah congregation adopted a provision among its regulations that called for an investigation of anyone accused of violating Sabbath or festival regulations; the guilty were to be barred from synagogue honors until they made amends. Less than one year later, the Georgians responded to allegations that one of their members had kept his store open on the Sabbath by summoning him for questioning, although later exonerating him. In 1820, the constitution adopted by Charleston's community authorized the withholding of religious privileges in the synagogue for Sabbath and holiday violators, as well as fines and any other penalties thought appropriate.[26]

In still other known instances, the leaders of the congregations of the early Republic endeavored to maintain traditional Judaism, but, as during the colonial era, they were laymen who were on their own, acting without rabbinic guidance in matters of Jewish law.[27] As before, they could turn to rabbinic authorities in Europe to rule in cases in which they had no knowledge of the law, as the Philadelphia congregation did in 1785 in a case arising upon the death of a man who had married a non-Jewish woman in a civil wedding ceremony. At issue was whether he could be buried in the community's cemetery. A committee designated by the congregation to render a legal decision authorized interment in the burial ground, but without the traditional washing and enshrouding of the corpse. However, a faction within the congregation disagreed with this ruling and managed to bury the deceased after washing and clothing the body in traditional manner, citing their own rabbinic texts in support of their position, This, in turn, prompted two members of the committee to write to the Ashkenazic leadership in Amsterdam for an authoritative religious ruling in such cases.[28]

In their letter to the rabbinic authority in Amsterdam, the two Philadelphians alluded to the other side of the coin regarding the state of traditional law and practice in American Judaism, writing that there was a "great lack of discipline that prevails in our generation."[29] Despite the fact that the Jews of the early Republic endeavored, as had their predecessors, to sustain traditional Judaism in America, defections were all too apparent. In addition to failures to observe the laws of kashrut, Sabbath, and festivals, there are hints that some people may have already questioned the exclusive use of Hebrew in the synagogue service, save for the occasional use of Portuguese to pledge donations.[30] (The issue of permitting English in the synagogue would become a staple of efforts to reform American Judaism in the nineteenth century.) Perhaps most troubling of all, marriage out of the faith appears to have been a growing phenomenon, or at least to have been perceived as such, to judge from repeated references to it in the congregations' constitutions and regulations. In New York in 1790, community membership was permissible only to adult men who married according to Jewish law; again in New York, any person who married a non-Jewish woman without approval by the community's leaders was to forfeit his membership; in Savannah in 1791, the hazan was to officiate only at weddings in which both parties were Jewish; in Philadelphia in 1798, any member who intermarried was to forfeit synagogue membership, have his name erased from the congregation's records, and be denied burial in the cemetery, unless first making "concessions" and paying a fine; and in Charleston in 1820, any person who married contrary to religious law was to be denied membership and burial in the congregation's cemetery.[31]

A significant change also occurred within the walls of the synagogue in the office of the hazan. The hazan's traditional function was to lead services; the requirements for the position were a good voice and knowledge of the liturgy. After 1780, however, the hazan's activities evolved to foreshadow those of the rabbi in modern American life.

For one, the hazan began to represent the Jewish community to the larger community. In 1788, for example, Philadelphia's hazan marched with two clergymen in the city's parade celebrating Pennsylvania's ratification of the Constitution. In New York, Gershom Mendes Seixas, America's first native-born hazan, sat on Columbia College's board of trustees for more than thirty years, thereby serving in a capacity similar to that filled by Protestant clergymen. In addition, he joined with the city's clergymen to help plan such citywide religious events as thanksgiving days and fast days. Seixas, it should be noted, was no trained clergyman: his formal Judaic training did not extend beyond the age of thirteen; his knowledge of Hebrew was rudimentary; and he had no rabbinic authority.[32]

It was inside the synagogue, however, that Seixas introduced the most novel feature of all when he undertook to preach sermons. This too amounted to an innovation of considerable import, one that was again predictive of the function and responsibilities of the rabbi in modern America, for rabbis did not traditionally preach in the synagogue except once or twice a year on major Sabbaths. For Seixas, the Protestant ministry, for whom weekly preaching was a major part of their responsibilities, was evidently the model rather than the rabbis of Europe. Indeed, he borrowed the rhetorical devices he used, as well as some of the Christian terminology he utilized in his speeches, from Protestant sermons.[33]

However, neither a public role for the hazan nor synagogue sermons violated religious law. These were not innovations that went to the root of the tradition. More radical ideas, in contrast, emerged in the middle of the 1820s from within the congregation in Charleston, ideas that may well be regarded as precursors to the development of Reform Judaism in the United States. There, reformers called for modifying the services conducted in the synagogue. This, in turn, potentially had a much greater implication, namely that of opening the door to change across the board, be it in theology, religious law, or ritual practice.

The forty-seven members of Charleston's congregation who in 1824 signed a petition for reform suggested that part of the liturgy be eliminated in order to shorten the synagogue service, with the retention of only the most important prayers. From the perspective of the Orthodox practice of Judaism, this was the most drastic of their proposals. The members advocated the addition of English, which was less confrontational to tradition, with the hazan to read an English translation of all the retained sections of the service after they had been chanted or recited in Hebrew. Further, they asked for an English sermon by the hazan, one based on the weekly Torah reading. Finally, they called for ending the practice in which people publicly pledged donations in the synagogue upon being called to the Torah.

To justify their program of reformation, a word they actually used in their petition to the community's officers, these advocates of change emphasized they did not seek alterations in religious fundamentals. They had no wish "to destroy long standing institutions, but to accommodate them to the progress of time, and change of situation and circumstances," and they assured the recipients of their memorial that they had no intention of eliminating important Jewish ceremonies or of compromising Judaism's bedrock principles. Instead, they sought first and foremost to overcome the widespread "apathy and neglect which have been manifested towards our holy religion," decrying the high rate of synagogue absenteeism that seemed to prevail. They hoped to achieve greater "decency and decorum" during services and greater understanding of Judaism's principles and practices, particularly among the young. In a passage reminiscent of Abigail Franks's brief expression of skepticism almost a century before, they asserted they could no longer expose their children to practices and ideas that were "only calculated to darken the mind, and withhold from the rising generation the more rational means of worshipping [*sic*] the true God." All in all, their program, they argued, was one that would reverse the decline in the level of commitment to Judaism they perceived on all sides.[34]

Rebuffed by the elders of the Charleston congregation, the reformers formed an organization they called the Reformed Society of Israelites, and they congregated separately between 1825 and 1833. Despite their disavowal of changing the fundamentals of Judaism, they developed a prayer book that, through the deletion of certain prayers and passages, espoused a number of theological innovations. Gone were references to belief in the Messiah, the restoration of sacrifices in Jerusalem, and a return to the Holy Land. And although their society disbanded in 1833, they ultimately did succeed in their efforts to steer a new course. Three years later, part of Charleston's congregation embarked on a course of reform modeled after one of Germany's Reform synagogues, thereby establishing the first reformed congregation in the United States, although the reforms were at first limited to a weekly sermon in English and the use of an organ during services.[35]

The impetus to reform Judaism in America, however, came not from Charleston but from among the Ashkenazic Jewish immigrants from Central Europe who entered the United States between 1820 and 1860. Thousands made their ways from the German states (including Polish Jews from Posen, which was then under Prussian rule), leaving behind them the economic dislocation and difficulties that arose as a consequence of growing industrialization, as well as the widespread restrictions on Jews that existed in many German jurisdictions. By 1860, the size of the Jewish population in the country probably reached 200,000. The newcomers settled not only on the eastern seaboard, where America's original Jewish communities existed, but also spread rapidly into the interior, striking roots throughout the Northeast, the South, and the expanding Midwest. Many began their careers in the New World as peddlers, fanning across the countryside with their wares on their backs. The more successful individuals eventually opened retail stores in small and midsized towns; many others settled in larger cities, where they too tended to concentrate in the retail trades. Ultimately, some established major department stores, while others became bankers who helped underwrite the country's growing industrial infrastructure.[36]

Wherever adequate numbers settled, they formally organized Jewish communities and erected synagogues. In the larger cities, a multiplicity of congregations developed, sometimes because of splits within existing synagogues and at other times because of the expanding size of the population. Given both the number of Jews and the number of synagogues they established, the prevailing rite in America shifted from Sephardic to Ashkenazic, with German and Polish variants, depending on the makeup of the membership in any given synagogue. Moreover, these new congregations were committed to traditional Judaism; the newcomers, as one historian of the emergence of Reform Judaism has argued, were not in any way drawn to or interested in bringing with them the innovations underway in Germany: "Not only did the bulk of the German Jewish immigrants reject Reform, but they resisted reforms." To be sure, many abandoned traditional ritual observance to varying degrees in their personal lives – it was difficult to observe the commandments as they peddled their wares through the countryside, or to provide kosher food in a small town deep in the Midwest – but the synagogues they established adhered to Judaism's established theology and practices. It was, therefore, traditional, Orthodox Judaism to which the new Ashkenazic congregations subscribed.[37]

Along with growing prosperity came acculturation to American life, and with it an emphasis on incorporating the English language into the synagogue, a transformation much in evidence during the 1850s. Although worship remained largely in Hebrew, sermons and congregational minutes and reports shifted from German and Yiddish to English. Moreover, modest reforms in ritual were adopted in the 1850s and 1860s, although in only in a small number of congregations and not in any organized fashion that would have been indicative of collective movement in any specific direction. The few synagogues ready to introduce a small measure of reform did so independently of each other. In one, for example, the hazan was authorized to face the congregation instead of the ark as he led services. In another, some seats faced north rather than east, the direction of prayer in traditional normative Judaism. Yet a third eliminated the second day of Yom Tov (a day of worship and no work that is somewhat less stringent than Sabbath) on the three pilgrimage festivals of Passover, Shavuot (Feast of Weeks), and Sukkot (Festival of Booths).

However, these developments were only tentative moves toward the creation of a reformed Judaism, inasmuch as few congregations were yet ready to explore such changes. As one observer noted in 1861, reform had been introduced in only 8 out of the more than 200 congregations in the United States. Indeed, six years before, at a small, national gathering of congregational leaders in Cleveland, the statement of ideology approved by the participants had affirmed that the Torah was of divine origin, that the Bible as a whole was divinely inspired, and that the Talmud was the valid, authoritative text for determining all matters of Jewish law. All of these points were in strict conformity with traditional Judaism; they were, and they remain, the bedrock principles of Orthodox Judaism.

By contrast, the impulse to change Judaism in America surged between 1860 and 1870. Congregations everywhere began to implement a host of innovations, including the incorporation of the organ into synagogue worship, the abolition of head covering for men during services, and the introduction of mixed seating for men and women. Other reforms included abolition of the second day of the pilgrimage festivals, abridging the weekly reading from the Torah, and the introduction of prayer books that made no reference to the return to the Holy Land, reconstruction of the Temple in the Messianic era, and the restoration of the sacrificial cult.

These changes in the prayer books were theological in nature, although no statement of theological principles, no formal ideological guidelines, as yet existed for the reformers to follow. That finally came in the year 1885, when a small group of rabbis convened in Pittsburgh and adopted a doctrinal platform that severed ties to the traditional Judaism that had been preserved by North America's Jews during the colonial era and by their successors from the German states when they first settled in the United States. Above all else, the new statement of principles omitted reference to – thereby in effect denying – any literal Revelation, that is, God's transmission of the Torah to Israel at Mount Sinai. There was, therefore, no divine imperative for the laws and practices of Judaism. Rejecting Revelation (except in a spiritual sense) meant there was now a theological basis for changing and replacing traditional beliefs and practices with new ones, for if the law was not literally from God then it possessed no eternal truth or validity. The principles approved in Pittsburgh, therefore, signaled a dramatic turning point, a profound shift from the preservation of the traditional Judaism that had been formulated ages ago to a wholesale embrace of innovation in theology and practice.

The fact that it was a group of rabbis who in effect codified theological justification for what had been evolving by way of practice in the American congregations attests to another important change wrought by the German immigrants and their offspring, namely, the emergence of rabbinical leadership after 1840. Not that the rabbis who came to America from Germany and England between 1840 and 1880 – there were as yet no American-trained rabbis – were able to assert untrammeled authority. They were, after all, employees who could be, and in not a few cases were, dismissed by the congregations that engaged them.[38] Few of them could be said to have mastered the traditional texts in which European rabbis were steeped prior to their ordinations; in fact, there is reason to question whether all of them had actually been ordained. This lack of traditional training and credentials bespoke the emergence of a new kind of rabbi. Rather than a scholar who was deeply learned in the law, qualified to rule on questions of religious law and even matters of Jewish civil law, the American rabbi was an employee of the congregation who officiated in the synagogue, delivered weekly sermons, ministered to the emotional and spiritual needs of his congregants, and represented the Jewish community to the larger surrounding community. In sum, the new American rabbinate formulated in the mid-nineteenth century by the German congregations embodied the kind of rabbinical office foreshadowed by Gershom Mendes Seixas between 1785 and 1815. It was, in fact, a reformed rabbinate.

In the realm of congregational leadership, therefore, significant change also characterized the Judaism that developed in the mid-nineteenth century in the wake of the advent of the thousands of Jews from Central Europe. In the emergence of the modern American rabbinate, innovation again trumped preservation. However, beginning in 1880, a great new wave of Jewish immigrants, this time from Eastern Europe, began to enter the United States, many of whom were unyieldingly committed to tradition. Out of the clash between the two options that would now be present in America – Reform and Orthodoxy – would ultimately come even more creativity, as well as controversy, in American Judaism.

Notes

1. The cemetery's site is unknown; see David De Sola Pool and Tamar De Sola Pool, *An Old Faith in the New World: Portrait of Shearith Israel, 1654–1954* (New York: Columbia University Press, 1955), 31–32. For the identities of the earliest Jews in New York, see the listing in Leo Hershkowitz, "Original Inventories of Early New York Jews (1682–1763)," *American Jewish History* 90 (2002), 246–47, n. 7.
2. See David De Sola Pool and Tamar De Sola Pool, *An Old Faith in the New World*, 34 and 303 for the later cemetery. See David De Sola Pool, *Portraits Etched in Stone: Early Jewish Settlers, 1682–1831* (New York: Columbia University Press, 1952) for Jews present during the 1680s.
3. For references to worship in the late 1690s in a private house, see David De Sola Pool and Tamar De Sola Pool, *An Old Faith in the New World*, 39. In 1730, the community still owed rent to the landlord of the building it worshiped in before relocating to its new synagogue. See "The Earliest Extant Minute Books of the Spanish and Portuguese Congregation Shearith Israel in New York, 1728–1786," *Publications of the American Jewish Historical Society* 21 (1913), 1–3, 9, 11–12, 14, 26.
4. "The Earliest Extant Minute Books of the Spanish and Portuguese Congregation Shearith Israel in New York, 1728–1786," *Publications of the American Jewish*

Historical Society 21 (1913), 14, 35, 54, 72, 81; David De Sola Pool and Tamar De Sola Pool, *An Old Faith in the New World*, 45.

5. Morris A. Gutstein, *The Story of the Jews of Newport: Two and a Half Centuries of Judaism, 1658–1908* (New York: Bloch Publishing, 1936), 28, 36–38, 82, 340–42.

6. Jacob Rader Marcus, ed., *American Jewry – Documents – Eighteenth Century* (Cincinnati: Hebrew Union College Press, 1959), 94.

7. Saul J. Rubin, *Third to None: The Saga of Savannah Jewry, 1783–1983* (Savannah: S. J. Rubin, 1983), 23–24.

8. The death of a member of the community outside Charleston in 1764 and the subsequent efforts to bring his body to the town for burial provide dating for the cemetery. See Thomas J. Tobias, "Charles Town in 1764," *South Carolina Historical Magazine* 67 (1966), 72.

9. The reader's desk was in the center of the structure rather than in the front near the ark, as is evident in Newport's still-standing Touro Synagogue, and from an early-nineteenth-century painting of Charleston's synagogue, reproduced in Eli Faber, *A Time for Planting: The First Migration, 1654–1820* (Baltimore: Johns Hopkins University Press, 1992). Women sat in an upstairs gallery, but this was not a feature of Sephardic synagogue architecture alone, inasmuch as women and men sat separately in Ashkenazic synagogues too, with the women often in a gallery.

10. Jacob R. Marcus, *Studies in American Jewish History: Studies and Addresses* (Cincinnati: Hebrew Union College Press, 1969), 52.

11. R. D. Barnett, "Dr. Samuel Nunes Ribeiro and the Settlement of Georgia," in *Migration and Settlement: Proceedings of the Anglo-American Jewish Historical Conference Held in London Jointly by the Jewish Historical Society of England and the American Jewish Historical Society, July 1970* (London: Jewish Historical Society of England, 1971), 60, 87, 94; Leo Hershkowitz and Isidore S. Meyer, eds., *The Lee Max Friedman Collection of American Jewish Colonial Correspondence: Letters of the Franks Family (1733–1748)* (Waltham: American Jewish Historical Society, 1968), 66–67, 75–76; Malcolm H. Stern, "The Function of Genealogy in American Jewish History," in *Essays in American Jewish History to Commemorate the Tenth Anniversary of the Founding of the American Jewish Archives Under the Direction of Jacob Rader Marcus* (Cincinnati: American Jewish Archives, 1958), 74–81.

12. Eli Faber, *A Time for Planting: The First Migration, 1654–1820* (Baltimore: Johns Hopkins University Press, 1992), 64.

13. On the subject of consultation between congregations in the English colonies and London in general, see R. D. Barnett, "The Correspondence of the Mahamad of the Spanish and Portuguese Congregation of London During the Seventeenth and Eighteenth Centuries," *Transactions of the Jewish Historical Society of England* 20 (1959–61), 1–50. For a request for a religious ruling made by Philadelphia to London in 1793, see Jacob Rader Marcus, ed., *American Jewry – Documents – Eighteenth Century* (Cincinnati: Hebrew Union College Press, 1959), 188–89.

14. "The Earliest Extant Minute Books of the Spanish and Portuguese Congregation Shearith Israel in New York, 1728–1786," *Publications of the American Jewish Historical Society* 21 (1913), 71, 74–75, 81. In Philadelphia, the community resolved around 1770 to bar Sabbath violators from receiving religious honors

without first satisfying a penalty. See Jacob Rader Marcus, ed., *American Jewry – Documents – Eighteenth Century* (Cincinnati: Hebrew Union College Press, 1959), 96.

15. "The Earliest Extant Minute Books of the Spanish and Portuguese Congregation Shearith Israel in New York, 1728–1786," *Publications of the American Jewish Historical Society* 21 (1913), 4, 13–15, 29, 30, 45, 48, 75–78, 80, 93–94, 106–07, 112, 113, 123–27, 135.

16. "The Earliest Extant Minute Books," 73, 84–85, 92, 100–01; Morris A. Gutstein, *The Story of the Jews of Newport: Two and a Half Centuries of Judaism, 1658–1908* (New York: Bloch Publishing, 1936), 72–73, 82, 116; Eli Faber, *A Time for Planting: The First Migration, 1654–1820* (Baltimore: Johns Hopkins University Press, 1992), 43, 104–05.

17. "The Earliest Extant Minute Books," 19, 20, 22–24, 81; Morris A. Gutstein, *The Story of the Jews of Newport*, 88, 94, 105–06; Eli Faber, *A Time for Planting*, 50.

18. Estimates of the Jewish population in the United States in 1790 range from 1,300 to 3,000. See Ira Rosenswaike, "An Estimate and Analysis of the Jewish Population of the United States in 1790," in *The Jewish Experience in America: Selected Studies from the Publications of the American Jewish Historical Society*, ed. Abraham J. Karp (Waltham and New York: American Jewish Historical Society 1969), vol. I, 401–2; and the ensuing discussion in Malcom Stern, "Some Additions and Corrections to Rosenswaike's 'An Estimate and Analysis of the Jewish Population of the United States in 1790,' " followed by Rosenswaike's "Comments on Dr. Stern's Additions and Correction," *American Jewish Historical Quarterly* 53 (1963–64), 289–92.

19. For examples of these transatlantic and intercolonial marriages, see Eli Faber, *A Time for Planting*, 47–49.

20. Leo Hershkowitz and Isidore S. Meyer, eds., *The Lee Max Friedman Collection of American Jewish Colonial Correspondence: Letters of the Franks Family (1733–1748)* (Waltham: American Jewish Historical Society, 1968), 7–8, 69; Jacob Rader Marcus, ed., *American Jewry – Documents – Eighteenth Century* (Cincinnati: Hebrew Union College Press, 1959), 134–36; Eli Faber, *A Time for Planting: The First Migration, 1654–1820* (Baltimore: Johns Hopkins University Press, 1992), 40, 91; and Morris A. Gutstein, *The Story of the Jews of Newport: Two and a Half Centuries of Judaism, 1658–1908* (New York: Bloch Publishing, 1936), 132. Joseph Simon's ark for his two Torah scrolls still exists; it is in the possession of the American Jewish Historical Society, New York City.

21. "The Earliest Extant Minute Books," 74–75. For the absence of male head covering and ladies' wigs, see the portraits reproduced in Richard Brilliant, *Facing the New World: Jewish Portraits in Colonial and Federal America* (Munich and New York: Prestel, 1997). Comments by the New York hazan and by non-Jewish observers are in Eli Faber, *A Time for Planting: The First Migration, 1654–1820* (Baltimore: Johns Hopkins University Press, 1992), 84, 92. The marriage contract of Solomon Myers-Cohen and Belle Simon is in the Gratz Family papers at the American Jewish Historical Society, New York City.

22. Malcolm H. Stern, "The Function of Genealogy in American Jewish History," in *Essays in American Jewish History to Commemorate the Tenth Anniversary of the Founding of the American Jewish Archives Under the Direction of Jacob Rader Marcus* (Cincinnati: American Jewish Archives, 1958), passim.

23. Leo Hershkowitz and Isidore S. Meyer, eds., *The Lee Max Friedman Collection of American Jewish Colonial Correspondence: Letters of the Franks Family (1733–1748)* (Waltham: American Jewish Historical Society, 1968), 66.

24. Ibid., 116–19, for Franks's reaction to her daughter's actions.

25. Jacob Rader Marcus, ed., *American Jewry – Documents – Eighteenth Century* (Cincinnati: Hebrew Union College Press, 1959), 116, 128, 149, 153–56, 177.

26. Jacob Rader Marcus, *American Jewry – Documents –* 166, 179–81; Joseph L. Blau and Salo W. Baron, eds., *The Jews of the United States, 1790–1840: A Documentary History*, 3 vols. (New York: Columbia University Press, 1963), vol. 2, 552.

27. Jacob Rader Marcus, *American Jewry – Documents –* 121, 123–24, for documentation of one such instance involving a cohen (a member of the priestly line of Aaron) who proposed to marry a convert. The records relate that the laymen examining the case heard a presentation reviewing the laws that governed in such an instance. In their ruling on the marriage's illegality, the community's leaders barred the hazan from officiating at the wedding and prohibited anyone else from attending it.

28. Jacob Rader Marcus, *American Jewry – Documents –* 139–41.

29. Ibid., 141.

30. "No language [is] to be made use of in synagogue but Hebrew, except the offerings," stated the New York congregation's regulations in 1790. Its bill of rights asserted that members had the right to make pledges "in the Hebrew language or in the Portuguese, and in those language only (the latter having been practiced from the establishment of this congregation)." In Savannah, in contrast, pledges had to be made in Hebrew. See Jacob Rader Marcus, *American Jewry – Documents –* 153, 156, 177.

31. Jacob Rader Marcus, *American Jewry – Documents –* 129, 150, 160–61, 179–80; Joseph L. Blau and Salo W. Baron, eds., *The Jews of the United States, 1790–1840: A Documentary History*, 3 vols. (New York: Columbia University Press, 1963), vol. 2, 551.

32. Eli Faber, *A Time for Planting: The First Migration, 1654–1820* (Baltimore: Johns Hopkins University Press, 1992), 119. On Seixas's limitations, see Thomas Kessner, "Gershom Mendes Seixas: His Religious 'Calling,' Outlook, and Competence," *American Jewish Historical Quarterly* 58 (1968–69), passim.

33. Thomas Kessner, "Gershom Mendes Seixas: His Religious 'Calling,' Outlook, and Competence," *American Jewish Historical Quarterly* 58 (1968–69), 468; Jacob Rader Marcus, "The Handsome Young Priest in the Black Gown: The Personal World of Gershom Seixas," *Hebrew Union College Annual* 40–41 (1969–70), 438, 445.

34. Morris U. Schappes, ed., *A Documentary History of the Jews in the United States 1654–1875*, 3rd ed. (New York: Schocken Books, 1971), 171–77.

35. Ibid., 171, 608, n. 5.

36. For a thorough treatment of this immigrant group, see Hasia Diner, *A Time for Gathering: The Second Migration, 1820–1880* (Baltimore: Johns Hopkins University Press, 1992).

37. The quotation is from Leon Jick, *The Americanization of the Synagogue, 1820–1870* (Hanover: University Press of New England, 1976), 49. The description here of the development of Reform Judaism in the United States in the mid-nineteenth century closely follows Jick's, passim, but it relies also on Michael

A. Meyer, *Response to Modernity: A History of the Reform Movement in Judaism* (New York: Oxford University Press, 1988), 225–70, and on Naomi W. Cohen, *Encounter with Emancipation: The German Jews in the United States, 1830–1914* (Philadelphia: The Jewish Publication Society, 1984), 161–94.

38. The emerging Reform movement established its seminary in the 1870s and ordained its first four graduates in 1883; Michael A. Meyer, *Response to Modernity: A History of the Reform Movement in Judaism* (New York: Oxford University Press, 1988), 263.

2 American Judaism, 1880–1945

LLOYD P. GARTNER

Denominations existed in American Judaism by about 1880, but only that of Reform was clearly defined and organized. The new period would see the continued growth of Reform and the expansion on a massive scale of Orthodoxy and Conservatism. Controversy and creativity were found within all these movements.

In 1880, there were about 260,000 Jews among the over 50 million inhabitants of the United States, constituting a small minority of only 0.5 percent of the population. They were an articulate and much-noticed group, as their communal activities and synagogue sermons were often reported in general newspapers. Moreover, numerous books, essays, and the weekly Jewish press kept them and their religion in the public eye.[1] America, as a deeply Christian country, could not ignore the Jews in its midst, the ancient denier and challenger of Christianity.

During this era, the Jewish religion as practiced in the America of 1880 was largely Reform Judaism. It had first appeared, but briefly, in 1828 and began its unbroken history around 1845. Of the dozens of Orthodox synagogues that immigrant German and Polish Jews founded in cities and small towns, all but a few "reformed" their worship by approximately 1870. Men and women no longer sat separately; prayers and the reading of the Torah were drastically shortened, and the *trop* (chant) of its reading was abolished; the two days of festivals were reduced to one; and the vernacular sermon by the rabbi became the center of the service. The rules of kosher diet were largely abandoned, and services were no longer held on weekdays. Still, the Sabbath was inviolate, although many worshipers went from services to their business, or only their wives attended the synagogue. The service itself was mostly in Hebrew. By 1880 this moderate Reform came as close as Reform ever came to being synonomous with American Judaism.

American Reform Judaism embraced an immigrant German Jewish community of hard-working businessmen at all levels, from country peddlers to solid urban merchants, most of whom had themselves started in America as peddlers. They were not men of learning or intellectual ambition. Their rabbis had been teachers and occasional preachers in Europe, seldom with rabbinical ordination, and very few among them could claim scholarly stature. Traditional Jewish life and worship were familiar to many immigrants from their European childhood, but rabbis as well as laymen held that the elaborate structure of Jewish law, *halakhah*, as erected by centuries of rabbis, was outdated and out of place in the free, emancipated environment of America. They were not in *galut* (exile) any more and saw in the new country their home, and they did not cherish the ideal of returning to a restored ancient homeland. Instead, reflective rabbis and laymen felt proud that they had successfully transplanted Judaism across the ocean to America.

From early Reform days, there had been a recurrent desire to state its credo. Rabbis traveled long distances on slow, rattling trains in order to meet and formulate declarations of Reform Judaism's principles. Although none of the platforms that were adopted claimed to be binding or authoritative, they received attention and exerted influence. The conference of Reform rabbis at Pittsburgh, 1885, led by the learned Kaufman Kohler (1843–1926), who had come from Germany in 1869, was the most influential of all. Its declaration of eight principles, known thereafter as the Pittsburgh Platform,[2] was more radical than the accepted Reform doctrines of their day, but the platform soon became the accepted standpoint of the movement. It viewed Judaism and the Bible as the highest expression of the "God-idea," and it recognized the Jews as the "priest people" charged with the mission of furthering this idea. Contrary to the national messianism of Jewish tradition, the platform optimistically foresaw the coming "universal culture of heart and intellect" as the true expression of Reform's universalist messianism. The Pittsburgh Platform declared the Jews "no longer a nation but a religious community," and it expressly rejected the return to Palestine and the restoration of the Temple and its priestly rites. It dismissed halakhah except for its moral content, while declaring that Reform intended to participate in solving the social problems of the age. The last point was an early statement of what became the social justice movement, a twentieth-century concern of Reform Judaism that it shared with liberal Protestantism.

The Pittsburgh Platform remained the accepted credo of Reform Judaism for half a century. There were some prominent dissenters, especially when the issue of Zionism arose, and at the other extreme a few Reform rabbis virtually left Judaism in order to join nontheistic religious movements. The mid-1880s, the period when the Pittsburgh Platform was promulgated, witnessed the sharpening of the cleavage between Reform and traditional Judaism. Hebrew Union College, the first American institution for training rabbis, became decidedly Reform. This was symbolized by the banquet at its first commencement exercises in 1883, at which the first course was nonkosher shellfish. Several invited traditional rabbis and laymen stalked out. An impressive series of addresses disputing Reform, known as *The Ethics of the Fathers*, was delivered in 1885 by the recently arrived scholar Rabbi Alexander Kohut (1842–94), and it was soon answered vigorously by Kohler's *Backwards or Forwards?* series. Both series of addresses were delivered in New York synagogues. Also in New York, a rabbinical school, The Jewish Theological Seminary, was founded in 1886. It was committed to upholding the sanctity and obligation of the Talmud and the oral law that Reform discarded.[3] From these years of controversy and counterorganizations, it was clear that the original conception of the founder and patriarch of Reform Judaism, Isaac Mayer Wise (1819–1900), which was that moderate Reform Judaism would be American Judaism as a whole, faded away.

Reform Judaism from the 1880s entered a period called Classical Reform, characterized by its remoteness from Jewish tradition. Classical Reform was defined by the tenets of the Pittsburgh Platform and by the mainly English liturgy of the semiofficial *Union Prayer Book*. It often called itself Prophetic Judaism, after the teachings of the Biblical prophets as Classical Reformers understood them. By 1900 and thereafter, Reform was composed largely of a bourgeois constituency of bankers, merchants, lawyers, and manufacturers, most of them the children and grandchildren of German immigrants, besides a stratum of later middle-class immigrants from Germany. German language and culture within Reform were in decline, with German Jewish theology and philosophy almost gone. Nevertheless, the two most influential contemporary leaders of Reform, Kohler and Emil G. Hirsch (1852–1923), his brother-in-law, had deep Germanic roots.

Meanwhile, the traditionalists and Orthodox gathered strength from a different source, the mass of immigrants from Eastern Europe who began to pour into the United States in 1881. There had been small-scale immigration from the empire of the tsars before 1881. However, the dozens of large and small pogroms in 1881 and 1882, ending only in 1883, and the added oppression of the "temporary" May Laws decreed by the new tsar Alexander III (1881–94) in 1882, inspired a great wave of emigration westward from Russia. It continued until the outbreak of war in 1914 and resumed after the war until the passage of the highly restrictive Johnson Act in 1924. During the five peak years of immigration from 1904 through 1908, at least 642,000 Jews entered the country. Jewish migration on this scale had never been seen. The Jews of Galicia, as part of the Hapsburg realm, had been emancipated in 1867, so the motive for their mass emigration was almost wholly economic. Like most immigrants, the Russian Jews came for a simple reason – to leave hunger and the oppressive regime and to realize the American promise of abundance and personal freedom. Legends about America, such as the streets paved with gold or golden apples growing on trees, demonstrated the hopes of immigrants. They could hardly have believed such stories, but many did know of men who had arrived penniless in America and achieved material comfort. Stories like those inspired newcomers to have faith in their own chances. Many also sought to practice Judaism unhindered, or, in contrast, to escape family and communal pressures that demanded Orthodox religious conformity. The enormous extent of the emigration, which was inspired by poverty and oppression, including pogroms, was made possible by the new awareness that oppression was not inevitable, to be endured. Jews could escape tsarist abuse by sailing in frequently scheduled though uncomfortable steamships and entering about ten days later almost without restriction into the land of freedom and abundance. The medical inspection that was required at the port of arrival (usually Ellis Island in New York harbor and also Boston and Philadelphia) for admittance to America was anxiously expected, but the fact remains that 98 to 99 percent of arriving Jews were admitted. Some two and a half million Russian, as well as Galician, Hungarian, and Romanian Jews, arrived until the gates of America[4] were almost shut by the Johnson immigration act of 1924; fewer than 8 percent returned to Europe. The realities of the life to be encountered in the new country had been embellished in Europe with legends that were obvious fictions, but underlying such tales there was the basic truth that the abundance of the land was accessible to immigrants. The promise of America also meant hard work and disappointments, and many immigrants barely made a living, lived poorly, and never partook of abundance. Letters back to the old country from relatives and fellow townsmen who had gone to America drew the picture.

Mass immigration had a revolutionary effect on American Judaism. The new immigrants had a much different background than their German predecessors. Like the Germans, the East Europeans came mainly from small cities and villages, but they had lived in an almost exclusively Jewish environment. On one hand, intense religious piety and concentration on Talmud study characterized East European Judaism, and a small measure of this was transplanted to America. On the other hand, the sects of Hasidic Judaism, each led by a *rebbe* or *zaddik*, did not establish themselves before the First World War. However, East European Judaism had burst the bounds of its Orthodox heritage by the time of its mass migration. Religious life remained Orthodox, but other intellectual streams also reached American shores. Yiddish was the immigrants' language, but an increasing number of individuals came with some Russian education and had come under the influence of Russian literature and social thought. Socialism and anarchism emerged in America from the Russian underground, and so did the idealization of agrarian life. Haskalah enlightenment and Hebraism had representatives, and the new Yiddish theatre, literature, and press found American soil fertile for their development. Out of these movements emerged the Jewish labor movement and Zionism.

Yet it was religious tradition, whether obeyed or rejected in whole or in part, that was the central Jewish experience of the immigrant generation. In America, the cherished beliefs and meticulous observances of Orthodox Judaism were confronted by urban, industrial society with its secular, pragmatic emphasis. Workers and small businessmen, as well as immigrant children in public schools, were drawn in this direction. In the ready-made garment trades, workers often abandoned religious observance as a result of the stern demands of the job and the Jewish labor movement's competing secular message of trade union solidarity and revolution to come. There were ambitious young women, who had been traditionally relegated in Judaism to the role of housewife and mother, who found a sense of personal liberation by participation in the Jewish labor and radical movements.

Fidelity to religious commandments had many shadings. The nature of the subject and the absence of statistical data make it nearly impossible to provide numerical data, but one can surmise that a large minority, perhaps 15 to 20 percent, adhered to Orthodox Judaism in full. At the other end of the spectrum, a smaller minority, perhaps 10 percent, rejected the beliefs and practices of Judaism entirely, for example never attending synagogue or fasting on Yom Kippur or eating only kosher foods. Only a very small number participated in occasional antireligious demonstrations. In contrast, conversion to Christianity was hardly known, despite the exertions of missionaries within immigrant Jewish neighborhoods. The great majority of Jewish immigrants found their place between these extremes. Thus, immigrant synagogues were not much frequented all year but full to overflowing on the High Holidays. The immigrants might not be meticulous about the food they ate, especially away from home, but on Passover they ate only matzah, not bread.

Pious immigrants soon realized the difficulties in maintaining religious ways. They had been warned by rabbis in Eastern Europe that America was no place for sincerely religious Jews, many of whom, it was reported, had gone astray there and violated basic religious laws. From a different perspective, Jewish community leaders in America repeated the warning against immigration and so did Zionists and revolutionary activists in Russia. Undoubtedly there were Jews who heeded these warnings, but more than 2 million, as we have seen, boarded emigrant ships anyhow. Among them were several hundred rabbis, who emigrated despite warnings from their colleagues. Rabbis were subject to the same pressures as ordinary Jews, and many saw their small-town communities dwindling away as a result of emigration to large cities such as Warsaw and Odessa, and especially overseas. The rabbis believed they could find positions and religiously influence the new immigrant congregations that were springing up throughout the United States. Many did find positions, but for all but a few their lot was not a happy one in the face of communal indiscipline and widespread religious impiety.[5]

Immigrant congregations in the largest cities were established as *landslayt* (home town) organizations, called *landsmanshaft*. Immigrants from the same town founded congregations composed of fellow-townsmen, at least at their beginning. Men from other towns also joined and sometimes became the majority. Women played no role, seldom attending except on High Holidays and preparing food and drink for the men's religious feasts. In New York City there were about 500 immigrant congregations at their peak around 1915. Often quartered in mean small premises, *landslayt* congregations sought to reproduce the worship they remembered from their hometown. Aside from the Hebrew of prayers, their language was Yiddish. Some of these congregations had a rabbi, but more often they could not afford the expense. All provided funerals and cemetery plots for members and their families. In smaller cities where the number of immigrants was limited, their congregations were usually based on an East European region, such as Lithuania or Galicia. These immigrant congregations seldom outlasted the immigrant generation. Their children, even those religiously observant, usually found the services and atmosphere unappealing and did not want to worship there. In any case, when young people married they usually quit the immigrant neighborhood and its congregations.

Two ancient functions of the synagogue passed into other hands. The immigrant synagogues still dispensed charity but in a small way, besides benevolent aid to members in distress. The larger demands were taken over by well-financed charitable institutions run by native Jews. Pious Jews lamented that America, the land of the dollar, was no place to practice the religious value of Torah study. Torah learning was limited to Talmud study sessions in synagogues, usually attended by a few older people who no longer worked. For children, general education of course belonged to the public school that virtually all Jewish children attended. Jewish education had to take place after school hours, and it was usually carried on in schools sponsored by private societies. Some of them were excellent, with modern teaching methods and learned pedagogues who inculcated the new, modern Hebrew. The old-time *heder* continued to exist and sometimes was held on the synagogue premises. Day schools, which combined Hebrew and general studies, lay in the future – after 1920 approximately. Coming from the poor masses in Eastern Europe, the majority of immigrants showed little interest in pursuing

Talmudic study, which led to no practical goal; it was for practical goals they had come to America. Nevertheless, in 1886 an advanced yeshiva, Etz Chaim, was established in New York. It was small and poor and subsisted on a shoestring for many years. In 1896 it merged with a new, still smaller school to establish Yeshivath Rabbenu Yizhak Elhanan, named after the recently deceased Rabbi Spektor mentioned in the paragraphs that follow. In 1913 it established a high school, the Talmudical Academy, and began the development that culminated as Yeshiva University.[6]

Immigrant congregations maintained a chummy but indecorous and bickering atmosphere. On one hand, congregational and *landsmanshaft* meetings, when held, served as an introduction to American democratic practices, but they were noisy and uncontrolled. Secessions were common. On the other hand, attempts were made to bring order to the Orthodox religious world. Bearing in mind European precedents, they usually proposed a local chief rabbi who would exercise religious authority over all cooperating congregations. The chief rabbi would also supervise animal slaughter (*shehitah*) and certify meat as kosher, and he would draw his salary mainly from the fees attached – a constant source of dispute and bitterness in the unregulated American market. Depending on his personal qualities, the immigrant chief rabbi would be a preacher and Talmud lecturer and a religious and moral unifier and conciliator. The first chief rabbi, Rabbi Jacob Joseph (1840–1902), an eminent religious scholar brought from Vilna to New York in 1887, possessed these qualities. Nevertheless, the kosher meat entrepreneurs as well as rival rabbis refused to accept his authority, and the entire project collapsed, ending in personal tragedy for the rabbi. Rabbi Bernard L. (Dov Aryeh) Levinthal (1865–1951), in contrast, was able to rule the Orthodox scene in Philadelphia for half a century. Rabbi Moses Simon Sivitz (1855–1936) of Pittsburgh overcame occasional rabbinical opponents and was recognized as the foremost rabbi in his city for many years. These rabbis were considerable scholars of the traditional type, and there were others among the thirty or so local chief rabbis, not to mention other East European rabbis, who did not hold such a position. Most of them came from Lithuania and had studied at its yeshivot. Quite a few had been fellows of the *kollel* of married young rabbis headed by the influential Rabbi Spektor of Kovno. A large number produced works of rabbinic learning in addition to editing collections of their sermons (*derashot*), delivered to audiences that preferred them to learned discourses on the Talmud and halakhah. In Eastern Europe, rabbis delivered sermons on a few special occasions, but in America they were expected to do so often, even weekly. The institution of chief rabbi (*rav ha-kollel*) in the United States went through many changes; in some cities, but not the largest ones, it continues to the present day. It was and remains

Orthodox. The immigrant, European-trained rabbis organized themselves in the Union of Orthodox Rabbis (*Agudath Ha-rabbanim*) in 1903.

The prime attraction of an Orthodox synagogue was not its rabbi, if any, but the cantor (*hazan*). Many had fine and sometimes brilliant voices and were sought out, especially for the High Holidays, by congregations who could afford their fee. Their lyric, emotional style thrilled and could inspire waves of fervent devotion in congregations. In the age before radio, when phonograph records were few and expensive, cantorial song also provided a form of musical entertainment. The average little *landslayt* synagogue could not afford a star cantor and utilized its own members, but "uptown" Orthodox synagogues engaged them and proudly announced their appearance. Many cantors were no more pious than appearances required, but the most famous among them, Josef (Yossele) Rosenblatt (1882–1933), was also admired for his strict Orthodoxy.

The immigrant congregations reached their peak around 1915 and then entered a long decline. Masses of immigrants, especially the next generation, moved away from the "neighborhood of first settlement," as sociologists have termed it, leaving its synagogues high and dry. Some of the people, however, succeeded in moving to the more agreeable "neighborhood of second settlement," where several might merge to build often attractive or pretentious synagogues. Within these neighborhood synagogues the uneasy transition began from Yiddish to at least partial use of English. These so-called second settlement synagogues believed it essential to employ rabbinical orators who could preach in English as well as Yiddish, besides fulfilling the traditional functions of halakhic authorities and teachers of Talmud. The synagogues' European-bred members bowed reluctantly to the necessities of American life, but they demanded that at least some sermons be in Yiddish. The synagogues employed a hazan; how illustrious he was depended on the congregation's inclinations and budget. A few maintained an after-school Talmud Torah on their premises, but most preferred to support a community Talmud Torah. The mortgages that many congregations undertook during the prosperous 1920s became an almost unmanageable burden during the depression of the 1930s.

As these congregations grew and changed, the ways of their members, the immigrants' next generation, also changed. During the 1920s, Hasidic Judaism established itself with the arrival of rebbes, especially from the pogrom-stricken Ukraine. For support in early years, the rebbes drew largely on the European memories of older immigrants. However, the impress of East European Judaism as a whole lessened. The new generation, going to American schools and taking part in American life, wanted the English language to replace Yiddish in the synagogue and generally in Jewish life. Religious observance weakened, and the Sabbath was not fully observed, sometimes even by men who were synagogue officers. A recurrent theme in contemporary rabbis' published sermons was the harmony between Judaism and American life and ideals, but the same sermons bitterly deplored American materialism and the tireless pursuit of the dollar. The Orthodox synagogue had new functions in America that were far more central than they had been in Europe. Memorial prayers (*yizkor*) four times annually during worship, eleven months of daily *kaddish* for deceased near relatives, and *bar mitzvah* for boys aged thirteen assumed a new importance. These, like many of the sermonic themes, responded to the new American reality. Yizkor, kaddish, and bar mitzvah (a *bat mitzvah* for girls was unheard of) symbolized, in contrast, the desire to overcome the break with previous generations that took place with immigration to America, and to be assured that the rising generation would stay within the fold. In their preaching, Orthodox rabbis pleaded to maintain the Judaism of their pious ancestors, whose hardships and sacrifices for religion and family were fervently extolled. The role of women in Orthodox synagogue life increased, although they took no part in conducting worship. Now there was a ladies' auxiliary or sisterhood, which aided the congregation by raising money, arranging social functions, and hearing occasional lectures on Jewish subjects.

Families who had recently attained American middle-class status often sought a modernized form of Judaism that, unlike Reform, would also retain much of the flavor and content of Jewish tradition. Orthodox synagogues in second settlement neighborhoods thus came into competition with Conservative synagogues nearby that presented their religion in a manner palatable to seekers after traditional yet modern Judaism. Conservative synagogues belonged to the movement based at the Jewish Theological Seminary in uptown New York City.[7] It had been reestablished in 1902 after several years of dormancy. The Seminary's sponsors, who included rich and prominent men, had brought the outstanding scholar and religious leader Solomon Schechter (1847–1915), by origin an East European Jew, from England to head it. Many of the sponsors were Reform Jews, who recognized that their Judaism was too distant from the familiar ways of Judaism to attract East European immigrants and their children. The renewed Jewish Theological Seminary began its career well supported. A large new building was erected near Columbia University, good salaries were provided for Schechter and the gifted young faculty he appointed, and a world-class Jewish library began to take shape. However, there were differences of emphasis over the Seminary's objectives. Its wealthy patrons desired the institution above all to produce modern rabbis and to be an "Americanizing" influence on immigrant Jews.

Schechter, whose dynamic direction of the institution was unchallenged even when he endorsed Zionism, scornfully rejected the object of "civiliz[ing] the downtown barbarians," as he put it in his characteristic sharp, epigrammatic style. Nevertheless, the Seminary did educate rabbis and serve the downtown Jews with modern Hebrew educators it trained. Schechter supported these purposes, but his conception of the Seminary was of a major institution of Jewish learning, one that he succeeded in building. A younger member of the Seminary faculty, Mordecai M. Kaplan (1881–1983), formulated a theology during the 1920s that he called Reconstructionism.[8] It defined Judaism as a "religious civilization," and its radical revision of basic religious principles, accompanied by Zionism and fidelity to many traditional ways, stirred controversy for decades. The Seminary faculty and student body remained religiously observant in the traditional sense as well as pro-Zionist.

The most significant institutional development in Orthodoxy was yeshivot. A small number of Americans went to study at European yeshivot, while two new yeshivot were founded in America, one in Chicago in a modern spirit and a more fundamentalist school in Brooklyn. A third yeshiva existed in Cleveland that moved to New Haven for several years. The development of Yeshivath Rabbi Isaac Elhanan, however, was without precedent. While continuing as a traditional yeshiva with its attached preparatory high school to include secular studies, under the direction of Rabbi Bernard Revel (1885–1940), a modern as well as a traditional rabbinic scholar, it undertook the controversial step of establishing the degree-granting Yeshiva College in 1928, housed in a large new building in uptown Manhattan. To many Orthodox people, a college combined with a yeshiva was an illegitimate mixing of the sacred and profane. Others attacked Yeshiva College as "a ghetto college," not giving its students a true liberal education. Decades of financial stringency passed before Yeshiva College gained academic respectability and financial stability. The immigrant European rabbis were denied the role that they sought for themselves in the training and ordination of these rabbis. They looked down on rabbis trained in America and would not admit them into their Union of Orthodox Rabbis. One outcome of their rejection was the establishment by "American" rabbis of their own Rabbinical Council of America.

At the other end of the Judaic spectrum, Reform Judaism in the early twentieth century was in its most "classical" period. By 1914 the large majority of Reform rabbis were graduates of Hebrew Union College, where so-called classical Reform was the prevailing doctrine under Kaufman Kohler's presidency. Reform services were almost all in English and held once weekly, and they were conducted by the rabbi who preached and prayed, with his congregation as a quite passive audience. Some congregations also held short

Sunday services featuring a sermon or lecture, but Sunday worship was a controversial issue within Reform. Social justice, as it was called, became a major concern of the movement, deriving its rationale from the words of the prophets and its agenda mainly from contemporary American liberalism. Reform's social justice was concerned mainly with the rights of labor, and in world affairs with endorsing pacifism before the Second World War. Some Reform rabbis took an active role in union labor struggles. Not the denomination as such but members within it directed Jewish charities. Reform Judaism with its message attempted to reach the Jewish immigrant masses through institutions of social service; the synagogues it sponsored in immigrant neighborhoods had little success. Significant for future developments, however, some East Europeans joined Reform congregations, and sons of immigrants studied to be Reform rabbis. Within Reform Judaism, the establishment of an authoritative "synod" to settle matters of principle and practice was deliberated at length for several years after 1900 but not acted on. To immigrant rabbis, Reform Judaism was anathema, a perversion of Judaism. In Reform Judaism's flourishing they saw the dangers that life in free America embodied.

Hebrew Union College moved in 1910 to a spacious new campus, in suburban (as it was then) Cincinnati. Despite its material prosperity and intellectual power, the movement felt malaise over its relative decline from the dominant position it had held in American Judaism in 1880 and thereafter, to its status by approximately 1905 as a well-off denomination isolated from the Jewish masses. Several Reform rabbis, notably Stephen S. Wise (1874–1949) and Judah L. Magnes (1877–1948) became important figures through activity in the larger Jewish community and the Zionist movement, with only slight attention to their Reform affiliation, while Abba Hillel Silver (1893–1963) did likewise but was also active within Reform Judaism. Reform laymen such as Louis Marshall and Jacob H. Schiff became major leaders of American Jewry, but their Reform connection played only a minor role in their Jewish activities. Reform Judaism lessened its emphatic anti-Zionism, especially after the Balfour Declaration, and the movement took up the cause of Palestine but without subscribing to Zionist ideology. Wise and Silver became famous Zionist leaders, and there were some Reform rabbis who did endorse Zionist ideology.

Inspired mainly by the vision of Jewish peoplehood, modern Hebraism, and Zionism, Stephen S. Wise founded the Jewish Institute of Religion in 1924 as a "nondenominational," but generally Reform, rabbinical school. The new school existed in clear opposition to Hebrew Union College. It possessed the advantage of location in New York City, the center of American Jewish life with its Jewish population of almost 2 million, while the senior school was rather isolated in provincial Cincinnati. Wise recruited a distinguished faculty who taught a talented student body. The Jewish Institute of Religion depended heavily on Wise's personal ability to raise its funds, and in 1948 its aging, ailing founder reluctantly merged his school in New York with Hebrew Union College in Cincinnati. By that time, the long-standing differences between the two institutions were blurred. The new Reform emphasis on Jewish peoplehood had reached official expression in its Columbus Platform of 1937, which essentially replaced the Pittsburgh Platform of 1885.[9] It spoke of the Jewish people as the source of Judaism, and declared it the "obligation" of all Jews to aid in the development of Palestine. Nevertheless, the currents of thought within Reform that emphasized Jewish peoplehood over a purely religious conception of Judaism were strongly resisted, and a powerful segment of rabbis and laymen remained unswervingly anti-Zionist. The clash between them and Zionists within Reform Judaism sharpened from the late 1930s onward.

The American Jewish religious scene during the 1930s was a cheerless one. The Great Depression, lasting until 1941, had a shattering effect on many Jewish institutions.[10] Unable to pay synagogue dues, thousands of members dropped out. Even after salaries were cut, many religious and educational institutions could not meet their payrolls. Hardly any new building was undertaken during the hard times. There were then about 3,700 synagogues, the majority of which were small Orthodox congregations remaining from immigrant days. One would estimate that only one third were sizeable, stable congregations.

The gathering world Jewish crisis of that decade drew American Jewish funds and energies into defensive efforts, relief for German Jewry under Nazi rule, and for threatened Jews in other European countries. These pressing responsibilities caused Jewish religious life to lose priority. The second generation of East European immigrants, then in its prime, did not provide a strong lay leadership for Orthodox Judaism. Hope came during the 1930s when important Orthodox rabbis arrived from abroad and others trained in America came to the forefront of Orthodox life, but its future nevertheless looked bleak. Immigrant Orthodox Jews were mostly unable to retain their children within that fold, and many yeshiva students also went over to Conservative Judaism. The attraction of Conservative Judaism lay in its modern scholarship and flexible, historical approach to religious life and practice. Young men who were candidates for the rabbinate realized that positions as rabbis of Conservative congregations were available and usually well paid, in contrast to the generally meager position of Orthodox rabbis. Many Orthodox rabbis served Conservative congregations while remaining

Orthodox in their personal lives. In general, most Conservative rabbis had been yeshiva students in their early years. The lines between Orthodoxy and Conservatism as a rule were blurred. Conservative Judaism had hardly any youth cohort, and it depended on the Orthodox world for its replenishment. Clear separation between the two denominations resulted from an Orthodox initiative that came in the 1950s.

Reform, burdened with its own issues, unlike the Orthodox was well established institutionally and not too harmed financially by the Depression. As already mentioned, it began a dynamic period of reorientation. The trend was toward a revival of traditional religious ways, but it was still slight. Long, strenuous effort was invested in hammering out their new platform of principles; the still-weak Conservatives, in contrast, debated the need or propriety of any platform at all for their movement. Some leading Conservative rabbis and the influential faculty of the Jewish Theological Seminary insisted that theirs was not a distinct denomination of Judaism but the heir of Jewish tradition as a whole. The movement would introduce the religious changes required by the needs of the time, as had been done in the past in accordance with traditional, accepted methods of interpreting halakhah. Nevertheless, the Conservative movement as such avoided actually introducing such changes. Faced with strong Orthodox objections, the individuals of the movement backed down from their proposal to solve the Agunah problem by halakhic measures. It was individual congregations led by their rabbis who sometimes took the initiative for change, usually in shaping their own liturgy and worship.

The refugee problem of the 1930s affected American Judaism only marginally. A stream of approximately 150,000 German and Austrian refugees overcame the stringent immigration laws and reached the United States during the 1930s, before World War II broke out in 1939. Mainly middle-class businessmen and professionals, these people underwent much difficulty in establishing themselves in America during the depression. Many refugees founded their own congregations in the German language, preserving the religious customs of their native land. Unique among the German congregations was Adath Jeshurun of Washington Heights in upper Manhattan, a transplantation of the separatist, rigorous Orthodoxy of Frankfurt-am-Main. Led in an almost sovereign manner by Rabbi Joseph Breuer (1882–1978), it was not only a congregation but also a community (*kehillah*) with all the necessary communal facilities. In Washington Heights and elsewhere in New York City, most of the German congregations were Orthodox, yet many German Jewish refugees, especially those who were Reform (Liberal in Germany), joined existing congregations.[11] The German refugees included notable rabbis and Jewish scholars, in addition to the scientists and scholars who included some of world renown. Some of the German Jewish intellectual heritage was of a previously unknown level of sophistication. There was a chasm between the writings in religious philosophy of such men as Martin Buber and Franz Rosenzweig and the halakhic directness of the rabbinic leaders of Orthodox Judaism in the United States. The newly arrived Orthodox rabbis during these prewar years included Joseph B. Soloveichik (1903–93), Moses Feinstein (1895–1985) and Joseph Isaac Schneersohn (1880–1955), the Hasidic rabbi of Lubavich, who arrived shortly after the war began.

In the two years between the onset of World War II in September 1939 and the entry of the United States into the war in December 1941, ever more horrifying accounts were received of Jewish suffering and death under Nazi domination. American Jews knew from the record of Nazi deeds in Germany that had climaxed in the vast "Crystal Night" pogrom of November 1938 that these accounts were not fictitious or exaggerated. They influenced Jewish attitudes to the national debate over isolation or intervention in Europe, although American Jews sought to stay on the sidelines for fear of being labeled warmongers and making the conflict appear a "Jewish war."

But the war came, and American Jews immediately expressed total commitment to the war effort. American Jewish soldiers numbered half a million (550,000) altogether, 10,500 of whom fell in the line of duty and 24,000 of whom were wounded. The American Jewish community did whatever it could do to aid its sons in uniform. The services of the Jewish Welfare Board, the prime organization for Jewish soldiers' special needs, provided kosher food packages and local hospitality near army camps. There were 310 Jewish chaplains, ordained rabbis of all denominations who were often young men recently graduated from rabbinical schools. Chaplains ministered to soldiers of all religions, but like the chaplains of other religions, Jewish chaplains first served mainly their own people. They not only conducted religious services but also aided Jewish soldiers in personal matters. As the Allied armies liberated western Europe and conquered Germany in 1944 and 1945, the Jewish chaplains played a valuable role in rebuilding the lives of the survivors of hiding and of Nazi concentration camps.

While the war was waged, significant issues in Jewish religious life were argued in a lower key. American Jews knew that the Holocaust (a later term) was consuming millions of Jews, but they felt impotent to do more than protest and ask, not too forcefully, for intercession and rescue from high government officials.[12] Within Reform Judaism, the issue of Zionism reached an explosive level when the Reform rabbis' Central Conference of American Rabbis endorsed the Zionist demand for a Jewish army in Palestine in 1942. A sizeable, embattled minority, invoking the memory of Reform's pioneers who rejected any idea of Jewish national restoration, in that year established the American Council for Judaism. Vehemently criticized, it soon had a significant contingent of rabbis and several thousand members who carried on its strongly anti-Zionist propaganda. The Jewish Theological Seminary of the Conservatives broadened its scope considerably during the war years under the new presidency of Rabbi Louis Finkelstein (1895–1991). Ambitious to couch the Seminary's religious message in terms not only of Biblical but also rabbinic Judaism, he established the Institute of Religious and Social Studies as an interreligious, intellectual center for considering the worldwide moral crisis of the day. It recruited an impressive roster of intellectuals and philosophers as participants and issued a string of publications. At the popular level, the "Eternal Light" began in 1944 as a successful dramatic series on the radio that conveyed a spiritual message. Finkelstein, on one hand, renewed the Seminary's aging faculty with several important appointments. On the other hand, he declined to involve his institution in rescue activity even of scholars and rabbis, declaring that its purpose was solely to study Torah, and by rescuing the study of Torah from Nazi clutches the Seminary was fulfilling its true mission. Finkelstein also steered the Seminary, with its strongly pro-Zionist faculty and student body, away from identification with the Zionist program. Conservative congregations and their rabbis, however, were all but unanimously Zionist.

Orthodox Judaism began to profit from its recently arrived intellectual forces. The teaching of Rabbi Soloveichik, philosophically trained and a brilliant Talmudist, inspired students at Yeshivath Rabbi Isaac Elhanan. He became the rabbinic mentor of American modernist Orthodoxy, which was engaged in self-definition and ending its overlapping closeness with Conservative Judaism. Rabbinical students, exempt from conscription as divinity students, became more numerous, especially among the ultra-Orthodox, as new yeshivot were established. At his recently founded yeshiva in Lakewood, New Jersey, the eloquent Rabbi Aaron Kotler, who arrived as a refugee during the war in 1943, became the leading advocate of yeshiva study as a career to the exclusion of secular studies. Rabbi Feinstein was gradually recognized as the foremost decisor (*posek*) of halakhic problems for Orthodox Jewry in and beyond America. Rabbi Schneerson led his Hasidic movement, *Habad* in its Hebrew acronym, in an unprecedented campaign to draw back to religious life those Jews who had left it or who were new to it.

Orthodox Jewry, particularly its extreme wing, labored at Holocaust rescue. Its Vaad Ha-Hatzoloh undertook with some success to save several thousand teachers and students of Lithuanian yeshivot with their families.[13] From 1944 the Vaad also sought to rescue Hungarian Jews. Reform and Conservative Jews did nothing comparable, since they contributed to the rescue efforts of the Joint Distribution Committee. When World War II ended with an overwhelming Allied victory but a catastrophic Jewish defeat, American Judaism realized that its prime efforts for years to come would have to be invested overseas. With religious fervor, it labored to rehabilitate the survivors of Nazi bestiality and to support Eretz Israel Jewry in the struggle to establish the state of Israel. Meanwhile the postwar hopes and needs of American Judaism patiently waited.

Notes

1. Many local Jewish community histories describe the condition of communities at this time. On Reform Judaism, the leading work is Michael A. Meyer, *Response to Modernity: A History of the Reform Movement in Judaism* (New York and Oxford: Oxford University Press, 1988).

2. The text of the Pittsburgh Platform with excerpts from debates on its text is given in W. Gunther Plaut, *The Growth of Reform Judaism* (New York: World Union for Progressive Judaism, 1965), 31–42. Sources on Reform thought are in Joseph L. Blau, ed., *Reform Judaism: A Historical Perspective* (New York: KTAV Publishing House, 1973).

3. Moshe Davis, *The Emergence of Conservative Judaism: The Historical School in 19th Century America* (Philadelphia: The Jewish Publication Society, 1963), gives the early history of the Seminary and Conservative Judaism.

4. On the great Jewish migration see Simon Kuznets, "Immigration of Russian Jews to the United States: Background and Structure," in *Perspectives in American History* 9 (Cambridge: Harvard University Press, 1975), 35–126; Irving Howe, *World of Our Fathers* (New York: Simon & Schuster, 1976); Lloyd P. Gartner, "Jewish Migrants en Route from Europe to North America: Traditions and Realities," *Jewish History* 1, 2 (Fall 1986), 49–66.

5. On religious observance among East European immigrants, see Irving Howe, *World of Our Fathers* (New York: Simon & Schuster, 1976), 190–200; Arthur Goren, *New York Jews and the Quest for Community: The Kehillah Experiment, 1908–1922* (New York: Columbia University Press, 1970), 76–85; and local histories such as Lloyd P. Gartner, *History of the Jews in Cleveland* (Cleveland: Western Reserve Historical Society, 1978), 162–85.

6. Jeffrey S. Gurock, *The Men and Women of Yeshiva: Higher Education, Orthodoxy, and American Judaism* (New York: Columbia University Press, 1988).

7. Marshall Sklare, *Conservative Judaism: An American Religious Movement*, new ed. (Lanham: University Press of America, 1985). A massive, lively history is Jack Wertheimer, ed., *Tradition Renewed: A History of the Jewish Theological Seminary*, 2 vols. (New York: Jewish Theological Seminary of America, 1997).

8. Mordecai M. Kaplan's philosophy is set forth in his *Judaism as a Civilization* (New York: The Reconstructionist Press, 1934).

9. The text is in W. Gunther Plaut, *The Growth of Reform Judaism* (New York: World Union for Progressive Judaism, 1965), 96–100.

10. Lloyd P. Gartner, "The Midpassage of American Jewry," in *The American Jewish Experience*, ed. Jonathan D. Sarna (New York: Holmes & Meier, 1986), 224–33.

11. Steven M. Lowenstein, *Frankfurt on the Hudson: The German-Jewish Community of Washington Heights, 1933–1983* (Detroit: Wayne State University Press, 1989).

12. This is a subject of bitter contention to the present day. See Henry L. Feingold, *The Politics of Rescue: The Roosevelt Administration and the Holocaust 1939–1945* (New Brunswick: Rutgers University Press, 1970).

13. Efraim Zuroff, *The Response of Orthodox Jewry in the United States to the Holocaust: The Activities of the Vaad ha-Hatzalah Rescue Committee 1939–1945* (New York: KTAV Publishing, House, 2000).

3 Trends in American Judaism from 1945 to the present

DANA EVAN KAPLAN

When the Second World War ended, the American Jewish community became aware that it had unprecedented responsibilities as the largest and most important Jewish community in the world. The Holocaust had not yet become a public concern, but it nevertheless had a sobering effect on American Jewry, who played an important role in assisting Holocaust survivors in Europe. During this time, American Jews provided economic as well as political support for the establishment of a Jewish state. Nevertheless, many American Jews understood that they needed to retain a religious as well as an ethnic identity. Although there was a renewed consciousness of their obligations, only a minority of American Jews had a clear conception of what religious beliefs they adhered to or had a consistent approach to ritual practice. Arthur A. Goren contends, "American Jews intuitively sensed that the functional consensus based on supporting Israel and defending a liberal America was not sufficient. What was needed was a doctrinal and ideological core that, while identifying the group, would also justify the operative elements of the consensus."[1] That doctrinal core would be supplied by the preservation and evolution of the Jewish religion in America.[2]

INCREASING SOCIAL ACCEPTANCE

In 1945, the United States was, in Will Herberg's words, a "three-religion country" consisting of Protestants, Catholics, and Jews. Religion rather than ethnicity was the primary distinction between Americans. "The newcomer is expected to change many things about him as he becomes an American – nationality, language, culture. One thing, however, he is not expected to change – and that is his religion. And so it is religion that . . . has become the differentiating element and the context of self-identification and social location."[3] Protestants, Catholics, and Jews all adhered to the "American way of life," which held to the values of political democracy, economic free enterprise, and social egalitarianism. These three religious groups all believed in and worked toward promoting the American way of life. Jews in particular,

embraced the post-World War II emphasis on goodwill, brotherhood, pluralism, and tolerance. What could be interpreted as a heretical indifference to
the core beliefs of one's religion was actually a pluralistic affirmation of the
common "Judeo–Christian heritage."

During the Eisenhower years, the American civil religion endorsed religious identification as an element of good citizenship. Thus, Americans stood
for democracy against the state-sponsored atheism that existed in the totalitarian communism of the Soviet Union. This atheism was one of the many
evils that had to be refuted, and thus it reinforced the importance of American
religiosity. President Dwight Eisenhower emphasized that "our government
makes no sense unless it is founded in a deeply felt religious faith –
and I don't care what it is." Religion was a "good thing" for the individual
American, the family, the local community, and the country as a whole. And
yet the decade was, in Robert S. Ellwood's words, "full of spiritual strife."[4]
On a daily basis, the adaptation to new lifestyles in new neighborhoods was
stressful for many American families. On a much grander scale, the threat
of nuclear annihilation was troubling to Americans. People of faith needed
to balance freedom with conformity in an effort to redefine their role in
American society. Many rabbis, such as Reform Rabbi Joshua Loth Liebman,
argued that Judaism could help Americans understand how to cope with this
dilemma. In his 1946 bestseller, *Peace of Mind*, Liebman suggested that religion could provide the tranquility to restore health, security, and prosperity
for Americans still recovering from the atrocities of World War II and only
beginning to adjust to the realities of the Cold War.

Even following the Allied victory over the Germans during World War II,
American Jews still perceived the world to be a hostile and frightening place
for them. Although the Holocaust was not discussed very often in the immediate postwar years, all Americans knew of Hitler's murder of 6 million
Jews; this shocking crime made any public expression of anti-Semitism dis-
reputable. Even as they reveled in the accomplishments of many of their coreligionists, American Jews remained suspicious, worrying about what their
neighbors thought of them – and justifiably so. Many corporations had a "No
Jews" policy firmly in place, and even many "Jewish fields" tried to ensure
that Jews hired would not carry identifiably ethnic names. American Jews
therefore placed much of their energies into the fight against anti-Semitism
both domestically and worldwide.

As it became more evident that it was no longer fashionable to overtly
express anti-Semitic views, American Jews began to feel an unprecedented
sense of security, self-confidence, and well-being. Nevertheless, in 1949,
Eli Ginzberg forewarned that the fight against anti-Semitism could not by

itself create a strong American Jewish identity, nor could it be the basis for building a vibrant Jewish community. "Today at least among large numbers of American Jews, the 'defense activities' have usurped a position of priority. This was more or less inevitable since many of these Jews have lost all interest in positive Jewish values; their entire adjustment is externally oriented."[5] Although many American Jews felt the need to affirm their Jewishness in public, this obscured the fact that their inner religious life was shallow. Thus, in the battle to protect their Jewish ethnicity, many Jews lost sight of what the Jewish religion truly meant.

AMERICAN JUDAISM ON THE SUBURBAN FRONTIER

Beginning in the mid-1940s, Americans of all faiths began seeking out a more independent existence away from the inherent pressures of city life, and they started establishing new communities in the suburbs. American Jews followed this trend, joining the exodus to suburbia and further accelerating the assimilatory process. Many Jews were exposed to Christianity, the dominant religion in America, for the first time. Considerable numbers were influenced by the allure of the commercial aspect, and some even accepted secularized Christian symbols, holidays, and ideas. The exposure to Christianity had tremendous implications for how Jews saw themselves and their religion. This resulted in creating a new form of Jewish identity that emphasized to them what they were not – Christians. While many American Jews had taken being Jewish for granted, they nevertheless struggled to find new ways to express their Jewish identities in the suburbs, which lacked the intense ethnic feel of the urban Jewish neighborhoods. The cutting of ties resulting from the move out of the urban neighborhoods, such as The Lower East Side in New York, led to the development of new paradigms in their religious and cultural life.

The newly suburban Jewish families needed houses of worship where they could meet people of a similar background. As a result, the 1950s and 1960s saw a massive building boom of synagogues, as it appeared that the American Jewish community had an "edifice complex." These suburban temples, many designed by architect Percival Goodman, featured an elevated Bimah (pulpit) that separated the rabbi and cantor from the congregants. The architectural plans provided plenty of space to expand for the High Holy Days by separating the social hall from the sanctuary with a removable partition. Increasing numbers of American Jews were joining these new synagogues. Whereas in 1930 only about 20 percent of the American Jewish population belonged to a synagogue, by 1960 this number had risen to almost 60 percent – a threefold increase in only thirty years. Scholars have cautioned that this increase did not mean that American Jews were becoming more devout. Herberg wrote in his classic work *Protestant, Catholic, Jew* that the suburban Jewish synagogue stood for "religiousness without religion." Rather, it was "a way of sociability or 'belonging' rather than a way of orienting life to God." Religious leaders tried to integrate their theological identities with the social and communal needs of their congregants. As believers in ethical monotheism and prophetic Judaism, Reform rabbis saw political activism as one of their functions. Orthodox rabbis saw themselves as teaching the practical implications of their belief in Torah Le-Moshe Mi-Sinai, the revelation from God to Moses at Mt. Sinai. Conservative rabbis suffered the most severe "confusion of roles," unable to successfully combine their self-image as Talmudic scholars with the communal expectation of them as therapeutic providers.[6] Most congregants participated in Jewish rituals on specific holidays (Rosh Hashanah, Yom Kippur, Hannukah, and Passover) and at life-cycle events (brises, baby namings, bar mitzvahs, weddings, and funerals). Despite their lack of piety, suburban Jews felt compelled to participate in the religious affiliation that was seen as a cornerstone of American citizenship.

Societal attitudes were evolving quickly, and the religious denominations struggled to respond with innovations that would attract congregants to attend synagogue services. With the exception of the High Holy Days, synagogue attendance was typically poor and it was hoped that religious change might inspire new devotion. Beginning in 1945, each of the movements produced new prayer books. With the exception of the Orthodox, they all introduced new liturgy that they felt reflected the current state of belief. Nevertheless, many congregants found the aesthetic dimension to be more important than the theological expression. The non-Orthodox movements began to make ritual changes, such as giving women greater roles in synagogue governance and ritual. The Reform movement experimented with traditional rituals that had been jettisoned in earlier decades and also pioneered innovative services that stressed creativity and originality. In a dramatic departure from the traditional interpretation of *Halacha* (Jewish law), the Conservative movement began allowing worshippers to drive to and from synagogue on Shabbat.

Conservative Judaism, which was "dedicated to the conservation and development of traditional Judaism in the modern spirit,"[7] dominated the American Jewish religious landscape during this period. While many American Jews fondly remembered attending small Orthodox synagogues in the urban ghetto, they considered the movement and its emphasis on the observance of Halacha too confining, as they yearned to be Americans in every sense of the word. However, many of these "fallen Orthodox" suburbanites felt uncomfortable in Reform temples, which they found to be "churchlike." They preferred the traditional prayers of the Conservative synagogue and its respect for Jewish ritual practice. Congregations nevertheless had difficulty generating religious commitment. As Rabbi Morris Adler told a United Synagogue Convention in 1948, "Multitudes of our people are untouched, uninformed, uncovenanted. They have not enough Judaism to live it, nor enough interest to reject it. They go on in routine indifference."[8] The suburban synagogues began organizing formal and informal educational programs. Family services proved very popular, as they attracted those eager to find constructive activities for their growing children. Because many parents became enthused when their children became involved, religious life became very child-centered, thus launching a short-lived trend that many leaders found disturbing. Still, the religious schools, which met on Sunday mornings and even on one or even two weekday afternoons, were unable to transmit much at all about Judaism, Hebrew, Jewish history, or Biblical studies to its young students. However, despite the many problems, some believed that the experience inculcated a pride in being Jewish and an understanding of the need to affiliate with the synagogue as an adult.

SHIFT FROM UNIVERSALISM TO PARTICULARISM

In the 1960s, there was a palpable diminution of interest in Jewish religious life, although the synagogue building boom continued. Many young people began joining the counterculture, listening to rock 'n' roll, imbibing drugs, and joining in "free love." Hippies, flower children, runaways, cult followers, and groupies searched for their own identity and destiny. Full of youthful idealism, activists and protesters sought to overturn the status quo. The New Left developed out of heavily Jewish community action groups that had supported various liberal social and political causes. Many idealized Chinese and Cuban communism, just as many leftists of an earlier generation had romanticized the Bolsheviks from Soviet Russia. Rabbis did their best to try to reach out to alienated Jewish youths. Rabbi Joseph R. Narot of Temple Israel in Miami wrote a series of letters to the "NOW generation," stating "I do not deplore much that you do and are. I applaud you. I approve of you ... but also understand the context of concern for other things, people, places, and hopes into which your rights must be set and seen."[9] Ellwood argues that both Jews and Protestants were rejecting the melting-pot leveling that had been promoted so heavily in the 1950s: "Protestant churches tended to lose something of traditional ethnic and denominational identities, picturing themselves either as parts – ideally as servants – of a larger society, or as collections of spiritually questing individuals. Jews, on the other hand, came out of the Sixties often more ready to affirm an ethnic and cultic identity that had been there all along."[10]

Both the Reform and the Conservative movements placed universalistic issues of ethical and moral concern high on their agendas. The laity as well as the rabbinate organized political action groups, established activist commissions, and worked closely with non-Jewish organizations for the benefit of the poor and the oppressed. American Jews responded with great enthusiasm to the civil rights movement, which formed in the mid-1950s under the leadership of Martin Luther King, Jr. Jews who had been raised equating Judaism with prophetic justice found King's stress on passive resistance rather than violence to be compelling, and they felt an obligation to help fight for Negro rights. However, the commitment of the American Jewish community to helping African Americans achieve equality was eventually damaged by what many Jews perceived as overt black hostility. The black leaders of the younger generation, such as Reverend Jesse Jackson and Louis Farrakhan, were quoted as making antagonistic remarks about American Jews as well as the State of Israel. Nevertheless, many Jewish religious leaders felt that it was very important for Jews to remain involved in the struggle for civil rights. In their view, this struggle reached the heart of what America means as an idea and as an ideal. Jews felt compelled to fight to keep America as a land of opportunity for all people, regardless of the color of their skin or the background of their families. Nevertheless, a gap developed between many of the Jewish communal leaders, who on the whole remained very liberal, and the Jewish population overall, which was becoming more politically conservative.

Social justice and other activist involvement reached a zenith during the 1960s, when many Jews participated in the civil rights movement, the anti-Vietnam War effort, the counterculture, feminism, and other causes. Leading rabbis such as Abraham Joshua Heschel tried to link social justice causes with Judaism. The Jewish communal agenda slowly shifted focus from universalistic issues such as civil rights and the Vietnam War to particularistic issues that directly affected the Jewish people. Much of this was due to the new interest in the Holocaust that followed the Adolf Eichmann trial of 1961. In the years following the trial, numerous books were published on the Holocaust and its aftermath. Elie Wiesel wrote the international bestseller *Night*, one of a series of gripping novels based closely on his own experiences as a youth in Auschwitz. In 1967, journalist Arthur Morse published *While Six Million Died*, which criticized the American government's failure to attempt to save more European Jews. While Morse's primary concern was President Roosevelt's apparent apathy, he also raised the question of whether American Jews had done enough to save their brethren. Perhaps gripped with "survivor guilt," many American Jews resolved to work diligently on behalf of oppressed Jewries throughout the world. Rabbi Meir Kahane, founder of the Jewish Defense League (JDL), publicized a Jewish activist response to the Holocaust and the apathy that surrounded it – "Never again!" Although communal leaders worried about Kahane's extremism, he was an inspiration to many lower-middle-class urban youth. Eventually, mainstream Jewish groups adopted similar, if less militant, activist approaches.

In the spring of 1967, American Jews underwent a mixture of emotions, as they feared for the very survival of the State of Israel. Arab nations had threatened to obliterate Israel and drive the Jews into the sea. Heschel recalls the sentiments that many had at that time: "Terror and dread fell upon Jews everywhere. Will God permit our people to perish? Will there be another Auschwitz, another Dachau, another Treblinka?... In the midst of that thick darkness there is one gleam of light: the return of our people to Zion."[11] Arthur Hertzberg commented in August of that year that "the mood of the American Jewish community underwent an abrupt, radical, and possibly permanent change [following the war]... the immediate reaction of American Jewry to the crisis [preceding Israel's preemptive strike] was far more intense and widespread than anyone could have foreseen."[12] In the face of the Israeli victory, American Jews felt an unprecedented pride. The State of Israel had redeemed them from being perpetual victims of persecution and destruction. Support for Israel now became a central pillar of the American Jewish civil religion. Jack Wertheimer explains: "Whereas American Jews had demonstrated sympathy in the past, Israel now was incorporated into the very structure of American Jewish identity."[13]

In the aftermath of the Israeli victory in 1967, many began to see the Holocaust as a catastrophic event that led up to miraculous victories. The Israeli victories in the Six Day War helped American Jews to put the Holocaust in a religious context. The Holocaust on its own was such a horrible event that it seemed impossible to give it religious meaning. Taking a radical view, Jacob Neusner argues that "the extermination of European Jewry could become the Holocaust only on 9 June when, in the aftermath of a remarkable victory, the State of Israel celebrated the return of the people of Israel to the ancient wall of the Temple of Jerusalem." He believes that the Six Day War transformed the political and military events into a sacred story with not only tragedy but also a miraculous conclusion, endowing a symbol with a "single, ineluctable meaning."[14] This "Judaism of Holocaust and Redemption" provided American Jews with a compelling myth.

NEW APPROACHES TO RELIGIOUS IDENTITY

A set of values and beliefs crystallized during the 1960s that Jonathan Woocher calls "civil Judaism" or "Jewish civil religion." Woocher argues that the core of this civil Judaism was a commitment to Jewish group survival as a sacred value. By the 1970s, though, many American Jews were finding this approach to be insufficient to keep them closely connected to the tribe. The majority, who Samuel Heilman refers to as "Jewish-Americans," made their Jewish involvement subordinate to their American identities. Heilman explains that their Jewish attachment was similar to that of other hyphenated Americans who also absorbed American values and cultural patterns. They had adapted themselves to the American way of life and observed only those rituals that would not compromise their personal autonomy.

Charles S. Liebman similarly argues that the "ambivalent American Jew" was torn between "integration and acceptance into American society" and "Jewish group survival."[15] Jews now felt they were able to integrate fully into American society, where they could work in most professions and participate in secular extracurricular activities. There was so little hostility from the outside that it now became very easy to break all connections with the Jewish community without experiencing any adverse repercussions. Many American Jews simply drifted off, needing Judaism neither for a social network nor for existential meaning. In an increasingly postmodern world, commitment to Judaism became a matter of personal faith rather than a question of fate.

A minority of American Jews was still deeply committed to perpetuating Jewishness not only as an ethnicity but also as a compelling religion. While not necessarily Orthodox, these Jews were more than likely to be highly observant and participate in Jewish activities on a weekly basis. Many attended synagogue regularly, studied in adult education classes one or more nights a week, and sent their children to Jewish day schools. Heilman writes that "one either took Jewish life and Judaism more seriously and actively engaged it" or "one let meaningless rituals and old traditions fade."[16] The gap between those who cared and those who did not grew. For those who chose to embrace Judaism, the paths leading toward religious practice were many and diverse.

One of the most innovative Jewish religious groups was the Havurah movement, which consisted of small, spiritually oriented communities that integrated joyous musical expression, creative religious readings, art and dance, and even left wing politics into their Judaism. Finding the mainstream congregations spiritually passive and overly materialistic, they searched for an opportunity to mold their own religiosity based on their emotional needs, personal experiences, and life expectations. Although men initially dominated the Havurah movement, the rising spirit of social equality soon had an impact. In fact, it has been an important source of inspiration for women. Judith Plaskow explains that, "Many women, myself included, had our first experiences of egalitarianism in the context of Havurot."[17]

For those looking for "cutting edge" Judaism, the Jewish Renewal movement provided a congenial setting for expressing heartfelt spirituality through innovative modern approaches such as folk crafts, music, and dance. Rabbi Zalman Schachter-Shalomi started his career as an emissary for the Lubavitch before becoming the spiritual elder of the Jewish Renewal movement. He favors what he calls "Davenology," the art of enhancing Jewish worship through meditative practices and mysticism taken from Hassidism and even other religious traditions. Former 1960s activist Arthur Waskow gave the Jewish Renewal movement its name in a 1978 article in his journal *New Menorah*. Waskow now directs ALEPH: Alliance for Jewish Renewal, which coordinates religious and organizational activities. The movement is characterized by nonconformity and creativity, and it attracts many "searchers" who are looking to find a spiritual path that they can claim as their own. Michael Strassfeld's *The First Jewish Catalogue* has become a Jewish Renewal "Bible" for the millions who have read it since its publication in 1974.[18] *The First Jewish Catalogue* was subtitled a *Do-It-Yourself Kit*, and the early Havurah movement emphasized that, as Strassfeld himself put it, "We don't need rabbis, we should just do it ourselves and rabbis get in the way."[19,20]

However, many young Jews were indeed looking for rabbinic authority. The followers of *Ba'alei Teshuvah* (singular: *Baal Teshuvah*), literally meaning "those who repent," embraced Orthodox Judaism in their search for religious meaning. These young Jews had not been raised in observant homes but sought the type of structure that the rigorous Halachic system provided. There seemed to be an explosion in the number of young American Jews proudly wearing their yarmulkes (head coverings) and tzitzith (ritual fringes). This phenomenon went against what most observers expected would be the momentum toward greater acculturation and higher levels of assimilation. *Rolling Stone* journalist Ellen Willis wrote a personal account about her brother Chaim, a Baal Teshuvah, who studied at Aish HaTorah Yeshiva and became an Orthodox rabbi. The article became a recruiting tool for the many Ba'alei Teshuvah yeshivas in Jerusalem and their associated institutions worldwide. Despite the great interest in this movement, the numbers involved were relatively small and a high percentage of Ba'alei Teshuvah reverted to their original levels of observance within a few years. Demographer Barry Kosmin has recently argued "the much heralded return to Judaism in the 1980s and growth of Orthodoxy turned out to be of little statistical significance."[21] Even so, the Ba'alei Teshuvah have had an enormous influence on Orthodoxy, generating interest among many Jews who have reembraced the religious tradition of their ancestors.

While many saw Judaism as a way to express Jewish particularity, others hoped that it could answer the big questions about life. Increasing numbers of Jewish thinkers began to speak and write, not only for committed Jews, but also for the masses. In 1981, Conservative Rabbi Harold S. Kushner published *When Bad Things Happen to Good People* to help him deal with the death of his young son.[22] Kushner stressed that he did not write an abstract book about God and theology, but rather a very personal book that helped him deal with the "deep, aching sense of unfairness. . . . If God existed . . . how could He do this to me?"[23] This question haunted Kushner and compelled him to document the important lessons he had learned through his years of emotional turmoil. He wanted to encourage people to maintain their belief in God regardless of adverse situations. Even though many theologians were less than impressed with Kushner's spiritual revelations, millions of Americans found comfort in his words.[24]

Another group of Jews found Judaism unfulfilling and joined new religious movements, or cults. Many of these cult members were from Jewish families, where they had likely received little religious direction. Even if some members had attended religious school, they had learned only what they did *not* want to find in religion. The result was that they looked elsewhere for authentic spirituality. New religious movements such as the Unification Church, the Church of Scientology, the Family, and the Church Universal and Triumphant all had disproportionate numbers of Jewish members. Eastern approaches to spirituality such as Transcendental Meditation (TM) and American Buddhism were also very popular.

American Judaism is presently characterized by eclecticism. Many Americans are following the approach of Sheila Larson, a woman interviewed in Robert Bellah's *Habits of the Heart.* "I believe in God. I am not a religious fanatic. I can't remember the last time I went to church. [Yet] my faith has carried me a long way. It's Sheilaism. Just my own little voice."[25] Many American Jews share Sheila's perspective. Whereas once an individual had to believe in order to belong, today Americans are freer than ever before to express their religious individualism. Religion is personalized, privatized, and voluntarized. Many different types of Jews have come forward with many different types of Judaism. Some stress the power of spiritual healing, others scrupulously observe the Mitzvot, while still others organize Jewish men's groups.[26] In an effort to feel spiritual, Americans attempt to incorporate a variety of approaches to achieve this goal.

INTRARELIGIOUS TENSIONS

Orthodoxy had been strengthened by the arrival, after World War II, of almost 150,000 immigrants between 1944 and 1952. Many of them were Holocaust survivors from Eastern Europe and came to America to rebuild their religious life. Using the Old World as their model, these immigrants contributed to the growth and development of Orthodox communities throughout the United States. Almost 100,000 additional Jews hailing from diverse locations such as Hungary, Egypt, Cuba, Iran, and Israel settled in the United States between 1952 and 1965. Many joined Orthodox congregations and established synagogues designed to cater specifically to their national group, although the main factor contributing to the "drift to the right" was the influx of Ultra-Orthodox Holocaust survivors who settled in urban neighborhoods in large cities such as New York and Chicago. Eventually some Haredi, Ultra-Orthodox groups, moved to the suburbs, always as a community.

Several surviving Hasidic leaders came to America, including Rabbi Joel Teitelbaum, the Satmar Rebbe. Many Satmar settled in Williamsburg, Brooklyn, while many Lubavitch, another Hasidic sect who followed Rabbi Menachem Mendel Schneerson, moved to Crown Heights. Other Ultra-Orthodox groups were Mitnagdim, fervent opponents of the Hasidim, who established yeshivot in Brooklyn. One of their highest priorities was the establishment of appropriate school facilities for their many children. Whereas before World War II there were less than 20 Jewish day schools, by 1963 there were 257 Orthodox day schools in the United States, of which about half instructed in Yiddish. This growth in Orthodox day schools contributed to the intensification of Orthodox Jewish life in the United States.

Lawrence Grossman argues that, beginning in the 1950s, "religious polarization became a serious concern of American Jewry."[27] The Orthodox in the United States became stronger and more extreme while the rest of American Jewry began intermarrying at very high rates and made religious decisions that affected the Jewish status of their offspring. Orthodox partisans saw this as violating an unspoken arrangement in which they would tolerate non-Orthodox violations of the Halacha and their belief in heterodox theology while the non-Orthodox would abstain from any decision that would affect personal status issues. The rate of intermarriage had begun to worry Jewish communal leaders, and they debated how best to respond. While the Orthodox refused to soften their opposition, most other Jews shifted their emphasis from prevention to outreach. Rejection slowly turned to acquiescence and then later acceptance. The Central Conference of American Rabbis (CCAR) of the Reform movement reaffirmed the position that "mixed marriage is contrary to the Jewish tradition and should be discouraged." They declared their "opposition to participation by its members in any ceremony which solemnizes a mixed marriage." However, given that all CCAR resolutions were nonbinding, rabbis were free to ignore this declaration. As early as 1973, Reform Rabbi Irwin Fishbein urged his colleagues to agree to officiate at intermarriages in order "not to slam a door that might be only slightly ajar." Indeed, the increasing social acceptance of intermarriage led many Reform and Reconstructionist rabbis to officiate at such ceremonies, even though the Orthodox were staunchly opposed. The Conservative rabbinical group (the Rabbinical Assembly) took a position similar to that of the Orthodox, refusing to allow its rabbis to officiate at intermarriages. However, many Conservative congregants held similar views as Reform Jews and agitated for their rabbis to help them in their moment of need, requesting that their rabbi officiate at such ceremonies.

By the beginning of the 1980s, relations between the Jewish denominations were deteriorating. This was not due to any one factor, but the Patrilineal Descent Resolution of 1983 was a crucial turning point. While patrilineality had been accepted informally in most Reform congregations for decades, Rabbi Alexander Schindler urged the Union of American Hebrew Congregations (UAHC) to formally adopt new criteria for establishing Jewish identity. The resolution, passed by CCAR, affirmed that a child born of a Jewish father and a gentile mother could be considered Jewish if he or she was raised in the Jewish religion. Orthodox leaders felt that this decision made it impossible to cooperate with the Reform movement on a wide range of issues, because they felt that the Reform movement had taken the first steps toward creating two Jewish peoples – accepting as Jewish those individuals who were not Halachically Jewish.

As a result of the perceived interdenominational "polarization," some Jewish leaders made attempts to encourage interdenominational dialogue, while others unequivocally rejected the notion. In 1986, the annual General Assembly of the Council of Jewish Federations and Welfare Funds (CJF) chose the theme *Klal Yisrael* (Jewish Unity). Rabbi Harold Schulweis of Encino, California, spoke heavy-heartedly about what he saw as the coming cataclysm between the Jewish religious streams. "The division is no longer between 'them' and 'us,' but within us." By March 1987, the situation had become so grim that the National Jewish Center for Learning and Leadership (CLAL) sponsored a conference, Will There be One Jewish People by the Year 2000? As a prerequisite for attending, the Orthodox insisted that speakers not appear on the same platform at the same time. Rabbi Norman Lamm, the President of Yeshiva University, spoke in favor of a joint Beit Din[28] to handle issues of personal identity, but his idea was rejected by most of the Orthodox rabbinical establishment, rendering that the last time he would attempt to suggest such a cooperative venture. The rift deepened further in June 1987, when Rabbi Louis Bernstein announced that the Orthodox were withdrawing from the Jewish Welfare Board (JWB) Commission on Jewish Chaplaincy because Reform Rabbi Joseph Glaser had certified a female rabbi without consulting them. Knowing that the Orthodox would never agree to certify any woman as a chaplain, Glaser explained that he went ahead on his own, feeling it was a matter of conscience to allow her to serve. Thus, in August 1987, a new system was put into place in which each movement's rabbinic organization would endorse its own candidate without the need for approval from the other denominations.

Interdenominational dialogue had always relied on the mediation of the modern Orthodox. However by the late 1980s, modern Orthodoxy was in decline, as the passing of the modern Orthodox mentor, Rabbi Joseph B. Soloveitchik, weakened their stature in the world of Talmudic scholarship. The word *modern* became so stigmatized that many began to refer to themselves as centrist Orthodox while others preferred the term *Open Orthodoxy*. Any word was acceptable as long as it did not connote modernity. There was increasing pressure on modern Orthodox rabbis to withdraw from organizations and activities in which there was theological discussion and social interaction with non-Orthodox leaders. Modern Orthodox rabbis who served on interdenominational committees were urged to resign, and many local rabbinical associations lost most or all of their Orthodox members. The Synagogue Council of America, a national organization headquartered in New York, had to disband because of Orthodox withdrawal.

In 2001, Samuel G. Freedman published a best-selling work entitled *Jew vs. Jew* that seemed to capture the feeling that a "civil war" was "tearing apart" the American Jewish community: "It is tragic . . . that American Jews have battled so bitterly, so viciously, over the very meaning of being Jewish."[29] However, while Freedman speaks of a "civil war," the reality is that there has been a gradual process of separation since 1945 that may rather be leading to a "divorce" between the Orthodox and all other American Jews. Some believe that the Orthodox will dominate American Judaism in the coming decades. In *Jew vs. Jew*, Freedman argues that, "in the struggle for the soul of American Jewry, the Orthodox model has triumphed." Not all scholars agree. Jonathan D. Sarna points out that this triumphalism has been seen before. In the mid-1870s, the Reform movement believed it would become "the custom of [all] American Jews," while the Conservative movement appeared destined to dominate American Judaism during the era after World War II. Nevertheless, both movements fell far short of expectations. Sarna stops short of predicting that Orthodoxy will follow the same trajectory, but he points out that there are a number of serious vulnerabilities that indicate that Orthodoxy's dramatic rise could be followed by an equally precipitous decline.[30]

THE SEARCH FOR ACCEPTANCE IN CONTEMPORARY JUDAISM

All of the American denominations faced increasing pressures to respond to the needs and wants of previously neglected groups, to include women, gays, and lesbians. The more liberal movements, namely Reform and Reconstructionists, granted full equality to women, gays, and lesbians with only a small struggle. In 1972, Sally J. Priesand was ordained as a rabbi at Hebrew Union College, thus paving the way in the more liberal movements. However, the Conservative movement had a much more protracted and bitter struggle over the women's rights' question as well as gay and lesbian rights. Indeed, when the Jewish Theological Seminary decided to admit women to the Conservative rabbinate, some right wing Conservatives left the movement in protest. Furthermore, even as Orthodoxy has faced persistent calls to allow women to take a larger role in religious life, it by definition refuses to countenance gay sexual behavior.

By the 1990s, women had achieved equal religious rights in most of the American Jewish religious denominations. Even some liberal modern Orthodox tried creative strategies for engaging women's spirituality without violating Halacha. Women's educational programs were established to allow women to study Talmud, and *minyanim* (prayer quorums) were set up in which women could read from the Torah. Despite the fact that the feminist Orthodox leaders ardently tried to ensure that they abided by all Halachic restrictions, many ultra-Orthodox and even a few centrist Orthodox rabbis condemned these innovations. Nevertheless, the changing status of women in American society has influenced even Haredi society, and male rabbinical leadership is taking women's perspectives into account.

Ultra-Orthodox women are now leading study sessions for other women and writing articles and books. Nevertheless, women must study for ordination privately, as the Orthodox remain opposed to women rabbis. In 1994, Rabbi Haviva Krasner-Davidson struggled with what she perceived to be the lack of equality in the Orthodox ritual system and eventually decided to accept upon herself the positive time-bound commandments such as wearing tzitzit, putting on tefillin, and praying three times a day. She applied for admission to Yeshiva University's rabbinical program, but she allegedly never received a response to her application. She later found a sympathetic Orthodox rabbi in Israel willing to train and ordain her. Few reputable Orthodox rabbis have recognized her as a colleague.

The Conservative movement similarly struggled with the women's issue, as they were in the middle religiously, caught in between following the
Orthodox standards but wanting to advance with the changing times. In
1955, the Committee on Jewish Law and Standards voted to allow women to
recite the blessings proceeding and following the reading of the Torah.[31] In
1975, a resolution submitted to the Rabbinical Assembly (RA) Convention
to admit women into the rabbinical school was tabled. Two years later, another resolution urging Jewish Theological Seminary chancellor Gerson D.
Cohen to establish an interdisciplinary committee to study the possibility of
ordaining women was tabled again. On October 24, 1983, Jewish Theological
Seminary faculty and the RA finally agreed to admit women and thus passed
the resolution that eventually allowed the first woman rabbi to be ordained
in spring 1985.

Gays and lesbians were also demanding that their voices be heard so
that they might enjoy their religious rights. In 1972, gay and lesbian Jews
inspired by the Metropolitan Community Church founded a Jewish religious
community in Los Angeles. In 1978, Rabbi Allen Bennett became the first
openly gay rabbi, serving as the first rabbi of Sha'ar Zahav, a gay and lesbian
outreach congregation founded in 1977 in San Francisco. Throughout the
1990s, the CCAR dealt with the issue of gay and lesbian rights. At their
annual conference in 2000, they voted to accept a resolution urging rabbis to
look favorably on same-sex commitment ceremonies. The Reconstructionist
movement had already taken similar steps and the Conservative movement
seems likely to follow suit. Rabbi Steven Greenberg has "come out" of the
closet as the first Orthodox gay rabbi, even though most Orthodox leaders
regard homosexual behavior and Orthodoxy as incompatible.

CONCLUSION

American Jewish identity in the period after World War II is a complex
one, with religious and ethnic elements intertwined. Nathan Glazer has argued "for the great majority of American Jews, Judaism means an *ethnic*
commitment more than a transcendent faith."[32] Arthur Goren has explained
that, despite the emphasis on Jewish ethnicity, religiosity has played an important role in how Jews identified themselves: "As individuals, Jews identified themselves as belonging to a religious community. As a group, they
acted like an ethnic minority."[33] This ethnic identity derived in large part
from the Eastern European Jewish background, and the cultural, religious
reinforcement by a steady stream of immigrant waves. These immigrants
enriched Jewish life and reinforced the ties that existed with the Old World.
However, at the beginning of the twenty-first century, American Jewry can no

longer count on continued Jewish immigration from traditional societies to replenish their numbers and bring them back in touch with their roots. Rather, they are going to have to develop strategies to produce indigenous American Jewish experiences that can excite and enthuse the next generation and the one after that.

American Judaism in the twenty-first century has to find its place in "A New Religious America." What was formerly seen as a Christian country has become one of the most religiously diverse nations in the world. Whereas the religious landscape of the 1950s that Will Herberg surveyed had three religions – Protestantism, Catholicism, and Judaism – contemporary America now has many other faiths, including Buddhism, Zoroastrianism, Islam, and Hinduism. Diana L. Eck comments that "not only is America changing these religions, but these religions are also changing America."[34] Judaism will have to take account of and respond to this new religious pluralism. How can Jews articulate the meaning of Judaism in a country that has opened up to so many new faiths? Judaism faces the challenge of reinterpreting what it means to be a religious minority that is composed primarily of adherents who are classified as part of the white majority. Can Judaism find a meaningful role to play in twenty-first-century American society?

American Jews have to answer this key question: Why would I want to forever maintain a distinct Jewish identity in an open, liberal society? Arthur Hertzberg argues that religious faith is the only answer. "After nearly four centuries, the momentum of Jewish experience in America is essentially spent. Ethnicity will no doubt last for several more generations, but it is well on the way to becoming memory. But a community cannot survive on what it remembers; it will persist only because of what it affirms and believes."[35]

Notes

1. Arthur A. Goren, *Studies in Contemporary Jewry*, vol. 8 (Oxford: Oxford University Press, 1992), 8.
2. I thank Lawrence Grossman, Charles S. Liebman (z"l), and Kayla Ship for critiquing this essay.
3. Will Herberg, *Protestant, Catholic, Jew: An Essay in Religious Sociology* (Garden City: Anchor/Doubleday, 1955), 23.
4. Robert Ellwood, *The Fifties Spiritual Marketplace: American Religion in a Decade of Conflict* (New Brunswick: Rutgers University Press, 1997).
5. Arthur Hertzberg, *The Jews in America: Four Centuries of an Uneasy Encounter* (New York: Simon & Schuster, 1989), 331.
6. Daniel J. Elazar and Rela Mintz Geffen, *The Conservative Movement in Judaism: Dilemmas and Opportunities* (Albany: State University of New York Press, 2000), 120–22.
7. Robert Gordis, *Understanding Conservative Judaism* (New York: The Rabbinical Assembly, 1978), 216.

8. Morris Adler, "New Goals for Conservative Judaism – An Address [1948]," in *Tradition and Change: The Development of Conservative Judaism*, ed. Mordechai Waxman (New York: Burning Bush Press, 1958), 280.

9. Joseph R. Narot, *Letters to the NOW Generation* (New York: Union of American Hebrew Congregations Press, 1969), 2, 72.

10. Robert S. Ellwood, *The Sixties Spiritual Awakening: American Religion Moving from Modern to Postmodern* (New Brunswick: Rutgers University Press, 1994), 248.

11. Melvin Urofsky, *We Are One: American Jewry and Israel* (Garden City: Doubleday, 1978), 31.

12. Arthur Hertzberg, "Israel and American Jewry," *Commentary 44*, 2 (August 1967), 69–73.

13. Jack Wertheimer, *A People Divided: Judaism in Contemporary America* (Hanover and London: Brandeis University Press, 1997), 30.

14. Jacob Neusner, *Death and Birth of Judaism: The Impact of Christianity, Secularism, and the Holocaust on Jewish Faith* (New York: Basic Books, 1987), 279.

15. Charles S. Liebman, *The Ambivalent American Jew: Politics, Religion, and Family in American Jewish Life* (Philadelphia: The Jewish Publication Society, 1973), vii.

16. Samuel C. Heilman, *Portrait of American Jews: The Last Half of the 20th Century* (Seattle and London: University of Washington Press, 1995), 72.

17. Rodger Kamenetz, "Has the Jewish Renewal Movement Made It Into the Mainstream?" *Moment* (December 1994), 42.

18. Michael Strassfeld, Sharon Strassfeld, and Richard Siegal, *The First Jewish Catalogue: A Do-It-Yourself Kit* (Philadelphia: The Jewish Publication Society, 1974).

19. Rodger Kamenetz, "Jewish Renewal Movement," 81.

20. Ironically, Strassfeld later became a rabbi and took on a congregation.

21. Barry Kosmin, "Politics of Blame Play into Jewish Population Study," *Jewish Bulletin of Northern California* (8 November 2002), 25A.

22. Harold S. Kushner, *When Bad Things Happen to Good People* (London: Pan Books, 1982).

23. Ibid., 10.

24. Abraham Cohen, "Theology and Theodicy: On Reading Harold Kushner," *Modern Judaism* 16, 3 (1996), 229–61.

25. Robert Bellah et al., *Habits of the Heart: Individuality and Commitment in American Life* (New York: Harper & Row, 1985), 4.

26. Julie Becker Grossman, "Heal! O Israel: A New Jewish Movement Discovers Spirituality Helps," *Moment* (December 1997), 62–64, 92–96.

27. Lawrence Grossman, "Jewish Communal Affairs," *American Jewish Yearbook* 88 (1988), 188.

28. A Beit Din is a rabbinical court consisting of three rabbis that is required or at least recommended to do conversions, divorces, and other technical Jewish legal processes.

29. Samuel G. Freedman, *Jew vs. Jew: The Struggle for the Soul of American Jewry* (New York: Simon & Schuster, 2000), 359.

30. Jonathan D. Sarna, "The Future of American Orthodoxy," *Sh'ma* (February 2001). Available from http://www.shma.com.

31. Aaron H. Blumenthal, "An Aliyah for Women," *Proceedings of the Rabbinical Assembly* 19 (1955), 168–81.
32. Nathan Glazer, *American Judaism* (Chicago: The University of Chicago Press, 1957), xii.
33. Arthur A. Goren, *Studies in Contemporary Jewry*, vol. 8 (Oxford: Oxford University Press, 1992), 9.
34. Diana L. Eck, *A New Religious America* (San Francisco: HarperSanFrancisco, 2001), 22.
35. Arthur Hertzberg, *The Jews in America: Four Centuries of an Uneasy Encounter* (New York: Columbia University Press, 1997), 374.

Part II

Themes and concepts

4 Jewish religious denominations
LAWRENCE GROSSMAN

Denominational Judaism did not yet exist when Jews began settling in the American colonies during the seventeenth century. The primary dividing line between Jews at that time was ethnocultural – between Sephardim, who traced their ancestry to Spain or Portugal where their families had in many cases been forcibly converted to Catholicism, and Ashkenazim, who originated from German-speaking lands. Although synagogue ritual for both groups was meticulously traditional, individual religious behavior varied widely. In keeping with European precedent, each American community maintained only one official synagogue, run by a lay board. Since there were no ordained rabbis in the country, knowledgeable congregants conducted services. Gradually, the natural growth and increasing heterogeneity of the Jewish population, internecine conflict, and the American penchant for individualism and freedom of association splintered the unified Jewish communities and led to the founding of multiple congregations in the same city.

REFORM, THE FIRST DENOMINATION

Beginning in the 1830s and continuing through the Civil War, a stream of Jewish immigrants from German-speaking lands planted the first Jewish "denomination" in America, Reform. Although it was technically the Sephardi congregation, Beth Elohim of Charleston, South Carolina, that first espoused so-called Reform Judaism in the 1820s, the German newcomers made this form of Judaism the primary American expression of the religion until well into the twentieth century.

Reform Judaism originated in German cities that had been occupied by Napoleon, whose armies had broken down ghetto walls and granted Jews equality. Eager to retain their rights under the restored German regimes after 1815, early advocates of Reform sought to bring Jewish life in line with contemporary notions of reverence and deportment. To merit full emancipation, they felt, Jews would have to shed the ways of the ghetto: Decorum must replace informality during worship; German must take its place along-side Hebrew as a language of prayer; organ music and regular sermons in German must become part of the services; secular and vocational education must take priority over the study of religious texts. Changes in practice were accompanied by criticism of the prayer book, and this, in turn, entailed challenges to doctrine. Virtually every principle of traditional Jewish theology was reexamined and revised. The old ghetto assumption that Judaism had an ethnic or national dimension was dropped or subordinated, and Jews were now viewed as Germans, Frenchmen, or Americans "of the Mosaic persuasion." Since Jews were now equal citizens, Judaism was seen simply as a religion. Furthermore, the Biblical covenant of God with the Israelites was reinterpreted to deemphasize traditional religious observances and highlight instead the mission of the Jews to spread monotheism and prophetic ethics to the world. The law of the land now superseded traditional Jewish law that had guided Jewish communities through centuries of exile. As good citizens, many Jews gave up any interest in an ultimate messianic "redemption" that included a return to the Holy Land. Messianism was now to be understood, in line with the liberalism of the time, as a process whereby mankind progresses toward a future of peace and harmony.[1]

In America, where most Jews had already shaken off the obligations of ritual observance, where there was no traditional rabbinic establishment that could counter innovation, and where Jews were accepted unreservedly as bona fide citizens, Reform Judaism enjoyed its greatest successes. Under the energetic leadership of Isaac Mayer Wise (1819–1900), who arrived in the United States from Bohemia in 1846 and served as rabbi in Cincinnati from 1854 until his death, an Americanized version of Reform spread rapidly, especially in the West and South. Wise built institutions that he hoped would come to represent *all* of American Jewry, and hence the word *Reform* does not appear in their names: the Union of American Hebrew Congregations (1873); Hebrew Union College, a rabbinical seminary (1875); and the Central Conference of American Rabbis (1889).[2]

The first official theological pronouncement of American Reform – the work not of Wise, who was indifferent to theology, but of Rabbi Kaufmann Kohler of New York – came in 1885. Known as the Pittsburgh Platform because it emerged from a rabbinical conference in that city, it described Judaism as "the highest conception of the God-idea," a "progressive religion ever striving to be in accord with the postulates of reason." Biblical law, called "Mosaic legislation," was understood as "a system of training the Jewish people for its mission during its national life in Palestine." However, the moral laws were primary, not the rituals; "only such ceremonies as elevate and sanctify our lives" were recommended. Regulations regarding eating, dress, and priestly purity were specifically mentioned as irrelevant to modern sensibilities. Asserting that Judaism was "no longer a nation," the document rejected any return to Palestine, reinauguration of the Jerusalem Temple, or "restoration of any of the laws concerning the Jewish state." In the 1890s, the Reform movement reacted with outrage to the rise of political Zionism, seeing it as a revival of an atavistic Jewish nationalism that threatened the acceptance of Jews as equal citizens in the nations where they lived. The messianic age, which the platform defined as "the kingdom of truth, justice and peace among all men," was close to realization. In the meantime, Jews were obligated "to participate in the great task of modern times, to solve ... the problems [that] presented the contrasts and evils of the present organization of society."[3]

Since personal religious observances had virtually vanished, Reform practice was limited to the temple – Reformers did not like the old-fashioned ghetto connotations of the word *synagogue*. The temple service was conducted in English with organ music, and a number of temples replaced Saturday prayer with Sunday services. Neither head coverings nor prayer shawls were worn, and men and women sat together. By the end of the nineteenth century, Classical Reform, based on the universalistic, rational, optimistic creed of the Pittsburgh Platform, had crystallized.[4]

THE EMERGENCE OF CONSERVATIVE JUDAISM

For all its success, Reform did not become synonymous with American Judaism, as Wise had anticipated. From the outset, there were pockets of resistance to its initiatives, and the drift of American Reform further away from tradition induced its opponents to organize. While the promulgation of the Pittsburgh Platform in 1885 was the last straw, an event two years earlier – the so-called Trefa [Unkosher] Banquet – made the break inevitable. At the dinner honoring Hebrew Union College's first graduating class, clams, crabs, shrimp, and frogs' legs (prohibited by the kosher laws) were served, and the traditionalist guests walked out. In 1886, leading traditionalists met in New York City to found the Jewish Theological Seminary of America, which stressed adherence to Jewish law in addition to study.[5]

Although the Jewish Theological Seminary would become the central institution of what would become known as Conservative Judaism, the roots of that movement traced back to Europe. Reform was not the only religious response to the onset of modernity and the promise of emancipation in Central Europe. A position known as Positive-Historical Judaism also developed, which agreed with Reform that changes were necessary in Jewish life to meet the new circumstances, but that Jewish ritual law, not only moral law, retains its binding character. The law, however, could be adapted to changed circumstances through a process of interpretation. It was argued that previous generations of Jews had done exactly this, albeit without the historical self-consciousness of the nineteenth century. Learned European Jews who espoused this approach studied the texts of the Jewish tradition by using the tools of modern scientific scholarship, on the assumption that an accurate understanding of how the religion changed in the past would provide guidance for legitimate change in the present and the future.[6] It was this ideology, emphasizing traditional practice in alliance with objective scholarship, that came to animate the Jewish Theological Seminary, especially after the accession of Solomon Schechter (1847–1915) to the presidency in 1902. A renowned rabbinic scholar, Schechter gathered a distinguished faculty and made the seminary a world-class center of Jewish learning.

However, the mass constituency for the nascent Conservative movement – the children of the millions of East European Jews who arrived in America between the 1880s and World War I – had little knowledge of, and even less interest in, the scholarly work done at the seminary. Eager to escape the immigrant slums they grew up in and attain middle-class respectability in America, relatively few of these Jews identified with the Old World Judaism of their parents. Neither were they drawn to Reform temples, which seemed forbiddingly un-Jewish to those who were but one generation removed from the *shtetl*. Instead, the steadily growing circle of synagogues served by graduates of the Jewish Theological Seminary, organized in 1913 as the United Synagogue of America, fit their needs.

These synagogues, increasingly called "Conservative" to differentiate them from Reform temples, on the one hand, and Orthodox congregations of the Old World style on the other, held on to enough of the Jewish tradition to make second-generation Jews feel at home, but not so much as to interfere with modern American values. The prayer service was basically traditional, in Hebrew, with English responsive readings. Men wore head coverings and prayer shawls, but the rabbi, who was clean shaven, would preach in English, often on present-day topics. In the great majority of such congregations, men and women sat together; the rabbi and cantor used a microphone; and organ music was rare but not unknown. The Conservative synagogue became especially popular in new areas of Jewish settlement, particularly the suburbs of large cities. Rabbis and lay leaders were optimistic that this Conservative synthesis of tradition and innovation was not simply the beginning of a new denomination, but would soon become the quintessential American form of traditional Judaism as the immigrant generation that clung to European forms passed from the scene. It is estimated that, by the 1930s, Conservative Judaism had outdistanced Reform as the most popular denomination.

However, just as Classical Reform had been wrong in presuming that it was the wave of the future, so Conservatism erred in assuming that it was the only form of traditional Judaism that could survive in America.[7]

The transformation of American Jewry from a community of Central European lineage to one predominantly East European in origin also affected Reform. Under the influence of a new generation of Reform rabbis, many of whom – like the new immigrants – had been brought up in religiously traditional or ethnically Jewish homes, Classical Reform began to adapt to the changing community. In 1937, it adopted the Columbus Platform, which differed from its Pittsburgh predecessor in its more positive evaluation of Jewish peoplehood and religious practice. While still citing "the doctrine of the One, living God" as the core of Jewish identity, it acknowledged "the group-loyalty of Jews" who were not religious. In addition, moving away from its old negative attitude toward ritual practice and ethnic expression, the document spoke affirmatively of "the preservation of the Sabbath, festivals, and Holy Days," and "the cultivation of distinctive forms of religious art and music, the use of Hebrew, together with the vernacular, in our worship and instruction." Noteworthy, too, was a more positive attitude toward Zionism. "Many of our brethren," the platform noted, would "behold the promise of renewed life" in a rehabilitated Palestine, and Jews were therefore obligated "to aid in its upbuilding... to make it not only a haven of refuge for the oppressed but also a center of Jewish culture and spiritual life." Reform, however, was not yet ready to make its peace with the idea of a Jewish state.[8]

ORTHODOXY AMERICANIZES

Orthodox Judaism as an ideology emerged in early-nineteenth-century Germany among traditionalist Jews who opposed the changes advocated by Reform. In fact, the term *Orthodox* seems originally to have been coined by Reformers as a pejorative epithet. By midcentury, under the leadership of Samson Raphael Hirsch (1808–88), there developed what became known as neo-Orthodoxy in Germany, which maintained a stance of resistance to religious change while embracing Westernization in dress, language, and culture. There were relatively few such German Orthodox Jews in America in the nineteenth century, and – since there was as yet no clear distinction between Orthodox and Conservative – they tended to associate with the anti-Reform forces that built the Jewish Theological Seminary. Indeed, the first national organization of Orthodox synagogues, the Union of Orthodox Jewish Congregations of America (founded 1898), was supported by many of the same people who backed the Seminary.

Orthodoxy in Eastern Europe was quite different. Jews there were not yet legally emancipated, and even among those acculturated enough to demand equal rights, relatively few yearned for acceptance as Poles or Russians. Reform had made no inroads to speak of. In Eastern Europe, Orthodoxy mobilized at the end of the century to fight a different enemy: the secularization of the Jewish community at the hands of socialists, assimilationists, and Zionists. When such Orthodox Jews arrived in America, the cultural modernity of the "traditional" Jewish Theological Seminary looked hardly more acceptable than outright Reform.

There is, in fact, considerable scholarly disagreement over the so-called Orthodoxy of the large waves of East European Jews who came to the United States beginning in the 1880s. While their Old World looks and manners identified them as Orthodox in the eyes of Jewish and non-Jewish observers, the swiftness with which so many of them jettisoned hallowed laws and traditions under the pressure of economic necessity and social convenience and the haphazard Jewish education most gave to their children have led some scholars to conclude that their Orthodoxy was more social than religious. It was not, after all, mainly the rabbis and scholars, nor the more Jewishly serious laymen, who came; they, heeding the warnings of their spiritual leaders that ungodly America would undermine their Judaism, tended to stay put. Most of the Jews who did come were those who had the least to lose in terms of social status and economic class, those least rooted in the old religious way of life.[9]

To be sure, the congregations that these immigrants founded looked like transplants from the old home: small, intimate synagogues, many of them organized by people who came from the same town or region in Europe. And large numbers of these Jews tried – despite the economic problems involved – to keep up the traditional Sabbath and holidays, and to observe the kosher laws. They even attempted to replicate the system of rabbinic authority they were used to: a community rabbi who was responsible for all aspects of Jewish religious life in a town, and whose major source of income came from supervising kosher food suppliers. Slowly, traditionally trained rabbis began to arrive to fill these posts. In 1902, these Orthodox rabbis – born and trained in Europe and all Yiddish speaking – formed the first Orthodox rabbinical organization in the country, Agudath Harabbonim (Union of Orthodox Rabbis). However, the institution of communal "chief rabbi" in America was only a pale shadow of its European model, in which the rabbi functioned as both legal authority and quasi-government official.[10]

With the rise of a second, American-born generation at the beginning of the twentieth century, the weakness of this nominally Orthodox community became evident, as the increasingly acculturated, public-school-educated youngsters deserted the "old-fashioned" synagogue in droves. This was the phenomenon that encouraged the embryonic Conservative movement in its aspiration to appropriate the banner of traditional Judaism in America, but it also provided impetus for the Orthodox to make adjustments in order to hold on to their children.

A significant step in the Americanization of the Orthodox synagogue was the establishment of the Young Israel movement in 1912. Without in any way altering the basics of the traditional service, Young Israel synagogues instituted changes that appealed to the American-born generation: decorum, congregational singing, the encouragement of young people to lead services, and the elimination of announcing monetary contributions in return for synagogue honors. Around the same time, an Americanizing trend developed in Orthodox education. A small European-style rabbinical school in New York City, the Rabbi Isaac Elchanan Theological Seminary, instituted a secular high school program in 1916, largely under pressure from students who felt that, unlike the case in Europe, they could not function in America as rabbis, or indeed as ordinary Orthodox Jews, with only a traditional Jewish education. In 1928, this institution opened a college as well. This new Yeshiva College, with the later addition of graduate schools, would become Yeshiva University. Yeshiva developed into a training ground for a new type of Orthodox rabbi, fluent in the English language, conversant with secular knowledge, dressed in modern garb, and yet committed to Orthodoxy and learned in its sacred books. The hope was that such rabbis could successfully compete with their counterparts in the Conservative movement for the allegiance of American-born traditional Jews. In 1935, the Rabbinical Council of America was organized to represent these modern Orthodox rabbis.[11]

KAPLAN AND RECONSTRUCTIONISM

Reconstructionism is the only stream within American Judaism whose roots are totally American and whose principles were the work of one man – Mordecai Kaplan (1881–1983). Brought up as an Orthodox Jew in a rabbinical family on the Lower East Side of New York City, Kaplan was ordained at the Jewish Theological Seminary. He abandoned Orthodoxy as a result of his studies in the social sciences. While serving on the Seminary faculty, Kaplan developed Reconstructionism, a system best described in his 1934 book, *Judaism as a Civilization*. Kaplan rejected supernaturalism, Biblical revelation, messianism, and the doctrine of the chosen people as incompatible with modern thought. Nevertheless, he sought to restore the old premodern collective Jewish identity that had been shattered by individualism. To do this, he suggested that Jewish peoplehood, not religion, be seen as the core of Jewish identification, thus substituting what we today call ethnicity (though he did not use that term) for faith in a supernatural being. On that basis, Kaplan tried to reorganize the institutions of American Jewish life – synagogues, schools, and Jewish centers – so that American Jewry might function as an organic community.[12]

Kaplan faced rejection and even attack from many sides. The institutions of Reform Judaism, still unenthusiastic about the notion that Jews were a people, could not accept his sociological approach. The Orthodox decried his abandonment of tradition; the Union of Orthodox Rabbis even "excommunicated" Kaplan after he published an innovative prayer book. His colleagues at the Jewish Theological Seminary, committed as they were to traditional Jewish law, were appalled at his radicalism, some even seeking to have him dismissed. In 1954, Kaplan finally gave up hope of capturing the Conservative movement; his followers launched an independent movement, founding the Reconstructionist Federation of Congregations (now called the Jewish Reconstructionist Federation). A Reconstructionist Rabbinical College was established in Philadelphia in 1968, and a Reconstructionist Rabbinical Association in 1974. Reconstructionism remained a small but influential movement. Its honest confrontation with twentieth-century thought attracted considerable enthusiasm from Jewish intellectuals, and it influenced the thinking of many Reform and Conservative rabbis who admired Kaplan and his vision of Jewish life but did not officially join the movement.[13]

POSTWAR JUDAISM

In the years following World War II, Judaism shared in the new popularity that religion enjoyed in American life. Many new synagogues were built and congregational memberships soared. In 1947, Hebrew Union College, the training school for Reform rabbis located in Cincinnati, merged with the Jewish Institute of Religion (founded by maverick Reform Rabbi Stephen Wise) in New York, and the combined institution maintained both campuses; seven years later a third branch was opened in Los Angeles. The trauma of the Holocaust tipped the balance within Reform in the direction of support for a Jewish state. In 1942, Reform Jews uncomfortable with the movement's increasing warmth toward Zionism founded the American Council for Judaism, which continued to argue the Classical Reform position that Judaism has no national dimension. The emergence of the State of Israel as fait accompli in 1948 weakened the Council considerably. To all intents and purposes, Reform Jewry had been Zionized.[14]

Soon after the end of World War II, Reform became heavily involved in social justice issues. In doing so, it saw itself as fulfilling the Biblical prophetic mandate to help the weak and provide justice to the oppressed. At a time when anti-communism was riding high, Reform took a principled stand in favor of civil liberties. The movement opened a Religious Action Center in Washington in 1961 to coordinate social action programs. The Civil Rights movement received strong support from Reform Jews, many of them giving large sums of money to fund Civil Rights organizations and participating personally in Civil Rights marches. A number of Reform rabbis in the South spoke out bravely against racial segregation. Reform leaders were among the first American religious figures to challenge the escalation of the war in Vietnam.[15]

Meanwhile, Conservative Judaism was growing exponentially, continuing the process that had begun before the war. From 1945 to 1960, the number of Conservative synagogues jumped from 350 to 800. The movement started a highly successful network of summer camps called Ramah, and a somewhat less successful network of Solomon Schechter day schools. A branch of the Jewish Theological Seminary was founded in Los Angeles in 1947, called the University of Judaism, which would later spawn its own rabbinical school.

Still targeting the Americanized children of Orthodox parents, Conservative Judaism, for the first time – through its Committee on Jewish Law and Standards – started issuing decisions on Jewish law that eased some of the more onerous restrictions and ended some perceived inequities imposed by Orthodox Jewish law. In the 1940s, a clause was inserted in the Conservative marriage contract that made it more difficult for a recalcitrant husband to deny his civilly divorced wife a get, which is a Jewish divorce. In 1950, Conservative Jews were allowed to drive to synagogue services on the Sabbath, a serious violation in the eyes of the Orthodox. This move reflected the reality that few suburban Jews lived close enough to the synagogue to be able to walk. A 1954 decision gave women the right be called up to the Torah, and beginning in 1973 women could be counted for a minyan, the quorum of ten people needed for communal prayer. Taken together, these steps began to clarify what had previously been a rather vague distinction between modern Orthodox and Conservative practices.[16]

It was Orthodox Judaism, transformed by a new wave of immigrants, that underwent the greatest change in the postwar period. Among the newcomers were rabbis and scholars of Eastern Europe, uprooted by communism in Russia and later the horrors of the Holocaust, who found their way to America. Some were leaders of Hasidic sects (the rebbes of Lubavitch and

Satmar are the best known) and others were prominent heads and promising students of the great Lithuanian yeshivas. Uninfluenced, indeed repelled, by a modernity they associated with a threatening non-Jewish world, they were unprepared to compromise with it.

The primary complaint that the more rigorous Orthodox had about the modern Orthodox was the latter's participation in umbrella organizations of a religious nature together with non-Orthodox denominations, such as local boards of rabbis and the Synagogue Council of America, set up in 1926 to represent the common interests of Orthodox, Conservative, and Reform Judaism. Orthodox participation, the more rigorous Orthodox individuals charged, granted unwarranted legitimacy to heterodox versions of Judaism. In 1956, ten heads of rabbinical seminaries issued an edict forbidding membership in such bodies. Ever since, this insistence that other denominations were not "real" Judaism has hampered the development of interdenominational relations.

By the 1960s it was evident that the new type of American Orthodox Jew was successfully withstanding the pressures of acculturation. While culturally isolationist, these Jews quickly caught on to the intricacies of the American political system, utilizing the ballot box to protect their interests. Agudath Israel of America, which had been around since the 1920s as the U.S. branch of a worldwide antimodernist Orthodox movement, took on a new life in the 1960s as a potent lobbying group in Washington and on the state and local levels for the sectarian Orthodox. Public relations was another modern tool that these Orthodox Jews learned to use with great skill. In 1963, Agudath Israel began publication of the *Jewish Observer,* a glossy and well-written English monthly that conveyed the antiacculturation message through a contemporary medium.[17]

CONTEMPORARY REFORM

How to address rising rates of intermarriage, a challenge that emerged in the 1960s, quickly became a bone of contention within and between the denominations. Reform rabbis split over the question of rabbinic officiation, or co-officiation together with non-Jewish clergy. Some believed that Jewish marriage was inappropriate when one party was not Jewish. Others suggested that refusal to officiate might alienate the couple, while officiation increased the likelihood that the bride and groom would maintain a Jewish connection and raise the children as Jews. Furthermore, among those rabbis who would not themselves participate in a mixed-marriage ceremony, many had no compunction about referring such couples to more liberal rabbinic colleagues. The matter was brought before the Central Conference of

American Rabbis in 1973, and a majority of roughly 60 percent passed a resolution stating "opposition to participation by its members in any ceremony which solemnizes a mixed marriage." Nevertheless, no sanctions were spelled out for those rabbis who did perform intermarriages, and their numbers have grown over the years.[18]

Another Reform response to the proliferation of mixed marriages was the "outreach" initiative first enunciated in the late 1970s by Rabbi Alexander Schindler, president of the Union of American Hebrew Congregations. Ostensibly directed at interesting "unchurched" Americans in joining the Jewish faith, its actual intention was to win over the non-Jewish spouses and children in mixed marriages for Judaism through specially targeted educational and social programs that would ultimately lead to conversion. The idea of outreach to the intermarried quickly spread beyond Reform, since it gave some hope of arresting demographic erosion. Increasingly, Jewish federations across the country earmarked funds for outreach projects in synagogues, Jewish community centers, and other sites.[19]

Rabbi Schindler then led the Reform movement into a far more controversial policy that altered the age-old definition of Jewish identity. In traditional Jewish law, the religion of the mother determines the religious status of the child: The son or daughter of a Jewish mother is Jewish, irrespective of the father's religion, but the child of a non-Jewish mother is not Jewish, even if the father is, unless that child is converted. Since the great majority of mixed marriages were between Jewish men and non-Jewish women, most offspring of these marriages were non-Jews, unless conversion took place. To ease the barrier to the identification of these children as Jews, the Reform acceptance of patrilineal descent – adopted in 1983 after several years of heated debate – meant that one was a Jew if either parent was Jewish, and the individual performed acts, not specifically defined, to identify himself or herself as a Jew. This change was justified historically on the grounds that the matrilineal criterion was not Biblically mandated.[20]

Predictably, this decision aroused criticism in Orthodox and Conservative circles for creating a population considered Jewish by Reform but not by the more traditional branches. Reform leaders were quick to note, however, that the Orthodox had never recognized Reform conversions anyway, so that the decision to eliminate the need for such conversions if the father was Jewish was hardly as revolutionary as it seemed.

Reform outreach, capped by the decision on patrilineality, has had an energizing effect on Reform as a movement. The influx of new Reform Jews – patrilineal, converted, and also unconverted spouses who join Reform temples – has played a major role in the numerical resurgence of Reform. According to the 1990 National Jewish Population Survey, the number of self-identified Reform Jews drew even with, or perhaps even surpassed, the number of self-identified Conservative Jews, with the Orthodox lagging far behind. To be sure, even with this Reform surge a greater percentage of synagogue members were Conservative in 1990. However, since Reform Jews tended to be younger than their Conservative counterparts, Reform continued to grow during the 1990s at the expense of Conservatism, eventually outstripping the latter even among synagogue members. The 2000–01 National Jewish Population Survey showed that 39 percent of members were Reform as compared with 33 percent who were Conservative.[21]

At the same time that Reform was abandoning the traditional definition of Jewishness, it also gave evidence of new interest in ritual practice. Using Hebrew in the services, wearing a prayer shawl and covering the head during prayer, adhering to the laws of kashrut at synagogue functions, and reciting the blessing over bread and the *havdalah* service after the Sabbath became more common. Rabbi Eric Yoffie, who replaced Rabbi Schindler as president of the Union of American Hebrew Congregations in 1996, made Torah study and "the poetry of faith" his priorities. In 1999, the Central Conference of American Rabbis, the Reform rabbinical organization, passed a resolution affirming the centrality of Jewish ritual, which it called "the means by which we make our lives holy."[22]

Reform has remained in the forefront of social change. Outspokenly feminist, American Reform broke its last religious taboo against women when it ordained its first female rabbi in 1972. It has also championed the freedom of women to choose abortions. Another case in point is gay rights. While Jews have traditionally rejected homosexuality on the basis of the biblical ban on it as an "abomination," in 1990, after four years of study and debate, the Central Conference of American Rabbis declared that sexual orientation was Jewishly irrelevant, and that gays and lesbians might be ordained as rabbis. Five years later it endorsed civil marriage for homosexuals, and in 2000 it passed a resolution that supported those of its members who conducted "commitment ceremonies" for same-gender couples through "appropriate Jewish ritual."[23]

CONSERVATISM DEFINES ITSELF

Until the 1960s, the preferences of second-generation Jews for a traditional yet Americanized Judaism gave strength to Conservative Judaism. However, by the middle of that decade the movement stopped growing, as many Jews who had been raised in Conservative families chose to affiliate with Reform. According to the National Jewish Population Survey of 1990, fully 26 percent of Jews who said they came from Conservative backgrounds now called themselves Reform. A much smaller number, about 5 percent, seeking greater religious consistency, opted for Orthodoxy.[24]

The battleground for constructing a new definition for Conservatism was the issue of ordaining women. With women already eligible to be called to the Torah and be counted for a minyan, the United Synagogue in 1973, and the Rabbinical Assembly in 1977, called for the admission of women to the Rabbinical School of the Jewish Theological Seminary. It took until 1983 for the faculty to approve the change, by a vote of 34 to 8. Two years later, the school graduated the first female Conservative rabbi, and soon the Cantorial School also began graduating women.[25]

A number of Conservative opponents of the change, rabbis and laypeople, organized the Union for Traditional Conservative Judaism in 1984. Originally intended to be a traditionalist lobby within the Conservative movement, it broke with Conservatism entirely by 1990, setting up its own rabbinical school (its first four rabbis were ordained in 1996) and deleting the word *Conservative* from its name. Unsuccessful so far in establishing a mass movement, the Union for Traditional Judaism sees itself as the continuation of what the Conservative movement was originally intended to be, genuinely loyal to tradition but open to the modern world. In that sense, little distinguishes it from modern Orthodoxy.[26]

The next matter of contention between the traditional and innovative forces in Conservative Judaism was theological. Hoping to address the criticism that Conservative Judaism had no clearly defined principles, the movement set up a commission in 1985 to draw up a statement of beliefs. What emerged in 1988 was a document titled *Emet Ve'Emunah* (Truth and Faith). On some points, the statement was quite untraditional, stating that the Torah was a human document and that Jewish law constituted human beings' understanding of what God wants. On other matters, Emet Ve'Emunah validated a plurality of views – for example, it asserted the centrality of belief in God while recognizing the right to challenge God's existence. The overall effect of this statement of principles was, like women's ordination, to strengthen the hand of the forces of change within the movement. This tendency was reaffirmed in 2001 with the publication of *Etz Hayim*, the first Bible commentary officially commissioned by the denomination, which fully accepted the findings of contemporary Biblical criticism.[27]

In confronting the phenomenon of widespread mixed marriage, the Conservative movement has not gone nearly so far as Reform. While there are Conservative voices that call for ambitious outreach programs on the Reform model, and even a number of Conservative rabbis who want the movement to at least look into the possibility of enacting patrilineal descent, the predominant view opposes initiatives to mixed-marrieds that might send a message that such marriages are condoned. Thus the movement has tended to concentrate on "inreach," meaning programs to strengthen the Jewish identity of young Jews so as to encourage marriage to fellow Jews.

The question of the Jewish status of gays and lesbians has embroiled Conservative Judaism in an intense internal struggle that could well prove as divisive as the controversy over the ordination of women. Unable, on the one hand, to follow the lead of the Orthodox and ignore or dismiss the change in societal attitudes toward homosexuality, and unwilling, on the other, to follow the Reform precedent of rejecting or reinterpreting Biblical strictures against it, the Conservative movement has so far not reached a consensus – other than to assert that synagogues should welcome gays and lesbians.[28]

A 1996 study of affiliated Conservative Jews in North America, sponsored by the movement, yielded ambiguous results. Unlike earlier generations of Conservative Jews, for whom the movement was often a compromise prompted by rejection of the Orthodox and Reform alternatives, today's Conservative Jews, especially the younger cohorts, identify positively with Conservative principles. Furthermore, the movement has succeeded in instilling allegiance to the idea of Jewish law: 62 percent of its synagogue members agree that Conservative Jews are obligated to obey the law. However, actual practice lags far behind, as only 24 percent say they keep kosher, and 37 percent say they light Sabbath candles (the percentages for self-styled Conservative Jews who do not affiliate with a synagogue are even lower). Despite the nominal allegiance to Jewish law, 76 percent say that a Jew can be religious without observance, a surprising 69 percent accept the patrilineal definition of Jewishness practiced by Reform but resisted by the Conservative leadership, and 28 percent feel that their rabbis should perform intermarriages – a position that even the Reform movement has never officially condoned.[29]

THE NEW RECONSTRUCTIONISM

Since the 1960s, Reconstructionism has radically transformed itself. The naturalistic Judaism of Mordecai Kaplan, based on the scientific and sociological assumptions of the early twentieth century and the philosophy of pragmatism that was so influential at that time, has been largely replaced by an emphasis on individual religious experience and, for some, mysticism. As a result, Reconstructionism has become the branch of Judaism least tied to the past and most willing to experiment. The Reconstructionist rabbi is viewed as a resource person, not an authority figure. Each Reconstructionist congregation decides policies by consensus or majority vote, so that there is great variation between congregations. There is also considerable lay participation in the liturgy, including leading services and delivering talks, tasks that are generally reserved for cantors and rabbis in Reform and Conservative Judaism.

Nevertheless, the central bodies of Reconstructionist Judaism have developed guidelines for the movement that are widely accepted by Reconstructionists. Some of these positions, when adopted, anticipated those taken later by Reform – ordination of women, patrilineal descent, outreach to intermarried families, and the ordination of gays and lesbians. In fact, the movement went beyond Reform in 1992 when it ended all distinctions based on sexual preference, including the right to a Jewish ceremony – not just a civil one – equivalent to marriage.

The distinctive features of contemporary Reconstructionism would have a far greater impact on the larger Jewish community if the denomination were larger. Despite the founding of many new Reconstructionist congregations in recent years, the 1990 Jewish Population Survey showed that only 1.4 percent of American Jews (2 percent of synagogue members) identified themselves as Reconstructionists. The 2000–01 Survey indicated that 3 percent of American synagogue members were Reconstructionists.[30]

RESURGENT ORTHODOXY

The ferment within Orthodoxy that began in the 1960s with the emergence of a sectarian, immigrant-led group resistant to Americanization has accelerated. A new adjective, *haredi*, came to be applied to this group. The word means "fearful," in this context referring to the awe that the Jew is supposed to feel toward God. The rigor and self-assurance of this element – buttressed by parallel developments within Israeli Orthodox society – has had a spillover effect on American Orthodoxy as a whole, making it both more extreme in religious expression and less willing to accept direction from, or to compromise with, non-Orthodox forms of Judaism.[31]

The increasing dynamism and heightened morale of American Orthodoxy is demographically puzzling. Between 1970 and 1990, the percentage of self-defined Orthodox Jews in the United States, as measured by national surveys, declined from 11.5 percent to just 6.6 percent. These numbers, of course, must be taken with some skepticism, since it is likely that the surveys undercounted the growing haredi element, whose insularity made it suspicious of interviews and questionnaires about religion. In addition, much of the decline was due to the heavy concentration of Orthodox in the older immigrant generation, which was rapidly dying off.

Whatever the truth about Orthodox numbers, the remaining pool of Orthodox Jews today are undoubtedly more ideologically committed to Orthodoxy than in any previous generation in America. It is this noticeably heightened intensity, not numbers, which may give some credence to Orthodox claims that theirs is the only denomination that is likely to escape the ravages of assimilation and survive as a recognizable Jewish community. Indeed, the qualitatively disproportionate impact of Orthodoxy was reflected in the 1990 survey data: Orthodox Jews made up 16 percent of all synagogue members, close to two-and-a-half times their proportion of all self-identified Jews, and in the 2000–01 Survey their percentage of synagogue members was up to 21 percent. Furthermore, while less than half of Reform and Conservative Jews join a synagogue, 80 percent of the Orthodox are synagogue members. There is also evidence of rising Orthodox numbers in specific communities. A 2002 survey of New York City Jewry showed 19 percent of respondents identifying as Orthodox, a rise of 6 percent since 1991, and the *American Jewish Year Book* reported a 152 percent increase in the Jewish population of Lakewood, New Jersey – a heavily Orthodox bastion – from the 17,500 previously reported to 29,000 in 2001. The next largest increase, 27 percent, occurred in the Satmar Hasidic village of Kiryas Joel in New York State.[32]

Determined to rebuild the Orthodox Jewish societies that had gone up in the flames of the Holocaust, the leaders of sectarian Orthodoxy concentrated on education, creating elementary and high school yeshivas in cities across the country. Largely thanks to haredi educational zeal, a Jewish day school education through high school, for boys and girls, has become virtually de rigueur in the broader Orthodox community as well. Furthermore, new schools of higher Jewish education have proliferated where young men (not women) study Talmud and related texts for twelve or more hours daily. Such institutions are not, strictly speaking, rabbinical schools, since they are not intended to prepare students for the profession of the rabbinate. They stress instead the traditional Jewish value of sacred learning for its own sake. Some of the graduates do indeed enter the rabbinate or the field of Jewish education, while others become professionals or businessmen.[33] The strides made by the sectarian Orthodox have created several points of tension with the older modern Orthodox, represented institutionally by Yeshiva University and the Rabbinical Council of America. Recent signs of a possible counteroffensive by the modern Orthodox have been the establishment of Edah, a self-consciously modernist national organization, and of a new rabbinical seminary in New York, Chovevei Torah, embodying modernist values.

The role of women is a primary focus of dispute between the two Orthodox camps. Modern Orthodoxy, having pioneered women's religious education in the United States – now including even study of the Talmud, which haredi Orthodoxy resists – has also begun exploring new possibilities within the bounds of Jewish law for enhancing women's religious expression. These have taken the form of women's prayer groups, women reading the Scroll of Esther for the congregation on Purim, women as presidents of synagogues, and even calling women up to the Torah for aliyot. Pressure for diminishing the husband's advantage in Jewish divorce law (a woman can only be divorced if her husband willingly grants her a get) also reflects a growing sensitivity within modern Orthodoxy to the status of women. The sectarian Orthodox generally view attempts to address women's grievances as illegitimate intrusions of secular feminist ideology into Judaism, threatening the traditional role of the Jewish woman as wife and mother.[34]

AMERICAN HASIDISM

The various Hasidic groups constitute a significant Orthodox subculture in America. Hasidism began in eighteenth-century Poland as a folk movement that stressed emotional religion as against what it perceived as the dry rationalism of the scholarly leadership of the time. The movement quickly spread through Eastern Europe. American Hasidism is overwhelmingly a post–World War II phenomenon, brought to these shores by refugees from the Holocaust.

While for the purposes of broad classification the Hasidim can be identified as part of American haredi Orthodoxy, they have certain characteristics that set them apart. For one thing, while leadership in non-Hasidic circles is primarily determined by superior Talmudic scholarship, Hasidic leadership is both charismatic and hereditary. Each Hasidic group gives allegiance to its own rebbe, who is viewed as the repository of God's will, and who, in most cases, descends from a long line of Hasidic masters. Hasidic Jews are generally more isolationist in relation to the outside world than other haredim, tending to live in self-contained neighborhoods in close proximity to their rebbe, either in urban centers or in suburban villages. Hasidic sects differ greatly from each other: those of Hungarian origin, for example, are more hostile to modernity than those from Poland. A case in point is the Satmar group, which remains adamantly opposed to the very existence of the State of Israel on the grounds that Jews may not create a state until the messiah comes.[35]

The best known Hasidic sect on the American scene has been Lubavitch, also known as Habad. Under the energetic leadership of Rabbi Menachem Mendel Schneerson (1902–94), who assumed control in 1951, Lubavitch has made Jewish outreach its priority. Avoiding an all-or-nothing approach, Lubavitch emissaries around the country (and all over the world) have influenced many Jews, if not to join Lubavitch or commit themselves to live by Jewish law, at least to perform certain rituals, feel positively toward Jewish tradition, and maintain a personal allegiance to the rebbe.

However, the movement is currently undergoing a crisis. Speculation began in 1991 among Lubavitchers that the elderly and ill Rabbi Schneerson was the messiah, and enthusiasm for the idea escalated steadily within the movement. Even the rebbe's death three years later did not resolve the issue. Many of his followers continue to hold out the hope that he will rise from the dead, and even those Lubavitchers who disagree are reluctant to condemn the messianists openly. Meanwhile, although no successor has been chosen, Lubavitch continues its outreach activities as before.[36] For its part, non-Lubavitch Orthodoxy has been shocked and embarrassed by the messianic fervor, especially since the ascription of redemptive powers to a dead man bears an all-too-close resemblance to early Christianity at the point where it began to diverge from its Jewish origins. In 1996, the Rabbinical Council of America issued a resolution declaring that the doctrine of a messiah who will arise from the dead has no basis in Jewish tradition.

DENOMINATIONAL PROSPECTS

Neither Reform nor Conservative Judaism, each of which previously aspired to become synonymous with American Judaism, makes that claim any longer. Both movements have changed the names of their synagogue bodies to reflect a more modest contemporary understanding of themselves. In 1991, the organization of Conservative synagogues abandoned the inclusive-sounding name United Synagogue of America in favor of the denominationally specific United Synagogue of Conservative Judaism. In 2003, the Reform movement followed suit, as the Union of American Hebrew Congregations became the Union for Reform Judaism. At the beginning of the twenty-first century it is Orthodoxy – still far smaller than its two competitors – that optimistically sees itself as the only form of Judaism able to withstand the assimilatory pressures of American society, a belief that only time can affirm or deny.

Meanwhile, there is reason to question the standard denominational framework for understanding American Judaism. On the one hand, an unknown number of Jews interested in greater spirituality choose to pray and study in nondenominational settings, often under the banner of Jewish Renewal. On the other, the fastest growing Jewish "religious" group consists, ironically, of self-styled secular Jews, for whom denominational identity has no meaning.[37] Over the next several decades, American Judaism may take on unanticipated new forms.

Notes

1. Michael A. Meyer, *Reponse to Modernity: A History of the Reform Movement in Judaism* (New York: Oxford University Press, 1988), Chapters 1–3.
2. Ibid., Chapter 6.
3. Ibid., 387–88.
4. Ibid., Chapter 7.
5. Hasia Diner, "Like the Antelope and the Badger: The Founding and Early Years of the Jewish Theological Seminary, 1886–1902," in *Tradition Renewed: A History of the Jewish Theological Seminary of America*, ed. Jack Wertheimer (New York: Jewish Theological Seminary, 1997), vol. 1, 7–12.
6. Ismar Schorsch, *From Text to Context: The Turn to History in Modern Judaism* (Hanover: University Press of New England, 1994), Chapters 8–13.
7. The definitive work on the sociology of Conservative Judaism in the first half of the twentieth century – and one of the classic books on American Jewry – is Marshall Sklare, *Conservative Judaism: An American Religious Movement*, new augmented ed. (New York: Schocken Books, 1972).
8. Michael A. Meyer, *Reponse to Modernity: A History of the Reform Movement in Judaism* (New York: Oxford University Press, 1988), 388–91.
9. Charles S. Liebman, "Orthodoxy in American Jewish Life," *American Jewish Year Book* 66 (1965), 27–30.
10. Jeffrey S. Gurock, "Resisters and Accommodators: Varieties of Orthodox Rabbis in America, 1886–1983," in *The American Rabbinate: A Century of Accommodation and Change*, ed. Jacob Rader Marcus and Abraham J. Peck (Hoboken: KTAV Publishing House, 1985), 10–37.
11. Jenna Weissman Joselit, *New York's Jewish Jews: The Orthodox Community in the Interwar Years* (Bloomington: Indiana University Press, 1990), chapter 2; Jeffrey S. Gurock, *The Men and Women of Yeshiva: Higher Education, Orthodoxy, and American Judaism* (New York: Columbia University Press, 1988), Chapters 2–4.
12. Mel Scult, *Judaism Faces the Twentieth Century: A Biography of Mordecai M. Kaplan* (Detroit: Wayne State University Press, 1993).
13. Charles S. Liebman, "Reconstructionism in American Jewish Life," *American Jewish Year Book* 71 (1970), 3–99.
14. Michael A. Meyer, *Reponse to Modernity*, 326–34.
15. Michael A. Meyer, *Reponse to Modernity*, 309–13, 364–68.
16. Neil Gilman, *Conservative Judaism: The New Century* (West Orange: Behrman House, 1993), Chapter 6.
17. Charles S. Liebman, "Orthodoxy in American Jewish Life," *American Jewish Year Book* 66 (1965), 67–79.
18. Michael A. Meyer, *Reponse to Modernity: A History of the Reform Movement in Judaism* (New York: Oxford University Press, 1988), 371–73; Dana Evan Kaplan,

American Reform Judaism: An Introduction (New Brunswick: Rutgers University Press, 2003), 177–79.

19. Dana Evan Kaplan, *American Reform Judaism: An Introduction* (New Brunswick: Rutgers University Press, 2003), 157–64.

20. Dana Evan Kaplan, *American Reform Judaism*, 171–72.

21. Walter Ruby, "Reform vs. Conservative: Who's Winning?," *Moment* (April 1996), vol. 21, 2, 30–37, 67; *The National Jewish Population Survey 2000–01: Strength, Challenge and Diversity in the American Jewish Population* (New York: United Jewish Communities, 2003), 7.

22. Dana Evan Kaplan, *American Reform Judaism*, 184–85, 238–40.

23. Ibid., Chapters 9, 10.

24. Walter Ruby, "Reform vs. Conservative: Who's Winning?," *Moment* (April 1996), vol. 21, 2, 32.

25. Neil Gilman, *Conservative Judaism: The New Century* (West Orange: Behrman House, 1993), Chapter 8.

26. Ibid., 145–48.

27. Ibid., Chapter 9.

28. Steve Israel, "How Halachic is Homosexuality? Conservatives to Debate Gays and Religion," *Manhattan Jewish Sentinel* (November 21–27, 2003), 2, 12.

29. Jack Wertheimer, ed., *Conservative Synagogues and Their Members: Highlights of the North America Survey of 1995–96* (New York: Jewish Theological Seminary, 1996).

30. Walter Ruby, "Reform vs. Conservative: Who's Winning?," *Moment* (April 1996), 32; *The National Jewish Population Survey 2000–01: Strength, Challenge and Diversity in the American Jewish Population* (New York: United Jewish Communities, 2003), 7.

31. Haym Soloveitchik, "Rupture and Reconstruction: The Transformation of Contemporary Orthodoxy," *Tradition* (Summer 1994), vol. 28, 4, 64–130.

32. Walter Ruby, "Reform vs. Conservative: Who's Winning?," *Moment* (April 1996), vol. 21, 2, 32; *The National Jewish Population Survey 2000–01: Strength, Challenge and Diversity in the American Jewish Population* (New York: United Jewish Communities, 2003), 7; *The Jewish Community Study of New York: 2002 Highlights* (New York: United Jewish Appeal – Federation of New York, 2003), 31; *American Jewish Year Book* 102 (2002), 249.

33. William B. Helmreich, *The World of the Yeshiva: An Intimate Portrait of Orthodox Jewry* (New York: The Free Press, 1982).

34. Sylvia Barack Fishman, *Changing Minds: Feminism in Contemporary Orthodox Jewish Life* (New York: American Jewish Committee, 2000).

35. Allan Nadler, *The Hasidim in America* (New York: American Jewish Committee, 1994).

36. Jonathan Mahler, "Waiting for the Messiah of Eastern Parkway," *New York Times Sunday Magazine* (21 September 2003), 42–47.

37. Egon Mayer, Barry Kosmin, and Ariela Keysar, *American Jewish Identity Survey 2001* (New York: Graduate Center of the City University of New York, 2001), 33–45; *The Jewish Community Study of New York: 2002 Highlights* (New York: United Jewish Appeal–Federation of New York, 2003), 31.

5 Patterns of American Jewish religious behavior

CHAIM I. WAXMAN

Historically, Jews have been defined as a religious group and continue to be so defined by scholars. Thus, an overwhelming majority of Jews define themselves accordingly. In fact, most major surveys conducted on America's Jews that pertain to religion typically inquire about denominational affiliation, synagogue or temple membership, attendance at synagogue or temple services, and performance of basic rituals. This follows from the classic definition of religion as defined by the French sociologist, Emile Durkheim (1858–1917), who suggested that religion is "a unified system of beliefs and practices relative to sacred things, that is to say, things set apart and forbidden – beliefs and practices which unite into one single moral community, called a Church, all those who adhere to them."[1] However, these questions and their corresponding responses do not provide sufficient information on the religious beliefs or religious behavior patterns of American Jews. Indeed, such a perspective misses much of what most American Jews view as their religious needs and character. This essay goes beyond those data and examines American Jewish patterns of religious behavior as well as belief in a sociohistorical context. In an effort to unravel the meaning behind these actions or convictions, I examine and interpret the various patterns, their changes over time, and their relationship with the broader patterns of religious behavior and belief within American society.

In the mid-twentieth century, several sociologists studied the initial manifestations of these Jewish patterns. On the basis of field research conducted on the Jews of Yankee City between 1930 and 1935, W. Lloyd Warner and Leo Srole[2] suggested that "the progressive defection of successive generations of Jews from their religious system in a process apparently nearly completed among the children of the immigrants themselves" was much more apparent than the defections among other groups. It was their observation that "the religious subsystem of [the Yankee City Jewish] community is apparently in a state of disintegration,"[3] primarily because of an economic factor. If Jews were to successfully compete in the economic sphere, Warner and Srole argued, they had to break with the traditional religious patterns that tended to be restrictive, such as Sabbath observance. Although they readily dropped those religious traditions that inhibited their successful participation in the competitive race, Yankee City Jews did not opt for mass identificational assimilation nor did their actions result in the disintegration of the Jewish community. As Warner and Srole noted, what developed was a process of basic change in the nature of the community:

> [T]he process of change is one of a replacement of traditionally Jewish elements by American elements. In the religious system of the Jews there is no such replacement. The Jews are not dropping their religious behaviors, relations, and representations under the influence of the American religious system. There are no indications that they are becoming Christian. Even the F^1 generation [the native-born generation] can only be said to be irreligious.[4]

The Jewish community, according to them, was culturally assimilating but not disappearing. Even as Yankee City's Jews shed their traditional Jewish norms, they did not eliminate the religious element from the group's self-definition. They did not cease to define themselves as a religioethnic group, nor proceed to become solely an ethnic group, nor seek to eliminate the ethnic component of Jewishness in order to define Jewishness as solely a matter of religion, as Reform had done.[5] Instead, they embraced Conservative Judaism, which they perceived as a progressive form of Judaism that was also rooted in tradition. It provided them with a framework within which they could behave as Americans while espousing an ideological commitment to tradition, so as to maintain an explicit emphasis on the ethnic character of Judaism. In other words, their Judaism was as much an expression of ethnicity as of religion.

In the 1950s, sociologist Will Herberg performed his own analysis of religion in the United States at the mid-twentieth century, arguing that the Americanization of Judaism "was characterized by a far-reaching accommodation to the American pattern of religious life which affected all 'denominations' in the American synagogue. The institutional system was virtually the same as in the major Protestant churches."[6] Herberg then proceeded to provide a vivid portrait of that Americanization as it manifested itself in a variety of American Jewish religious patterns, including the organizational structure of the synagogue as well as the structure of the synagogue edifice itself, the patterns of worship, ritual observance, and Jewish education. He further suggested that "by mid-century, all three of the 'denominations' were substantially similar expressions of this new American Jewish religious pattern, differing only in background, stage of development, and institutional affiliation."[7] That Herberg's observations about American Jewish denominationalism were either incorrect at the time he made them or that the denominational patterns have subsequently changed radically is evidenced in the detailed analyses of Lazerwitz, Winter, Dashefsky, and Tabory[8] and Waxman.[9] Nowadays, it is less likely that one's denominational affiliation is a matter of sociology rather than ideology. Contemporary American Jewish Baby Boomers in different denominations are much more similar to each other socioeconomically than they have ever been. Denominational affiliation is increasingly a matter of personal choice, presumably based on decisions about theological issues as well as a desire for structure in one's life and the lives of one's family members.

Nevertheless, there are some important insights in Herberg's central thesis about religion in America at midcentury. When concurring with theologian Reinhold Neibuhr, Herberg provides a conclusion that is reminiscent of Durkheim's theory of religion and society:

> What Americans believe in when they are religious is . . . religion itself. Of course, religious Americans speak of God and Christ, but what they seem to regard as really redemptive is primarily religion, the "positive" attitude of *believing*. It is this faith in faith, this religion that makes religion its own object, that is the outstanding characteristic of contemporary American religiosity. . . . Prosperity, success, and advancement in business are the obvious ends for which religion, or rather the religious attitude of "believing" is held useful.[10]

This kind of religion, Herberg argues is, in essence, not religion but crass secularism, in that it is worship not of God but of the goals and values of American society, the "American way of life." Thus, even though there were increases in the rates of religious identification and affiliation, and increases in the percentage of Americans who placed importance on religion, it was not really religion and religious values but secular American social and cultural values that they were revering. Perceptive as he may have been, Herberg's critique was more theological than sociological and was a reflection of his personal spiritual transition from secularism to religion.[11] However, he was far from alone in deciphering the basic secularism of America's Jews, even as they continued to affiliate with American Jewish religious institutions.

Despite the many changes in American society and culture, including changes in patterns of identification and affiliation with formal institutions including religious ones, there are certain striking similarities between American Jewish religion at midcentury as depicted by Herberg and the more contemporary patterns. On the one hand, they do not manifest strong commitment to traditional Jewish religious ritual or belief. On the other hand, they are very strongly committed to the principle of social justice and the belief that it is the core of Jewish identity. For example, when a survey for the

Los Angeles Times asked respondents to indicate the quality most important to their Jewish identity, half of the respondents answered "social equality."[12]

On the heels of the first edition of Herberg's work, Herbert Gans, in line with Warner and Srole, again portrayed the religion of America as, actually, an expression of ethnicity, in his analysis of the acculturation and secularization of the Jews of Park Forest.[13] As he saw it, the temple was the center of most of the community's activities, but not because of its sacred status and the centrality of religiosity in the members' lives. On the contrary, it was the focal point because of ideological and institutional diffusion and its ability to adapt itself to the wishes and desires of its members. This is very much akin to what Peter Berger later portrayed as religious institutions being subject to consumer preferences.[14] As Gans saw it, in the case of America's Jews, the consumer preferences were essentially ethnic; that is, the temples, synagogues, and Jewish schools were, in the final analysis, manifestations "of the need and desire of Jewish parents to provide clearly visible institutions and symbols with which to maintain and reinforce the ethnic identification of the next generation."[15] At a later point, Gans broadened his analysis of both ethnicity and religion in America and concluded that they are "symbolic," in much the same way that Charles Liebman used the term, as distinct from ritualistic.

Rituals, Liebman argues, are *mitzvot*, meaning "commandments," whereas ceremonies are symbolic acts that derive from and appeal to personalism, voluntarism, universalism, and moralism. He focused on the non-Orthodox, who constitute about 90 percent of American Jewry, and detailed how they create a uniquely American Judaism by both reinterpreting and transforming traditional rituals into ceremonies, and by producing entirely new ceremonies, all of which are performed within the context of the aforementioned modern doctrines or "isms." These isms, he concluded, "now have become major dimensions or instruments through which American Jews interpret and transform the Jewish tradition."[16]

Contemporary American Judaism is replete with the manifestations of the transformation of Jewish rituals into ceremonies. Perhaps one of the most prevalent is the Bar and Bat Mitzvah, which is traditionally a rite of passage at age thirteen for boys and twelve for girls, during which time the youngster becomes adult for the purposes of religious observances. In American Judaism, this ritual been transformed into ceremonious affairs where, even among Conservative synagogue members, approximately half have a nonkosher Bar or Bat Mitzvah reception.[17]

Another ritual that has been recently transformed is the gay marriage ceremony, during which the spouses wear *kipot* and *talitot*, the traditional skullcaps and prayer shawls worn by Jewish men and, more recently, by some Jewish women. The ceremony is replete with the breaking of the glass, similar to the traditional ceremony, symbolizing the incompleteness of the joy so long as Jerusalem has not been ultimately redeemed.

The initial manifestations of the privatizing and personalizing of American Judaism were evident in the Havurah, a late-1960s movement that represented alienation from the institutionalized synagogue and its substitution in the form of countercultural prayer and study groups. In one of the few ethnographies of a Havurah, the Kelton Minyan, Riv-Ellen Prell provides important insight into its basic objective. As she found, its members sought to synthesize Jewish religious tradition as they understood it with their own modern American norms and values, and the Minyan functioned as the place where prayer and study were meant to be experienced in an egalitarian manner.[18] However, things did not always turn out as they had been envisioned, as Prell's analysis of the "prayer crisis" – members' inability at times to accept or find meaning in certain liturgy – clearly demonstrates.

One of the Havurah movement's founders and spiritual gurus was Rabbi Zalman Schachter-Shalomi, who, having been ordained as a Lubavitch-trained rabbi, parted with Orthodox Judaism and developed his own non-Orthodox brand of Hasidic spiritualism in the hopes that it would bring about a "Jewish Renewal." As he saw it,

> Jewish Renewal is based on the Kabbalah, Hasidism, and other forms of Jewish mysticism. These sources support a transformational and developmental reading of our current place in history.... Restoration is ultimately not a viable option because of the impact of the paradigm shift.... This expresses itself in the emergent voices of the emerging cosmology, in which old reality maps are scrapped and new ones emerge that are, if not identical, at least parallel to the intuitions and traditions of Jewish mysticism ... augmented and at times even reshaped by feminism.... This in turn leads to a kind of healthy planetary homemaking and is concerned about ecology. This also calls for an eco-kosher *halakhah* and ethic. In order to become the kinds of Jews/persons who can effect the needed changes, the intra- and interpersonal work related to meditation and liturgy that are the laboratory of the spirit need to be renewed, and this leads to making prayer and meditation into a science as well as an art. Hence the need for a davvenology that is (1) an art and a science, (2) based on the Kabbalah, and (3) a generic empiricism.[19]

Among Schachter-Shalomi's proteges is Arthur Waskow, who was an early 1960s antiwar activist who adapted Hasidism to his social and political ideologies. He is currently a rabbi and director of a center committed to spiritually healing the world, and he is also a leader of the Alliance for Jewish Renewal. He introduced an alternative Passover Haggadah, *The Freedom Seder*,[20] which transformed the Jewish Seder ritual into a universalistic one. He later created a unique Jewish festival commentary, *Seasons of Our Joy*.[21] In all of his works, he puts a Jewish–Hasidic–spiritual cloak on his political and social radicalism. For example, in his more recent work, *Down-To-Earth Judaism; Food, Money, Sex, and the Rest of Life*,[22] Waskow adopts Schachter-Shalomi's concept of ecokosher and argues for expanding the definition of *kosher* to include not only food but every kind of product that Jews "ingest." Rhetorically, he asks a series of confrontational questions, such as whether it is kosher to use newsprint in a Jewish newspaper when it was created by cutting down an ancient forest, or whether a bank that invests its money in an oil company that pollutes the ocean is a kosher place for either an individual or the United Jewish Appeal to keep accounts. Moreover, Waskow's views on sexuality are anything but traditional. He asserts that a religion that sanctions sex only within marriage is not a realistic one, and instead he looks for ways in which Judaism can celebrate all human sexual relationships, whether within marriage or without, whether heterosexual or homosexual.

Schachter-Shalomi and Waskow may be unique, but their influence is significant. They were among the major figures in the neo-Hasidic and mystical movement that emerged alongside the Havurah movement.[23] Most of those involved in the Havurah movement were not as radical as Waskow nor as neo-Hasidic as Schachter-Shalomi, but they were interested in spiritualism in nontraditional ways. It was within that context that *The Jewish Catalogue* was written. Patterned after the *Whole Earth Catalog*, a work that was very popular in the 1960s counterculture, *The Jewish Catalogue* quickly became a bestseller and a publishing phenomenon in American Judaica[24] and was the first of two additional such catalogs. In a critical review, Marshall Sklare expressed his disdain for the "new personalism" represented in the work. Although, he asserted, "in most areas of life discussed . . . the relevant Jewish law is scrupulously reported, where applicable . . . the dominant stress quickly shifts to the experiential side of the subject in question, the side connected with issues of personal style, of taste, and aesthetic pleasure."[25] It was not just one book that Sklare was reacting to; for him, it was another line in the transformation of American Judaism that had begun in the Palmer, Massachussetts branch of Conservative Judaism's Camp Ramah, then to the *havurot*, and then to the creation of a guide for the privatization of Judaism. It was not this book that disturbed him so much as its further impact on American Judaism. Whether or not Sklare was correct in his specific criticisms of that volume is beside the point. In the final analysis, the empirical evidence appears to confirm the transformation, the privatization of much of American Judaism. This is even the case, to some degree, with some varieties of Orthodox Judaism,[26] such as the "nominally Orthodox," who are much more selective in their ritual observance and religious beliefs than the "centrist" Orthodox, who in turn are more selective than the "traditional" Orthodox. Although there are neither Orthodox who overtly assert the non-binding character of *Halakha* nor any who overtly legitimate nonconformity with basic requirements of dietary and family purity rituals as well as Sabbath, there are those who are selective in their own personal conformity with Orthodox beliefs and norms and are thus described as "behaviorally modern Orthodox."[27]

The increased personalism and privatization of not only Judaism but religion in general appears to be a phenomenon that transcends America's geographic boundaries and is, in fact, much more pervasive in other, mostly Western, countries. The political sociologist, Ronald Inglehart, has conducted comprehensive cross-national surveys, and his analyses reveal broad international patterns for which he provides a penetrating sociological explanation. In his analysis of survey data gathered in twenty-five industrial societies primarily in Western Europe and the United States between 1970 and 1986, Inglehart argues that "economic, technological, and sociopolitical changes have been transforming the cultures of advanced industrial societies in profoundly important ways."[28] Following Maslow's need hierarchy, according to which the need for food, shelter, and sex are on the lowest rung and must be satisfied before a person can move up the pyramid to its apex, self-actualization, Inglehart maintains that individuals are most concerned with the satisfaction of material needs and threats to their physical security. "Materialist" values, which are characteristic of less secure, economically and otherwise, societies, Inglehart avers, are values that emphasize material security. In the area of politics, these would focus on such needs as strong leaders and order. In the realm of economics, the values emphasize economic growth and strong individual achievement motivation. In the area of sexuality and family norms, the emphasis would be on the maximization of reproduction within the two-parent family. Within the realm of religion, the emphasis is on a higher power and absolute rules. However, once the basic material needs are satisfied and physical safety is ensured, individuals strive for "postmaterialist" values; these entail the satisfaction of more remote needs, many of which are in the spiritual, aesthetic, and interpersonal realms. Their focus becomes self-fulfillment and personal autonomy, rather than identifying themselves with their families, localities, ethnic groups, or even nations. The "culture shift" is manifested in a declining respect for authority and increased mass participation; an increasing emphasis on subjective well-being and quality-of-life concerns; an increasing emphasis on meaningful work; greater choice in the area of sexual norms; declining confidence in established religious institutions, as well as declining rates of church attendance; and an increasing contemplation of the purpose and meaning of life. This shift, which entails a shift from central authority to individual autonomy, has taken place in a "postmaterialist" society, that is, the West in the late twentieth century.

For institutionalized religions, this has meant they can no longer count on traditional allegiance. In modern society and culture, religion's ability to locate us and provide that order and meaning is greatly diminished. As Peter Berger puts it, the intricately interrelated processes of pluralization, bureaucratization, and secularization that are endemic to modernity have greatly shaken the religious "plausibility structures."[29] Although "a rumor of angels" prevails, it is but a rumor in modern society, and it coexists with a "heretical imperative." In other words, the pluralistic character of modern society impels us to make choices, including religious ones.[30] We are no longer impelled to believe and act. We choose, even when we choose to be religiously Orthodox. From the standpoint of traditional religion, Berger points out that this is heresy because it "comes from the Greek verb *hairein*, which means 'to choose.' A *hairesis* originally meant, quite simply, the taking of a choice."[31]

The growth of fundamentalism and *haredism* in advanced Western societies in no way disproves Inglehart's thesis. He argues that it is precisely the conditions of postmodernity that foster religious fundamentalism, which is typically reactionary and arises as a defense mechanism in reaction to the deep fears and anxieties inherent in the situation. It is, as Inglehart suggests, a reaction to the growth of postmaterialism,[32] and, in most advanced societies, fundamentalists are a minority who can, at most, slow down some of the impact of postmaterialism. It may be predicted that the greater the size of the fundamentalist constituency in a given society, the more it will be able to have an impact on consequences of postmaterialism in that society. In their most recent study, Inglehart and Wayne Baker found that, although attendance at religious services is declining in postmaterialist countries, including the United States, close to half of the Americans surveyed say that they often think about the meaning and purpose of life, and fully half rate the importance of God in their lives as very high. They found that allegiances to the established religious institutions are continuing to decline in postmaterialist countries, but spiritual concerns are not.[33]

Indeed, during the closing decades of the twentieth century, there was a significant increase in spirituality in the United States as a whole. As reported by the Religion Editor of *Publishers Weekly*,

[I]n February 1994, the Association of American Publishers...had already reported that the sales of books in the Bible/religion/spirituality category were up 59 percent nationally over sales for February 1992.

Earlier, in June 1992, *American Bookseller*, the official publication of
the American Booksellers Association, had devoted six pages to this
emerging pattern, declaring that "the category's expansion is
indisputable." An even earlier Gallup study had projected that the
largest sales increase in nonfiction books in the twenty-first century
would be in religion/spirituality books (82 percent growth by 2010 over
1987), to be followed at a considerable distance (59 percent) by
second-place investment/economic/income tax books. As if in
preparation for that predicted pattern, the American Booksellers
Association in 1995 opened for the first time a special section of its
annual convention and trade show for what it categorizes as
"religious/spiritual-inspirational" books.[34]

It is not only in books but in television as well that Americans demonstrate a deep involvement with spiritualism. One highly popular weekly
show – indeed, it was among the ten most-watched television shows in the
country in 1999 – was *Touched by an Angel*, a show that featured the well-
known singer and actress Della Reese as an angel who oversees the work
of her angels in the field. Each week, these angels, who look like ordinary
humans, would help people who are in trouble, undergoing a crisis, or otherwise unhappy by convincing them that God loves them and that, if they only
seek Him out, He will respond and help them to change their lives for the
better. The numerous references to God and His mercy were completely out
of character with what American prime-time network television had previously been. It simply had not been considered proper to mix religion, which
had been relegated to the private sphere, into the mass media public sphere
in any serious way. This was not just mysticism or spirituality, but rather traditional Biblical notions about God and His ways, something that the mass
media have long avoided like a plague.

In 1999, Andrew Greeley and Michael Hout analyzed survey data from
the past several decades and found that an increasing majority of Americans
responded affirmatively to this question: "Do you believe there is a life after
death?" Between 1973 and 1998, the figures rose from 77 to 82 percent. In
fact, the increases have been across the board, among various religions as well
as among those claiming no religious affiliation, and have been the greatest
among America's Jews. These figures appear to indicate an abandonment of
secularism and a return to religious consciousness and religiosity.

In the summer of 2000, Senator Joseph I. Lieberman, an Orthodox Jew,
was nominated as the Vice Presidential running mate on the Democratic
ticket. He so frequently made reference to God and traditional religion that
he was asked, by a number of national organizations – including a Jewish

one – to tone down those references, lest he weaken the separation of religion and state. Nevertheless, his very nomination suggests that traditional religion is viewed positively among the American public. There has also been a proliferation of books about Kabbalah and, as a book critic for the widely circulated Jewish weekly newspaper, the *Jewish Week*, found, "new titles are coming from Jewish publishers and university presses as well as mainstream commercial houses that only a few years ago would have found the subject too much on the fringes."[35]

Whatever else the rise in spirituality in American culture may mean, however, it does not mean a return to religiosity in the sense of normative, institutionalized religion. As both Robert Wuthnow and Wade Clark Roof argue, the contemporary spirituality is largely a search or "quest" by the individuals of the Baby Boomer generation and their children to find "purpose" and "meaning" in the individuals' personal existence. As Wuthnow suggests, the sacred has been transformed into something fluid. The Baby Boomers are the first to have "opportunities to explore new spiritual horizons," and in the past two decades they sought it within themselves, in their "inner selves," rather than within the church.[36] On the basis of his analyses of religion and spirituality among Baby Boomers, Roof argues that Americans' ideas and practice of religion is motivated by a search for a sense of spirituality and personal fulfillment. Americans are looking beyond traditional religious institutions and identities and are on a spiritual quest, borrowing different elements from a variety of practices now available to them in the ever-expanding spiritual marketplace.[37] The rise in spirituality was, thus, part and parcel of the pattern of personalism and privatization that is increasingly characteristic of American religion, in general, and American Judaism, in particular.

The increased personalism and privatization present powerful challenges not only to established religious institutions but also to all institutions. For Jews, these are challenges to the very unity of the Jewish people. As Charles Liebman has penetratingly analyzed it, the privatization of Judaism weakens the basic nature of ethnic Judaism. The "new spiritualism" thus weakens the basic Jewish notions of peoplehood, community, and solidarity.[38] His argument appears to receive support from a broad analysis by political scientist Robert Putnam, who amassed a wide array of empirical evidence indicating that Americans are increasingly less likely to be involved in civic activities and are detached from social groups such as community. They are less likely to join parent–teacher associations, unions, political parties, and a host of other social groups, all of which, he argues, has serious implications for the future of American society.[39] For Jews, it also has serious implications for Jewish peoplehood and the Jewish community.

The connection between commitment to tradition, commitment to institutions, and commitment to the group are apparent in the intense involvements in the haredi community with charity and social welfare, or *zedaka* and *gemilut hasadim*. For example, Netty Gross reported on a major study of volunteerism in Israel by Benjamin Gidron of Ben-Gurion University, who had found that "nearly 45 percent of ultra-Orthodox Jews volunteer...compared to 15 percent of secular Israelis."[40] Moreover, the greater propensity for charity is not limited to haredim. As the Guttman Center 2000 study of Israeli Jews found,

> Comparison of the civic and social priorities of the various sectors highlights an interesting phenomenon that has been noted in earlier studies: "religiosity" is associated with altruistic social values. For example, "contributing to society" is very important for 64% of the religious/strictly observant, as compared to 55% of the traditional/somewhat observant, 48% of the non-religious/somewhat observant, 41% of the non-religious/non-observant, and only 33% of the anti-religious. A similar pattern is evident for "being a good citizen" and "understanding another person's point of view."...The altruistic Jewish values of "helping the needy" and "giving charity" are also more important to the religious/strictly observant (81%) and the traditional/observant-to-a-great-extent (as high as 70%) than to the non-religious/non-observant (31% and 16%) and the anti-religious (28% and 12%). The pattern noted above, that religious and traditional respondents attribute greater importance to helping others than do the non-religious and anti-religious, recurs here. However, there has been a significant rise in the importance of these two altruistic Jewish values among Israeli Jews in general – from 32% to 42% ("giving charity") and from 41% to 56% ("helping the needy").[41]

In a similar vein, my analysis of American Jewish Baby Boomers indicates that patterns of charity vary denominationally. Of the Orthodox Baby Boomer respondents, 80.5 percent reported contributing to Jewish charities, compared with 56.4 percent of the Conservative, 43.5 percent of the Reform, and only 40.7 percent of the denominationally unaffiliated. Almost 95 (94.4) percent of the small number of Reconstructionists in the sample reported that they contributed to Jewish charities. The significance of affiliation within the three major denominations becomes even sharper when family size and family income are considered. Orthodox Baby Boomers reported larger families and lower annual family incomes than those who are Conservative or Reform (an average of about $10,000 a year less than the Conservative and $20,000 less than the Reform). However, 70.8 percent of the Orthodox reported contributing $500 or more to Jewish charities, as compared to 18 percent of the Conservative and 15.7 percent of the Reform. Of the unaffiliated, only 11.4 percent reported contributing $500, and none contributed more than $1,000 to Jewish charities.[42]

For all of their beneficial qualities, the postmaterialist values conflict with the traditional religioethnic bases of the Jewish community. Although membership in the American Jewish community was always voluntary, from the legal–political perspective, it was much less voluntary before the denominational institutions of America were overtaken by what Berger calls religious free enterprise and consumer demands, which are today guided by individualistic values. Religious authority has declined even as the so-called spiritual quests of the Baby Boomers intensify. Spiritualism is consistent with postmaterialist values; institutional religious loyalties and religious authority are not. It is for these reasons that Reform and Reconstructionism are the denominations most appealing to those Jewish Baby Boomers that wish to identify religiously. Reform and Reconstructionist Judaism reflect and reinforce many of the postmaterialist values to a greater extent than the more religiously conservative denominations do. In addition, Reform Judaism, in particular, has incorporated, in a nondogmatic manner, many more of the rituals and customs of traditional Judaism than it had in the past and, thus, attracts those who, for one reason or another, find those rituals and customs appealing.[43] Orthodoxy and, to some extent, Conservative Judaism, by contrast, profess the notion of religious law, tradition, and authority; in this way, they do not speak to those for whom the values of individualism are primary.

Nevertheless, these denominations are not immune to the impact of the larger culture. Conservative Judaism was, from its inception, a bold attempt to enable adherence to tradition while not restricting participation in the larger American society and culture. As Elazar and Geffen indicate, however, many have opted out of the denomination altogether and most of those who have not have religiously liberalized it from within.[44] Within Orthodoxy as well, although the dominant trend is one of increasing fundamentalism,[45] there appears to be an opposite, although smaller, movement within Modern Orthodoxy. Both in the United States and in Israel there are increasingly organized public challenges by individuals and groups within Orthodoxy to the established rabbinic elite and their interpretation of correct Jewish law, Halakha. In the United States, these manifest themselves in the now-annual conferences of the Jewish Orthodox Feminist Alliance (JOFA) and Edah, an organization whose motto is "the courage to be modern and Orthodox" and that seeks "to give voice to the ideology and values of modern Orthodoxy and to educate and empower the community to address its concerns."[46] These conferences attract many hundreds of attendees and appear to grow larger each year. Although they are not quite as organized, there have been similar developments in Israel.[47] What the impact of these developments will be on the broader Orthodox community remains to be seen. It is also not clear that the numbers of such Orthodox have actually increased. It may well be that they are the same proportion of the Orthodox population that they had previously been; the change is that they are now more vocal and attempting to organize. Be that as it may, it alone is a reflection of the larger cultural patterns of postmaterialism.

Since September 11, 2001, however, there may have been another significant shift, this time in the opposite direction. The bombing of the World Trade Center in New York City, the subsequent anthrax terrorism, the "Al Aksa Intifada" with its suicide bombings, and the increasing struggle with Iraq appear to have shaken the sense of complacency that characterized much of the West in recent years. There is now a significantly heightened sense of fear and anxiety concerning the future of global terrorism. There is a decreased sense of security in the United States, and there have been increased manifestations of civic involvement, some of which Putnam himself indicated shortly after the destruction of the Twin Towers.[48] For America's Jews, the shift is much more profound. In addition to all of the aforementioned stresses, there is a sense of growing anti-Semitism "out there," as eloquently and powerfully expressed by Jonathan Rosen in *New York Times Magazine* article after September 11.[49]

All of this has almost certainly impinged on the religiosity of America's Jews. The questions that remain are how long-lasting will the effects of these events be and to what extent will they slow down or even reverse the trend of postmaterial culture, including religion and spirituality.

Notes

1. Emile Durkheim, *The Elementary Forms of Religious Life* [1912], trans. Karen E. Fields (New York: The Free Press, 1995), 44.
2. W. Lloyd Warner and Leo Srole, *The Social Systems of American Ethnic Groups*, Yankee City Series, vol. III (New Haven: Yale University Press, 1945).
3. Ibid., 199–200.
4. Ibid., 202.
5. Chaim I. Waxman, *America's Jews in Transition* (Philadelphia: Temple University Press, 1983), 15–17.
6. Will Herberg, *Protestant–Catholic–Jew: An Essay in American Religious Sociology*, rev. ed. (Garden City: Anchor Books, 1960), 191.
7. Will Herberg, *Protestant–Catholic–Jew: An Essay in American Religious Sociology*, rev. ed. (Garden City: Anchor Books, 1960), 195.
8. Bernard Lazerwitz et al., *Jewish Choices: American Jewish Denominationalism* (Albany: State University of New York Press, 1998).

9. Chaim I. Waxman, *Jewish Baby Boomers: A Communal Perspective* (Albany: State University of New York Press, 2001).

10. Will Herberg, *Protestant–Catholic–Jew: An Essay in American Religious Sociology*, rev. ed. (Garden City: Anchor Books, 1960), 265–66.

11. Will Herberg, *From Marxism to Judaism: The Collected Essays of Will Herberg*, ed. with an introduction by David G. Dalin (New York: Markus Wiener, 1989).

12. Robert Scheer, "Serious Splits: Jews in U.S. Committed to Equality," *Los Angeles Times* (13 April 1988), 1.

13. Herbert J. Gans, "The Origin and Growth of a Jewish Community in the Suburbs: A Study of the Jews of Park Forest," in *The Jews: Social Patterns of An American Group*, ed. Marshall Sklare (New York: The Free Press, 1958), 205–48.

14. Peter L. Berger, *The Sacred Canopy: Elements of a Sociological Theory of Religion* (Garden City: Doubleday, 1967).

15. Herbert J. Gans, "The Origin and Growth of a Jewish Community in the Suburbs: A Study of the Jews of Park Forest," in *The Jews: Social Patterns of An American Group*, ed. Marshall Sklare (New York: The Free Press, 1958), 247.

16. Charles S. Liebman, "Ritual, Ceremony, and the Reconstruction of Judaism in the United States," in *Art and its Uses: The Visual Image and Modern Jewish Society*, ed. Ezra Mendelsohn, vol. 6 of *Studies in Contemporary Jewry* (New York: Oxford University Press, 1990), 272–83; Charles S. Liebman and Steven M. Cohen, *The Two Worlds of Judaism: The Israeli and American Experiences* (New Haven: Yale University Press, 1990).

17. Jack Wertheimer, *Conservative Synagogues and Their Members: Highlights of the North American Survey of 1995–96* (New York: Jewish Theological Seminary, 1996), 42.

18. Riv-Ellen Prell, *Prayer and Community: The Havurah in American Judaism* (Detroit: Wayne State University Press, 1989).

19. Zalman Schachter-Shalomi, *Paradigm Shift: From the Jewish Renewal Teachings of Reb Zalman Schachter-Shalomi*, ed. Ellen Singer (Northvale: Jason Aronson, 1993), xx.

20. Arthur I. Waskow, *The Freedom Seder; a New Haggadah for Passover* (New York: Holt, Rinehart & Winston, 1970).

21. Arthur I. Waskow, *Seasons of Our Joy: A Celebration of Modern Jewish Renewal* (New York: Bantam Books, 1982).

22. Arthur Waskow, *Down-To-Earth Judaism: Food, Money, Sex, and the Rest of Life* (New York: William Morrow, 1995).

23. Jack Nusan Porter and Peter Dreier, eds., *Jewish Radicalism: A Selected Anthology* (New York: Grove Press, 1973), xlii–xliii.

24. Richard Siegel, Michael Strassfeld, and Sharon Strassfeld, eds., *The Jewish Catalog* (Philadelphia: The Jewish Publication Society, 1973).

25. Marshall Sklare, *Observing America's Jews* (Hanover: Brandeis University Press, 1993), 82.

26. Samuel C. Heilman and Steven M. Cohen, *Cosmopolitans and Parochials: Modern Orthodox Jews in America* (Chicago: University of Chicago Press, 1989).

27. Chaim I. Waxman, "Dilemmas of Modern Orthodoxy," *Judaism* 42, 1 (Winter 1993), 68.

28. Ronald Inglehart, *Culture Shift in Advanced Industrial Society* (Princeton: Princeton University Press 1990), 3.

29. Peter L. Berger, *The Sacred Canopy: Elements of a Sociological Theory of Religion* (Garden City: Doubleday, 1967), 126 ff.

30. Peter L. Berger, *A Rumor of Angels: Modern Society and the Rediscovery of the Supernatural* (Garden City: Doubleday, 1969).

31. Peter L. Berger, *The Heretical Imperative: Contemporary Possibilities of Religious Affirmation* (Garden City: Anchor Press, 1979).

32. Ronald Inglehart, *Modernization and Postmodernization: Cultural, Economic, and Political Change in 43 Societies* (Princeton: Princeton University Press, 1997).

33. Ronald F. Inglehart and Wayne E. Baker, "Modernization, Cultural Change and the Persistence of Traditional Values," *American Sociological Review* 65, 1 (February 2000), 19–51.

34. Phyllis A. Tickle, *Rediscovering the Sacred: Spirituality in America* (New York: Crossroad, 1995), 18.

35. Sandee Brawarsky, "Into the Mystic," *Jewish Week* (19 November 1999), 57.

36. Robert Wuthnow, *After Heaven: Spirituality in America Since the 1950s* (Berkeley: University of California Press, 1998).

37. Wade Clark Roof, *Spiritual Marketplace: Baby Boomers and the Remaking of American Religion* (Princeton: Princeton University Press, 1999).

38. Charles S. Liebman, "Post-War American Jewry: From Ethnic to Privatized Judaism," in *Secularism, Spirituality, and the Future of American Jewry*, ed. Elliot Abrams and David G. Dalin (Washington, DC: Ethics and Public Policy Center, 1999), 7–18.

39. Robert D. Putnam, *Bowling Alone: The Collapse and Revival of American Community* (New York: Simon & Schuster, 2000).

40. Netty C. Gross, "Salvation Army," *Jerusalem Report* (14 February 2000), 22.

41. Elihu Katz, Hanna Levinsohn and Shlomit Levy, *Beliefs, Observances, and Values Among Israeli Jews 2000: Highlights from an In-Depth Study* (Jerusalem: Israel Democracy Institute and AVI CHAI Foundation, 2000), 11.

42. Chaim I. Waxman, *Jewish Baby Boomers: A Communal Perspective* (Albany: State University of New York Press, 2001), 92.

43. Dana Evan Kaplan, *American Reform Judaism* (New Brunswick: Rutgers University Press, 2003).

44. Daniel J. Elazar and Rela M. Geffen, *The Conservative Movement in Judaism: Dilemmas and Opportunities* (Albany: State University of New York Press, 2000).

45. Chaim I. Waxman, "The Haredization of American Orthodox Jewry," *Jerusalem Letter/Viewpoints* 376 (Jerusalem Center for Public Affairs, 15 February 1998).

46. Edah, www.edah.org;JOFA www.jofa.org.

47. Yair Sheleg, *The New Religious Jews: Recent Developments Among Observant Jews in Israel* (Jerusalem: Keter, 2000).

48. Robert D. Putnam, "A Better Society in a Time of War," *New York Times* (19 October 2001), 19.

49. Jonathan Rosen, "The Uncomfortable Question of Anti-Semitism," *New York Times Magazine* (4 November 2001), 148 ff.

6 Thinking Judaism through: Jewish theology in America

BYRON L. SHERWIN

Ignored at best, deemed irrelevant or divisive at worst, theological thinking has never been a priority item on the American Jewish communal agenda. American Jewry has expressed its largesse in many ways, but the training and support of Jewish theologians has not been one of them. Until recently, even Jewish theological seminaries in the United States were exceedingly lax in teaching Jewish theology or in training Jewish theologians. If the presence of trained theologians indicates a precondition for the production of theology, then their absence would seem to preclude the very existence of an American Jewish theology.[1] Nevertheless, American Jewish theology has developed in spite of, rather than because of, the interest or support of American Jewry.

According to the British Jewish theologian, Louis Jacobs, Jewish theology may be defined as "an *attempt* to think through consistently the implications of the Jewish religion."[2] Although *theology* literally means "discourse about God," American Jewry has resisted this and other such attempts for many reasons. One reason is because Americans tend to embrace activism and pragmatism, often neglecting and opposing doctrinal or ideological discourse. If Americans are basically activists, pragmatic and atheological, then American Jews are as well, and even more so. American Jews have tended to understand Judaism as a religion primarily concerned with doing things rather than thinking things, as a religion of action rather than doctrine, as an ethnic commitment rather than adherence to a transcendent faith.[3]

Another reason why American Jewry has resisted attempts to develop an American Jewish theology is because American Jews tend to be secular; indeed, they are even more so than other Americans. Obviously, the more secular a community, the less likely it is to be concerned with theological thinking. As sociologist Steven Cohen put it, "American Jews are among the most religiously inactive, the most theologically skeptical, in short, the most secular [group in America]."[4] In fact, sociological studies and opinion polls consistently reveal that American Jews are more tenuous in their belief in God than other Americans. American Jews not only tend to pray less and less regularly than other Americans, but there is also a higher proportion of agnostics or atheists among American Jews than among other groups of Americans. Furthermore, faith in God does not play a major role either in Jewish identity or in Jewish communal activity.

AMERICAN CIVIL RELIGION

In 1967, sociologist Robert Bellah published his seminal essay on the American "civil religion." According to Bellah, besides various forms of denominational religious faith, Americans also embrace a common "civil religion" with certain fundamental beliefs, values, holidays, and rituals.[5] In 1986, Jonathan Woocher extended Bellah's insight to American Jewry by formulating and examining "the civil religion of American Jews." While Bellah found that belief in God plays a central role in American civil religion, Woocher found that it plays a "thoroughly insignificant role in the civil religion of American Jews. . . . [The civil religion of American Jews] is atheological – not atheistic – religion."[6] Indeed, the God-idea is perceived as a cause for potential divisiveness among American Jews, who embrace a substantial diversity of views on the subject, ranging from intransigent atheism to fervent religious faith. Rejecting or ignoring traditional Jewish theological affirmations, the civil religion of American Jews had to posit an alternative basis for Jewish belief, identity, ethics, and communal life. According to Woocher, the fundamental "dogma" of the civil religion of American Jewry became "Jewish survival." The biological survival of the Jewish people became the ideological foundation for Jewish communal life in America. The people of Israel replaced the God of Israel as the foundation upon which Jewish existence was based. Particularly in the last decades of the twentieth century, the doctrine of Jewish survival became the prime directive and basic dogma of Jewish communal life.[7]

The consolidation of Jewish communal power in the late 1960s and 1970s by Jewish federations gave the civil religion of American Jews a position of centrality and authority in Jewish communal life. A prominent dogma of American civil religion, closely connected to Jewish survivalism, became the Holocaust–Israel, death–rebirth idea. This exceedingly Christian-sounding motif of death and resurrection demonstrated how the awareness of a certain understanding of the nexus between the Holocaust and the existence of the State of Israel had become a fundamental feature of American Jewish identity.[8] Awareness of the Holocaust was used as the rationale for why Jewish biological survival had now become the prime directive for Jewish existence. In this way, Israel became the symbol of Jewish survival and the antidote to threats to Jewish survival. Jewish powerlessness was considered a condition that permitted anti-Semitism and the Holocaust to occur. Jewish power, such as the military power of Israel and the political power of American Jewry, was now considered to be the primary tool for helping to ensure Jewish survival. Consequently, political activity and fundraising on behalf of Israel became central "sacred" activities according to the prevailing civil religion. Israel became not only the foundation for the Jewish identity of American Jews, but also a foundation of their faith. Commitment to the dogmas of the civil religion of American Jews replaced classical Jewish theological beliefs for many American Jews, both secular and religious.

The neglect of, opposition to, and marginalization of Jewish theological concerns precipitated the inception of alternative secular "faiths" to Judaism. For many Jews, there were one or more of the substitute "Jewish" faiths, like Jewish nationalism, or one or more of the "isms" of the twentieth century (e.g., Socialism, Communism, Humanism, and Rationalism). Louis Jacobs identifies three such substitute Jewish faiths: (1) worshipping the Jewish people rather than exclusively worshipping God; (2) making Jewish survival the ultimate goal of Jewish existence rather than the service of God; and (3) replacing the Torah with Jewish culture. These three approaches exclude the need for a Jewish theology.[9]

The Judaism of American Jewry was further recast so as to become consonant with the ideals and teachings of American political liberalism. As Steven Cohen has written, "for many American Jews, politics – in particular pro-Israel and liberal activity – have come to constitute their principle working definition of Jewishness. In this sense modern Jewish political movements have served as functional alternatives to conventional religion.... Many American Jews were raised with the understanding that liberalism or political radicalism constituted the very essence of Judaism, that all the rest – the rituals, liturgy, communal organizations – were outdated, vestigial trappings for a religion with a great moral and political message embodied in liberalism."[10]

The publication of the *1990 National Jewish Population Study* sent a seismic tremor throughout the organized Jewish community. This study showed that Jewish identity along ethnic lines, secularization, intermarriage, and the exiting of Jews from Judaism through formal conversion to another religion had severely diminished the number of American Jews professing Jewish religious faith of any variety. The strategy of Jewish survivalism clearly had failed in helping to ensure the survival of Jews as Jews, especially the survival of Jews as adherents to Judaism.

As the twenty-first century dawned, studies of American Jewry found that concern for and commitment to Israel was not as robust as it was assumed to be or as it actually had been in the 1970s. A decline of Jewish liberalism and social action as central determinants of Jewish self-identity was also found to be the case. Jews increasingly began to identify themselves in religious rather than ethnic categories, by spiritual rather than secular criteria, thereby providing a hospitable environment for Jewish theological thinking to develop. As the dogmas of the civil religion of American Jews began to lose their grip, and as Jews began to look to the intellectual and spiritual resources of their tradition as a source of wisdom, personal meaning, and Jewish identity, the long-standing marginalization of Jewish theology promised to come to an end. Many Jews now began to ask the kinds of questions with which theologians are concerned: What is Judaism? What is Jewish faith? What does Judaism believe? What does Judaism teach about God, the meaning of life, and life after death? Writing in 1994, Arthur Green observed that "the Jewish people is ready for theology, needs it urgently. . . . Indeed thinking about our own Jewishness is precisely what we Jews need most to do. . . . We need to define our goals for the continuity of Jewish life. What we do mean by a Jewish future in America."[11]

Despite the neglect and the marginalization of American Jewish theology for many years, and despite attempts to suppress Jewish theological thinking and writing when it challenged the secular assumptions, the Jewish communal agenda, and civil religion of American Jewish communal life, a long-standing tradition of American Jewish theology actually exists.

THEOLOGICAL TRENDS

Intradenominational and interdenominational theology

Five distinct trends in the history of American Jewish theology may be identified. The first is intradenominational and interdenominational Jewish theology. Many studies of American Jewish theology focus exclusively on certain individual Jewish thinkers but neglect theological discussion both within and across "denominational" lines. In reality, American Jewish theology begins with the attempts of Reform Jewish theologians not only to define and to clarify the nature of Judaism but also to define and clarify the nature of American Judaism. The issues that preoccupied Reform Judaism as it developed were not only social and demographic but also profoundly theological. They were not only matters of liturgy and ritual; they were also matters of theology. Indeed, changing theological perspectives in American Reform Judaism, represented by its various so-called platforms (especially those of 1885, 1937, and 1999), had a direct impact on the role of liturgy, ritual, ethics, and observance within that movement.[12]

As Conservative Judaism emerged in America in the early decades of the twentieth century, it became increasingly clear that the differences between

Conservative and Reform Judaism were not simply sociological or demographic; they were theological as well. As Orthodox Judaism experienced a resurgence in the period after World War II, the three movements – Reform, Conservative, and Orthodox – could be distinguished, not only on the basis of differences in religious practice but also on the basis of visceral theological claims. While individual Jewish theologians produced works that were mostly read by an intellectual elite, and therefore had only a circumscribed impact, the theological discussions within and across so-called denominational lines undoubtedly have had a direct impact on the extensive professional and lay constituencies of the movements that largely represent American Judaism.

Kaufmann Kohler, who played a central role in the development of Reform Judaism in the late nineteenth century and in the first decades of the twentieth century, may be considered the first significant American Jewish theologian. Kohler (1843–1926) was a German rabbi who arrived in the United States in 1869. After serving a number of congregations, he was appointed president of Hebrew Union College in 1903. At that time, Reform Judaism was the dominant form of American Judaism. For Kohler, Reform was not a movement within American Judaism; rather, it *was* Judaism in its most highly evolved and contemporary form. In 1918, Kohler published *Jewish Theology*, the first systematic work on Jewish theology in the English language.[13] In this bold pioneering effort, Kohler locates the essence of Judaism in the ethical monotheism of the Biblical prophets rather than in what he considered to be the legal particularism of the Talmudic and Medieval rabbis. From this perspective, the mission of the people of Israel is to preserve and perpetuate the ethical message of the prophets until the time when it can become the uniting basis of a religion for all of humankind. Kohler's presentation of a socially and intellectually "progressive," universalistic, ethical (i.e., nonlegal), aggressively optimistic (e.g., evil really does not exist) portrait of Judaism is paradigmatic of early-twentieth-century American Reform Judaism. So is his rejection of Zionist aspirations. It is not surprising that the theological posture Kohler adapts in his lengthy *Jewish Theology* is an expansion of the views he succinctly set down in the 1880s for his proposed draft of the Pittsburgh Platform.[14] In 1885, leaders of Reform Judaism largely adapted Kohler's draft as the definitional statement of American Reform Judaism. To the seven "planks" of the Pittsburgh Platform, basically drafted by Kohler, an eighth was added, affirming liberal political progressivism and calling for an active program of social reform. The Pittsburgh Platform represents a precise statement of views on a wide variety of theological issues, including the nature of God, the nature of the Torah, the mission of the people of Israel, the afterlife, the Messianic Era, and the relationship of Judaism to other religions.

The adoption in 1937 of the Columbus Platform by Reform Judaism represented not only a shift in policy but also a change in theology from the positions represented by the Pittsburgh Platform. Just as Kohler was the major force behind the Pittsburgh Platform, another significant Reform Jewish theologian, Samuel S. Cohon (1888–1959), was the primary author of the Columbus Platform. As Professor of Jewish Theology at Hebrew Union College for over three decades, Cohon would play a decisive role in the shaping of Reform Jewish theology. Unlike Kohler, Cohon does not begin his theology with general theological principles, but with the religious consciousness of the individual, specifically with the personal experience of the sacred. This encounter with the holy was, for Cohon, the basis of all religion. According to Cohon, Judaism shaped this primal religious experience into its own unique forms, symbols, values, beliefs, and rituals. Unlike Kohler, Cohon had a positive view of Jewish particularism, Hebrew language, Jewish mysticism, religious observance, and Zionism. These views are embedded in the 1937 Columbus Platform.[15]

While not a systematic theologian like Kohler or the author of a Jewish theology for the contemporary American Jew like Cohon, Solomon Schechter (1849–1915), the "father" of Conservative Judaism in America, did address Jewish theological issues throughout his many published works. Both implicitly and explicitly, Schechter polemicized against the views of Reform, particularly those represented in the Pittsburgh Platform. Schechter also formulated and articulated theological positions that would serve as the ideological foundation for Conservative Judaism, particularly in America.[16] However, from its inception, Conservative Judaism had resisted a clear and precise statement of its teachings. Indeed, it was not until 1988, when *Emet Ve-Emunah: Statement of Principles of Conservative Judaism* was published, that the Conservative movement issued a statement of its theological beliefs and principles.[17]

By 1999, when Reform Judaism in America adapted the second Pittsburgh Platform, most of the ideological and theological differences between Reform and Conservative Judaism that had existed in the days of Kohler and Schechter had been resolved and were now passé. Like early American Reform, early Conservative Judaism operated on the premise that it would eventually emerge as the dominant form of American Judaism. The Conservative Jewish leaders anticipated that Orthodoxy was too linked to European Jewry to survive in America beyond an immigrant generation. They also believed that Reform would dissipate through the inevitable assimilation and secularization of its constituency. However, these beliefs proved incorrect. By the period after World War II, three Jewish religious groups, Reform, Conservative, and Orthodox, rather than one, characterized American Judaism. Like Christian denominations that distinguished themselves from others by theological stances, liturgy, and religious practice, each of the three Jewish denominations was obliged to do the same. Though various theological issues divided the three movements, in none has their differences been more pronounced than in their views of divine revelation and religious authority.

Many Orthodox Jews maintain that there is no Jewish theology and that Judaism is essentially a system of religious law. However, underlying this claim is a theological presupposition that differentiates Orthodoxy from other contemporary forms of Judaism. That theological presupposition, called *Torah min ha-shamayim*, "Torah from Heaven" in classical Hebrew, asserts that God has directly revealed the Torah in its present form to the people of Israel, and that its contents are therefore inerrant. Revelation is viewed as a monologue of God to Israel. The role of the Jewish people is obedience to the word of God as found in the Torah and as interpreted by ongoing authoritative rabbinic tradition. This view of revelation and authority stands in sharp contrast to the views of non-Orthodox American Jewry.

For Schechter, there is both revelation to Israel and revelation through Israel. God's word and God's will become manifest through and within *Kelal Yisrael*, which Schechter translates (following Isaac Leeser) as "Catholic Israel." In this view, revelation is more of a dialogue with God than a monologue of God. Judaism is more of a creation of the interaction of the people of Israel with the revealed word of God than a system of divinely given dictates. For Schechter, the Jewish people is the final authority in determining the nature of Judaism. Historical research can determine which beliefs, practices, and institutions have been and continue to be essential to Judaism. Though oversimplified here, Schechter's view on revelation and authority represents early Conservative Judaism, contrasted not only with that of Orthodoxy but also with that of Reform. Throughout the history of Reform Judaism, first in Europe and then in America, the Kantian idea of individual autonomy served as the basis for religious and moral decision making. In more recent Reform, individual autonomy and the authority of the tradition remain in a constant state of tension, as Eugene Borowitz has discussed in considerable detail.[18]

The classical Reform view of "progressive revelation," influenced by Hegelian philosophy, claimed that, as history unfolds, human beings automatically move to a higher perception of truth than they had held previously. The current generation, in this view, knows more than any previous generation, and consequently has the knowledge and hence the authority to reform the teachings of past traditions. Orthodoxy took the opposite view of revelation, identifying the revelation at Sinai as the apogee of revealed truth. From this perspective, the more proximate a religious authority is to Sinai, the greater his authority. Conservative Judaism embraced the idea of continuous revelation; that is, the revelation of the divine will continues through *Kelal Yisrael*, the community of Israel.

These approaches to revelation directly influenced each of the movements' philosophies of Jewish law. For Reform, the law (*halakhah*) is no longer binding and authoritative. For Conservative Judaism, the law remains binding but is subject to change based on certain historical and other meta-halakhic considerations, such as the ethical principles of Judaism as well as certain socioeconomic conditions. For Orthodoxy, not only is the law binding, but the last authoritative code of Jewish law, the *Shulhan Arukh,* representing the quintessence of the Jewish legal tradition, is binding as well. Since the greater scholars dwelt in the past rather than in the present, change is discouraged and halakhic alterations are viewed as "deviationist."[19]

The Reform notion of progressive revelation is predicated on ideas rooted in the European Enlightenment, such as unbridled optimism, individual autonomy, rationalism (since that which is rational is that which is true, and Judaism is true, Judaism can be defined and shaped only by that which is rational), and universalism. However, as the horrors of the twentieth century, particularly the Holocaust, became evident, Jewish theologians in America, including Reform theologians, began to back away from the foundational assumptions that had animated liberal Judaism since the Enlightenment. The combination of the naïve optimism characteristic of American culture coupled with the unrestrained optimistic tenor of Enlightenment thought was shattered by a confrontation with the effects of two world wars, the Depression, and the post–World War II threat of nuclear annihilation. American Jewish theologians confronted the grim realities of history by breaking with the presuppositions of Enlightenment thought that had been incorporated into earlier American Jewish theology.

Existential theology

In the era after World War II, American Jewish theologians began to formulate new approaches to understanding the nature of Jewish faith and to understanding the particular nature of American Judaism.[20] Until the 1950s, American Jewish theology had been largely confined to intradenominational and interdenominational thinking and writing. Few works of a Jewish theological nature had been produced by individual thinkers. However, the 1950s began with a salvo of works on Jewish theology. Although the authors of these works, such as Will Herberg (1901–77) and Abraham Joshua Heschel

(1907–72), were different in many ways, they shared an existentialist approach to thinking Judaism through.[21] It has been suggested that Jewish existentialist theology constitutes a second trend in the development of American Jewish theology. Though some American Jewish existentialist theologians were affiliated with one of the movements of American Judaism, their thought is not particularly denominationally oriented.

American Jewish existentialist theologians shifted the focus, agenda, and presuppositions of American Jewish theology. Rather than initiating theological discourse by merely stating principles of religious belief, or by defining the "essence" of Judaism, the existentialists began with questions about the meaning of human life and Jewish existence. This approach took a more positive view of past Jewish intellectual and theological tradition and of Jewish historical experience than had previously been the case in American Jewish theology. Earlier modern Jewish thought tended to subordinate classical Jewish literature, especially Talmudic and Kabbalistic literature, to modern European philosophy and to science. The Jewish existentialists, in contrast, sought to articulate an "authentic" Judaism, rooted in classical Jewish religious sources and ideas.

The Jewish existentialist theologians rejected the unbridled optimism, secularism, rationalism, the acquiescence to science and technology, and other ideas drawn from Enlightenment thinking that had dominated earlier American Jewish life and thought. In their view, recent history, particularly the two world wars, the Holocaust, and the terrors of Stalinism, had adequately demonstrated the failures of the various secular isms that had been pervasive in their times. No longer was rationalism or humanism considered to be viable foundations for Jewish life and thought. Historical events had demonstrated that neither human nature nor human history could provide a viable foundation for unbridled faith in the automatic improvement of the human condition or for the belief in the innately beneficent nature of humankind. In formulating their theological positions, the Jewish existentialists saw Jewish religious faith as holding the answer to the existential questions posed by the post–World War II period. Their approach focused not on theological principles or dogmas, but on the implications of a personal commitment to Judaism. Consequently, much of their thinking focused on the divine–human relationship. Their approach was less humanistic and more theocentric than that of their immediate predecessors.

A major theme of existentialist thought is the problem of how to overcome loneliness, absurdity, and alienation. In a complex treatise combining Neo-Kantian, Jewish legal and philosophical, and existentialist approaches, the leading Orthodox Jewish scholar and theologian, Joseph B. Soloveitchik

(1903–95) offers faith in God, commitment to traditional norms, and social interaction within a religious community as paths to individual fulfillment and redemption.[22]

For Abraham Heschel, a basic question confronting Jewish religious thought was this: What characterizes authentic Jewish thinking? What is *Jewish* about Jewish theology? Heschel maintained that Judaism is a way of thinking as well as a way of living, and that Jewish thinking is characterized by uniquely Jewish categories that are radically different from those of western philosophy. Furthermore, for Heschel and others, only an authentically Jewish way of thinking can serve as the basis for an authentically Jewish way of living. Thus, Judaism is a personal and existential commitment that is not verified or refuted by philosophical argument but is rather articulated by one's lifestyle.

Will Herberg identified religious faith as a matter of personal existential commitment, rather than as the intellectual affirmation of certain specific theological principles. For Herberg, there exist two alternatives: faith in God or idolatry. Herberg defines idolatry as treating as ultimate that which is not ultimate, such as committing to a secular ideology like Communism. For Herberg, only God is ultimate.

For Jewish existentialists, ours is an unredeemed world where the human capacity for irrationality and evil is manifest in human experience. For Heschel, the doctrine of human self-sufficiency is spurious. Human beings require the wisdom and insight rooted in divine revelation. For Heschel, revelation serves as the paradigm for the divine–human relationship, as the basis for religious authority, and as the bedrock of moral values and religious practice. It was not coincidental that revelation became the key issue in the theological works of Jewish existentialists.

Kaplanian thought

Mordecai M. Kaplan (1881–1983) represents a discrete trend in American Jewish theology not only in terms of his longevity but also in terms of his thought and its impact on American Judaism. Kaplan's thought in itself may be considered a third trend in American Jewish theology.[23] Though Kaplan considered himself more of a sociologist than a theologian, his theology of Judaism is particularly American. Kaplan used the endemically American philosophy of pragmatism in producing a philosophy and a program for the reconstruction of American Judaism. Kaplan's life and thought had a profound impact on American Jewish life, institutions, thought, and thinkers such as Milton Steinberg, Richard Rubenstein, and William Kaufman.[24] Just as the leading American philosopher, John Dewey, sought "reconstruction" in philosophy, Kaplan sought to reconstruct Judaism. Kaplan's goal was to provide a variety of reconstructed Judaism that would be relevant and challenging to modernized American Jews. Kaplan's ultimate hope was for a renaissance of Judaism in America. Eventually, Kaplan's work developed into a fourth movement in American Judaism, Reconstructionist Judaism, which was the first native form of American Judaism.

For Kaplan, what American Judaism needed was a more "organic," comprehensive view of Judaism than was then being offered by Jewish nationalism, culturism, secularism, or the religious movements of American Judaism. For Kaplan, that need could be best fulfilled by understanding Judaism as an "evolving religious civilization." This meant that Judaism is a total civilization, including religion, culture, and nationality. It is developing and evolving; hence, it is not static. It is religious, whereby religion is not its totality but its core.

By severing them from their traditional theological meanings, Kaplan radically reconstructs the three major issues of Jewish theological thinking: God, Torah, and Israel. For Kaplan, *God* is no longer an abstract noun; it is a functional noun. What is important for Kaplan is not so much the nature of God but how God functions in our lives. The pragmatic application supersedes the theological concept. God, for Kaplan, is not a "person" but a "force" or a "process" that operates in the universe and human life for goodness, meaning, and salvation. Similarly for Kaplan, the Torah is not the product of a supernatural, divine revelation. God does not give us commandments. Rather, Judaism and Torah are expressions of the creative religious genius of the Jewish people. Jews observe certain practices not because God has dictated them but because they express the "sancta" of the Jewish people. Kaplan's reconstruction of Jewish theology led him to a reformulation of Jewish liturgical texts so that they might be correlative with the teachings of his reconstructed American Judaism. Furthermore, for Kaplan, the idea of Israel as a chosen people is obsolete.

Focus on the Holocaust and Israel

As a result of the perceived threat to the Jewish population in Israel during the 1967 Israel–Arab Six Day War, American Jewry experienced a deeper awareness of the Holocaust than it had until then. In addition, American Jews began to manifest a deeper commitment to Israel as a symbol of Jewish survival and rebirth than they had done previously. With an almost exclusive focus on the Holocaust and Israel in the 1970s and 1980s, American Jewish theology entered a fourth phase. For the first time, American Jewish theology and the civil religion of American Jewry came together, as in the teachings of Irving Greenberg.

As a German rabbi and naturalized Canadian citizen who later emmigrated to Israel, Emil Fackenheim made a substantial contribution to American Jewish theology and to Holocaust theology in particular.[25] Like the American Jewish theologian, Arthur Cohen (1928–86), Fackenheim sees the Holocaust as a seismic, unprecedented event in human history.[26] However, in contrast to Richard Rubenstein, Fackenheim reaffirms faith in the supernatural God. For Cohen, not only is God supernatural, but the people of Israel are also supernatural in their mission in the world, which includes bearing witness to the evil that infects humankind through the abuse of human freedom. Like Cohen, the eminent Orthodox Jewish scholar and theologian, Eliezer Berkovits (1908–92) considers the Holocaust the result of a perversion of human freedom. However, Berkovits also utilizes the early notion of *hester panim*, the "hiding face of God," to address the Holocaust. God mysteriously and inexplicably, and without any obvious cause such as human sin, hides from human beings. It is precisely this absence that makes human freedom and hence human tragedy possible. Further, Berkovits sees the Holocaust as proof of the endemic failure of western civilization and Christianity. Unlike Rubenstein and Fackenheim, who utilize the unprecedented nature of the Holocaust to call for unprecedented Jewish responses, Berkovits deals with the theological issues posed by the Holocaust, particularly theodicy (the problem of evil), by using traditional Jewish theological categories.[27]

Postmodern trend

A fifth phase in American Jewish theology began to emerge in the 1990s. According to Peter Haas, it is a "post-modern" trend represented for the first time by all American-born and American-trained Jewish theologians.[28] Haas correctly indicates that with the emergence of this trend the legacy of the Enlightenment heritage has been completely discarded. The Holocaust and the State of Israel are dealt with, but neither is considered central to Jewish theological thinking. Neither rationalism, nor science, nor secularism, nor Jewish survival is considered to be a sine qua non for either human or Jewish meaning. While the insights of Jewish mystical tradition are embraced, classical Jewish sources are the raw materials out of which these theologians attempt to re-create an understanding of Judaism for the twenty-first century.

An issue that concerns postmodern theologians is how a Jew goes about living out his or her commitment to the Jewish covenant with God. This concern leads to formulations of views concerning issues such as revelation; philosophies of Jewish law; ethical behavior; and the nature, interpretation, and application of Jewish law. For postmodern Jewish theologians, the task of theology is to provide a response and an alternative to the secularization of American Jewish life. Theological polemics with other faiths is not an issue, as interreligious dialogue is presumed to be important and theologically enriching. The polemic here is against a despiritualized American Jewish community that suffers from spiritual anemia and yet that has begun to manifest a deep hunger for things Jewish and things spiritual. The goal is to produce a re-created yet authentic and traditional though non-Orthodox American Jewish theology. The theological, mystical, spiritual, ethical, and halakhic elements of Judaism must be re-created and restated in a contemporary idiom, and then applied to the existential, social, and communal problems confronting American Jews. For these theologians, Jewish theology is the key to providing American Judaism with a creative and meaningful future.[29] An important feature of this latest trend in American Jewish theology has been the beginning of the emergence of Jewish theological thinking and writing by women. Early works, such as those of Judith Plaskow, have opened new agendas and have added new insights into the theological discussion of Judaism.[30] They have stimulated new liturgies, a new sensitivity to the sexist use of religious language, the formulation of theologies of the human body, and new approaches to pastoral theology and counseling.

Finally, what might be considered the ground rules for formulating and for evaluating a theology of Judaism? What are some criteria for evaluating past, present, and future expressions of Jewish theology? In my view, there are four such criteria: authenticity, coherence, contemporaneity, and acceptance by the faith community. Authenticity depends on the nature and the use of traditional Jewish religious texts consulted, and on the faith commitment of the individual consulting them. A Jewish theologian is an individual committed to Jewish faith, conversant with classical Jewish religious texts, who seeks to restate and re-create that tradition. Coherence relates to the cohesion, clarity, and communicability of a formulated theological perspective out of the textual and historical resources of that tradition. Contemporaneity pertains to the successful application of past traditions to present situations. As Louis Jacobs puts it, "The theologian asks the more personal question: what in traditional Jewish religion continues to shape my life as a Jew in the here and now?"[31] Communal acceptance refers to the ratification of a theological posture by committed members of the faith community. Communal acceptance does not mean acceptance by a consensus of the Jewish community as a social unit, but by those committed to the vocation of the people of Israel that is divine service as understood by the Jewish interpretive tradition.[32]

One would hope that American Jewish theologians of the present and the foreseeable future will be able to produce Jewish theology in a less hostile and more appreciative Jewish communal environment than their predecessors did. Indeed, the future of American Judaism might depend on precisely that. As the twenty-first century unfolds, new trends in American Jewish theology will inevitably develop. Just as the various past and present trends presented herein were largely unpredicted in the periods that preceded them, so are future trends currently uncertain. However, certain issues may possibly preoccupy American Jewish theologians in the decades to come.

The relationship between science and religion will be a growing concern of American, including Jewish, theologians, such as the unfolding theories of cosmology and astrophysics as well as developments in genetics and biotechnology. The reshaping of Jewish theological and social attitudes toward Christians and Christianity will continue in the twenty-first century. In addition, theological reconsideration of and dialogue with Islam, Buddhism, and other religions will increase as America continues to become more religiously pluralistic. As theologies of feminism influenced Jewish theology in the late twentieth century, theologies related to sexual preference are likely to develop in the first decades of the twenty-first century. The greatest challenge to American Jewish theologians in the near future may not be the isms of the past, nor the secularism of the present, but the American trend toward custom-made individualized forms of religion in general and of Judaism in particular. What sociologists have called "the sovereign self"[33] will increasingly define the religious identity of many American Jews. Ideas and practices from other religions and ideologies will increasingly become elements of individual American Jews' religious identity. Whereas in recent decades, individual Jews wanted to autonomously decide which aspects of classical Jewish belief, ethics, and ritual were meaningful for themselves, already emerging trends indicate that individual Jews now believe they can determine for themselves what Judaism is. This trend threatens to undermine both the continuity of Judaism as a historical theological tradition as well as the cohesion of the Jewish community.

Jewish theology historically has been open to change and innovation. It has been responsive throughout its history to contemporary social, cultural, and philosophical trends. It has continuously reshaped its ideas because of significant historical events. In all this, Jewish theology has nonetheless been characterized by a certain continuity and as an inextricable link with the Jewish people. It has withstood the onslaught of religious disputation, historical trauma, and ideological attacks from all sides, including those from within the Jewish community itself. How it will meet the challenges to continuity and community posed by individualized "boutique" Judaisms, by the "brave new world" of the unfolding so-called biotech century, and by the dangers to America in a post–9/11 world remains to be seen.

Notes

1. Arnold Eisen, "Theology, Sociology, Ideology: Jewish Thought in America, 1925–1955," *Modern Judaism* 2, 1 (February 1982), 91–104.
2. Louis Jacobs, *A Jewish Theology* (New York: Behrman House, 1973), 1.
3. Norman Frimer, "The A-Theological Judaism of the American Jewish Community," *Judaism* 11 (1962), 144–54.
4. Steven Cohen, *Content or Continuity?* (New York: American Jewish Committee, 1991), 26.
5. Robert Bellah, "Civil Religion in America," *Daedalus* (Winter 1967), 1–21.
6. Jonathan S. Woocher, *Sacred Survival: The Civil Religion of American Jews* (Bloomington: Indiana University Press, 1986), 92.
7. Ibid., 72–76.
8. Ibid., 132–36.
9. Louis Jacobs, *A Jewish Theology* (New York: Behrman House, 1973), 281–83.
10. Steven Cohen, *American Modernity and Jewish Identity* (New York: Tavistock Publications, 1983), 32, 35.
11. Arthur Green, "New Directions in Jewish Theology in America," in *Contemporary Jewish Theology*, ed. Elliot N. Dorff and Louis E. Newman (New York: Oxford University Press, 1999), 487.
12. For the texts of the various platforms, see Michael A. Meyer, *Response to Modernity: A History of the Reform Movement in Judaism* (New York: Oxford University Press, 1988), 387–94.
13. Kaufmann Kohler, *Jewish Theology: Systematically and Historically Considered* [1918]. 2nd ed. (New York: KTAV Publishing House, 1968).
14. Michael A. Meyer, *Response to Modernity: A History of the Reform Movement in Judaism* (New York: Oxford University Press, 1988), 264–73.
15. Michael A. Meyer, *Response to Modernity: A History of the Reform Movement in Judaism* (New York: Oxford University Press, 1988), 317–20; Samuel S. Cohon, *Jewish Theology* (Assen: Royal Van Gorcum, 1971); Samuel S. Cohon, *Judaism: A Way of Life* (New York: Union of American Hebrew Congregations Press, 1948).
16. Solomon Schechter, *Aspects of Rabbinic Theology* (New York: Macmillan, 1909).
17. *Emet ve-Emunah* (New York: Jewish Theological Seminary, 1988).
18. Eugene Borowitz, *Renewing the Covenant: A Theology for Post-Modern Jews* (Philadelphia: The Jewish Publication Society, 1991).
19. Byron L. Sherwin, *In Partnership with God: Contemporary Jewish Law and Ethics* (Syracuse: Syracuse University Press, 1990), 16–46.
20. Robert G. Goldy, *The Emergence of Jewish Theology in America* (Bloomington: Indiana University Press, 1990).
21. Will Herberg, *Judaism and Modern Man* (New York: World Publishing, 1951); Abraham J. Heschel, *God in Search of Man* (New York: Farrar, Straus & Cudahy, 1955).
22. Joseph B. Soloveichik, *Halakhic Man*, trans. Lawrence Kaplan (Philadelphia: The Jewish Publication Society, 1983).
23. Mordecai M. Kaplan, *Judaism as a Civilization* (New York: Macmillan, 1934); Mordecai M. Kaplan, *The Meaning of God in Modern Jewish Religion* (New York: Jewish Reconstructionist Foundation, 1947).
24. Milton Steinberg, "The Theological Issues of the Hour," *Proceedings of the Rabbinical Assembly* 13 (1949), 356–408; Richard Rubenstein, *After Auschwitz*

(Indianapolis: Bobbs-Merrill, 1966); William E. Kaufman, *The Evolving God in Jewish Process Theology* (Lewiston: Edwin Mellen Press, 1997).

25. Emil Fackenheim, *God's Presence in History* (New York: New York University Press, 1970); *The Jewish Return into History* (New York: Schocken Books, 1978).

26. Arthur A. Cohen, *The Tremendum* (New York: Crossroad, 1983); *The Natural and the Supernatural Jew* (New York: McGraw-Hill, 1964).

27. Eliezer Berkovits, *Faith After the Holocaust* (New York: KTAV Publishing House, 1973).

28. Peter J. Haas, "The Making of a New American Jewish Theology," *Central Conference of American Rabbis Journal* 39, 3 (Fall 1992), 1–13.

29. Eugene Borowitz, *A New Jewish Theology in the Making* (Philadelphia: Westminster Press, 1968); Arthur Green, *Seek My Face, Speak My Name* (Northvale: Jason Aronson, 1992); Neil Gillman, *Sacred Fragments* (Philadelphia: The Jewish Publication Society, 1990); Byron L. Sherwin, *Toward a Jewish Theology* (Lewiston: Edwin Mellen Press, 1991).

30. Judith Plaskow, *Standing Again at Sinai* (San Francisco: Harper & Row, 1990).

31. Louis Jacobs, *A Jewish Theology* (New York: Behrman House, 1973), 1.

32. Byron L. Sherwin, *Toward a Jewish Theology* (Lewiston: Edwin Mellen Press, 1991), 9–32; cf. Jacob Neusner, "The Tasks of Theology in Judaism," *Journal of Religion* 59, 1 (1979): 71–86.

33. Steven M. Cohen and Arnold M. Eisen, *The Jew Within* (Bloomington: Indiana University Press, 200), 13–42.

7 The essence of American Judaism

CHARLES S. LIEBMAN

The term *American Judaism* is not as clear as it might seem at first glance.[1] Not too long ago the term *Judaism* seemed clear enough. People might disagree about its specific contents but agree that Judaism referred to the norms, values, and beliefs that characterized the Jewish religion. There were those who argued that Judaism was basically a culture rather than a religion, and some even argued that the term *civilization* was more suitable. However, at its core, Judaism – whether a religion, culture, or civilization – contained a set of norms, values, and beliefs, many of which, all would agree, referred to God and to the relationship between the Jewish people and God. These norms, values, and beliefs existed independently of how individual Jews behaved or what individual Jews believed. In other words, there was a structure or an essence called Judaism, and the behavior or beliefs of individual Jews could be measured by the extent to which they conformed to or deviated from the norms and beliefs of Judaism.

Within the confines of these norms existed differences between Judaism in different societies. *American Judaism* meant the particular customs, or emphases, or variations that were characteristic of the manner in which Judaism was practiced in the United States, distinct from the practice of Polish or German or Yemenite Judaism. This set of understandings had important implications, most especially for differences between the various Jewish denominations, that is, the Orthodox, Conservative, Reform, and more recently the Reconstructionist movements. As long as Jews believed that there was an *essence* called Judaism, then it was incumbent in the competition between the various denominations for each to argue that it had not deviated from Judaism. Whatever its differences with other denominations might be, these differences, each denomination would argue, were reasonable, fair, and legitimate interpretations of Judaism. In other words, whereas a belief in a construct called Judaism did not reduce all differences about what Judaism meant, it did dictate the nature of the debate about the legitimacy of each denomination and of decisions reached within each denomination. Furthermore, it provided a limit or boundary of sorts to such decisions – they had to be arguably within the boundaries of Judaism. Each group seeking its particular definition of Judaism was required to describe, at least in general, what Judaism meant in its eyes. It went without saying that Jews, if they were to be good Jews, were obliged by this definition. Still, these definitions have proved to be less of a limitation on some denominations than on others. Reform Judaism was radically innovative in the late nineteenth century, declaring that Jews were no longer obliged to observe the ritual laws of Judaism. Nevertheless, Reform did maintain that Jews were bound by its moral and ethical law. While this statement carried little practical weight, the logic of religion dictated such an affirmation. What else could a religious movement declare – that it projected a set of religious principles that its followers were *not* obligated to observe?

It is sometimes difficult to recall the consensus that once existed around the notion of a Jewish essence. When Israel Friedlander published his essay "The Problem of Judaism in America" 100 years ago, he defined the problem as Jewish assimilation: the abandonment of Judaism. Neither he nor I assume his readers doubted that there was an essence called Judaism. Until recently, the questions posed by survey researchers seeking to measure Jewish identity queried respondents about their ritual behavior, synagogue affiliation and attendance, Jewish friendship patterns, Jewish family patterns, relationships with non-Jews, and attitudes toward Israel. The assumption of these survey researchers was that since these are the components of Judaism, Jewish identity could be measured by the respondent's attitudes and behavior toward these components.

In one sense, the view of Judaism as an essence is still adhered to by many, if not most, Jews. It requires a high level of intellectual agility to consider oneself as acting in accordance with Judaism if there is no such thing as Judaism. However, a new wave of critical studies by social psychologists, social scientists, and Jewish historians dealing with questions of identity challenge the notion that there is an entity or essence called Judaism. In my opinion, whether a scholar decides that there is or is not an essential Judaism depends very much on what that scholar wishes to find. The conclusion rests on how much weight one gives to one set of facts rather than another set of facts, or on how one interprets one or another set of facts. What the scholar is looking to demonstrate may be a function of that scholar's own religious behavior (religious scholars are notoriously deviant in their religious behavior, and even more so in their beliefs), but no less important, currents within the wider world of scholarship. If debunking the existence, much less the longevity, of a religion or a nation or an ethnic group is the current fashion, we can anticipate that studies of Judaism and of the Jewish people will come up with similar conclusions, which do not automatically render them false. True or false, though most Jews have constructed a myth of an essential Judaism. It is unlikely that Judaism, or for that matter any religious, national, or ethnic tradition, could sustain itself without such a myth. Lest the reader mistake the intention of this discussion, my topic is Judaism, not Jewishness. There is much to be said for exploring how American Jews behave and what American Jews believe. Not everything that would be included under this rubric is Jewishly relevant. Nevertheless, studies of what might be called the *lived religion* or the *lived culture* of American Jews are important, yet we presently lack such research.

The efforts of deconstructionist and contemporary critical theory to undermine the notion of an essential, that is, an authentic, Judaism coincides with the notion that there is no one Judaism. This is not quite the same as arguing that Judaism as understood by any one group is as legitimately or authentically Jewish as the Judaism of some other denomination. That would leave groups such as Jews for Jesus in a theoretically unassailable position. However, it certainly encourages such sentiments. This, in turn, is not the same as arguing that anything an individual chooses to call Judaism is in fact Judaism, but at the popular level it encourages such notions. Our contemporary emphases on the value of individual autonomy seem to include the right – indeed, the desirability – of each individual to provide his or her own interpretation of what Judaism means. In the process, the representation of Judaism has undergone radical changes.

One consequence of changing ideas about the existence of a Judaic essence is that denominations no longer need to legitimize the innovations and changes they introduce in terms of how they fit into basic norms of Judaism. American Judaism is increasingly defined, in practice and sometimes in theory (it is true of a number of authors in this collection), as that which American Jews do. Such definitions of Judaism are not confined to the United States. In fact, to the best of my knowledge, these definitions were preceded by secular Israelis who argued that Judaism was defined by whatever it was that Jews in Israel did. Today one finds such sentiments in other Diasporas as well. Increasingly, leaders of American Jewry are inclined to the position that each individual is free to choose how Judaism is to be interpreted and no one has the authority to issue judgments in this regard. Once again, this is least true of the Orthodox Jews, increasingly true of Conservative Jews, and most true of Reform, Reconstructionist, and secular Jews.

In reality, however, the situation is actually more complex and inconsistencies prevail, since the notion of a boundless or limitless Judaism undermines the very notion of Judaism. Hence, Jews seek some essence, which is sometimes articulated in negative terms; for example, one cannot believe in the divinity of Jesus and still be Jewish. Here I only observe that, given our present cultural climate, boundaries are difficult to formulate. In the case of American Jews, these boundaries are mainly reflected in sentiments that are felt to be true and expressed emotionally but rarely articulated. This is partially because they lack theoretical justification and partially because they run against the prevailing liberal American culture that has exerted such a profound influence on American Jews.

In returning, however, to the issue of denominations, we can broadly distinguish Orthodox and non-Orthodox on the acceptance or rejection of the notion that however one chooses to practice or celebrate one's Jewishness is beyond the pale of judgment and that whatever one practices and calls Jewish is a legitimate expression of Judaism. This may help explain the growing divide between Orthodox and non-Orthodox to which a number of authors allude. Even when the Orthodox refrain from criticizing the non-Orthodox (and they seem to revel in doing so), their behavior, characterized by their insistence on adhering to Jewish law as the true expression of Judaism, stands as a silent criticism of the non-Orthodox. I use the term *silent criticism* because Orthodox Jews who follow the prescriptions of *halakha* are likely to find some prescriptions burdensome, as they do not seem to make any sense or provide any meaning to one's life. Nevertheless, the fact that Orthodox Jews continue to adhere to them suggests that, in their minds, one does not *choose* how to be Jewish.

The Orthodox–non-Orthodox divide is most apparent at the level of religious organizational life. For example, not too long ago, leaders of the Conservative movement were sensitive to how the Orthodox might react to their innovations. The potential reaction of the Orthodox was certainly a factor in their decisions. Even a few Reform leaders, as late as the 1970s, considered how the Orthodox might respond to this or that change in practice. This is no longer the case for a number of reasons. First, there is a sense that, regardless of what the Conservative, much less the Reform movement, might do or refrain from doing, this will not spare them from Orthodox criticism. Second, and this is no less important, the Conservative and Reform movements increasingly recruit their rabbinic and lay leadership from those who were raised in Conservative or Reform – not in Orthodox – families. Family and friendship ties between the leaders of Conservative or Reform and Orthodox Jews are less and less common. This means that the Orthodox are no longer significant referents for the non-Orthodox. Conservative rabbis and lay leaders, for example, are now products of Conservative homes, Conservative camps, and Conservative schools. They take Conservative practice for granted as normative Jewish practice. They do not feel that they need to apologize or act defensively about their brand of Judaism, much less turn to the Orthodox as role models. However, in certain Conservative synagogues, in certain urban neighborhoods, this is not entirely the case. There, one finds within some Conservative synagogues a core of members who are regular Sabbath attendees, who walk rather than ride to the synagogue, observe *kashrut*, and send their children to day schools. They are the most likely to have friendship networks with Orthodox synagogue members and view their Orthodox friends as role models of a sort. Furthermore, a disproportionate number of professionals in nondenominational Jewish organizations are Orthodox and serve as role models for some of the lay members. However, as the authors in this collection have noted, the tendency is for a growing division between Orthodox and non-Orthodox. What consequences, if any, stem from the divide? The consequences are related to what I described earlier as the absence of boundaries or standards beyond those of individual preferences. This is evident in the interdenominational relationships in the development or evolution of denominations' beliefs, with the Orthodox influencing the Conservative and the Conservative likewise influencing the Reform.

The Conservative movement has a key role in establishing standards for what is or is not Judaically proper, although the Reform movement does not adhere to these standards. However, the Conservative standards provide, indirectly at least, benchmarks for many rabbis in the Reform movement. For example, as long as the Conservative movement forbids its rabbis to perform marriages in which one of the partners is non-Jewish, or prohibits its rabbis from performing marriages together with Christian clergy, this acts as a brake on the Reform movement that continues, at the official level, to oppose such marriages. Although the Reform movement will not sanction Reform rabbis who perform such ceremonies, it is clear that the movement is officially unhappy when such marriages are performed. This official unhappiness provides space for Reform rabbis who prefer not to perform such marriages but also fear the ire of congregants who insist they do so. Should the Conservative movement, for example, change its policy in this regard, the Reform movement would surely do so as well. This is only one example of the manner in which the Conservative movement, at the national level, and individual Conservative rabbis, at the local level, serve as models of sorts for the Reform movement. (This is not to suggest that they are exclusive models or to deny the impact that Reconstructionism and Jewish Renewal have had on the Reform movement.)

Up until twenty or thirty years ago, the same influence was true in the Conservative movement's relationship to Orthodoxy. The Conservative movement, to use an expression common among its leadership, was constantly looking over it right shoulder to see how Orthodoxy would respond to its innovations in Judaic norms. Among the more right wing, that is, more strictly observant wing of the movement, Orthodox standards were identical to their own at the level of personal observance. Conservative rabbis, in turn, served as models for their own congregants, who allowed themselves far greater latitude in determining what was or was not permitted. As long as this was the case, the notion of ordaining gays, for example, would have been unthinkable. How can a theological seminary that pretends to uphold standards of Jewish law ordain committed homosexuals when homosexual acts are in clear violation of Jewish law? Nevertheless, the pressure today to ordain gays and lesbians in the Conservative movement is very strong, and there is every reason to believe that within the next decade they will be ordained. This can be explained as a function of changing standards within liberal American society, where attitudes toward gays and lesbians have become a touchstone of one's commitment to personal liberties. Because Orthodoxy no longer provides a model for the Conservative leadership and its members, the vast majority are no longer concerned with what the Orthodox will think or say. Other examples extend to areas such as Sabbath or kashrut observance and the manner in which each is to be observed, and even to curriculum models within Conservative schools.

It is not surprising that whereas the Conservative movement has both a centrist and a left wing, it lacks an outspoken articulate right wing. It has no ballast to the right, because there is no longer any base on which a right wing can seek to impose standards. Standards are increasingly derived from individual preferences, the individual's own sense of what is right or wrong and proper or improper, and the culture of American liberalism. (Cynics already quip that the editorial pages of the *New York Times* compete with Torah as the source of standards within the Conservative movement.) The absence of Judaic standards may work in theory, but this places any religious movement that makes a claim to ultimate truth and standards in an impossible predicament. Furthermore, as the Conservative movement abandons the notion of objective or outside standards to which members or at least rabbis must adhere, it will inevitably have an impact on the rest of American Jewry.

At the present time, there is something of a revival of ritual within American Jewish life and this is especially evident in the Reform and Conservative movements. Nevertheless, we should not be misled about the scope of the Judaic renaissance in the United States. The Jewish population study of 2000 indicates that, whereas members of the American Jewish community count their number at roughly 5.5 million, many of these people no longer consider themselves Jewish. According to the American Jewish Identification Survey of 2000, as reported in the *American Jewish Year Book 2002,* the number of Jews who identified with a religion other than Judaism more than doubled in the past decade, and an additional 1.4 million individuals of Jewish parentage or ethnicity said they were secular or had no religion. On one hand, the leakage out of Judaism, particularly through intermarriage, is numerically significant. On the other hand, among those who identify themselves as Jews and identify themselves with the Jewish community, there are, within many core groups, an increased interest in Jewish matters and a revived interest in Jewish ritual practice. Whether this is a matter of personal choice, or very much related to fears of family disintegration, or to a desire to keep children from marrying non-Jews, or to an increased interest in *spiritual* matters following similar trends in the general American culture remains to be seen. It may be somewhat utilitarian or faddish if it does not rest on the traditional bedrock of religion – the sense that one performs rituals regardless of whether one likes them or not because one is commanded by God to do so. Hence, just as there is a revival of ritual interest and practice, a decline may ultimately follow.

I realize that this paints a rather gloomy picture of the condition and outlook for American Judaism. Although I confess that I am by nature a pessimist, it would certainly be a mistake to overstate the tendencies I have described or to imagine that they alone comprise an adequate description of contemporary American Judaism. As was already pointed out, American Jews have established markers, if not boundaries, for what is or is not Judaically legitimate, although the line between denying one individual as Jewish and judging another to be a bad Jew is somewhat blurred. Support for Israel and remembrance of the Holocaust are among the key markers. A Jew may confess that he or she does not observe kashrut or the Sabbath or even attend a synagogue on the holiest of Jewish days and offer as a reason that he or she is uncomfortable with the rituals or the synagogue or sees no point in their observance. Having said so, that Jew will not fear accusations of having abandoned Judaism or of being a Jewish self-hater. However, this is not true of Jews who refuse to identify with Israel or with the suffering Jews underwent in the Holocaust. Once again, not all American Jews accept these markers but virtually every Jewish organization, religious and nonreligious (indeed even intermarriage support groups), do so. These are more ethnic than religious markers, a point to which I will return. Nevertheless, there are other, albeit less emphasized, boundary lines or markers, some of a more specifically religious variety, that the vast majority of those Jews, who choose to identify as Jews, recognize as obligatory. They certainly include a major negative marker – not being a believing Christian. There is virtual unanimous consensus across all the denominations that Jews for Jesus are not Jewish. Other points of consensus include the celebration of the Passover Seder and the observance, in some form or another, of Yom Kippur, the holiest of Jewish holy days. They probably still include circumcision, although within the Reform movement some objections to circumcision have been raised. Individuals who observe none of the aforementioned markers may be defined as Jews, but they are unlikely to be thought of as "fellow Jews."

In light of the presence of markers or boundary lines, it is less than clear how they are formed or, if one considers them as obligatory, to whom Jews are obligated. The notion of obligation is itself problematic. It is undermined by the increased quest for *spirituality* to which a number of authors refer. As a number of authors have noted, ethnic interests and concerns appear to have declined; interests in Judaism as a religion and the search for *spiritual* fulfillment have increased. I have emphasized the term *spiritual* because no concrete definition has been developed, especially in the American Jewish context. It mainly refers to the search for uplift, for a sense of transcendence, for a greater legitimacy for and expectation of emotional expression, for getting outside oneself or feeling something beyond the everyday and the mundane. There is certainly a language of spirituality that one hears with increasing frequency. Elsewhere, in a somewhat different context, it has been noted that ethnic Judaism has retreated before a form of privatized religion that I now think is indistinguishable from what American culture terms *spirituality*. It is formulated in a language of hushed, soft terms of individual meaning, journeys of discovery, and the search for fulfillment. Its emphases are interpersonal rather than collective. Its favored qualities are authenticity and sincerity rather than achievement or efficiency. Typically it is consoling, nonjudgmental, intuitive, and nonobligating. There are distinct signs that privatized Jewishness is having a substantial impact, especially on Jews in the younger age brackets. Contributions to the Federations of Jewish Philanthropy – a major form of public Jewish expression – are stagnating, if not actually declining. Mobilization for political causes of all kinds is reported to be more and more difficult to justify and sustain. The current Intifada and the challenges to Israel's legitimacy may have halted this development, but there is no reason to doubt that this is anything other than a temporary respite.[2]

There are two models to explain the Jew's relationship to Judaism in the modern era. I believe that we can identify most Jews by the paradigm that best describes their relationship to Judaism. I do not suggest that these two modes of relationship, which I have referred to as "public" and "private," are mutually exclusive but rather that they are conceptually distinct. By public Judaism, I mean the Judaism that conceives of the Jew as part of a collective entity – the Jewish people – with obligations and responsibilities toward other Jews and toward the collective interests of the Jewish people. Most nonsectarian Jewish organizations define their Judaism in public terms. Concern for Israel, Soviet Jewry, or the political interests of American Judaism is a reflection of public Judaism. Private Judaism, in contrast, reflects a regard for the meaning Judaism has for the individual Jew. The Jew who defines his or her Judaism in private terms is concerned with what patterns or answers Judaism provides for stages of life, for calendar events, for personal crises, and for a need to celebrate aspects of life. The Jew who sees his or her Judaism in personal terms is more likely to think of Judaism in religious terms, whereas the Jew who defines his or her Judaism in primarily public terms is more readily categorized as an "ethnic" Jew. Although there is presently an evident emphasis on private Judaism, I believe that this not only may shift but, in a related development, the very nature of Judaism as interpreted in the private realm is likely to undergo reformulation.

In place of the declining public face of Jewishness, a burgeoning private (spiritual) sphere offering a new understanding of the Jewish tradition has begun to make itself felt. It is the voice of a distinctively American cohort whose initial inspiration can be traced back to the counterculture of the Sixties. Since then, it has lost many of its rebellious qualities but it still presents a picture of creative diversity and moral enthusiasm. This emphasis on the self and its realization, which have been interpreted as spiritual quests rather than obligations transcending the individual person, entails a turning away from the kinds of commonplace commitments that lack the special cachet of personal authenticity or inner growth. Responsibilities toward abstract collectivities such as the Jewish people, therefore, decline in significance. From the perspectives of one searching for the spiritual experience, true love, the spiritual and personal experience far outweighs it. Indeed, to the degree that love needs to overcome obstacles, ethnic or religious, in order to be realized, it is considered the more authentic and marvelous. Understood in terms of personal meaning, Jewishness becomes – even for Jews – an acquired taste. Moreover, experience-based religiosity has no intrinsic justification for exclusion or boundaries; it necessarily includes all who are partner to the inspirational moment.

One can be strongly ethnic without being religious. This was characteristic of the second generation of American Jews. However, ethnicity, in addition to its intrinsic importance in Judaism, rendered religion credible. To borrow a formulation of Durkheim, ethnic Judaism posed an ineffable and transcendent presence, that of the collective Jewish people, which imposed itself on the lives of individuals. In this manner, it made the core notion of the religion, the notion of a transcendent God, meaningful and real. The traditionally religious Jew is, by definition, an ethnic Jew as well. One need not be religious in order to be an ethnic Jew, but to move from strong ethnic to strong religious commitments is a natural transition. Moving from the privatized or spiritualized religion, which I have just ascribed to ethnicity, is less natural and less likely. On the contrary, the more likely move is from spiritualized, that is, privatized, Judaism to Christianity or some other form of New Age religion that uplifts the individual spiritually.

In the past two years the Palestinian Intifada and the threat to Israel's security, accompanied by increased signs of anti-Semitism in Europe and even on American college campuses, has strengthened the bounds of ethnicity among American Jews. This is especially true of older Jews and less true of college-age students. While the portrait of diminished ethnicity is perhaps overstated, this depiction of the dangers of spirituality is also incomplete. Many may have exaggerated the spirituality of American Jews and its impact on ethnic sensitivities. Shortly after Steven M. Cohen and Arnold Eisen completed their study, *The Jew Within*, which documented the decline of ethnic sentiment and the increase in the spiritual quests among American Jews, Cohen noted during a private conversation that at least some of this apparent spirituality that he and Eisen uncovered might serve as a cover for ethnicity. Perhaps one reason Jews increasingly utilize the language of spirituality to explain their Jewishness is because it is consistent with dominant trends in American culture, trends that American Jews generally absorb unthinkingly. Terms such as *love, feeling, God, healing, inclusivity, soul, inner self,* and *journeys* have become part of the jargon of American religious life, and Jews have adopted this language. It is important for them to believe that these are terms that are central to Judaism and that Judaism "empowers" spirituality. In other words, the language of spirituality justifies and explains what are ethnic choices. Obviously these terms have consequences. Language creates its own reality, and if Jews talk about the "healing" power of religion, they become more open to a "healing" experience, such as the reliance on Jewish songs and music to alleviate, if not heal, physical ailments. The religious–spiritual dimension has indeed been strengthened, but the choice of Jewish songs and the rejection of Christian hymns must be understood as an ethnic rather than a religious choice. As long as the context is a Jewish one, and as long as Judaism is a distinctly minority religion in the United States, choosing a set of Jewish rather than Christian symbols must be understood, at least partially, as an ethnic choice.

The Reform movement, for example, has gone much further than the Conservative movement in embracing intermarried couples and permitting non-Jews to become members of Reform synagogues, even delegates to national Reform synagogue conventions, and to participate in religious services.

The question of the degree of non-Jewish participation has become a matter of dispute within the movement. Their participation is most problematic when a young boy or girl from an intermarried family celebrates the bar or bat mitzvah (when the adolescent reaches the age of 13), and the youngster's family members anticipate participating in the ceremony. It is instructive to quote from a recent paper by Michael A. Meyer, the foremost historian of Reform Judaism, on the topic.

> The most interesting result of the non-Jewish participation in *bnai mitzvah* ceremonies [*bar* and *bat mitzvah* ceremonies] has been the creation of hierarchies of holiness with regard to objects that play a role in the service. These hierarchies have been created differentially in various congregations, but in each instance they have been established in order to discreetly mark off an inner boundary. Some of the boundaries are constructed on the basis of traditional distinctions, other are novel and contrary to tradition. In the former category is the provision that non-Jews may (and in some cases if they ascend the *bimah* should) wear a *kipah* [head covering]. [The *bimah* is the platform where the ark containing the Torah scrolls are kept and were the rabbi, the Cantor, and the President of the synagogue sit]. But the wearing of the *talit* [prayer shawl] is restricted to Jews. The *kipah* indicates worshipfulness, the *talit* is seen as a specific symbol of Jewishness.
>
> In a few congregations the *aron hakodesh* [the ark where the Torah scrolls are kept] assumes actual *kedushah* [sanctity] and gentiles are not permitted to come into contact with it. In 7 percent [of congregations], according to the survey, non-Jews may not even approach it by ascending the *bimah*, in another they may come up to the *bimah* but not sit on it, the latter representing permanent and complete belonging. However in general the privilege of opening or closing the ark, which is properly seen as a *kibud* [honor] rather than as a *mitzvah* [a commandment] and which is exercised silently, has been seen as a way to involve the gentile members of the *bnai mitzvah* family without creating dissonance. Symbolically they stand at the portal but they have no contact with what lies within it, the scrolls of the torah. To touch the religious symbols of Judaism, one policy statement makes explicit, one must be Jewish.[3]

These restrictions strike me as ethnic as well as religious. They suggest to me that, even in a strictly religious context, even within that denomination which has been, historically, the least ethnically driven, the ethnic dimension is still very much a presence.

Notes

1. I am grateful to Steven M. Cohen, Riv-Ellen Prell, and Jonathan Sarna for their illuminating comments on an earlier draft.
2. Charles S. Liebman and Steven M. Cohen, *Two Worlds of Judaism: The Israeli and American Jewish Experience* (New Haven: Yale University Press, 1990).
3. I am indebted to Michael A. Meyer, who provided me with his English-language text of the article "The Place and the Identity of the Non-Jew in the Reform Synagogue," *Gesher* 146 (Winter 2003, in Hebrew), 66–74. The bracketed insertions are my own.

8 Contemporary Jewish education

ISA ARON, MICHAEL ZELDIN, AND SARA S. LEE

Learning and teaching have been central to the Jewish tradition since its early beginnings.[1] Deuteronomy 6:6–7 states the following: "These words, which I myself command you today, are to be upon your heart. You are to repeat them with your children and are to speak of them in your sitting in your house and in your walking in the way, in your lying down and in your rising up." Building on this dictum, the tradition held that Jewish study was both a *mitzvah* (commandment) in its own right and a prerequisite for the observance of all other *mitzvot*. The Talmud abounds with legends and sayings emphasizing the power and importance of education; later rabbinic authorities, such as Maimonides, included communal expectations about learning in their codes of Jewish law.

With the Emancipation, as European Jews entered more fully into the larger society, the value of Jewish learning began to recede while the value of secular learning increased. Schools in Western Europe in the eighteenth and nineteenth centuries strove to offer the right mix of traditional text study, Hebrew language instruction, and secular subjects; not surprisingly, each educator's view of the correct proportions of these elements varied with his (they were all men) religious and political ideology.

As Jews immigrated to North America, the process of adapting to the values of secular society accelerated. The earliest immigrants took care to provide for the Jewish education of both their own children and the indigent children of the community; there was even a brief period, from about 1845 to about 1865, when Jewish day schools sprouted in eighteen cities. By 1870, when public schooling became the norm, Jewish parents enthusiastically enrolled their children in public schools, and Jewish education was relegated to supplementary settings. Jewish schools sponsored by congregations and communal agencies met anywhere between one and four times per week; in addition, private classes and tutors were widely available. Early on, most of these institutions were perceived to be problematic, plagued by undereducated and unskilled teachers, poor discipline, a paucity of curricular materials, and a lack of parental support. In 1880, Professor B. A. Abrams wrote in the Milwaukee Jewish paper:

> It is a strange fact that parents who take great care to see to it that their child attend public school regularly and punctually keep the very same children at home for nonsensical reasons, since it is only Sabbath School that they are missing.[2]

Twenty years later, a survey of Jewish educational establishments in the New York area came to this conclusion:

1. The demand for Jewish education is comparatively small.
2. Small as the demand is, the means and equipment which we possess at present are far too inadequate to meet it.
3. Wherever that demand is met there is a lack either of system or of content.[3]

Though communal leaders continued to pay lip service to the value of Jewish education, they were, in truth, preoccupied by other, more immediate, causes. Immigrants were concerned, above all, with their economic survival; more established groups were concerned with the welfare of new immigrants and fighting anti-Semitism. In the twentieth century, the attention of the organized Jewish community focused, in turn, on rescuing European Jews, assisting Holocaust survivors, founding and supporting the State of Israel, and helping Jews in crisis from diasporic countries such as the Soviet Union and Ethiopia.

Out of the spotlight, quiet but significant changes in Jewish education were underway during the second half of the twentieth century. While the primary form of Jewish education for the vast majority of Jewish children remained the supplementary school, day schools, Jewish summer camps, Jewish early childhood education, Jewish family education, and educational trips to Israel flourished. In a 1988 article on the state of Jewish education, Professor Barry Chazan of the Hebrew University saw a great deal of promise in these new forms of education. Nonetheless, he bemoaned this fact:

> The Jewish educational community has been thirsty for vision.... During the past decade, the Jewish educational community . . . has devoted most of its energies . . . to solving immediate problems (funding, staff, programs). . . . While Jewish education seems to be a mature and relatively well-equipped ship, it is not always clear where it is sailing or who is its captain.[4]

By the 1990s, the need to provide more intensive and effective Jewish education of higher quality to a larger percentage of the Jewish population assumed greater urgency. While communal leaders were steadfast in their concern for the State of Israel and diasporic communities in need, they realized that a different kind of danger lay at home. As anti-Semitism receded and America became more hospitable, Jews were losing their connection to the Jewish tradition and the Jewish people.

A stunning realization of this problem came with the publication of the 1990 National Jewish Population Study (NJPS), which found an alarming rate of intermarriage (52 percent). The rate of intermarriage was not the only problem identified by the NJPS and other demographic studies. For example, only 32 percent of NJPS respondents were members of a synagogue, less than 20 percent lit Shabbat candles on a regular basis, and only 40 percent gave to a Jewish cause.

One hopeful finding among all this bad news was that higher levels of Jewish education were correlated with more active participation in Jewish life. The more intensive the Jewish education of NJPS respondents, the more likely they were to join a Jewish organization, give to a Jewish cause, marry a Jewish partner, and practice Jewish rituals.[5] As leaders of the Jewish community searched for positive steps they could take in response to this study, their catchword became, "Jewish education is the key to Jewish survival."

As Jack Wertheimer notes, "NJPS and other demographic studies...did not invent the issue of 'continuity'; rather, they dramatized the dire nature of the problem and impressed upon the wider Jewish public, including its lay leaders, the need to develop a strategy to confront the serious issues."[6] While previous studies pointing to the correlation between Jewish education and active participation in Jewish life had gone largely unremarked on, the alarm raised by the 1990 NJPS led people to focus on Jewish education as they never had before. As stated in a 1991 report, "The responsibility for developing Jewish identity and instilling a commitment to Judaism...now rests primarily with education."[7]

Suddenly, the spotlight was aimed at the heretofore unheralded successes of the 1980s and 1990s: preschools, day schools, Israel trips, and innovations in family education. The Commission on Jewish Education in North America (an independent national entity funded by the Mandel Associated Foundations) spawned dozens of local "continuity" commissions.

The result has been a decade of sustained concern and support for Jewish education that is without precedent in American Jewish life. Each of the denominations has issued new curricular frameworks, produced new curricular materials, and provided increased opportunities for professional development. Umbrella organizations such as the Jewish Education Services of North America and the Coalition for Advancement of Jewish Education have served as catalysts for new initiatives, convened task forces and conferences, and sponsored research and publications. New foundations, such as the Covenant Foundation and the AVI CHAI Foundation, have been established, and existing foundations have increased their funding for educational projects.

Much has been accomplished, though much more remains to be done. Fortunately, the interest in Jewish education shows no signs of abating. This article, then, should be considered an interim report on a work in progress. It focuses on six key points:

1. Jewish education is now seen as a lifelong endeavor. The spectrum of educational activity has been extended at both ends to include early childhood, late adulthood, and everything in between.

2. Increasingly, Jewish education is seen as encompassing an array of activities and programs beyond formal schooling, including family education, camping, youth groups, and trips to Israel. It is now conventional wisdom that a complete Jewish education requires a variety of different experiences in a variety of different settings, throughout one's life.

3. It is difficult to predict whether the growth of day schools, particularly in the non-Orthodox world, will continue. Even at their current level, day schools are now de rigueur for the Orthodox and have transformed sectors of both the Conservative and Reform movements.

4. Despite the growth of day schools, it seems likely that the majority of Jewish children will continue to receive a much less intensive education in congregational religious schools; however, new initiatives have led to dramatic changes in congregational education.

5. All these new programs require staff that is knowledgeable in Judaica and versed in educational theory and practice. To address this need, a variety of new programs has been created for the preparation of Jewish education professionals. Nonetheless, the field faces a tremendous shortage of personnel.

6. Finally, the cost of Jewish education, to both the sponsoring institutions and the individual consumers, is rising. One can only hope that the Jewish community will be able to meet these costs.

1. JEWISH EDUCATION IS A LIFELONG ENDEAVOR

The injunction "to repeat them with your children" is only the first part of Deuteronomy 6:7. In addition, the Torah enjoins us, "to speak of them in your sitting in your house and in your walking in the way." *All* Jews are expected to continue learning throughout their lives. In contrast with secular education, which focuses on the mastery of subject matters, Jewish education sees learning as an end in itself. Thus, while no one would expect to have to return to sixth-grade math or tenth-grade American history, Jewish learning is centered on the repeated reading, year after year, of the Torah. Commentaries on, and further elaborations of, the laws of the Torah are also considered Torah in a larger sense. The *siddur* (prayer book) speaks of study as a mitzvah, and the study of selected biblical and rabbinic texts is an integral part of the morning prayer service.

In their concern first with economic survival, and then with assimilating into American society, American Jews neglected this obligation to study Torah. Their interest in Jewish learning was limited to the education of their children; and, in keeping with the Western paradigm, the education of children focused more and more on achievement, particularly their performance in the *bar* or *bat mitzvah* ceremony at the age of thirteen. In contrast, one of the most significant developments in Jewish education today is that it is, increasingly, seen as a lifelong activity.

Early childhood programs

As more women have entered the workforce and as American society has placed a higher value on preschool education (without providing many publicly funded venues for this education), it is not surprising that programs for young children in Jewish settings would increase. Early childhood programs (primarily preschools, but also day care for infants and toddlers, and family programs such as Mommy and Me) are commonly found in both synagogues and Jewish Community Centers (JCCs). In 1990, it was estimated that 50,000 children aged eighteen months to five years were enrolled in Jewish early childhood programs[8]; by 2002 the number had doubled. In that year, 20 percent of Jewish two-year-olds, 25 percent of three- and four-year-olds, and 41 percent of five-year-olds spent between thirty and forty hours per week in Jewish early childhood centers. Summarizing research on this area of Jewish education, Wertheimer writes the following:

> A limited amount of research has substantiated the claim that family
> observance of Jewish religious rituals increases when parents enter
> their children into child-care programs rich in Jewish content. One
> study found greater observance of home rituals, such as lighting
> Friday-night candles and reciting the *kiddush*, and even increases in the
> number of Jewish friendships reported by parents.[9]

Wertheimer argues that there is considerable pent-up demand for these programs but that their expansion is limited by the severe shortage of teachers (a topic to which we will return in Section 5). Similarly, there are relatively few

Jewish day care programs for children under the age of two, and existent programs have long waiting lists.

The education of adolescents

For decades, most marginally identified Jewish parents have viewed Jewish schooling as bar or bat mitzvah preparation; it is no surprise, then, that the dropout rate after bar or bat mitzvah has been, on average, 50 percent.[10] As the Jewish community has focused more intently on both Jewish continuity and Jewish education, it has come to realize the critical importance of the high school years, and it has redoubled its efforts to create compelling programs for teens. Attracting participants, however, continues to be a challenge. A survey of thirteen- through seventeen-year-olds conducted by researchers at Brandeis University in 2000 found that these teenagers' time out of school was taken up with homework, extracurricular activities, and after-school jobs, which left little time to participate in Jewish activities of any kind. More sobering still was the finding that few teenagers viewed Judaism as an important part of their lives: "As expected at this developmental stage, three-quarters of the teenage respondents were preoccupied with a search for meaning in life. Among these, only 40% thought it important to find that meaning through their Jewishness."[11] With these findings in mind, efforts are underway to help Jewish teens stay connected to the Jewish community. Many of these efforts have utilized informal venues – including camping, youth groups, and especially Israel trips – and these are discussed in the next section.

College Judaica courses

Prior to the 1960s, it was rare to find a Judaic studies course of any kind at a college or university. Today the situation is reversed, as it is rare to find a major institution of higher learning that does not offer at least a few Judaica courses. According to Hillel: The Foundation for Jewish Campus Life, over 400 college-level courses in some aspect of Jewish studies are offered annually.[12] A 1991 study of Jewish adults in the New York area under the age of 40 found that 18 percent of them had taken at least one such course.[13]

Among the Orthodox, it has become common for high school graduates to study at a *yeshiva* in Israel for a year or two prior to attending college. By the mid-1990s it was estimated that 3,000 students (well over half of both male and female high school graduates of Orthodox day schools) were studying in Israel for at least a year.[14]

Adult learning

Most dramatic of all has been the growth of adult Jewish learning. Once limited to synagogues and JCCs, programs for adult learning are now offered by a panoply of institutions in a variety of settings. The most ambitious and fastest growing of these is the Florence Melton Adult Mini-School, the first branch of which opened in 1986. Students enroll for thirty weeks per year, two and one-half hours per week, over a four-year period. The course of study, which is the same for all branches, deals with Jewish history, Jewish texts, Jewish ethics, and the Jewish life cycle. In an effort to attract a range of students, both daytime and evening classes are offered. In the summer of 2002, the school claimed over 20,000 graduates and had sixty branches in cities throughout North America. A majority of its students are either retirees or women with school-aged children, but other sectors of the Jewish community are also represented.

The Melton Mini-School shattered two of the prevailing preconceptions about Jewish adult learning: (1) that adults were interested only in short-term courses or one-shot lectures and would not enroll in a sustained program; and (2) that adults were more interested in trendy topics than a basic, in-tegrated curriculum. With these limiting assumptions challenged, the field was open to a variety of different programs: the Wexner Heritage Program, a national program for young adult leaders; Boston's Me'ah program, in which students study for 100 hours over a two-year period; and a variety of others.

Other models of innovative adult learning have also been developed. The San Francisco Bay Area's Lehrhaus program is famous for its wide-ranging course offerings. The Union for Reform Julaism's summer Kallah offers a week of intensive learning with Judaic scholars in a retreat-like setting. The adult education opportunities within JCCs have also increased dramatically. Many JCCs now have at least one Jewish educator on staff. A 1994 survey found that all offered some adult learning opportunities, and over half offered an introductory Judaism class. Three-quarters sponsored some form of family education, and one-third sponsored educational trips to Israel.[15]

A small but growing number of synagogues also have an adult educator on their staff, which enables them to offer a range of learning opportunities: courses of varying length and duration; day-long Hebrew marathons; week-end retreats; parallel learning for parents of school-aged children; and ongo-ing family education, in which parents and children study together (learning opportunities for parents of religious school children are discussed at greater length in Section 4).

These new programs are attracting new audiences, many of whom have little prior experience with Jewish learning of any kind. As widespread and successful as these programs are, many Jewish adults have yet to be reached. A 2001 national survey by Steven M. Cohen and Aryeh Davidson found that "about half have never participated in a Jewish study group, about half have never studied Jewish texts on their own, and about half have never even taken a class with a Jewish theme."[16]

2. THE CONFLUENCE OF FORMAL AND INFORMAL EDUCATION

It is by now a truism that a single summer in a Jewish camp can teach campers more Hebrew, more Jewish prayers, and more Jewish concepts than several years spent in an afternoon supplementary school. What is more important is that Jewish camps have a strong affective component; they create intense Jewish communities with their own culture, which can exert a strong influence on the camper's Jewish identification. Similarly, a summer or a semester spent on an Israel trip can have a profound effect on a heretofore uninvolved Jewish adolescent:

> When compared with other studies of Jewish adolescents . . . research indicates that there is no other Jewish experience that is as positively regarded by Jewish teens as the Israel Experience. No less important is the finding that for many Jewish teens the Israel trip ranks among the most positive life experience of any kind – Jewish or general – that they have had.[17]

Not surprisingly, then, Jewish educational experiences that were once viewed as ancillary are now considered to be of critical importance. It is now conventional wisdom among Jewish communal leaders that a complete Jewish education requires a range of different experiences, formal and informal, throughout one's life.

Unfortunately, the conventional wisdom of the leadership has not yet reached *amcha*, "the ordinary people," as no more than 55,000 children between the age of eight and seventeen attend a Jewish summer camp of any kind, out of a total population of 600,000.[18] It seems likely, however, that the demand for summer camps is greater than the supply. Though expensive (with an average fee of $625 per week, according to a 2002 study), the average Jewish camp is filled to 96 percent capacity; in some, parents pay a deposit in August to ensure a place for their child the following summer.[19]

From 1992 to 1996 (years of relative peace and stability in Israel), only 14 percent of Jewish teens between the ages of thirteen and nineteen (a total of 36,500) went to Israel on an organized educational trip.[20] In an attempt to maximize the educational potential of the Israel Experience, philanthropists

Charles Bronfman and Michael Steinhardt created "birthright israel," a program aimed at bringing 100,000 young adults (aged eighteen to twenty-six) a year on a ten-day trip to Israel. During its first two months (December 1999 to January 2000) the program had 6,000 participants. Unfortunately, continuing political unrest in Israel has made it difficult to recruit large numbers of additional participants, especially those who had not previously been to Israel. As of January 2002, a total of 20,000 young adults had participated in the program.

Family education

In the early decades of the twentieth century, Jewish education professionals looked to the public school as their model for a modern Jewish education. They assumed that their students were observing basic Jewish rituals and practices at home and that they did not need to attend a Jewish school to learn about the Jewish holidays or to gain a sense of Jewish identification.[21] The schools established in this era saw their primary goal as instruction in such subjects as modern Hebrew, Bible, and Jewish history.

Today, many educators espouse a model in which instruction is just one part of the overriding goal of enculturation, the induction of children into a culture. In families that live active and rich Jewish lives, enculturation occurs gradually over the course of a child's upbringing. Children in these families do not need to be taught the *kiddush* (the blessing over wine on Shabbat) or the *motzi* (the blessing over bread); they absorb these and many other rituals, customs, and values over the course of their childhood. As demographic studies in the past three or four decades have shown, however, the majority of non-Orthodox families (and a minority of Orthodox ones) do not live life in a Jewish rhythm, practicing few rituals and participating only marginally in synagogue life.

In the absence of enculturation, instruction in Hebrew, Bible, or Jewish history is as alien as instruction in Japanese, and a good deal more foreign than instruction in math. Slowly, over the course of the twentieth century, Jewish educators began to adapt their goals to the changing population, focusing, first and foremost, on enculturation.

It was not long before educators took this shift in goals a step further, viewing parents as part of their target audience because parents are the most powerful agents of enculturation. If a child's parents embrace the goals of Jewish education, she or he will bring a more positive attitude to the Jewish school. If Jewish rituals become incorporated into a family's weekly and yearly rhythm, the children will come to school with a wealth of knowledge, both tacit and explicit. If, in addition, the parents are studying the same

Torah portion (or Talmudic legend or period of history) as the child, they can not only reinforce what the child has learned but also serve as role models without parallel. No wonder, then, that Jewish educators began in the 1970s to focus more of their energies on the family as a whole. From modest attempts (holding an annual family day) to more ambitious ones (creating a track for parents or an entire "family school"), educators have spent the past few decades experimenting with a wide range of family education modalities. Communal agencies and foundations have championed this notion and have supported it financially. For example, the Combined Jewish Philanthropies of Greater Boston has created the Sh'arim Family Educator Initiative, in which congregations, day schools, and Jewish community centers receive funding to hire a family educator. Similarly, the AVI CHAI Foundation has funded family education programs for day schools. The Whizin Institute of the University of Judaism has pioneered the training of congregational and day school teams to introduce family education in synagogues and schools. The teams include educators, rabbis, and significant volunteer leaders.

Even when an outside source of funding is available, incorporating family education into a school can be challenging. Parents accustomed to dropping off their children at the parking lot may be resistant to the notion that they attend themselves. The institution's most senior and influential leaders (both lay and professional) must signal their support for family education and explain why it is so important; if the programs prove to be engaging, the school's culture will change over time and parent participation will come to be taken as a given. To be engaging, family programs must have staff members who can work with both children and adults; in addition, the programs must be structured to accommodate a variety of participants, from those with little or no Jewish education attending for the first time to those with an excellent Jewish education attending with their third child. The ways in which family education has transformed the congregational school will be discussed in section four.

The programs discussed in this section offer a glimpse of the many ways that formal and informal Jewish education, which in an earlier era were seen as separate entities, have, in recent years, informed and enriched each other. Programs such as the Institute for Informal Jewish Education at Brandeis University have begun to raise the level of professionalization among those who work in informal settings; as a result, professionals in these settings have begun to curricularize their offerings and borrow methodologies from formal education. For their part, formal institutions have benefited from importing techniques and learning modalities that had heretofore been the province of informal educators.

3. THE GROWTH OF JEWISH DAY SCHOOL EDUCATION

Over the past few decades, Jewish day schools have come to occupy a central place among the options for Jewish education. A day school provides a complete secular education in line with the requirements of the state in which it is located, along with a Jewish education consistent with the institution or organization that sponsors it. The most significant development in the past decade has been growth in the number of such schools and in the number of students who attend them, and a broadening of the spectrum served by the schools, including Jewish affiliation and student age group.

In the nineteenth century, Jewish day schools developed in almost every city in the United States large enough to support a school. Since most of the Jews who lived in the United States before 1880 were of central European origin, these schools combined a basic Jewish education with numeracy (basic arithmetic skills) and reading and writing in English and German. These schools often bore names such as the Hebrew English German Academy, signaling their commitments to help students develop a basic working knowledge of Jewish worship, to prepare students for life in the United States, and to familiarize students with high culture (for these immigrants, German culture). As free universal public education became the norm throughout the United States in the 1870s, as public schools reduced the overtly Protestant teaching that characterized their early days, and as some public schools in neighborhoods heavily populated by immigrants from Germany offered German language electives, the Jewish day schools closed their doors one after another.[22] By 1870, all these schools had closed, and Isaac Mayer Wise, a leader of the American Jewish community, reported this to the U.S. Commissioner of Education:

> It is our settled opinion here that the education of the young is the business of the State, and the religious instruction, to which we add the Hebrew, is the duty of religious bodies. Neither ought to interfere with the other. The secular branches belong to the public schools, religion in the Sabbath schools, exclusively.[23]

The first Orthodox *yeshivot*, Yeshibath Etz Chaim and Yeshibath Rabbi Yitzchak Elchanan, opened several decades after the closing of the last nineteenth-century day schools (1886 and 1897, respectively). These schools were Orthodox in orientation and patterned after yeshivot in Eastern Europe, but they added secular studies "from four in the afternoon [for] two hours."[24] Twenty-eight additional yeshivot opened by 1939, but the "era of expansive growth" of Orthodox day schools started after World War II and the destruction of European Jewry and European centers of learning. The Torah Umesorah movement fanned out to establish schools wherever modern Orthodox Jews moved, and they were so successful that by 1963 there were 308 such schools.[25] These modern Orthodox day schools put into practice the philosophy of Samson Raphael Hirsch, the European founder of modern Orthodoxy: Torah U'mada, Jewish studies alongside modern secular studies.

Beginning in 1958, other segments of the Jewish community began opening day schools of their own to provide Jewish education in a full-time environment. The Solomon Schechter Schools of the Conservative movement blazed the way for others and were soon followed by pluralistic "community day schools." The last segment of the organized Jewish community to establish day schools was the Reform movement. The first two Reform day schools opened in 1970, but the official approval of the movement did not come until 1985.[26]

During the 1998–99 school year, 185,000 children were enrolled in Jewish day schools. Eighty percent of this enrollment was in Orthodox day schools. Virtually all Orthodox children of school age attend day schools, identified as Centrist Orthodox, Chabad, Chasidic, Immigration and Outreach, Modern Orthodox, or Yeshiva.[27] Most Jewish communities where Orthodox Jews live are home to at least one elementary day school, though often children must go to other cities (notably New York and Chicago) for an Orthodox high school education.

The growth in day school enrollment in the 1990s was dramatic, increasing by approximately 20,000 to 25,000.[28] In terms of numbers, the largest growth was in Orthodox day schools of various affiliations, primarily because of the high fertility rate among Orthodox Jews. In terms of percentage growth, non-Orthodox day schools (Conservative, Community, and Reform) increased more dramatically, growing by some 20 percent (reaching 37,000) between 1992 and 1998. As the enrollment in day schools has grown and as the number of schools has increased, day schools have banded together in associations either because their founding was spearheaded by a national movement (Chabad, Satmar Chasidic, or Torah U'mesorah) or the schools shared a common ideology (Schechter–Conservative, Ravsak–Community, and PARDeS–Reform). In recent years, day school growth was fueled by the Partnership for Excellence in Jewish Education, which offered challenge grants to local community groups contemplating the establishment of new elementary day schools or expanding existing elementary schools into middle schools. The AVI CHAI Foundation also stimulated the growth of day schools through its building loan program and its many funded programs and projects aimed at developing curriculum, providing continuing education for personnel, or enhancing the Jewish culture of day schools.

The most recent area of growth in day school education is the expansion of community (all-day) high schools. A handful of such schools that were firmly rooted in their communities for many years (notably Akiba in Philadelphia and Charles E. Smith in Rockville, Maryland) were joined by the Milken Community High School of Stephen S. Wise Temple in Los Angeles (the only community high school sponsored by a Reform temple, which attracts significant numbers of Reform and Conservative children) and the New Jewish High School in Boston. These schools were followed by a spate of smaller schools in cities across America.

The impact of day schools on the children who attend them and on their families is well established and widely accepted among leaders of synagogues, federations, and foundations. The 1990 NJPS indicates that day school graduates are more likely to join a synagogue or other Jewish organization, give to a Jewish cause, marry a Jewish partner, and practice Jewish rituals.[29] These factors led many in federations and foundations to see day schools as "the answer to the continuity crisis" and to increase financial support to unprecedented levels. As the 1990s came to a close and the twenty-first century began, this conventional wisdom was shifting toward the view that day schools can have a significant impact – perhaps even the most significant impact – on the future Jewishness of their students, but that Jewish education has its greatest impact when children participate in a variety of types of Jewish education – including youth groups, camps, and Israel trips – in addition to day school education. As one educator explained, "Day school teaches their minds, but we need camps to touch their hearts."[30]

The greatest challenge facing all day schools is financial. Tuition can be as high as $18,000 per year, and these schools must rely heavily on nontuition income to sustain their programs. They also face the personnel problem that is ubiquitous in Jewish education, including the challenge of providing benefit packages that would attract educators to choose to teach in a day school.

Educationally, day schools face the challenge of providing an answer to the question historian Jonathan Sarna says all schools must address:

> Schools serve as a primary setting, along with the home, where American Jews confront the most fundamental question of American Jewish life: how to live in two worlds at once, how to be both American and Jewish, part of the larger American society and apart from it. This question ... is what Jewish education in America is all about.[31]

How a school arranges the relationship between Jewish studies and general studies represents a day school's response to Sarna's question, whether explicitly, self-consciously, or both.

Many schools, notably the yeshivas and other Orthodox day schools not considered modern Orthodox, see their task as providing a complete Jewish education, focusing on rabbinic texts and providing the minimum secular education required by the state. Their mission is to prepare their students to live as educated Jews and to take their place in a literate, traditional, often separatist Jewish community.

Modern Orthodox, Conservative, Community, and Reform day schools all provide an education in which general and Jewish studies are brought into relationship with one another. While "integration" of general and Jewish studies often functions more as a slogan than a guiding educational principle, beginning in the late 1970s integration was carefully researched and thoughtfully planned as a way to prepare children to see the relationship between their identities as Americans and as Jews.[32] Often the goal of integration is to reinforce the "coalescence" of values that Sylvia Barack Fishman sees as pervasive in American Jewish life: "The 'texts' of two cultures, American and Jewish, are accessed simultaneously.... These value systems merge, or coalesce."[33] There are other modern Jewish thinkers and educators who argue that "the notion of the 'melting pot' that fostered the model of 'integration' (the notion that there is a comfortable synthesis between the teachings of Judaism and the values of the West) no longer seems compelling."[34] In response, these advocates of "interaction" present a different view of the role of schools in preparing children to live as Jews in America: "By creating schools, and providing a model of Judaism that is not identical, but interacts, with the larger world of values and culture of which we are a part, Judaism may make its greatest contribution to individual Jews and our larger society."[35] Thus, the structure and content of a day school's curriculum presents a unique message about what it means to live as a Jew in America.

4. FROM THE AFTERNOON RELIGIOUS SCHOOL TO THE CONGREGATION OF LEARNERS

Although much of the publicity surrounding Jewish education has focused on day schools, Israel trips, and family education, significant change has also come to the supplementary congregational school, the institution that enrolls the largest number of Jewish students – nearly three-fifths of those who receive any Jewish education. In the nineteenth century these schools were modeled after Protestant Sunday schools, and in the twentieth century after public schools. While their curricula changed gradually over time (for example, prayer Hebrew replaced modern Hebrew, and the study of Jewish holidays replaced the study of Jewish history), their structure remained essentially the same for nearly a century.

By the 1970s the failures of congregational schools were universally acknowledged. Their problems ranged from a chronic shortage of qualified teachers,[36] to lax discipline on the part of teachers and disruptive behavior on the part of students,[37] to a low level of student achievement[38] and a dropout rate of approximately 50 percent after bar or bat mitzvah.[39] A 1977 task force convened by the American Jewish Committee (AJC) observed that supplementary schools "produce graduates who are functionally illiterate in Judaism and not clearly positive in their attitudinal identification.... [M]ost graduates look back without joy on their educational experience."[40]

In the same vein, a 1989 study of thirty-nine supplementary schools in the New York area, conducted by the Board of Jewish Education of Greater New York, concluded, "Schools do a very poor job in increasing Jewish knowledge in all subject areas; they show no success in guiding children towards increased Jewish involvement; and they demonstrate an inability to influence positive growth in Jewish attitudes."[41]

During these decades, many educators chose to ignore the problems of the religious school, focusing their attention on settings they deemed more effective, such as day schools and Israel trips. Others attempted to improve supplementary education by developing new curricula and creating new textbooks. As the theory and practice of family education assumed greater currency and as the goal of enculturation, rather than instruction, was embraced, an increasing number of educators concluded that what was needed was a paradigm shift from the supplementary religious school to a Congregation of Learners.[42]

A famous dictum from Pirkei Avot (Ethics of the Fathers) says, "the world stands on three things – on Torah (learning), *Avodah* (worship) and *G'milut Hasadim* (good deeds)." A Congregation of Learners is a congregation that lives by this dictum – a congregation in which learning is seen as being on a par with worship, community building, and *tikun olam* (the repair of the world). In a Congregation of Learners there is a prevailing expectation that everyone, not just children in the religious school, should be learning. If this ideal is to become a reality, then active, engaging learning must be built into as many synagogue activities as possible. Rather than listening to a sermon at every service, worshippers might be divided into small groups to study the weekly Torah portion. Rather than a two-minute *d'var torah* at the beginning of a meeting, a portion of the agenda might be devoted to the study of a relevant Jewish text. Synagogues aspiring to become Congregations of Learners have found ways of incorporating learning into Mitzvah Day, the new members' orientation, and similar congregational gatherings. They have increased the variety of study opportunities for adults and have recruited and trained congregants to become part of the teaching staff in the religious school.[43]

Most dramatically, congregations espousing the ideal of a Congregation of Learners have begun to reenvision and restructure their religious schools, creating some exciting new models. Among them are the Shabbat community, in which parents and children come together to worship and study on either Shabbat morning or Shabbat afternoon; congregation-led experiential education, in which the entire student body focuses on the same topic, taught by members of the congregation who have, themselves, studied the topic in depth; and a home-schooling *havurah* model, in which family *havurot* worship and celebrate together, hold book discussions, engage in tikun olam projects, and undertake independent Torah study.[44] While relatively few congregations have adopted these models in their purest form, many have adapted aspects of these programs to enrich their existing model.

At their best, religious schools are only one element of a full program of congregational education. A congregation aspiring to become a Congregation of Learners should offer all its members a variety of learning experiences throughout their lives, including preschool, family education, adolescent programs, retreats, Israel trips, and adult classes, in addition to religious school. These programs should have as their overriding goal the enculturation of congregants of all ages – enabling congregants to encounter the richness of the Jewish tradition and to develop strong Jewish identities, commitments, and practices. In a saying popularized by Hillary Clinton, "it takes a village to educate a child" – the Jewish equivalent of this is "it takes an entire synagogue to educate a Jew."

5. THE SHORTAGE OF JEWISH EDUCATION PERSONNEL

The new developments described in this chapter are exciting and invigorating and have already begun to yield fruit – a sector of the Jewish community that is better educated, more involved, and more committed to Jewish life. All these new programs, however, face a common challenge, which is the shortage of qualified Jewish educators. This shortage is not new, as it goes back at least sixty to seventy years,[45] but its severity is now more keenly felt, as the Jewish community focuses greater attention on, and demands more of, Jewish education.

To reach their full potential – day schools whose graduates are literate, practicing Jews; religious schools whose students become fully enculturated into Jewish life; preschools that inspire parents as well as children; family programs that change the culture of the congregation; camps and Israel trips that transform their participants – each of these institutions and programs must be led by at least one highly qualified professional and be staffed by well-trained teachers and counselors. The good news is that exciting part-time work and full-time professional opportunities are available and that administrative positions offer relatively high salaries.[46] The bad news is that the shortage of qualified personnel is as great, or perhaps greater, than ever. The following items indicate the depth of this problem:

1. A 1998 study of teachers in Jewish schools in three communities found the following:

   Only 19% of the teachers we surveyed have collegiate or professional training in both Jewish studies and education. Another 47% have formal training in one field or the other but not both, including 35% with backgrounds in education and 12% certified in Jewish subjects. The remaining 34% of teachers in Jewish schools in the three communities lack collegiate or professional degrees in both areas.

   Even more shocking is the finding that 29 percent of supplementary school teachers had no Jewish education after the age of thirteen.[47]

2. The same study found that "more than half of early childhood teachers had no Jewish education beyond the age of 13, and nearly a quarter had received no Jewish education before age 13 either."[48] The Jewish Early Childhood Education Partnership Study found that over 30 percent of teachers are not Jewish.[49] Anyone familiar with the economics of Jewish preschools would not be surprised by these findings; it is universally acknowledged that preschool teachers are appallingly underpaid. Wertheimer writes this:

   A survey conducted by the BJE of New York found in 1998–99 that nearly one third of *full time* early childhood teachers earned less than $20,000 a year and another 43 percent reported earning less than $26,000. 82 percent lacked health benefits and 83 percent received no pension benefits. In Detroit, early-childhood teachers earn around $16,000 per year with no benefits.[50]

3. Barry Chazan and Steven Cohen write that "many Jewish Community Centers still engage a high proportion of non-Jewish staff. Most Jewish staff remains Jewishly ignorant or modestly knowledgeable at best."[51]

4. A high proportion of education directorships in congregational schools in the Reform and Conservative movements are filled by individuals

without professional training, because there is a serious shortage of candidates with the appropriate credentials in education and Judaica.

5. Each year, day schools struggle to find administrators and teachers, often turning to executive search firms (head hunters) who work in the public education sector in order to fill these positions. The most dire needs are at the level of heads of school and teachers to teach the Jewish studies curriculum.

In response to this shortage, a host of new initiatives have sprung up – some aimed at teachers, others at educators. At the local level, a wide range of programs, usually under the auspices of a central agency for Jewish education, have focused on the recognition of excellent teaching, as well as the recruitment and training of new teachers for preschools, day schools, and congregational schools.[52]

The following are just some of the efforts that are more national in scope.

1. New graduate-level training programs for teachers and educational administrators have been established, bringing the total of these institutions to fourteen.[53] Most enroll both full-time and part-time students, though some accept only full-time students; some offer a distance learning component. Overall, enrollment in these programs has increased, but they are far from being filled to capacity.

2. A consortium of philanthropists created DeLeT: Day school Leadership through Teaching, a national fellowship program in which recent college graduates and midlife career changers combine study either at Hebrew Union College–Jewish Institute of Religion, Los Angeles or at Brandeis University with mentored internships in day schools in order to become teachers who see their primary identity as Jewish educators (whether they go on to teach general studies, Jewish studies, or both). Other recent teacher preparation efforts include Hashaa'ar, Jewish Teachers Corps/Eidah, and Maimonides' of Boston's school-based program. All these are designed to prepare teachers to teach Jewish studies in day schools.

3. The Day School Leadership Training Institute enrolls current day school administrators to prepare them for top leadership positions through summer courses at the Jewish Theological Seminary and other institutes and through year-round mentoring.

4. The Mandel Associated Foundations created the Teacher Educator Institute to prepare education directors and staff members of central agencies to provide more intensive and continuous staff development at school sites.[54]

5. The Covenant Foundation created the Covenant Awards to honor excellence in both teaching and educational leadership.

6. Jewish Education Services of North America (JESNA) and the Covenant Foundation established the Jewish Educator Recruitment/Retention Initiative, which aims to conduct research on existing practices, publicize "best practices" at the local level, and devise new recruitment strategies.

7. A number of important programs were created in Israel, including the Pardes/Hebrew University program for the training of day school teachers, the Melton Senior Educators Program,[55] and the Jerusalem Fellows.[56]

6. THE RISING COST OF JEWISH EDUCATION

All the new initiatives described in this chapter add considerable cost to an already expensive educational system. Since Jewish educational institutions operate independently without any central coordination, it is difficult to know with any precision the total annual budget for Jewish education. A 2001 study estimated the annual cost of supplementary schools at $750 million (an average of $1,500 per student), of day schools at $2 billion ($10,000 per student), and of camps at $200 million ($4,000 per camper).[57]

As a voluntary, private endeavor, Jewish education does not receive public funding of any kind and is financed by a combination of tuition and charitable contributions. The proportion of the institution's budget that is covered by tuition, compared with that covered by donations, varies. In Conservative and Reform day schools, for example, tuition covers between 88 and 89 percent of the operating budget; in Community day schools that figure is only 68 percent. Orthodox schools, which constitute the majority of day schools, vary greatly, with anywhere between one-third and two-thirds of the budget being covered by tuition. It is more difficult to arrive at comparable calculations for congregational schools for several reasons: first, the number of hours that children attend these schools varies from two to six hours a week; second, a percentage of the school's staff serves in other capacities at the same synagogue; and third, many congregations charge little or no tuition above membership dues.

Periodically, articles in the Jewish press decry the "high cost of being Jewish." A recent study by the AJC found that a family with two children that belonged to a synagogue and a JCC; made a small gift to the federation (of $200); and sent its children to day school, day camp for two weeks, and residential camp for two weeks would be spending a total of $25,000–$35,000 a year on these expenses alone.[58] Demographic studies indicate that the median income of American Jewish families with children is $80,000 a year.[59] Thus, over half of American Jewish families cannot afford to give their children a "complete" Jewish education without financial assistance. Even families whose income is well over the median must still consider whether they want such a large percentage of their disposable income devoted to Jewish education. The AJC report commented:

> Attention must be paid to the significant minority for whom cost is not a barrier but the desirability of the product has to be "sold." Naturally, the desires of most middle-class and upper-middle-class Jews are not focused only on Jewish matters. Those who formulate the cost of Jewish living cannot ignore the other expenses families face, including the need to save for college.[60]

Over and above what they receive in tuition, Jewish educational institutions may receive subsidies from federations or other communal agencies. Federations have tended to direct their funding to day schools, but the amounts given to each school vary widely. The federations of Baltimore, Detroit, and Cleveland, for example, all give between $25 and 30 million to day schools. In Baltimore (which has 5,400 students enrolled in day schools), the subsidy comes to only $280 per child. In Detroit (with 2,100 students), the subsidy is $810 per child. In Cleveland (with only 1,400 students), the subsidy is $1,362 per child.[61] In addition, foundations in western Massachusetts, Seattle, and Tulsa have made grants to day schools for the purpose of capping their tuition.

As the interest in Jewish education has intensified, the role of philanthropists and foundations has increased. The AVI CHAI Foundation, for example, has funded day school education in a variety of ways – from an experimental program that gave vouchers for four years of day school tuition to students in Atlanta and Cleveland; to family education programs in day schools; to Jewish Day Schools for the 21st Century, a project that helped liberal day schools reenvision and strengthen the Jewish component of the education they offer.[62] A national consortium of donors, the Partnership for Excellence in Jewish Education, makes substantial funds available for the founding of new day schools. In addition, nearly every day school is supported by large contributions from a handful of wealthy donors and smaller contributions from parents and members of the community.

We have already mentioned the creation of Birthright Israel, which provides free Israel trips to young adults. In comparison with day schools and Israel trips, educational institutions such as preschools, camps, JCCs, and supplementary schools have received much less attention and much less outside funding. Nonetheless, financial support from communal agencies, foundations, and philanthropists has gone toward teacher training, curriculum development, and other innovative efforts in these settings. The JCC Association, for example, has developed a two-year course of study (including a subsidized trip to Israel) for preschool teachers in eighteen JCCs. A group of national and local foundations – including the Mandel Associated Foundations, the Nathan Cummings Foundation, the Koret Foundation, the Commission on Jewish Identity and Renewal of the UJA – Federation of Greater New York, and the Covenant Foundation – has funded the decade-old Experiment in Congregational Education, which helps synagogues become Congregations of Learners.[63]

7. IS THE GLASS HALF EMPTY OR HALF FULL?

As of the winter of 2005, the future of Jewish education looks much more promising than it did a decade ago. Clearly, however, significant challenges remain – high expenses, a shortage of personnel, the need for continual reevaluation and revitalization, and the need to convince its potential clientele of its importance. While acutely aware of the work that lies ahead, we are encouraged and inspired by the accomplishments of the past decade, by the dedication of so many lay leaders, and by the wisdom and talents of so many professionals. Jewish education is more than the key to Jewish survival; it is the bridge to a robust Jewish future.

Notes
1. We thank Beth Nichols and Dena Kahn for their research assistance and John Merriman for his editorial assistance.
2. B. A. Abrams, "The Discipline in Our Sabbath Schools," reprinted in *Jewish Education in the United States: A Documentary History*, ed. Lloyd. P. Gartner (New York: Teachers College Press, 1969), 100.
3. Mordecai M. Kaplan and Bernard Cronson, "A Survey of Jewish Education in New York City," reprinted in *Jewish Education in the United States: A Documentary History*, ed. Lloyd. P. Gartner (New York: Teachers College Press, 1969), 126.
4. Barry Chazan, *The State of Jewish Education* (New York: Jewish Education Service of North America, 1988), 14.
5. Sylvia Barack Fishman and Alice Goldstein, *When They Are Grown They Will not Depart: Jewish Education and the Jewish Behavior of American Adults* (Waltham: Cohen Center for Modern Jewish Studies at Brandeis University and the Jewish Education Service of North America, 1993), 7.
6. Jack Wertheimer, "Jewish Education in the United States: Recent Trends and Issues," *American Jewish Year Book* 99 (1999), 43.
7. The Commission on Jewish Education in North America, *A Time To Act* (Lanham: University Press of America, 1991), 15.
8. Ibid., 33.
9. Jack Wertheimer, "Jewish Education in the United States," *Year Book*, 74.
10. The dropout rate increases from the eighth to the tenth grade, and it varies tremendously from congregation to congregation and city to city.

11. Charles Kadushin et al., *Being a Jewish Teenager in America: Trying to Make It* (Waltham: Cohen Center for Modern Jewish Studies at Brandeis University, 2000), 74.

12. Steven M. Cohen and Aryeh Davidson, *Adult Jewish Learning in America: Current Patterns and Prospects for Growth* (n.p.: The Florence G. Heller/JCC Association and the Jewish Theological Seminary, 2001), 5.

13. Bethamie Horowitz, *1991 New York Jewish Population Study* (New York: United Jewish Appeal–Federation of Jewish Philanthropies of New York, 1993).

14. Jack Wertheimer, "Jewish Education in the United States," *Year Book*, 76.

15. Barry Chazan and Steven M. Cohen, *Assessing the Jewish Educational Effectiveness of Jewish Community Centers – The 1994 Survey* (New York: JCC Association, 1994).

16. Steven M. Cohen and Aryeh Davidson, *Adult Jewish Learning in America: Current Patterns and Prospects for Growth* (n.p.: The Florence G. Heller/JCC Association and the Jewish Theological Seminary, 2001), 8.

17. Barry Chazan, *What We Know About the Israel Experience* (n.p.: Israel Experience, n.d.), 2.

18. Jack Wertheimer, "Jewish Education in the United States," *Year Book*, 90.

19. Amy L. Sales and Leonard Saxe, *Limud by the Lake: Fulfilling the Educational Potential of Jewish Summer Camps* (New York: The AVI CHAI Foundation and the Cohen Center for Modern Jewish Studies at Brandeis University, 2002), 5.

20. Barry Chazan, *What We Know About the Israel Experience* (n.p.: Israel Experience, n.d.), 5.

21. As later research uncovered, this assumption was not altogether warranted. Many first-generation immigrants abandoned their Jewish practices shortly after arriving in the United States. Though their children were raised in Jewish neighborhoods, they were largely ignorant of Jewish customs and rituals.

22. Michael Zeldin, "The Promise of Historical Inquiry: Nineteenth Century Jewish Day Schools and Twentieth Century Policy," *Religious Education* 83, 3 (1988), 438–52.

23. Isaac M. Wise, "Jewish Education in Cincinnati," reprinted in *Jewish Education in the United States: A Documentary History*, ed. Lloyd P. Gartner (New York: Teachers College Press, 1969), 86.

24. Alvin Schiff, *The Jewish Day School in America* (New York: Jewish Education Press, 1966), 30.

25. Ibid., 49.

26. Michael Zeldin, *The Status of a Quiet Revolution* (New York: Union of American Hebrew Congregations Press, 1985).

27. Marvin Schick, *A Census of Jewish Day Schools in the United States* (New York: The AVI CHAI Foundation, 2000).

28. Ibid., 12.

29. Sylvia Barack Fishman and Alice Goldstein, *When They Are Grown They Will not Depart: Jewish Education and the Jewish Behavior of American Adults* (Waltham: Cohen Center for Modern Jewish Studies at Brandeis University and the Jewish Education Service of North America, 1993).

30. Helene Schlafman, private communication (Summer 1990).

31. Jonathan D. Sarna, "American Jewish Education in Historical Perspective," *Journal of Jewish Education* 64, 1–2 (1998), 10.

32. See Bennet Solomon, "A Critical Review of the Term 'Integration' in the Literature on the Jewish Day School in America," *Jewish Education* 46, 4 (1978), 4–7; Mitchel Malkus, "Portraits of Curriculum Integration in Jewish Day Schools" (Ph.D. diss., Jewish Theological Seminary, 2001); Michael Zeldin, "Integration and Interaction," in *The Jewish Educational Leader's Handbook*, ed. Robert E. Tornberg (Denver: A.R.E. Publishing, 1998), 579–90.

33. Sylvia Barack Fishman, *Negotiating Both Sides of the Hyphen: Coalescence, Compartmentalization, and American Jewish Values* (Cincinnati: Judaic Studies Program, University of Cincinnati, 1996).

34. David Ellenson, "An Ideology for the Liberal Jewish Day School: A Philosophical-Sociological Inquiry" (Malibu: HUC-PARDeS Symposium on Rethinking Integration, 1994); Michael Zeldin, "Integration and Interaction," in *The Jewish Educational Leader's Handbook*, ed. Robert E. Tornberg (Denver: A.R.E. Publishing, 1998), 579–90.

35. David Ellenson, "An Ideology for the Liberal Jewish Day School: A Philosophical-Sociological Inquiry" (Malibu: HUC-PARDeS Symposium on Rethinking Integration, 1994).

36. Isa Aron and Adrianne Bank, "The Shortage of Supplementary School Teachers: Has the Time for Concerted Action Finally Arrived?" *Journal of Jewish Communal Service* 63 (1987), 264–71.

37. David Schoem, *Ethnic Survival in America: An Ethnography of a Jewish Afternoon School* (Atlanta: Scholars Press, 1989); Samuel Heilman, "Inside the Jewish School," in *What We Know About Jewish Education*, ed. Stuart Kelman (Los Angeles: Torah Aura Productions, 1992), 303–30.

38. Board of Jewish Education of Greater New York, *Jewish Supplementary Schooling: An Educational System in Need of Change* (New York: Board of Jewish Education, 1988).

39. Sylvia Barack Fishman, *Learning About Learning: Insights on Contemporary Jewish Education from Jewish Population Studies* (Waltham: The Cohen Center for Modern Jewish Studies, 1987).

40. American Jewish Committee, preface to *Does Jewish Schooling Matter?* Geoffrey Bock (New York: American Jewish Committee, 1977), i.

41. Board of Jewish Education of Greater New York, *Jewish Supplementary Schooling: An Educational System in Need of Change* (New York: Board of Jewish Education, 1988), 119.

42. *A Congregation of Learners: Transforming the Congregation into a Learning Community*, ed. Isa Aron, Sara S. Lee, and Seymour Rossel (New York: Union of American Hebrew Congregations Press, 1995).

43. For additional examples, see Isa Aron, *Becoming a Congregation of Learners: Learning as a Key to Revitalizing Congregational Life* (Woodstock: Jewish Lights Publishing, 2000), chapter 3.

44. Isa Aron and Robert Weinberg, "Rethinking and Redesigning the Religious School," *Sh'ma* 32 (March 2002).

45. Susan Shevitz, "Communal Responses to the Teacher Shortage in the North American Supplementary School," in *Studies in Jewish Education*, ed. Janel Aviad (Jerusalem: Magnes Press, 1988), vol. 3, pp. 25–61.

46. Some teachers' salaries have risen, in response to the shortage, while others remain low. Unfortunately, the salaries of preschool teachers continue to be extremely low, as will be discussed.

47. Adam Gamoran et al., *The Teachers Report: A Portrait of Teachers in Jewish Schools* (New York: Council for Initiatives in Jewish Education, 1998), 6–7.

48. "Jewish Education in the United States: Recent Trends and Issues," *American Jewish Yearbook* 99 (1999), 75.

49. Ilene C. Vogelstein and David Kaplan, *Untapped Potential: The Status of Jewish Early Childhood Education in America* (Baltimore: Jewish Early Childhood Education Partnership, 15, 2002). Available from http://www.caje.org/earlychildhood/UntappedPotential.pdf., p. 7.

50. Jack Wertheimer, *Talking Dollars and Sense About Jewish Education* (New York: American Jewish Committee, 2001), 15.

51. Barry Chazan and Steven M. Cohen, *Assessing the Jewish Educational Effectiveness of Jewish Community Centers – The 1994 Survey* (New York: JCC Association, 1994), 16.

52. Coalition for the Advancement of Jewish Education, *Jewish Education News* (Summer 2001).

53. Together, these fourteen schools have formed the Association for Higher Learning in Jewish Education.

54. Research in public education indicates that this model of professional development for teachers is the most effective.

55. This program is under the auspices of the Melton Centre for Jewish Education at the Hebrew University.

56. This program is under the auspices of the Mandel Institute in Jerusalem.

57. Jack Wertheimer, *Talking Dollars and Sense About Jewish Education* (New York: American Jewish Committee, 2001), 3–5.

58. Gerald Bubis, *The Costs of Jewish Living* (New York: American Jewish Committee, 2001), 16.

59. Ibid., 2.

60. Ibid., 26.

61. Ibid., 15.

62. Jewish Day Schools for the 21st Century (JDS-21) is a project of the Rhea Hirsch School of Education, Hebrew Union College–Jewish Institute of Religion, Los Angeles.

63. The Experiment in Congregational Education (ECE) is a project of the Rhea Hirsch School of Education, Hebrew Union College–Jewish Institute of Religion, Los Angeles. More information on this is available at www.eceonline.org.

9 The place of Judaism in American Jewish identity

DEBRA RENEE KAUFMAN

- More Jews than most other Americans respond "None," when asked "What is your religion, if any?"
- More Jews than members of most other American religious groups think of themselves as "secular" rather than as "religious."
- Fewer Jews than members of most other American religious groups belong to a temple, synagogue or any other religious institution.
- Fewer Jews than members of most other American religious groups agree with the essential proposition of religious belief that "God exists."

These items were taken from one of the most recent studies on religious identity in the United States among contemporary Jews.[1] Compared with other Americans, it appears that American Jews "are not a very religious lot."[2] The survey further reveals the following:

> Vast numbers of Americans who regard themselves as Jewish or who are of Jewish parentage and upbringing simply have no faith in the conventional religious sense of that term. They adhere to an identity that is rooted in an ancient faith. But their claim to that identity implies little or no commitment to its religious roots.[3]

The task of this chapter is to move beyond the survey data themselves to explore how social scientists come to their interpretative findings of the data. While doing so, we will discover that statements about religiosity and religion in the lives of contemporary Jews are not as straightforward as they might first appear.

Let us begin by exploring the dominant models and measures of religious identity (Judaism) and then look to a selective group of contemporary studies that challenge these models and measures. Most social science investigations, especially large survey studies, are designed to measure religiosity as if it existed in some objective and measurable reality within individuals.[4] In such studies, behavior, beliefs, and patterns of belonging (thought to measure religiosity) are placed on a continuum of more or less, or they are measured as better or worse in comparison with other generations or with other contemporary Jews. "Doing Jewish" in such models is equated with being Jewish.[5] Critics are suggesting that studies framed to gauge more or less and better or worse, cannot, for the most part, capture the many complex, sometimes contradictory, if not ambivalent, expressions of religious identity among American Jews today. Moreover, critics are challenging the use of more or less distance from an "authentic" and "traditional" Judaism as a valid and reliable measure of religiosity. Finally, in most studies it is difficult to distinguish between patterns of ethnicity and religiosity.

Survey studies, such as the National Population Studies (1990 and 2000), are particularly vulnerable to such criticisms. While surveys offer reliable evidence about the patterns of Jewish experience in contemporary America, they lack the rich ethnographic and qualitative data needed to interpret the meaning of those patterns for respondents and, for the purposes of this chapter, to our understanding of the place of Judaism among contemporary Jews. Qualitative studies help us reflect on the subjective meanings respondents give to such terms as *religiosity* and *ethnicity*. Being a "member of the tribe" today may include new religious foci and meanings, especially from the perspective of those once not visible or represented in the traditional "core" or "canon," but who were, nonetheless, a part of it and who are today finding their voices.

The data, as reported by some of the leading researchers of the past decade, suggest that religion plays an important part in contemporary Jewish identity, albeit, perhaps, to a less extent than among other religious groups.[6] However, data do not speak for themselves. Different theoretical and methodological approaches change the meaning and the message of research findings. The concept of identity, as it is generally conceptualized in large-scale surveys, treats categories of difference (e.g., greater or lesser, weaker or stronger, and more intense or less intense) as if they "corresponded to something concrete and real in people themselves."[7] Mayer and Horowitz[8] warn that behavioral measures may or may not correspond to the psychological measures of a personal sense of Judaism (religiosity) or Jewishness (ethnicity).

The intended effect of this selective review is to illustrate that the place of religiosity, or, as Feingold[9] puts it, those things Judaic, within contemporary American Jewish identity cannot be answered by simply reading the data. To address the nature and expression of religiosity among contemporary American Jews, we must ask whose experiences, whose lives, whose "Judaism" serve as the yardstick from which we measure authenticity, decline, intensity, or strength of contemporary religious Jewish identity.

ETHNICITY OR RELIGIOSITY: WHAT ARE WE MEASURING?

Reflecting on the idea of faith and belief as important measures of religiosity in Judaism, Michael Meyer compares Reform and Orthodox Jews:

> For Orthodox Jews . . . the principles of faith as set forth by Maimonides and based entirely on God's revealed will, require no modification. In their view, Judaism is self-contained and hence independent of historical vicissitudes. . . . Reform Jews are in a different position because we recognize historical change as *religiously* important. In contrast to the Orthodox, we do not say that Judaism stands above history. . . . It therefore becomes our task to determine the realm of the holy within the totality of human experience and within that realm to indicate what sets Judaism, *as we understand it*, apart from other faiths and ideologies, and especially, *from other forms of Judaism* [italics mine added].[10]

Key to Meyer's argument is that religiosity is understood differently among different denominational sectors of Judaism. As Meyer notes, in contrast to Orthodoxy, historical change is recognized as "religiously important" among Reform Jews. Meyer is responding to the implicit assumption that denominational differences represent only responses to modernity rather than platforms for belief and theology. In an insightful coverage of the theological responses to the American experience, Susannah Heschel[11] reminds us that the challenges presented by assimilation and acculturation do not simply result in "accommodation," but in theological reinvigoration and re-creation as well.

In much identity research, practices (behavior and belonging) and beliefs are given precedence over other indicators when a person's religiosity is measured. However, measuring a person's religiosity by his or her practices, without controlling for the person's denominational affiliation, can be misleading. For instance, while synagogue attendance, holiday observance (and the rites and rituals associated with each), *kashrut* (dietary laws), and the observance of the Sabbath are certainly observable measures of at least one expression of Jewish religiosity, different denominational communities attribute different meanings and priorities to such practices. Moreover, affiliation and frequency of synagogue attendance, when used as measures of religiosity, may obfuscate the ethnic (social, communal and even political) functions such practices may also serve, thereby confounding our measures of religiosity and ethnicity.

The twin concepts of symbolic ethnicity and symbolic religiosity, often used to understand the effects of assimilation and acculturation on contemporary Jewish identity, bring into focus the difficulty we may have in differentiating between expressions of ethnic and religious identity.[12] Gans defines symbolic ethnicity as "a love for and pride in a tradition that can be felt without having to be incorporated in everyday behavior."[13] He reminds us that Jewish ethnicity is different from other groups in that Jews not only "share elements of a common past or present non-American culture," but that the "sacred and secular elements of the culture are strongly intertwined."[14] Symbolic religiosity, for Gans, is the "consumption of religious symbols, apart from regular participation in a religious culture and in religious affiliations – other than for purely secular purposes."[15] For many scholars, symbolic ethnicity and religiosity represent an accommodation to existing conditions, or, put another way, a bumpy rather than a straight-line theory of assimilation into the larger culture. From the third generation on, symbolic ethnicity and religiosity represent what some have referred to as "stand-ins" for the substantive process and practices associated with ethnicity or religion. Given this description, there is an implicit assumption that stand-ins are weaker expressions of "authentic" ethnicity or religiosity.

The following evaluation about the celebration of Chanukah provides an insight into the ways in which symbolic religiosity may appear as a less authentic or a weaker expression of religiosity. Gans writes that Chanukah represents symbolic religiosity "if it is introduced into the home by otherwise non-observant parents to strengthen their children's interest in a Jewish identity once a year; not if it is celebrated *regularly as one among many religious holidays of the year*" [italics added].[16] Unless he means quite literally by *nonobservant* that the only Jewish holiday celebrated is Chanukah and only for one motivation, the children, then this example presents several problems. According to Gans' formulation, the greater the number of observances over the year, the less symbolic or more authentic the celebration of any one holiday. However, why should we automatically assume that the motives for observing the holidays, including the celebration of Chanukah, are less symbolic (or, put another way, more authentic) among those who observe many or most of the other holidays? Might there not be mixed motives for those who celebrate religious holidays, all of the time, some of the time, or inconsistently? Whether intentional or not, symbolic religiosity ultimately represents a construct that measures distance and difference from those who are more observant or traditional in their practices. Symbolic religiosity is then best reflected in the behavior of those who fall "at the *lower* end of the practice spectrum" or by those who are "minimal religious participants."[17] We then run the risk of measuring religious identity by distance from Orthodox practices and beliefs rather than as a measure of religiosity per se. Symbolic religiosity or ethnicity are no more value free or merely descriptive measures than are the terms *lower* and *minimal.* If we neglect to measure (as most large surveys by design often must) respondents' subjective understandings of identity, we cannot readily distinguish between that which is symbolic or not symbolic, or, for that matter, between religiosity and ethnicity.

A. Jerry Winter cautions that "there is a need to determine the extent to which religious observances among contemporary American Jews are cere-monies linking them to their community rather than rituals linking them to God."[18] For Winter, a link to God is a symbol of religiosity, while a link to the community is a symbol of ethnicity or civil religion. However, without respondents' self-understandings present in the data, such distinctions are difficult to make. Like Gans, Winter acknowledges the need for different methodological approaches to the study of symbolic ethnicity and religiosity (such as fieldwork, ethnographic studies, and intensive interviews) to distin-guish between the two. Future research, writes Winter, will have to "tease out the religious aspects of Jewish ethnicity as well as the ethnic aspects of Jewish religiosity in order to understand better the ethnoreligion which this study finds importantly related to integration into the Jewish community in America."[19] Sharot argues that our point of reference determines how we understand religiosity. He contends that, as ethnicity becomes more a mat-ter of feelings and identity, religious institutions assume importance for the "salience and continuation of those feelings and identity."[20] Arguing that "the subjective feelings of ethnicity appear to determine the objective existence of religious institutions and behavior," Sharot concludes that "ethnicity and religion are in a relationship of symbiosis or complementarity." He reasons that sociologists have tended to analyze the religiosity of American Jews as an "epiphenomenon of ethnicity."[21] Kunkelman coined the term *religion of ethnicity* to express this peculiar phenomenon.[22]

WHAT DOES IT MEAN TO BE JEWISH IN AMERICA?

Sharot summarizes the situation for most American Jews today: "Where an all-encompassing religion has lost its strength, and where non-religious ethnic cultural sources are no longer available, instead of rejecting reli-gious symbols, secularized Jews tend to reinterpret them, extracting their supernaturalist meanings and making them suitable for familial and ethnic celebrations."[23] The majority, he claims, continue to mix religious and ethnic components in their identities. On the face of it, the data seem to support Sharot's contentions. In 1990, the National Jewish Population Survey asked this question: What does it mean to be Jewish in America? In response, 70 percent of the sample said it was a cultural group, 57 percent said it was an ethnic group, and 49 percent said it was a purely religious group.[24] However, what American Jews mean by these labels is not evident from the data. Sharot writes the following:

> That there is a religious element in the identity of most of the American Jews who prefer the labels cultural, national, or ethnic to purely religious can hardly be doubted: four-fifths identify with one of the Jewish religious denominations, and many of the remainder who termed themselves "just Jewish" were no doubt stating the absence of a religious preference within the orbit of Judaism rather than a Jewish identity without a religious element.[25]

Similarly, while we may agree with Heilman that most American Jews do not associate their identity exclusively with religion, almost half agree that Jews in America are a purely religious group.[26]

Responses to large-scale studies, such as the 1990 or 2000 National Population Surveys, focus largely on the *things* Jews do as indicators of Jewish identity. Behaving in recognizably Jewish ways has been a cornerstone of Jewish identity research.[27] However, the "Jewish way" and "recognizably Jewish" are a by-product of ongoing processes and perceptions. New contexts for old content, and new content in old contexts, shake our understanding of that which is recognizably Jewish or Judaic. For instance, a young man in Kaufman's[28] study of post-Holocaust Jewish identity among twenty- to thirty-year-old adults reveals the following when he recounts his typical Shabbat experience. After engaging in many of the traditional Friday night rituals, he and his other Jewish friends usually end the evening by singing "Amazing Grace." For this respondent, the Jewish Sabbath includes a Protestant hymn, written by a slaveholder in retribution for his part in slavery. "When I hear Amazing Grace," says this young man, "I think Shabbos!"

Whose life, whose rituals, and whose experiences legitimately make up the core of Jewish tradition and knowledge? For instance, could the trend toward privatism, reported by key identity researchers,[29] represent a movement, by both men and women, away from the public, male sphere that has, until the past few decades, represented so-called authentic Judaism? Could the breakdown of grand identity narratives and the focus on personal choice in a multicultural America account for much of the revisioning and reimagining of what constitutes tradition and religiosity among contemporary Jews?

THE JEW WITHIN, OUTLOOK, JOURNEYS, AND CONNECTIONS: RESPONSES TO THE IDENTITY ISSUES

As one of the most prolific and insightful writers on contemporary Jewish identity, Steven M. Cohen has been a contributor to the identity literature and a critic of it. In an unpublished paper, Cohen gives credence to the thinking that contemporary American Jews see themselves, and are seen, in primarily religious terms. He claims that in the United States *"it is not at all surprising that Jews have largely refrained from defining themselves outwardly as ethnic, even as they have established and supported institutions that are seemingly both ethnic or religious in character* [italics mine].[30] As with earlier findings, Cohen's review of the identity literature leads him to suggest that, at the same time there appears to be a "slow retreat" in ethnicity, "indicators of specifically religious involvement seem to be holding their own, and in some cases rising."[31]

Cohen incorporates, into his nationwide study of attitudes and behavior among American Jews, qualitative data gathered earlier and reported in his coauthored book, *The Jew Within*. In attempting to distinguish ethnicity from religiosity, he measures religiosity as "faith in God, religious commitment, and the practice of rituals and ceremonies sanctified by the religious tradition."[32] Ethnicity is measured by "attachment and commitment to various aspects of the Jewish collective from the most intimate and concrete to the most remote and abstract: marriage and family, friends, local institutions, Israel, and Jewish peoplehood."[33] Almost immediately, however, Cohen's findings begin to trouble his categories of religiosity and ethnicity:

> Thus while a cursory glance at some of the findings may suggest a positive attachment to the religious conception of Judaism, several factors indicate a much weaker – or perhaps more narrowly based – religious commitment. For example, the survey points to widespread indifference to several elements of Jewish religious life that are more "traditional." These include the Sabbath, Jewish law, keeping a kosher home, and the study of religious texts. When compared with other items (for example, the High Holidays, Passover, giving one's children a Jewish education), these more traditional items elicit relatively little enthusiasm.[34]

While Cohen adjusts his language from *weaker* to *narrower*, we do not obtain a corresponding clarification of just what such a distinction might mean for respondents. *Weaker*, for Cohen, clearly indicates a seeming indifference to tradition. *Narrower*, however, may indicate a different locus for religious expression more appropriate, perhaps, to the respondent's specific life-cycle stage or denominational preference. Cohen sees another example of weak religious commitment in the difference he notes between his respondents' attitudes toward synagogue attendance and their actual behavior. He reports "that most of those who look forward to going to religious services, as well as most of those who find them interesting, fail to attend them even once a month. This apparent contradiction calls into question the veracity of the respondents' claims about the importance of religious aspects of being Jewish."[35] Perhaps, however, veracity is less the issue than perspective. Respondents may look forward to and enjoy services when they do attend, even if they do so infrequently or inconsistently. Moreover, the frequency of attendance at formal religious services does not reveal what they may read, recite, and relish outside of the synagogue or other informal practices that function to reinforce the religious component of their Jewish identities.

In teasing out the relationship between ethnic and religious commitment, Cohen reports that only one-fourth of respondents indicate that religion was very important in their lives, while one-half claimed that being Jewish was very important. Alluding to his earlier work, Cohen reflects on religious commitment: "Indeed, the interviews Arnold Eisen and I conducted further support the notion that American Jews are not a particularly religious lot, at least in the way that 'religious' is normally understood."[36] Here again we have an issue of perspective. If we measure religiosity as it is "normally understood," then Cohen's analysis stands. However, if our intent is to explore the dimensions of religiosity as they exist and as they are expressed by respondents for whom normal may or may not be defined in the same way, we might wish to ask different questions. Religiosity as normally understood is an empirical question, not an empirical fact. For instance, what is a woman's "normal experience" within religious Judaism? Is it in appropriating the male experience with ritual and rites as her own, or is it in the search for, or making of, a "usable" tradition of her own?[37]

While most respondents in Cohen and Eisen's study did report a belief in God, the authors conclude that the only thing Jewish about God in the interviews they conducted was the absence of Jesus. Cohen concludes that the American Jews he and Eisen interviewed have a faith in a "universal God, both very distant from traditional Jewish conceptions and very much in keeping with images shared by other Americans."[38] In response to Cohen and Eisen's conclusion that there is nothing particularly Jewish about the God the interviewees describe, Deborah Dash Moore asks this: "Is the only Jewish God a supernatural revealer of the Torah or a Commander of mitzvot? . . . The naturalistic God preferred by many American Jews is . . . very Jewish in the American context."[39] Finally, while Cohen may be in doubt about the kind of religiosity his respondents proffer, his cross-sectional studies reveal that "younger Jews maintain their elders' levels of religious commitment and practice," thus leading him to conclude that Jewish religiosity is not in decline "either in prospect or in retrospect."[40]

Cohen and Eisen recognize that, for the moderately affiliated Jews they interviewed, Judaism is a subjective experience. In their analysis of the forty-five solo interviews and two group interviews (fifteen each) they conducted, they write that Judaism "cannot be increased or lessened by observance, in-marriage, communal affiliation, or any other normative behavior."[41] In addition, they write that their respondents "feel no need to express or enact their identity in regular activity. Judaism is rather an 'inner thing,' a point of origin, a feature of experience, an object of reflection."[42] This recognition of an inner thing as a key feature of religious identity among contemporary Jews reflects a new focus for inquiry in the social sciences.

Aware of past limitations, Bethamie Horowitz explores the nature of people's Jewish engagement with a focus on the subjective meaning of such behaviors to respondents. Subcategories within what Horowitz calls a "mixed pattern of Jewish engagement"[43] reveal some interesting twists on the way in which subjective understandings expand identity and our conceptions of religiosity. Horowitz points to a "subjectively engaged" constituency who, she claims, were not discernible in prior identity studies because, despite their "intensely internal, personal mode of expression," they exhibited little "conventional Jewish behavioral expression."[44] Horowitz believes that the strength of their internal connections to Judaism and their pride in being Jewish are among the highest in her sample. The second subgroup within this mixed pattern expresses their identity through strong cultural–communal engagement, rather than in particularly religious ways. The last subset, the "tradition oriented," express their Jewishness in ritual ways, but they are not as well integrated into the Jewish community as the second subgroup. Although Horowitz does not directly address the symbolic ethnicity or religiosity issues in her discussion, the responses of those in the mixed pattern of Jewish engagement reflect the feeling and emotional components so critical to the symbolism arguments. Horowitz stresses that those who have mixed patterns of Jewish engagement are not indifferent to being Jewish, but that they "experience their Judaism as a set of values and historical people-consciousness rather than as a mode of observance."[45] Here perhaps we see the most explicit recognition, through respondents' narratives of the multiple ways in which religiosity can be expressed, of the ways in which ethnicity and religiosity may be mutually constitutive. Moreover, we can see how the meaning of religiosity varies, depending on the models and measures used.

By concluding with narratives taken from a sample of contemporary American Jews between the ages of twenty and thirty years, we can see how expressions of those things Judaic (religious), as well as those things Jewish (ethnic), move in and out of respondents' identity stories. We can see the appropriation and reappropriation of text and history in ways that are both traditional and innovative. The following identity stories mirror claims made by respondents in Cohen and Eisen's sample and those reported by Horowitz. That is, contemporary Jews are often uncomfortable with some of the basic tenets of what were once understood as the "traditional expressions of Judaism." We can hear in the following narratives those things that are particular and universal, individual and collective. Like those in Cohen and Eisen's sample, the respondents in Kaufman's research pick and choose expressions of their religiosity with impunity, seemingly unworried about issues of so-called authenticity. The expression of their Judaism takes place as much in the private sphere as in the public sphere. Traditional measures of tribalism, such as the Holocaust, Israel, and organized Jewry, do not necessarily take center stage in their structured conversations about Jewish identity.

The following narratives about post-Holocaust identity, mostly representative of fourth-generation Jews in America, are taken from a sample of seventy young adults. The data suggest that these young men and women are highly committed to Jewishness, but not necessarily to those things Judaic.[46] If we listen carefully, we can detect many mixed and sometimes contradictory motives in their claims to being Jewish. For them, there is no necessary tie between being Jewish American and a Jew in America, except perhaps through memory. Often their autobiographical searches turn out to be, as Fischer writes in another context, "revelations of traditions."[47] Finally, while the symbols of ethnicity may seemingly be on the decline, and religious expression stable, motivations to hold onto ethnicity and to establish a new arena for its expression appear important to these respondents. Religion and ethnicity move in and out of their narratives in expected and unexpected ways.

"It's very hard to think that you are part of a chosen people and still feel you are part of all people," complains one twenty-seven-year-old female. Another twenty-two-year-old suggests that she intellectually understands what *chosen* means, "a light unto nations," but worries that "actually" it is expressed as a feeling of "superiority." "This is no way to be a light," she concludes.[48] One twenty-seven-year-old male states that the most comfortable part of being Jewish is that he identifies with a "community and a history and a tradition. . . . Notice, I didn't bring up God. . . . Whether God exists, or doesn't . . . gave us the Torah or didn't, or brought us out of Egypt or didn't . . . it doesn't change our history or tradition."[49] Responding to a probe about Jewish identity, a twenty-two-year old male responds with a question:

> What's identity? I mean I feel very Jewish even if I don't practice the religion very much. It's kind of very hard to explain, I mean, about feeling Jewish. I know one thing, we are bound by our history. It [history] sort of affects how we feel about ourselves today, if you know what I mean . . . it's about being an American too. . . . I am both Jewish and American, they can't be separated.[50]

On the issue of belief in God, the following twenty-eight-year-old male says this:

> It is not just a matter of history, a matter of working things out historically, but the idea that we are a people of God, that we are a chosen people, and that we represent God's working in history. We [Jews] represent God working through history. While I don't understand or can I really explain fascism, murder, or oppression, I do know that evil exists and, it too, is a part of the working out of history. We must choose to act on the ideas and ideals that lead away from evil, but it is finally a matter of choice. Man's choice, that too, is a part of God's working in history.

A twenty-five-year-old Orthodox bisexual woman recounts her experiences with Orthodoxy accordingly:

> I think there's something about being a woman and also being bisexual that are not dealt with. . . . That whole thing's being cast as a Jewish issue and as a religious issue, and as a . . . Orthodox issue. It's *not*. It's a feminist issue. It's a misogynist issue. It's an issue of control of women. It happens to be happening with a Jewish community and taking on the trappings of Jewish religious law. . . . But do I think that's authentically Judaism? No, I don't think that Judaism authentically prohibits women from singing . . . or from reading the Torah. . . . It's not my understanding of Judaism nor of a growing body of feminist scholars.[51]

JEWISH IDENTITY, AUTHENTICITY, AND SHIFTING PARADIGMS

Worries that future trends in Jewish identity research will "take lightly" or "abandon the matter of Jewish authenticity" are only reinforced by the postmodern shift in identity studies.[52] Although tensions and conflict over

canon, authority, and authenticity are not new and have always been a part of
so-called Jewish tradition, they are made even more evident and troubling in
a postmodern setting.[53] Cohen warns that "we cannot allow our fascination
with the current turn toward personalism and subjectivity to lead us to
ignore the Jewishly authentic, whatever that may be."[54] Della Pergolla has
less trouble defining what he means by *Jewishly authentic*. He describes it in
the following way:

> Judaism involves complying with relatively rigorous behavioral rules
> coupled with submitting oneself to possible sanctions by a recognized
> authority or by the whole community. Numerous Jewish ritual acts
> require the presence of a quorum of other Jews. Active Jewish
> identification through religion necessarily involves the simultaneous
> presence of a unique complex of values, norms, and behaviors, and by
> belonging to an exclusive community.[55]

However, the notion that the same sets of rituals have the same set of meanings to contemporary Jews dismisses many of the issues raised in this selective review. The data suggest that there has been a turn toward personalism
and the private sphere in expressions of religiosity. Moreover, age, denomi-
ination, and gender color such expressions. The boundaries that mark the
exclusive community have shifted and the expressions of both religiosity
and ethnicity are found in many recombinant ways.

While many postmodernists might agree with Charles Liebman[56] that
perceptions of the past guide current traditional content, Liebman does not
elaborate on the power issues that dictate whose understandings, teachings,
and perceptions guide that reappropriation. Many scholars and researchers
have begun to challenge assumptions about who and what represents Jewish
tradition. New voices and new traditions are in the making. For instance,
Sylvia Fishman[57] has devoted a whole book to the reclamation of women's
rituals within Jewish orthodoxy. Judith Plaskow, one of the most important
of contemporary feminist thinkers, advocates many faith communities, each
with its own normative stance on what tradition means for its constituents.[58]
Jack Wertheimer brings together a series of essays addressing the ways in
which contemporary Jews appropriate aspects of Jewish tradition for "radically new purposes."[59] The struggles contemporary Jews have with appropriating traditional sources or rituals to contemporary needs or contexts are
often fraught with difficulties. For instance, new rituals and programs for
feminist and not-so-feminist women, trying to reclaim a "tradition" in a religion that is markedly male in almost every aspect, poses particular challenges.
We need only to recollect Cynthia Ozick's[60] classic observation that it is only
in the synagogue that she does not feel that she is a Jew, to make this point.

CONCLUSION

Not unlike the population at large, the data suggest that religion is key in American Jewish identity, although Jews may not be very *religious* in the conventional sense of that word or identify with religion as much as others in the population. We have seen throughout this chapter that religious identification is fraught with conceptual and methodological questions. New questions have entered our research: "*How* are American Jews Jewish? In what ways, if any, do they connect to Jewishness and Judaism?"[61] Bethamie Horowitz writes the following:

> American Jewry is more diverse and dispersed than before, and the Jewish group in America today is characterized by a degree of integration and social acceptance that contrasts sharply to the situation 50 years ago or to Europe in the 18th century. In this new environment no one is either forced to be Jewish or to escape from being Jewish. . . . Jewish continuity of the group as a whole has come to depend on the individual's commitments and decision-making. For this reason, in addition to looking at Jewish practices and involvements in Jewish life, it is essential to examine the subjective, inner experience of being Jewish.[62]

The data presented sensitize us to patterns of engagement that do not fit comfortably within any one of the so-called two identity packages (ethnicity and religiosity) that currently dominate inquiry into contemporary Jewish identity. Horowitz urges us to explore different journeys toward Jewish identity that fit American patterns of engagement across the life course and across time. Therefore, an understanding of contemporary Jewish identity demands more than adding qualitative to quantitative data, or of adding "other" voices to the responses, or of even adding subjective feelings to the findings, although all are ways of exploring identity and ultimately religious identity. If the data are collected in response to categories already understood to represent "authentic" Judaism or a "known" path,[62] it makes no difference if the method used was quantitative or qualitative. We run the risk of repeating what we already know and of missing new categories and new spaces and modes of religious expression. If we let go of fixed theoretical constructs and definitions of *authentic* and *traditional*, we might see how recent identity narratives provide new dimensions to the ever changing boundaries of "normal" religious commitment and identity among contemporary American Jews. The identity narratives and the qualitative data of the past decade qualify quantitative findings. They clarify the ways in which religion is relevant to contemporary American Jews and the manifold, if not ambivalent, ways it is expressed. In conclusion, the data, from this selected review, indicate that religion plays an important role in the identity narratives of many American Jews. Expressions of religiosity among American Jews are an interesting mix of the old and the new, if not the unexpected, in the making of what is yet to be.

Notes

1. E. Mayer and B. A. Kosmin, *American Jewish Identity Survey 2001: AJIS Report: An Exploration in the Demography and Outlook of a People* (New York: The Graduate Center of The City University of New York, February 2002), 9.
2. S. M. Cohen, "Religiosity and Ethnicity: Jewish Identity Trends in the United States" (unpublished paper, 2002), 38; see n. 30 for related information.
3. E. Mayer and B. A. Kosmin, *American Jewish Identity Survey 2001*, 8.
4. E. Mayer, "Secularism Among America's Jews" (paper delivered to the Association for Jewish Studies, Washington, DC, 2001).
5. B. Horowitz, "Reframing the Study of Contemporary American Jewish Identity" (paper delivered at the conference convened by the North American Jewish Data Bank, October 1999); J. A. Winter, "The Transformation of Community Integration Among American Jewry: Religion or Ethno-Religion," *Review of Religious Research* 33, 4 (1992), 360, 349–63.
6. S. C. Heilman, *Portrait of American Jews: The Last Half of the Twentieth Century* (Seattle: University of Washington Press, 1995); S. M. Cohen, "Religiosity and Ethnicity: Jewish Identity Trends in the United States" (unpublished paper, 2002); E. Mayer, "Secularism Among America's Jews" (paper) delivered to the Association for Jewish Studies, Washington, DC, 2001); E. M. and B. A. Kosmin, *American Jewish Identity Survey 2001: AJIS Report: An Exploration in the Demography and Outlook of a People* (New York: The Graduate Center of The City University of New York, February 2002).
7. E. Mayer, "Secularism Among America's Jews," 3.
8. B. Horowitz, "Reframing the Study of Contemporary American Jewish Identity" (paper delivered at the conference convened by the North American Jewish Data Bank, October 1999); E. Mayer, "Secularism Among America's Jews" (paper delivered to the Association for Jewish Studies, Washington, DC, 2001.
9. H. Feingold, "The American Component of American Jewish Identity," in *Jewish Identity in America*, ed. D. M. Gordis and Y. Ben Horin (Los Angeles: Susan and David Wilstein Institute of Jewish Policy Studies, University of Judaism, 1991), 69–81.
10. M. A. Meyer, "Our Collective Identity as Reform Jews," in *Platforms and Prayerbooks: Theological and Liturgical Perspectives on Reform Judaism*, ed. D. E. Kaplan (New York: Rowman & Littlefield, 2002), 93.
11. Susannah Heschel, "Imagining Judaism in America," in *The Cambridge Companion to Jewish American Literature*, ed. Michael Kramer and Hana Wirth-Nesher (Cambridge, MA: Cambridge University Press, 2003), 31–49.
12. H. Gans, "Symbolic Ethnicity: The Future of Ethnic Groups and Cultures in America," *Ethnic and Racial Studies* 2 (1979), 1–20.
13. Ibid., 8–9.
14. Ibid., 7.

15. H. Gans, "Symbolic Ethnicity and Symbolic Religiosity: Towards a Comparison of Ethnic and Religious Acculturation," *Ethnic and Racial Studies* 17, 4 (1994), 577–92.
16. Ibid., 585.
17. E. Mayer, "Secularism Among America's Jews" (paper delivered to the Association for Jewish Studies, Washington, DC, 2001), 18–19.
18. J. A. Winter, "Symbolic Ethnicity or Religion Among Jews in the United States: A Test of Gansian Hypothesis," *Review of Religious Research* 37, 3 (1996), 144.
19. J. A. Winter, "The Transformation of Community Integration Among American Jewry: Religion or Ethno-Religion," *Review of Religious Research* 33, 4 (1992), 360.
20. S. Sharot, "A Critical Comment on Gans' 'Symbolic Ethnicity and Symbolic Religiosity' and Other Formulations of Ethnicity and Religion Regarding American Jews," *Contemporary Jewry* 18 (1997), 39.
21. Ibid., 39.
22. G. A. Kunkelman, *The Religion of Ethnicity: Belief and Belonging in a Greek-American Community* (New York: Garland Publishing, 1990).
23. S. Sharot, "Judaism and Jewish Ethnicity: Changing Interrelationships and Differentiations in the Diaspora and Israel," in *Jewish Survival: The Identity Problem at the Close of the Twentieth Century*, ed. E. Krausz and G. Tulea (New Brunswick: Transaction Publishers, 1998), 94.
24. S. C. Heilman, *Portrait of American Jews: The Last Half of the Twentieth Century* (Seattle: University of Washington Press, 1995), 105.
25. S. Sharot, "Judaism and Jewish Ethnicity: Changing Interrelationships and Differentiations in the Diaspora and Israel," in *Jewish Survival: The Identity Problem at the Close of the Twentieth Century*, ed. E. Krausz and G. Tulea (New Brunswick: Transaction Publishers, 1998), 94.
26. S. C. Heilman, *Portrait of American Jews*, 135.
27. B. Horowitz, *Connections and Journeys: Assessing Critical Opportunities for Enhancing Jewish Identity* (New York: Commission on Jewish Identity and Renewal, United Jewish Appeal Federation, 2000), 9.
28. D. Kaufman, "Gender and Jewish Identity Among Twenty-Somethings in the United States," in *Religion in a Changing World: Comparative Studies in Sociology*, ed. Madeleine Cousineau (Westport: Greenwood Press, 1998), 49.
29. B. Horowitz, "Reframing the Study of Contemporary American Jewish Identity" (paper delivered at the conference convened by the North American Jewish Data Bank, October 1999); S. M. Cohen and A. M. Eisen, *The Jew Within: Self, Family, and Community in America* (Bloomington: Indiana University Press, 2000).
30. In this chapter, references to Cohen (2002) are from an unpublished paper wherein he revisits some of the issues he and his coauthor, Arnold Eisen, raised in their landmark book, *The Jew Within: Self, Family, and Community in America* (2000). S. M. Cohen, "Religiosity and Ethnicity: Jewish Identity Trends in the United States" (unpublished paper, 2002), 3.
31. Ibid., 5.
32. Ibid., 14.
33. Ibid., 14.
34. Ibid., 14.

35. Ibid., 22.
36. Ibid., 38.
37. Paula Hyman (1983) was the first to coin this term. "The Jewish Family: Looking for a Usable Past," in *On Being a Jewish Feminist*, ed. Susannah Heschel (New York: Schocken Books, 1983).
38. S. M. Cohen, "Religiosity and Ethnicity," 18.
39. D. D. Moore, "Commentator," in *The Jew Within: Self, Community and Commitment Among the Variety of Moderately Affiliated*, ed. by S. M. Cohen and A. M. Eisen (Boston and Los Angeles: The Susan and David Wilstein Institute of Jewish Policy Studies, 1998), 68–71.
40. S. M. Cohen, "Religiosity and Ethnicity," 38.
41. S. M. Cohen and A. M. Eisen, *The Jew Within: Self, Family, and Community in America* (Bloomington: Indiana University Press, 2000), 184.
42. Ibid., 184.
43. This mixed pattern of identification looks much like Cohen and Eisen's "moderately-affiliated" respondents. S. M. Cohen and A. M. Eisen, *The Jew Within: Self, Family, and Community in America* (Bloomington: Indiana University Press, 2000).
44. B. Horowitz, *Connections and Journeys: Assessing Critical Opportunities for Enhancing Jewish Identity* (New York: Commission on Jewish Identity and Renewal, United Jewish Appeal Federation, 2000), 187.
45. Ibid., 187.
46. D. R. Kaufman, "Gender and Jewish Identity Among Twenty-Somethings in the United States," in *Religion in a Changing World: Comparative Studies in Sociology*, ed. M. Cousinea (Westport: Greenwood Press, 1998), 49–56.
47. M. Fischer, "Ethnicity and the Post-Modern Arts of Memory," in *Writing Culture: The Politics and Poetics Ethnography*, ed. J. Clifford and G. E. Marcus (Berkeley: University of California Press, 1986), 185.
48. D. R. Kaufman, "Embedded Categories: Identity Among Jewish Young Adults in the United States," in *Race, Gender & Class: American Jewish Perspectives* 6, 4 (1999), 86.
49. Ibid., 79.
50. D. R. Kaufman "Ethnicity, Collective Memory and Post-Holocaust Identity Narratives," in *De-ghettoizing the Holocaust: Lessons for the Study of Diaspora, Ethnicity, and Collective Memory*, eds. Judith Person and Diane Wolf, Duke University Press (forthcoming 2005), 8.
51. D. R. Kaufman, "Gender and Jewish Identity Among Twenty-Somethings in the United States," in *Religion in a Changing World: Comparative Studies in Sociology*, ed. Madeleine Cousineau (Westport: Greenwood Press, 1998), 55.
52. S. M. Cohen, "Response to Charles Liebman," *Contemporary Jewry* 22 (2001), 118.
53. See also, Riv-Ellen Prell, "Response to Charles Liebman" in *Contemporary Jewry* 22 (2001), 120–25.
54. S. M. Cohen, "Response to Charles Liebman," 119.
55. Sergio Della Pergola, "Arthur Ruppin Revisited: The Jews of Today 1904–1994," in *National Variations in Jewish Identity*, ed. S. M. Cohen and G. Horenczyk (Albany: State University of New York, 1999), 66.

56. Charles S. Liebman, "The Reappropriation of Jewish Tradition in the Modern Era," in *The Uses of Tradition: Jewish Continuity in the Modern Era*, ed. J. Wertheimer (New York: Jewish Theological Seminary, 1992).

57. Sylvia Barak Fishman, *A Breath of Life: Feminism in the American Jewish Community* (New York: The Free Press, 1993); D. Kaufman, *Rachel's Daughters* (New Brunswick: Rutgers University Press, 1991).

58. J. Plaskow, *Standing Again at Sinai: Judaism from a Feminist Perspective* (San Francisco: Harper & Row, 1990).

59. J. Wertheimer, "The Reappropriation of Tradition in Contemporary Judaism," in *The Uses of Tradition: Jewish Continuity in the Modern Era*, ed. J. Wertheimer (New York: Jewish Theological Seminary, 1992), 471–77.

60. C. Ozick, "Notes Toward Finding the Right Question," in *On Being a Jewish Feminist*, ed. S. Heschel (New York: Schocken Books, 1983), 120–51.

61. B. Horowitz, "Reframing the Study of Contemporary American Jewish Identity" (paper delivered at the conference convened by the North American Jewish Data Bank, October 1999), 19.

62. A. Dashefsky et al., "Journey of the 'Straightway' or 'Roundabout Path': Jewish Identity in the United States and Israel," in *Handbook of the Sociology of Religion*, ed. M. Dillon (Cambridge, MA: Cambridge University Press, 2003).

10 The Holocaust in American Jewish life

LYNN RAPAPORT

AMERICA AND THE HOLOCAUST

Beginning in the 1930s, as Hitler's Germany persecuted and eventually murdered Jews, America turned a blind eye. Until the Japanese attack at Pearl Harbor, Americans were unwilling to be drawn into European power struggles or take sides between Hitler and his intended victims. Gallup polls from the 1930s show that Americans regarded "staying neutral" as their most important concern.[1] Even after the *Anschluss*, *Kristallnacht*, and the Evian conference, the United States government refused to lift immigration restrictions for frantic Jewish refugees. In 1939, America refused to accept 20,000 German-Jewish children from the *Kindertransport*, and it also turned back the Hamburg-American Line's *SS St. Louis*, a ship carrying 900 Jewish refugees that reached American shores after being stranded in the Caribbean when their Cuban visas were canceled. America also refused to press Britain to rescind the British White Paper of May 1939 that limited immigration to Palestine by European Jews fleeing Hitler.[2] By 1942, the governments allied against Hitler were well informed about concentration camps and the tragic fate of the Jews, but they did little to mitigate it. Toward the end of the war, the United States and its Allies refused to bomb the gas chambers or the railroad tracks to Auschwitz and other killing centers.

The reluctance of the Roosevelt administration to respond to the Jewish tragedy has been documented forcefully by a variety of scholars. Books with the following titles are revealing: *The Abandonment of the Jews, The Failure to Rescue, While Six Million Died, No Haven for the Oppressed, Beyond Belief,* and *The Jews Were Expendable.*[3] Some scholars cite anti-Semitism as the key reason for abandonment, while others are more moderate, taking into account the larger social and political context of the 1930s and 1940s. Most importantly, they cite the impact of the Depression, a strong isolationist position and reluctance to enter the war in Europe, a deep-seated anti-immigration sentiment, and disbelief that the plight of European Jews was desperate.[4]

Furthermore, during World War II, the American Jewish community was ineffective at mobilizing American Jews and their organizations to rescue European Jewry. During that period, most American Jews lacked influence or power, and their organizations were small, understaffed, and underfinanced. American Jewry was organizationally incohesive and internally divided about how to respond to the Holocaust. The differing perspectives of Jewish leaders hampered an all-out mobilization of American Jews and their organizations for massive rescue.[5] Efforts to unify a Jewish response were not sustained. Moreover, Jews in Roosevelt's administration, with the exception of Henry Morgenthau, failed to make rescuing European Jewry a war priority.

Because of their fears for American Jewry's future in a still anti-Semitic America, many Jewish leaders downplayed specifically Jewish concerns. During that period, American Jews held cautious political attitudes fashioned by centuries of the Diaspora. By Spring 1943, when an Allied victory was more certain, this complacency changed. There emerged a greater willingness to confront genocide, and Jews mounted concentrated pressure both inside the Roosevelt Administration and in Congress and public opinion to establish the War Refugee Board in January 1944. With the cooperation of the Red Cross and the Swiss and Swedish governments, the War Refugee Board saved thousands of Jews in Hungary – the sole surviving European Jewish community whose numbers had swelled with Jews fleeing other liquidated centers. However, had the War Refugee Board been founded earlier, it might have facilitated additional rescues.

By the end of World War II, the Nazis had murdered approximately 6 million European Jews, reducing the world Jewish population to fewer than 11 million. Little remained of the great centers of Jewish life. When the allies liberated Nazi-occupied territories, only half a million Jews remained in Europe, casting the burden of Jewish leadership on the Jews in North America and Palestine. Between 1944 and 1952, 137,450 European Jews immigrated to the United States.[6] Most were Eastern European Jews who survived Nazi slave labor and death camps. On December 22, 1945, then-President Truman enacted emergency legislation that made immigration policy more flexible. The majority of Jewish immigrants came after June 1948, when President Truman signed into law a Displaced Persons Act allowing 205,000 refugees to enter the United States.[7] This was followed by the Displaced Persons Act of 1950, and the Refugee Relief Act of 1953. During the postwar period, the Jewish population in the United States was approximately 5 million. The immigrants, mostly Holocaust survivors, constituted about 2.5 percent of this postwar Jewish population.

The experiences of Jewish Holocaust survivors during World War II varied markedly. Some survived ghettos and concentration camps, enduring slave labor and severe deprivation. Others lived out the war in hiding. Some survived above ground on false papers by passing as Gentiles. Thousands more were exiled and confined in work camps in the Soviet Union. A small number fought in the forests as partisans. Most survivors (especially those from Eastern Europe) experienced the murder of their immediate and extended families.

While American Jews were unable to help rescue European Jewry, they contributed significantly to postwar relief. Through philanthropic institutions, American Jews provided food, clothing, shelter, medical care, education, transportation, and resettlement for the Jewish refugees in Europe. In 1948, when Israel's existence hung in balance, American Jews raised over $200 million through their federated campaigns. From 1939 through 1967, American Jews raised over $3 billion for philanthropic Jewish needs, more than half of which went to Israel.[8]

As Jewish Holocaust survivors tried to assimilate into American and American Jewish life, they faced a postwar nation recovering from war. Some Americans were unable to listen to the tales of woe recounted by survivors. The postwar victory spirit pervading America discouraged confronting wartime atrocities. Moreover, the impact of new Cold War alliances between West Germany and the United States limited public discussion of the Holocaust. For example, Moritz Feldman, a survivor, was told by his aunt: "If you want to have friends here in America, don't keep talking about your experiences. Nobody's interested and if you tell them, they're going to hear it once and then the next time they'll be afraid to come see you. Don't ever speak about it."[9] After immigrating to the United States, Benjamin Meed, president of the American Gathering/Federation of Jewish Holocaust Survivors and Warsaw Ghetto Resistance, recalls being told, "Forget the past; it can only hurt you."[10]

Whereas today, victim status has been appropriated as a political resource, in the postwar period few survivors wanted to think of themselves as victims for it symbolized their life in the Old World and evoked pity and contempt.[11] Most Holocaust survivors were reluctant to talk about the war, thus silencing themselves, and often rationalizing their silence by saying the stories were too horrible to be believed.[12]

As Holocaust survivors tried to integrate into American Jewish life, they faced a Jewish community characterized by upward mobility, assimilation, and suburbanization. Anti-semitism in postwar America had declined. Colleges and universities with former exclusionary and anti-Jewish policies changed their admissions criteria to merit based. Like other Americans during the postwar years, American Jews had expanded access to previously restricted professional, educational, and cultural opportunities. Between 1940 and 1957, the share of Jews in white-collar jobs soared from 10 percent to 55 percent. Between 1945 and 1965, one-third of the American Jewish population moved from cities to suburbs.

Postwar America was also characterized by the growth of religious affiliation. American Jews shared in this trend. During the Eisenhower years, previously unaffiliated Jews flocked into the Jewish community. Moving from cities to suburbs, young Jewish couples joined newly constructed temples, mostly Reform and Conservative, raising congregation membership by 60 percent from the1930s.[13] Indeed, Jews spent approximately $1 billion building 1,000 new synagogues, most of them Conservative and Reform.[14] Nevertheless, American Jews were "belonging without believing," celebrating a symbolic ethnicity whereby Jews could be Jewish without being religious. In *Jewish Identity on the Suburban Frontier*, Marshall Sklare and Joseph Greenblum show how Jews were relying increasingly more on Jewish communal organizations – the synagogue, the Jewish school, and the Jewish camp – to provide Jewish training and a sense of identity that religious doctrine, family, and Jewish neighborhoods once offered.[15]

The Holocaust influenced American Judaism in the postwar period by revitalizing its more religious branches – Orthodoxy and Hassidism. As a result of dislocations that accompanied and followed the Second World War, many leader-oriented Orthodox immigrant groups arrived in the United States and re-created the Talmudic scholarship and insulated spirit of their Old World. For instance, in 1939, Rabbi Joseph Breuer moved from Frankfurt am Main by way of Belgium to New York's Washington Heights, and he quickly attracted a following of German immigrant Jews. In 1940, Rabbi Joseph Isaac Schneersohn, leader of Lubavitcher Hasidim, arrived in Brooklyn's Crown Heights, beginning a process of resettlement of wartime and postwar Russian Hasidic refugees. Rabbis Mordechai Katz and Elijah Meir Bloch, driven from their yeshivas in Telz, Romania, led their community from western Russia through Siberia to Japan and then to Seattle, Washington before reassembling their lives and Telshe Yeshiva in 1941 in Cleveland. That same year, after a similarly arduous escape, Rabbi Aaron Kotler, head of the Polish Kletzk Yeshiva, resettled in New York. Two years later, he opened up a yeshiva in New Jersey and his graduates went on to lead yeshivas and rabbinical colleges in Philadelphia, St. Louis, and Denver. The alumni established Talmudic centers in Los Angeles and Detroit and operated several Orthodox publishing houses. Other Orthodox scholars and rabbis, like Abraham Kalmanowitz, established the Mirrer Yeshiva, named for his former academy in the Russian town of Mir, and Joel Teltelbaum replanted the Satmar Hasidic dynasty he led as grand rabbi. Committed to re-creating the lost communities of Europe on American soil and resisting the pressure of immigrant acculturation, these leader-oriented groups quickly established their own network of schools, self-help charitable institutions, and social organizations. These new, growing, and confident Orthodox elements dramatically affected the status, thinking, and practice of indigenous Orthodox groups. All told, fewer than 100,000 Orthodox Jews entered the United States in the decade after the war, yet their impact on Orthodox Jewry was profound. By the end of the 1950s, there was once again a first generation of Orthodox Jews on American soil.[16]

In the 1940s and 1950s, the Holocaust had not yet been conceptualized as a discrete "event." During the Nuremberg Trials in November 1945, where the highest Nazi officials captured were tried for murdering European Jewry, the killings were considered one of many war crimes. Until the 1960s, Holocaust survivors and the general public used terms such as *catastrophe, disaster,* or *recent Jewish catastrophe* to describe the genocide of Europe's Jews.

Moreover, American Jewish Holocaust accounts decalamatized the murders by emphasizing heroic imagery and downplaying Jewish suffering and persecution. Simultaneously, Jewish educators focused on building positive Jewish identity. During this period, Jewish history textbooks, collections of plays, and children's literature presented highly selective versions of wartime events. They privileged acts of physical resistance and rescue such as the Warsaw ghetto uprising, the life of Hannah Senesh, and Jewish rescue efforts in Palestine.[17] They also focused on a line of continuity among heroes throughout Jewish history. For instance, educational texts cast the Warsaw ghetto uprising as a David and Goliath struggle – the small against the large, the weak against the strong, the few against the many. "We glorify, above every other phase of the tragedy, the uprising in the Warsaw ghetto," writes Jewish historian Salo Baron. Commenting on the disproportionate attention paid to physical resistance and heroic imagery in Holocaust narratives of the 1940s and 1950s, Baron called for a more balanced view in writing Jewish history – one that addresses Jewish tragedies as well as triumphs.[18]

Zionist conceptions of Jewish history and of the Holocaust also gained prominence in American Jewish life. The creation of a Jewish state in 1948 inspired for all Jews new heroes, stories, poems, songs, and dances. Israeli narratives of the Holocaust focused almost exclusively on examples of Jewish physical resistance and rescue. What emerged was the image of the heroic Jew – empowered and masculinized – that contrasted with the notion of the victimized Holocaust survivor.[19] Israeli narratives of the Jew focused on his or her physical strength and endurance, and these characterizations affected American Jewish Holocaust narratives.

One primary theme in postwar American Jewish accounts was that the Nazis never "broke the Jewish spirit."[20] This dovetailed with the more general upbeat postwar mood in the country. In the 1950s a young girl, Anne Frank, became the quintessential icon capturing this spirit. Her diary, first published in Dutch in 1952 as *Het Acherhuis*, (The Annex), turned her story of victimhood into a life-affirming triumph.

The Diary of Anne Frank has been translated into fifty-five languages and has sold over 24 million copies worldwide.[21] In 1952, Doubleday published the first English translation; more than 45,000 copies were sold in a matter of days, and around 100,000 copies were sold in its first year of publication.[22] Frances Goodrich and Albert Hackett, a husband and wife writing team from Hollywood, wrote a popular play based on the diary that opened in 1955 on Broadway. The play was a box-office smash; it won a Pulitzer Prize, the Tony Award, and the New York Drama Critics Circle Award. In 1959, a successful film version of the Goodrich–Hackett play was released, followed by several popular television adaptations.[23]

Ironically, many analysts attribute the success of *The Diary of Anne Frank* to the story line that downplays her Jewishness and turns her into a universal figure representing all martyred innocents. This universalistic framing emphasizes the diversity of the victims rather than focusing singularly on Jewish victimhood. "It is the story of the gallant human spirit," John Chapman wrote of the play in the Daily News.[24] Anne offers forgiveness and hope, is faithful to the spirit of optimism celebrated in American culture, and inspires others through her moral courage. With her redemptive promise, "In spite of everything, I still believe people are really good at heart," she embodies the most prevalent American and Jewish values of the early postwar decades. Moreover, her legacy has endured. To date, *The Diary of Anne Frank* is the most widely read book about the Holocaust in the United States. Indeed, it was named as the predominant source of Holocaust education in a 1996 University of Michigan survey, as it was required reading for over half the high school students surveyed.[25]

Some scholars have argued that the early postwar decades were characterized by a conspiracy of silence surrounding the genocide of European Jewry. The general impression was that the Holocaust disappeared from movies, plays, television productions, books, and public discourse.[26] However, by the late 1950s, television had presented several dozen broadcasts that dealt in some way, though perhaps indirectly, with the subject. These included original dramas for prime-time "playhouses," programs for ecumenical religion series, documentaries on the history of the Second World War or the Third Reich, and several installments of popular shows that featured Holocaust survivors.[27] Moreover, by 1959, William Shirer's *The Rise and Fall of the*

Third Reich appeared and sold over 1 million copies in its first year. The book stayed on the best-seller list for over a year, and when condensed and serialized in *Reader's Digest*, it became one of the best-selling nonfiction historical works of all times.[28] Furthermore, *The Diary of Anne Frank*, already mentioned, was a successful book, play, and Hollywood film.

Nevertheless, the Holocaust did not permeate public discourse and its commemoration wasn't institutionalized. While remembering that the murder of European Jewry is central to the importance of remembering and mourning within Jewish culture, American Jews were not creating monuments or tributes marking the Holocaust. Most commemorative activity took place within the Jewish survivor community. The language of the ceremonies was Yiddish, and outsiders were painfully aware of their peripheral status. Indeed, Rabbi Irving Greenberg, then president of the National Jewish Center for Learning and Leadership, recalled attending Holocaust remembrance services in the late 1950s and early 1960s. "It felt," Greenberg said, "like we were crashing a funeral."[29] Furthermore, although Shirer was successful at finding a publisher, Elie Wiesel, now the most celebrated American writer on the Holocaust, and Raul Hilberg, author of *The Destruction of European Jews*, had trouble getting American presses to publish their Holocaust work.[30] In a 1957 study of American Judaism, sociologist Nathan Glazer observed that the Holocaust "had remarkedly slight effects on the inner life of American Jewry."[31] American Jews seemed uninterested in the Holocaust. In a 1961 symposium sponsored by *Commentary* magazine on "Jewishness and Younger Intellectuals," only two of thirty-one participants cited the Holocaust as having a significant impact on their lives.[32] Likewise, a 1961 roundtable on "My Jewish Affirmation," convened by the journal *Judaism*, almost completely ignored the subject.[33] There was only one university course on the Holocaust in the United States.[34] Reviewing various Jewish local newspapers and publications from the period, Deborah Lipstadt found little mention of the Holocaust or its impact on Jewish identity.[35]

The awakening of Holocaust consciousness

In the early 1960s, the death of Stalin, the end of McCarthyism, the cooling of relations between China and the Soviet Union, and the stabilization of postwar alliances resulted in a cultural shift more open to Holocaust exploration. The catalyst for awakening Holocaust consciousness came when then-Prime Minister of Israel David Ben-Gurion announced to the Knesset that Israeli agents had captured Adolf Eichmann in Argentina and secretly transported him to Israel to stand trial. The Eichmann trial in Jerusalem District Court consisted of one hundred and fourteen sessions from April 11 through August 14, 1961. The trial was broadcast around the world and amounted to a retelling of the events of the Holocaust – the Nuremberg Laws, the ghettos, deportations, mobile killing units on the Eastern Front, the Final Solution, the death camps, and forced marches. Although the grim facts had been available to those who cared to know them, the trial resulted in making names and numbers common knowledge. For many Americans, including American Jews, it was the first time they grasped the full account of the Nazi campaign to murder European Jewry.

The trial's public nature transformed the status of the Holocaust into a landmark event and a turning point in defining what humanity is capable of. Historians and critics describe the trial as generating new interest in the experiences of European Jewry during the Nazi era. Moreover, Raul Hilberg's *The Destruction of the European Jews* appeared about the same time, in 1961. Eichmann was formally charged with committing "crimes against the Jewish people," "crimes against humanity," "war crimes," and being a member of a hostile organization. The agenda and protocols of Eichmann's case were widely debated in public forums within Israel and internationally.

The American news media treated the Eichmann trial as an important story. During the two years between Eichmann's capture and his eventual execution on May 31, 1962, his case appeared repeatedly on multiple American television channels. Regular reports also appeared in the nation's major daily newspapers and news magazines. The trial was covered in theatrical news-reels and radio broadcasts, and it was followed closely by the press outlets of various Christian denominations, along with heavy coverage in American, Yiddish, German Jewish, and Anglo-Jewish press.[36]

The Eichmann trials introduced the term *Holocaust* to the American public. This happened when Paul Jacobs, an American journalist in Israel covering the trial, wrote in a dispatch to America of "the Holocaust, as the Nazi annihilation of European Jewry is called in Israel."[37] It would take until the late 1960s before Elie Wiesel and countless others popularized the term to mean the suffering and genocide of European Jewry.

During the Eichmann trial, the status of Holocaust survivors was also transformed. The survivors took on the role of expert witnesses with cru-cial testimony to offer. After being silenced for the preceding fifteen years, and embodying a victim status that evoked pity, Holocaust survivors were now asked to render precise accounts of their experiences and encouraged to disclose even the most horrifying details. "The trial was the first event to awaken survivor consciousness, to touch even some non-survivor Jews deeply," said Michael Nutkiewicz, then director of the Martyrs Memorial Museum of the Holocaust in Los Angeles, and the son of survivors.[38] "It was really the first time survivors were telling their stories in public, expressing their pain on television, before the world," he continued.[39] Because of the trial, these individuals were not shameful about what they endured; their status as Holocaust survivors gave them distinctive voices of authority.

In 1963, Hannah Arendt published a series of articles on the trial in *The New Yorker*. The articles were published the same year in book form as *Eichmann in Jerusalem: A Report on the Banality of Evil*. Arendt introduced the world to "the banality of evil," concluding that Eichmann was not a monster and that the perpetrators were normal bureaucrats. She also argued that the *Judenräten* (Jewish Councils) in Germany, in the occupied countries of Western Europe, and in the ghettos of Eastern Europe had cooperated "in one way or another, for one reason or another, with the Nazis." "The whole truth was that if the Jewish people had really been unorganized and leaderless, there would have been chaos and plenty of misery but the total number of victims would hardly have been between four-and-a-half and six million people," she wrote.[40]

Arendt's writings created a public furor. The theses provoked many Jewish intellectuals into passionate and critical responses. Gershom Scholem, the eminent scholar, described her work in a letter to her as "heartless, frequently almost sneering and malicious." Martin Buber criticized her for misrepresenting his position on the trial. For Irving Howe, the book affected his own thinking and aroused "overwhelming" passions among other New York Jewish intellectuals. The press also had a field day. "Self-Hating Jewess Writes Pro-Eichmann Series for New Yorker Magazine," headlined one Jewish newspaper. The Anti-Defamation League sent its branches defamatory reviews of her "evil book," as they called it. The Jewish Publication Society of America distributed a 400-page criticism of the book.[41] Norman Podhoretz, writing in *Commentary*, accused Arendt of replacing the "confrontation between guilt and innocence" with "collaboration" between perpetrator and victim. For weeks the *New York Times*, the *New Republic*, the *National Review, Commentary*, and *The New Yorker* continued their analysis of both the book and responses to it.[42]

The Eichmann trial also prompted the Christian community in America, both within and outside the Church, to scrutinize Christian responsibility and collaboration.[43] In 1963, the premiere of Rolf Hochhuth's play *The Deputy* began a controversy by raising troubling questions about the relationship between the Vatican and the Third Reich. The play portrayed Pope Pius XII as an aloof, calculating diplomat, more concerned with the war's financial impact on the Vatican's holdings than with saving Jewish lives. The controversy became so great that Pope Paul VI came to Pius's defense, arguing that a papal protest against the Nazis would have caused even greater suffering.[44]

The Eichmann trial, along with the controversies over Hannah Arendt's book and Hochhuth's play, broke fifteen years of near silence in American public discourse. The trial focused American attention on the attempt of the Nazis to murder European Jewry, yet public opinion polls suggest that the trial and the debate over Arendt's book didn't generate sustained interest in the Holocaust among Americans and American Jews. An analysis of Jewish magazines and periodicals from the period show a momentary flurry of interest in the Holocaust in general and Eichmann in particular. Furthermore, in 1964, New York City's Arts Commission rejected a design for a Holocaust memorial from survivors of the Warsaw Ghetto uprising, because, among other reasons, they had to ensure that "monuments in the parks . . . be limited to events of American history."[45] In 1966, when *Commentary* conducted another symposium on the "Condition of Jewish Belief," the Holocaust was not mentioned in the five lengthy questions distributed to thirty-eight rabbis and theologians. Only a small number of the respondents made reference to the Holocaust.[46]

While in the 1940s and 1950s American Jewish culture emphasized the motifs of rescue and resistance in their Holocaust narratives, the trials, scholarship, and literature arising out of the early 1960s highlighted Jews' brutalization, suffering, and victimization. Indeed, much discussion among Holocaust educators during that period centered on how to present tragic events to young Jews. Educators began presenting the Holocaust as a distinct subject, requiring special pedagogical methods and a separate place on the curriculum. They stressed the Holocaust, as well as the founding of Israel, as pivotal events in twentieth-century Jewish history, and they viewed narratives of Jewish wartime victimization, in addition to Jewish heroism, as conducive to forming a positive Jewish identity.[47] The Six Day War, the domestical upheavals associated with the Vietnam War, and the rise of politics of victimization all contributed to this change.

Mainstreaming the Holocaust into American and American Jewish life

Egyptian President Gamal Abdel Nasser mobilized his army on May 15, 1967, and declared on May 26 that his goal was to annihilate Israel. Abraham Joshua Heschel, the distinguished Jewish theologian, captured the sense of foreboding: "Terror and dread fell upon Jews everywhere. . . . Will there be another Auschwitz, another Dachau, another Treblinka . . . In those days many of us felt that our own lives were in the balance of life and death . . . that indeed all of the bible, all of Jewish history was at stake, the vision of redemption, the drama that began with Abraham." It was, Heschel continued, "an awesome time, the collapse of complacency."[48]

On June 5, 1967, Israel launched a preemptive strike against Egypt, Jordan, and Syria. In six days of warfare, Israel defeated these Arab forces and occupied the Gaza Strip and the Sinai peninsula of Egypt, the Golan Heights of Syria, the West Bank of the Jordan River, and the Old City of Jerusalem, which Jordan had annexed back in 1949. While the prospect of defeat triggered despair among Jews worldwide, Israel's stunning victory empowered the American Jewish community and brought American Jewish concern for Israel to a peak. There was a renewed sense of Jewish interdependence and a resolve that, unlike the unresponsiveness during the Second World War, this time there would be an aggressive Jewish American commitment.

After 1967, Jewish thinkers began to absorb the full meaning of Auschwitz. Jews and Israel had almost disappeared, fitting with Hitler's intentions. Jewish theologian Richard Rubenstein argued that God was silent at Auschwitz and in 1967, and that Jews must now rely on themselves and their own physical power for survival. When addressing what the legacy of Auschwitz demands, "Jews are forbidden to hand Hitler posthumous victories," responded Jewish philosopher Emil Fackenheim. "They are commanded to survive as Jews, lest the Jewish people perish. They are commanded to remember the victims of Auschwitz lest their memory perish," Fackenheim writes.[49] Indeed, "Never again," with reference to the Holocaust, became the slogan of the nascent Jewish Defense League, officially formed by young militant Jews in 1968.

Israel's stunning victory also enabled the creation of a salvation myth – a folk theology of "Holocaust and Redemption." Jews with any shred of religious belief struggled with why God allowed the brutal death of 6 million innocent Jewish men, women, and children. This salvation myth enabled them to reconcile the Holocaust with the Covenant that God would protect Jews and integrate the Holocaust into Jewish religious consciousness. According to Jacob Neusner, it was a myth "of darkness followed by the light; of passage through the netherworld...then, purified by suffering and by blood, into the new age." Neusner writes,

> The extermination of European Jewry could become *the Holocaust* only on 9 June when, in the aftermath of a remarkable victory, the State of Israel celebrated the return of the people of Israel to the ancient wall of the Temple of Jerusalem. On that day the extermination of European Jewry attainted the – if not happy, at least viable – ending that served to transform events into a myth, and to endow a symbol with a single, ineluctable meaning.[50]

Jonathan Woocher argues that the story of "Holocaust to rebirth" became central to secular Judaism's beliefs and values, providing a moral paradigm for Jewish history and inspiration for Jewish survival and social justice. American civil Judaism treats recent Jewish history as beginning in

death – the Holocaust – and ending with resurrection, or rebirth – the establishment of the State of Israel.[51]

Moreover, with the growth of Holocaust awareness in the 1960s,
American Jews began connecting Jewish persecution under Nazism with
current issues affecting American society – the Civil Rights movement and
the Vietnam War. Some analysts suggest that the disproportionate Jewish
involvement in the New Left and the decade's political, social, and cultural
movements was a reaction of Baby Boomers to their parents' unresponsiveness to the Holocaust.[52] "For Jewish adolescents in particular," asserts Todd
Gitlin, "the Nazis were not so long defeated. . . . We were going to be active
where our parents' generation had been passive."[53] Jewish studies programs
began to emerge, and Jewish educators introduced courses on the Holocaust,
linking them to current social issues such as social justice and civil and human
rights. Two popular films, Stanley Kramer's *Judgement at Nuremberg* (1961)
and Sidney Lumet's *The Pawnbroker* (1965), also analogized the Holocaust
with American concerns of democracy, civil and human rights, and the struggles of African Americans and other minorities. In addition, Jewish leftists,
among others, repeatedly invoked Holocaust imagery in anti-Vietnam War
protests, using terms such as *genocide* and *race war* to describe American
actions there.

In 1973, the year that America withdrew direct military intervention
from Vietnam, Israel was taken by surprise when Egypt and Syria coordi-
nated an attack on October 6, Yom Kippur, the holiest day in the Jewish calendar. At least nine Arab states, including four non-Middle Eastern nations,
actively aided the Egyptian–Syrian war effort in a long, drawn-out battle.
While Israel appeared on the brink of defeat, it eventually mobilized forces
and defeated its foes. Nonetheless, the Yom Kippur War was considered a
diplomatic and military failure, with significant Israeli casualties.

The Yom Kippur War further transformed American Jews' relationship
to Israel and, ultimately, to the Holocaust. While the Six Day War helped create a triumphant salvation myth, the Yom Kippur War shattered the illusion
of Israeli military invincibility and signaled that Jews were still vulnerable to
mass murder. The Yom Kippur War heightened Israel's feelings of isolation
in the international community, and it inspired similar feelings of abandonment among American Jews. While the United States was still Israel's
greatest supporter, that relationship threatened to exacerbate tensions with
the Soviet Union and oil-producing Arab nations.

Both Arab–Israeli wars coincided with the emerging economic success of the survivors in America. By the mid-1960s, many Holocaust survivors had accumulated significant wealth and were eager to use it for
causes close to their hearts. By the mid-1970s their children – the "Second

Generation" – became politically active and established numerous organizations in different cities across the United States. In June 1981, about 1,000 individuals of the Second Generation joined their parents at the first World Gathering of Holocaust Survivors in Jerusalem. The political engagement of the Second Generation prodded survivors to become more politically active.

Moreover, the growth of "identity politics" in the 1970s, legitimating the victim experience as a basis of group difference, mobilized American Jews to accept victimization as a basis of group identity, and the Holocaust as a historical experience that set Jews apart. Jewish educators no longer shied away from teaching Jewish suffering – on the contrary, they embraced it.[54] In light of the politics of victimization in which American society validated ethnicity and the victim experience, American Jews sought to strengthen their inner community by raising the Holocaust to heightened levels of Jewish consciousness.[55]

In the late 1970s, several events catapulted the Holocaust from American Jewish consciousness into mainstream American life. In 1978, the Office of Special Investigations was created to prosecute and deport Nazi war criminals living in the United States. Simultaneously, from April 1977 through June 1978, Americans witnessed Holocaust survivors in direct conflict with American neo-Nazis, to protest the neo-Nazis' proposed march through Skokie, Illinois.[56] The Skokie incident received frequent and prominent news coverage. In 1981, CBS produced a two-and-a-half hour docudrama, *Skokie*, that, unlike other television dramas dealing with the Holocaust, "offers a forthright performance of American Jewish communal pride, in which the Holocaust figures as a central moral touchstone," writes Jeffrey Shandler.[57]

Moreover, in *Popular Culture and the Shaping of Holocaust Memory in America*, Alan Mintz shows the pivotal role popular culture played in spreading Holocaust awareness from the Jewish community to the larger American society.[58] Indeed, in April 1978, NBC broadcast a nine-and-a-half hour miniseries, Gerald Green's *Holocaust: The Story of the Family Weiss*. NBC envisioned *Holocaust* as an epic work similar to Alex Haley's *Roots*, the saga of an African-American family over the course of five generations. *Holocaust* focused on the experiences of a cosmopolitan, upper-middle-class, German Jewish family, the Weiss's, from the mid-1930s until the end of the war. Educators and community leaders across the country made watching the miniseries an educational imperative. The American Jewish Committee prepared an accompanying study guide for NBC, which the National Education Association distributed to teachers across the country. The United States Catholic Conference Division of Film and Broadcasting and the Communications Division of the National Council of Churches prepared study guides for use in parochial schools.[59] Close to 120 million Americans watched all or most of *Holocaust* as it aired over four evenings, and it inspired a deluge of articles – both critical and supportive – in the mainstream press.

Then, on November 1, 1978, President Carter announced plans to create the President's Commission on the Holocaust. Its purpose was to recommend an appropriate memorial to those who perished during the Holocaust, examine funding for such a memorial, and recommend appropriate ways of commemorating April 28 and 29, 1979, which Congress declared as "Days of Remembrance of Victims of the Holocaust."[60] A Commission report asserted in 1979 that it was "essential that all Americans, not just Jews, confront this event," and encouraged schools to teach the Holocaust, in hopes of "making a better moral, political order for the future."[61] Elie Wiesel headed the commission and, with other commission members, argued for creating a living memorial, which culminated fifteen years later in the United States Holocaust Memorial Museum.

From the 1970s on, there were additional events that kept the Holocaust in the news. In 1985, then-President Ronald Reagan created a controversy when, as a celebratory act of reconciliation between the United States and West Germany, he planned to visit Bitburg, a German military cemetery where Waffen SS members were buried. Reagan's much publicized remark that "German soldiers buried in the Bitburg cemetery were victims of the Nazis just as surely as the victims in the concentration camps," created a furor.[62] Upon receiving the U.S. Congressional Gold Medal in 1985, Elie Wiesel publicly implored President Reagan not to visit Bitburg. A compromise was struck, and on May 5, 1985 Reagan visited both the Bitburg cemetery and Bergen-Belsen concentration camp, to honor the victims of the Holocaust and World War II.[63]

A year later Kurt Waldheim made headlines when the former Secretary-General of the United Nations, in the course of his successful campaign for the Austrian presidency, was exposed as having participated in Nazi war crimes. In April 1987, the U.S. Justice Department barred Waldheim from entering the United States, and controversy erupted again two months later when Pope John Paul II received Waldheim at the Vatican with open arms. Meanwhile, a major Jewish–Catholic dispute erupted over the presence of a Carmelite convent at Auschwitz. In 1985, Jewish organizations protested their presence as a misappropriation of Jewish victimhood. On February 22, 1987, Jewish and Catholic leaders signed an agreement to raise substantial funds to move the convent outside the area of "Auschwitz–Birkenau camps" and become part of a new interfaith center devoted to fostering mutual understanding and trust.[64] Simultaneously, John Demjanjuk, the retired Cleveland automobile worker, made headlines when he was identified by Holocaust survivors as "Ivan the Terrible" of Treblinka and extradited to Israel to face trial.

In 1987, Israeli authorities found him guilty and sentenced him to death. In 1993, however, on the basis of reasonable doubt, the Israeli Supreme Court reversed the decision. Demjanjuk was freed and returned to the United States, and, after much legal arguing, he had his citizenship restored.

In the past three decades, interest in the Holocaust among Jews and American society has soared. The Holocaust has become an important phenomenon in American consciousness and is constantly in the news. There has been a swelling of books, plays, articles, films, television programs, museums, and memorials devoted to Holocaust education and commemoration. This process of remembrance culminated in 1993, which was dubbed "the year of the Holocaust." In that year, Steven Spielberg's film *Schindler's List* was released, grossing slightly less than $1 million in its first weekend. The film went on to win seven Academy Awards, including Best Director and Best Picture, and grossed a total of $95 million in the United States and over $221 million at foreign box offices, not including video sales. When *Schindler's List* had its television debut on Sunday, February 23, 1997, an estimated 65 million viewers watched the film. It had by far the biggest audience of any nonsports program on television that season; according to Nielsen Media Research, 34 percent of the homes watching television than night were tuned to *Schindler's List*.[65]

Later that year, the United States Holocaust Memorial Museum opened in Washington, DC, placing the Holocaust firmly within the official state-sponsored memory of the United States. The Holocaust museum boasts the largest attendance in history for a national museum – 5,000 persons visit daily. In its first year, it had 2 million visitors, of whom only 38 percent were Jewish.[66]

By the end of the twentieth century, the Holocaust had been firmly planted in American and American Jewish consciousness. In the mid-1990s there was a flurry of Jewish compensation claims against German corporations and Swiss banks, as well as lawsuits to retrieve art stolen by the Nazis. Daniel Goldhagen's *Hitler's Willing Executioners* sold over 500,000 copies worldwide and made the *New York Times* Best Seller List; Goldhagen appeared on the cover of the *NY Times* magazine, on *McNeil–Lehrer News Hour*, and various other public venues. Art Spiegelman's illustrated memoir *Maus* won the Pulitzer Prize. The Holocaust is omnipresent in popular culture, education, and discussions of religion and intolerance. In 1996, Clark University established the first doctoral program specifically in Holocaust history. Holocaust survivors have become celebrities, telling their stories on *Oprah, Geraldo, Sallie Jesse Raphael,* cable television, and in schools and museums.[67] Indeed, Elie Wiesel was given the honor of throwing the ceremonial first pitch of the New York Mets' 1988 home season.

This Americanization of the Holocaust – whereby the Holocaust moved into mainstream American life – influenced American Jews in several ways. It confirmed the importance of the Holocaust in building Jewish identity. Holocaust awareness was now a pillar of Jewish faith, and it provided a moral framework to explore atrocities and social injustice. Some hoped that it would encourage Jewish Americans to rediscover the religious core of Judaism, but instead the Holocaust has become central to secular Judaism, or American Jewish civil religion, which gives Jews their sense of identity. Simultaneously, Jewish Americans constructed a collective memory that would speak to their concerns. Jewish philanthropy endowed memorials, museums, libraries, and professorships devoted to the Holocaust. Hundreds of memorials appeared, ranging from a single cemetery tablet commemorating a destroyed Eastern European Jewish community in Eastern Europe to rooms set aside in community centers devoted to Holocaust education. As membership waned in Hadassah and B'nai Brith – for decades bastions of communal life – the Simon Wiesenthal Center of Los Angeles, founded by and named for the Nazi hunter, grew into the largest organization in American Jewry.

In *The Jew Within*, Steven Cohen and Arnold Eisen demonstrate the significance of the Holocaust for American Jewish identity in the nineties. In a 1997 national survey, they asked about the relative importance of several concepts and symbols to respondents' sense of being Jewish; 85 percent marked the Holocaust as "very important" or "extremely important." This combined percentage exceeded all other items in the survey, including God, the Jewish family, the Jewish people, and American anti-Semitism. Elsewhere in the survey, 65 percent agreed that "my feelings about the Holocaust have deeply influenced my feelings about being Jewish."[68]

Likewise, in the 1997 Annual Survey of American Jewish Opinion conducted by the American Jewish Committee, 94 percent of respondents believed that Jews should "keep the remembrance of the Holocaust strong, even after the passage of time." Three years later, 81 percent of respondents rated "remembering the Holocaust" as either "extremely important" or "very important" in defining their Jewish identity. Nothing else ranked higher, not even "celebration of Jewish holidays (68 percent) or "participating in synagogue services."[69]

Some critics have argued that this Americanization of the Holocaust has been fueled by a "Holocaust industry" or "Shoah business" operated by Jews and Jewish organizations to exploit Holocaust memory for Jewish interests. These interests range from fostering Jewish identity to justifying Israeli policies against Palestinians (and U.S. support for these policies) and extorting money from Europe for compensation claims.[70] Others pose this question: Is healthy to base American Jewish identity on a consciousness of victimization? For example, Shlomo Avineri argues that the strong link between the Holocaust and Jewish identity in the Diaspora is problematic because the Holocaust was something done by non-Jews to Jews rather than something Jews did themselves.[71] Rabbi Chaim Seidler-Feller argues that, in the absence of a positive motivation, Holocaust films, novels, memorials, and museums are the institutional resources sustaining Jewish identity.[72] The emphasis on victimology, perceived and real anti-Semitism, and the Holocaust reinforces what historians Cecil Roth and Salo Baron objected to more generally as the "lachrymose" conception of Jewish history.[73] Historian Deborah Lipstadt feared that "if our image is only of suffering, we will have robbed ourselves of the joy and replenishment that Jewish tradition has always fostered."[74] Writing after the release of *Schindler's List*, Harvard Professor Ruth Wisse makes this observation:

> There is something disturbing about the way American Jews have lately appropriated the Holocaust to their own needs of self-identification, and begun to wrap themselves in its historical mantle. Commemorating the Holocaust does not require its placement at the center of Jewish experience. A community otherwise so ignorant of its sources that it becomes preoccupied with death and destruction is in danger of substituting a cult of martyrdom for the Torah's insistence on life.[75]

Although the Holocaust lasted only several years, it has profoundly influenced the twentieth century. The Holocaust is the leitmotif for genocide, and the moral paradigm through which good and evil are refracted. In the post-9/11 world, with the advent of terrorism, the escalation of the Israeli–Palestinian conflict, and the rise of anti-Semitism worldwide, there is a reemergence of the "Jewish question" as a cultural and intellectual phenomenon. While scholars agree that the Holocaust has affected American Judaism, they differ in their interpretations of what that impact is. Nonetheless, as American Jews enter the twenty-first century, they face major challenges regarding their future – a high intermarriage rate, assimilation, a declining birthrate, and the disappearance of Jewish neighborhoods. They face growing factionalism among Orthodox, Reform, and Conservative movements, as well as political and religious division regarding the state of Israel and its government's policies. American Jews face worldwide anti-Americanism, anti-Zionism, and increasing anti-Semitism. How American Jews respond to this challenge, as Americans and as Jews, will be paramount for the future of American Judaism. Ultimately, it will be American Jews who determine the role the Holocaust plays in their lives and future by what they consider important and how they handle the challenges that lie ahead.

Notes

1. Deborah Lipstadt, *Beyond Belief: The American Press and the Coming of the Holocaust 1933–1945* (New York: The Free Press, 1993), 108.
2. American Jewish leaders were unsuccessful in getting the United States government to put pressure on the British to relax immigration restrictions. The British, in turn, urged the United States to liberalize its immigration quotas. Jewish leaders were reluctant to lobby against liberalizing United States immigration restrictions for German and Eastern European Jews out of fear that it would inflame anti-Semitism and raise fear of job competition.
3. David S. Wyman, *The Abandonment of the Jews: America and the Holocaust* (New York: Pantheon Books, 1984); Herbert Druks, *The Failure to Rescue* (New York: Robert Speller & Sons, 1997); Arthur D. Morse, *While Six Million Died* (New York: Random House, 1968); Saul Friedman, *No Haven for the Oppressed: United States Policy Towards Jewish Refugees, 1938–1945* (Detroit: Wayne State University Press, 1973); Deborah Lipstadt, *Beyond Belief* (New York: The Free Press, 1986); Monty Penkower, *The Jews Were Expendable: Free World Democracy and the Holocaust* (Urbana: University of Illinois Press, 1983).
4. For instance, even as late as December 1944, 12 percent of the American public believed that the mass murder accounts were false, 27 percent believed only about 100,000 people were killed, and only 4 percent believed that over 5 million Jews had already been murdered; Haskell Lookstein, "American Jewry's Public Response to the Holocaust 1934–44" (Ph.D. diss., Yeshiva University 1979), 349–51 as cited in Seymour Maxwell Finger, *American Jewry During the Holocaust* (New York: Holmes & Meier, 1984), 43.
5. For instance, Ben Gurion and Stephen Wise were concerned about helping European Jewry within the context of how this aid would affect the future of their own communities.
6. For a breakdown on their ages, occupational groups, and the states and cities where they resettled, see Leonard Dinnerstein, *America and the Survivors of the Holocaust* (New York: Columbia University Press, 1982), 287–90.
7. William Helmreich, *Against All Odds: Holocaust Survivors and the Successful Lives They Made in America* (New York: Simon & Schuster, 1992), 21. For other accounts of Holocaust survivors' integration in the United States, see Aaron Hass, *The Aftermath: Living with the Holocaust* (Cambridge, MA: Cambridge University Press, 1995).
8. Lucy Dawidowicz, *On Equal Terms: Jews in America 1881–1981* (New York: Holt, Rinehart & Winston, 1982), 129.
9. Ibid., 38.
10. As cited in Edward Tabor Linenthal, *Preserving Memory* (New York: Viking Press, 1995), 6.
11. Ronald J. Berger, *Fathoming the Holocaust: A Social Problems Approach* (New York: Aldine de Gruyter, 2002), 159.
12. William Helmreich, *Against All Odds: Holocaust Survivors and the Successful Lives They Made in America* (New York: Simon & Schuster, 1992), 38.
13. According to the Union of American Hebrew Congregations, there were 400 congregations in 1949; by 1960 there were more than 600; see Michael Meyer, "What a Difference a Century Makes," *Reform Judaism* 28, 2 (Winter 1999), 24.

14. Samuel Freedman, *Jew vs. Jew: The Struggle for the Soul of American Jewry* (New York: Simon & Schuster, 2000), 40.

15. Marshall Sklare and Joseph Greenblum, *Jewish Identity on the Suburban Frontier: A Study of Group Survival in the Open Society* (New York: Basic Books, 1967).

16. Samuel Freedman, *Jew vs. Jew*, 37–39; Jeffrey Gurock, *American Jewish Orthodoxy in Historical Perspective* (Hoboken: KTAV Publishing House, 1996), 52–54.

17. Roma Sheramy, "Defining Lessons: The Holocaust in American Jewish Education" (Ph.D. diss., Brandeis University, 2001), 25–54.

18. As cited in Roma Sheramy, "Defining Lessons: The Holocaust in American Jewish Education" (Ph.D. diss., Brandeis University, 2001), 62–63.

19. Yael Zerubavel, *Recovered Roots: Collective Memory and the Making of Israeli National Tradition* (Chicago: University of Chicago Press, 1995); Tom Segev, *The Seventh Million: The Israelis and the Holocaust* (New York: Owl Books, 2000).

20. Roma Sheramy, "Defining Lessons: The Holocaust in American Jewish Education" (Ph.D. diss., Brandeis University, 2001), 41.

21. Tim Cole, *Selling the Holocaust: From Auschwitz to Schindler, How History is Bought, Packaged, and Sold* (New York: Routledge, 1999).

22. Tim Cole, *Selling the Holocaust: How History is Bought, Packaged, and Sold* (New York: Routledge, 1999), 29.

23. Ronald Berger, *Fathoming the Holocaust: A Social Problems Approach* (New York: Aldine de Gruyter, 2002,) 144.

24. As cited in Joyce Angler, "Three Thousand Miles Away: The Holocaust in Recent Works for the American Theater," in *The Americanization of the Holocaust*, ed. Hilene Flanzbaum (Baltimore and London: Johns Hopkins University Press, 1999), 125.

25. As cited in Hilene Flanzbaum, ed., *The Americanization of the Holocaust* (Baltimore and London: Johns Hopkins University Press, 1999), 1.

26. More recent scholarship is challenging this view, presenting more nuanced analyses showing that Holocaust consciousness was nascent, albeit in more subtle and indirect ways. For example, in *While American Watches*, Jeffrey Shandler shows how American television indirectly touched on the Holocaust in the early postwar years, as the industry was building a national audience for the medium. In "Defining Lessons: The Holocaust in American Jewish Education," Roma Sheramy shows how Jewish educators responded to pressure to downplay the tragic features of the European Jewish wartime experience by constructing heroic narratives of the war.

27. Between 1953 and 1961, the popular television show, *This is Your Life*, devoted nine segments to the successful postwar lives of Holocaust survivors, including that of Hanna Bloch Kohler, who survived Westerbork, Theresienstadt, Auschwitz, and Mauthausen. Lili Meier, a survivor of Birkenau, was chosen as *Queen for a Day*, another popular show of the 1950s, when she said, "Each time I look down at my left arm and see my tattoo I am reminded of my terrible past.... If only I could have my tattoo removed." Moreover, in the late 1950s, *Playhouse 90*, the American television drama, presented an average of one Holocaust-related drama for each of its five seasons. One of its most famous episodes, *Judgement at Nuremberg*, aired on April 16, 1959, and two years later it was made into a Hollywood movie; see Jeffrey Shandler, *While America Watches:*

Televising the Holocaust (New York and Oxford: Oxford University Press, 1999), 50.

28. Deborah E. Lipstadt, "America and the Memory of the Holocaust," *Modern Judaism* 16, 3 (1996), 204.

29. Edward Tabor Linenthal, *Preserving Memory: The Struggle to Create America's Holocaust Museum* (New York: Columbia University Press, 2001), 6.

30. Wiesel finally found a publisher willing to take a chance on his Holocaust memoir, *Night*, which appeared in 1960. Hilberg's manuscript, which grew out of his doctoral dissertation, was eventually published by Quadrangle Books, after a Holocaust survivor family agreed to subsidize the press $15,000 "in payment for copies that were to be shipped as donations to libraries." See Ronald J. Berger, *Fathoming the Holocaust: A Social Problems Approach* (New York: Aldine de Gruyter, 2002), 148–49.

31. Nathan Glazer, *American Judaism* [1957] (Chicago: University of Chicago Press, 1989), 172.

32. As cited in Deborah E. Lipstadt, "America and the Memory," 196.

33. Stephen J. Whitfield, "The Holocaust and the American Jewish Intellectual," *Judaism* 28 (Fall 1979), 391–401.

34. Rochelle E. Saidel, *Never Too Late to Remember: The Politics Behind New York City's Holocaust Museum* (New York: Holmes & Meier, 1996), 32.

35. Deborah E. Lipstadt, "America and the Memory," 196.

36. Jeffrey Shandler, *While America Watches: Televising the Holocaust* (New York and Oxford: Oxford University Press, 1999), 81–132.

37. As cited in Novick, *The Holocaust in American Life* (Boston: Houghton Mifflin, 1993), 133.

38. As cited in Judith Miller, *One by One by One* (New York: Simon & Schuster, 1990), 222.

39. Ibid., 222.

40. As cited in Novick, *The Holocaust in American Life* (Boston: Houghton Mifflin, 1993), 139.

41. Novick, *The Holocaust in American Life*, 134.

42. Deborah E. Lipstadt, "America and the Memory," 206.

43. Alan Mintz, *Popular Culture and the Shaping of Holocaust Memory in America* (Seattle and London: University of Washington Press, 2001), 11–15.

44. He also ordered the publication of documents from the Vatican Secretariat of State archives to show that, contrary to Hochhuth's portrayal, Pius was not guilty of moral cowardice and "silence" in the face of the Nazi onslaught.

45. James Young, "America's Holocaust: Memory and the Politics of Identity," in *The Americanization of the Holocaust*, ed. Hilene Flanzbaum (Baltimore: Johns Hopkins University Press, 1999), 70.

46. Deborah E. Lipstadt, "America and the Memory," 207.

47. Roma Sheramy, "Defining Lessons: The Holocaust in American Jewish Education" (Ph.D. diss., Brandeis University, 2001), 57.

48. As cited in Edward Tabor Linenthal, *Preserving Memory: The Struggle to Create America's Holocaust Museum* (New York: Columbia University Press, 2001), 9.

49. As cited in Nathan Glazer, *American Judaism* [1957] (Chicago: University of Chicago Press, 1989), 184–86.

50. As cited in Peter Novick, *The Holocaust in American Life* (Boston: Houghton Mifflin, 2000), 150.

51. Jonathan S. Woocher, *Sacred Survival: The Civil Religion of American Jews* (Bloomington: Indiana University Press, 1986), 131.

52. In the summer of 1961, Jews made up two-thirds of the white Freedom Riders who traveled into the South to desegregate interstate transportation. In 1964, Jews constituted between one-third and one-half of the Mississippi volunteers; see Chaim I. Waxman, *Jewish Baby Boomers: A Communal Perspective* (Albany: State University of New York Press, 2001), 6.

53. As cited in Chaim I. Waxman, *Jewish Baby Boomers: A Communal Perspective* (Albany: State University of New York Press, 2001), 5.

54. Roma Sheramy, "Defining Lessons: The Holocaust in American Jewish Education" (Ph.D. diss., Brandeis University, 2001), 108.

55. Stuart Rosenberg, "The New Jewish Identity in America," in *The Challenge of America: Can Judaism Survive in Freedom*, ed. Jacob Neusner (New York: Garland Publishing, 1993), 289.

56. A series of legal confrontations between the municipal government of Skokie and the National Socialist Party of America (NSPA) garnered national attention as a test of American civil liberties. The neo-Nazis enlisted the American Civil Liberties Union to sue the village of Skokie over violations of the neo-Nazis' First Amendment rights to freedom of speech and assembly. Subsequent court cases and appeals to the Illinois Supreme led to an eventual victory for the NSPA.

57. Shandler, Jeffrey, *While America Watches: Televising the Holocaust* (New York and Oxford: Oxford University Press, 1999) 185.

58. See Alan Mintz, *Popular Culture and the Shaping of Holocaust Memory in America* (Seattle and London: University of Washington Press, 2001).

59. Roma Sheramy, "Defining Lessons: The Holocaust in American Jewish Education" (Ph.D. diss., Brandeis University, 2001), 98.

60. Edward Tabor Linenthal, *Preserving Memory: The Struggle to Create America's Holocaust Museum* (New York: Columbia University Press, 2001), 25.

61. Roma Sheramy, "Defining Lessons," 98.

62. As cited in Peter Novick, *The Holocaust in American Life* (Boston: Houghton Mifflin, 2000), 227.

63. For an interesting set of discussions on the controversy, see Ilya Levkov, ed., *Bitburg and Beyond: Encounters in American, German and Jewish History* (New York: Shapolsky Publishers, 1987).

64. The controversy continued, though, when in November 1987 a large cross was installed on the convent building; it was subsequently removed, but another cross was planted in the convent garden. Six more years elapsed before the Pope asked the nuns to move. In 1995, eight years after the deadline, the convent was gone but the cross remained.

65. Lynn Rapaport, "Hollywood's Holocaust: *Schindler's List* and the Construction of Memory," in *Film and History* 32, 1 (2002), 55.

66. Hilene Flanzbaum, ed., *The Americanization of the Holocaust* (Baltimore and London: Johns Hopkins University Press, 1999), 7.

67. Jeffrey Shandler argues that, over the past two decades, television dramas and documentaries have contributed to the "rise of the survivor" as a distinctive ideal

type embodying exceptional courage, nobility, rectitude, and moral authority. See Jeffrey Shandler, *While America Watches: Televising the Holocaust* (New York and Oxford: Oxford University Press, 1999), 183–210.

68. Steven Cohen and Arnold Eisen, *The Jew Within: Self, Family, and Community in America* (Bloomington: Indiana University Press, 2000), p. 138.

69. Andrew Wallenstein, "Shoah Business," *Moment* 27, 2 (April 2002), 51–55.

70. Most notable are Peter Novick, *The Holocaust in American Life* (Boston: Houghton Mifflin, 1993); Normal G. Finkelstein, *The Holocaust Industry: Reflections on the Exploitation of Jewish Suffering* (London and New York: Verso, 2000); and Tim Cole, *Selling the Holocaust: From Auschwitz to Schindler, How History is Bought, Packaged, and Sold* (New York: Routledge, 1999).

71. Remarks made at "The President's Conference on Jewish Culture and Identity in the 21st Century," Hebrew University in Jerusalem, May 2002.

72. As cited in Debra Kaufman, "Post Holocaust Identity Narratives: A Sociological Approach to Collective Consciousness, Memory and History," (unpublished conference paper).

73. Berel Lang, "Jewish Culture," *American Jewish Yearbook* 98 (1998), 153.

74. As cited in Edward Shapiro, *A Time for Healing: American Jewry Since World War II* (Baltimore: Johns Hopkins University Press, 1992), 216.

75. As cited in Samuel Freedman, *Jew vs. Jew: The Struggle for the Soul of American Jewry* (New York: Simon & Schuster, 2000), 344.

11 Long-distance nationalism: American Jews, Zionism, and Israel

STEVEN T. ROSENTHAL

Even in comparison with the rest of the history of the Diaspora, the relationship of Zionism and Israel to American Jews has long been notable for its ironies and contradictions. In the prestate era, even though Zionism was largely irrelevant to American Jews, their extraordinary efforts at fundraising and political support made possible the very birth of the Jewish state. Since 1967, once Israel was established, there has been no other country whose citizens have been as committed to the success of another country as American Jews have been to Israel. Nevertheless, the vast majority of American Jews have remained astonishingly ignorant of the object of their devotion. In spite of all of their support for and obsession with Israel, the Jewish state has had relatively little effect on the religious and cultural life of American Jews. The key to these apparent contradictions lies in the fact that, from the beginning to the present, American Jews' response to Zionism and Israel has been circumscribed by American priorities and needs. From their early indifference to Zionism, through a quarter century of unequivocal support for Israel following its foundation, to the breakdown of consensus in the 1970s and 1980s leading to the present fragmentation, American Jews have related to Israel primarily through their American identity.

Beginning in the nineteenth century, European Zionists and American Jews were diametrically opposed in spirit, ideology, worldviews, and lifestyle. Classical Zionism saw anti-Semitism as all pervasive, ineradicable, and impervious to the liberalism in which American Jews had placed their trust. Believing that diasporic life was inevitably doomed, Zionists maintained that the only solution was for all Jews to emmigrate to Palestine and form a state of their own where they could fully and safely live out authentic, Jewish lives. As Zionism competed with the Diaspora-based doctrines of socialism, bundism, and assimilation, it began to emphasize that life for Jews in exile was degrading and humiliating. Herzl's colleague, Max Nordau, sounded these themes at the first Zionist Congress of 1897.

The emancipated Jew is insecure in his relations with his fellow man, timid with strangers and suspicious even of the secret feelings of his friends.... He has become a cripple within and a counterfeit person without, so that like everything unreal, he is ridiculous and hateful to all men of high standards.[1]

In retrospect, this proved to be a moderate statement of condemnation, as later Zionist "negation of the Diaspora" became so bitter as to be nearly indistinguishable from the anti-Semitism to which it was presumably an antidote.

Zionist ideology had little effect on American Jews, whose optimistic pragmatism and already half-fulfilled hopes in America contradicted the jeremiads of European Zionism. At best, Zionism appeared irrelevant; at worst, it raised the specter of dual loyalties. In 1864, the burgeoning American Reform movement had repudiated the messianic restoration of the old Jewish state; three decades later its leading figure, Isaac Meyer Wise, referred to political Zionism as the result of "the momentary inebriation of morbid minds."[2] The small American Zionist movement that arose in response to the increased persecution of East European Jews rejected the notion of total ingathering and the revolutionizing of Jewish life, emphasizing instead the charitable task of alleviating the misery of their East European brethren. The fact that Emma Lazarus, whose poetry so celebrated America as a refuge for the oppressed, was an early Zionist underscores the gap between the European and American movements.

Only when American Zionism was able to demonstrate its compatibility with American patriotism did it gain broad appeal. The principal architect of this change was Louis Brandeis, a Supreme Court judge, whose personal example and intellectual formulations reassured American Jews that their adherence to Zionism did not compromise their primary identity. For Brandeis, the Zionist ideal was a reflection of both the American spirit and of the progressive political and social programs with which he identified in the larger society. A Jew became a better American as he or she worked to further the principles of freedom in Palestine. Ignoring Zionist ideology, Brandeis directed the American movement to concentrate on the tasks of economic and agricultural development in Palestine. The success of "practical Zionism" only reinforced the American movement's priorities. However, when asked by Chaim Weizmann, then-president of the Zionist Organization, to give up his Supreme Court seat in order to devote himself full time to Zionism, Brandeis refused. During a 1927 visit to the United States on a fundraising mission, Weizmann felt it necessary to imply to potential donors that no Jewish state was contemplated.[3] In accepting at face value Weizmann's assurance, most American Jews began a pattern of willful ignorance for half a century that enabled their vast ideological differences with Zionism to be submerged in the practical work of relief and development.

American Jews' response to the rise of Hitler demonstrated that their American priorities extended to other areas of Jewish concern. Although American Jews agitated against the 1939 British White Paper that effectively closed Palestine as a refuge and pushed for increased immigration quotas to America, their efforts were limited by fears of alienating their fellow citizens. As one frustrated Zionist leader noted, "The American Jew thinks of himself first and foremost as an American citizen. This is a fact whether we like it or not."4 The war and the horror of the Holocaust transformed American Jews' relationship to Zionism. A Jewish state could provide a haven for survivors, help assuage American Jews' guilt at their failure to save European Jewry, and provide a powerful counterweight to the image of Jewish passivity. American Jews now embraced the idea of a Jewish state en masse and acted with an unprecedented communal self-assertiveness. By 1945, over 2.5 million American Jews, almost half of the population, belonged to organizations that endorsed the goal of a Jewish state. Between the end of the war and 1948, they contributed an astonishing 400 million dollars for Israel's relief, development, and defense. In fact, it was American influence in the World Zionist Organization (WZO) that helped move Zionism to a policy of noncooperation with Great Britain. Abandoning their fears of dual loyalty, American Jews launched a campaign of mass publicity that convinced the American public to endorse the creation of a Jewish state. It was their equally persistent lobbying that induced President Truman to disregard the advice of the State Department and support the creation of Israel at the United Nations and to use American influence to urge others to do so.

The emergence of the state of Israel had an immense effect on American Jews. It provided new pride and self-respect, a model of progressive liberalism, a source of Jewish identity, and a reason for belief in the post-Auschwitz age. Mesmerized by the state's symbolic power, most American Jews were content to support Israel without question and to enthusiastically provide whatever financial and political aid the Israeli government deemed appropriate. While to some degree this was the natural result of Israel's assuming responsibility for its own affairs, the new state strove to demonstrate its independence from its principal supporters by trumpeting the antidiasporic rhetoric it had long deemphasized in the name of unity. Almost immediately after independence, Prime Minister David Ben Gurion, who may have been seeking to deflect demands by American Zionist leaders for power sharing, launched a bitter verbal assault informing American Zionists that they must emigrate to Israel because life in the Diaspora was doomed and that, despite all America's freedom, it was a spiritual exile. He went on to say that any Zionist who remained in America was not a Zionist and any Jew who lived in exile was an inferior Jew. Having reduced American Zionism to a defensive posture, Ben Gurion now moved against its power base. By transferring fundraising from the WZO to the newly formed United Palestine Appeal, he replaced knowledgeable, sophisticated Zionist veterans with a community-based leadership largely unfamiliar with the issues of state building.[5] While this mobilized a vast constituency, it left the American Jewish relationship with Israel largely in the hands of those emotionally committed to the state, but intellectually equipped to do little more than sincerely write checks for its support.

Most American Jews were simply oblivious to these changes precisely because they related to Israel emotionally and symbolically. They perceived the Jewish state as a collection of clichés – as a secular nation of go-getters who made the desert bloom, as religion in progressive action, and as a Middle Eastern outpost of American values. These somewhat contradictory but always benevolent images were vital to American Jews' self-conception and to their presentation of Israel to the larger society. An even more powerful myth for American Jews was the Zionist notion that Israel was the culmination of Jewish history. Unlike most of Zionist ideology, this belief was enthusiastically embraced as appropriate to the social and psychological needs of American Jews. As American Jewry was assimilating its way toward what Charles Silberman would call "the first free Diaspora society,"[6] overt religious expression declined and Judaism became increasingly nostalgic and emotional. To equate Israel with Judaism was a comforting way to avoid the encumbrances of religion by focusing ones' Jewishness on a secular state 8,000 miles from home.

If Zionism had not tempted American Jews with a physical refuge, it at least provided a psychological one. Synagogues, the new mainstay of American Jewish life in the postwar era, became Israel-centered. A new class of Jewish professionals, such as educators, community relations specialists, and fundraisers, arose in the suburbs. They soon discovered that Israel was the most effective means to counter the growing religious indifference of their constituencies. Primarily in response to Israel's overwhelming need for financial and political support, new institutions such as the Jewish Federation and the Conference of Presidents of Major Jewish Organizations arose, and fundraising and lobbying increasingly defined American Jews' relationship to Israel. The sheer worthiness of the former and the general community of interest between Israel and the United States ensured that there was little resistance to taking direction from the Jewish state. However, the relationship may have been less deep than broad. *Aliya* (Jewish immigration to Israel), the sine qua non of Zionist commitment, was so low as to be a source of embarrassment to Zionists. Moreover, in the one major instance of deep disagreement between Israel and the United States regarding whether Israel should withdraw from the Sinai after the 1956 war, American Jews predominantly endorsed the position of their own government.

The Six Day War of 1967 was no less a watershed for the American Jewish relationship with Israel than for the Jewish state itself. Egypt's annihilatory threats, the magnitude of Israel's victory, and the Jewish state's new status as a target of the left wing all served to greatly strengthen the ties between American Jews and Israel. Any number of rapturous histories maintain that American Jews' unprecedented mobilization for and contributions to Israel represented a discovery of their deepest roots and feelings.[7] As unbounded relief and pride replaced dread, American Jews became conscious of their "real" priorities. Such accounts are correct yet incomplete. The Six Day War coincided with an identity crisis for American Jews. The Vietnam conflict and the rise of the Black Power movement had discredited the liberalism with which American Jews had so identified and destroyed the political coalition by which they related to the rest of America. American Jews saw that the same forces that attacked them as exploiters also castigated Israel as conquerors. They subsequently felt more politically and socially vulnerable than at any time since the Second World War. Their sense of parallel beleaguerment further strengthened identification with the Jewish state. Because the Black Power movement had made overt ethnicity acceptable, American Jews now felt free to express their commitment to Israel in ethnic as well as religious terms.

Feelings of pride and vulnerability determined the American Jewish relationship to Israel for the next fifteen years. Scholars spoke of Israel as "the very center of concern"[8] whose total and unquestioning support had become the principal component of "the new civil religion of American Jews."[9] Stephen Cohen's surveys for the American Jewish Committee (AJC) found one-third of American Jews to be passionately pro-Israel, one-third to be reflexively so, with 28 percent relatively indifferent, and only 5 percent antagonistic. Israel's new political vulnerability meant that lobbying increased in importance. The professionals of the Federation and the Conference of Presidents generally took their cues from the Israeli government. Emotional issues such as the infamous 1973 United Nations' vote equating Zionism with racism mobilized a large percentage of the community. Enforcing a unity of opinion among the rank and file was little problem for the Federation, since secular veneration of the Jewish state was combined with a kind of intense superficiality. For many non-Orthodox Jews, Judaism was increasingly defined as singing "Hava Nagila" but not learning Hebrew, visiting Israel with no thought of actually settling there, and generously giving to the Jewish state without getting involved in the issues surrounding its development. Israel's fierce internal debate over the establishment of Jewish settlements in the West Bank and Gaza after the Six Day War found little reflection among American Jews. For millions of American Jews, criticism of Israel was a worse sin than marrying out of the faith. They generally accepted the notion that diasporic criticism of Israel was immoral or dangerous and further supported world anti-Semitism. Even a small dissident organization such as Breira, which in the early 1970s called for negotiations with the Palestinians on the basis of Israeli security, elicited shock and loathing from the mainstream Jews, who often strove to demonstrate the impropriety of raising such issues rather than debate the issues among themselves. It was telling that the only issue that did elicit American Jewish establishment criticism of Israel was Prime Minister Golda Meir's instructions to American Jews to vote for Nixon in the 1972 election. Jewish leaders regarded this as unwarranted interference in American affairs.

The tenure of Prime Minister Menachem Begin (1977–83) marked the beginning of a new independence for American Jews in their relations with Israel. On the one hand, the end of the Labor Party's political monopoly and the emergence of the right-wing Likud meant there was no longer one Israel from which to take direction. On the other hand, new political developments such as the peace treaty with Egypt increased Israel's security and presented its government with a range of controversial choices. As American Jews responded to these new conditions, consensus gave way to a gradually widening fragmentation: first, private criticism of Israel, as public expression was still inhibited by old fears; then, public disagreement with the Jewish state by individuals. New political conflicts then gave rise to an overt split between American Jewish organizations and various Israeli governments, and finally to attempts by some American Jewish organizations to actually override the policies of the Jewish state by lobbying Congress and appealing to the American Jewish public.

While Prime Minister Begin reaped great and justifiable praise for concluding a peace treaty with Egypt, his harsh interpretation of the Camp David Accords and his continued establishment of Jewish settlements on the West Bank caused the first cracks to appear in the united front of mainstream American Jewry. Although hardly reflecting the level of conflict within Israel, internal debate grew and various groups placed newspaper advertisements supporting or condemning settlement building and the peace process as a whole. In a July 1980 *New York Times* advertisement, fifty-six mainstream Jewish leaders urged that land should be traded for peace.[10] Still, such rising public expression of criticism was limited by the tripartite relationship among Israel, American Jews, and the rest of society. Whenever the Jewish state was criticized by outsiders – by the United Nations for settlement policy or by the media for bombing PLO headquarters in Beirut – American Jews, equating Israel's vulnerability with their own, would usually swallow their private misgivings and circle the wagons.

A series of political and cultural crises or flash points over two decades helped strip away the idealized image of Israel and gradually redefined the relationship between American Jews and the Jewish state. Israel's invasion of Lebanon in 1982 led to the first mass show of independence by American Jews. Although the campaign was presented by Israel as a limited incursion, Israeli forces, directed by Defense Minister Ariel Sharon, soon pushed toward Beirut with the objective of routing out the PLO. American Jews felt increasing anxiety about Israel's disregard of its self-imposed geographical limits and the large number of civilian casualties. Once again, the American Jewish establishment publicly supported the invasion, and world criticism of Israel inhibited most public outcry. The massacre of hundreds of Palestinian civilians in the Sabra and Chatilla refugee camps by Christian rightist forces allied to Israel elicited unprecedented anxiety, soul searching, and public criticism by American Jews. To supporters of the Israeli government, this criticism stemmed from American Jews' embarrassment at Israel's failure to reflect American values and bespoke a dangerous naïveté about Middle Eastern realities. American Jewish critics responded by noting the unprecedented amount of criticism *within* Israel and feared that the massacre imperiled American support. At the very least, Sabra and Chatilla and its aftermath called into question the cherished notion that Israel was qualitatively different from other states and revealed to American Jews that Israeli leaders were just as prone to stupidity, arrogance, and mendacity as any other politicians.

The Pollard affair three years later led to the most serious breach yet in the history of the American Jewish–Israeli relationship. In November 1985, Jonathan Jay Pollard, an American Jewish civilian employed by the U.S. Navy, was arrested on charges of spying for Israel. The international relations equation was reversed, and enraged American Jews took the lead in not only denouncing the operation as monumentally stupid for imperiling special relations between both countries, but also in demanding punishment of those responsble. Unaccustomed to being lectured by their American cousins, Israelis reacted bitterly. Shlomo Avineri, political scientist and former director-general of Israel's Ministry of Foreign Affairs, accused American Jews of demonstrating a "cringing" exile mentality and of being motivated by fears of dual-loyalty. It was not simply American Jews' fear of dual-loyalty accusations that had elicited such emotion, but anger that Israel had put at risk its special relationship with America, a connection that was so vital to American Jews. Many leading American Jews wrote "replies" to Avineri, emphasizing the courage of American Jews in defending settlement building and the invasion of Lebanon. As Abraham Foxman, the head of the Anti-Defamation League, wrote, "However much we were disconcerted by those policies we never shrank from our Jewishness nor did we waver in our support for Israel. And we aren't 'cringing' when we disavow Israeli espionage against the U.S. in the strongest terms."[11]

As successive Israeli governments seemed beset by failure and paralysis, independent words turned to deeds. In late 1985, a delegation of American Jews under AJC auspices met with Jordan's King Hussein and Egypt's President Hosni Mubarek. In responding to right-wing Likud criticism that "the world must know that Israel represents the Jewish people on Jewish problems," the AJC reply demonstrated the growing new perspective of American Jews. Besides trying to find openings to peace, the mission also served "the not unimportant purpose of reaffirming the independence of Jewish communities everywhere and our commitment to the democratic character of American Jewish life."[12]

The Palestinian Intifada, which began in December 1987, vastly increased American Jewish criticism of Israel. American Jews were appalled by images of Israeli repression of the rebellion. Convinced that the revolt demonstrated the hopelessness of continued occupation of the West Bank and Gaza, increasing numbers of American Jews began to criticize not simply specific government actions but the whole thrust of its foreign policy. American Jews became sharply divided, with the left side criticizing Israeli repression and calling for a peace conference, and the right side in turn accusing the left of political naïveté and self-hatred. For almost two months, enraged American Jews visited Israel to express their concerns and Jewish periodicals were filled with polemics against Prime Minister Shamir. On a daily basis, individuals and organizations announced their withdrawal of financial support. Reflecting these divisions, an ad hoc group of American Jewish activists and academics engaged in an unprecedented initiative on December 7, 1989. After meeting unofficially with Yasir Arafat, they announced that the members of the PLO were sincere about peace and the United States should end its ten-year ban on talking to them. Given that one week later the administration decided to renew discussions with the PLO, it appears that the most radical of American Jews had acted as a catalyst in influencing American policy against Israeli desires. By 1990, about three-quarters of American Jews declared themselves to be in favor of talks with the PLO, and the traditional consensus among Israel, American Jewish leaders, and the rank and file had broken down.

The Intifada had greatly expanded the permissiveness of open display of American Jewish dissent. The increase in Israeli security resulting from the collapse of the Soviet Union and the defeat of Iraq during the 1990–91 Gulf War further encouraged disunity within the American Jewish community. American Jews were divided when, in September 1991, President Bush tied a loan for the absorption of Soviet Jews to an Israeli suspension of the West Bank settlement building. While the American Jewish Committee told Israeli Prime Minister Shamir that he had to choose between settlements and guarantees, the American Israeli Public Affairs Committee (AIPAC), which by the mid-1980s had become the principal pro-Israel lobby, worked so furiously for both as to earn a later rebuke from Yitzhak Rabin when he became Prime Minister.[13] Not even an attack by Bush on the power of the Jewish lobby led to the kind of automatic clinging to Israeli policy as in the past. Eighty-five percent of American Jewish leaders rejected Prime Minister Shamir's refusal to give up one inch of territory. Even more portentous for the Israeli right wing was the fact that seventy-five percent of American Jewish leaders were in favor of a settlement freeze.[14] The new political openness was indicated by the reception given by the mainstream to the New Jewish Agenda, whose advocacy of a Palestinian state was much more radical than Breira's program of two decades earlier. Instead of total rejection, the New Jewish Agenda was given a hearing and even a place on some Jewish community councils.

By raising the possibility of a peace treaty with the Palestinians, the election of Yitzak Rabin in August 1992 led to new levels of public disagreement. In America, the religiously Orthodox and politically conservative, who had long equated public Jewish criticism of Israel with treason, now excoriated the Rabin government as too willing to trade land for peace. As conflict within Israel approached a bitterness that would result in Rabin's assassination, Israeli politicians, especially on the right, moved to co-opt American Jews into the rough and tumble of Israeli politics. Many came to America to raise funds and build new constituencies, which were only a fax transmission away. Israel's ambassador to the United States, Itamar Rabinovich, found himself in the unfamiliar position of "having to argue with our own supporters on the merits of the peace process."[15] The now-public display of intra-Jewish conflict at times assumed an *opera buffa* quality. In July 1993, Tom Dine, the longtime head of AIPAC, was forced to resign for referring to Orthodox Jews as "smelly and low class,"[16] while two weeks later one of his vice presidents met a similar fate for calling dovish Deputy Prime Minister Yossi Beilin "a little slime ball."[17] Those who valued community discipline above all could only look with nostalgia on the recent past when the prohibition against washing dirty laundry in public was enough to keep conflict private. American Jews had evidently become secure enough in their own position and that of Israel so as not to worry so much about "what will the gentiles say?"

Yitzhak Rabin's conclusion of the Oslo Peace Treaty with the Palestinians in October 1993 mobilized the right wing in both Israel and America. The political importance of American Jews, especially to Israel's right, became evident when opposition leader Benjamin Netanyahu chose the Op-Ed page of the *New York Times* to condemn the proposed Israeli–PLO Peace Treaty as another Munich.[18] The Oslo Accords elicited almost universal condemnation among the American Orthodox, while the support of the mainstream, who were nervous about security issues, was broad but less than enthusiastic. In a further overturning of traditional boundaries, the opposition Likud directed its American supporters to lobby Congress to cut off aid to the PLO and to transfer the American Embassy to Jerusalem by May 1999. The passage of either measure would sabotage peace negotiations, and the Rabin government opposed both proposals. Nevertheless, even such a mainstream an organization as AIPAC endorsed the Jerusalem bill. American Jewish politics were in such disarray that Rabin complained, "Never before have we witnessed an attempt by U.S. Jews to lobby Congress against the policies of a legitimate democratically elected Israeli government."[19]

The assassination of Rabin and the election of Benjamin Netanyahu exacerbated divisions in the United States no less than in Israel. The extremely harsh criticism of the right wing, which had accused Rabin of selling out Israel, was replaced by the more moderate criticism of the left wing, which accused Netanyahu of sabotaging the peace process. However, it was Netanyahu's religious policies that led to the most bitter and protracted split between Israel and American Jews. In April 1997, the Orthodox parties in the Knesset, without whom Netanyahu could not govern, proposed the passing of a law in which conversions to Judaism performed by non-Orthodox rabbis would not be recognized. American Jews, 85 percent of whom are non-Orthodox, reacted with unbridled rage. As Rabbi Eric Yoffie, one of the leaders of the American Reform movement, fumed, "if Reform rabbis in Israel are not rabbis and their conversions are not conversions, that means our Judaism is not Judaism, and that we are second-class Jews."[20] The American Jewish media filled with indignant letters and editorials, which expressed resentment that the legal power of the state was used against American Jews. Many Jews withheld their customary donations, and the United Jewish Appeal experienced a $20 million shortfall. As the Israeli ambassador reported, "Jewish organization leaders have warned us clearly that this will lead to the worst crisis ever between American Jews and Israel."[21] While even after more than five years the dispute has yet to be resolved, the Knesset's failure to pass the "conversion law" is directly the result of American Jewish pressure.

American Jewish displeasure with Netanyahu over religion and his negative attitudes toward the Oslo Accords produced the widest split between
mainstream American Jewry and an Israeli administration. As the United
States pressured Israel to move the Oslo process forward by further withdrawal from the West Bank, the principal American Jewish lobbies, AIPAC
and the Conference of Presidents, refused three direct appeals from the
Netanyahu government to issue statements supporting him in his opposition. At the Wye River Peace Conference convened in October 1998 to
implement the provisions of the Oslo Agreement, Netanyahu rejected a
13 percent withdrawal from the West Bank in return for Palestinian promises
to fight terrorism, and he threatened to desert the conference. When the Conference of Presidents refused to support his departure, the prime minister
reluctantly signed the Wye Agreement.[22] This evolution of American Jews'
relationship with Israel from one of obedience to self-assertion is the product
of the independent judgment that they have developed in the past quarter
century.

The traumatic events of the first two years of the twenty-first century
have superficially reinvoked old patterns. At the July 2000 Camp David Conference convened to reach a final settlement, Prime Minister Ehud Barak
offered the Palestinians 94 percent of the West Bank, autonomy in East
Jerusalem, and religious control of portions of the Temple Mount. When
Yasir Arafat refused to budge from his maximalist demands or even offer
counterproposals, peace, which seemed so close, remained as elusive as ever.
A few weeks later, sustained rioting erupted in response to a visit by opposition leader Ariel Sharon to the Muslim Holy Places. Rock throwing gave way
to gunfire, and the so-called second Intifada spread across the West Bank,
Gaza, and into Israel itself. Scores of Palestinians were killed by Israeli gunfire and, in an incident that symbolized the utter failure of peace, two Israeli
reservists who made a wrong turn in Gaza were stabbed and beaten to death
by a mob that then mutilated their bodies. As Prime Minister Barak continued
his desperate and futile negotiations with the Palestinians, his conciliatory
approach was rejected by the Israeli people in favor of the presumed firmer
policies of Ariel Sharon, elected as Prime Minister in March 2001.

American Jews, who had placed so much hope in the Oslo Agreements,
felt betrayed by Arafat, who made no effort to restrain the violence, and
were angry at European criticism of Israel's alleged "overreaction." They now
united around Israel with a renewed fervor. Ironically, they found themselves
supporting Ariel Sharon, the man whose policies in Lebanon had led to the
first great revolt of American Jews against Israel in 1982. Their suspicions of
Sharon and their uneasiness with the civilian casualties caused by the Israeli
response to terrorism at first served to moderate their political support. As

Palestinian terror groups began a campaign of suicide bombing, the whole-sale cancellation of trips to Israel by Jewish organizations and individuals caused widespread Israeli resentment.[23]

The World Trade Center catastrophe in September 2001 provided new complexities and dilemmas for American Jews, but it did not fundamentally alter their patterns of independence from Israel. In the days after the attack, fear that American support of Israel would be blamed for the tragedy vied with the hope that the attack had demonstrated the danger of Muslim ter-rorism to the whole world. However, America's war planning soon revealed a more complex reality. In order to build a Muslim coalition against terror, the United States befriended Israel's enemies and pressured the Jewish state to moderate its response to Palestinian terrorism. By and large, the majority of American Jews supported President Bush's call for Israeli restraint.[24]

By Spring 2002, the accumulation of suicide bombings, capped by the massacre of twenty-nine people at public seder in Netanya, led American Jews to give even greater support to the Israeli government. The seemingly endless suicide bombings, European condemnation of the resulting Israeli assault on the West Bank, and the execution of Jewish journalist Daniel Pearl by Muslim terrorists convinced some American Jews that Israel and per-haps even all Jewry were in existential crisis.[25] However, for the majority, it was their independent evaluation of the situation on the ground that led them to support Sharon's harsh retaliatory measures against the Palestinians, whatever their reservations concerning his ultimate vision for the West Bank.

On April 15, the largest pro-Israel rally in three decades took place in Washington, D.C. Organized by the Conference of Presidents and the United Jewish Communities, it drew well over 100,000 people. With speakers in-cluding Benjamin Netanyahu, Rudolph Giuliani, and Deputy Secretary of Defense Paul Wolfowitz, the gathering had an unmistakably pro-Sharon bias. The prevalent siege mentality led many Jewish organizations to re-frain from publicly expressing any internal dissent from Israeli policy.[26] Rabbi David Saperstein, head of the Religious Action Center for Reform Ju-daism, expressed the dilemma of the liberal camp. "This has been a difficult time. Palestinian suicide bombers and Yasser Arafat's moral and political bankruptcy in terms of leading the path back to the diplomatic table has not left the people who believe in [former Prime Minister] Rabin's vision with a political program to follow."[27] Those who publicly disagreed with the Is-raeli government's policies such as *Tikkun* editor and activist Rabbi Michael Lerner and former president of the American Jewish Congress, Henry Sieg-man, made little impact on the mainstream. However, American Jews' rally-ing around the Sharon government was different from the kind of knee-jerk support that existed in the 1970s and 1980s. American Jews now backed

Israeli policy because of their independent reading of the military and political situation. Their general belief that harsh retaliation was the most appropriate and effective defense against suicide bombers became the lowest common denominator of political support.

In late June, President Bush stunned even the strongest supporters of Israel by taking the Israeli position that if any progress were to be made toward peace, Arafat, as an incorrigible supporter of terrorism, would first have to be removed. In contrast to the heavy requirements for change placed on the Palestinians, this speech made few immediate demands on Israel with regard to the occupation and West Bank settlements.[28] As suicide bombings began to abate, and Israel, now unequivocally supported by the world's only superpower, seemed to be less imperiled, the line of public communal solidarity began to waver. Small groups of Jews, concerned about the morality and effectiveness of the Israeli policy, began to place newspaper ads and to mount demonstrations against the Sharon government. When Israel killed fifteen civilians, including nine children, by using an aircraft-deployed "smart bomb" to assassinate the military commander of Hamas, mainstream Jewish organizations did not hesitate to criticize the Jewish state. In the months after the Bush speech, the world and American Jewish focus on the Israeli–Palestinian conflict abated. Israel's reoccupation of much of the West Bank greatly reduced the incidence and severity of suicide bombing. Instead of implementing a program to remove Yasir Arafat, the Bush administration became far more concerned with ousting Saddam Hussein; the possibility of war with Iraq replaced the Israeli–Palestinian conflict on the front pages. While American Jews still rallied to the strong defense implemented by Ariel Sharon, beyond that lowest common denominator the community remained extremely divided over any vision of ultimate peace. When Israel ultimately finds a credible negotiating partner, there is no doubt that American Jews will revert to their now-customary public fractiousness.

It is again ironic that their general support of Israeli policy may mask a decline in the importance of Israel to American Jews. While the volume, intensity, and variety of public discussion of Israel has increased among the committed American Jews, fewer may be listening or caring. American Jewish support of Israel has declined, and the percentage of funds allotted to Israel by American Jewish fundraising has similarly dropped. These trends are especially pronounced in the younger generation. Stephen Cohen has found that, for every ten-year drop in age, there is a 5 percent decline in support for Israel.[29] One of the principle concerns of fundraisers is how to build bridges to the younger generation.

Such trends are in part the inevitable result of the passage of time. Those who experienced the Holocaust and the birth of Israel are passing on. The emotions associated with these events, even those memories of unimaginable horror and boundless ecstasy, lose potency over generations. Israel's heroic age has similarly passed. The desert *has* bloomed. Millions of immigrants have been absorbed, the country has defended itself against great odds, and it has produced a high culture with democratic values. Fractious normalcy has replaced the emotional high points of the founding of the state, the Six Day War, and the Entebbe raid. A contemporary video clip of young Israeli soldiers manning a checkpoint in East Jerusalem simply lacks the emotional resonance of the image of their fathers praying at the newly liberated Western Wall.

In a larger sense, this new distancing is the result of the failure of Israelis and American Jews to create any great common cultural bonds. The prediction of Zionist thinker Ahad Ha Am that a Jewish state would serve as a spiritual center for a Jewishly revived Diaspora has remained much more of a dream than a reality. As Arthur Hertzberg noted, "little has been written about Israeli culture and it remains a mystery except perhaps to Israel itself."[30] The existing gulf in world view, history, and daily life between Israeli and American Jews may be nearly impossible to bridge, even without the additional obstacle of different languages. The empowerment of Israel's Sephardic population, of different cultural heritage than most American Jews, has only widened the separation. Far from being internally transformed by Israel, the majority of American Jews remained ignorant and skeptical. A 1989 poll indicated that less than 66 percent of American Jews knew the year Israel was founded, and less than 40 percent knew when the West Bank was acquired.[31]

Other bases of the bond between American Jews and Israel are also weakening. The secular, humanistic Zionism with which American Jews have so identified has become passé – commentators readily speak of a "post-Zionist" era[32] – and the religious nationalism that seeks to replace it inspires few American Jews but the ultra-Orthodox. Fundraising, long the centerpiece of the relationship, is becoming less vital as American Jewish contributions now equal less than 1 percent of Israel's Gross National Product. In January 1994, Deputy Prime Minister Yossi Beilin shocked a gathering of American donors by stating that their charity was no longer needed.[33] Nevertheless, Israeli economic development *has* made fundraising less crucial while the end of political consensus has hindered the unified political lobbying that has historically been the other major task of American Jews. Lacking a sense of urgency and of common purpose at least until the second Intifada, American Jews have increasingly focused on their own internal problems.

The problems of American Jewry are considerable. The fact that less than half of American Jews belong to a synagogue, that most spend less than three days a year there, and the existence of a 50 percent rate of intermarriage have raised doubts about the future of the American Jewish community. Among many Jewish professionals, there has been a belated recognition that a half-century of obsession with Israel has prevented the laying of the spiritual, cultural, and intellectual bases for future generations. This is something of a false dichotomy. Even the vicarious identity that Israel provides is, for many Americans, the major focus and expression of their Jewishness. Indeed, the most publicized "solution" to the problem of "Jewish continuity" has been the foundation of "Birthright Israel," a program that hopes to stimulate Jewish identity by providing college students with a free ten-day trip to Israel. At the very least, Israel has, for two generations, furnished what might be a rearguard defense against the cultural and social forces that have assimilated almost all immigrant groups. However, American Jews' identification with Israel has largely failed to reinforce other aspects of Jewishness, and the strength of that identification is by no means assured. This is precisely where a great irony may lie – that for all American Jews' concern and obsession, their evolving relationship with Israel might be simply a way station on the road to assimilation.

Notes

1. Max Nordeau, "Address before the First Zionist Congress," in Arthur Hertzberg, *The Zionist Idea* (New York: Greenwood Publishing, 1970), 239.
2. Walter Laqueur, *A History of Zionism* (New York: Holt, Rinehart & Winston, 1972), 402.
3. Yonathan Shapiro, *Leadership of the American Zionist Organization* (Chicago: University of Illinois Press, 1971), 126.
4. Ibid., 420.
5. Samuel Halperin, *The Political World of American Zionism* (Detroit: Wayne State University Press, 1961), 327.
6. Charles Silberman, *A Certain People* (New York: Summit Books, 1985).
7. Melvin Urofsky, *We Are One* (Garden City: Doubleday, 1978), 358–59.
8. Daniel Elazar, *Community and Polity* (Philadelphia: The Jewish Publication Society, 1976), 107.
9. Jonathan Woocher, *Sacred Survival* (Bloomington: Indiana University Press, 1986), chapter 3.
10. "Key U.S. Jews Back Israeli Peace Move," *New York Times* (2 July 1980), A1, A3.
11. Abraham Foxman, "Israeli hutzpa," *Jerusalem Post* (17 March 1987), 10.
12. Henry Siegman, "Independence of the Diaspora," *Jerusalem Post* (26 September 1985), 8.
13. Clyde Haberman, "Rabin and Pro-Israel Group off to Testy Start," *New York Times* (22 August 1992), 2.
14. Sabra Chartrand, "On Visit To U.S., Shamir to Find Jews are Dovish," *New York Times* (21 November 1991), D-23.
15. Thomas L. Friedman, "Writing New Rules for Criticizing Israel from Afar," *New York Times* (11 July 1993) Section 4, p. 3.

16. Thomas L. Friedman, "A Second Top Pro-Israel Lobbyist Is Forced Out After Insulting Jews," *New York Times* (2 July 1993), A4.

17. Ibid.

18. Benjamin Netanyahu, "Peace In Our Time," *New York Times* (5 September 1993), E11.

19. Marilyn Henry, "PM Blasts American Jews For Lobbying Congress Against Government," *Jerusalem Post* (1 October 1995), 1.

20. Joel Greenberg, "Orthodox Conversion Bill Gains In Israel," *New York Times* (2 April 1997), A6.

21. Haim Shapiro, "Ben-Elissar Warns of a Rift With U.S. Jews," *Jerusalem Post* (22 October 1997), 1.

22. Stephen Erlanger, "Israel Threatens to Abandon Talks, Then Backs Down," *New York Times* (22 October 1998), A1, A12.

23. Julie Wiener, "Israel Summer Teen Programs Push ahead Despite the Hard Sell," *Jewish Telegraphic Agency* (19 March 2001), 1. Yigal Schleifer and Ina Friedman, "Not This Year in Jerusalem," *The Jerusalem Report* (20 May 2002), 12–18.

24. Janine Zacharia, "Is the Enemy of My Enemy My Friend?" *Jerusalem Post* (6 November 2001), B2.

25. Jodi Wilgoren, "Unnerved," *New York Times* (22 April 2002), A12. American Jewry To Launch Emergency Campaign For Israel, *Jewish Telegraphic Agency* (2 April 2002), 1.

26. (Israeli Consul General) Allon Pinchas interview by author, 19 June 2002.

27. Anthony York, "Endangered Species: The Jewish Dove," *Salon Magazine* (25 April 2002), 1 (salon.com/politics).

28. Elisabeth Bugmiller and David Sanger, "Bush Demands Arafat's Ouster Before U.S. Backs A New State: Israelis Welcome Tough Line," *New York Times* (25 June 2002), A1, A10.

29. Stephen Cohen, "Israel in the Jewish Identity of American Jews: A Study in Dualities and Contrasts," in *Jewish Identity in America*, ed. David Gordis and Yoav Ben-Horin (Los Angeles: Susanand David Wilstein Institute of Jewish Policy Studies, 1991) 132.

30. Arthur Hertzberg, "One Hundred Years Later a Jewish Writer's Time Has Come," *New York Times* (31 March 1991) sec VII, 1.

31. Stephen Cohen, "Israel in the Jewish Identity," 124.

32. Laurence J. Silberstein, *The Post Zionism Debates* (New York: Routledge, 1999).

33. Clyde Haberman, "Israel Debates Taking Charity," *New York Times* (1 February 1994), A-3.

12 Life cycle rituals: Rites of passage in American Judaism

RELA MINTZ GEFFEN

Every religion, ancient and modern, has special rites of passage tied to both biological and sociological events that typify life. These rituals flow seamlessly from birth through puberty, marriage, and death. During the past half-century, rites have been created to match newly recognized passages. As people live longer and, in America, become more affluent and thus gain leisure time, newly conceptualized stages emerge, such as adolescence, midlife, empty nest, menopause, and golden age. In addition, family formations have shifted, leading to new rituals.[1] In Judaism, special life cycle rituals have surrounded birth, puberty, marriage, death, and mourning. At the same time, traditional rites have been revised and expanded, particularly as a result of the influence of the women's movement. Mothers, as well as fathers, have sought and even demanded inclusion in birth, adolescent, and marriage rituals for themselves and for their daughters.

This essay is focused on factors within and outside of the communal life of twentieth-century American Jewry that enhanced the salience of the traditional rites of passage accompanying birth, puberty, marriage, and death. Particular attention is paid to developments in the American Jewish cultural and religious context of the last quarter of the twentieth century.[2] The contraction, expansion, and transformation of rites of passage is explored within several of the many expressions of American Judaism. The impact of the Jewish feminist movement that grew out of the Conservative movement and spread to Modern Orthodoxy and Reform, the empowering of laity through the *Havurah* and New Age spirituality movements, and the reintroduction of traditional rituals to Reform Judaism are considered as formative elements enhancing the significance of life cycle rituals in contemporary American Jewish life.[3] Conversely, the impact of the feelings of alienation and exclusion generated in those Jews who do not "fit" the typical life cycle or who lack Jewish social circles with whom they can celebrate or mourn is addressed.

THE UBIQUITY AND POWER OF
LIFE CYCLE RITUALS

The existence of passages and rites to mark them is a universal characteristic of human civilization. Communal rituals that mark special moments
are part of the life story of those who attend the ceremony as well as of those
in the extended family of the celebrants. In theory, the rituals belong to all
who are present, reminding them of similar rites held by strangers at far-off
times and places as well as personal ones that they have attended. Thus,
participating in a public Jewish ritual links individuals to other Jews across
space and time, tying their personal histories to that of the Jewish people.

Emile Durkheim, the great French sociologist, wrote about the importance of public ritual life for the maintenance and strengthening of group
norms. He noted, for instance, that people who would have attended the
wedding feel cheated when a bride and groom elope. During Jewish wedding ceremonies, many couples relive their own special moment and may
even mouth the words of the wedding formula or of the seven benedictions
being recited under the *huppah* (wedding canopy). The religious community
is conceptualized as the extended family writ large, a clan or tribe. Communal norms are reaffirmed for all as the onlookers vicariously relive their own
most intense moments of commitment through public ritual. When there is
no public ritual, the norms of the community are not reaffirmed.

The familiarity of the ritual enhances its power, infusing it with communal and historical meaning for the celebrants and reinforcing memories
of similar moments in the lives of the onlookers. Understanding this aspect of human nature, the rabbis ordained that many of life's passages be
marked in the presence of a quorum, the minimum definition of community. For this reason, circumcision, marriage, and recitation of *kaddish* (the
mourner's prayer) require the presence of a *minyan* (ten Jews over the age of
thirteen).

The communal context is further reinforced through the prescription of
a *seudah shel mitzvah* (commanded feast) at circumcisions and weddings,
with special introductions and interpolations added to the *birkat hamazon*
(grace after meals) to mark the occasion. Commensality, the sharing of a
communal meal, often with special foods included in the banquet, is the
focal point of religious events in many ancient and modern religions. The
Jewish calendar is replete with customs linked to consumption of special
food, the epitome of which is the Passover Seder. The connection between
life cycle rituals and food is less remarked but equally powerful. For example, chickpeas, a symbol of fertility, are customarily served at circumcision
feasts.

Some life cycle events such as birth, puberty, illness, and death are biologically determined, whereas others, including adolescence, marriage, divorce, and midlife owe more of their identities to social invention. Over time, these differentiations tend to blur and even disappear as social convention gains precedence over biological determinism.

For example, the fact that the celebration of Bar and Bat Mitzvah originally marked the onset of puberty has become irrelevant to their celebration in the present day. In large suburban American synagogues, shared celebrations often occur, giving rise to the sometimes amusing spectacle of *bnai mitzvah* of vastly differing physical and intellectual maturity sharing the honors. Nevertheless, the celebrants are still within an age range close to puberty, maintaining the legal fiction of the biological connection. This is so despite the failed attempt late in the nineteenth and early in the twentieth centuries by the Reform movement to replace Bar Mitzvah with Confirmation at age sixteen or eighteen to be more consonant with American high school graduation, which symbolized adulthood at that time. One of the first confirmation ceremonies in America took place at Temple Emanu-El of New York on Shavuot in 1848. As in the case of the public wedding rite, holding a public confirmation on Shavuot became a reenactment of the Sinai Covenant for the entire congregation. The logic of social maturity occurring much later than physical maturity was not powerful enough to overcome the attachment to traditional practice.

Actually, within *halacha* (Jewish law), attaining the status of Bar and Bat Mitzvah was always fixed to a certain age regardless of the physical maturity of an individual child. This suggests that, even in ancient times, there was a sociological as well as a biological dimension to reaching the age of responsibility for fulfilling the commandments.

THE DEMOCRATIC NATURE OF JEWISH RITES OF PASSAGE

Life cycle commemorations are, arguably, the most democratic of Judaism's rituals. Assuming a society in which most Jews are born, reach puberty, marry, birth children, and die, each man or woman is entitled to celebrations or commemorations surrounding each event. Traditionally, men and women were not entitled to the same public ritual marking of each of these stages, but at least within gender all were theoretically equal. Concerned that this fundamental egalitarian principle not be compromised, the rabbis of the Talmud (*Mo'ed Katan* 27a–b) decreed that rich and poor alike should be buried on the simplest of biers in plain shrouds. Like the Amish code, the rabbinic message conveyed the sense that "plain" is the highest accolade.

However, there were clearly problems with maintaining these standards. In late medieval and early modern times, rabbis in some European Jewish communities invoked sumptuary laws restraining ostentation at life cycle events. They limited the number of guests, the number of food courses, and even the jewels that could be worn by the host families. Clearly, the temptation of conspicuous consumption is not a contemporary invention.

Demographic and sociological changes in the life patterns of many American Jews have posed more recent challenges to the democratic nature of Judaism's rites of passage. On the one hand, the democratic nature of these rituals has been enhanced by the breakdown of the gender differentiations in most of the Jewish community. On the other hand, the diminution of the number of Jews who go through the passages of marriage and childbirth and the increase in those who experience them but in circumstances alien to the Jewish tradition, such as with Christian or same-sex partners, makes for a fragmented community in which many Jews are always onlookers but never personally experience the traditional rites. In fact, they may be alienated from Judaism by the constant emphasis on and centrality of life paths from which they are, whether by choice or happenstance, excluded. Nevertheless, the dominant trend of the past quarter century has been toward increased observance of traditional Jewish rites of passage, albeit with contemporary embellishments.

LATE TWENTIETH-CENTURY EVOLUTION OF LIFE CYCLE RITUALS

As a result of a confluence of factors internal to Jewish life and community, and of contextual trends in American society more generally, rites of passage have become an important vehicle for exploring and evoking religious community, identity, and spirituality in contemporary American Judaism. There are several internal factors promoting the new rites of passage.

The first is the increased level of Jewish education of American Jewish adults and their consequent familiarity with existing life cycle rituals. Not only are many more Jewish children attending supplementary religious schools, but there has been a dramatic increase in day school attendance from kindergarten through Grade 12. The first individuals who were part of this increase are now forming their own families. Many of them have also been to Jewish summer camp, participated in youth movements, and gone on extended educational trips to Israel. The burgeoning of Jewish studies on the college campus has also enlarged the number of adult Jews who have studied Jewish law on a higher level. Finally, the last decade of the twentieth century saw an explosion of adult learning across all of the religious movements. Many of these courses took as their subject matter the Jewish calendar and life cycle rituals.[4]

The second factor promoting new rites of passage is the lessening of clericalism and enfranchisement of the laity exemplified by the Havurah movement. From its inception in the 1960s, leaders of the Havurah movement insisted that every member of the community was responsible for leading rituals, or, at the very least, being an active participant in worship. The role of the rabbi and cantor were deemphasized and innovation in liturgy was encouraged.

A third factor was the Reform community's greater acceptance of and education toward the practice of home ritual, including openness to such practices as the dietary laws and *mikvah* (immersion in the ritual bath). While during its classical phase, Reform Judaism eschewed ritual practice as vestigial, beginning in the 1960s a range of customs were gradually reintroduced to public and private liturgy.[5] For example, Bar and Bat Mitzvah, *aliyot* to the Torah for lay people, carrying the Torah around the synagogue for congregants to touch and even to kiss, and the use of Hebrew in the liturgy are now commonplace in Reform congregations, along with lively communal singing and chanting of liturgy, such as Debbie Friedman's settings of the traditional healing prayer and the *Havdalah* ritual ending the Sabbath. With the adoption of the newest version of the Pittsburgh Platform in 1999, Reform Jews officially embraced *mitzvot* (observance of ritual commandments) between people and God in a way that could not have been predicted even twenty-five years ago.[6]

The fourth factor leading to innovations in rites of passage is the growing openness to conversion to Judaism of the past quarter century. The outreach movement and the sophisticated, compelling introduction to Judaism classes for adults that the Jewish partner attended with the potential convert brought with it experimentation in the ritual arena.

The drive of the feminist movement to include women in traditional rituals and to create new ones, where none previously existed, to mark moments of significance in women's lives was the fifth factor promoting innovation.[7] There is some evidence that coming-of-age rituals for girls of the age of twelve gradually developed in Europe during the past 200 years. However, the idea was not crystallized in America until Judith Kaplan celebrated with her family in the synagogue of her father, Rabbi Mordecai Kaplan, in New York in 1922. In the late 1950s and during the sixties and seventies, synagogue Bat Mitzvah rituals were more fully developed in Conservative and then Reform synagogues.

Although Bat Mitzvah emerged in the first half of the century, it was with the women of *Ezrat Nashim*, literally, "the help of women," the Jewish feminist consciousness-raising group that emerged out of the New York Havurah in the early 1970s, that more intensive reworking of life cycle rituals began. The traditional liturgy had to be expanded to include mothers' names in circumcision and naming ceremonies and to create covenantal ceremonies to welcome baby girls to the world. Sometimes the focus was bringing women in; in other instances, such as the creation of childbirth or menopause rituals, the aim was to enable women to give expression to the power of their experience when the rabbis had failed to recognize passages salient to them.

A sixth internal factor spurring ritual innovation was the emergence of new family forms. Lifelong singlehood, single-parent households, remarried couples with children in tow who were "yours, mine, and ours," gay and lesbian couples – all of these configurations have led to the development or modification of rituals.

Finally, partly through a neo-Hasidic influence and partly as a result of societal factors, a greater search for spirituality among liberal as well as traditional Jews in the closing decade of the past century provided a framework within which experimentation was welcomed. Taken together, these seven trends have led to innovative rituals for passages for which no rites existed in the tradition. They have also led to the reconceptualization and reinterpretation of existing rites of passage.

Contextual, external factors have also enhanced or led to innovative expressions of spirituality. The first of these is the fluidity of American society and the growth of a generalized search for meaning through personalized religion. Wade Clark Roof, an important scholar of American Protestantism, has dubbed Americans "switchers."[8] He opines that, in contradistinction to people in the rest of the world, Americans view religion as changeable. This willingness to experience religion in a fluid way has profoundly influenced American Jews.

The second external factor mirrors an internal one. It is the legitimation of new family forms in U.S. society. The ability to celebrate the differences in "alternative lifestyles" is made possible by their growing acceptance in the society at large. Thus, if gay marriages are at issue in general elections, or if surrogate mothering makes it possible for gay men to father children through artificial insemination, or if the law of the land permits adoption by lesbian couples, then it is easier for Jewish gays and lesbians to follow suit.

The third and final external factor leading to the creation of new rites of passage is the multicultural and individualistic ethos that has led non-Jews to explore *Kabbalah* (Jewish mysticism) and other aspects of Judaism as a path for their own spiritual growth. If it is good enough for Madonna and Michael Jackson, then it becomes the vogue for Jews to follow non-Jews and take their own heritage more seriously.[9]

Having briefly sketched out the internal and external factors encouraging the burgeoning of life cycle ritual in the context of the universal cultural and religious import of rites of passage, the remainder of this essay is devoted to concrete examples of new or embellished rites of passage.

WELCOMING BABY GIRLS INTO THE JEWISH COVENANTAL FOLD

One of the first active steps taken by the burgeoning Jewish feminist movement in the mid-1970s was to write ceremonies to publicly sanctify the entry of Jewish baby girls into the covenant. Jewish baby boys had benefitted from multiple ceremonies for generations – *ben or shalom zachor* on the Friday night after birth – a party with protective Torah study and special foods before the boys were named; the actual covenantal ceremony, *Brit Milah*, with all of its elaborate mystery and joy; and, for firstborn sons of non-priest-related mothers, the rite of *pidyon haben*, the redemption of the firstborn son from sacred service, on the thirtieth day after birth.

Daughters, in contrast, often had no ceremonial welcome at all, or were named in a brief ceremony on a Torah reading day as soon after the birth as possible, and often with few family members or friends present and almost never in the presence of the baby girl or the new mother. Over the past thirty years, numerous versions of *Brit Bat* (the covenant of a daughter) or *Simhat Bat* (the joy of a daughter) ceremonies have been developed for home and synagogue usage by parents and rabbis alike. It has become necessary for parents to explain why they are not having a ceremony, rather than why they are having one. In other words, public welcomes for baby girls have become normative in American Judaism.[10]

Typical ceremonies include these: a formal welcome by those present as the baby is carried in; spelling the Hebrew name out with biblical verses; explaining the rationale for the names given to the child; the priestly benediction; the traditional naming prayer; an expression of thanks for return to good health by the mother; and a series of short blessings including the one over wine and sometimes in the format of the seven benedictions of the traditional Jewish wedding ceremony (*sheva brachot*) and special added benedictions to the grace after meals after the festive meal (*seudah shel mitzvah*) that accompanies the ritual. Usually booklets are printed and distributed that announce the name and provide a "script" for the ceremony so that all present may participate.

THE PROLIFERATION OF EXPLANATORY MANUALS

The development of printed scripts for birth ceremonies for baby girls has had ramifications for other life cycle rituals. These manuals serve as vehicles for innovation and as educational tools to enable assimilated Jews and the growing number of non-Jews who attend Jewish life cycle rituals to understand and follow what is going on before them. Booklets in honor of baby girls led to similar ones for Brit Milah (circumcision) ceremonies.

These, in turn, led to bridal manuals that announce the names and relationships of the participants as and explain the nuances of all aspects of the traditional Jewish wedding ceremony along with any special prayers or props unique to a particular wedding. Thus, a wedding booklet might include the fact that the bride's mother made the huppah or that the bride is carrying a Bible given to her grandparents. In the case of interfaith marriages, booklets are now written expaining symbols utilized from the different faiths. Gay and lesbian wedding booklets note their uses of and modifications of traditional passages.

A later addition to the booklet phenomenon has made its appearance at Bar and Bat Mitzvah ceremonies. Here the service at the particular synagogue is detailed along with the names of the individual family and friends participating in the service and sometimes the names of charitable organizations to which the celebrant has donated a percentage of his or her gifts or for whom he or she has done a Mitzvah or service project.[11]

Finally, the first generation of booklets for funerals are now available. These typically include a brief biography of the deceased, his or her favorite charities, a psalm, the address where the family is sitting *shiva* (the seven-day period of traditional Jewish mourning), and service times and printed driving directions to the house of mourning from MapQuest. I was told by one Jewish funeral director that this idea was copied from Catholic funeral homes, who pioneered the map idea.

The proliferation of explanatory manuals of various types has been a by-product of: the search for roots; the reclamation of public ritual by the laity; the availability of technology; the deliberate "push" of the Jewish feminist movement; and the recognition that both Jews and a growing number of non-Jews want to be active listeners and participants in these rituals.

THE TRANSFORMATION OF WEDDING CUSTOMS

By the middle of the twentieth century, most American Jewish weddings had become Protestant in character. The signing of the *Ketubah* (marriage document) usually took place in private and brides marched down the aisle on their father's arm to the strains of Lohengrin's famous "Here Comes the Bride." Rabbis in black robes added English vows to the ceremony, and bride and groom carefully chose popular music for their first dance.

By the end of the century, a revolution had occurred. Elaborate neo-Hasidic groom's "tishes" with speeches interrupted by song and shnapps; dancing the groom to the bride who sat on a thronelike chair where he publicly performed the "badeken" and veiled her for the ceremony; the wearing of a *kittel* (white robe) by the groom over his formal American suit; the commissioning of elaborate calligraphied *ketubot*; the bride and groom each marching down with their parents to recognizably Jewish music and the proliferation of Klezmer bands and Jewish dancing – all attested to the new era.

In addition to the reinstitution of traditional rituals, albeit with a more egalitarian cast (e.g., brides circled the grooms and then the grooms circled the brides), innovations abounded. Brides and grooms from the more liberal movements in Judaism immersed themselves in the mikvah (ritual bath), fasted, and read the confessional the morning before the wedding in a spirit of renewal prior to beginning a new life. Some couples wrote the words of their own marriage documents and spoke to each other under the huppah. Whereas in the traditional ceremony the bride was passive, it became normative for the bride and groom to exchange rings and for the ceremony to be more reciprocal. Family members and friends participated in addition to clergy, sharing in the recitation of the traditional seven benedictions. The breaking of the glass that closed traditional weddings was invested with new meaning after Jerusalem was reunified, and clever marketers of Judaica urged couples to gather the shards and send them to special craftspeople who turned the broken glass into *mezuzot* for the first home of the newlyweds.

Finally, at some interfaith weddings and gay and lesbian commitment ceremonies, Jewish traditions were adapted to the new situations. Interfaith couples were wed under canopies and broke glasses at the close of the ceremony, often in syncretistic rites that included Christian clergy, ceremonial readings, and ritual objects. At commitment ceremonies, the last of the seven benedictions was rewritten to reverberate with the joy of *kol kallah v'kol kallah* – "the voice of the bride and the voice of the bride" instead of the voice of the groom and the voice of the bride. Inclusion was clearly the dominant trend, though it was difficult to know which of these trends would persist and which would wither during the next twenty-five years.

CONCLUSION

The flow of the life cycle affords an opportunity for human beings to mark off time and express the meaning in their lives through rites of passage celebrated in community. For American Jews, living in an era of impersonality and immersed in the corporate life of the world of work, these moments based on sentiment, family ties, and friendships enhance life immeasurably. Experiencing special moments by participating in ancient rituals in the context of a religious community and within the horizontal and vertical connections with Jews in other times and other places across time and space deepens the joy and mitigates the sadness of life and death.

Within contemporary American Judaism, life cycle rituals have also become a major vehicle for the expression of the social and political trends in communal life. Thus, the politics of Jewish feminism, the reclamation of public worship and ceremonials by the laity, the embrace of new family constellations, and the recognition of new stages such as adolescence and midlife have all been marked by innovative or enhanced rites of passage.

Notes

1. For an expansion of these ideas, see Rela M. Geffen, "Introduction," in *Celebration and Renewal: Rites of Passage in Judaism,* ed. Rela M. Geffen (New York: The Jewish Publication Society, 1993), 3–10.

2. Discussions of findings about the nature of the American Jewish Community in the last quarter of the twentieth century may be found in various analyses of the National Jewish Population Survey of 1990 and a variety of community studies completed during the decade of the nineties. See, for example, Sidney Goldstein, "Profile of American Jewry: Insights from the National Jewish Population Survey," *American Jewish Year Book* 92 (1992), 77–177. For an excellent analysis of these trends in one community, see Sherry Israel, *Community Report on the 1995 Demographic Study* (Boston: Combined Jewish Philanthropies, 1997). For a popular treatment of the developments in the decades of the 1960s and 1970s, see *The Jewish Catalog,* 3 vols., ed. Michael and Sharon Strassfeld (Philadelphia: The Jewish Publication Society, 1973–80).

3. For more about the Havurah movement, see Bernard Reisman, *The Chavurah: A Contemporary Jewish Experience* (New York: Union of American Hebrew Congregations Press, 1977), and Riv-Ellen Prell, *Prayer and Community: The Havurah in American Judaism* (Detroit: Wayne State University Press, 1989).

4. The recently released findings of the UJC National Jewish Population Survey of 2000–01 clearly document the expansion of participation in the more intensive forms of Jewish formal and informal education. For details, see the section on Jewish Connections in *Strength, Challenge and Diversity in the American Jewish Population, A United Jewish Communities Report of the NJPS 2000–01* (city: publisher, 2003), 7–15.

5. For the text of the original Pittsburgh Platform of 1885 and later platforms of the Reform movement from Columbus and Los Angeles, see the classic work, Michael A. Meyer, *Response to Modernity: A History of the Reform Movement* (New York: Oxford University Press, 1988).

6. In striking contrast to earlier platforms, the 1999 Pittsburgh Platform states this:

> Through Torah study we are called to mitzvot, the means by which we make our lives holy. We are committed to the ongoing study of the whole array of mitzvoth and to the fulfillment of those that address us as

individuals and as a community ... We bring Torah into the world when we seek to sanctify the times and places of our lives through regular home and congregational observance ... And we mark the milestones of our personal journeys with traditional and creative rites that reveal the holiness in each stage of life.

7. On the development of the Jewish feminist movement, see, for example, Sylvia B. Fishman, "The Impact of Feminism on American Jewish Life," in *American Jewish Year Book* 89 (1989) and Rela Geffen (Monson), "The Impact of the Jewish Women's Movement on the American Synagogue; 1972–1985," in *Daughters of the King-Women and the Synagogue*, ed. S. Grossman and R. Haut (Philadelphia: The Jewish Publication Society, 1992) 227–37.

8. Wade Clark Roof, *A Generation of Seekers: The Spiritual Journey of the Baby Boom Generation* (New York: HarperCollins, 1993).

9. For a discussion of the power of individualism in American religion and in American Judaism in particular, see the explication of the concept of the sovereign self in chapter 2 of Stephen M. Cohen and Arnold M. Eisen's book, *The Jew Within – Self, Family, and Community in America* (Bloomington: Indiana University Press, 2000).

10. I have a collection of about sixty such ceremonies. Several graduate students have analyzed them to see which forms persist and which innovations did not "make it." The latest book about birth ceremonies for baby girls is Debra Nussbaum Cohen's *Celebrating Your New Jewish Daughter: Creating Jewish Ways to Welcome Baby Girls into the Covenant: New and Traditional Ceremonies* (Woodstock: Jewish Lights, 2001).

11. A recent (2003) addition to the literature on Bat Mitzvah is *Traditions and Celebrations for the Bat Mitzvah*, ed. Ora Wiskind Elper; this is an Orthodox guidebook published in conjunction with MATAN, The Sadie Rennert Women's Institute for Torah Studies and Urim Publications in Hebrew and English editions in Jerusalem and New York.

13 Choosing lives: Evolving gender roles in American Jewish families

SYLVIA BARACK FISHMAN

Jews have often regarded themselves as being exceptionally family oriented. In historical, premodern Jewish communities, and in many contemporary traditionalist societies, the family has been the basic building block of society. Societies have encouraged men and women to marry early, stay married, and remarry in the case of divorce or widowhood. A congruence of religious values, economic necessities, and cultural and societal pressures within traditional Jewish cultures have promoted marriage as the preferable marriage status providing a productive and salutary state in adulthood. This belief or conviction makes married adults and their families central, while it marginalizes the unmarried. This essay explores the impact of revisioning gender roles within the Jewish family within three contexts: the impact on society, the impact on the family, and the impact on the individual woman and man.

Jewish law prescribes specific behaviors for all members of the family unit, and thus it plays an important part in gender role divisions. For instance, little boys are socialized into the rigors of study and public prayer, while little girls are socialized into the endless demands of family and household. This dictates that women and men should share the vast majority of behaviors prescribed through a complex network of *mitzvot* (commanded behaviors). Thus, before Passover, males scour rabbinic texts and sources for new interpretations of Haggadic materials to bring to the Seder table, while females scour floors, cabinets, and closets.

Even though gender roles in traditional Jewish societies have been constructed around covenantal responsibilities, rabbinic law traditionally excuses women from many significant ceremonies and rituals. Sociological reasons are given for prohibiting women from activities such as leading or being a member of a *minyan* (prayer quorum). One reason is that many rabbis assume that the demands of family life make women unable to commit themselves to prayer on a regular basis throughout their lives. Another rabbinic explanation is that the presence of praying women among praying men could create sexual chaos. Both psychological and sociological reasons are given for discouraging women from participating in activities such as studying complex rabbinic texts. Some rabbis suggest that women as a group do not have the intellectual capacity to grasp the intricacies of Jewish law, or that they will trivialize what they study. Other rabbis worry that exposing women to textual materials of a sexual nature might teach them how to evade prescriptions for marital monogamy.

Despite these gender role constructions, traditional Jewish societies have not necessarily inculcated their members with the idea that women are incapable of being doctors, lawyers, or accountants. Jewish tradition does not socialize Jews to believe that men lose status if their wives earn more money than they do. The "public" spheres from which women are barred are the males-only religious arenas of the synagogue and study hall. The marketplace activism that might have seemed shockingly unfeminine to middle-class Americans has historically been an accepted female behavior among many pious Jews.

WESTERNIZED GENDER-ROLE CONSTRUCTION REPLACES HISTORICAL JEWISH PATTERNS

In the decades before and after the turn of the twentieth century in Imperial Germany, Eastern European Jews accommodating to German bourgeois values and behaviors "accepted middle class mores for the family and made them their own," as Marion Kaplan has convincingly demonstrated. Devoting themselves to the creation of obedient, soft-spoken, educated children and spotless, orderly homes, German Jewish women eschewed female labor force participation along with the shrillness and slovenliness that they associated with Eastern European households.[1] When Eastern European families emigrated to the United States, the Germanic values carried through, thereby discouraging married women to work outside the home for pay. These immigrants, now German Jewish Americans, became doubly adapted to life as full-time homemakers: first as German Jews assimilated to the bourgeois German pattern,[2] and second as German Jews adapted to the United States.[3] Eastern European Jewish women quickly adopted the Americanized pattern of looking down on outside employment for married women. Indeed, when financial necessity forced them to work, they often reinterpreted reality so that they could reply that they were not working outside the home for pay.[4]

The addition of voluntarism to domestic concerns among American Jewish women followed the Christian American and German Jewish pattern as the twentieth century proceeded. Like German Jewish bourgeois homemakers who acculturated by "adapting to styles of dress and manners of speech, moving out of predominantly Jewish neighborhoods into new ones, and accommodating to contemporary middle class attitudes toward work and achievement,"[5] American Jewish women absorbed American middle-class values into their notions of Jewish domesticity. In the United States, as in Germany half a century earlier, "women who did not work outside the home and who focused on the creation of domesticity were the *de facto* symbols of having 'made it' into the bourgeoisie." Focusing on home, children, and communal voluntarism, Jewish women "integrated" the "spirit" of two cultures. Partially because Christian middle-class society both in the United States and in Western Europe had high regard for women who devoted themselves to voluntary efforts on behalf of culture, education, and social welfare, Jewish women, like their Christian sisters, "found work, demonstrated competence, and built self-esteem" in Jewish local and national organizations.[6]

GENDER EQUALITY IN CONTEMPORARY JEWISH FAMILIES

What has made Jewish families "Jewish" in traditional societies is not their adherence to bourgeois norms of gender-role construction. Jewish family values have been expressed through the family's adherence to prescribed social behaviors, grounded in a perception of covenantal responsibilities. Within this matrix, clearly defined gender roles historically contributed to highly married and unusually stable societies. Some argue that families in which gender roles are clearly defined also contributed to marital serenity within the family unit and the mental health of individuals: men and women, boys and girls all knew what was expected of them. While some individuals might have had moments of chafing or rebellion, they had few occasions to confront the terrors of indecision afflicting many contemporary Americans with too many choices.

Today, American Jewish culture has adapted its norms of gender-role construction and has relocated its ethnic boundaries vis-à-vis many gender issues so completely that it can arguably be said to have reached a postfeminist state. The most completely mainstreamed changes in American Jewish gender-role construction focus on personal aspects of life: women's health issues, friendship circles, erotic liaisons, marriage, family relationships, childbearing, and childrearing. The attitude of American Jews toward women has been sweepingly more liberal than that of other American ethnic groups and than that of Jews in some other areas of the world, such as Israel and Latin America. American Jews, for example, are overwhelmingly committed to equal educational and occupational opportunity for women, and to reproductive choice. Thus, in the realm of personal choice, marriage, and family planning, the American community has by and large relocated its ethnic boundaries. Rather than being defined as a community that is highly prescriptive in its gender-role construction, American Jewish men and women today, especially outside of Orthodox communities, tend to be characterized by more permeable gender-role constructions than those found in many other groups.[7] Other societal changes involve professional development, such as education, vocational choice, and career advancement. While these are areas of feminist impact that Jewish women share with other American women, their attitudes are sometimes influenced by Jewish communal norms and values.

Many observers believe that nonmarriage is the greatest challenge to the population of the American Jewish community today, more so than changing gender roles or intermarriage.[8] A striking decline over the past three decades in the proportion of married Jews and in the fertility level of American Jewish women reflects the responsiveness of American Jews to middle- and upper-middle-class American culture. When American Jews married early and had their children early in the 1950s, they were following American and traditional Jewish patterns, which at the time had considerable overlap. When they married later in the 1980s and 1990s, they followed American patterns only. American Jews today are overwhelmingly likely to work toward graduate or professional training and to begin establishing their careers before they make a permanent romantic commitment. While Jewish young men and women were more likely than the general public to acquire a college education in the 1950s, 1960s, and 1970s, their eventual rates of marriage were almost universal. Today, while a substantial number of American Jews are marrying late, it is not clear whether many others will ever marry.

Recent research indicates that film and television can be contributing factors to extended singlehood in the Jewish community. The negative image of Jewish men and women that prevails in literature, the media, and popular culture is absorbed by Jewish men, coloring the way they look at Jewish women.[9] Thus, stereotypical images of Jewish women are more than insulting: They produce toxic relationships among Jewish singles, which work to undermine feelings of erotic attraction between Jews.[10]

The social trends that create large numbers of Jewish singles also affect the assumptions that wives and husbands bring to the family enterprise. Partially because they marry later, and partially because, even within marriage, career goals often initially take precedence over starting a family, contemporary Jewish families are smaller than they were in the 1950s and 1960s. Most American Jewish couples hope to have children "some day." Furthermore, research indicates that the vast majority of Jewish women still place an enormous value on having children and are less likely than any other religious or ethnic group to state that they wish to remain childless.[11] Unlike women of other ethnic groups, where higher education is associated with lower expectations of childbearing, the more highly educated a Jewish woman is, the more children she expects to have.[12]

Nevertheless, according to 1990 National Jewish Population Survey (NJPS) household data, highly educated Jewish women do not actually have as many children as they once expected to. Although Jewish career women are more committed to the idea of having families than any other group of career women, they are at least as likely as other white middle-class women to postpone the onset of childbearing until they have reached what they consider to be an appropriate level of financial or occupational achievement. Expectations do not always give way to reality, and, "as education increases among both Jewish men and women, the proportion with no children increases." Indeed, "among those with a masters degree . . . Jews have significantly higher levels of childlessness than non-Jews."[13] Working with the 1970 NJPS and the 1990 NJPS, Frank Mott and Joyce Abma point out that Jewish women between the ages of sixteen and twenty-six years who were interviewed in a national study in 1969–70 expected to have an average of 2.5 children. Today, that cohort ages thirty-five to forty-four, have in fact born an average of 1.5 children, and expect an average of 1.7 children completed family size.[14]

While one cannot measure with exactitude the impact of gender-equal family roles on the shrinkage of the Jewish family, egalitarianism in the form of women's career aspirations is certainly a factor, along with economic realities and changing social mores. However, egalitarian career goals do not necessarily correlate with smaller families. In households in which wife and husband have a high level of Jewish education and high levels of ritual observance, careers and family sizes of three, four, and more children coexist. A highly significant predictor of family size – independent of educational and career accomplishment – is Jewish traditionalism. Religiously traditional women have children earlier and have more children than less traditional women, as in the past. However, contradicting the patterns of past generations, ritually observant young Jewish women do not have less secular education or more modest career accomplishments than their less observant sisters.

Jewishly committed younger Americans, including many centrist and modern Orthodox Jews, do not substantially differ from the educational patterns characteristic of other Jews in their cohort. Indeed, as Moshe and Harriet Hartman have painstakingly demonstrated in their recent monograph, "the more involved in formal and informal Jewish social circles, the collective celebration of Jewish identity, and the closer to Orthodox affiliation, the higher is the educational achievement." Not only does traditionalism no longer have a negative impact on secular educational levels, but, even within individual households, "contrary to popular opinion, Orthodoxy is not associated with more spousal inequality: educational differences are even smaller than among the Conservatives, Reforms, and Reconstructionists." Simply put, younger Orthodox couples are the group most likely to be educationally matched sets.

When the narrowed gender gap and the positive relationship between secular education and Jewish connections are considered together, secular education for women emerges as being associated with stronger, not weaker, Jewish bonds. As the Hartmans note, "the relationship between Jewishness and education is slightly stronger for women than for men."[15] For many decades, Jewish women received more secular education than most non-Jewish women, but less education than Jewish men. The generally high level of secular education among American Jews resulted in an ironic disparity: among most non-Jewish Americans, the majority of men and women did not go much beyond high school, so the gender gap in secular education was relatively modest; among Jews, in contrast, men were far more likely and women somewhat more likely than other Americans to continue their education. Because of their higher levels of secular education in general, the educational gender gap among Jews was more striking. In contrast, in the 1990 NJPS data, a pattern of exceptional levels of educational achievement is characteristic of both men and women. Before and after the childbearing years, younger women's educational achievement more closely resembles their brothers than their Jewish mothers or non-Jewish sisters.[16] Only during childbearing years, ages thirty to thirty-nine, do Jewish women's mean years of secular education lag by half a year or more below that of Jewish men their age.[17] Among Jewish women ages thirty-five to forty-four, 24 percent have not gone beyond high school, 7 percent have some college or a two-year degree, 32 percent have completed their bachelor's degrees, 28 percent have master's degrees, and 10 percent have doctorate or professional degrees.

Just as the gender gap is closing in terms of secular education, it is also closing in terms of Jewish education. The Jewish educational profile of American Jewish women and men shifts across generational lines, with higher education overall among younger American adults than among the older cohort, which is due to the dramatic increases in the proportion of Jewish women who are receiving a Jewish education. The closing of the gender gap also offers some striking and perhaps surprising information along denominational lines. Among women ages twenty-five to forty-four, substantial (six or more years of multiday schooling) Jewish education was received by 53 percent of Orthodox women, compared with 26 percent of Conservative women, and 10 percent of Reform women. Among men the same age, 61 percent of Orthodox, 40 percent of Conservative, and 25 percent of Reform men received substantial Jewish education. In terms of substantial Jewish education, the gender gap is now smallest among the most traditionalist portions of the population. This may be tied to the high emphasis placed on Jewish education by traditionalist religious groups, and the prevalence of elementary through high school day school education among those populations.

For much of the twentieth century, high levels of secular education were tied to assimilationist lifestyles. Today, however, contradicting decades of earlier statistical data and lingering folk wisdom, contemporary young American Jews who have extensive secular education are, on average, more likely to participate in Jewish activities and establish Jewish homes, while modestly educated young Jews are more often estranged from Jewish organizations and behaviors, married to current non-Jews, and not rearing their children as Jews. Data from the 1990 NJPS show that high levels of educational and occupational achievement are frequently tied to current Jewish involvement. The positive correlation between high secular education and more Jewish lifestyles is especially dramatic when levels of Jewish education are also high. As a result, highly educated Jewish women, who represent the group most likely to have career aspirations, are not necessarily less Jewishly affiliated than stay-at-home mothers. This is an important point, because the majority of Jewish mothers do indeed work outside their homes for pay.

CONTEMPORARY QUESTIONS

Today, many Americans are agonizing over the health of the family, and a surge of "familist"[18] feeling has appeared repeatedly in both intellectual and popular venues. Many writers blame changing gender roles, specifically those induced by feminism, for the "decline" of the American family. "New familists" have mourned shifting trends in American marital status, and they have warned that these trends accompany social and moral decline and perhaps even the decline of Western civilization as we know it. To these observers, the normative two-parent, single wage-earner, monogamous, fertile family unit requires and instills the qualities of character that are necessary for the physical and moral vitality of individuals, households, communities, and states. Blankenhorn summarizes the six social functions of the family as procreation, socialization, affection, sexuality, cooperation, and pluralism, and he posits that normative family units are best designed to provide the context for balancing larger social needs with individual diversity.[19]

Familists of many faiths believe that contemporary preoccupations with the rights and material success of individuals have undermined a more productive emphasis on social groupings and their interwoven responsibilities. Bruce Hafen makes this argument:

> In familistic relationships, shared commitments and mutual attachments transcend individual self-interest. These relationships are rooted in *unlimited* personal commitment – not merely to another person, but to the good of the relationship and to the family entity as a larger order. Because of the unlimited nature of such commitments, detailed lists of rights and duties can neither describe nor prescribe a familistic relationship.

Contractual relationships, by contrast, combine solidaristic and antagonistic elements. By definition, these relationships are *always limited* in both scope and intensity. Parties enter a contractual relationship primarily because of self-interest, weighing their commitment to the relationship and calculating the return of profit, pleasure, or service.[20]

Profamily sentiments are brought to a broader audience by conservative media figures such as Dr. Laura Schlessinger, once "the most successful radio therapist in America," described as "an intense 49-year-old size 2 with permed hair, a jeweled Star of David around her neck, red-lacquered nails and the unmistakable air of someone who is always sure she's right." Schlessinger urges callers to think about spouses, children, and other family members – and about the family as a whole – rather than to focus on their own narrow needs. She asserts that religious guidance is a healthier influence on people than psychological counseling, which "promotes self-centeredness. . . . My morality is based on the Old Testament and the Talmud. Whenever I can, I try and push people toward religion."[21]

Other policy analysts and writers refute the familist vision of history and society, insisting that the mid-twentieth-century notion of the family is neither ancient nor universal, but instead shaped by modern economic, political, and social transformations. Moreover, they point out that unlimited personal commitment was expected only of women in most traditional societies. Women, not men, were expected to sacrifice personal goals for the good of the family unit. In contrast, Barbara Ehrenreich suggests that American men prided themselves on rugged individualism in the supposed heyday of family values, and they frequently neglected families and abandoned relationships as the spirit moved them. Ehrenreich charges that it was men's "flight from commitment" in the 1950s and 1960s that provided fertile ground for feminist growth in the 1970s.[22] Judith Wallerstein and Sandra Blakeslee, themselves supporters of the traditional family unit because of the corrosive effect that divorce often has on children, observed that the men they studied who initiated divorce proceedings always had an extramarital romantic involvements, whereas the women they studied who initiated divorce almost never did but instead were unhappy with the quality of the marital relationship.[23]

In analyzing the impact of changed gender-role construction on the Jewish family, one of the difficulties in proceeding with these questions is that axiomatic assumptions about men, women, and families in traditional Jewish societies have often differed from those of society at large. Notions of what comprises the "public" and "private" spheres, for example, have been radically different among Jewish traditionalists than among their Westernized neighbors. In modern Western societies, women were often perceived as being innately more religious and churchgoing than men, while commercial arenas were perceived as dangerous public spaces inappropriate for delicate females. In contrast, in many traditional Jewish communities, synagogues were primarily male domains, while women were assumed to have practical skills for the world of commerce.

Many observers within the Jewish community share a sense that Jews have something extra at stake in the dialogue about gender equality in family life. Within traditional Jewish families in traditional Jewish societies, fathers and mothers have clearly defined, complementary, and largely diverging roles. Upon hierarchical distinctions, including gender distinctions, Judaism has built and reinforced a concept of the sacred family absorbed in sacred tasks.

It is therefore not surprising that underlying the practical, social, sociological, and psychological concerns, existential questions sometimes surface. Isaac Bashevis Singer, in his subversive story *Yentl the Yeshiva Boy*, has his boyishly clad heroine look into the mirror miserably one night:

> Only now did Yentl grasp the meaning of the Torah's prohibition
> against wearing the clothes of the other sex. By doing so one deceived
> not only others, but also oneself. Even the soul was perplexed, finding
> itself incarnate in another body.

It is appropriate to acknowledge the fact that many people are, at least occasionally, touched by uneasiness with the concept of total gender equity in families and society. Some wonder whether men and women are capable of enough unselfishness for families to thrive without one partner taking on the task of the designated enabler.

DIVORCE AND CHANGING GENDER ROLES

One practical concern about the impact of changing gender roles is the possible repercussions such flux has on the viability of relationships in married households. The American Jewish family not only is formed later than in the recent past but also is often less durable as well. National data show that Jewish women with master's degrees have the highest overall level of divorce, although the data do not indicate whether these degrees were earned before, during, or after divorce proceedings were initiated. The overall divorce rate among Jewish males is 6 percent, compared to 7 percent of all white American males. The overall divorce rate for Jewish women is 10 percent, compared with 9 percent of all white American women. The disparity in divorced status for women and men illustrates the fact that divorced men remarry more quickly than women, and that many second wives are not Jewish.

Divorce has increased in all segments of the Jewish community, although there is an inverse relationship between the traditionalism of the household and the likelihood of divorce, with households strongly connected to Jewish behaviors and community showing lower rates of divorce than those with weak connections. Divorce is twice as likely to terminate a mixed-married relationship as an in-married Jewish household. Conversely, once a Jewish–Jewish couple has divorced, the ex-spouses are twice as likely to marry non-Jews the second time around than they were when entering into a first marriage.

Almost one-third of American Jewish children live in homes that have been affected by divorce: about one-fifth of Jewish children live in two-parent households in which at least one parent has been divorced, and one-tenth of them live in single-parent households. More children are living in single-parent households and in "blended" families as stepchildren. The number of Jewish single-parent families, like the number of divorces, seems deceptively small at first glance, but because of the generally low Jewish birthrate, they are a significant factor in the number of households with children. In single-parent households, usually headed by women, annual income is in general severely diminished, when compared with the income of both divorced men and married couples. These financial discrepancies indicate that gender equality has certainly not been achieved where money is concerned.

GENDER EQUALITY CAN ENHANCE MARITAL RELATIONSHIPS

While more marriages may fail today because women are less likely to be trapped socially and economically than in the past, marriages that succeed have been shown to incorporate much more fulfilling roles and choices for women. Marital stability between certain kinds of people can arguably be strengthened rather than disrupted by feminist social change. Indeed, Wallerstein and Blakeslee found that egalitarianism enhanced marital relationships:

> [Couples'] marriages had benefited from the new emphasis in our society on equality in relationships between men and women. However they divided up the chores of the household and of raising the children, the couples agreed that men and women had equal rights and responsibilities within the family.... [M]arriages today allow for greater flexibility and greater choice. Today's men and women meet on a playing field that is more level than ever before.[24]

It is worth noting that traditional Jewish cultures and rabbinic prescriptions put significant emphasis on female sexual satisfaction within marriage, during pregnancy, and even past menopause, when reproduction is no longer a possibility. Erotic pleasure was encouraged as an important facilitator of harmonious companionship between husband and wife, within the boundaries of *taharat ha-mishpakhah* (Jewish family law). In a kind of assymetrical arrangement, husbands were responsible for providing their wives with sexual enjoyment, while wives always had veto power on when such activities took place. Marital rape was recognized and forbidden. Even within arranged marriages, couples were expected to and often did form affectionate, romantic bonds. Husbands were enjoined to pay attention to their wives' emotional signals, and women who initiated sexual activity with their husbands were highly praised. Thus, while the *ketubah* (the traditional Jewish marriage contract) promises the husband exclusive access to his wife's sexuality, he does not own her sexuality as men did previously in many Western countries until relatively recently.

In marriages that have a gender-equal approach to relationships, daily life and "maintenance" tasks can also be a source of relationship building rather than friction. Dana Vannoy-Hiller and William W. Philliber found that husbands who were perceived as sharing familial responsibilities were participants in extraordinarily satisfying relationships.[25] The success of these gender-equal marriages stands in stark contrast to the larger context of troubling findings on the general emotional status of women in married households. Married women report 20 percent more depression than single women, more nervous breakdowns, and more physical symptoms of somatized mental disease.[26] In contrast, married men enjoy far better mental health than single men. Some social historians suggest that households differing from popular perceptions of past families have shouldered the blame for many developments that precede and extend far beyond them. Stephanie Coontz warns that familists harken back to dangerously mythologized households and cautions today's American families to avoid "the nostalgia trap" that can blind them to the truths of the past and present.[27]

CONTEMPORARY FATHERS ARE MORE INVOLVED IN CHILDREN'S LIVES

Partially as a result of the working-mother syndrome, American Jewish fathers have reportedly become more involved with the detailed daily raising of their young children. These changes have taken place throughout mainstream populations and across denominational lines. One recent issue of *The Jewish Parent Connection*, a publication of the Orthodox Torah Umesorah National Society for Hebrew Day Schools, makes the assumption that "Due to today's high cost of living . . . it is frequently necessary for both Jewish parents to pursue careers." The author considers the "pros and cons" of "nanny, au pair, babysitter, or day care center," without instilling guilt in the working mother or assuming that she should remain at home while her children are in school all day long.[28] Other articles suggest ways for women with small children to find time for their spiritual lives, urging mothers to hire a babysitter or establish "channels for communication without recrimination" with the children's father, presumably to engage him in the task of enabling spiritual time for his wife.[29]

Today, teachers at traditionally oriented Jewish day schools report that they are almost as likely to see working fathers as working mothers of young children at midday programs such as plays, ceremonies, and special parties – a situation that differs markedly from parental gender-role divisions in the past. The fact that both parents have to juggle work and home responsibilities and make a special effort to be available for such programming means that female parents are not uniquely designated within the family unit for events that disrupt the workweek.[30]

TRADITIONALIST MODELS FOR EGALITARIAN JEWISH FAMILIES

The data clearly indicate that changing lifestyles of Jewish mothers and fathers have not automatically led to a waning of Jewish vitality. Today, dual-career Jewish households have become the new normative Jewish family. The readiness of contemporary American Jewish women to pursue higher education and high-powered careers may be seen as an extremely complicated kind of coalescence, which is built on a rejection of earlier coalescence. Jewish women stayed home and took care of their families not because this was originally a Jewish value, but because it was originally an outside cultural value. Eventually, American Jewish women came to believe that they avoided work force participation because it was a Jewish value for married women to stay home. Indeed, when they finally left their homes to go to work, many felt that they were disobeying Jewish norms. Contemporary Jewish women have been at the forefront of feminist striving, almost universally acquiring higher education and pursuing career goals. Educational accomplishment for women became a coalesced American Jewish value decades ago, and now, occupational accomplishment for women is becoming a coalesced American Jewish value as well.

Demographic trends make it virtually inescapable that Jews living in married-with-children households will also probably continue to have attitudes and expectations of marriage and parenthood that differ from those of Jewish spouses and parents in other historical eras and societies. As Norman Linzer suggests, "in a heavily institutionalized, traditional society, institutions narrow choices for decision-making." With the institutions of Jewish law and communal approbation in place, "clarity of roles" and "consistency of behavior" were reinforced. The authority of family, community, and Jewish tradition discouraged individualistic, transgressive behavior.[31] When such external forces cease to effectively reinforce familism and communalism, connections to Jewish and Jewishness are more likely to grow out of personal considerations.

Individualism may well be historically antithetical to traditional Jewish family and communal values, but American Jews, for better and for worse, have coalesced the individualistic ethos into their concept of Judaism. Many American Jews perceive Judaism as a possible source of personal, spiritual renewal rather than as a social construct. In an atomized community, religion is atomized as well. Because the cohesiveness of the Jewish community has diminished, the impetus to make one's household into a Jewish home, regardless of marital status, arises from within the individual.

This is not necessarily bad news. We can learn much about how to create a specifically Jewish form of gender equality in the family by looking within the covenantal framework that guided individuals and family units in traditional Jewish societies. As we have seen for a small, but significant, highly activist portion of the American Jewish population, gender equality in the family has been combined with impressive adherence to Jewish behaviors, and to what one might call "Jewish family values." Within these families, women receive extremely high levels of both secular and Jewish education and have ambitious career aspirations. They get married and start their families at ages that enhance the possibility of fulfilling their goals for expected family size. As married women and mothers, they go to work as physicians, lawyers, teachers, and businesswomen. Within such households, both mother and father negotiate leaving offices early enough to "make Friday night into Shabbat," and they create Jewishly meaningful holiday environments. Household tasks are often split with a rough equality, by sheer necessity if not by conviction. One could easily argue that these households are a departure from patterns of gender-role construction within Jewish families of the past.

However, one could also argue that these egalitarian Jewish households derive much of their success from ancient formulas for social responsibility. Families that make room for both husband and wife to grow and develop and that are deeply committed to Jewish activities and learning provide us with significant new models for the Jewish family and Jewish family values. These gender-role equality values can be made compatible with traditional Jewish values, in which Jewish knowledge, skill, and commitments are also part of the package.

It is significant that Jewish culture does not assume that women are responsible for doing the kindly deeds that make societies, and the families upon which societies are built, function smoothly. On the contrary, rabbinic law includes numerous familial and societal tasks among the sacred responsibilities of men, responsibilities that extend to society's most vulnerable. According to *Mishnah Peah i*, a key passage included in the *Birchot Ha-Shakhar*, the early morning worship liturgy which most Jewish men (and some Jewish women) recited for many hundreds of years, commandments about social responsibility are so significant that one can never finish fulfilling them: "These are the commandments in which a man enjoys their fruits in this world, and still has their fruit to enjoy in the world to come . . . And the study of Torah leads to all of these."

Within this Mishnaic formulation, social responsibility crosses gender lines. A complex network of social activism is grounded in passionate prayer to a God who transcends selfish strivings, and in lifelong devotion to the study of Jewish texts that teach that activism. In such Jewish texts, society is viewed as one large family; within that family, women and men share many responsibilities, such as caring for aging parents. They are also equally responsible for caring for those individuals whose more limited nuclear families cannot meet their needs, either on a temporary or a permanent basis.

Paternal sharing of household tasks and child rearing can be perceived as contemporary, gender neutral, and sensitive. However, the child-involved father is actually more in keeping with certain aspects of the historical hands-on role of the Jewish father: praying and studying with his young sons, or leading all his children around the house in an educational charade with feather, candle, and spoon, searching for *hametz* on the night before Passover. The traditional Jewish father was enjoined to be the moral educator of his family. In their entrepreneurial economic strivings, many American Jewish immigrants and second-generation males abandoned this role. It was Westernization, and then America, that taught Jewish fathers to replace piety, scholarship, and family involvements with secular ambitions.

Society may indeed require designated enablers, but historical Judaism places the burden of enabling social good equally on men and women. Neither men nor women are encouraged by traditional Judaism to focus exclusively on their own personal aspirations. Households in which fathers are as involved as mothers with the needs of children and parents, societies in which men and women donate time and energy to meet social needs, may be utopian, but it is a utopian vision mandated by Jewish law and tradition.

Notes

1. Marion A. Kaplan, "Gender and Jewish History in Imperial Germany," in *Assimilation and Community: The Jews in Nineteenth-Century Europe*, ed. Jonathan Frankel and Seven J. Zipperstein (Cambridge, MA: Cambridge University Press, 1992), 199–224.
2. Marion A. Kaplan, *The Making of the Jewish Middle Class: Women, Family and Identity in Imperial Germany* (New York: Oxford University Press, 1991).
3. Paula Hyman, *Gender and Assimilation in Modern Jewish History: The Roles and Representations of Women* (Seattle: University of Washington Press, 1995).
4. Susan Glenn, *Daughters of the Shtetl: Life and Labor in the Immigrant Generation* (Ithaca: Cornell University Press, 1990), 76–78.
5. Kaplan, "Gender and Jewish History," 199–224.
6. Ibid., 199–224.
7. Sid Groeneman, "Beliefs and Values of American Jewish Women" (report by Market Facts, Inc., presented to the International Organization of B'nai B'rith Women, 1985).
8. Sylvia Barack Fishman, *A Breath of Life: Feminism in the American Jewish Community* (New York: The Free Press, 1993), 255–56.
9. *I of the Beholder: Jews and Gender in Film and Popular Culture* (International Research Institute on Jewish Women Working Paper Series, no. 1, May 1998).
10. Susan Weidman Schneider, "Detoxifying Our Relationships: An Interview with Esther Perel," *Lilith*, 17 (oooo), x.
11. Calvin Goldscheider and Frances K. Goldscheider, "The Transition to Jewish Adulthood: Education, Marriage, and Fertility" (paper for the 10th World Congress of Jewish Studies, Jerusalem, 1989), 92–98.
12. "Transition to Jewish Adulthood," 17–20.
13. Frances K. Goldscheider and Calvin Goldscheider, "The Changing Transition to Adulthood" (Thousand Oaks: Sage Publications, 1999).
14. Frank L. Mott and Joyce C. Abma, "Contemporary Jewish Fertility: Does Religion Make a Difference?" *Contemporary Jewry* 13 (1992), 74–94.
15. Moshe Hartman and Harriet Hartman, *Gender Equality and American Jews* (Albany: State University of New York Press, 1996), 219–25.

16. Ibid., 38–39.
17. Ibid., 38–39.
18. *Family Affairs* 5, 1 and 2 (Summer 1992).
19. David Blankenhorn, "Introduction," in *Rebuilding the Nest: A New Commitment to the American Family* (Milwaukee: Family Service America, 1990), vii–xv.
20. Bruce C. Hafen, "Individualism in Family Law," in *Rebuilding the Nest: A New Commitment to the American Family* (Milwaukee: Family Service America, 1990), 161–77.
21. Rebecca Johnson, "The Just-Do-It Shrink," *The New York Times Magazine* (17 November 1996), 41–45.
22. Barbara Ehrenreich, *The Hearts of Men: American Dreams and the Flight from Commitment* (Garden City: Anchor Press, 1983).
23. Judith S. Wallerstein and Sandra Blakeslee, *Second Chances: Men, Women, and Children a Decade After Divorce – Who Wins, Who Loses, and Why* (New York: Ticknor & Fields, 1989), 35–53, 296.
24. Judith S. Wallerstein and Sandra Blakeslee, *The Good Marriage: How and Why Love Lasts* (Boston: Houghton Mifflin, 1995), 330.
25. Dana Vannoy-Hiller and William W. Philliber, *Equal Partners: Successful Women in Marriage* (Newbury Park: Sage Publications, 1989), 120–22.
26. Walter R. Grove, "Sex Differences in Mental Illness Among Adult Men and Women," *Social Science and Medicine*, 12B (1978).
27. Stephanie Coontz, *The Way We Never Were: American Families and the Nostalgia Trap* (New York: Basic Books, 1992).
28. David Zigelman, "Babysitter or Day Care Center: That Is the Question," *The Jewish Parent Connection* (September/October 1995), 22.
29. Deena Garber, "Mom and the Machzor: Balancing Spirituality and Maternal Realities," and Sharon First, "8 Ways to Help Make the High Holy Days More Meaningful for the Whole Family," *The Jewish Parent Connection* (September/October 1995), 9, 13.
30. Sylvia Barack Fishman, *Changing Minds: Feminism in Contemporary Orthodox Jewish Life* (New York: American Jewish Committee, 2000).
31. Norman Linzer, "Self and Other: The Jewish Family in Crisis," in *Crisis and Continuity: The Jewish Family in the 21st Century*, ed. Norman Linzer, Irving N. Levitz, and David J. Schnall (Hoboken: KTAV Publishing House, 1995), 1–21.

14 The body and sexuality in American Jewish culture

DAVID BIALE

Over the past several decades, historians have come to recognize the body as a central site for defining and contesting identity. At the end of the nineteenth century, modern nationalism sought to mobilize the body – most typically the *male* body – to serve the nation, as soldier, worker, or citizen.[1] The classical ideal of a strong, healthy body promoted movements of physical fitness, while the modern nation's need for population fostered efforts at sexual eugenics. Jewish nationalism, a product of the same trends, took up this cult of the body with such expressions as Max Nordau's "muscle Judaism" as well as projects to cure the alleged sexual degeneration of the Jewish people.[2] However, Zionism was by no means unique in this attempt to "modernize" the Jewish body. American Jewish culture, too, following, and, in some cases, leading trends elsewhere in the Jewish world, fostered new images of the body. Whether in the prominence of certain Jews in sports such as boxing and baseball or in athletic institutions such as the Young Men's Hebrew Association, Jews in America refashioned their bodies as part of the overall struggle for integration in their new homeland. At the same time, though, persistent stereotypes of physical weakness and imperfection, as well as sexual neurosis, betrayed Jewish anxieties about the limits of assimilation for both men and women. The dialectic between contradictory perceptions of the body and sexuality and tensions between the genders around both of these issues remain, to this day, ongoing preoccupations of American Jewish culture.

The stereotypes of sickly, bookish, sexually neurotic Jews, to which we shall return in a moment, are belied by the realities of Jewish immigrant life in America. To be sure, Jews eventually achieved prominence in cultural, professional, and commercial fields that were removed from the life of the body. It is easy to forget in light of the rapid transformation of their occupation and class profile that the vast majority of Jews who came to America were originally working class. Few yeshiva students and even fewer rabbis accompanied the mass migration to America; only after the Holocaust would the remnants of the traditional intellectual class – always a small minority, even in Eastern Europe – transplant themselves to the New World.

Jews who relied more on brawn than brains had always been part of European Jewish communities, and, by the early twentieth century, a number of Yiddish and Hebrew writers, such as Sholem Asch and M. Y. Berdichevsky, celebrated their existence as a critique of the more traditional scholarly ethos. Such Jews were, if anything, even more disproportionately represented in America and became the subject of works such as the Communist writer Michael Gold's *Jews Without Money* (1930). In this memoir, Gold also draws attention to the American Jewish underworld, a phenomenon that had existed in Europe since the Middle Ages and, with the upheavals of urbanization and industrialization, gained new life both in the cities of the Russian Pale and in the immigrant communities of America.[3] Like the Jew as proletarian, the Jew as gangster represented a very different type from that of the pale *yeshiva bocher*.

Perhaps the most important novel of the immigrant period, Abraham Cahan's *Rise of David Levinsky*, first published in 1917, captures this new type of Jew. Levinksy abandons the traditional Eastern European world for the materialism of America. His drive for riches in the New World is symbolized by his outsized libido, as he succumbs repeatedly to the temptations of "Satan" by seducing his landladies and other available women. To be sure, Levinsky's sexual and material conquests leave him lonely and spiritually bereft by the end of the novel, which, of course, is the moral of Cahan's story. However, in identifying David Levinksy as an authentic Jewish American "type," Cahan constructed a new image of the Jew as sexually vital and dynamic. Cahan's Levinsky would become the prototype for later Jewish fictional characters, such as the Canadian writer Mordecai Richler's Duddy Kravitz.

If the immigrant Jews were not as weak and sickly as contemporary observers often saw them, programs developed to "Americanize" them were typically based on just such perceptions. The Young Men's Hebrew Association (begun as a cultural organization for German Jews in 1874) advocated athletics as a way of turning the newly arrived East European Jews into Americans, which it defined in both physical and moral terms.[4] The Y spawned the Atlas Athletic Club, which became an independent organization in 1907. The Settlement House movement also saw athletics as a way of turning the immigrants into a fit and disciplined work force. The immigrant Jews internalized these values. A Chicago Yiddish daily put it this way in 1923: "We have been branded as weak and physical cowards.... While we are proud to emphasize our interests in matters intellectual, we must not brand ourselves as physical weaklings.[5]

A classic example of the use of physical prowess as a vehicle toward Jewish integration was boxing, a sport that was dominated by Jews, at least in the divisions other than heavyweight, during the interwar period.[6] Benny Leonard was the lightweight champion of the world between 1917 and 1925 and became a kind of folk hero to immigrant Jews. By 1928, Jewish fighters comprised the largest ethnic group of title contenders. Even Max Baer, the world heavyweight champion in 1935, who was apparently not Jewish, affected to be Jewish by wearing a Magen David on his shorts. The rise of Jewish boxing came during the most virulent period of American anti-Semitism and clearly fulfilled a need, both in the ring and among the audience, for Jews who could use physical force to defend Jewish honor. Boxing fulfilled the same role that dueling had a generation earlier as acculturated Jews in Europe ran into barriers blocking social integration. As the novelist Budd Schulberg recalled about Leonard, "to see him climb in the ring sporting the six-pointed Jewish star on his fighting trunks was to anticipate sweet revenge for all the bloody noses, split lips and mocking laughter at pale little Jewish boys who had run the neighborhood gauntlet."[7] Following World War II, boxing declined as a Jewish sport, in part as Jews themselves no longer felt as strongly the need to prove themselves physically in the face of anti-Semitism.

The other sport that produced Jewish folk heroes was baseball, the quintessential American pastime and thus the symbolic key to integration. The greatest of these heroes, and probably the most celebrated American Jewish athlete of the twentieth century, was Hank Greenberg, whose career started in the 1930s. Greenberg served as a lightning rod for anti-Semitic insults from the stands, but he won wide admiration for spending Yom Kippur, 1935, in synagogue rather than on the field, anticipating Sandy Koufax's similar decision not to pitch in the World Series on Yom Kippur three decades later. A Jew might thus affirm both his body and spiritual legacy; the two need not be alienated from each other.

Sports such as boxing and baseball served as surrogate fantasies for Jewish men and boys eager to prove that their bodies were as American as those of the native born. Comics served a similar function, albeit in a more disguised fashion. Two Depression-era Jewish youths from Cleveland, Jerry Siegel and Joe Shuster, invented Superman in the summer of 1934 in a context whose Jewish meaning has recently been explored in fictional form by Michael Chabon in his Pulitzer-Prize-winning *The Amazing Adventures of Kavalier and Klay*. As the Nazis consolidated their power in the 1930s and anti-Semitism grew more menacing at home, Superman seemed an expression of the desire for Jewish power in a strange land. He was a "Krypto-American immigrant" whose Hebraically loaded name on his home planet was *Kal-El*, literally "the god who is light" and metaphorically "the god who can fly".[8] Clark Kent was, in name and appearance, hardly the stereotype of a Jew, but his glasses clearly marked him as less than physically imposing. Nevertheless, underneath his unassuming demeanor lay a Man of Steel, although one devoted to the cause of the oppressed. Later, cartoonist Jules Feiffer wrote this about the Jewish semiotics of Superman: "We were aliens. We didn't choose to bé mild-mannered, bespectacled and self-effacing. We chose to be bigger, stronger, blue-eyed and sought-after by blond cheerleaders. *Their* cheerleaders. We chose to be *them*."[9] Superman was the assimilationist's fantasy, but one whose Jewish roots were still quite visible.

Clark Kent never quite consummates his relationship with Lois Lane, the comic's version of the mythic Gentile "cheerleader," but the quest for sexual acceptance frequently did accompany the search for a new Jewish body. The theme of intermarriage, typically of Jewish men with non-Jewish women, lies at the heart of Jewish sexual dilemmas in American culture. As early as 1908, Israel Zangwill's play, *The Melting Pot*, made relations between its Jewish hero and the daughter of a Russian pogromist the cornerstone of Zangwill's celebration of America's ability to overcome European differences. In a subtle way, though, the play calls less for Jews to give up their distinctiveness as for the American melting pot to take on specifically Jewish characteristics: by marrying Gentiles, Jews will not so much lose their identities as convert the non-Jews to a new Jewish American "religion."[10]

So, too, the first talking motion picture, *The Jazz Singer* (1927), conflated the hero's desire to make it in the entertainment world with his relationship with a Gentile dancer, Mary Dale, explicitly labeled a *shikse*. The images of this film are ambiguous. The jazz singer, a cantor's son, cannot finally renounce family and religion: Although he has professed that his career is more important to him than anything else, he cancels the opening night of his first big Broadway show to sing Kol Nidre in place of his dying father. Like Hank Greenberg a few years later, Jackie Robin (nee Rabinowitz) reconciles with his religion on the most solemn day of the Jewish year, making a statement that the price of acceptance in America need not be total assimilation. Indeed, the song with which he achieves his greatest success in blackface is "My Mother," clearly demonstrating that the most important woman in his life is not his shikse sweetheart. As a tale of sexual transgression, *The Jazz Singer* hardly lives up to its initial promise.

The jazz singer puts on black face in his climactic performance. By taking on the erotic energy of the black music he has made his own, the erstwhile cantor's son implies that Jews and Blacks share a common sensuality. However, in this complex rendering of American Jewish identity, *The Jazz Singer* suggests that it is through the culture of the black minority that the Jews can paradoxically achieve acceptance as whites, ultimately leaving their erstwhile black allies behind.[11]

In portraying the allure of the non-Jewish woman – the proverbial shikse – Hollywood movies such as *The Jazz Singer* and its many successors initially generalized to all Jews a problem that afflicted primarily their own social class. The interwar period saw very little intermarriage, especially among the East European immigrants and their children; the rate would only begin to rise significantly in the 1960s and 1970s. However, the Hollywood stereotypes struck roots and persisted. While earlier European myths of Jewish–Gentile romance typically featured a non-Jewish man in love with a *belle juive*, the American pattern was most often the opposite: the Jewish man proving his Americanization with his Gentile mate, the "blond cheerleaders" of Feiffer's remembrance. Jewish women were left out of the erotic equation. When they were treated, it was either as mothers (in *The Jazz Singer*, Jackie's mother is much more sympathetic to his aspirations than his father) or as their grasping, materialistic daughters.

The mythic image of young Jewish women, going back to the pre–World War I "ghetto girl," was of ostentatious desire for material luxury.[12] By demanding more than her potential mates might be able to provide, she implicitly reproached them for failing to achieve the only success that counted in America. As icons of consumption, these (later-named) Jewish American Princesses (JAPs) typified the American dream, but their excessiveness and bad taste suggested that Jews would never quite make it culturally in America, even if they made it economically. As a grotesque caricature of consumption, they symbolized Jewish ambivalence about assimilation. When this particular negative stereotype developed in the hands primarily of Jewish comedians, both male and female,[13] it acquired additional features. In some representations, the Jewish woman is either physically repulsive or has no interest in sex. The only eroticism this female stereotype knows is consumption. One particularly tasteless joke puts it this way: "How does a JAP achieve orgasm? By yelling, 'charge it to Daddy.'" The female Jewish body is also the site for corporeal assimilation; rhinoplasty, the "nose job," was developed first in Europe to erase the sign of Jewish difference that anti-Semites considered most prominent.[14] It migrated to America, where it became not only a symbol of assimilation but also of its impossibility: No matter how successful the nose job, the archetypical Jewish woman could not be concealed.

This particularly unsavory stereotype found its most complex expression in the period after World War II, with such works of fiction as Herman Wouk's *Marjorie Morningstar* (1955) and Philip Roth's *Goodbye Columbus*

(1957). Here, the movement of Jews to the affluent suburbs is represented by the materialism of Jewish women. In both novels, young Jewish men rebel against the path middle-class Jewish life sets for them, represented by the beautiful, affluent, but emotionally entrapping Wouk's Marjorie and Roth's Brenda Patimkin. As opposed to the JAP stereotype, though, these women are neither physically repulsive nor sexually inert. However, in refusing these daughters of the middle class, despite their allures, the male protagonists in these novels opt out of the task of reproducing the Jewish family.

Works like these do not pillory only Jewish women; indeed, they are perhaps even more critical of their male figures. Earlier images of the Jewish male as physically puny were transmuted in certain postwar fiction into sexual *shlemiels*. Perhaps the best-known expression of this stereotype is Philip Roth's outrageous *Portnoy's Complaint* (1969), published at the height of the sexual revolution.[15] His "complaint" is precisely that the more he thinks – and speaks – about sex, the less he is able to achieve satisfaction. This is a book about how words can replace sex and how the Jews, the quintessential People of the Book, are eternally in exile from their own bodies.

Since the repressive Jewish tradition suffocates sexuality, Gentiles are seen as having a monopoly on healthy eroticism. The Jewish male is forced to look for erotic fulfillment in the arms of the shikse, but since the result of Jewish childhood and adolescence is psychological castration, the shikse can never fulfill her mythic role. Nevertheless, Jewish women as sexual possibilities do not exist in the novel. Although the myth of the sexless JAP is not articulated in *Portnoy*, it clearly hangs in the background. *Portnoy* reflects such a thoroughgoing misogynist view of the world that not only are Jewish women impossible as potential partners, but even Gentile women must be robbed of their names and turned into cardboard stereotypes.

If the American Jewish woman has no sexual potential and the Gentile has too much, perhaps the solution for Portnoy lies in the allegedly healthy sexuality of the Jewish state, which he visits at the end of the novel. However, Portnoy cannot escape his diasporic fate, and he becomes impotent in the Promised Land. The Israeli women, it turns out, are depressingly puritanical and Zionism offers no sexual liberation. In an attempt to avenge himself on Zionism and believing that he has gonorrhea, Portnoy tries to infect a healthy kibbutz woman in order to poison "the future of the race" with a dose of diasporic disease. With this bizarre twist on the anti-Semitic motif of Jewish race pollution, *Portnoy* comes to its ending that also promises the needed therapy: Portnoy's analyst, the audience for his complaint, proclaims in a Viennese accent that it is time now to begin.

Portnoy is a very shrewd work that consciously manipulates a variety of myths about Jewish sexuality, from the anti-Semitic belief in Jewish hypersexuality to fantasies about the suffocating Jewish mother and the seductive shikse. Roth plays on contradictory images of Jewish respectability, as he himself has written:

> [T]he man confessing to forbidden sexual acts and gross offenses against the family order and ordinary decency was a Jew.... Going wild in public is the last thing in the world that a Jew is expected to do.... He is not expected to make a spectacle of himself, either by shooting off his mouth or by shooting off his semen and certainly not by shooting off his mouth about shooting off his semen.[16]

Like this reflection by Roth on his own book, Portnoy's monologue, in the form of a psychoanalytic confession, is really a Borscht-belt *shtik* and is thus heir to a long tradition of self-deprecatory Jewish humor. It represents the nihilistic culmination of this tradition and is particularly striking, coming as it does at the moment when Jews were finally at home in America. With the postwar waning of American anti-Semitism, the entry of Jews into many hitherto blocked professions, and their social integration (including rising rates of intermarriage), it would seem a peculiar time for such a work of Jewish self-doubt. It may be, though, that the lacerating self-criticism of *Portnoy* paradoxically reflects self-confidence, rather than doubt, for only with the acceptance of Jews in America might it be possible to expose satirically the myths about Jewish sexuality to a larger public.

Roth's *Portnoy* was published at about the same time that Woody Allen popularized a similar, if somewhat less outrageously offensive, stereotype of the shlemiel as antihero. In the sexual self-doubt and obsession with Gentile women of his characters, he not only typified but was centrally responsible for disseminating many of the popular stereotypes of the Jewish male. From the first movie he wrote and acted in, *What's New Pussycat?*, he portrayed what was to become a stock figure, the little man with the big libido and the even bigger sexual neurosis. What was typical of this character was his comic inability to consummate his desire. In *Pussycat*, we first encounter Allen helping Parisian strippers dress, fumbling ridiculously with their costumes as they parade half-naked around him; later, the girl he tries to bed falls asleep on him. The sexual insecurities of the characters Allen plays are quintessentially Jewish. Even the sperm he portrays in the funniest scene of *Everything You Wanted To Know About Sex* turns out to be Jewish, worrying compulsively before the grand moment whether he will be hurt going in and whether he will be stymied by birth control pills. Allen's characters are not, however, merely impotent. They are also highly erotic. Jews have the libidinal energy to win over Gentile women from their desiccated WASP culture, but they can never seem to consummate their conquests. In many of Allen's movies, the Jew's sexual ambivalence infects the female Gentile characters and turns them into mirror images of himself: even Gentile Americans become "Jewish," thus making America safe for the Jews.

A film from roughly this period that brings together many of the themes of sexual insecurity, misogyny toward Jewish women, and idealization of the shikse is *The Heartbreak Kid* (1974). After their ostentatiously Jewish wedding, Lenny Cantrow and Leila Kolodny set out on their honeymoon to Miami Beach. The new marriage immediately turns sour as Leila appears increasingly coarse and unerotic. When she becomes sunburned after the first few hours on the beach, she retreats to her room and covers herself with unsightly cream. This explicitly rendered JAP is so divorced from nature and alienated from her body that, not only can't she stand a bit of sun, but she doesn't even know how to swim! Alone on the beach, Lenny is seduced by a spectacularly beautiful blonde from Minnesota named Kelly Corcoran. As he knowingly puts it, "a girl like you *would* have a name like Kelly Corcoran." Kelly accosts him as he lies on the beach and informs him, "that's my spot," suggesting that the Jews have intruded into the metaphoric American heartland. Dropping his marriage "like a bomb," Lenny sets off in pursuit of the mythical shikse, following her all the way to Minnesota. Although he wins her hand in marriage by outsmarting a muscular Gentile competitor and by denouncing her father's anti-Semitic prejudices, the film ends with Lenny as an empty shell, deracinated in the land of the Gentiles. He gets the prize, but his search for sexual fulfillment leaves him emasculated. Billed as a comedy, *The Heartbreak Kid* is an American Jewish tragedy, a cautionary tale about the fate of the Jewish parvenu who succumbs to Gentile temptation in order to climb out of the ghetto.

These stereotypes of American Jewish men and women leave the impression of a culture thoroughly self-critical in its sexual identity. However, there are significant countertraditions that suggest much greater complexity and ambiguity. Lenny Bruce's comedy, for example, often treated the Jews as the most sexually liberated and healthy individuals. Jews are the archetype of the nonrepressed, representing the margins of American culture:

> To me, if you live in New York or any other big city, you are Jewish. It doesn't matter even if you're Catholic; if you live in New York you're Jewish. If you live in Butte, Montana, you're going to be goyish even if you're Jewish. . . . Negroes are all Jews. Italians are all Jews. Irishmen who have rejected their religion are Jews. Mouths are very Jewish. And bosoms.[17]

To be Jewish means to be outside the American mainstream both verbally ("mouths") and erotically ("bosoms"). Jews, Bruce declares, have no concept of obscene words or pornography because they put no value on celibacy:

> There are no words in Jewish that describe any sexual act – *emmis* – or parts or lusts.... Are Jews pornographers? Or is that the Jew has no concept? To a Jewish f-u-c-k and s-h-i-t have the same value on the dirty-word graph.... And the reason for that is that – well, see, rabbis and priests both s-h-i-t, but only one f-u-c-ks. You see, in the Jewish culture, there's no merit badge for not doing that.... And since the leaders of my tribe, rabbis, are *schtuppers*, perhaps that's why words come freer to me.[18]

Jews are promiscuous with words because they have no puritanical restrictions on sex: As opposed to *Portnoy*, the verbality of Jewish culture is a sign of – and not a contradiction to – its sexuality.

A number of novels and films dealing specifically with the State of Israel deliver similarly positive messages about Jewish male sexuality. When, at the end of *Portnoy's Complaint*, Alexander Portnoy discovers that he is impotent in the Jewish state, he represents the mythic tension between Israel as the imagined site of Jewish erotic health and the neurosis of the Diaspora, a projection of what American Jews might desire but perhaps believe themselves unable to achieve. The Israeli heroes and heroines of a host of popular American novels are portrayed as highly erotic, "tough Jews" who have overcome the impotence of the Diaspora and are now able to wreak vengeance on ex-Nazis and Arabs alike.[19]

The archetype of this fiction was Leon Uris's best-selling novel *Exodus*, first published in 1958 and made into a highly successful movie in 1960. Uris's hero is named Ari Ben Canaan, a quite deliberately non-Jewish name, indeed, a name that conjures up the ancient Canaanites as opposed to the Jews. Ben Canaan is ascetic and fanatical, but, as a prototypical *sabra*, has his hidden romantic side, which is revealed in his affair with Kitty, a Gentile American nurse. Zionism, it seems, has not only liberated the Jew from sexual neurosis but has turned him into a quasi-*goy*. Where the characters of much of American Jewish fiction cannot realize healthy erotic relationships with the Christian women they pursue, the Israeli has no such difficulty. However, the film also avoids the assimilationist theme so common to the Jewish–Gentile romance of Hollywood tradition. The affair between Ari and Kitty reaches a dead end when Kitty, in a scene overlooking the Jezreel Valley, tells Ari "all these differences between people are made up." He disagrees: "Don't ever believe it. People are different. They have a right to be different." Although they kiss, their romance goes no further: the Jew and the Gentile *are* different and can never become totally one. Thus, the very eroticism of

Ari Ben Canaan, played by the Jewish actor Paul Newman, is in the service of Jewish difference; while set in Israel, the story also conveyed a powerful message of identity to American Jews.[20]

An even more remarkable film in terms of the American–Israeli sexual connection, although it was a commercial and critical failure, is *Cast a Giant Shadow* (1966), starring another Jewish actor, Kirk Douglas, as Mickey Marcus, the American Jewish colonel who volunteered for the Israeli Army during the 1948 war. The historical Marcus played an important role in opening up the famous Burma Road to break the siege of Jerusalem. In the film, however, his role is inflated into the virtual savior of the young Jewish state, who takes command of the disorganized, even hapless, Israelis and forces them to seize the offensive. Made just before the Six Day War, which would transform the Israeli soldier into a superhero, *Cast a Giant Shadow* depicts the Israelis in a surprisingly unflattering light, as fearful and physically unimpressive, unable to save themselves without the intervention of the invincible American: Douglas, playing the American giant of the movie's title, literally towers above the Israelis.

The movie concocts a romantic potboiler. Married to a classically WASP woman who cannot understand his need for military adventure, Marcus falls in love with a beautiful female Israeli soldier, Magda. In a significant scene, she confesses that her husband, who conveniently dies later in battle, is not very good in bed. In response to her question, Marcus assures her that he has no such problems. His American wife has given him a divorce, so Marcus is free to consummate his romance with Magda; unfortunately, his life is cut short when an Israeli sentry mistakenly kills him. The subtext of the film thus contradicts much of American Jewish mythology: Here is an American Jew who is physically and sexually powerful and who comes to liberate the Israelis militarily and erotically. Marcus' fictional journey from intermarriage to the arms of a Jewish Israeli lover traces a path that contradicts the dominant narrative. Far from a projection of sexual fantasies onto the Jewish state, *Cast a Giant Shadow* suggests a very different myth.

Two other films that contradict the common stereotypes are *Norma Rae* (1979) and *Crossing Delancy* (1988). In *Norma Rae*, a New York Jewish union organizer, Reuben Warshawsky, comes to the South to unionize textile workers. Reuben is earthy, effusive, and unabashedly proud of being Jewish. He is the closest Hollywood has come to portraying a thoroughly attractive Jew, although his breed of Jewish union organizers is probably on the way to the museum. While erotically compelling, Reuben is not allowed to play a sexual role in the movie. He and his native protégée, Norma Rae, acknowledge their attraction to each other, but they deliberately avoid any entanglement as Reuben has a woman, presumably Jewish, offscreen in New York. The allure of the Jewish–Gentile connection is recognized, but the fundamental differences between Jews and non-Jews articulated by *Exodus's* Ari Ben Canaan are now brought home to America.

Crossing Delancy, made by a female Jewish director, Joan Micklin Silver, takes the next step of portraying an erotic relationship between Jews. Isabelle, a high-powered professional Jewish woman, is frustrated in her attempt to find a suitable man and finds herself repeatedly in problematic relationships with non-Jews. Her Lower East Side grandmother arranges for a matchmaker to fix her up with a traditional pickle vendor and, after the predictable cultural malapropisms, love blossoms. Nevertheless, this celebration of love between Jews sends an implicitly ambiguous message. The pickle vendor is out of another era, the period of the immigrant, caught in a time warp in the late twentieth century. For *Crossing Delancy*, the American Jew's sexual salvation comes by a leap in time to a vanished age.

One female writer who has constructed an explicitly Jewish erotic fiction is Erica Jong. Jong's work deliberately challenges the male mythologies of a Woody Allen or a Philip Roth with a countermythology of her own. In her madcap first novel, *Fear of Flying*, her protagonist, in search of the mythical purely physical "zipless fuck," encounters an Englishman who seduces her with this line: "It's just that Jewish girls are so bloody good in bed."[21] So much for the myth of the asexual JAP! In *Any Woman's Blues*, Jong's protagonist is Leila Sand, a middle-aged "sexoholic" Jewish artist who, in a gender reversal of *Portnoy*, pursues one Gentile man after the other. She says of her greatest obsession, Dart: "I must admit that my Dyckman Street Jewish childhood had left me with a lifelong fascination for old WASP ways. I was not just fucking a man when I fucked Dart. I was fucking American history, the Mayflower myth, the colonial past."[22] However, Sand is no unadulterated assimilationist. The one man with whom she has children is a Jew: "I realized that they had to be fathered by a hirsute Jew of my blood and bone. . . . I could no more have brought WASP babies into the world than I could have stopped drawing and painting." She recounts seeing a documentary on Auschwitz while pregnant and "weeping with joy and pain to be replenishing the Jewish race. . . . [W]here having babies is concerned, all our conservatism seems to burgeon."[23] Procreation, as opposed to pure sex, must somehow remain Jewish.

Jong's strategy in these novels is deliberately outrageous, a kind of female Lenny Bruce, in which the outrageousness is specifically Jewish. Nevertheless, despite this seeming erotic liberation through outrageous language, Jong's characters remain mired in sexual confusion and frustration. Leila Sand in *Any Woman's Blues* has no more resolved her "sexoholism" by the end of the novel than does Portnoy at the end of his complaint or Allen's characters after nearly two decades of films. Jong's answer to the male stereotypes is to create a female version of the same syndrome. Still, Jong's work represents an explicit attempt by a woman to shatter some prevalent myths and create an erotic Jewish woman, stereotyped, perhaps, but still refreshingly subversive.

Some similar subversions of the depiction of Jewish sexuality in popular culture can be found in *Seinfeld*, the most popular sitcom in television history. The Jewish semiotics of *Seinfeld* are enormously complex, since a number of the characters bear all the stereotypical markings of Jews but are explicitly labeled as something else. Only Jerry Seinfeld himself is avowedly Jewish (Jerry Stiller, who plays George Castanza's father, has quipped that the Castanzas, who are presented as Italian, are really Jews in a witness protection program). Most of his romantic possibilities, few of whom last more than one show, would appear to be Gentiles, but Seinfeld's inability to maintain any lasting relationship with these women has less to do with some stereotyped Jewish neurosis than with the bizarre idiosyncrasies of the main characters of the show. Rather than focusing on Jerry's pursuit of the proverbial shikse – the obvious comic route – *Seinfeld* lampoons the myth in an episode in which the Gentile character, Elaine, has trouble fighting off, first, a Bar Mitzvah boy, then her Jewish boss, and, finally, a rabbi. Her problem, she is told, is her "shiksappeal." The success of this satire depends on the persistence of the myth of the shikse, but also on the belief that the myth itself has begun to lose its hold.

Although Seinfeld's relationships are typically not Jewish, there are two episodes in which we find him with Rachel, who is not only Jewish but Orthodox to boot. In the most iconoclastic of them, Jerry and Rachel, unable to have sex because she lives with her parents and his parents are staying in his apartment, "make out" during *Schindler's List*, a film that had become a sacred cow when the episode aired. Jerry becomes as an ethnic outlaw for refusing to take the iconic Holocaust film with the proper seriousness, but the fact that, for once, his partner is also Jewish suggests that the show's satirical treatment of *Schindler's List* must be read as an internal Jewish debate: Should the sexual desire of these two Jews, no matter how adolescent, take back seat to the Holocaust? *Seinfeld* may therefore reflect a new stage in the representation of Jewish sexuality in which the old myths and stereotypes may provide some comic fodder, but they no longer bespeak the same underlying anxieties.

Indeed, the generations of Jews who have grown up since the waning of American anti-Semitism and the rise of cultural phenomena such as assimilation, feminism, and sexual liberation have often broken free of the old stereotypes, even as they acknowledge their persistence in memory. Female writers and film makers, such as *Crossing Delancy*'s Silver, set out to create new, more positive images of Jewish women and of the possibility of relationships between Jewish men and women. Novels such as Susan Lukas' *Fat*

Emily, Myrna Blythe's *Cousin Suzanne*, or Louise Rose Blecher's *The Launch-ing of Barbara Fabrikant* subvert the JAP stereotypes by explicitly satirizing the body images of those jokes: Big breasts or noses become the subjects of a self-consciously burlesque humor that confronts head on the price that the stereotypes have exacted.[24]

While these fictions from the 1970s never actually *affirm* the allegedly grotesque features of the female Jewish body, a new generation of writers and artists evidently feel no compunction in challenging traditional body images. In a recent anthology, *Yentl's Revenge*, contributor Ophira Edut celebrates the virtues of being "a Jewess with a caboose," a black cultural ideal that *zoftig* Jewish woman can now legitimately embrace.[25] To be sure, her hilarious autobiographical reminiscences show that Jews have still not accepted this ideal, but, written in hip-hop style, Edut argues that Jews who want to be culturally "with it" have no choice but to embrace their own large posteriors: What's black *is* beautiful. Al Jolson's blackface has made a long journey indeed.

Another tongue-in-cheek gesture to black culture is the "Jewsploitation" film, *The Hebrew Hammer* (2002), in which an Orthodox Jewish hero, dressed in long leather coat, *payot*, a *tallit*, and an oversized gold Chai, does battle with the evil "son of Santa" to save Chanukah. The "Hammer," dubbed "the baddest Heeb this side of Tel Aviv," is both a rejection and exaggeration of Jewish stereotypes – ultracool and ultraneurotic – just as the Blaxploitation films of the 1970s created outrageous characters who satirically exaggerated Black stereotypes. This guerrilla warfare against the myths of sexually neurotic and physically impotent Jews demonstrates, on the one hand, the persistence of the myths, but, on the other, the diminishing of their debilitating grip on the Jewish imagination.

No longer is the Jewish body a taboo subject. For example, despite the traditional prohibition of tattooing, a short-lived underground 1990s Jewish periodical from San Francisco, *Dafka*, attracted controversy by depicting on the cover of its first issue the back of a naked, tattooed woman wearing a tallit. Similarly, the actor Leonard Nimoy has exhibited photographs of naked or partially naked Jews wearing Jewish symbols.

Equally subversive are female writers who have attempted to infuse a Jewish feminist agenda with sexual liberation. The poet Irina Klepfisz writes the following:

When you ask me to say something about being a Jewish lesbian, what can I say? You know of course that there are no Jewish lesbians because to begin with Jews are not supposed to be sexual. Especially Jewish women.[26]

To adopt a sexual identity, and even more to adopt a lesbian identity, for a Jewish woman is to challenge the myths of the asexual Jewish woman and of an asexual Judaism. The poet Adrienne Rich suggests that Yiddish women poets represent a tradition "more sexually frank that [that of] the men."[27]

The Jewish feminist movement has also challenged the boundaries of the dominant discourse of American Jewish sexuality. By contesting male definitions of Jewish women and by rereading classical texts such as the Bible from a feminist point of view, feminist theologians, such as Judith Plaskow, hope to recapture a healthy eroticism that some believe characterized Jewish women more than men in the past. Plaskow writes this in *Standing Again at Sinai*:

> Feminist images name female sexuality as powerful and legitimate and name sexuality as part of the image of God. They tell us that sexuality is not primarily a moral danger... but a source of energy and power that, schooled in the values of respect and mutuality, can lead us to the related, and therefore sexual, God.[28]

Despite her critique of male theology, Plaskow's own hopes to resurrect a healthy sexuality are actually remarkably similar to those of a range of American Jewish male theologians. Representatives of all religious movements of Judaism, from Orthodox to Conservative and Reform, have commonly argued that Judaism preaches affirmation of the body and of sexual relations, especially within marriage.[29] These authors all tend to base their arguments on contrasting Judaism – or, better, their *interpretations* of Judaism – with Christianity, which they view as sexually repressive.

Norman Lamm, president of the Orthodox Yeshiva University, for example, denounced the sexual revolution of the 1960s as a modern form of the sacred prostitution of the Canaanites and the debauchery of the ancient Romans. Ancient "hedonism" gave birth to ascetic Christianity, so that Christianity became a kind of inverted paganism. The contemporary "renaissance of paganism" treats sex as nothing but a biological urge that must be stripped of its shroud of mystery. Against this new paganism, Lamm holds that Judaism stands as the only plausible bulwark; the contemporary debate over sexuality thus becomes nothing less than the modern version of the age-old struggle between monotheistic Judaism and idolatry. As opposed to the modern religion of openness, Judaism advocates restoring the mystery to sex. At the same time, however, Judaism rejects any association of sex with guilt, as long as sex takes place within the framework of marriage. Men and women must enter marriage with a positive attitude toward sex: "Any attitude brought to the marital chamber that... regards sex as evil and identifies desire with lust, can only disturb the harmonious integration of the two forces within man: the moral and the sexual."[30] By rendering marital sex so unproblematic, Lamm implicitly echoes a peculiarly American discourse: The Jews believed in sex without guilt long before the 1960s. Indeed, these religious writers on sexuality have to be understood in the context of the broader American Jewish culture of sexuality and the body traced in this essay. The challenge of the self-critical stereotypes of sexual neurosis lies implicitly behind these apologetic arguments, not just for Jewish "normality," but even its superiority.

The primary theological texts on Jewish sexuality are from the 1960s to the 1990s, largely in response to the feminist and sexual revolutions in American culture. With the growth of academic gender studies, a similar body of scholarly literature has emerged over the past decade. The aptly named anthology, *People of the Body*, edited by Howard Eilberg-Schwartz in 1992,[31] represents a group of scholars dedicated to resurrecting discourses around the body and sexuality in historical Jewish texts. Although this new school of body and gender studies rejects the apologetic scholarship of an earlier age,[32] some of these writers engage in their own acknowledged apologetics. Thus, Daniel Boyarin, one of the most prominent representatives of this school, confronts the apologetic question head on in his pathbreaking work, *Carnal Israel*.[33] He constructs Talmudic Judaism in opposition to Hellenistic culture, where he finds the origins of modern sexism and hostility toward the body. The rabbis constitute a counterculture that affirms the body and sexuality, although in ways that are never without struggle and conflict.[34] Turning to the issue of the male Jewish body in a later work, *Unheroic Conduct*,[35] Boyarin argues that rabbinic culture offers an ideal of masculinity that is the opposite of the Western model. The pale, "feminized" yeshiva scholar, whose image fed the stereotypes of popular American Jewish culture, represents an alternative form of masculinity. Rather than overturning this image or arguing that it had never really existed, Boyarin transvalues what a century of jokes, movies, and novels had satirized: Instead of sexual neurosis and physical impotence, he finds *edelkeit*, the traditional virtue of scholarly refinement.[36]

The range of sources discussed here – movies, novels, and theological and scholarly works – demonstrates that the question of sexuality and the body has engaged all registers of American Jewish culture over the past century. The body and its erotic desires have frequently been the site for conflicting visions of assimilation versus ethnic self-assertion. Gender, too, has proved to be a powerful location for the expression of assimilationist anxieties in a country that itself has undergone important transformations on matters of gender and sexuality. Whether Jews will find marital and sexual fulfillment with other Jews or with Gentiles, key questions for the future of the American

Jewish community, cannot therefore be divorced from the images of the body, sexuality, and gender with which Jewish culture in America has wrestled throughout its recent history.

Notes

1. George Mosse, *Nationalism and Sexuality* (Madison: University of Wisconsin Press, 1988).
2. On Zionism as an erotic revolution, see David Biale, *Eros and the Jews* (Berkeley: University of California Press, 1997), chapter 8. On modern images of the Jewish body, see Sander Gilman, *The Jew's Body* (New York: Routledge, 1991).
3. On Jewish gangsters in America, see Rich Cohen, *Tough Jews* (New York: Simon & Schuster, 1998); Albert Fried, *The Rise and Fall of the Jewish Gangster in America* (New York: Columbia University Press, 1980); Jenna Weissman Joselit, *Our Gang: Jewish Crime and the New York Jewish Community* (Bloomington: Indiana University Press, 1983); and Robert Rockaway, *But He Was Good to His Mother: The Lives and Crimes of Jewish Gangsters* (Jerusalem: Gefen, 2000). More broadly, for a discussion of both Jewish underworld violence and sports such as boxing, see Elliott Horowitz, " 'They Fought Because They were Fighters and They Fought Because They Were Jews': Violence and the Construction of Modern Jewish Identity," *Jews and Violence, Studies in Contemporary Jewry*, 17 (2002), 23–42.
4. Peter Levine, *Ellis Island to Ebbets Field: Sports and the American Jewish Experience* (New York: Oxford University Press, 1992), 14–15.
5. Ibid., 16.
6. Levine, *Ellis Island to Ebbets Field*, chapter 8; Allan Bodner, *When Boxing Was a Jewish Sport* (Westport: Praeger, 1997).
7. Levine, *Ellis Island to Ebbets Field*, 155.
8. Stephen J. Whitfield, "Declarations of Independence: American Jewish Culture in the Twentieth Century," in *Cultures of the Jews*, ed. David Biale (New York: Schocken Books: 2002), 1109–10.
9. Jules Feiffer, "The Minsk Theory of Krypton: Jerry Siegel (1914–1996)," *New York Times Magazine* (29 December 1996), 14–15.
10. For an analysis of the play along these lines, see David Biale, "The Melting Pot and Beyond: Jews and the Politics of American Identity," in *Insider/Outsider: American Jews and Multiculturalism*, ed. David Biale, Susannah Heschel, and Michael Galchinsky (Berkeley: University of California Press, 1998), 17–33.
11. Michael Rogin, *Blackface, White Noise: Jewish Immigrants in the Hollywood Melting Pot* (Berkeley: University of California Press, 1996).
12. For a detailed study of these images from the early twentieth century to the present day, see Riv-Ellen Prell, *Fighting to Become American: Jews, Gender and the Anxiety of Assimilation* (Boston: Beacon Press, 1999).
13. The comedian Joan Rivers is proof that the JAP stereotype is not only limited to male voices.
14. Sander Gilman, *Making the Body Beautiful: A Cultural History of Aesthetic Surgery* (Princeton: Princeton University Press, 1999) and *The Jew's Body* (New York: Routledge, 1991).

15. For an analysis of the sexual semiotics of *Portnoy's Complaint*, see David Biale, *Eros and the Jews* (Berkeley: University of California Press, 1997), Introduction and chapter 9. The pages that follow were substantially drawn from this work.

16. Philip Roth, "Imagining Jews," in *Reading Myself and Others* (New York: Penguin Books, 1985), 278.

17. Lenny Bruce, *How To Talk Dirty and Influence People* (Chicago: Playboy Press, 1963), 5.

18. John Cohen, ed., *The Essential Lenny Bruce* (New York: Ballantine Books, 1967), 32–33.

19. Paul Breines, *Tough Jews* (New York: Basic Books, 1990).

20. Stephen J. Whitfield, "Declarations of Independence: American Jewish Culture in the Twentieth Century," in *Cultures of the Jews*, ed. David Biale (New York: Schocken Books: 2002), 1134–35.

21. Erica Jong, *Fear of Flying* (New York: Holt, Rinehart & Winston, 1973), 30.

22. Erica Jong, *Any Woman's Blues* (New York: Harper & Row, 1990), 32.

23. Ibid., 59.

24. Riv-Ellen Prell, *Fighting to Become American: Jews, Gender and the Anxiety of Assimilation* (Boston: Beacon Press, 1999), chapter 7.

25. Ophira Edut, "Bubbe Got Back: Tales of a Jewess with a Caboose," in *Yentl's Revenge: The Next Wave of Jewish Feminism*, ed. Danya Rutenberg (Seattle: Seal Press, 2001), 24–30. As two indications of this book's iconoclasm, it contains a defense of marrying "a nice Jewish boy" (A. C. Hall, "The Nice Jewish Boy," 3–13) *and* a defense of intermarriage (Sarah Coleman, "A Jewish Feminist Atheism Meditates on Intermarriage," 67–76).

26. Irena Klepfisz, "Resisting and Surviving in America," in *Nice Jewish Girls: A Lesbian Anthology*, ed. Evelyn Torton Beck (Trumansburg: Crossing Press, 1982), 106.

27. Adrienne Rich, "Stepmother Tongues," *Tikkun*, vol. 5, no. 5 (September–October 1990), 36.

28. Judith Plaskow, *Standing Again At Sinai: Judaism from a Feminist Perspective* (San Francisco: HarperSanFrancisco, 1990), 210.

29. For three examples from each of the movements, see Norman Lamm, *A Hedge of Roses: Jewish Insights into Marriage and Married Life*, 1st ed. (New York: Feldheim, 1966). Lamm's books went through at least five editions. Robert Gordis, *Love and Sex: A Modern Jewish Perspective* (New York: Farrar, Straus & Giroux, 1978), and Eugene Borowitz, *Choosing a Sex Ethic: A Jewish Inquiry* (New York: Schocken Books, 1969).

30. Norman Lamm, *A Hedge of Roses: Jewish Insights into Marriage and Married Life*, 1st ed. (New York: Feldheim, 1966), 31–32.

31. Howard Eilberg-Schwartz, *People of the Body: Jews and Judaism from an Embodied Perspective* (Albany: State University of New York Press, 1992).

32. An example of such "traditionalist" scholarship would be Louis Epstein, *Sex Laws and Customs in Judaism* (New York: Bloch Publishing, 1948).

33. Daniel Boyarin, *Carnal Israel: Reading Sex in Talmudic Culture* (Berkeley: University of California Press, 1993), 20.

34. Not all scholars have accepted Boyarin's view. Some have demurred by pointing out the significant strands of asceticism that can be found in historical Judaism. See David Biale, *Eros and the Jews* (Berkeley: University of California Press, 1997).

35. Daniel Boyarin, *Unheroic Conduct: The Rise of Heterosexuality and the Invention of the Jewish Man* (Berkeley: University of California Press, 1997).

36. For two important dissents to Daniel Boyarin, see Allan Arkush, "Antiheroic Mock Heroics: Daniel Boyarin Versus Theodor Herzl and His Legacy," *Jewish Social Studies* n.s. 4; 3 (1998) and Hillel J. Kieval, "Imagining 'Masculinity' in the Jewish Fin de Siecle," *Jews and Gender: The Challenge to Hierarchy, Studies in Contemporary Jewry*, 16 (2000), 142–55.

15   The American Jewish urban experience
NATHAN GLAZER

To evoke the American Jewish urban experience may seem like an exercise in nostalgia, indulging in a history whose bearing on the lives of American Jews today is debatable.[1] What, after all, is urban about American Jews today? Presently, almost all Jews live in cities, towns, suburbs, and metropolitan areas that are officially considered "urban" by U.S. census standards. However, nowadays, *urban* holds a rather different meaning from that used in the census; it refers to the central city of a metropolitan area. More specifically, it refers to the dense and historic inner city, which has been steadily eclipsed demographically by the growth of suburbs and exurbs and by migration to developing new cities in the South, Southwest, and West. In fact, *urban* today has an even narrower meaning and often evokes the city of minorities, the Hispanics and African Americans, who tend to make up the greater part of the central city population. This kind of urban city brings to mind the social problems, regardless of their origins, currently associated with inner-city minorities. With this kind of city, American Jews today have little direct experience.

THE AMERICAN JEWISH URBAN EXPERIENCE

At the close of World War II, two great migrations began emptying the inner cities of Jews, leaving these areas for the most part without a substantial Jewish population. These two migratory waves resulted in a radical redistribution of the Jewish population of the United States in the thirty years after World War II.[2] The first migration was to the suburbs; the second was to cities in California and Florida. The demographic change can be traced in the annual Jewish population statistics of the *American Jewish Year Book*. The data show a steady rise of the cities of the South and Southwest to the point where the second and third largest Jewish population concentrations today are no longer Chicago and Philadelphia, but Los Angeles and Miami. Substantial Jewish populations are still listed for cities such as Cleveland and Detroit, which are actually almost without Jews; but this is because the statistics of city population presently refer to the metropolitan area of each city and not to the politically defined city alone.

In 1962, in the midst of this population transformation, two leading figures in Jewish communal affairs wrote a book on Jewish communities in the United States. It contained a chapter on the Jewish community in Cleveland alarmingly entitled "City without Jews," which suggested that Jews had somehow been eliminated or driven out of Cleveland. Indeed, virtually no Jews lived within the city limits of Cleveland by that time.[3] The steady movement of the center of Jewish population eastward and southeastward had moved the Jews of Cleveland out of the city, into Cleveland Heights, Shaker Heights, and similar communities. There were a substantial number of Jews in the metropolitan area, and Cleveland remained a leading center of Jewish communal activity.

Like many other midwestern and northeastern Jewish communities, the city of Detroit was similar to the city of Cleveland in numbers and character. The Dexter area located in Detroit "housed 49 percent of Jewish families in 1949; but by 1958" – less than ten years later – "the number had drastically decreased to only 9 percent."[4] There was a concurrent boom in the Jewish population of the new suburban areas of Jewish migration. "In 1952 only 3 percent of the Jewish population lived in Oak Park.... By 1965, 46 percent resided in Oak Park." In a sense, the population changes that occurred in Cleveland and Detroit are not surprising. America itself was suburbanizing and moving South and West in the era after World War II, which constituted years of prosperity and economic growth for the most part. Jews were also part of this trend, yet their rate of mobility out of the central city far surpassed that of any other group.

Perhaps the best-studied case of the rapid Jewish migration out of the central city is in Boston, where no less than three books have been written describing and analyzing what happened to its main Jewish neighborhood. Yona Ginsberg, an Israeli sociologist, was at Harvard while the flight was in process and described it in her doctoral thesis, *Jews in a Changing Neighborhood*,[5] which was published as a book in 1975. Hillel Levine and Lawrence Harmon told the story in their book *The Death of an American Jewish Community: A Tragedy of Good Intentions*,[6] published in 1992. A third book has recently been published, *Urban Exodus: Why the Jews Left Boston and the Catholics Stayed*,[7] which further highlights the special circumstances that led to the rapid emptying of the classic Jewish section of Boston. In particular, there was a mortgage program designed to make it easier for blacks to own homes. This program targeted the Jewish area and contributed to the sudden abandonment of the largest Jewish area of Boston.

The Jewish movement out of the central cities across America was so rapid and so complete that it inevitably raises the question, why? In the case of other ethnic groups, the migratory movement was significantly slower. Even as a significant portion of an ethnic group relocated as a result of improved economic circumstances, it was typical for the businesses and institutions that served the ethnic community to still remain in the area of first settlement and form a node of group activity. This was the case with the largest inner-city Jewish area, the Lower East Side in New York. However, in most cities, the first areas of Jewish settlement lost any indications of Jewish presence. This did not happen to the same degree with other ethnic groups, and so we find Chinatowns, Little Italies, and Greektowns in various central cities even though the majority of the ethnic community has moved off to other parts of the city or to the suburbs. Jewish mobility was an extreme form of ethnic mobility, the movement outward from the area of first settlement that we have seen for all ethnic groups. The mobility of Jewish Americans speeded up to the point where it might remind us of the parody of a Hasidic song in which whatever the rabbi does, the followers go to excess in imitating him. Thus, when the rabbi walks, the followers jump; when he eats, they gorge themselves; when he sings, they shriek; and so forth. Other ethnic groups moved; the Jews fled.

This more rapid movement of American Jews may be attributed to three factors. The first is that Jews were more economically successful than other ethnic groups, and so they had the wherewithal to move to newer and better areas than the dense central city. The second is that Jews formed weaker attachments to specific areas and did not form the same sentimental connection to a plot of land or home that immigrants from other groups, with rural and peasant backgrounds, did. Where apartment house living was common, more Jews rented than bought, and this made it easier for them to move. In Sidney Bolkosky's rich historical account of the Jews of Detroit, he observes that the houses of Jews in the Hastings Street area "were easily identified as Jewish-occupied. One former resident of the old neighborhood joked that 'the non-Jews grew flowers, the Jews grew dirt in front of their houses.' Tidy gardens with picket fences seemed to be a low priority in the Jewish agenda around Hastings Street."[8]

The third factor in Jewish mobility can be found in the organization of Jewish religion. Catholics – who formed the chief neighbors of Jews in central cities – based their neighborhoods on parishes, with church and school identified as the heart of a neighborhood. As the newest account of what happened to the old Jewish neighborhoods of Boston by Gerald Gramm emphasizes, this structure helped anchor the varied Catholic ethnic groups strongly to a given geographical section of the city. In contrast, Jewish inner-city neighborhoods contained a multiplicity of synagogues, each with no formal relation to the other, with no or weak relationships to a central body, each standing alone, with an independent government, dependent on its own financial resources. Synagogues did not create neighborhoods but instead followed neighborhoods. "Other considerations besides religion, having to do with more material, social, and educational needs, seemed to take priority [in the movements of Jews]. In the name of those needs, congregants moved; if the synagogue wanted to survive, it would have to follow them."[9] Thus, the grand Temple Beth El in Detroit, built in 1903 and designed by the famous architect Albert Kahn, lasted less than twenty years as a Jewish place of worship. It was replaced in 1922 by the new Temple Beth El, which was also designed by Kahn, further out in the suburbs. Although it lasted surprisingly for fifty years, a new Temple Beth El, further out in the suburbs, has also replaced it.

The movement of the Jewish community in city after city can be marked by a trail of impressive but abandoned synagogues and temples, which now often serve as African American churches. It seems to have been the norm for the Jewish community to be succeeded by a black community in city after city. One reason was that the black populations of the Northern cities were growing rapidly in the 1920s and 1930s, and in the years after World War II. Another reason was that the Jewish communities offered the least resistance – indeed, no resistance at all – of any ethnic community in the inner city to blacks moving in. The urban sociologist Ernest W. Burgess wrote about this as early as 1928: "No instance has been noted where a Negro invasion succeeded in displacing the Irish in possession of a community. Yet, frequently..., Negroes have pushed forward in the wake of retreating Jews." Analyzing the Jewish flight from Boston, Gerald Gramm writes that "Malcolm X, in his autobiography, emphasizes how quickly and completely Jews abandoned neighborhoods in which African Americans had begun settling. 'Who would always lead the whites' exodus? The Jews!' he observed. 'Generally in these situations, some whites stay put – you just notice who they are: they're Irish Catholics, they're Italians; they're rarely ever Jews.' " There is an implication in Malcolm X's remarks that Jews were more prejudiced than others, but clearly that was not the explanation. As Gramm points out:

Jews also tended to greet new African-American neighbors with higher levels of tolerance and with little violence. In Chicago, racial change in the large Jewish district of North Lawndale occurred with none of the anti-black violence that routinely characterized the city's working-class Catholic neighborhoods. The same pattern prevailed in Detroit, where African Americans encountered little resistance in Jewish neighborhoods, but where homeowners' associations, dominated by Catholics, became organized vehicles of rabid, antiblack violence in the 1940s, 1950s, and 1960s.[10]

While this tolerance is to the credit of the American Jewish community, it also meant the nearly complete abandonment of the political inner city as Jews relocated to the suburbs, with substantial consequences for American Jewish life. Indeed, there were a variety of implications of this shift from central city to suburb, from the northeastern and midwestern centers of Jewish population to the South and Southwest. There are three aspects of American Jewish life that were substantially transformed by this movement out of the inner city: the nature of Jewish education, the nature of Jewish organizational life – in particular, religious life – and the political orientation of American Jews.

JEWISH EDUCATION

The great age of public-school achievement in America can be dated to the time when large and dense Jewish communities still lived in the central city. While the public school was not a Jewish institution, it was the dominant educational institution, indeed the dominant institution, of the old neighborhood, taking the place in many respects of the church–parochial school complex for Catholics. Jews were by far the most earnest and committed clients of the public schools. However, despite their strong orientation to education, Jews were not initially prominent among teachers and principals and higher officials of the inner-city public schools they attended. These posts were generally in the hands of the ethnic groups that had preceded Jews, and of those groups that were also more politically effective than Jews in gaining the spoils of public office and public jobs. Typically, in each Jewish neighborhood, there were certain public schools and high schools dominated almost entirely by Jewish students. Moreover, in each city, the schools that were overwhelmingly Jewish were academically among the best in the city. Jewish students in cities such as New York and Boston dominated the special public schools for the academically achieving, to which entry was by examination. In effect, when the quality of urban public schools was considered to be superior – as was the case in the twenties and thirties and forties of the twentieth century – it was because they were filled with eager Jewish students.

A bond was created among those Jewish students who attended the public high schools, as is evident in the present day alumni gatherings of graduates of New York City high schools in Los Angeles and Miami. However, the role of the public school as a common binding experience has sharply declined in the new areas of Jewish settlement that have replaced the central city Jewish communities. First, one effect of the move outward was that Jewish neighborhoods were not so exclusively Jewish anymore. Thus, the public schools in the suburbs are nowhere as dominantly Jewish in composition as they were when Jews congregated in the central city. A New York City account tells us this: "Given the residential concentration of immigrant Jews and the local character of the public schools, Jewish children often discovered that they constituted 90 percent of a school's enrollment."[11] At Central High School in Detroit, which became known as the "Jewish school," more than half the graduates in 1938 were Jews.[12] This kind of concentration is simply not possible in the suburbs. The ambience previously created by this Jewish concentration along with the intensity with which academic achievement was pursued is no longer as commonly found. Second, the public school in the Jewish communities of today now have significant competitors, in the form of Jewish day schools and private schools.

The most striking development since the age of urban Jewishness is the rise of the Jewish day school, which had previously played a very minor role in the education of children. In fact, "[w]ell into the 1930's, Jewish parochial schools attracted only 2 percent of the city's Jewish children."[13] Those who attended the few Jewish day schools, typically known as *yeshivas*, were generally from Orthodox families. The explosion of the Jewish day school took place simultaneously with the Jewish migration out of the central city. One reason for the growth of the Jewish day school was the decline of the public school and the simultaneous increase in the number of black pupils in these schools. Whether it was the academic decline of urban public schools or the growing number of black pupils, or a combination of both, Jewish parents increasingly felt their children deserved better than a public school education. This resulted in the astonishing growth of Jewish day schools, which today enroll perhaps one-third of all Jewish youth of school-going age.[14] There were certainly other reasons than the growing minority population of the urban schools that were responsible for the rise of the Jewish day school. This rise is as prominent in the suburbs, where the public schools have (on the whole) a good reputation and where there are a smaller number of black students, as in the inner cities. One such reason was that there was a growing concern among many parents as assimilation proceeded over what kind of Jews their children would become. In contrast to fifty years ago, parents felt less capable either because of ignorance or ambivalence of creating a Jewish environment or experience for their children, and so they hoped the Jewish day school, which always had some religious educational component, would do so in their stead.

Whatever the reasons, one kind of binding Jewish experience was undoubtedly broken, to be replaced by a much greater diversity in educational experience. A case in point is the impressive variety of Jewish backgrounds to be found among students presently enrolled at Harvard University. Some students are closely identified with Israel and with Jewish interests, others are very distant from any kind of Jewish experience or interest. Attendance at Jewish schools plays a large role in differentiating these students into such very different types. This is in contrast with my personal experience in the national student Zionist organization in the 1940s, when the Jewish students at Harvard were much more of one type – bright students from the public schools of Boston. They were not very different from the students at City College, who were also the products of the public schools.

One unifying experience in the diverse Jewish life of the city has passed: the large public school with its culture of eager commitment to a larger life beyond the *shtetl* of the Jewish inner city, a life open to new culture, new intellectual challenges, and offering the possibility of social and economic advancement and a wider intellectual and cultural horizon. This world can be sensed in Alfred Kazin's writing on growing up in New York and in Norman Podhoretz's *Breaking Ranks*, and in other Jewish memoirs. It can be seen in Joseph Dorman's documentary film and book, *Arguing the World*, about four inner-city Jewish youths who grew up in the thirties (one of them the author of this chapter). The public school represented the common experience of a whole generation of Jewish students in every major Jewish community.

ORGANIZATIONAL LIFE

The shift to the suburbs has had a very different effect on Jewish organizational life from that on education. Instead of increasing divergence, it has reduced divergence and created one common, overriding kind of Jewish organizational life for suburban Jews. One of the striking characteristics of central-city and first-settlement Jewishness was the astonishing range of Jewish ideologies and organizations that were then available, such as Socialist and Communist, Zionist and anti-Zionist, Hebraist and Yiddishist. There were Jewish afternoon schools, day schools, and community schools, each of a different persuasion. There were also synagogues of every kind, from tiny *shtiblach* to grand buildings with an array of synagogue-related groups and activities. One signal effect of the move from the inner city was the death of most of these movements and tendencies and organizations. Of course, many factors contributed to the decline and death of so many Jewish ideologies, organizations, and institutions, thus reducing the types and styles of Jewishness. This variety of movements and organizations depended on a large and dense Jewish population, living in close proximity, from which any specific tendency could draw the few adherents of its ideology or perspective that made it possible for it to exist. In contrast, where was one to find in the suburbs enough families with an interest in, for example, secular Yiddishism, to maintain a Sholem Aleichem school? The move from the inner city and the breakup of dense Jewish concentrations was only one reason for this decimation of the types of Jewish ideology and Jewish organizational life. Certainly assimilation and distance from Europe was a more important cause, yet it is likely that this variety of Jewish organizational life could have survived longer had there not been such a hasty abandonment of the inner city and Jewish density.

What has replaced the diversified Jewish organizational life? The characterization of present-day Jewishness is not easy. It is the Jewishness of an upper-middle-class community composed of businessmen, executives, professionals, and academics, with very few workers, even in New York City, where a fragment of a Jewish working class still survives. Socially, the community does not reach much below the occupational categories of teachers, civil servants, small businessmen, or various kinds of white-collar employees. The relatively restricted occupational range of the Jewish community contributes to one single, dominant style of being Jewish, that is, the style of the large suburban synagogue.

Ideologically, Israel is at the center of Jewish concerns and presently forms the key, unifying element for Jewish organizational life, whether religious or nonreligious. During the first twenty years of Israel's existence, the issue of Israel did not dominate American Jewish organizational life as it has since the 1970s. Prior to the Six Day War and the conquest of the West Bank, there was no major successful American Jewish lobby for Israel or major American government aid for Israel. In fact, even as Israel was coming into creation as a state, there were still important intellectual and organizational currents in Jewish life that did not support statehood. Israel became central for American Jewishness some time after its creation and after the years of its greatest peril.

Another important unifying element of the current dominant style of Jewishness is the overwhelming role of the Holocaust. There were no Holocaust museums or memorials, no major public ceremonies to mark the Holocaust, and no state educational requirements that the Holocaust be taught in schools until two to three decades after the end of the war. The centrality of the Holocaust came relatively late to American Jewish life. Along with Israel, it now shapes contemporary Jewish concerns.

In contrast to the prior Jewish life in the central city, current Jewish life appears to be of a more homogenous type and more limited in its variety.

Rebellions against this uniformity were raised by Jewish youth organizations in the 1970s and by the Havurot movement of the same period. Discontent was expressed in the creation of alternative smaller congregations, sometimes within the framework of the large synagogue. For better or worse, Jewishness in the United States is now centered in the large suburban synagogue. The alternative and competitive forms that once existed have virtually disappeared. The various forms of secular Jewishness that flourished in the inner city have been lost, as well as the Jewishness that came of itself, as a matter of course, from living in such dense Jewish neighborhoods. In the autobiographies of those who grew up in the Jewish central city, such as Irving Howe, it is striking that there is little overt reference to Jewish interests marking their growing up. However, certain aspects of Jewishness, such as the knowledge of Yiddish, of the varieties of Jewish political ideological positions, of the order of the religious services, were so ingrained that when Jewish interests awoke in them in later life, they had much on which to draw. Although the Jewish education provided today is much more professional than it was in the old Jewish central city, it cannot offer the same acquaintance with Jewishness in an intimate form, as that can only be gained from living in it rather than from studying it. The Jewish historian Hasia Diner, in her study of the role of the Lower East Side in Jewish memory, makes a similar point:

> Lower East Side Jews could "be" Jewish by belonging to a
> *landsmanshaft*, for example, or just by virtue of living in the
> neighborhood. After all, independent *mohelim* would usher their
> newborn sons into the covenant of Abraham; rabbis without
> congregations would marry them;... if they felt the call to worship
> during... Rosh Hashanah and Yom Kippur, dozens of makeshift
> services sprang up in rented halls.... These Jews did not need
> synagogues to service their religious needs.[15]

POLITICAL CHANGES

Another aspect of change that seems related to the move out of the central city was the change in the political attitudes of American Jews. From one perspective, there has been surprisingly little change: Jews were liberal then, and they are liberal now. They supported Franklin D. Roosevelt then, and, despite the sharp economic and social rise among today's Jews, they still support the Democrats. They remain the only white ethnic or religious group that is consistently liberal in its political attitudes and heavily Democratic in its voting. Indeed, the expectation that with suburbanization, which inevitably brings more home ownership and more concern with taxes, Jews would move to the right, has not been fulfilled – at least for most Jews. There has, however, been one significant change. The Jews of the central city were often reluctant Democrats, and ideologies to the left had a strong pull among them. So, in New York, the American Labor Party and the Liberal Party were created to permit these reluctant Democrats, only recently and perhaps still Socialist and Communist, to vote Democratic. Today many Jews may also be called reluctant Democrats, but the pull that makes them reluctant is from the right. Indeed, many are no longer reluctant: the neoconservatives, a tendency of the 1970s among a few intellectuals, whose dominant voice was *Commentary*, were mostly Jews who had grown up in the dense central-city Jewish neighborhoods. Today, their children – William Kristol, John Podhoretz, and many others – are no longer neoconservatives but simply conservatives. A change of some kind was inevitable as people rose economically and occupationally and, as a consequence, changed their residences from the central city to the suburbs. Nevertheless, the change was less sharp among Jews than among other groups, such as the Irish Americans and Italian Americans.

THE URBAN RESPONSIBILITY OF AMERICAN JEWS

In the late 1960s, as urban problems surfaced and as riots swept through the inner sections of American cities, the question inevitably arose: What is the responsibility of American Jews for these urban problems, for the disaster of the American city, with which Jews had been so closely identified and from which they had so recently departed? More than thirty years later, does this question make any special sense for American Jews? What does the move out of the central city mean for current Jewish attitudes toward urban problems? How does a suburbanized Jewish community today connect with the urban problems of impoverished minorities, housing projects, inadequate school systems, and crime-ridden neighborhoods? Should the suburban Jewish community be more closely connected with them?

Following their mass departure out of the inner city, American Jews maintained one ironic connection with the urban problems of today by way of the Jewish businesses they left behind. These included the liquor stores and groceries, pawnshops and clothing stores, which were all the target of inner-city rioters. At least one Jewish defense organization then pondered whether Jewish–black relations could be improved if there was some program to make possible the turnover of such endangered businesses to blacks, but nothing ever transpired as a result of this interest. The Jewish stores were succeeded by Chinese or Korean stores.[16] The fate of these businesses and their owners was one basis for Jewish concern with central cities during the urban riots of the sixties. However, the so-called urban crisis was, and remains, far from the top of the public concerns of the current American Jewish community, and it falls ever lower on the general political agenda as the population and political power of the large cities of the Northeast and Midwest decline.

The great age of urban Jewish life constitutes the background against which American Jews inevitably see their life today. Is the Jewish urban experience simply a matter for history now, or can a new kind of urban experience for Jews be anticipated? After all, Jews have historically been an urban people and still feel an attachment to the areas in which the Jewish communities of today were spawned. There is modest evidence of something of a renewal in interest in the central city as a place to live among some suburbanites. In city after city, some minimal revival of sections of the inner city is visible, as couples and individuals without school-aged children begin to find parts of the inner city more attractive than the suburbs. The inner cities still have a concentration of facilities – cultural, educational, athletic, entertainment, and the like – that suburbs cannot match.

CONCLUSION

Older inner city areas are becoming somewhat more residential, as factories and warehouses turn into condominiums, and some new construction is visible; here and there a small synagogue surprisingly sprouts in the inner cities to serve the new returning population. This urban return is, as of yet, on a very small scale. Nevertheless, just as Jews exceeded their neighbors in the celerity with which they left the inner city, so too are they more prominent in this movement to return. They are prominent as developers trying to restore the livability of inner city areas in which a grand architectural heritage, surpassing in interest and quality anything available in the suburbs, still can be found. As middle-class people with an interest in urban facilities return, there is some promise that Jews will have to engage themselves more deeply, because of immediate connection, with the problems of the inner city. Perhaps the Jewish urban experience in America need not be limited to history and nostalgia alone.

Notes

1. An earlier version of this paper was presented at a conference held at the Cohn-Haddow Center for Judaic Studies at Wayne State University in 1999.
2. Generalizations such as these exclude the city of New York, where almost half of American Jewry resided.

3. Eugene J. Lipman and Albert Vorspan, eds., *A Tale of Ten Cities: The Triple Melting Pot in American Religious Life* (New York: Union of American Hebrew Congregations Press, 1962).

4. Sidney Bolkosky, *Harmony and Dissonance: Voices of Jewish Identity in Detroit, 1914–1967* (Wayne State University Press, 1991), 298, 301.

5. Yona Ginsberg, *Jews in a Changing Neighborhood* (New York: The Free Press, 1975).

6. Hillel Levine and Lawrence Harmon, *The Death of an American Jewish Community: A Tragedy of Good Intentions* (New York: The Free Press, 1992).

7. Gerald Gamm, *Urban Exodus: Why the Jews Left Boston and the Catholics Stayed* (Cambridge, MA: Harvard University Press, 1999).

8. Sidney Bolkosky, *Harmony and Dissonance*, 59.

9. Sidney Bolkosky, *Harmony and Dissonance*, 30, 72, 98. All this, of course, can be paralleled in other communities, which have also left a trail of synagogues abandoned by their communities and now most commonly serving black congregations. See Sidney Z. Vincent and Judah Rubenstein, *Jewish Life in Cleveland: A Contemporary Narrative 1945–1975; A Pictorial Record 1839–1975* (The Western Reserve Historical Society and The Jewish Federation of Cleveland, 1978), 115, 207, 209, 223, 269, 275.

10. Gerald Gamm, *Urban Exodus: Why the Jews left Boston and the Catholics Stayed* (Cambridge, MA: Harvard University Press, 1999), 3.

11. Deborah Dash Moore, *At Home in America: Second Generation New York Jews* (New York: Columbia University Press: 1981), 95.

12. Sidney Bolkosky, *Harmony and Dissonance*, 185.

13. Ibid., 95.

14. Jack Wertheimer, "Current Trends in American Jewish Philanthropy," *American Jewish Year Book 97* (1997), 29, reports 181,000 Jewish students enrolled in Jewish day schools in 1994; the chart of Jewish population by age on p. 60 of this article suggests this may be as much as one-third of all Jewish children of school age.

15. Hasia Diner, *Lower East Side Memories* (Princeton: Princeton University Press, 2000), 139.

16. Sidney Bolkosky, *Harmony and Dissonance*, 268, 464.

16 "Sacred survival" revisited: American Jewish civil religion in the new millennium

JONATHAN WOOCHER

Among the questions posed by sociologists of American Jewry, there is one that is perennial and basic but that has always seemed to elude easy answer: What is the *content* of American Jews' "Jewishness"? What beliefs and behaviors, self-understandings and commitments do Jews embrace as a consequence of being Jewish?

Writing from the vantage point of the early 1980s, I suggested that, for a large number of American Jews, and especially for those most active in the institutional structures of the American Jewish community, many of the answers to these questions were provided by what I called an American Jewish "civil religion."[1] This civil religion defined a way of being Jewish that enabled its adherents to give meaning to their identities as Jews by connecting them to a great historic drama of destruction and rebirth. Such Jews made the survival of the Jewish people their sacred cause. They supported Israel and marched to free Soviet Jews. They gave generously to philanthropies in order to express their solidarity with fellow Jews and their commitment to the Jewish value of *tzedakah* (philanthropy and social justice). They educated their children as Jews, and they gathered at key points during their lives and during the year to publicly acknowledge and celebrate their Jewishness and their attachment to Jewish tradition. They celebrated as well their success as Americans, always wary of anti-Semitism, but feeling that in America they had found a congenial home, not just another way station in a long journey. With mostly good humor, these Jews accepted the fact that, when it came to theology and observance of Jewish law, two Jews meant three opinions. They were divided denominationally, but they were substantially united on what "really mattered": remembering the past (especially the Holocaust), sustaining and caring for other Jews, living both as part of and slightly apart from the American mainstream, and sharing in the special destiny – difficult to name, but proudly affirmed nonetheless – of a noble people.

In the two decades since this portrait was drawn, much has changed.[2] American Jews have become even more diverse in their beliefs and behaviors. For many, biography (self and family) has replaced history as the arena in which they seek meaning and significance in their Jewishness. Jewish life has become privatized and personalized. Institutions, especially those of the federation–United Jewish Appeal system where "civil Judaism" was centered, no longer carry the authority they once did. *Spirituality* has replaced *solidarity* as a watchword. Jewish ethnic identity is eroding, even as religious identity holds its own. For large numbers of Jews, the boundaries separating them from the larger American society and culture have collapsed to the point where their Jewishness and Americanness are not only compatible but virtually indistinguishable (at least in their minds). Internally, the divisions between denominations loom far more salient, as cooperation among their leaders is far more difficult to sustain even as many American Jews manifest a growing disenchantment with or indifference to any formalized version of Judaism that impinges on their autonomy in choosing when, how, and even whether to "be Jewish."

Does this mean that the Jewish civil religion that was so potent a force on the American Jewish landscape in the 1970s and 1980s is now just a historical memory? And, if so, how are we to assess its flowering and withering? Was it ever of any real consequence, worth having a book written about it in the first place? Is its passing from prominence to be celebrated, bemoaned, or merely acknowledged with a shrug of the shoulders?

I believe that the answers to these questions – like that of the content of American Jews' Jewishness – are rather more complex than may be evident at first blush. At a minimum, it is worth revisiting what Jewish civil religion was and what has happened to it and to the Jewish community over the past twenty years before deciding whether to bury it, praise it, do neither, or do both.

JEWISH CIVIL RELIGION: A SECOND LOOK

The idea that American Jews have created and practice a form of Jewish civil religion is founded on two major insights. The first, popularized if not originated by the sociologist Robert Bellah, holds that some nations, the United States being a prime example, develop an understanding of their identity and history that depict these in transcendent terms. That is, the nation (or at least its political leadership) views itself as living out a sacred story, one that connects it to ultimate values that the nation embodies (or ought to embody) and that give its political institutions their purposes. The citizens of a nation (or group) that so sees itself as living out a sacred drama can derive meaning for their individual lives through their participation in this drama. They are called on to live the values being celebrated, to acknowledge symbols of these values, and to join in appropriate rituals that celebrate the nation's attachment to them. This civil religion is distinguishable from, though it may often be intermingled with, the specific religious beliefs and practices of the nation's churches. Its focus is not on any denominational creed, but rather on the life of the nation itself, which is seen as embodying a religious message.[3]

Bellah's argument for the presence and persistence of an identifiable American civil religion meeting these criteria excited considerable controversy. Nevertheless, the concept has proven to be a durable one, applicable in a number of different contexts. While it is clear that civil religious rhetoric and impact wax and wane, it is also clear that imagining American politics without the sense of American mission or the belief that our core political values are "self-evident" is a futile task. If the United States is indeed, as many scholars claim, the most "religious" of the Western nations, then this is partly due to the fact that we have enjoyed a "common faith" in the form of the civil religion that has been threaded through our political life since colonial days.

The second critical insight that underlies the identification of an American *Jewish* civil religion is that of political scientist Daniel Elazar (z"l). In his now-classic book, *Community and Polity*, Elazar argued persuasively that American Jews (like Jews before them throughout the world) have formed a polity through which they carry out important collective tasks.[4] The American Jewish polity is voluntaristic; it has no coercive authority and no one is compelled to participate in it. It is a true polity nonetheless. During the course of the twentieth century, the shape of this polity evolved in such a way as to place the local Jewish community federations and their national organizations, now unified in a single body called the United Jewish Communities, in a pivotal position. These federations do not "control" the American Jewish organizational system. They are, though, the single most encompassing and powerful expression of the self-organizing thrust of American Jewry. Elazar called them "framing institutions" for the polity. Today, we might think of them more as hubs in the multiple intersecting and overlapping networks of organizations that carry out the "public" business of the Jewish populace – providing health and welfare services to Jews and others, domestically and abroad; defending Jewish political interests and managing relationships with non-Jews; Jewishly educating the next generation; and maintaining settings for Jews to come together for a myriad of other purposes, including private ones, such as worship and ritual celebration.

As with Bellah, Elazar's conception of an American Jewish polity has not been without its critics. Certainly, the shape of that polity has changed since Elazar first advanced the concept more than a quarter century ago. Federations are not nearly as dominant, and the priorities of the public agenda have shifted and shifted again over time. Here too, though, Elazar's fundamental insight seems unassailable: American Jews have organized themselves to function as a political system, to allocate resources, and to use power and influence to achieve collective purposes. Much, if not most, of this organizational activity takes place outside the domain of identifiably religious institutions. The American Jewish community is clearly more than a church or even a denomination, and certainly more than an ethnic group. Though it is not a nation or a nationality, it is indeed a voluntary polity with an identity that transcends its formal religious dimensions.

All that remained to generate the idea of an American Jewish civil religion was to put these two insights and claims together and to test empirically whether the concept fit the case. This I did in my book, *Sacred Survival: The Civil Religion of American Jews*. My conclusion was that there was indeed an American Jewish civil religion with readily identifiable tenets, some public rituals, and three powerful stories that provided its mythic core. This civil religion was most visible in the rhetoric of the leaders of the institutions of the Jewish polity, but, I argued, it was not limited to these institutions. Its tenets were widely affirmed by American Jews, if not in their minds as a civil religion, then certainly as embodied in its "popular" version, the American Jewish "folk" religion described by Charles Liebman at around the same time.[5] It may be useful to recall the seven major tenets of "civil Judaism" as I then identified them:

1. The unity of the Jewish people;
2. Mutual responsibility;
3. Jewish survival in a threatening world;
4. The centrality of the State of Israel;
5. The enduring value of Jewish tradition;
6. Tzedakah, or philanthropy and social justice; and
7. Americanness as a virtue.[6]

In support of these affirmations, the American Jewish civil religion told three primary stories.

The first was the story of destruction and rebirth, that is, how the Jewish people were nearly destroyed in the Holocaust but were now determined to survive, to build the State of Israel, and to keep its tradition and values alive in a still-threatening world.

The second was the story of American Jewish exceptionalism, which is the notion that America and American Jews are different, uniquely privileged to live in two great cultures, and therefore responsible for using their power and good fortune purposefully for the sake of Jewish survival and repair of the world.

The third was the story of Jewish chosenness, the conviction, difficult to understand rationally, but felt deeply, that Jews have a special destiny and mission, and that these can give our individual lives profound meaning and purpose.[7]

The American Jewish civil religion is an institutional ideology that functioned effectively to buttress the position and claims of the polity that sponsored it. It unified Jews across denominational and organizational boundaries. It legitimated the activities of the institutions of the polity itself, especially the federations. It also mobilized Jews to give and to work on behalf of the purposes defined by the polity.[8] However, it was more than that as well. "Civil Judaism" clearly responded to a desire on the part of many American Jews to give their Jewishness a larger significance, and to do so in terms that allowed for, but did not require, elaborate theological affirmations or religious observances. It was in many ways an ideal religious stance for Jews who, as they moved to the suburbs in the 1950s, had rushed to build synagogues in order to fit in well with their church-building Christian neighbors, but who were uncertain about the content with which to fill these synagogues, other than life-cycle celebrations and an annual pilgrimage of public reaffirmation of the faith at the High Holidays. Jewish civil religion both provided a content, a religion of support for Israel, for social justice, and for preservation of the faith (however ill defined), and a set of alternative venues, for some more compelling than the synagogue, from which to practice this religion.

THE DECLINE AND FALL OF JEWISH CIVIL RELIGION

I continue to believe that, as a work of descriptive sociology, *Sacred Survival* holds up well. Even at the time of its publication (1986), few critics took issue with the portrait it painted of the values and beliefs animating the federation system and its activists. A number, however, sharply attacked what they perceived as a gross overestimation of the importance of the phenomenon and any attempt to accord it legitimacy as a serious religious stance, civil or otherwise.[9] I will return to the issue of the religious seriousness of American Jewish civil religion later, but what seems certain is that the centrality of this ideology in defining the content of American Jews' Jewishness has declined, perhaps dramatically, since *Sacred Survival* was published. As described in the introduction to this chapter, American Jewish identity appears to have undergone a decisive shift in the 1990s away from a focus on the collective, historical experience of the Jewish people and toward a highly individualized appropriation of Jewish symbols, beliefs, and practices as part of the search for personal meaning.

This shift has been widely documented. Drawing on survey research, Steven M. Cohen has described a broad phenomenon of "religious stability and ethnic decline" affecting American Jewry. Nearly all expressions of Jewish identity rooted in a sense of "peoplehood," from proportion of Jewish friends to membership in Jewish organizations (except the synagogue) to attachment to the State of Israel, have declined, especially among younger Jews. At the same time, more conventionally religious expressions of Jewish identity, including ritual observance, have held steady.[10] This shift parallels those in the larger society. The same Robert Bellah who wrote in the 1960s and 1970s about American civil religion turned his attention in the 1980s and 1990s to the growing "privatization" of American religion and the threat to community in *Habits of the Heart*.[11] Numerous other observers of American religious, social, and political life have echoed this fundamental theme of Bellah's later work: Americans today are less "collectivist" in every dimension of their lives, including religion.[12] "Freedom of choice" is the watchword of contemporary American social life, and with it comes a diversity and fluidity of identity and values that militates against all efforts to unify society around overarching ideas or institutions.

Using in-depth interviews, Cohen and Arnold Eisen have fleshed out this portrait of "religious personalism" among American Jews. They examined the Jewishness of so-called moderately affiliated Jews (the kind of Jews, I would suggest, who a decade or two earlier certainly embraced Liebman's folk religion and quite likely the tenets of Jewish civil religion as well) in their book, *The Jew Within*. For these Jews in the late 1990s, being Jewish was a personal project of meaning making, with self and family as the primary reference points. Institutions play a secondary role, and contemporary Jewish history even less. These Jews tend to be universalistic in their outlook. They value being Jewish, but they are reluctant to draw hard boundaries between Jews and non-Jews, or between Jewish values and those of any other religion. They also reserve the right to decide on when and how to be Jewish to themselves (what Cohen and Eisen call "the sovereign self"). Jewish norms, even those of the civil religious variety (support Israel, give to Jewish philanthropies) lack authority for these Jews. They do not necessarily repudiate the behaviors, but neither do they see these as externally mandated. In fact, they resent any attempt to make binding demands or to impose value judgments regarding desirable or undesirable Jewish behaviors – even those that might be made by ostensibly nonreligious institutions. These Jews, the Jews whom Cohen and Eisen describe, are unlikely to be strong adherents of Jewish civil religion.[13]

If Jewish civil religion is "too much" – too collective in its orientation, too anchored in large, distant institutions, too demanding in its activist ethos – for the Jews of *The Jew Within*, there is also a growing segment of the American Jewish populace for whom it is clearly too little. Civil Judaism avoided theology and an emphasis on the spiritual dimensions of Jewish life because they were inherently divisive and largely unnecessary for its purposes. However, what was once a strength became a decided weakness in a period when more Jews sought a deep connection to their tradition and its intellectual and spiritual dimensions. The Jewish civil religion always represented a version of Judaism that was secularized and somewhat superficial, a selective reading of Jewish tradition that left out at least as much as it took in. Even if this did not make it inauthentic, as some have charged, its truncated appropriation of the multiple dimensions of Judaism rendered it vulnerable when new issues, concerns, and American cultural trends came to the fore and began to shape the American Jewish religious sensibility. Today's Jewish Renaissance is noteworthy for its embrace of serious Jewish learning, for its efforts to revitalize synagogue life and other forms of spirituality, for its emphasis on creating intimate, caring communities built around personal acts of *gemillut hesed* (acts of kindness), and for the wide-ranging artistic and cultural creativity that is beginning to flourish. The Jewish Renaissance is not against civil religion, but the Jewish civil religion of the late 1960s, 1970s, and 1980s seems passé and almost irrelevant as a defining characteristic of the contemporary Jewish scene.

The mirror image of the decline in the ethnic and historical sensibility that undergirds American Jewish civil religion is the weakening of the institutions of the Jewish polity to which the civil religion is so closely linked. Political systems thrive when they are effectively able to perform certain critical functions. They must be able to extract resources from the populace and return these to meet agreed-on needs. They must be able to protect those whom they serve from external threats and at the same time maintain internal order and cohesion. They must be able to adapt to changing demands from the citizenry. Finally, they must offer symbolic rallying points, helping their citizens (or subjects) feel that they are pursuing a higher purpose worthy of their loyalty, exertions, and obedience.[14]

On all these fronts, one must conclude that the American Jewish polity, and especially the federation system, lost ground over the past two decades. The reasons are many, some having to do with a general decline in the credibility of political systems (viz., declining voter turnouts), and some with changes internal to the Jewish community. American Jews feel less threatened, less needy of a strong polity to protect them and look out for their well-being. They are less willing to accept voluntary "self-taxation," and they want to preserve greater control over their own resources. They resist calls for unity; division and contest over values and policies are more frequent. They are more critical of institutions for their perceived rigidity and slowness to adapt. They are also less likely to be stirred by appeals to higher purpose. The result is that the American Jewish polity can no longer expect and no longer receives the same deference and support that it once did. Its ideology, the American Jewish civil religion, is, therefore, less compelling as well. American Jews have gone to other things, and quite possibly for the better.

THE CIVIL RELIGION REBORN?

So one might have written with confidence until Rosh Hashanah 2000, September 11, 2001, and, even more, Pesach 2002. Now, the picture is not so certain. The condition of Israel, the Jewish people, and the world are again, it seems, on American Jewish minds. During the past year, hundreds of thousands of American Jews have rallied publicly for Israel; hundreds of millions of dollars have been donated to Israel emergency campaigns; and the war against terror and the struggle against perceived anti-Semitism have become continuing preoccupations. It would appear that American Jewish civil religion has made a comeback; sacred survival is again a source of unity, legitimacy for the Jewish polity, and a rallying cry for action.

Does the change in mood and priorities since the outbreak of the second Intifada represent a genuine resurgence of the American Jewish civil religion of the 1970s and 1980s? Will the events of the past two years, which show every sign of continuing to be with us for the foreseeable future, precipitate a turn back from privatized and personalized religiosity toward a more ethnically and communally grounded Jewishness and a renewed sense of history as a critical arena within which the meaning of being Jewish is played out? It is too early to say.

In life, the clock is never simply turned back. Even if the current situation in Israel and the world has brought up short those who believed that Jewish civil religion, with its focus on Jewish unity, mutual responsibility, endangerment, and activist ethos of repairing the world, was passé, we cannot, nor should we wish to, unlearn the lessons of the past decade. Empirically, evidence for a dramatic resurgence of civil religious sentiment – even for a substantial broadening and thickening of American Jewish popular support for Israel – is simply not yet available. That the most committed Jewish activists have rallied to Israel's cause with renewed vigor is clear. Whether a broader sweep of the American Jewish population is in the process of fundamentally rethinking the nature of its Jewish commitment and reembracing the myth and ethos of the Jewish civil religion is more doubtful. Even if such a recalibration is underway, it is unlikely that we will ever see a simple return to the post-1967 era, and that the effects of a decade and more of privatization, ethnic decline, and religious diversification will simply disappear.

REASSESSING JEWISH CIVIL RELIGION

The key question, then, is not whether American Jewish civil religion is experiencing a reprieve or even a resurgence, but what we should want its historical legacy to be. Let us postulate that civil Judaism is neither as vibrant and dominating as it once was nor as irrelevant and discarded as it more recently seemed. So what, and what then?

I continue to believe that, for all its limitations, the emergence and growth of an American Jewish civil religion in the twentieth century was an important and positive phenomenon. Whereas its critics saw it as a distortion or bastardization of "true" Judaism, I see it as a modern restatement of central Judaic themes. By itself, civil Judaism is a one-sided and truncated version of Judaism. *But, Jewish civil religion was never intended to be, nor over time did it function as, a self-sufficient statement of what it means to be Jewish.* Although some of its adherents may have tried to make it such, the vast majority of its proponents treated it otherwise – as a vital component of a larger, deeper, and (most important) developing Jewish commitment, not as a total or time-locked definition of what being Jewish entails either in belief or behavior.

Evidence for this proposition lies in the evolution of the Jewish polity, and especially the federation system, over the nearly two decades since *Sacred Survival* was written and in the lives of those who comprised the Jewish civil religion's staunchest adherents. If the American Jewish polity has grown weaker during this period, it has also grown more encompassing in its understanding of what a vibrant Jewish commitment entails. This is clear in the rhetoric of the polity's key spokespersons, in the beliefs and behaviors of its most vigorous activists, and in the public agenda of its institutions. Compare the level of support for Jewish education and synagogue life in the federation world today – including the personal involvement of leadership in these arenas – with that of two decades ago.[15] The difference is obvious.

The ideology of today's polity has been decisively informed and transformed by more than a decade of immersion in the so-called Jewish continuity and, more recently, the Jewish Renaissance agenda. The American Jewish civil religion of 2002 is not the same as that of the early 1980s. We have moved, as Barry Shrage has described it, from an era dominated by concern for sacred survival to one that is now seeking to create "sacred communities."[16] What was then a somewhat single-minded focus on support for Israel and value of tzedakah has become an embrace of *Torah, Tzedek,* and *Hesed* (in Shrage's language) or of *Torah, Avodah,* and *Gemillut Hasadim* (in *Pirkei Avot's* classic version) as the animating vision for contemporary Jewish identity and community building.

How shall we interpret this change? From one perspective, it might be seen as a retreat by the polity and its civil religion from the "battlefield" of Jewish meaning making, an acknowledgment of defeat in the struggle for Jewish hearts and minds. However, I believe that the shift is far better understood as a strategic advance. The civil religion proved itself capable of adapting to a new era by broadening and deepening its own message, by adding to its focus on Jewish survival, security, well-being, and good works a new appreciation of Jewish learning, spiritual life, and interpersonal connection as building blocks of a "Jewish life worth living."

What this suggests is that the American Jewish civil religion remains what it has been from its inception: an attempt to articulate the Jewish meaning and significance of those experiences and activities that are shared by a substantial portion of American Jewry. In another generation, these experiences and activities focused on immigration and adjustment to American life, on the destruction of European Jewry, and the rebirth and rebuilding of the State of Israel. More recently, the shared experiences and activities have included the efforts to forestall assimilation, to build a vibrant Jewish culture in America, and to support individual Jews in their quests to fashion meaningful, engaged Jewish lives. American Jewish civil religion has taken on new tropes and new symbols, but it continues to provide a rallying point for those seeking common purposes that can unite and inspire Jewish activism and a language to tell the American Jewish story that links it to the broad sweep of Jewish history.

To be sure, the transformation of the civil religion is neither complete, seamless, nor universal. There are those who prefer the less complex, more single-minded civil Judaism of the past. The past two years have been marked by a resurgence of older rhetoric and more traditional polity priorities in the federation system. This should not surprise us, given the circumstances in Israel and the world. Nevertheless, there is no sign that we will simply return to what was (even if some might wish this). The genie is out of the bottle – whether we see the evolution of the Jewish civil religion as a defensive effort to hold its ground against the rise of "personalist" Judaism, or as a positive growth to embrace a richer, broader vision of the content of Jewishness, the reality is that what was in the 1970s and 1980s is no more. Jewish civil religion has not disappeared, but it has been reshaped to better fit a new era in Jewish life.

This reading of what has happened still begs one important question: Does Jewish civil religion still have an important role to play qua civil religion in twenty-first-century American Jewish life? I contend that it does. Not only, therefore, am I suggesting that American Jewish civil religion is still alive and even reasonably well. I am arguing that it is still needed – perhaps even more than it was in the 1970s and 1980s. When I first described the civil religion, there seemed a danger that this public and detheologized version of Judaism might actually crowd out the Judaisms of the synagogue and the school. Had this happened, it would have been tragic indeed. But, as we know now, this was never a real danger. Judaism is too multidimensional, too rich substantively and symbolically, to be encompassed in a civil religion. American Jews are far too diverse and creative to limit the content and meaning of their Jewishness to the relatively few themes that even an expanded civil religion will inevitably emphasize. Only in totalitarian societies can one imagine a civil religion becoming the predominant form of religious life, and, as we have learned from the experience in the former Soviet Union, as soon as the coercive force of the state is removed, religious life again flourishes in all its variety.

In fact, we have seen, the real danger facing American Jewish religion over the past decade is precisely the opposite: that the central thrust of the civil religion – inspiring collective action to foster Jewish survival and efforts to improve the world – will be eclipsed by an inward-looking, laissez faire Jewish sensibility that places the pursuit of personal meaning and good feeling at the apex of its value system. Most serious Jews recoil from the notion that Judaism is whatever one chooses to make of it or take from it. However, it is this notion, not Jewish civil religion's legitimation of a public agenda focused on building a stronger Jewish community and people, that represents the predominant ideological alternative today to a holistic Jewish commitment to living a life of *kedushah*, of sanctity, and of "commandedness." Jewish civil religion is an ally, not the enemy, of those who are seeking to help American Jews speak Robert Bellah's "second" religious language of community, memory, and responsibility alongside the first of self-fulfillment.[17]

Critical to my argument is the belief that I articulated in *Sacred Survival* that Jewish civil religion, for all its limitations, is *not* simply a species of Jewish secularism. Civil Judaism was very much about finding genuine, life-shaping meaning in one's Jewishness. This meaning was not exclusive or all encompassing. However, the number of Jews for whom any form of Judaism provides the total framework through which they understand and guide both their personal and their public lives is relatively small, far fewer than the number of those who would willingly call themselves religious. In my reading, the Jewish civil religion provided many Jews with a genuine sense of transcendence and an authentic connection to dimensions of the Jewish tradition that became powerful forces shaping their behavior and defining deeply felt, perhaps even ultimate, commitments. Civil religion, however flawed it may be, is religion.

Furthermore, it is, as already noted, religion of a particular type, religion that is resolutely communal in its ethos. I do not believe that the communal ethos of the American Jewish civil religion is merely the product of a particular set of historical events, or reflective of a stage in the evolution of American Jewish life that should simply be put behind us. The civil Jewish message of solidarity and mutual responsibility, its insistence that we have obligations to one another, to the Jewish community, and to society as a whole expresses an authentic Jewish religious conviction. It is not the totality or even the essence of Judaism's message, as some civil religious adherents might have argued, but it is an important message whose weakening we ought not to celebrate. The pervasive assumption today that religion is a personal thing – highly individualized and valuable to the extent that it contributes to one's personal growth and fulfillment – is itself highly problematic from a traditional Jewish standpoint. To the extent that Jewish civil religion positions itself against this assumption and its consequences, it is helping to articulate a countercultural message about what Judaism teaches that ought to be welcomed widely, even by those who have little concern for the civil religion per se. Judaism is about family celebrations and spiritual seeking *and* about mutual responsibility and social justice. At a time when the latter concerns appear to have been eclipsed, at least among some Jews, civil Judaism's voice reiterating their significance is worth being heard.

Is such a voice, though, really necessary? Perhaps we have reached a point where Jewish civil religion qua civil religion is no longer needed. If the themes of its message are in fact authentically Jewish ones and if, as is undoubtedly the case, they are being articulated as well by other, more fully formed Jewish religious voices, then what role is there for a Jewish civil religion, especially a less powerful and focused one? My answer takes us back to the key functions that a civil religion plays for a polity: integration, legitimation, and mobilization.

I believe that there is a real loss for the American Jewish community if these functions are not being performed effectively. American Jewish life will not flourish if Jews do not continue to regard themselves as part of a religiously and ethnically based polity. We cannot thrive merely as a set of denominations in the sense that these are conventionally understood in American religious life – we are too small, our influence will be dissipated, our divisions will become too obvious, and our cultural heritage and creativity will be too circumscribed. What Elazar described as the Jewish polity, which includes but is not limited to our religious institutions, is vital to the well-being of Jewish life on this continent and, one could argue, around the world. Its weakening over the past twenty years should be a cause for concern, not relief. A strong Jewish civil religion in turn makes the Jewish polity more effective. I am not arguing that no polity can survive or function effectively without an explicit civil religion. I am arguing that, in twenty-first-century America, the voluntary Jewish polity that remains so important to our overall well-being as a community continues to draw strength from a civil religion – a set of widely shared beliefs, values, symbols, and rituals – that is effective in integrating, legitimating, and mobilizing Jews for its work. Even if the challenges facing the Jewish collectivity have changed from survival to renewal, the reasons that brought civil Judaism into being in the first place are still operative. We may indeed no longer need or want *the* Jewish civil religion of the 1970s and 1980s, but we still need *a* civil religion for American Jews.

We also need a civil religion precisely to add its voice to those who are seeking to speak more persuasively in Robert Bellah's second language of community, memory, and responsibility as part of a religious discourse increasingly dominated by America's first language of individualism, personal choice, and self-realization. Civil Judaism alone will not change the vocabulary of American Jewish life, but the absence of its voice would be felt, even by those who are most skeptical of its enduring worth. Jewish civil religion neither wishes nor has the capacity to supplant synagogue Judaism. However, it is unclear whether synagogue Judaism alone has the ability to win the struggle for a holistic Jewish spirituality – public and private, activist and inward, historical and biographical – without an articulate, even if softer, civil religious voice speaking alongside it.

The triumphal age of Jewish civil religion is over (if, indeed, it ever existed). This is so, however, not only because the times have changed, but because the civil religion was ultimately successful in launching thousands of Jews and hundreds of Jewish institutions on a quest to rediscover why the survival of Jews and Judaism in fact mattered so much to them. That the answers they found went beyond the bounds of the civil religion itself, at least in its version of two decades ago, does not render the Jewish civil religion either a failure or an irrelevancy. Civil Judaism remains with us. It is not what it was, but why would we want it to be?

American Jewish life as a whole is both stronger and weaker than it was two decades ago. The opportunities we see today for a Jewish Renaissance are real. So too, are the challenges that stand in the way of the realization of these opportunities. Jewish civil religion is a part of both stories. Its power in the 1970s and 1980s helped pave the way for the Jewish Renaissance, both because of what it was – a source of energy and self-confidence – and what it wasn't – an adequate vision of Jewish purposes and potentialities for the postmodern period. So too, its decline tells us much about the forces threatening the Jewish community's vitality, even as its continuing articulation of an ethos of solidarity and responsibility reminds us of some of what we must seek to reinvigorate.

I come, therefore, neither to bury Jewish civil religion nor to praise it, because its story is not yet over. The era of sacred survival may indeed have passed, but we may hope that the era of sacred community and of whatever will come after has only begun.

Notes

1. Jonathan S. Woocher, *Sacred Survival: The Civil Religion of American Jews* (Bloomington and Indianapolis: Indiana University Press, 1986).
2. These changes have been described in a number of books and articles. See, for example, Steven M. Cohen and Arnold M. Eisen, *The Jew Within: Self, Family, and Community in America* (Bloomington and Indianapolis: Indiana University Press, 2000); Bethamie Horowitz, *Connections and Journeys: Assessing Critical Opportunities for Enhancing Jewish Identity* (New York: United Jewish Appeal – Federation of Jewish Philanthropies of New York, 2000); Sylvia Barack Fishman, *Jewish Life and American Culture* (Albany: State University of New York Press, 2000); Sidney Schwarz, *Finding a Spiritual Home: How a New Generation of Jews Can Transform the American Synagogue* (San Francisco: Jossey-Bass, 2000); Charles S. Liebman, "Post-War American Jewry: From Ethnic to Privatized Judaism," in *Secularism, Spirituality, and the Future of American Jewry*, ed. Elliott Abrams and David G. Dalin (Washington, DC: Ethics and Public Policy Center, 1999), 7–17; Jack Wertheimer, *A People Divided: Judaism in Contemporary America* (New York: Basic Books, 1993).
3. Robert N. Bellah, "Civil Religion in America," *Daedalus* (Winter 1967), 1–21; Russell B. Richey and Donald G. Jones, eds., *American Civil Religion* (New York: Harper & Row, 1974); Robert N. Bellah, *The Broken Covenant: American Civil Religion in Time of Trial* (New York: Seabury, 1975); Robert N. Bellah and Phillip E. Hammond, *Varieties of Civil Religion* (San Francisco: Harper & Row, 1980).
4. Daniel J. Elazar, *Community and Polity: The Organizational Dynamics of American Jewry* (Philadephia: The Jewish Publication Society, 1976).
5. Charles S. Liebman, "Reconstructionism in American Jewish Life," in *Aspects of the Religious Behavior of American Jews* (New York: KTAV Publishing House, 1974), 254, 276.
6. Woocher, *Sacred Survival*, 67–68.
7. Ibid., 131–46.
8. The idea that civil religions perform the three functions of integrating the polity, legitimating its activities, and mobilizing citizens to support these is discussed in Charles S. Liebman and Eliezer Don-Yehiya, *Civil Religion in Israel: Traditional*

Judaism and Political Culture in the Jewish State (Berkeley: University of California Press, 1983).

9. See Trude Weiss-Rosmarin's review in *The Jewish Spectator*.
10. Steven M. Cohen, *Religious Stability and Ethnic Decline: Emerging Patterns of Jewish Identity in the USA* (New York: JCC Association, 1998).
11. Robert N. Bellah et al., *Habits of the Heart: Individualism and Commitment in American Life* [1985] (Berkeley and Los Angeles: University of California Press, 1996).
12. Wade Clark Roof, *Generation of Seekers: The Spiritual Journeys of the Baby Boom Generation* (San Francisco: HarperSanFrancisco, 1993); Mary C. Waters, *Ethnic Options: Choosing Identities in America* (Berkeley: University of California Press, 1990).
13. Steven M. Cohen and Arnold M. Eisen, *The Jew Within: Self, Family, and Community in America* (Bloomington and Indianapolis: Indiana University Press, 2000).
14. Compare Gabriel A. Almond and G. Bingham Powell, *Comparative Politics: A Developmental Approach* (New York: Little, Brown, 1966).
15. One example is this: One of the highlights of the 2002 General Assembly of the United Jewish Communities was a preassembly institute entitled Hadesh: Renewing Jewish Communities; it attracted 225 participants for two days of sessions dealing with Jewish Renaissance and education.
16. Barry Shrage, "Sacred Communities at the Heart of Jewish Life: 20 Years of Federation/Synagogue Collaboration and Change in Boston," *Agenda: Jewish Education* 15 (Summer 2002), 3–14.
17. Bellah et al., *Habits of the Heart*, 154.

17 Judaism and democracy in America

ALAN MITTLEMAN

In the mid-nineteenth century, the aptly named Know Nothings exempted America's Jews from their suspicion of Catholics and recent immigrants. The Know Nothings felt that "however repugnant their religion may be, their religion is Republican.... Indeed, the Jews were the first Republican people in the world."[1] In their view, the Jews posed no threat to American democracy, having conformed their communal life and religious world view to American democratic norms and standards. With no clerical hierarchy or manifest loyalty to a foreign power, the Jews were able to accept and embrace the values of a free republic. Indeed, this Know Nothing author believed that the intrinsic and historic form of Jewish polity was republican, because of the Jews' affinity for freedom and self-government.

Despite the tarnished source, this dyspeptic compliment was correct in pointing out that the vast majority of American Jews had internalized the ethos of American democracy in a thoroughgoing way. Fundamental themes of constitutional democracy such as the derivation of authority from the consent of the governed, equality before the law, and the primacy of rights figure early on in American Jewish communal life and correspondence. The constitutions of early American synagogues, for example, transparently reflect the constitutional norms of the young democracy, often moderating earlier Jewish and republican motifs in favor of democratic egalitarianism. American Jews postulated a unique affinity between Jewish political and social ideals and those of the United States to such a degree that one scholar discerns a "cult of synthesis" as a persistent focus of American Judaism.[2]

Jews had entered the American world with a proclivity toward republican ideas that derived from their own historic political tradition. This fundamental political and moral orientation allowed for compatibility with American republicanism. However, unlike America, the republicanism of the historic Jewish polity resembled a classic *res publica*: small in size and with emphasis on the sacrifice of individual prerogatives for the common good. In the American experiment, republicanism was moderated by both size and a commercial orientation. By the nineteenth century, American republicanism took an egalitarian turn, transforming itself into democracy. Jews too embraced the democratic turn, muting some of the republican elements in their tradition while continuing to embrace republican rhetoric to characterize, like the Know Nothing author, their Judaism.[3]

In this chapter I explore the putative affinity between historic Jewish society and polity and America's democratic culture by using insights into that culture from one of its most astute observers, Alexis de Tocqueville. I begin with a general consideration of how the democratic turn affected American religion as a whole, and then I look at its influence on the Jewish community. With religion, rather than general Jewish affairs, as the prominent idea, I consider the effects of democracy on the synagogue and on the republican elements of Jewish religious thought. I then show how Jews constructed a republican image of Judaism, harmonizing the ancient Jewish polity with an idealized America. Finally, I explore the aftereffects of this American–Jewish coalescence, as Sylvia Barack-Fishman terms it, on the political theology of contemporary American Jews.

RELIGION IN THE AGES OF EQUALITY

The historian Nathan Hatch writes of the "democratization of American Christianity" in the half-century after the Revolution. "The American Revolution and the beliefs flowing from it," Hatch writes, "created a cultural ferment over the meaning of freedom. Turmoil swirled around the crucial issues of authority, organization, and leadership."[4] The democratic revolution and its attendant political convulsions undermined the old conventions of deference to authority and tradition. It engendered a radically egalitarian culture in which challenge to authority, "widespread disdain for the supposed lessons of history and tradition, and a call for reform using the rhetoric of the Revolution" prevailed.[5] The Revolutionary upheaval in politics struck deeply into American religious culture as well. "Christianity was effectively reshaped by common people who molded it in their own image.... Increasingly assertive common people wanted their leaders unpretentious, their doctrines self-evident and down-to-earth, their music lively and singable, and their churches in local hands."[6] Groups such as the Methodists and Baptists, and later utopian communities such as the Mormons, challenged existing clerical elites and asserted the rights of the common man to control his own religious experience. They undermined inherited models of authority and leadership, eroding (or reinventing) the distinction between clergy and laity. Religion became populist and intensely pluralist. Sects proliferated and competed with each other on equal footing, freed of legal encumbrances. The constitution had cleared the way for a free market of religious ideas and institutions.

Hatch's analysis echoes that of the most famous nineteenth-century observer of American manners and morals, Alexis de Tocqueville. Experiencing this religious ferment first hand, Tocqueville became the great chronicler and analyst of religion in what he called the "ages of equality." Among the many themes that emerge in Tocqueville's treatment of American religion, I focus on three and apply them to Judaism,[7] a religion that Tocqueville did not observe or mention: religion's self-understanding as supportive of freedom, its propensity toward simplicity and moral emphasis, and its ambivalence toward authority.

Tocqueville was deeply impressed by the civic purposes that American Christianity served. All of the religious denominations and institutions, including his own Catholicism, conformed themselves to democratic norms. So congenial was Christianity to democratic culture that Tocqueville observed that "in the United States religious zeal constantly warms itself at the hearth of patriotism."[8] The underlying reason for this, sensed by both the American people and the foreign observer alike, was that "religion is much more necessary in [a] republic . . . than in [a] monarchy, and in democratic republics more than all others. How could society fail to perish if, while the political bond is relaxed, the moral bond were not tightened? And what makes a people master of itself if it has not submitted to God?"[9] The revolutionary upheaval and its resulting freedom relaxed the political bonds of hierarchical society. The ages of equality, in which every man had a like liberty to pursue his self-interest rightly (or wrongly) understood, deprived the new republic of the tight political bonds sustained by ancient loyalties. Thus Tocqueville's oft-quoted conviction that "religion, which, among Americans, never mixes directly in the government of society, should therefore be considered as first of their political institutions; for if it does not give them the taste for freedom, it singularly facilitates their use of it."[10] Religion facilitates their use of freedom by containing their stubbornly egoistic instincts, tempering their individualism, and cultivating those "habits of the heart" that lead to voluntary association and civic engagement. The capacity for moral restraint under such circumstances became all the more urgent. In Tocqueville's judgment, the necessity of religion for the "maintenance of republican institutions" was the shared belief of "the entire nation."[11] George Washington, in his 1796 Farewell Address, said as much:

> Of all the dispositions and habits which lead to political prosperity,
> Religion and morality are indispensable supports. . . . And let us with
> caution indulge the supposition that morality can be maintained
> without religion. Whatever may be conceded to the influence of
> refined education on minds of peculiar structure, reason and

experience both forbid us to expect that National morality can prevail in exclusion of religious principle."[12]

Granted that American religion conceived of itself as an aid to freedom and self-government, what specific features did it have in the ages of equality? In Tocqueville's view, religion in a democracy tends toward simplicity. "Even if equality does not shake religions, it simplifies them; it turns attention away from secondary agents to bring it principally to the sovereign master [i.e., God]."[13] In a nonhierarchical society, he reasoned, the religious imagination will not populate the space between man and God with angelic intermediaries or saintly intercessors. The nonmediated relationship between the individual and his or her God will be paramount. Furthermore, the relationship will not be freighted with ritual intermediation. "Another truth appears very clear to me: that religions should be less burdened with external practices in democratic times than in all others. . . . [For] men who live in these times . . . the sight of ceremonies leaves them cold, and they are naturally brought to attach only a secondary importance to the details of worship."[14] With this deemphasis on ritual and sacramental mystery, religion in a democracy takes on a moral, worldly cast: "[E]quality of conditions makes men conceive a sort of instinctive incredulity about the supernatural and a very high and often much exaggerated idea of human reason."[15]

A distaste for the supernatural and an exaggerated appraisal of reason lead to a complex, contradictory attitude toward authority, both divine and human. On the one hand, only with difficulty can democratic citizens "place the intellectual authority to which they submit outside of and above humanity. It is in themselves or in those like themselves that they ordinarily seek the sources of truth."[16] Their view of God tends toward naturalism. This ambivalence toward divine authority is mirrored by uneasiness with human authority. On the other hand, people cannot live without authority. Democratic man flees in anxiety from the prospect of complete independence in religious matters. He recognizes intuitively that certain consensual religious doctrines must be accepted. Deferring to the mass, he acquiesces in a rudimentary, common faith. "The disposition to believe the mass is augmented, and more and more it is opinion that leads the world."[17] Although Tocqueville seems to concede that religious visionaries and intellectuals will not develop under these circumstances, he prizes the stability that consensual religion affords.

Bowing uneasily to the need for some authority in religious belief, practice, and institutional life, democratic citizens will want to keep this authority within strict bounds. In democratic centuries, "religions ought to keep themselves discretely within the bounds that are proper to them and not seek to leave them; for in wishing to extend their power further than religious matters, they risk no longer being believed in any matter."[18] Tocqueville offers Islam as an example of a religion that does not stay within its bounds and that consequently has no hope of flourishing in a democratic age. Islam, unlike the Gospels, mixes "political maxims, civil and criminal laws, and scientific theories."[19] While he does not mention Judaism directly in *Democracy in America*, the reader could easily substitute traditional Judaism for Tocqueville's Islam, for Judaism, like Islam, also mixes "civil and criminal laws" into its religion. In addition, while its medieval philosophical heritage of "scientific theories" had no enduring hold on its American incarnation, Judaism did retain if not "political maxims" then a political culture of historic communal organization. How, then, did Jews come to modify their inherited Judaism to conform to the democratic norms of the ages of equality?

DEMOCRATIC JUDAISM: COMMUNAL ORGANIZATION AND AMBIVALENCE TOWARD AUTHORITY

The theopolitical tradition that the Jews brought with them to the New World was republican to its core. The *kehillot*, the Jewish communities of the Middle Ages, were essentially aristocratic republics governed by their leading citizens at the behest of Gentile authorities.[20] The republican element subsisted in the view that the community was constituted by the consent of its members and was intended to serve their common good. In exchange, the members were obligated to participate in the life of the community. The earliest Jewish communities in colonial America tried to replicate the communitarian values and coercive authority of their predecessor European models. Communities of Jews and religious congregations were coterminous. There were too few Jews in colonial America to divide into different congregations within a given city.

Following historic Sephardi and Ashkenazi patterns, the congregation–communities were governed by elected boards (*mahamad* in Ladino; *parnassim* in Hebrew) of leading citizens. The parnassim managed the community for the good of all its members and were responsible to them. The earliest North American community constitution, that of New York's Shearith Israel (1728), was accepted by "the common consent" of its members, signed by them, and read aloud in English and in Portuguese twice a year in the synagogue so that both members and trustees could reaffirm its authority.[21] These essentially covenantal practices link the community with the historic Jewish political tradition. As in Europe, the republican community was also aristocratic. Only the wealthier members, who, in America, were leading merchants, had a chance of being elected as community trustees. The trustees then elected one of their members to serve as the chief *parnas*. Anyone who refused to serve, in line with European Jewish norms, could be fined. Furthermore, the parnas appointed his own successor, thus attempting an "aristocratic" succession. Regarding the power of the parnas, historian Hasia Diner writes that "he could deny individual Jews the right to marriage, circumcision of sons, burial, kosher meat, matzo, and charitable assistance during times of need."[22]

Nonetheless, the power of the parnas, indeed of the attempt to replicate the coercive community of European Jewry in British North America, proved abortive. The London community, to which North American Jews turned for religious advice, was already much looser in its governance than the classic kehillot of the Middle Ages. As Daniel Elazar points out, "the constitutions of the 17th and 18th century Jewish communities in England, and even more so in British North America, are littered with provisions that turned out to be unenforceable, ranging from Sabbath observance to maintaining *kashrut*, to issues of intermarriage, and whether or not Jewish prostitutes can be accepted into the community."[23] Thus, by the end of the eighteenth century, membership in a Jewish community was largely a voluntary matter, as was acceptance of the community's strictures and the trustees' authority. By the early nineteenth century, as Ashkenazi immigrants arrived in greater numbers, they established their own synagogues rather than worship in ones dominated by Sephardi customs.[24] With multiple synagogues in the cities of the East Coast, the illusion of a unified, European-style community came to an end. Ultimately, the abortive attempt to establish compulsory, authoritative communities foundered on the fact that, unlike Europe, Jews were not required to live under their own law in their own legal and social enclaves. The *kehillah* was not necessary as an official representative to the host government, as a "state within a state." Jews were free to trade as they wished, associate with whomever they wished, eat, drink, and marry as they wished, and voluntarily affiliate with the community or not. Thus even before the institutionalization of American democracy, Jews modified their historically republican, albeit aristocratic, communal organization in a loosened, democratic direction. They constituted authority on the basis of a broader and more voluntary consent than was known in Europe. If they did not accept its dictates, nothing constrained them from leaving the community and moving on.

After the Revolution, Jewish congregations adopted new bylaws, which, for the first time, were called by the very American name *constitution*. (Earlier bylaws, in keeping with Sephardi tradition, were called *haskamot* or *askamot*.) These constitutions "broke from the old Sephardic model, incorporated large dollops of republican rhetoric, and provided for a great deal of democracy – at least on paper."[25] The new constitutions, such as that of

New York's Shearith Israel, incorporated "bills of rights," asserted that popular sovereignty is the source of civil and religious authority, and made it easier for the nonelite to become officers, who would now be known, reflecting the new democratic openness, as president and vice president rather than parnas and *hatan*.[26] While colonial bylaws, like their European precedents, listed dozens of behavioral and religious infractions for which members had to pay fines, postrevolutionary and nineteenth-century constitutions diminished or eliminated these altogether. The limits on authority in a purely voluntary society, which is what the congregation had become, were severe. Summing up the progressive attenuation of religious authority by the mid-nineteenth century, Sarna writes the following:

> With church-state separation, the growth of religious voluntarism, the spread of religious liberalism, the decline of synagogue-community, and the development of competing congregations in all major American Jewish communities, synagogues now found their authority severely weakened: they now needed members more than members needed them. This, over time, led to a drastic change in the relationship of synagogues to congregants, for rather than threatening to throw existing members out, synagogues suddenly had to learn how to attract new members in. Such was the American pattern, and it affected churches, synagogues, and all other "voluntary associations" (the term itself is significant) across the land.[27]

The democratizing trends in early Jewish congregational life only strengthened with time. While early constitutions began with procedures for the election of officers and then stated the criteria for and duties of membership, more recent constitutions begin (democratically) with issues of membership. Furthermore, the range of duties imposed on members virtually vanished, such as obligatory attendance at services and obligatory voting or standing for election, and conformity with Jewish law and custom shrank to the vanishing point. In modern constitutions, synagogues portray themselves more as adjuncts of the service economy than as traditional holy communities. In addition, membership entails the mere payment of dues in order to be qualified to use synagogue facilities. Whatever one contributes to the community as a volunteer is left to one's own discretion. The republican elements of the traditional kehillah, the tight bonds of mutual obligation and public responsibility, have been almost entirely dissolved in the democratic culture of liberal individualism. The "habits of the heart" of which Tocqueville spoke that equip citizens to govern themselves in a free republic have no institutional expression in modern synagogue constitutions.

Even as synagogues in the nineteenth century were moving away from classic Jewish republicanism, the trend was further spurred by the growth of popular, extrareligious, Jewish voluntary organizations. These "lay" led, social, and charitable organizations responded to the practical and secular needs of ordinary Jews and competed with the synagogues. Traditionally, the European kehillah had provided a comprehensive life world for its members, some of whom were organized into *havurot* (confraternities) as a means of both service provision and social life.[28] The congregation–community had never been without subgroups and mediating institutions. In America, however, a range of extrareligious options – lodges, clubs, and benevolent societies – proliferated that were based solely on "fellowship rather than [religious] obligation."[29] Contemporary rabbis bemoaned the American Jewish penchant for joining nonsynagogue institutions. The Jews, they complained, saw groups such as B'nai B'rith (founded in 1843) as surrogates for religious life and accessories to religious indifference. In retrospect, such groups represent the triumph of American democratic values within Jewish communal life. They represent the claim of laypersons to take charge of their own Jewish lives and freely form associations that express their own vital concerns. The extrareligious associations did not repudiate traditional religious authority and obligations as much as democratize and harmonize them with the normative culture of American voluntarism. Hasia Diner writes this:

> [The] societies made few distinctions between "secular" and "sacred" functions. Not only did they perform *tahara*,[30] give charity, and play cards; without rabbinic leadership or sanction, these associations often held worship services and in many cases helped create a congregation as a separate entity.... The community structures of American Jews in the 19th century can be seen neither as a break with the past, nor as the tradition's unbroken "chain of iron." American Jews believed they were both responsible to the past and unfettered by it.[31]

The unself-conscious blending of secular and sacred suggests a folk religion that is mindful of traditional obligations but relaxed and voluntaristic in its discharge of them. It is a religion that embeds obligations not in the commandments of an austere, demanding God but in the self-assumed responsibilities of moral men and women. It suggests the simplification of religion that Tocqueville foresaw, a religion of charitable acts and benevolent dispositions. With a few essential rituals freely assumed, it is a religion fit for the ages of equality. Rather than the encompassing sacramental cosmos of Old World Judaism (or Catholicism for that matter), religion in America would be simple, practical, and moral. "We look not to the antiquity of rites and ceremonies as a just criterion for their observance by us," an early proponent of Reform Judaism wrote in 1826, "but to their propriety, their general utility, their peculiar applicability to the age and country in which we live, to the feelings, sentiments and opinions of Americans." Among those sentiments and opinions – and democratic peoples were before all else prone to follow the tides of opinion according to Tocqueville – was the view that religion was meant to serve civil and republican purposes. Another Reformer, Isaac Cardozo, expressed this taken-for-granted assumption in 1827: "As all civil institutions are here founded on rational and equal principles, and look chiefly to the public benefit, those of a religious nature should partake of the same simplicity, and possess the same direct and positive good in their effects on society."[32] Religion, as civil society, is a product of rational choice and democratic deliberation. Religion, no less than the institutions of government, is meant to relieve the estate of man and promote the general welfare. It should be as malleable as necessary to secure this end. No undemocratic deference to the usages of the past should stand in the way of the progress of the present.

For Jews, democratic religion, simple and moral as it might be, would not resolve into a means of salvation for individuals alone. Rather, it would put the needs of the community, and of Jewish communities elsewhere, in the forefront of religious obligation. The still-vital sense of religion as obligation to other Jews moderated the excessive tendencies of democratic individualism with republican attention to the common good – at least until the late twentieth century, when group embeddedness became attenuated and frayed for almost all groups in America. This too was anticipated by Tocqueville in his analysis of how voluntary association could work to contain self-interest. He was not, however, entirely convinced that it would succeed.[33]

The tension between democratic individualism and civic republicanism emerges with particular sharpness in one of American Judaism's most prolific thinkers, Mordecai M. Kaplan. Kaplan advocated a thorough democratization of Jewish life. He posited that Jewish religion functions as a solidarity-building body of practices for Jewish society, or as he called it, "civilization." Religion, as an element of culture, is first among equals vis-a-vis other Jewish cultural expressions. However, all of the cultural expressions of the Jewish people have equal legitimacy. Consequently, synagogues must transform themselves into synagogue centers where prayer and study, their traditional activities, have a place alongside a diverse social and cultural offering. Unlike the Reform rabbis who criticized the so-called secular activities of their nineteenth-century congregants, Kaplan provided a theological valorization of ostensibly nonreligious activities. In his theology, democratic inclusiveness trumps traditional Judaism.

Kaplan would reconstitute Jewish communities as democratic bodies to which all Jews in a locality would join. Rather than suffer the messy pluralism of competing synagogues, benevolent societies, and other groups, all would be brought, in good Progressive fashion, under a common bureaucratic umbrella. However, unlike the kehillot of old, the governmental practices would be strictly democratic with as broad a franchise as possible. In some ways, Kaplan's proposal for regional kehillot-like communities, articulated in the decade after the collapse of the New York kehillah experiment, is a throwback to the democratically discredited forms of European and early American Jewish life. Kaplan was careful, however, to advocate for "organic communities" on a remarkably democratic basis: the satisfaction of self-interest. His masterwork, *Judaism as a Civilization*, sanctifies self-interest to such an extent that Tocqueville himself might blush. "The success of any proposed program of Jewish living," he writes, "will depend entirely upon the extent to which it leads to the salvation of the individual."[34] By salvation, Kaplan implies a radically worldly program of human flourishing based on the psychological satisfaction derived from creative self-expression and integration into a moral collectivity. Expressive selfhood, a key element of late modern democracy, uneasily coexists with the republican elements of kehillah-like community and a strong sense of obligation to the Jewish people. He rejects an ethos of pure identification of the individual with the collectivity, of pure sacrifice of the one to the other, in favor of self-interest rightly understood.

Self-interest rightly understood would lead the Jew to associate with others for his or her own salvation:

> The normal individual does not want to be a law unto himself. In his actions and in his impulses, he requires the sanctions and restraints imposed by a will which is supra-individual. Human nature demands that some pressure be brought to bear from without, and does itself create the source of that pressure – community life. Social life has as much need of a measure of involuntarism as physical life.[35]

The strains between the discourse of democratic voluntarism and older republican currents, here evocative of Rousseau, are evident. Individuality is the "ultimate criterion," but individuals who use their freedom wisely, who rightly understand their self-interest, will associate with the community and work for its common good. Kaplan's view is based in part on a theory of human nature, and in part on the empirical belief that anti-Semitism was so intractable that Jews could flourish only within the supportive framework of their own community. In either case, the volitional quality of associational life that is so strong a theme in Tocqueville is moderated by a necessitarian impulse: Both human nature and social prejudice drive the Jews into one another's arms. In Kaplan's later thought, affirming the need for group identification somewhat displaces the earlier emphasis on individualism.[36]

His attempt to "reconstruct" Jewish communal cum-religious life in a democratic key could not escape the old impulses of republican obligation. The
contradictions in Kaplan's work, the uneasy balance between self-interest
and disinterestedness, reflect the fate of a republican religion in the democratic ages of equality.

REPUBLICAN JUDAISM: THE RHETORIC OF TORAH AND CONSTITUTION

The construction of Judaism as a democratic political theology with
strong republican tendencies was a staple of rabbinic sermons, popular literature, and even folk art.[37] Perhaps the most systematic articulation of
this theme is found in Oscar Straus's *Origin of Republican Form of Government*, a dissertation on the indebtedness of the American founders to ancient
Judaism's "Hebrew commonwealth: the first federal republic."[38] As in other
examples of this literature, Straus goes beyond the claim that American ideals and institutions resemble Jewish ones. He argues rather that American
values *derive* from Jewish practices, in this case through the intermediation
of Puritan Biblicism. After tracing the channels by which the Puritans me-
diated Biblical ideas, he turns to an exposition of the constitutive ideas of
the classical Jewish polity – "the form of government outlined by Moses and
practically developed under Joshua and his successors, [which] first embodied the principles upon which the rights and liberties of a people should
rest and be sustained."[39] Moses, as a statesman, anticipated James Madison
in a remarkable way. "Having crossed the Red Sea, the first significant step
taken by Moses is the separation of Church and State, by causing the priestly
duties to devolve upon Joshua, while Moses retains the entire charge of the
civil administration."[40] After Moses' death and the conquest of the land, the
form of government instituted by the Judges becomes both fully republican and federal. "The government under the Judges was very much like our
own Federal Government: each tribe had its own tribal or state government,
which had jurisdiction over all local affairs, and it sent its duly elected representatives to the national congress."[41] The Hebrew commonwealth had an
executive branch and the functional equivalent of a bicameral legislature. Executive power was constitutionally limited. "That the Chief Executive might
not wield arbitrary power, and at the same time to divide the responsibility
of government and thereby to aid him in conducting the affairs of state, a
Senate was elected of seventy elders."[42] In addition to the "Senate," which
Straus attempts to show functioned, with interruptions, as both a legislative
and judicial body down into Roman times, there was a popular assembly,
equivalent to the House of Representatives. Straus builds his case not on

wishful fantasy but on a long tradition of Protestant and humanist political theory that applied Biblical materials to an argument in favor of limited government.

> [One thousand] years before Plato had dreamed of his ideal republic, when all of Western Europe was an untrodden wilderness, the children of Israel on the banks of the Jordan, who had just emerged from centuries of bondage, not only recognized the guiding principles of civil and religious liberty that "all men are created equal," that God and the law are the only kings, but also established a free commonwealth, a pure democratic-republic under a written constitution, "a government of the people, by the people, and for the people.[43]

Although the tradition of the "cult of synthesis," as Jonathan Sarna argues, has waned as Jewish insecurity lessened and as American patriotism, from the Vietnam War on, became less ingenuous, the project of linking the Jewish polity (and hence Judaism) with American founding principles persists. In a way, the work of the late Daniel J. Elazar may be seen as the latest example of Straus's form of argument. In Elazar's many works, especially his four-volume magnum opus, *The Covenant Idea in Politics*, we have a sustained attempt to ground modern federal republics, particularly that of the United States, in the practices and values of ancient Biblical covenantalism.[44] Like Straus, Elazar stressed the Reformed Protestant adaptation of Jewish covenantal theology as the key to American separation of powers, constitutionalism, and derived authority. In his writings on the Jewish political tradition, particularly *Community and Polity*, he emphasized the compatibility of enduring Jewish political traditions with American ones as a consequence of fundamental, shared values. Both systems rely on "federal principles" to organize communal life:

> [This system is] as old as the Jewish people itself, having its origins in the federation of the twelve tribes under Moses. The very term "federal" is derived from the Latin *foedus*, which means covenant and is an expression of the biblical idea of *brit* (covenant), which defines the basis of political and social relationships among humans as well as between man and God.[45]

By linking Jewish (and American) political organization to the covenant, Elazar connects republican politics to the innermost structure of Judaism.

As a scholarly project based on research and reasoned argument, Elazar's work cannot be lightly dismissed. It might still be considered, however, a form of systematic self-delusion driven by interests so deep as to be all but invisible. This, in essence, is the implied critique of Jerold Auerbach, who stresses the fundamental dissimilarity of Torah and Constitution. Those who would harmonize the dissonance between them fall prey to an artfully constructed, Americanized Judaism of which they are scarcely aware. For Auerbach, the Torah is (and should remain) a comprehensive sacred law, while the Constitution is a mere charter of governance:

> While the Torah defines an intimate covenantal relationship with God, the Constitution, in many respects, was designed to assure the absence of close relationships . . . constitutional ratification depended upon a Bill of Rights to insulate citizens from their own national governing institutions. In a legal system governed by divine rule, by contrast, there can be no bill of rights to protect individual autonomy from divine authority; nor can sacred law, divine and eternal, be amended.[46]

Auerbach sharply contrasts the *ur*-form of Judaism, holy life according to law, with the pale surrogate that American Jews created, a mimicry of Protestant Biblicism in which the prophetic themes of social justice predominate over the rigorous demands of sacred law. Those Jews who worship at the shrines of American democracy have forgotten the shrines of their real ancestors. Auerbach's criticism, which hits the mark in many ways, may well represent the end of the discourse of Judaism and republicanism.

The American discourse of religion and republicanism was meant to provide moral restraint for a self-governing, frontier, free society. In the estimation of Tocqueville and others, the republic required religion in a nonestablishmentarian form to survive. It is, of course, controversial whether this widely held view was true then or is still true now. American Jews were once part of the Tocquevillian consensus. Today, however, as persistent liberals they are more skeptical than most that the republic needs religion in any public form for its moral well-being. Nevertheless, despite their penchant for secularism, American Jews continue to shape their Judaism into a kind of democratic political theology that gives testimony to the implicit faith that religion has a vital public role to play in the republic. Since the 1960s, surveys show that Jews believe that "fidelity to the tradition [has] less to do with ritual observance or support for Israel and [is], instead, largely a matter of supporting worthy social causes. Though rarely stated as such, it seems that many American Jews regard liberalism as applied Judaism."[47] This identification of religion with the support of worthy social causes suggests that, then as now, American Jews affirm a Judaism that is simple, practical, and moral.

It is a long way from the early republican discourse to the rights-based liberalism of our own time. Nonetheless, the persistence of highly political ideas at the heart of what American Jews affirm as their religion attests to the ineluctable politicization of their faith. Judaism, like the other religions that have flourished in the United States, has been and continues to be profoundly affected by democracy in America.

Notes

1. Stephen Macedo, *Diversity and Distrust: Civic Education in Multicultural Democracy* (Cambridge, MA: Harvard University Press, 2000), 62.
2. Jonathan Sarna, "The Cult of Synthesis in American Jewish Culture," *Journal of Jewish Social Studies* n.s. 5, 1–2 (1999), 52–79.
3. By *republican* I refer to a political culture that prizes the commonwealth above individual liberties. Classic republicanism privileges duties to the whole over the rights of individuals. The duty to participate in self-government is more salient than the freedom to neglect public life in favor of private life, which, from a republican point of view, is deplorable. On the republican account, freedom is to be found in political participation. Authority in a republic can be strong and centralized, as long as it derives from consent. Republicanism and the custodianship of elites (aristocrats of one sort or another) are compatible, often typical. In so-called democracy, however, authority is diffused; egalitarianism reigns supreme; deference to elites is discarded; and rights trump duties. *Republican* and *democratic* are intended as ideal types in this analysis. Needless to say, the terms should not be taken to refer to political parties.
4. Nathan O. Hatch, *The Democratization of American Christianity* (New Haven: Yale University Press, 1989), 6.
5. Ibid., 7.
6. Ibid., 9.
7. While not observing Jews or Judaism in the present, Tocqueville did comment, critically, on Biblical Judaism as a source of law for the Puritans. See Alexis de Tocqueville, *Democracy in America*, trans. Harvey C. Mansfield and Delba Winthrop (Chicago: University of Chicago Press, 2000), 38.
8. Ibid., 281.
9. Ibid., 282.
10. Ibid., 280.
11. Ibid., 280.
12. James H. Hutson, *Religion and the Founding of the American Republic* (Washington, DC: Library of Congress, 1998), 80.
13. Alexis de Tocqueville, *Democracy in America*, 59.
14. Ibid., 421.
15. Ibid., 408.
16. Ibid., 408.
17. Ibid., 409.
18. Ibid., 419.
19. Ibid., 419.
20. Daniel J. Elazar, *Community & Polity: The Organizational Dynamics of American Jewry* (Philadelphia: The Jewish Publication Society, 1995), 10–17.
21. Eli Faber, *The Jewish People in America: A Time for Planting: The First Migration 1654–1820*, vol. I (Baltimore: The Johns Hopkins University Press, 1992), 56.
22. Hasia R. Diner, *Jews in America* (New York: Oxford University Press, 1999), 20.

23. Daniel J. Elazar, "The Jewish Political Tradition and the English Speaking World," in *Jewish Polity and American Civil Society: Communal Agencies and Religious Movements in the American Public Square*, ed. Alan Mittleman, Jonathan D. Sarna, and Robert Licht (Lanham: Rowman & Littlefield 2002), 3.

24. Faber, *The Jewish People in America*, 125.

25. Daniel J. Elazar, Jonathan D. Sarna, and Rela G. Monson, eds., *A Double Bond: The Constitutional Documents of American Jewry* (Lanham: University Press of America, 1992), 37.

26. Ibid., 39.

27. Ibid., 42–43.

28. Jacob Katz, *Tradition and Crisis: Jewish Society at the End of the Middle Ages*, trans. Bernard Dov Cooperman (New York: New York University Press, 1993), 132–40.

29. Hasia Diner, *The Jewish People in America: A Time for Gathering: The Second Migration, 1820–1880*, vol. II (Baltimore: The Johns Hopkins University Press, 1992), 87.

30. *Tahara* refers to the traditional preparation of the dead for burial.

31. Hasia Diner, *The Jewish People in America: A Time for Gathering, 1820–1880*, (Baltimore: The Johns Hopkins University Press, 1992), 97, 112.

32. Michael A. Meyer, *Response to Modernity: A History of the Reform Movement in Judaism* (Detroit: Wayne State University Press, 1988), 231.

33. Alexis de Tocqueville, "On the Use that the Americans Make of Association in Civil Life," in *Democracy in America*, vol. II, part two, chapter 5, 489–92.

34. Mordecai M. Kaplan, *Judaism as a Civilization: Toward a Reconstruction of American Jewish Life* (Philadelphia: The Jewish Publication Society, 1981), 282.

35. Ibid., 292.

36. Mordecai M. Kaplan, *The Religion of Ethical Nationhood* (New York: Macmillan, 1970), 136–47.

37. Jonathan Sarna, "The Cult of Synthesis in American Jewish Culture," *Journal of Jewish Social Studies*, n.s. 5, 1–2 (1999), 56–59.

38. Oscar Straus, *Origin of Republican Form of Government in the United States* (New York: G. P. Putnam's Sons, 1901).

39. Ibid., 101.

40. Ibid., 104.

41. Ibid., 108.

42. Ibid., 110.

43. Ibid., 117.

44. Daniel J. Elazar, *The Covenant Tradition in Politics*, vols. I–IV (New Brunswick: Transaction Publishers, 1996–98).

45. Elazar, *Community and Polity*, 154.

46. Jerold S. Auerbach, *Torah and Constitution: The Journey from Torah to Constitution* (Bloomington: Indiana University Press, 1990), 44–45.

47. Kenneth Wald, "The Probable Persistence of American Jewish Liberalism," in *Religion as a Public Good: Jews and Other Americans on Religion in the Public Square*, ed. Alan L. Mittleman (Lanham: Rowman & Littlefield, 2003), 75.

18 The economics of American Judaism

CARMEL U. CHISWICK

Most American Jews today are the descendents of immigrants who arrived about a century ago, especially during the decades between 1880 and 1920. They came from Tzarist Russia and the countries of Eastern Europe, politically repressive and anti-Semitic societies with little religious freedom for Jews. While the United States and much of Western Europe were experiencing rapid industrialization and economic modernization, the countries where Jews lived were still characterized by intense poverty and the virtual absence of economic opportunity. Russian Jews were also subject to religious persecution that took the form of severe crowding and restrictions on economic activity, with the result that their standard of living was among the poorest in a poor country. Even in the less repressive countries, when Jews moved to the cities, their economic advancement was often blocked by anti-Semitism or even legal restrictions on Jews.

The journey to America was both difficult and costly, but it was an investment in the future for the Jewish immigrants and their children. The United States at the turn of the twentieth century was arguably the most technologically advanced and fastest growing economy in the world. New York, the most common port of entry for Jewish immigrants, led the country in both respects. Although anti-Semitism was present, it was not nearly as prohibitive as in Europe and Jews could move up the socioeconomic ladder. The American economy was large enough for the Jews to be absorbed without difficulty; it was vigorous enough for them to find prosperity; and it was sufficiently open for them to unleash their latent creativity and in turn make some important contributions to economic development.

As both producers and consumers, American Jews transformed themselves from penniless, tenement-dwelling immigrants to upper-middle-class suburbanites in no more than three generations, and often less. This is the dominant economic story of twentieth-century American Jewry. It is a story that includes not only occupational mobility but also linguistic change, changes in consumption patterns and family life, and changes in Jewish communal structures and religious practice. These changes were achieved in part by purposeful design and creative response to new opportunities and in part by trial and error. While the entry of Jews into the suburban middle class was already evident by the 1950s, economic adjustment in other dimensions of Jewish life would continue throughout the rest of the century.

IMMIGRATION

In recent decades, economists have given much attention to the adjustment of immigrants with respect to employment and earnings.[1] The decision to move from one country to another is viewed as an investment with a lifelong time horizon, for which the rate of return is determined by comparing benefits – usually an increase in earnings – with the cost of moving and adjusting to the new country. New immigrants might not realize these benefits immediately on arrival if their skills are not readily transferable to the new country. The most important of these skills is language (English fluency), but immigrants may also be unfamiliar with consumption patterns (how to shop efficiently for goods and services), with residential patterns (how to find affordable housing in a good neighborhood), with labor markets (how to find a good job), with workplace culture (how to get along with employers and co-workers), and with job skills that differ between the two countries.

Like other immigrants who came to America from impoverished European populations, Jews could not fully realize their economic expectations without investing in human capital appropriate to production and consumption in their new country. These investments, popularly labeled "Americanization," had a very high rate of return and were undertaken with enthusiasm by Jewish immigrants. Night-school English classes, settlement houses, and Jewish immigrant-aid societies prepared the immigrants to move on from their low-paying jobs in sweatshops and pushcarts. As they learned the ways of their new country, they found better earning opportunities, whether wage work or self-employment, and evolved into an upwardly mobile ethnic community. Most of these opportunities required more investments to acquire occupational skills or to build a business. The economy was growing, however, and rates of return to learning English and to skills relevant to the American economy were high. Those immigrants who invested heavily were typically rewarded with improved incomes and higher consumption levels.

While all immigrants faced these same incentive structures, Jews seem to have invested more heavily in American forms of human capital than most non-Jewish immigrant groups.[2] Part of the reason may be that they knew from the outset that they would remain in the United States, so they had a high stake in learning English and other America-specific skills, in contrast to some other immigrant groups whose goal was to return to the origin country with enough money to improve their standard of living there. Part of the reason may be that Jews arrived with more human capital than other immigrants – they were more literate in non-English languages, were often comfortable in a multilingual environment, had experience with urban life and self-employment, had a variety of self-help traditions associated with minority status, and were familiar with study from their religious training in the old country. Part of the reason may also have been that they were more enthusiastic about participating in the American Dream, quicker than other groups to jettison their old-country traditions in favor of the new. There is also some evidence that Jews may have been more attuned to market signals and better able to interpret their implications for the future.[3] Whatever the reason, it seems clear that Jews faced higher rates of return to investments in human capital than most other groups, both immigrant and native, and they acted accordingly.

OCCUPATIONAL MOBILITY

Although Russian and East European Jewish immigrants may have come with better skills than other immigrants arriving during this period from Eastern and Southern Europe, they were unskilled by American standards and this affected their immediate opportunities for work. At first, they typically found housing and jobs within the Jewish immigrant enclave, a community where they could be understood in Yiddish, find kosher foods, and participate in familiar religious observance with other Jews from the old country. The most common employer of recently arrived immigrant Jews was the garment industry and its ancillary occupations. Although hours were long and wages were low, these jobs allowed immigrant men, women, and children to support themselves during their early years in a new country.

As Jewish immigrants learned their way around, they moved upward into better jobs and invested in their own businesses. Many Jewish entrepreneurs remained within the garment industry, taking a leading role in its transformation into the production of upscale ready-made clothes.[4] Others moved from pushcart peddling to shopkeeping to department store ownership. Some established the modern kosher food industry, while others nurtured the new motion picture industry. The common pattern was finding a niche in the growing American economy, and then applying creativity, entrepreneurship, and hard work to move into the middle class.

Although Jewish women and children worked during the early years of sweatshops and low wages, their role as income earners declined precipitously as men moved into better-paying occupations.[5] Young women typically worked both before and after marriage, but they withdrew from the labor force during childbearing years. The wife of a storekeeper might work beside him in the business, while wives in other industries might contribute informally as secretary, accountant, or sales representative. During the child-rearing years, however, most Jewish women worked primarily at homemaking and only secondarily as "unpaid family labor" in their husbands' businesses.

Jewish children – both boys and girls – were removed from the sweatshops and sent to school as soon as the immigrant family could forgo their wages. The immigrants understood the American public school as a good investment in human capital: any sacrifice in present income would pay off in terms of better future earning opportunities for their children. Jewish parents were especially desirous that their children acquire white-collar skills and were willing to support their schooling accordingly. As the Jews left poor immigrant neighborhoods in search of better living conditions, the quality of public schools would be an important criterion for them in choosing a new location. Most children of Jewish immigrants were able to complete high school; many continued through college or professional school, and a significant fraction earned professional degrees.

The speed with which American Jewry moved up the occupational ladder was impressive. In 1910, over three-fourths or 75 percent of the Jewish men still worked in crafts and other blue-collar occupations, while only 6 percent were owners or managers and less than 4 percent were professionals. By 1950 – a mere forty years later – there were 26 percent in management and 8 percent in the professions, for a total of 34 percent or over one-third in these high-level white-collar occupations. The next generation stayed in school even longer and was even less likely to enter a business. By 1990, nearly two out of three American Jewish men were in high-level occupations: nearly 50 percent were professionals and about 17 percent were in management.[6]

Jewish immigrants and their children invested in the education of their daughters as well as their sons. Although the daughters of Jewish immigrants did not attend college and professional school at the same rate as their brothers, they were more likely to do so than U.S.-born women and the women in other immigrant groups at the same income level. As Jewish men became doctors, lawyers, and college professors, Jewish women became public school teachers, social workers, and administrators in Jewish communal organizations. By the third generation in America, Jewish women were nearly as well educated as Jewish men, a substantial proportion had professional careers, and two-career couples had become the norm for young Jewish families.

Investments by American Jews in occupation-related education were accompanied by other human capital investments in a package that dramatically affected Jewish lifestyles. Investments in health by Jewish immigrants included an early concern with modern standards of good nutrition, hygiene, and sanitation as well as access to high-quality medical care, and these investments increased over time with rising income. The immigrants learned to enjoy American music and art, theater and literature, and they became sophisticated consumers of modern culture. They purposely chose to have small families so they would be able to afford heavy investments for their children in all these dimensions. There would be a "baby boom" in mid-century when Jews, like most other Americans, had more children than usual, but this was a temporary phenomenon in a population for which the two-child family was typical. The Jewish fertility rate is generally lower than that of non-Jews in the population and is currently below replacement (the 2.1 children per woman needed to maintain the Jewish population at its current size).[7]

JEWISH HUMAN CAPITAL

The emphasis on Americanization tended to crowd out more traditional forms of Jewish human capital investment. Torah study was not a high priority, and few American children learned enough Hebrew to engage in it with any sophistication. This may have been because the more religiously inclined were less likely to leave Eastern Europe, making the immigrants to America a self-selected group that was not especially interested in religious matters. However, even for those concerned with the Jewish education of their children, the rewards to Americanization were so great, and the process so all-consuming, that investments in Jewish religious skills seemed like a costly diversion of time and other resources. It was much easier to take religious skills for granted, adapting Jewish observance to an American version that merged with family life and conflating it with nostalgia for a romanticized version of the old country.[8] The development in America of many distinctive Jewish customs and rituals was accompanied by a marked decline in Jewish religious sophistication.

As is typical of immigrant religious groups, synagogues in immigrant neighborhoods were small (often storefront) establishments where language and practice replicated the old-country experience.[9] At a time when immigrants were still struggling to learn the ways of their new country, the synagogue was a haven of familiarity where old-country human capital could still have value. However, the investment priorities of American Jews lay elsewhere as they struggled toward economic security and upward mobility. Religious life was relatively neglected, synagogue attendance was low except on major holidays, and the Jewish education of American children was minimal. Instead, many of the immigrants turned to such secular activities as theater, political or labor organizations, and occupation-related social life to express their Jewish identity in America.

As Jews acquired their American skills and found occupational niches in the American economy, they left the crowded immigrant neighborhoods for better housing and, importantly, good public schools for their children. Religious observance in the old country had been very time intensive, perhaps reflecting the low wages and poor economic opportunity of Jews in Russia and Eastern Europe. These practices became more and more costly with higher wages, and people responded by spending less time in the synagogue and especially in religious study. The storefront synagogue was left behind, to be replaced by a synagogue that was more American in its style of observance. What was most important was that the new synagogue practices reduced the time intensity of Jewish observance not only by shortening services but also by relying more heavily on the professional rabbinate and by substituting English for Hebrew, both of which greatly reduced the amount of prior study required for full participation. The popularity of Reform and Conservative synagogue movements among upwardly mobile immigrants and especially their American-born children was thus a direct consequence of economic success.[10]

Despite their reduced observance of Jewish ritual, most immigrants were not rejecting Judaism itself and expected to educate their children as Jews. Jewish schools were established and attendance was widespread, but typically only for a few years before the *Bar Mitzvah* and even then for far fewer hours than the "regular" schools.[11] Whether the Jews of that generation underestimated the challenges of American pluralism or were simply responding to a high potential for upward economic mobility, education in American (i.e., secular) subjects clearly dominated Jewish subjects in the competition for study time.

By the second half of the twentieth century, most American Jews were living comfortably in middle-class suburbs, beyond the struggles of their immigrant parents and grandparents. Jewish families were typically small, and secular education was seen as the basis of both personal fulfillment and economic security. Jewish residential choices emphasized communities with high-quality public schools and good medical facilities. Jewish parents strove to send their sons and daughters to college, preferably to institutions with high academic standards.

Jewish education in the suburbs was facing a new set of challenges. Jewish children still attended after-school programs, but their home environments reflected the low Jewish education of their parents. Most adult children of immigrants had received only a perfunctory Jewish education and many viewed religion itself as an anachronistic old-country phenomenon. Despite their earlier reputation for secularism and irreligiousity, the grandparents whose youth had been spent in the old country or in immigrant neighborhoods where old-country customs prevailed became virtual repositories of Jewish tradition in the affluent suburbs. It was they who maintained ritual in the synagogues and in the home, while their adult children either scoffed or accepted passive religious roles in keeping with their low level of Jewish skills. Judaism in such families became associated with the elderly, and the nostalgia associated with many holiday traditions did little to counter this impression.

The grandchildren of immigrants, as the first generation that was native to suburban Jewish communities, typically reached adulthood with very high levels of secular human capital and very low levels of Jewish human capital. This meant that time spent in secular pursuits would be very productive – an implication born out by the high wage rate commanded by high skills – while time spent in religious activities would have very low productivity. For example, a man virtually illiterate in Hebrew and unfamiliar with the rhythms and ritual of the Shabbat synagogue service might find the experience more irritating than comfortable, generating a sense of low achievement utterly foreign to his weekday experience in a professional or social setting. In such a situation, synagogue attendance would be perceived as a "waste" of time, and perhaps also Jewish observance in general.

From an economic perspective, a large imbalance in the level of different kinds of human capital – in this case secular and religious – is inherently unstable. It gives an incentive either to align the two types of skill more closely by investing in Jewish knowledge or to reduce drastically the time spent on Jewish observance. The former incentive stimulated a revival of interest in Jewish learning and a creative Jewish Renaissance that began in the later decades of the twentieth century and continues today. The latter incentive underlies the somewhat larger concurrent trend toward assimilation of many American Jews and the consequent rapid rise in the rate of outmarriage. From an economic perspective, the paradoxical combination of "apathy and renewal" observed in the later decades of the twentieth century is an unintended consequence of the very same economic decisions responsible for the dramatic upward mobility of Jewish immigrants and their children earlier in the century.[12]

JEWISH COMMUNITY AND PHILANTHROPY

Together with their strong emphasis on individualism and upward mobility, American Jews were very successful at establishing communal organizations to facilitate their progress and share their wealth with the less fortunate. Like the religious institutions, self-help organizations in the immigrant community were largely imported from the old country where Jews had to depend on themselves for communal institutions. In addition to the familiar methods of charity to care for widows, orphans, and the truly indigent, they set up a variety of other institutions such as burial societies and mechanisms for the certification of *kashrut* (dietary laws) in factories and restaurants. Of major importance were the Hebrew Free Loan Societies that made many small short-term loans, often with no interest.[13] As Jews moved up the socioeconomic ladder, these institutions became organized along American lines and acquired a professional staff of their own.[14]

The much better opportunities for men in the American marketplace meant that women filled many positions in Jewish organizations, including jobs in Jewish education and in the administration of synagogues and charities, that were previously held exclusively by men. This brought women into new roles in Jewish communal life that eventually came to rely on them as social workers and middle-level administrators, as volunteers at first but later as paid employees.

American Jews were greatly affected by – and responsive to – major events in the Jewish world outside the United States. The immigrant community sent remittances to family remaining in the old country, encouraging them to immigrate by sending payment of passage and arranging for lodging and jobs in America. Organizations were formed to help new immigrants with their adjustment on arrival, the best known of which was the Hebrew Immigrant Aid Society (HIAS). American Jewry's concern with anti-Semitism led to political activities and support for the fledgling Zionist movement to establish a Jewish homeland in British Palestine. Although Jews shared with other Americans alarm at the rise of Nazism in Germany and the events that were to culminate in World War II, their concern was intensely personal since the families they left behind had been singled out for destruction. They contributed substantial sums to refugee relief and later to the support of displaced persons. They also contributed generously to the State of Israel, both before and after it became independent, providing money to resettle people from Jewish communities at risk, to provide social services, to purchase and develop land, to improve public health facilities, and to build and maintain modern medical and educational institutions. The financial and political support of American Jewry complemented the hard work of Israeli Jewry to establish Israel as an important center of Jewish life.

The funding of these large tasks was itself a major undertaking. At a time when Jews were preoccupied with Americanization and the vicissitudes of upward mobility, they were far more willing to be generous with money than with time. This was the strength of umbrella organizations (such as the United Jewish Appeal) that raised funds to be distributed among many recipients. Apart from streamlining the fundraising process, thus keeping administrative costs relatively low, these organizations made decisions about how to distribute funds. They enabled individual Jews to give money to general causes, such as "the poor," "refugee relief," or "Israel," without themselves having to invest in expertise on the worthiness of individual recipients or causes. This was especially important for overseas causes, where information would have been difficult to develop, but it was also useful in local communities where the needy might not be well known to the potential donors or where confidentiality might be an important concern.

The success of American Jewish fundraising activities, especially during the second half of the twentieth century, is legendary. The umbrella organizations functioned optimally when the causes were clear and when there was consensus among donors and administrators on fundamental criteria for evaluating the worthiness of recipients. This consensus has been breaking down in recent decades with increased diversity in the interests of American Jews. They are more secure in their socioeconomic situation, better integrated into American society, and better informed about many of the recipient organizations. With the acceptance of Jews into the American mainstream, local Jewish organizations have had to compete for funds with non-Jewish causes, as in the arts or in medical research, which Jews also feel a responsibility to support. The cost of acquiring information about Jewish recipients abroad has declined dramatically, whether in Israel or in other Jewish communities such as the former Soviet Union, in part because of new information technology and in part because foreign charitable organizations have learned to advertise directly in the American market. As a consequence, American Jewish philanthropy has been experiencing a shift away from the major federation fundraising campaigns toward non-Jewish charities and toward direct giving to selected Jewish organizations.[15]

CONCLUSION

The story of American Jewry in the twentieth century is the story of an immigrant group that successfully met the enormous challenges of social and economic adjustment in a new country. Faced with an economic environment radically different from any they had known before, and with little relevant experience from the past available for guidance, these Jews transformed Jewish practice even as they transformed nearly everything else in their lives. In the process, Judaism itself has entered a new phase in its long history. American Jews were responsive in creative ways to major events in the Jewish world outside the United States. However, the most important religious contribution of American Jews lies in their attempts to adapt Jewish observance to a community of highly educated, economically engaged members for whom time is a scarce and high-valued resource. In this context the distinctively American synagogue movements – Reform, Conservative, Reconstructionist, and Modern Orthodox – can be viewed as alternative solutions to this problem. Whether or not they survive the test of time in their current forms, they have surely laid the foundation for the Jewish community of the future to engage meaningfully in an ancient religion in an economic environment totally unlike the past.

Notes

1. Barry R. Chiswick, "The Economic Progress of Immigrants: Some Apparently Universal Patterns," in *Contemporary Economic Problems 1979*, ed. William Fellner (Washington, DC: American Enterprise Institute, 1979), 357–99; "Are Immigrants Favorably Self-Selected?," *American Economic Review* 89, 2 (1999), 181–85; Barry R. Chiswick and Paul W. Miller, *The Economic Cost to Native-Born Americans of Limited English Language Proficiency* (report for the Center for Equal Opportunity, city, 1998).

2. Barry R. Chiswick, "Differences in Education and Earnings Across Racial and Ethnic Groups: Tastes, Discrimination, and Investments in Child Quality," *Quarterly Journal of Economics* 103 (1988), 571–97.

3. Barry R. Chiswick, "Labor Supply and Investment in Child Quality: A Study of Jewish and Non-Jewish Women," *Contemporary Jewry* 9, 2 (1988), 35–53.

4. Andrew Godley, *Jewish Immigrant Entrepreneurship in New York and London 1880–1914: Enterprise and Culture* (New York: Palgrave, 2001).

5. Barry R. Chiswick, "Labor Supply and Investment in Child Quality: A Study of Jewish and Non-Jewish Women," *Contemporary Jewry* 9, 2 (1988), 35–53; "Working and Family Life: The Experiences of Jewish Women in America," *Papers in Jewish Demography 1997* (2001), 277–87.

6. This rate of increase from low- to high-skilled occupations was much faster than in the general population. See Barry R. Chiswick, "The Occupational Attainment and Earnings of American Jewry, 1890–1990," *Contemporary Jewry* 20 (1999), 68–98.

7. Carmel U. Chiswick, "The Economics of Contemporary American Jewish Family Life," in *Coping with Life and Death: Jewish Families in the Twentieth Century*, ed. Peter Y. Medding, vol. 14 of *Studies in Contemporary Jewry* (New York: Oxford University Press, 1998), 65–80.

8. Jenna Weissman Joselit, *The Wonders of America: Reinventing Jewish Culture 1880–1950* (New York: Hill and Wang, 1994).

9. R. Stephen Warner and Judith G. Wittner, eds., *Gatherings in Diaspora: Religious Communities and the New Immigration* (Philadelphia: Temple University Press, 1998).

10. Carmel U. Chiswick, "The Economics of American Judaism," *Shofar* 13, 4 (1995), 1–19.

11. Jack Wertheimer, "Jewish Education in the United States: Recent Trends and Issues," in *American Jewish Year Book* 99 (1999), 3–115.
12. Carmel U. Chiswick, "Economic Adjustment of Immigrants: Jewish Adaptation to the United States," in *Jews in America: A Contemporary Reader*, ed. Roberta Rosenberg Farber and Chaim I. Waxman, Brandeis Series in American Jewish History, Culture, and Life (Hanover: Brandeis University Press, 1999), 16–27; "The Economics of Jewish Immigrants and Judaism in the United States," papers in *Jewish Demography 1997* (2001), 331–44. See also Jack Wertheimer, *A People Divided: Judaism in Contemporary America* (New York: Basic Books, 1993).
13. Shelly Tenenbaum, *A Credit to Their Community: Jewish Loan Societies in the United States 1880–1945* (Detroit: Wayne State University Press, 1993).
14. For a general analysis of this phenomenon in American religious communities, see R. Stephen Warner, "Work in Progress Toward a New Paradigm for the Sociological Study of Religion in the United States," *American Journal of Sociology* 98, 5 (1993), 1044–93.
15. Helen Roberts, "American Jewish Donations to Israel," *Contemporary Jewry* 20 (1999), 201–13; Jack Wertheimer, "Current Trends in American Jewish Philanthropy," in *American Jewish Year Book* 97 (1997), 3–92.

19   American Judaism and interfaith dialogue

YAAKOV ARIEL

Momentous transformations have taken place in the relationship between the Jewish community and other religious groups in America throughout the twentieth century. Tentatively beginning at the turn of the twentieth century, a movement of interfaith dialogue between Jews and non-Jews served as a catalyst that helped to bring about the changes. This dialogue gained more ground in the decades between the two world wars and advanced considerably following the Second World War. It reached a "golden age" in the late 1960s and 1970s, when an unprecedented momentum for reconciliation and dialogue between the faiths flourished in America. Despite occasional setbacks, the interfaith dialogue helped to improve the relationship between Jews and non-Jews in America, thus helping to advance the well-being of the Jewish community in America.

THE BEGINNING OF THE DIALOGUE

Interfaith dialogue between Jews and non-Jews in America began in the latter decades of the nineteenth century, primarily between liberal Protestants and Jews. Jewish and Christian clergymen cooperated over civic issues, invited each other to give talks in their congregations, and, at times, participated in interfaith conferences.[1] Such interactions were on a sporadic basis and usually entailed personal friendships between Jewish and Christian religious leaders. A special occasion in the history of interfaith dialogue in America took place in 1893, when the World Parliament of Religions (WPR) convened in Chicago, bringing together Protestants, Catholics, Greek Orthodox Christians, Jews, Buddhists, Hindus, Bahai, Muslims, Native Americans, and representatives of other faiths as well. It offered Jewish religious leaders, such as Alexander Kohut, Isaac M. Wise, Kaufmann Kohler, Emil G. Hirsch, and Marcus Jastrow, an opportunity to present their views to a non-Jewish audience and make a case for Judaism. While Hirsch, a Reform rabbi from Chicago, spoke about the need to overcome parochial differences and create one world religion, other Jewish representatives defended Judaism against what they considered to be erroneous and degrading Christian views on the Jewish faith. In the wake of the WPR, some liberal Jewish and Protestant religious leaders further engaged in dialogue. In particular, Hirsch and Jenkins Lloyd Jones, a Unitarian minister and an architect of the WPR, were committed to interfaith dialogue.[2]

While the WPR gave Judaism a voice and put its representatives on the podium with other leaders of world religions, its long-range effects were limited. In theory, the unprecedented conference reflected a recognition and sense of respect of all religions. However, the WPR was a Protestant initiative, and the Protestant liberal activists who presided over it did not really view non-Protestant religions as equal to their faith.[3] Influenced by theories of religious evolution, which prevailed in the late nineteenth century, liberal Protestants had put their faith at the top of the religious evolutionary ladder. In spite of their relative openness to dialogue and their more critical reading of their own sacred Scriptures, liberal Christians held to a triumphalistic vision of Christianity, which they saw as a faith destined to become the world's all-encompassing religion. Adhering to a messianic view, liberal Christians were certain that they were building the kingdom of God on earth.

In spite of its many limitations, the WPR was a daring act, and in some ways ahead of its time. The liberals who led the event drew fire from conservative Protestants who strongly objected to a dialogue with non-Protestants. In the conservative Protestant view, only those persons who had accepted Jesus as their Savior would be "saved" and could expect eternal life. They insisted that Protestants should look at members of other religious traditions exclusively through missionary lenses and concentrate on spreading the Christian gospel instead of wasting precious time and resources on dialogue. Influenced by a more literal reading of the Bible, conservative Protestants saw special merit in evangelizing the Jews. Similarly, other Christian groups in America during that period were busy propagating Christianity among the Jews.[4] This caused much resentment among Jewish leaders, who viewed the missions as a demonstration of contempt toward Judaism and Jews. As a result, a number of Jewish religious leaders during the late nineteenth century concentrated on defending Judaism against what they considered to be unjustified defamation resulting from the unwillingness of Christians to relate to Judaism as a legitimate faith in America. Jewish tracts from this period point to huge frustrations on the part of Jewish religious leaders in their relation to liberal Christians, whom they had met and from whom they had expected a more respectful attitude toward Judaism.[5]

While interfaith dialogue at this point was limited, certain characteristics of the dialogue were already laid out at this early stage. Many of the issues discussed were not spiritual or theological, yet the dialogue between

Jews and non-Jews was entrusted to clergymen. Representing Judaism and the Jewish community in dialogue with members of other faiths would become an important component of rabbis' work in America and would add to the prestige of the American rabbinate. Rabbis would become the representatives of Judaism and Jewish causes vis-à-vis other faiths in America as well as American society at large. Another feature of the dialogue was that the willingness to meet with Jewish representatives and converse with Jews did not necessarily mean that Christians accepted Judaism as a religion equal to their own, or that Jews gave up on triumphalistic elements of their faith. Christian participants in the dialogue would continue to be representatives of liberal wings of their faith. Most Jewish participants at this early stage of the dialogue were Reform rabbis or rabbis of the fledgling Conservative movement. However, contrary to a prevailing myth, Orthodox rabbis and communities were also engaged in dialogue with Christians. While the very attempts at dialogue during that period should be viewed as a form of recognition and goodwill, it did not bring about any breakthroughs in the relationships between the faiths. Evidently, both Jews and Christians were not yet ready for such a transformation. This changed in the following decades.

MORE SYSTEMATIC DIALOGUE (1920–1960)

Attempts at dialogue took a more organized form in the 1920s, thus leading to more permanent results. In 1924, Roman Catholic, Protestant, and Jewish activists established the Committee on Good Will. The motivation for the creation of the committee was more social than theological, as it was due in part to the alarming rise of hate groups in America during the early 1920s. This rise in organized bigotry alarmed Roman Catholics and Jews, who were often targets of such attacks, as well as some liberal Protestants who were also concerned.[6] In 1928, interfaith dialogue took an additional step with the creation of the National Council of Christians and Jews (NCCJ). While the Committee on Good Will concentrated on fighting bigotry, the NCCJ concentrated its efforts on improving the relationship between Jews and Christians and acted as a major vehicle for dialogue between Jewish religious leaders and representatives of Protestant churches and Roman Catholicism. Similar attempts at establishing organized dialogue between Christians and Jews took place in other English-speaking countries.[7]

Even as the interfaith dialogue in America progressed from the 1920s to the 1950s, the relationship between the faiths in America as a whole was far from ideal and the developments in this realm were mixed. During the 1920s and 1930s, America witnessed the rise of virulent anti-Semitic expressions. A number of Catholic and Protestant groups and individuals joined in attacking

Jews, blaming them for the nation's problems. One of the most noted Roman Catholic clergymen during the period, Father Charles Coughlin, a pioneer of radio preaching, used his radio program as a vehicle to attack the Jews and blame them for the troubles of the age.[8] Another promoter of anti-Semitism during this era was Henry Ford, Sr., who financed the distribution of anti-Semitic publications, including an English translation of *The Protocols of the Elders of Zion*, a fabricated document alleging that the Jews were conspiring to take over the entire world.[9] Protestant ministers who promoted a reactionary political agenda, such as Gerald L. K. Smith, included attacks on Jews in their rhetoric. Jewish organizations responded to this anti-Semitic wave by institutionalizing their involvement with interfaith dialogue. Realizing that building a good relationship with Christian groups was of utmost importance, they turned it into one of the main items on their agenda. Groups such as the American Jewish Committee, the American Jewish Congress, and the Anti-Defamation League engaged in interfaith dialogue, with their leaders serving as representatives in interfaith forums. Similarly, Jewish federations throughout the nation created communal relationship divisions to combat bigotry and build cordial relationships with other local communities of faith.

While some Christian representatives in the dialogue were sympathetic to Jewish feelings, they did not necessarily represent their denominations as a whole. The mainstream Christian denominations of the time, not to mention the more conservative churches, were far from recognizing Judaism as a legitimate faith. The general standing of mainstream churches in America at that time was that, while Christians should establish cordial relationships with their Jewish neighbors, Judaism was not equal to Christianity and could offer its members neither spiritual comfort and moral guidelines, nor salvation for their souls. Conservative groups and mainstream Christian churches continued their efforts at evangelizing Jews. Not surprisingly, the missions became a major point of contention whenever Christians and Jews engaged in dialogue. From the Jewish point of view, Christian attempts at evangelizing Jews were a stumbling block to a relationship of trust and goodwill. They could not accept the idea that Christians could sincerely express respect toward Jews while at the same time seeking to convert them away from their ancestral faith. Committed to an improvement in the relationship between Christianity and Judaism, Christian participants in the dialogue began distancing themselves from the efforts to evangelize Jews.

An early proponent of a new liberal attitude that recognized Judaism as a legitimate religious tradition was the Unitarian minister John Haynes Holmes of the Community Church in New York. Holmes, who advocated a progressive social and political outlook, became a close friend of Steven

S. Wise, an independent Reform rabbi who shared Holmes' social agenda. As early as the 1920s, the influential minister related to Judaism as a religion that deserved respect and as a faith able to offer its adherents spiritual content and moral guidance. A more systematic advocation of Holmes's same opinion was offered by Reinhold Neibuhr, one of Protestant America's leading theologians between the 1930s and 1960s. Neibuhr's groundbreaking outlook offered recognition and acceptance of Judaism as a religious tradition equal in worth to Christianity.[10] Through his work as a minister in a working-class neighborhood in Detroit, where he encountered socially active Jewish religious leaders and visited Jewish congregations, Neibuhr concluded that Jews had high moral standards and social consciousness and were therefore not in need of the Gospel. He rejected the triumphalistic Christian Protestant attitudes and consequently militated against the propagation of the Christian gospel among the Jews. With few exceptions, mainstream Protestant theologians, as well as church councils of the early twentieth century, followed in the traditional Christian belief, according to which God's promises to Israel were inherited by the Christian church. Christians reasoned that once the Jews had rejected their Messiah, thereby losing their position as the covenant people and God's first nation, Judaism had no reason to exist except as a group holding witness to the triumph of Christianity. Niebuhr's attitude, which he expressed as early as 1926, signified a revolution in Christian Protestant thinking about Jews and Judaism. He pioneered an approach that accepted the legitimacy of a separate Jewish existence alongside Christianity and the idea that Jews, holding a valid religious tradition of their own, did not have to convert to Christianity.

During the same period, a number of Jewish thinkers also began to change their opinion on the relationship between Judaism and other faiths. In the years following World War I, the triumphalistic Reform Jewish theology of the late nineteenth century weakened considerably and virtually disappeared. A younger generation of Reform thinkers opened up to Christian–Jewish equality as never before. Few followed Stephen Wise when he called on Jews to adopt Jesus as one of their own, or Mordecai Kaplan's Reconstructionist program that suggested that Jews give up on their claim to be the chosen people and move to bless God for having chosen them together with all other nations. However, like their Christian counterparts, Jewish thinkers of the era were laying a foundation for further recognition and dialogue.[11]

While Holmes's and Niebuhr's positions during those years were a minority opinion, the majority of mainline Christians did not yet accept the stance adopted by the progressive ministers. Matters changed after World War II. The camaraderie that developed between Jewish and non-Jewish soldiers serving in the armed forces, as well as among Jewish, Protestant, and

Catholic chaplains, helped to change the relationships between the faiths.[12] Virulent forms of anti-Semitism decreased significantly during the postwar years and the public image of Judaism improved considerably. The social and economic changes that came about in the postwar years were also congenial to progress in the relationship between the faiths. Helped in part by the G. I. Bill, many Jews moved from the working class and immigrant quarters into the middle class and suburbia. To a growing number of Christians, Jews seemed like ordinary law-abiding middle-class citizens who were not to be blamed for America's social, political, or economic problems.[13]

The new atmosphere, which spelled more inclusiveness and acceptance, brought about changes on the theological level as well. Other leading Protestant thinkers followed Niebuhr in advocating the idea that Jews had a vital religious tradition of their own and were not in need of the Christian gospel. During the 1950s and 1960s, prodialogue groups within mainline churches, such as the Presbyterian Church USA or the United Methodist Church, gained the upper hand and a growing number of Protestant denominations decided that they had no more interest in evangelizing Jews. In New York, the Village Presbyterian Church and the Village Temple shared the same house of worship. In the atmosphere created by such an experiment, there was less room for the traditional Christian Replacement Theology and the missionary agenda.[14]

Paradoxically, the Cold War enhanced the atmosphere of interfaith reconciliation, as it helped legitimize middle-class religious expressions in all their varieties, including Judaism, in the American public arena. During the 1950s, the United States was engaged in an intensive global struggle and ideological debate with communism. Participation in religious life became equated with the "American way." Jews participated in the spirit of the age, building hundreds of suburban synagogues, architecturally in line with the tastes and values of middle-class America. Dwight Eisenhower, whose presidency took place during this period, expressed the new mood when he stated that he expected good Americans to be church or synagogue goers. In the 1950s, Judaism became one of the three "public religions" of America.[15] The dialogue between Jews and Christians intensified during this period. The scope of participation in the dialogue considerably enlarged, reaching the mainstream of the religious communities. In New York, Cardinal Francis Spelman, the Roman Catholic leader of the Archdiocese of New York, made interfaith dialogue and reconciliation between the faiths a high priority. Leaders and activists of the Conservative movement played a major role in the reinvigorated dialogue. Influenced by the opinions of Yosef Dov Soloveitchik, Orthodox Jewish leaders were more reluctant to take an active part in the dialogue. They asserted that, while civic cooperation between members of different faiths was acceptable, theological give and take was forbidden.

Nevertheless, the improved relationship between the faiths made open anti-Semitism in America less and less socially acceptable, although covert forms of anti-Jewish sentiments still ran strong. A sociological survey conducted at the initiative of the Anti-Defamation League in the early 1960s discovered that prejudices against Jews were prevalent among the majority of Christians in America, and they were especially strong among members of the more conservative Christian groups. Members of groups taking part in dialogue with Jews were relatively more tolerant.[16]

ADVANCEMENT OF THE DIALOGUE (1960S–1970S)

The 1960s marked an important turning point in the relationships between Jews and members of other faiths in America. The changes were brought about in part by the rise of a Christian ecumenical movement, which revolutionized the relationship between the different Christian churches and between Christianity and other faiths as well. In 1948, mainline Protestant churches had established the World Council of Churches (WCC) with the objective of Christian unity. Initially composed of mainline, mostly national Protestant churches, the WCC's membership grew to include Greek Orthodox, Middle Eastern, and Third World churches as well. In its early years the WCC promoted missions among Jews, but, by the 1960s to 1970s, most affiliated churches changed their approach toward the Jewish community and abandoned their missions among the Jews, instead emphasizing dialogue and recognition.[17]

The most profound global breakthrough that strongly affected the interfaith relations between the religious communities in America occurred during and following Vatican II, the Roman Catholic general council that convened intermittently between 1962 and 1965. The council was initiated by Pope John XXIII (1881–1963), who wished to reform the church, change its relationship to contemporary culture, and bring about a historical reconciliation between the Roman Catholic Church and other faiths. The council attempted to put to rest some of the old hostilities between the different Christian churches, as well as between Christianity and other religions, in order to promote an atmosphere of forgiveness and mutual recognition. In its first stages, the council concentrated on inner reform and intra-Christian relationships. However, the council's ability to influence Jewish–Christian relations was not lost on American Jewish leaders who lobbied for the inclusion of Judaism and the Jewish people in the council agenda for reconciliation.[18] The Anti-Defamation League and the American Jewish Congress sent representatives to Rome to keep in touch with the council and its leaders. Influenced by the developments in America in the relations between the faiths, American Catholic bishops and dignitaries, such as Monsignor John M. Oesterreicher, were instrumental in advancing the reconciliatory agenda regarding the Jews. Toward its very last sessions, Vatican II unveiled a historic resolution on the relationship between Christianity and Judaism. Among other things, it warned against the accusation of deicide and stated that "the Church... cannot forget that she received the revelation of the Old Testament through the people with whom God in His inexpressible mercy concluded the Ancient Covenant.... the Jews should not be presented as rejected or accused by God."[19]

The resolution opened a new phase in Jewish–Christian relationships and served as a stepping-stone for further dialogue and additional declarations on the part of Christian Churches in their relation to Jews.[20] The Catholic Church's attitude influenced not only American Roman Catholics but also American Protestant groups and even Christian Orthodox churches. A number of Protestant churches as well as American ecumenical groups issued statements on their relations with Jews, including a denial of the deicide charge.[21] Among the first of the Protestant groups to issue such a statement was the Synod of Bishops of the Episcopal Church in the United States:

> The charge of deicide against the Jews is a tragic misunderstanding of the inner significance of the crucifixion. To be sure, Jesus was crucified by *some* soldiers at the instigation of *some* Jews. But, this cannot be construed as imputing corporate guilt to every Jew in Jesus' day, much less the Jewish people in subsequent generations. Simple justice alone proclaims the charge of a corporate or inherited curse on the Jewish people to be false.[22]

One immediate result of the new atmosphere in interfaith relationships affected missions. The Roman Catholic Church as well as mainline Protestants churches decided to shut their missionary enterprises among Jews. The position Niebuhr had advocated in the 1920s became much more accepted by liberal Christian thinkers and developed further during the 1960s and 1970s by liberal Protestant theologians such as Roy A. Eckardt, Paul M. Van Buren, and Franklin Littell, and by Catholic thinkers such as David Tracy and John T. Pawliakowski.[23] For the most part, liberal segments of American Christianity gave up on their previous claim to be the sole possessors of the road to salvation. They accepted the idea that other churches and even non-Christian religions could offer moral guidelines and spiritual meaning to their adherents. Nevertheless, evangelizing the Jews has remained the declared agenda of the more conservative Protestant churches that did not take part in the dialogue, such as the Lutheran Church–Missouri Synod or the Southern Baptist Convention, who believe Christianity is the only viable religion and only its adherents have truly found the path to salvation.[24]

The new climate of interfaith dialogue embodied a greater degree of mutual recognition and legitimacy, motivating a keen Christian attempt to eradicate prejudices and establishing a new basis for a relationship between the faiths. Having acquitted the Jews of deicide, liberal Protestants and Catholics went a step further to clear the atmosphere of the hatred that these charges had created. During the late 1960s, Protestants and Catholics systematically examined textbooks that had been used in their religious schools and removed passages with anti-Semitic overtones or that drew a negative portrait of the Jews. A 1972 survey found that the charge of deicide had almost completely disappeared from Christian textbooks in America.[25] Not only liberal churches but conservative ones as well became more sensitive to the manner in which they presented Jews in their publications. A number of American Christian theologians, historians, Biblical scholars, and writers have traced the negative attitudes adopted toward the Jews in the early centuries of Christianity or to theologians in the Middle Ages and the Reformation.[26]

Like their counterparts in Europe, American Christians, both Protestants and Catholics, were motivated, at least in part, by a sense of guilt over the historical role of Christian anti-Jewish accusations in bringing about the mass murder of Jews during World War II. Numerous Christian thinkers determined that Nazi hatred of Jews had been fed by ages of anti-Semitic incitement stemming from Christianity's adverse and hostile attitude toward Judaism and Jews. This has led Christian theologians to examine the significance of the Holocaust for Christianity, in an attempt to ascribe a universal significance to the murder of millions of innocent people.[27] However, this has prompted uneasy feeling among Jewish participants in the dialogue.

Perhaps the most impressive development following the interfaith dialogue has been the growing curiosity among Christian thinkers, scholars, clergy, and students about the Jewish tradition. Many Christian scholars have come to view Judaism as a tradition worth studying because the history of Jews sheds light on the origins of Christianity. Scholarship at the turn of the twenty-first century concerning early Christianity tends to speak about rabbinical Judaism and Christianity as two traditions that developed during the same period, emerging from the same cradle.[28] Christian scholars have also taken an interest in the study of Jewish thought, mysticism, and religious law from the post-Biblical period to the present. The openness on the part of Christians toward the study of Judaism has had an impact on American universities, where it has been incorporated as a discipline of study.

In the atmosphere of reconciliation that developed in the aftermath of the Vatican Council, numerous regional groups of Christians and Jews organized around the nation. Liberal and mainstream Protestants of various denominations, together with Roman Catholics, Greek Orthodox, and Monophysite churches, formed meeting groups with Jews to discuss issues of mutual concern and engage in shared community projects. Congregations would invite each other to visit their sanctuaries and participate as observers in the services. Visiting other communities of faith became a standard feature of Sunday school curriculums in liberal Jewish and Christian communities in America. Likewise, it became customary for Protestant or Catholic congregations to pay visits to Jewish synagogues during services, even though previously synagogues had been, territories reserved exclusively for Jews. While some of the visitors came at the invitation of Jewish friends or as part of interfaith visits or study tours, many were simply curious or in search of a new community of faith.

While the interfaith dialogue has had remarkable achievements in decreasing negative stereotypes and improving relationships between Jews and Christians in America, Jewish observers have noted that official recognition did not necessarily equal true acceptance, and old accusations against Jews did not completely disappear in Christian popular culture. Still others have complained that old anti-Jewish sentiments have at times been replaced by anti-Israeli ones.[29] During the same years of the rapid advancement of the dialogue, many liberal American Christians have become pro-Arab, strongly criticizing Israeli policies. Ironically, the same churches and organizations that take part in the dialogue and recognize Judaism as a legitimate faith have become supporters of anti-Israeli lines. This has become increasingly evident since the 1970s, as liberal Christian groups and organizations in America, including the National Council of Churches, developed a strong commitment to national liberation movements, identifying the Israelis as oppressors. Thus, the relations of liberal Christian churches toward Jews can be defined as somewhat paradoxical – offering Judaism growing recognition, but objecting to the Jewish state and its policies as well as to the political agenda of Jewish organizations in America on Middle Eastern issues. Within the same churches, there are many different voices. On one hand, there are theologians committed to dialoguing with Jews and striving to build an appreciation for Judaism. On the other hand, there are activists who are concerned over Palestinian rights, who view Israel as an oppressor, and who do not necessarily take an interest in improving Christian–Jewish relationships. Nevertheless, Jewish representatives in the dialogue have often seen it as their mission to include Israel on their agenda and to try to convince the non-Jewish participants in the dialogue of the importance of the Land of Israel and the well-being of the Jewish state for the Jewish people.

CONSERVATIVE CHRISTIAN DIALOGUE WITH JEWS

The relationship between conservative Protestants and Jews in America developed along somewhat different lines than the relationship between Jews and liberal Christians. Although they were initially more hesitant to join official dialogue groups, the attitudes of conservative evangelicals toward the Jews have undergone huge transformations throughout the twentieth century. A major component of the evangelical theology is the belief that only those individuals who undergo a personal religious experience of conversion in which they accept Jesus as their savior will be saved and granted eternal life. Conservative evangelicals look on the Christian Bible as the message of God to humanity and as the source of authority on how to live a Christian life. Thus, they are committed to spreading the Christian gospel both in America and abroad. In evangelical eyes, granting legitimacy to the religious beliefs of others is an act of neglect toward them, and so conservative evangelicals do not lend themselves easily to dialoguing with representatives of other faiths. According to the evangelical understanding, neither can Judaism grant salvation to its believers nor can the observance of its precepts have any value or serve any purpose after Christ's death on the Cross.

Many in the evangelical Christian camp subscribe to a premillenialist messianic hope in the Second Coming of Jesus and his thousand-year reign on earth. In contrast to traditional Christian claims to be "true Israel," evangelicals have viewed the Jews as historical Israel and the object of the Biblical prophecies about a glorious future, when the Messiah arrives and Israel is restored to its land. Evangelical Christians have even welcomed the rise of the Zionist movement and the Jewish waves of immigration to Palestine as "signs of the time," indicators that the current era was ending and the apocalyptic events were about to begin.[30] They have seen in the establishment of the State of Israel the beginning of the fulfillment of prophecy and a preparation of the ground for the eventual building of the kingdom of God on earth. The Six-Day War in 1967 had a very different effect on the evangelical–Jewish relationship than on liberal Christian–Jewish attitudes. The war, in which Israel conquered the historical parts of Jerusalem, served as a proof that Israel was indeed born for a purpose, that the messianic times were near, and that the Jewish people would play a crucial role in the events of the End Times. Evangelical support for Israel increased throughout the period from the 1970s to the present, and the Christian Right has become an important component of the pro-Israel lobby in America. While many Jews have been suspicious of conservative Christians, viewing them as a threat to an open pluralistic society, a number of Jewish leaders and activists have come to appreciate the conservative Christian support.

Until the 1970s, evangelicals and Jews did not have many opportunities to encounter each other, thereby further contributing to the perpetuation of stereotypes on both sides. In conservative Protestant writings, Jews have often been portrayed as the perpetrators of secular ideological and political movements such as communism, socialism, or secular humanism, which, in the conservative view, have aimed to destroy Christian civilization. In the early 1960s, a study by sociologists commissioned by the Anti-Defamation League pointed to more anti-Jewish prejudices among conservative evangelicals than among liberal Protestants or Roman Catholics.[31] However, a similar study in the mid-1980s showed a drastic decline in the extent of such prejudices among the conservatives.[32] This change should be accounted for by the increased evangelical interest and involvement with Jewish and Israeli affairs since the Six Day War in 1967 and the subsequent increase in information available on these topics.

During the 1970s and 1980s, evangelicals warmed up in their relation to Jews even while many Jews suspiciously viewed this evolution. Evangelical missions to the Jews persisted and brought about an evangelical–Jewish movement: Jews who have adopted the evangelical Protestant faith yet have wished to retain their Jewish identity.[33] Missions to the Jews, and the movement of messianic Jews, have become important agents in shaping the evangelical–Jewish relationship, as missionaries have been active in lecturing to evangelical Christians on Israel, distributing pertinent material in churches, and organizing tours to the Holy Land. Ironically, missions to the Jews and the messianic–Jewish community serve as pro-Jewish interest groups within the larger evangelical community, promoting support for Israel and requesting a high priority to evangelization efforts among the Jews. While messianic Jews have strived for recognition as legitimate Jews, mainstream Jewish organizations have refused, as a rule, to dialogue with such groups.

Although conservative Protestants do not recognize the legitimacy of a religious faith not founded on the acceptance of Jesus as a savior, there have been some minor attempts at an evangelical–Jewish dialogue.[34] Leaders and activists who have participated in the dialogue, such as Marvin Wilson or Douglas Young, did not represent missionary organizations but rather voices of intellectuals and academics within evangelical Christianity. On the Jewish side, participants included leaders of Jewish organizations, hailing from different Jewish denominations, including even Orthodoxy. The Holy Land Fellowship of Christians and Jews, founded by the Orthodox Rabbi

Yehiel Eckstein, is among the organizations established in America in the 1980s to promote understanding between conservative Christians and Jews. Eckstein has emphasized the importance of the Holy Land and the State of Israel to Jews and evangelical Christians alike and viewed support for Israel as a common basis for cooperation and understanding between the two groups. Right-wing Orthodox Jews have also come to appreciate the conservative evangelical political agenda. In 1991, Rabbi Daniel Lapin founded a group called Toward Tradition, "a national coalition of Jews and Christians seeking to advance the nation toward traditional, faith based, American principles of limited government, the rule of law ... free markets, a strong military, and a moral public culture."[35] Orthodox rabbis such as Lapin decided that they have more in common with conservative Christians than with liberal ones. With the establishment of such new organizations, rabbis such as Eckstein and Lapin have created alternative dialogue groups unaffiliated with more institutionalized mainstream groups.

ENLARGING THE SCOPE OF THE DIALOGUE

From the 1960s to the present, the racial and ethnic scope of the dialogue has grown considerably, with non-Western Christians as well as African-American and Asian-American religious leaders joining the dialogue groups. While Jewish and Christian veteran participants in the dialogue welcomed representatives of old established communities, such as African-American churches or the fledgling communities of Muslim immigrants, they were not, as a rule, open to new religious movements that came up on the American scene at that time. The Jewish and Christian mainstream related to new religious groups suspiciously as "cults" and did not consider them partners for serious dialogue. Jews, like their Christian counterparts, looked on many of the new religious movements as illegitimate groups that conspired to capture innocent Jewish souls.[36]

Somewhat unexpectedly, observant rabbis, leaders of the emerging neo-Hasidic and Renewal movements in Judaism, were happy to converse with leaders of new religious movements. Zalman Schachter, the "Zeide" (grandfather) of the Renewal movement, and the neo-Hasidic rabbi Shlomo Carlebach participated in conferences with leaders of "alternative" religions, communicating and offering each other recognition and support. The cooperation between the Jewish neo-Hasidic and Renewal rabbis and leaders of new religious movements manifested itself in mutual gatherings and joint publications, and it presented an alternative dialogue based on mutual interest. Representing a Jewish movement of religious revival and return to tradition, Carlebach and Schachter had realized that Judaism needed to compete in an open market of religions even for the loyalty of its own children. They were interested in learning "the secret" of the new, alternative, religious movements that had successfully attracted young Jews into their midst. Thus, the new advocates of Jewish outreach felt they needed to associate with and learn from those relatively successful groups in order to revitalize their own tradition.

While refusing to engage in dialogue with what they considered to be marginal and disruptive religious groups, the more established dialogue groups nonetheless enlarged their scope considerably. From the 1980s to the present, dialogue with Muslims, although not easy, has become a major item on the Jewish interfaith agenda. For many Muslims, American Jews were associated with Israel and were the supporters of a country that they often resented. Official representatives of Jewish organizations, as well as local Jewish religious leaders, saw it as their duty to represent Judaism without compromising their concern for Israel. However, not all forms of interfaith dialogue between Jews and Muslims in America have come to an end. New modes and forums of what could be called alternative interfaith dialogue developed between Jews and non-Jews. The impetus for a number of Jewish religious leaders to be engaged in alternative avenues of dialogue with Muslims and Christians resulted from their dissenting opinions on Israeli policies and their exception to the extensive backing that the established American Jewish organizations have offered the Jewish state. Representatives of major Jewish organizations, such as the American Jewish Committee and the Anti-Defamation League, have viewed it as their mission to promote recognition and support for Israel and turn the Israeli cause into a major part of the interfaith agenda.

However, not everybody in the Jewish community agreed. In the early 1980s, in the wake of the Israeli war in Lebanon, a number of rabbis, including Jacob Arnold Wolf from K.A.M.-Isaiah Israel in Chicago, founded alternative forms of dialogue in which Jewish leaders came together with Christian and Muslim critics of Israel in an attempt to promote peace negotiations as well as safeguard civil rights in Israel and its occupied territories. Christian and Muslim clergy and laity who had concluded that they could not dialogue with Jewish representatives in official interfaith forums found a common language with Jewish leaders who deviated from the official policy of the Jewish establishment.[37] Alternative forms of dialogue grew throughout the 1990s to the present, correlating with larger developments within the Jewish community in America. On the Jewish liberal side, a growing discontent with the older established representative bodies of American Jews gave rise to the creation of new, alternative ones. With the growing effect of the Intifada in

Israel in the late 1980s and early 1990s, interfaith groups concerned with human rights have developed in America and in Israel.

In the wake of the attack on the World Trade Center on September 11, 2001, a number of Jewish religious leaders raised their voice against the vilification of Islam and the harassment of Muslims in America. Similarly, a number of Muslim leaders denounced the suicide bombings and the killing of innocent civilians in Israel. Such good intentions notwithstanding, the institutionalized Jewish–Muslim dialogue became virtually impossible amidst the continuous reports on killings and death in both the Israeli and Palestinian communities.[38]

CONCLUSION

As the interfaith dialogue in America heads into the twenty-first century, one can look back at over a century of Jewish intensive involvement in dialogue and reach some conclusions. The interfaith dialogue, essentially a liberal Christian initiative that concentrated on unresolved old-time issues as well as more current Jewish–Christian concerns, grew toward the latter part of the twentieth century to include discussions among Jews, Christians, and representatives of other religious communities as well. While the interfaith dialogue affected all members of the Jewish community, it remained overwhelmingly the domain of rabbis who became the official representatives of the Jewish community, its organizations, issues, and interests. Dialogue became part of the rabbis' communal responsibility, leaving out, at times, more secular, counterculture, or dissenting voices.

The interfaith dialogue groups have reached impressive achievements, serving as a vehicle to improve the relationship between Jews and non-Jews in America and thus advance the status of Jews in America and elsewhere. The dialogue has been particularly effective in putting to rest old prejudices and animosities and bringing about reconciliation between the communities. It has been somewhat less successful, however, when its agenda turned toward the Israeli–Arab conflict. Most liberal Christians refused to tie pro-Israeli sentiments to reconciliation between the faiths. Paradoxically, just when the dialogue reached a historical peak in the late 1960s to 1970s, bringing an unprecedented improvement in the relationship between Christians and Jews, the dialogue reached a crisis and even a partial dead end. Christian groups that showed willingness to transform and reverse their opinion on Judaism and Jews refused to accept what seemed to them a noncritical Jewish enchantment with the State of Israel. Toward the end of the twentieth century, some Jews and non-Jews alike created alternative dialogue groups, in which they voiced their more critical opinions or dialogued with groups that the Jewish and Christian establishments had excluded from the official dialogue.

The history of the interfaith dialogue and interfaith relationship in general has been that of progress, as the Christian majority has become more and more open toward Judaism and Jews. However, while interfaith relations have progressed dramatically, they have not brought about a full reconciliation between Jewish and non-Jewish groups in America, and pockets of bitterness and suspicions have certainly remained. Muslim–Jewish relations, for example, have developed much less favorably than Jewish–Christian relationships. Interfaith dialogue in one form or another will therefore continue to be an important mechanism for renegotiation of communal relationships in America.

Notes

1. Lawrence G. Charap, "Accept the Truth from Whomsoever Gives It: Jewish Protestant Dialogue, Interfaith Alliance and Pluralism, 1880–1910," *American Jewish History* 89, 3 (September 2001), 161–78.

2. Marcus Braybrooke, *Pilgrimage of Hope: One Hundred Years of Interfaith Dialogue* (New York: Crossroad, 1992).

3. Martin E. Marty, *Modern American Religion, Vol. 1: The Irony of it All, 1893–1919* (Chicago: University of Chicago Press, 1886), 17–24.

4. Compare Yaakov Ariel, *Evangelizing the Jewish People: Missions to the Jews in America, 1880–2000* (Chapel Hill: University of North Carolina Press, 2000).

5. Yaakov Ariel, "Christianity Through Reform Eyes: Kaufmann Kohler's Scholarship on Christianity," *American Jewish History* 89, 2 (June 2001), 181–92.

6. Benny Kraut, "A Wary Collaboration: Jews, Catholics, and the Protestant Goodwill Movement," in *Between the Times*, ed. William R. Hutchison (Cambridge, MA: Cambridge University Press, 1989).

7. Marcus Braybooke, *A History of the Council of Christians and Jews* (London: Valentine Mitchell, 1911).

8. Jay P. Dolan, *The American Catholic Experience* (Garden City: Image Books, 1985), 403–04; Glen Jeansonne, *Gerald L. K. Smith, Minister of Hate* (New Haven: Yale University Press, 1988).

9. Neil Baldwin, *Henry Ford and the Jews: The Mass Production of Hate* (New York: Public Affairs, 2001).

10. John Haynes Holmes, *Judaism and Christianity* (New York: Community Pulpit, 1928); Reinhold Niebuhr, "The Rapprochement Between Jews and Christians," *Christian Century* (7 January 1926), 9–11.

11. Richard Libowitz, *Mordecai Kaplan and the Development of Reconstructionism* (New York: Edwin Mellen Press, 1983).

12. Deborah Dash Moore, "Jewish G.I.'s and the Creation of the Judeo-Christian Tradition," *Religion and American Culture* 8, 1 (Winter 1998), 31–53.

13. Jonathan D. Sarna, *American Judaism: A History* (New Haven: Yale University Press, 2004), 272–93.

14. Ben Merson, "The Minister, the Rabbi and Their House of God," *Collier's* (17 February 1951), 27, 36–37.
15. Will Herberg, *Protestant, Catholic, Jew* (New York: Anchor Books, 1960); Stephen Whitfield, *The Culture of the Cold War* (Baltimore: Johns Hopkins University Press, 1991).
16. Charles Y. Glock and Rodney Stark, *Christian Beliefs and Anti-Semitism* (New York: Harper Torchbooks, 1966).
17. "First Assembly of the WCC, Amsterdam, Holland, 1948, The Christian Approach to the Jews," in *Stepping Stones to Further Jewish–Christian Relations*, ed. Helga Croner (New York: Stimulus Books, 1977), 72–85.
18. Arthur Gilbert, *The Vatican Council and the Jews* (Cleveland: World Publishing, 1968).
19. Helga Croner, ed., *Stepping Stones to Further Jewish–Christian Relations* (New York: Stimulus Books, 1977), 1–2.
20. Helga Croner, ed., *More Stepping Stones to Jewish Christian Relations* (New York: Stimulus Books, 1985).
21. *The Theology of the Churches and the Jewish People: Statements by the World Council of Churches and its Member Churches* (Geneva: World Council of Churches, 1988).
22. Helga Croner, ed., *Stepping Stones to Further Jewish–Christian Relations* (New York: Stimulus Books, 1977), 87.
23. Franklin Littell, *The Crucifixion of the Jews* (New York: Harper & Row, 1975); Roy A. Eckard, *The Elder and Younger Brother* (New York: Scribner's, 1967); Paul M. Van Buren, *Discerning the Way: A Theology of the Jewish Christian Realities* (New York: Seabury Press, 1980); John T. Pawlikowski, *Christ in Light of the Jewish–Christian Dialogue* (New York: Paulist Press, 1982).
24. Bruce J. Lieske, *Witnessing to the Jewish People* (St. Louis: Board for Evangelism, the Lutheran Church, Missouri Synod, 1975), 11–17, 46–48.
25. Gerald Strober, *Portrait of the Elder Brother* (New York: American Jewish Committee and the National Conference of Christians and Jews, 1972).
26. Rosemary Ruther, *Faith and Fratricide: The Theological Roots of Antisemitism* (New York: Seabury Press, 1974); James Carroll, *Constantine's Sword: The Church and the Jews* (New York: Houghton Mifflin, 2001).
27. Eva Fleischner, *Auschwitz – Beginning of a New Era: Reflections on the Holocaust* (New York: KTAV Publishing House, 1977); Stephen R. Haynes, *Reluctant Witnessess: Jews and the Christian Imagination* (Louisville: Westminster John Leno Press, 1995).
28. Jon D. Levenson, *The Death and Resurrection of the Beloved Son: The Transformation of Child Sacrifice in Judaism and Christianity* (New Haven: Yale University Press, 1995).
29. Judith Hershcopf Banki, *Christian Responses to the Yom Kippur War: Implication for Christian Jewish Relations* (New York: American Jewish Committee, 1974).
30. Yaakov Ariel, *Evangelizing the Chosen People: Missions to the Jews in America, 1880–2000* (Chapel Hill and London: University of North Carolina Press, 2000).
31. Charles Y. Glock and Rodney Stark, *Christian Beliefs and Anti-Semitism* (New York: Harper Torchbooks, 1966).
32. Lynne Lanniello, "Release for Press," Anti-Defamation League, New York (8 January 1986).

33. David Stern, *Messianic Jewish Manifesto* (Jerusalem: Jewish New Testament Publications, 1988).
34. A. James Rudin and Marvin R. Wilson, eds., *A Time to Speak: The Evangelical Jewish Encounter* (Grand Rapids: Eerdmans, 1987).
35. See www.towardtradition.org.
36. Harvey Cox, "Deep Structures in the Study of New Religions," in *Understanding the New Religions*, ed. Jacob Needleman and George Baher (New York: Seabury Press, 1978), 122–30.
37. Otto Maduro, ed., *Judaism, Christianity and Liberation* (New York: Orbis Books, 1991).
38. Yigal Schleifer, "No Dialogue, Only Mutual Distrust," *The Jerusalem Report* (23 September 2002), 16–17.

20 American midrash: Urban Jewish writing and the reclaiming of Judaism

MURRAY BAUMGARTEN

By the end of the tumultuous 1960s, a new vision of American Jewish writing emerged. Instead of the sociological fiction and psychological critique of immigrant assimilation, at the heart of novels such as Abraham Cahan's *The Rise of David Levinsky*,[1] religious issues and a Judaic rather than a secular Jewish perspective began to inform American Jewish fiction. As the father tells his son, Reuven Malter, in 1967 in Chaim Potok's *The Chosen*, "It is strange what's happening. And it is exciting. Jack . . . joined a synagogue. He is helping . . . put up a new building so his grandchildren can go to a modern synagogue and have a good Jewish education. It is beginning to happen everywhere in America. A religious renaissance, some call it."[2,3]

As American Jews rediscovered their roots and planted new synagogues throughout the land, they founded Jewish schools, developed Jewish summer camps, visited Israel in increasing numbers in the heady days after the triumph of the Six Day War, and funded Jewish Studies programs at colleges and universities. These events and activities reinforced the new agenda for American Jewish literature, which took hold in the 1970s in a renewal of interest in classical Jewish texts, including the Bible, traditional parables, Hasidic tales, and *midrashim*. The rekindled interest in classical Jewish learning had an American turn and developed into an American midrashic style, which began to inform the fiction of the younger generation of writers.

AMERICAN MIDRASH

In reclaiming classical Jewish learning, the Jewish intellectuals of the 1960s and 1970s did not simply follow traditional storytelling habits at work in parables, midrashim, and Hasidic tales. They did not directly engage classic texts; rather, they discovered that what was missing in their explorations of American Jewish life were central meanings articulated in those texts and that traditional culture. They expressed this not in a literature of allusion but in an innovative strategy that brought the subtext of classic learning into the foreground of secular experience. Their midrashim and parables here share habits with late Hasidic practice though they differ in narrative strategy.

David Stern notes that "the early rabbis, though they doubtless believed themselves to be the sole authentic heirs of the biblical tradition, never attempted to write narrative in the style of the Bible." Rather they "channeled their imaginative energies into the type of commentary known as *midrash* – literally 'study' but more accurately 'interpretation.' Contradictions in the scriptural text, discontinuities, lacunae, silences, inexplicable motives, lexical peculiarities, awkward or unusual syntactic constructions – any one of these 'irritants' became for the rabbis either an occasion for recounting a narrative of their own invention or a peg on which to hang an extrabiblical legend or tradition." The Biblical narrative "thus became for the rabbis a giant screen on which they projected the story of their own existence. Responding to the most subtle, latent possibilities of meaning in Scripture, these exegetes allowed their narrative imaginations to blossom in the cracks of the Biblical text, sometimes literally inside the empty spaces separating words or atop the wavy scribal crowns adorning letters."[4]

A religious imagination, fueled by a brief acquaintance with traditional Jewish texts and classic midrashic practice, took hold of American Jewish writers. These younger American Jewish writers had powerful allies in an earlier generation. Henry Roth's novel, *Call It Sleep* (1934),[5] a syncretistic commentary on Isaiah 6:1–7, was acclaimed at the end of the 1960s as an unknown masterpiece of American Jewish writing. Reissued in paperback, it became required reading in college courses. Cynthia Ozick had already called for the creation of a Biblically inspired Jewish literature in English in 1959, which she claimed could be considered the new Yiddish,[6] and Saul Bellow brought Biblical themes into his writing in *Mr. Sammler's Planet.*[7]

Consider the conclusion of the novel, a eulogy for Elya Gruner, a relative of Mr. Sammler, who has defended him against a mugger in New York City:

> Remember, God, the soul of Elya Gruner, who, as willingly as possible and as well as he was able, and even to an intolerable point, and even in suffocation and even as death was coming was eager, even childishly perhaps (may I be forgiven for this), even with a certain servility, to do what was required of him. At his best this man was much kinder than at my very best I have ever been or could ever be. He was aware that he must meet, and he did meet – through all the confusion and degraded clowning of this life through which we are speeding – he did meet the terms of his contract. The terms which, in his inmost heart, each man knows. As I know mine. As all know. For that is the truth of it – that we all know, God, that we know, that we know, we know, we know.

This conclusion of the novel echoes and comments on a famous passage in Deuteronomy 30:11–14.

> Surely, this Instruction which I enjoin upon you this day is not too baffling for you, nor is it beyond reach. It is not in the heavens, that you should say, 'Who among us can go up to the heavens and get it for us and impart it to us, that we may observe it?' Neither is it beyond the sea, that you should say, 'Who among us can cross to the other side of the sea and get it for us and impart it to us, that we may observe it?' No, the thing is very close to you, in your mouth and in your heart, to observe.

To read the conclusion of *Mr. Sammler's Planet* against this passage from Deuteronomy is to recognize a different trajectory to the novel than the sociological or the psychological acuity for which it has been praised. It resituates the novel in a Judaic tradition of Scriptural commentary and parable rather than the Jewish, secular narrative of immigration and assimilation. Furthermore, it articulates connections between Judaic views of the covenant between God and the Jews, as well as between God and humanity, that foreground them over and against the secular Enlightenment notions of the social contract. As a member of the Committee on Social Thought of the University of Chicago, Bellow must have delighted in this turn the novel provides to the practice of urban anthropological observation. And what a witty flourish for the writer who claimed he happened to be a Jew who was a writer, rather than a Jewish writer.

Read with the Scriptural text next to it, the conclusion of the novel thus turns into an interpretation of the meanings of the cited passage from Deuteronomy as the latter is seen to inform the former. In effect, they are reciprocal interpretations, commenting on and elaborating each other, and thus articulating subtexts in and of each. The two passages illuminate each other. I am not arguing for Bellow's novel as a classical midrash or parable. Rather, I want to emphasize the ways in which *Mr. Sammler's Planet* brings this passage from Deuteronomy into play and thereby shifts our expectations. It is poised against the sociological and psychological accounts of situation and character in the novel, with their vocabularies of social status and personal needs. Instead, the Biblical passage calls up the notion of moral responsibility and familial connectedness, and it locates it in the heart and soul. The genre of realistic fiction is here undermined by mythological reference in a generic upheaval: The text now points to the Jewish covenant with God as an innate faculty that cannot be denied. This dialogue between Jewish fiction and Scriptural text, set in the urban historical context, defines a Judaic literary movement and cultural history.

The Deuteronomic text invades the world of Bellow's characters and expresses what the reigning modernism and secularism of their world has left out. Bellow's strategy is paradigmatic and articulates a way of engaging the Biblical text, in this mode of American midrash, and making it operative in a realistic fiction. Neither Elya Gruner nor Jacob Sammler directly cite or interpret the Biblical text. Nor do they follow religious or ritual traditions. Nevertheless, that text shapes the meanings they find in their lives. That is why the conclusion of *Mr. Sammler's Planet* functions as an American midrash. Biblical text is not directly engaged, but it emerges as an informing mythic subtext of this realistic fiction.

Much contemporary Jewish writing is part of a recovered tradition of such innovative midrashic storytelling. Rebecca Goldstein's fiction, especially *Mazel*,[8] connects the midrashic impulse to the telling of stories. Her fiction is explicitly linked to Hasidic parable and storytelling habits, which grow out of classical midrash. What was peripheral has taken over the center of the literary imagination.

This innovative midrashic impulse reinscribes the dialogue with God in contemporary Jewish fiction. Note how E. L. Doctorow's *City of God* weaves relativity theory and quantum physics into a novel of conversion to Judaism.[9] Such Judaic concerns made explicit in this fiction also change our understanding of earlier Jewish writing. It makes the writing of the story into one of the central issues of the tale, which no longer exists in the past tense of historical narration but the present tense of lyrical imagining. Here it connects with "classical Jewish literature," in which Mark Mirsky notes this:

> [S]torytelling has not only an oral folk tradition but an oral intellectual one. As Rabbi Soloveitchik retold the biblical narrative, glossing it with a hundred commentaries, it was not primarily a literary performance, but it was certainly one that engaged the narrative itself. I recall the Rav rising from his seat to intone, as the self-conscious narrator, that the gift of reading Bible is to see it not as text but as the present drama of your life. It is happening now and you are an actor in it.

Furthermore,

> [T]he riddle not only of what we have been and what we are but what we can be lies in the stories we tell and understand – the stories in whose light we see ourselves. Serious and playful by turns, Jewish narrative has subsumed in it the old task of prophecy, not only to puzzle out the future but to show a way toward a better one and to hold out impossible hope by imagining it.[10]

What is being imagined is, among others, the epic sweep of an entire culture not only in geographic or national space but space–time. As Jonathan Safran Foer notes in his brilliant novel, *Everything Is Illuminated* (2002), for "Jews memory is no less primary than the prick of a pin, or its silver glimmer, or the taste of the blood it pulls from the finger. The Jew is pricked by a pin and remembers other pins. . . . When a Jew encounters a pin, he asks: *What does it remember like?*"[11] This turn to memory and the charting of a communal and religious psychic geography in time–space not only marks Foer's novel as part of this stream of Jewish writing but also connects him in its deployment of stream-of-consciousness to Henry Roth and his great novel, *Call It Sleep.*

Foer also draws, as does Nathan Englander in his story collection, *For The Relief of Unbearable Urges* (1999), on the achievement of Isaac Bashevis Singer.[12] This Nobel Laureate of 1978 engages his characters with the irrational, with questions of good and evil, and has them encounter in religious ritual and experiences forces and powers outside reason yet raging in history. Like Rebecca Goldstein's, Foer's characters live not in linear but stochastic time, and they function under the sign of *Mazel.* Like Malamud's heroes they live on the edge of, and occasionally straddle, what Foer calls the Jewish–human fault line. They are obsessed by the power of the Jewish imagination to change everyday life, as are the protagonists of Myla Goldberg's *The Bee Season.*[13] One of the defining characteristics of each of these works of fiction is the way in which explorations of the everyday life of sharply etched individuals turn out to be accounts of how classical texts inform modern tales, in effect making them versions of ancient stories. Instead of the ideology of (rugged) individualism central to the conventional view of mainstream American literature, the new Judaic fiction focuses on the communal implications of the actions of individuals. It is no accident that many of these Judaic fictions conclude with marriage and the blessing of children.

URBAN CULTURE AND THE RECLAIMING OF JEWISH LEARNING

The reclaiming of Jewish learning in this new mode, and its impact on American Jewish writing, runs counter to the conventional view of American Jewish fiction,[14] which locates it as a literary reflection of the process of Jewish assimilation. From that perspective, writers in the sociological and psychological modes are paradigmatic and the decline of Yiddish is cited as further evidence of assimilation.

However, this new Judaic turn in American Jewish literature changes that historical trajectory. The literary history of Jewish writing in America, in tandem with the larger history of Jewish American experience, is not a linear process; it is marked by complicated transitions and changes in the cultural work of this writing. The continuities and significant differences in the history of American Jewish literature are linked to the changing pressures of Diaspora, exile, homecoming, and Zionism, among others. They are thus connected to the long history of Jewish writing from the Bible onward, which makes their charting a complex and difficult task. This is not to deny American exceptionalism, though it does resituate that perspective by viewing it through the lenses of traditional Jewish writing.[15]

The Jewish Street, which has served so often as the dominant scene of this writing, has become a site for exegesis, interpretation, and commentary. It is not surprising, therefore, that there are traces of ritual Jewish experiences in the writing of Isaac Bashevis Singer and Henry Roth, and that Biblical passages function as informing presences in novels by Chaim Potok, Saul Bellow, and Philip Roth, while Allen Hoffman's, Michael Chabon's, Allegra Goodman's, and Rebecca Goldstein's historical fiction represent the Jewish imagination at work on the materials of modern experience. These fictions elaborate multiple layers of meaning, appropriate to the city worlds they evoke and the mixing of genres they deploy. They articulate an indeterminacy of meaning that invites the reader into the play of Judaic interpretation and exegesis. The conversation among these writers and the texts they have produced define the outlines of a Judaic literary movement.

The work of this younger generation elaborates a new subject. Rather than the novel of family dysfunction amid the dynamics of assimilation and the siren call of American modernity, which defines the writing, for example, of Ludwig Lewisohn, Jerome Weidman, and Daniel Fuchs, this new generation devises fictions articulating the return to communal traditions and a liturgical literature advocated by Cynthia Ozick. Rather than the marriage plot of the sociological and psychological novel with its emphasis on romantic love, family legacies, and the missteps of adultery in a supposedly monogamous and stable neighborhood, these writers chart the problematics of a diffuse and polymorphous sexual energy in brilliant travel narratives.

In their fiction, Jewish agency is reclaimed: their characters choose lives centered on Judaic tradition. Thus, for example, Phoebe makes the point throughout Rebecca Goldstein's novel, *Mazel*, as she chooses a traditional marriage, *kashrut*, and life in the Jewish suburb, Lipton, rather than her grandmother Sasha's dynamic New York.[16] The nostalgia for the environmental Judaism of the *shtetl* and neighborhood that made the 1971 film *Fiddler on the Roof* a popular success is absent from their writing. Rather than the conflicts of oedipal development, their tales focus on the engendering of desire, the birth of children, and the privileging of Jewish experience.

The crystallization as well as the disintegration of the ephemeral bonds of a fluid, mobile community focus their explorations of Jewish travelers seeking to unravel an ambiguous fate and construct a Judaic existence for themselves. Their protagonists are not anchored in local time and space as the site of a (diasporic) homeland, but encounter the changing possibilities of urban time and religious discovery. They give up Diaspora's anxieties and the success of "making it" for the reclaiming of the personal and communal meanings of the experience of exile. Exploring such a Judaic realm, in contrast to the secularizing fiction of Jewishness, these tales engage writer, reader, and critic in teasing out the impact of scripture rather than the analysis of psychic need or sociological function.

These younger writers define a third wave of American Jewish writing: the first was sociological; the second was psychological in orientation; and this third one is religious – in effect, a Judaic writing. This literary movement and history emerge in tandem with and connected loosely to the renewal movement that took hold of American Jewish culture from the 1970s on. It is important to note, however, that all three waves – sociological, psychological, and religious – elaborate an urban literature, drawing in various ways on the city as fateful setting and defining agent for their fictions even in the recent eras of suburbanization.

FROM JEWISH TO JUDAIC FICTION

The transition from Jewish to Judaic literature is already evident in Delmore Schwartz's *In Dreams Begin Responsibilities*.[17] In it he dramatizes the immigrant's anxieties of citizenship and independence, fusing inner and outer worlds into a stunning trope: The past is a first-run film we want to stop. As the internal images of desire and external environment are overlaid on each other in this urbane fiction, they remind us of the simultaneous rise of the modern western city and the way of seeing brought on by photography. Thus they help recover the informing force of the past as part of the work of the present moment, as Schwartz constructs a narrator who projects his tale against the imaginary screen of an old movie house. He sees his parents courting in that dream film, and he is terrified he does not measure up to their high hopes for their impending family.

Schwartz's story manages a near-tragic Freudian evocation that also has its comedic moments, articulating a mixed form. Try as he might, Schwartz's narrator cannot escape into the "soft darkness of the theatre." Though "the organist peals out the obvious and approximate emotions on which the audience rocks unknowingly," he is uneasy. "I am anonymous, and I have forgotten myself. It is always so," he thinks; "when one goes to the movies, it is, as they say, a drug."[18]

Delmore Schwartz's unnamed narrator relives the obdurate unyielding prehistory of his life, as he watches the dreamed film of his parents' courtship, which he desperately attempts to halt. In Schwartz's story, the narrator's father is "impressive, yet he is very awkward."[19] When the waltz music reaches its climax in Schwartz's story, the father proposes marriage and the mother sobs her acceptance: "'It's all I've wanted from the moment I saw you.'" Echoing Job's curse of the day he was born, the son stands up and tries to stop the film, yelling at his parents not to marry, not to bring him into the world. The discovery of personal interdependence endows him with a sharp sense of his own limitations: Their scenario has determined his. With Schwartz's narrator we readers shout at our parents, giving vent to oedipal rage, in a psychic echo of the Talmudic discussion that yields as one of its conclusions that it would have been better had God not created humanity. Nevertheless, Schwartz's story also moves us toward accepting the contradictions that define human beings. Thereby his fiction acknowledges that continuing rabbinic conversation that leads beyond present anger to the understanding that our presence, the very fact of human existence, even so, obliges us to praise Creation and the Creator.

Meyer Liben's "Homage to Benny Leonard" elicits a Judaic perspective through its evocation of Jewish history.[20] In this deft tale, the young David Flaxman, child of immigrants, must recover the honor of his hero, the great Jewish boxer, Benny Leonard. Leonard has just lost a boxing match, one of only three defeats he would suffer in his remarkable career. The morning newspapers are full of the event, which David cannot shrug off. Unlike his friend Chick – "who took for granted the prevailing freedom, was not drawn to the ancient midnight," nor "disturbed by vague and monstrous presentiments, menacing shadows" of "nighttime assaults and terrors" and the news of "the bearded Jew shot to death in the tunnels under the New York Central Railway up on Park Avenue" – Davey cannot put the event aside with his friend's accepting "So what, you can't win them all."[21]

Unlike Chick, who is "well-adjusted historically," Davey has one foot in the Jewish past. Thus, for Davey, Benny Leonard, the Jewish fighter, stands between his family and the pogroms of the Old World, defending them from "some unknown future enemy, even against the monstrous foes of the past – Haman, Antiochus Epiphanes, the thundering Black Hundreds."[22] Whereas they prefer evasive strategies, other Jews fought back with their fists. These include the "battling" Jews of the boxing ring, including Benny Leonard, as role models, as well as Isaac Babel's Benya Krik in his Odessa stories.[23] Woody Allen's shlemiehl is arrayed on one end of the spectrum of characters generated by American Jewish fiction, and it is connected at the other end to fighter, warrior, and criminal by means of their history, as part of the Jewish self-adaptation to the circumstances in which they have lived.

AMERICAN CHARACTER AND JEWISH AGENCY

The spectrum of characters evoked by astute observers of American Jewish life includes the street-smart cynic, Neil Klugman, of Philip Roth's prize-winning *Goodbye, Columbus*,[24] Saul Bellow's brash, urban, energetic adventurer Augie March,[25] the older suffering servant role taken by Morris Bober in Bernard Malamud's *The Assistant*,[26] as well as the perplexed convert, Frank Alpine. Non-Jews appear in the sociological and psychological novel as power-wielding figures with little depth. The engagement with the non-Jewish world especially in Philip Roth's fiction occurs in the encounter with the *shiksa* – the mysterious (usually) blonde American woman. She is simultaneously attracted to and repelled by the Jewish male protagonist. Often he shares her ambivalence, but he must conquer her to assert his right to America.

The younger generation of writers, however, in tandem with the women's movement beginning in the 1960s in which Jewish women played a prominent role, constructs a wider range of women characters. They claim the right to all the roles that had been reserved for American and for Jewish males.

Responding to Roth's and Bellow's views of women, Renee – woman, philosopher, and narrator of Goldstein's first novel, *The Mind-Body Problem* – acknowledges their power as she defines their limitations.[27] She recalls how in the course of a love affair, her partner has revealed the shape of his assimilationist understanding: "He was worshipful, offering me again and again the highest praise of which the Jewish male is capable: You don't look at all Jewish." Goldstein dramatizes what an earlier generation, including Bellow and especially Philip Roth, expressed about American Jewish men, and then opposes it: Her narrator defends what Portnoy and Herzog, potential Jewish American Princes, have done their best to escape from – the beauty and power of the Jewish woman.

> Our brothers always expect us to thrill at the words, because of course in their scheme of things there's nothing so desirable as a *shiksa*. I've never understood it. Jewish women seem to me so much juicier and more *betampte* (tasty). It's like the difference between a Saltine cracker and a piece of Sacher cake. The latter may be a bit much at times; but it's moist, it's rich, and it's layered. My symbolic logic professor in college, who regarded himself as a great connoisseur of women, once

told me that I was his first Jewish lover and that, judging from me, he had made a great mistake in never sampling from his own kind before. I recognized the compliment, although I was pricked by its suggestion that my qualities could be duplicated in any other daughter of Jacob. And I certainly didn't respect my professor any the more for it. It was as if someone who professed a great love and knowledge of wines told me he had just sampled a Bordeaux for the first time and thought these wines merited further investigation.[28]

In the analogy of Bordeaux wine to the complexity of the sexuality of the Jewish woman, we discover what Portnoy's implacable reductive logic has led him to miss. Unlike Portnoy, who journeys to Israel only to discover the extent of his inner confusion and personal malady, Renee encounters the sweetness of the Sabbath even amid the devastating memories of post-Holocaust Vienna. Her philosophic and sexual explorations lead Renee to discover the meaning of the Jewish idea. Edward Alexander notes this:

> [It is the view] that the Jews were called into existence as a people by a covenant with God that is as real and living today as it was at its inception. "I will establish My covenant," says God to Abraham, "between Me and thee and thy seed after thee throughout their generations for an everlasting covenant (Genesis 17:7)." According to this simple and traditional idea, the Jews were chosen by God in order to achieve the universal salvation of mankind: "In thy seed shall all the nations of the earth be blessed; because thou hast hearkened to my voice (Genesis 22:18)." Israel has been chosen, but chosen by a God who keeps admonishing Israel to love the stranger "as thyself; for you were strangers in the land of Egypt (Leviticus 19:34)." The chosenness of Israel, therefore, is directed toward the ultimate unity of mankind.[29]

Renee discovers the central purposes of Jewish tradition through the process of remembering and retelling. The turn to a first-person rather than a third-person narration is typical of these Judaic writers; in the first-person narrative voice they are free to explore the subjective experience that leads to spiritual enlightenment and the reconnection to Judaic traditions. Theirs is a voice relying not only on first-person narration but a narrative that shifts among and moves through first-, second-, and third-person narrative by means of free indirect discourse. The text thereby opens to a variety of forms, including parables, legends, poetry, and reportage. Rebecca Goldstein's fiction establishes a model for this narrative indeterminacy.

What is striking about *Mazel* is the powerful dialogue between and among shtetl, suburb, and city around which it is constructed.[30] In this novel, suburb, shtetl, and city spaces illuminate an abiding concern of Jewish life, that of the relation of exile and Diaspora. *Mazel* is in part a response to the American suburban appropriation of some of the central values of the shtetl. However, the shtetl is a world obsessed by the dislocation of exile, while the city provides the chance to construct an empowering, diasporic homeland within the larger condition of differing ranges of Jewish powerlessness – and the suburb, though similar to the shtetl, perhaps unknowingly and unself-consciously partakes of both conditions. Goldstein's central characters are caught dancing at two weddings, unable to abandon either world. Living in shtetl, suburb, and city they are marked by the political, sociological, spiritual, and cultural values of each, and thus enact the experience of modern Jewish life. They are forced to negotiate its contradictions for they are caught between exile and Diaspora.

Rather than the individualist character of the realistic novel, we encounter a different literary mode. *Mazel* lacks the narrative challenge thrown at the reader by a Bellow novel, or the strategy of entrapment of the reader in the seemingly autobiographical narrative characteristic of Philip Roth's fictions. Rebecca Goldstein's novel invites us into the conversation of the woman's world of sharing discourse. Instead of being forced with Bellow's Herzog to confront contradictions at the heart of western culture, or struggling with Roth's Portnoy in the middle of a Jewish joke to avoid becoming a scapegoat for an immigrant family's and community's habits, Goldstein's characters move through a landscape of possibility.

Most of these characters are at home in cities. Having abandoned their *shtetlach*, they respond to the dynamism of modern city life with energy and enthusiasm. Some characters – with exceptions such as Phoebe and Nachum – retreat into themselves in part perhaps as a result of the urban overload analyzed by Georg Simmel in his classic work, *The Metropolis & Mental Life*,[31] but most of the central personages in this novel, among them Sore, Hershel, Rosalie, Feliks, and Maurice, respond to the incessant urban stimulation by seizing city opportunities. Embracing Emancipation, they abandon religious practice and study and instead, frequent coffee houses, create a theater company, compose music, write learned articles, fall in and out of love, study at the university, and devour and devise the cultural treasures of urban life. What they discover when they get to Warsaw they carry with them and use to reshape all the cities they inhabit: "Jewish Warsaw, which was roughly a third of Warsaw proper was a city of rabbis and swindlers, capitalists and poets, but, most of all, it was a city of talkers. There were so many ideas in the air you could get an education simply by breathing deeply."[32] In the city, they make ideas into realities, and in the process turn themselves from *luftmenschen* into cosmopolitan citizens.

While their experience in Warsaw crystallizes their characters, never-theless, the deep structure of their personalities has been shaped by the environmental religious Judaic experience of the shtetl. *Mazel* explores the range of experience offered by that world, revealing its determining power at the critical moments of their life histories: birth, the onset of puberty, mar-riage, career decisions, childbearing, old age, and death. Shluftchev-on-the Puddle, to cite its full name, a central site in the novel, occupies more than a third of *Mazel.* It does not relinquish its hold on its characters, even when they are elsewhere, belying its name, which roughly translates into "Sleepy Hollow." Furthermore, this shtetl world is doubled in the novel in suburban Lipton, New Jersey – where the opening and closing sequences take place. Recall how Sasha characterizes Lipton, as the Sabbath before the prepara-tions for Phoebe's wedding comes to an end, with a sarcastic remark: "Lipton is Shluftchev with a designer label."[33] The sarcasm of her comment recalls the satire of Mendele Moycher Seforim, and it is echoed in Shluftchev, the name of his generic shtetl.

Whether positive or negative, Shluftchev forms the structure of their memory as well as provides the content of its images; it is the material their urban street-smarts will have to contend with, sort out, and make sense of. Shluftchev is a bounded world, governed by Jewish law and tradition, Jewish habits and ways of life. In it, the logic of Halakha holds. Dominated by that religious system, Shluftchev shapes the personalities, choices, and life histories of its inhabitants. For them, exile is the constant condition of their experience. The fiction of these younger writers thus engages and revises expectations defined by earlier writers. Their critique, however, is not just a matter of trading places; instead, they articulate differing literary modes in which realism leads, by an analysis of what is left out, to a mythic universe. In effect, they carry forward the project first articulated by Cynthia Ozick in her essay, "Toward A New Yiddish," which outlines the possibility of a "liturgical literature."[34]

Cynthia Ozick's insight articulates the difference between Jewish and Judaic writers: "Inspiration has no memory. Inspiration is spontaneity; its opposite is memory, which is history as judgment."[35] The Judaic writers parallel Ozick's effort to recover the conditions that make fictions more than secular stories, turning them into midrash by endowing them with the engendering power of the Biblical imagination.[36]

Rather than a stable subject these urban fictions foreground the nomad, whose identity meanders in step with the geography of wandering. Neverthe-less, they reclaim exile by giving us the diasporic hope of a temporary home. In his cartoons and films, Ben Katchor notably resumes this cultural history, parallel to the work of Rebecca Goldstein. Isaac Bashevis Singer, Henry Roth,

Saul Bellow, Philip Roth, Delmore Schwartz, and Meyer Liben, among others, all live inside the cartoon strip of this writer. His writing foregrounds the ache of exile and the dissatisfactions of Diaspora. The unease of urban life, shocked by the promise of plenitude and the delivery of fragments, thrusts his hero, Julius Knipl, Real Estate Photographer, into the arms of memory and desire.[37] His fiction thus reclaims the fabulous Jewish street, be it of Bruno Schulz, A. B. Yehoshua, David Grossman, Cynthia Ozick, and Ariella Deem. Along with Rebecca Goldstein's work, Katchor's articulates the abiding dimensions of the writing of a powerful and continuing urban Judaic culture.

JUDAIC EXPERIENCE AND THE IRONY OF SECULAR JEWISH IGNORANCE

Nowhere is this Judaic strategy more surprising than in Philip Roth's novel, *Operation Shylock*.[38] It is not just that Philip Roth has perhaps taken on the role of judge in traditional Jewish prophetic terms. He is not just a skilled recorder and satirist of suburban life and language; rather, he shows how the lives Jews lead in the suburbs no longer connect to Judaic traditions nor to any Jewish root experiences, and are empty without them. Perhaps he is a Juvenalian precursor of this innovative American midrashic impulse, or a satiric writer echoing the critique of Deuteronomy. Roth's satire reconnects Jews to their cultural and religious heritage by indicating their absence. Despite himself, for personal, political, and cultural reasons, Roth cannot simply ignore or jettison the baggage of classical Jewish religious life and experience. *Operation Shylock* invokes the sociological and psychological stereotype of the Jew articulated by Western culture to serve as its other, in order to articulate a different view of character and personal agency as part of a Judaic experience.

Operation Shylock gathers the prooftexts of modern Jewish life into a bundle of desperate queries. Kafka's famous question, "what have I in common with the Jews? I have hardly anything in common with myself," is balanced against the quote, in Hebrew, that Philip Roth the narrator encounters on the blackboard of the room into which he is hustled by the Israeli secret service at the turning point of the novel. Roth, narrator and character, does not understand this passage, despite his years of after-school Hebrew lessons and his sophisticated, finely honed modern knowledge of methods of decoding texts. He cannot read the incisive Hebrew account of Jacob wrestling with the angel, which serves as epigraph and central image of the novel. In his rote-learned cursive, he copies the sentence into his notebook, to stand there as another assessment of his ignorance: *Vayivater Ya'akov levado vayeavek ish imo ad a'lot hashachar.* What the character Philip Roth in the novel experiences but does not understand is the meaning of this phrase from Genesis 32:25: "Jacob was left alone. And a man wrestled with him until the break of dawn."

We read in the Biblical account that Jacob, fearing his brother Esau will kill him when they meet after a separation of many years, has divided his camp and sleeps alone. That night a stranger wrestles with him. As the next phrases in the Biblical story elaborate, Jacob does not relinquish his hold on his opponent, and he gains a blessing: as a result, in Genesis 30:39 he is renamed Israel. "Your name shall no longer be Jacob, but Israel, for you have striven with beings divine and human, and have prevailed." *Operation Shylock* similarly elaborates the complexities, difficulties, and power of the reconnection with his people of its protagonist. Even more fully than Bellow's novel, Roth's novel turns on a Biblical passage. It resituates Roth, the narrator, in a literary and cultural history hitherto ignored by these characters. Subtext becomes foundational text.

There is another element to this novel that connects it to the Judaic literary tradition I have been elaborating. Not only do we have the discovery that the protagonist of the novel is living a life that demands the Biblical passage for its decoding – the American midrash theme – but in a more dispersed mode he encounters a series of religious experiences that he cannot acknowledge because of his ignorance. This moment in *Operation Shylock* also functions as an emblem of the Judaic ignorance of Roth's generation: It is an exemplary scene.

This ironic move is also characteristic of writers such as Allen Hoffman and Jonathan Foer. Reader and character discover the knowledge the protagonist has been evading, in a series of dramatic discoveries. By contrast with Roth's generation, theirs is connected more directly to classical Jewish learning and culture. Perhaps it is the impact of Israeli culture, where that learning is the acknowledged and taught inheritance, reinforced by the Renewal movement, and the rise of Jewish Studies programs at American universities where these younger writers have been educated. Allen Hoffman, for example, cites traditional texts and then goes away from them to devise parables that reveal their implicit meanings; Nathan Englander and Michael Chabon put these texts into play in subtexts that define patterns of Judaic meaning; and enigmatic Allegra Goodman, steeped in classic Jewish texts, uses them implicitly as part of her critique of organized traditional Jewish life from a feminist perspective that analyzes the relation of gender to Judaism's traditional patriarchal religious hierarchy. This literary strategy may also turn on the example of Israeli Nobel laureate, S. Y. Agnon, whose fiction bridges the secular concerns of the great European novelists and the religious concerns of classical Jewish learning.

Modern Jewish writing has tended to focus on either Europe or Israel or America. What Roth has done brilliantly in *Operation Shylock* is to bring them together here, thereby helping us understand how they are all part of the same Jewish condition. It is a move also made by Rebecca Goldstein, Alan Hoffman, and Jonathan Safran Foer. Their narratives lead character and reader into the present and future of the action, yet they circle back into the past of the immigrant. The smells and sights of Europe, and the Holocaust, meet the world of modern Israel and America.

This exploration of the hallucinatory politics of the dominant sites of modern Jewish life reveals each to be at once both central and marginal. Neither New York nor Jerusalem, Washington, D.C. or Ramallah are independent entities; each urban location is implicated in the experiences located in the others. The novel plunges readers into a virtual testing experience in asking them to sort out these issues. Can the readers do what the narrator cannot and reclaim their own fate, their own judgment, by understanding it as part of a dialogue with ancient unacknowledged Jewish sources that tell us how the wily Jacob turned into the struggling Israel?

Born in Newark in 1933, Roth's knowledge of the Bible begins in the after-school lessons of a New Jersey synagogue. The older Bellow, by contrast, was an immigrant, steeped in his familial Yiddish-speaking milieu. Their literary connection to classical Jewish culture, like that of many of their contemporaries and the younger writers including Goldstein and Foer who follow them, is through the work of Isaac Bashevis Singer. Singer grew up in the traditional Jewish world of Eastern Europe. So did his older brother, Isaac Joshua Singer, also a novelist. Where the older Singer wrote epic novels of sociological and class analysis in a powerfully realistic Yiddish idiom, the younger brother turned to religious and kabbalistic psychological probings and a Yiddish prose that draws on folk traditions. There is a further difference. Bashevis Singer's fiction draws on classical Jewish sources. Ancient texts come alive in this writing of an American Jewish author always aware of the complex, ambivalent, and indeterminate habits of his modern audience.

Bellow played a central role in bringing Singer to the attention of an English-speaking audience. Translating "Gimpel – tam" into "Gimpel, the Fool," that is, a Yiddish fable into a modernist English tale, in 1953,[39] Bellow was the cultural mediator between a traditional Judaic realm and an exotic American–Jewish experience and writing. The tension between them suggest how intimately involved Bellow was in the immigrant cultural world and how much he needed to distance himself from it in order to become an

English writer. Bellow had to locate himself within the (Protestant) English and American literary tradition, from the perspective of the left-wing intellectuals of *Partisan Review*, like Lionel Trilling who tended to be more at home with Wordsworth than the Rabbis, though proud of his having been the first Jew to gain tenure in an Ivy league English department. Yet Bellow's involvement in Jewish learning as the son of a European immigrant (and himself a Canadian immigrant) was part of his familial cultural upbringing. Judaic experience paralleled his multicultural knowledge of tough guys (such as Elya Gruner), and the bootlegging underworld in which Bellow's father could not quite manage to achieve success. Bellow's Judaic learning is dispersed throughout his fiction and yet informs the sweep of Bellow's writing. What Bellow, like Roth, managed was to write out of the Jewishness Alfred Kazin identifies as the cultural milieu of the left-wing immigrant children, and at the same time evoke the Judaic experience that was its bedrock and from which it took its moral standards.

The accepted notion of modern Jewish literature conceives it as the writing of a secular civilization inspired by Enlightenment ideals – the literature of a people, a folk, a nation. The writers articulating an American midrash emphasize other aspects, including the urban, religious, diasporic, exilic, multilingual, multicultural, and even Zionist aspects, reveling in instead of evading these contradictory impulses. They explore the impact of this Judaic storytelling mode. Rather than a tale of political or social success, Judaic writing is a lens that refocuses the values, range, and doubled consciousness of Jewish experience and reclaims its religious sources.

Jewish writing in the 1950s and 1960s did not explicitly engage classical texts. It was a secular literature, defining itself in part in response to the Holocaust by declaring God irrelevant. The new generation of Jewish writers is rethinking modern Jewish history and using this innovative American midrash to speak to the existence of God in their own lives – or at least to the ways traditional stories and archetypes speak to their lives. Rather than a secular perspective, this new Jewish writing elaborates a Judaic vision.

JUDAIC FICTIONS AND MIDRASHIC PRACTICE

To have Mr. Sammler echo Deuteronomy 30:11–14 suggests that Bellow is not writing the history or sociology of immigrants but is exploring the engagement, and disengagement, of modern Jews, consciously and unconsciously, with the founding texts of their experience. Bellow's work is then in dialogue with centuries of Jewish writing, with the midrashic tradition that responded to the Hebrew Bible. It locates him and *Mr. Sammler's Planet* as a modern precursor of Judaic American writing.

Bellow's novel is pessimistic about many things. Blind in one eye, Mr. Sammler, a Holocaust survivor and witness, struggles to see clearly, and what he sees is not the celebratory optimism of American Jewish boosters. He sees not success but misery, the costs of assimilation, and the tragedy of the destruction of European Jewry. Nevertheless, his work has the optimism of writing even about misery, the power of acknowledgment of tragedy. Unlike other writing, Bellow's novel is not emplotted as comedy; it engages the murderous history of the twentieth century not only to lament but to warn of what may lie ahead. Here his novel strikes a note characteristic of the conclusion of Deuteronomy, when Moses tells us that this song he is chanting, his last will and testament, will serve as a witness against us if we lose our way. That is part of the purpose of this new Judaic writing.

Notes

1. Abraham Cahan, *The Rise of David Levinsky* (New York and London: Harper & Brothers, 1917).
2. Chaim Potok, *The Chosen* (New York: Simon & Schuster, 1967), 217.
3. Hugh Nissenson, "Choosing the Chosen: A re-Appraisal of Chaim Potok's *The Chosen*," in *Chaim Potok and Jewish-American Culture: Three Essays*, A Memorial Symposium (Jewish Studies Program, University of Pennsylvania, 2003), 7.
4. David Stern and Mark Jay Mirsky, *The Rabbinic Fantasies: Imaginative Narrative from Classical Hebrew Literature*, ed. David Stern and Mark Jay Mirsky (Philadelphia and New York: The Jewish Publication Society, 1990), 6, 7.
5. Henry Roth, *Call It Sleep* (New York: Robert O. Ballou, 1934).
6. Cynthia Ozick, "Toward a New Yiddish," in *Art and Ardor* (New York: Knopf, 1983), 151–77.
7. Saul Bellow, *Mr. Sammler's Planet* (Greenwich: Fawcett Publications, 1970).
8. Rebecca Goldstein, *Mazel* (New York: Penguin Books, 1996).
9. E. L. Doctorow, *City of God* (New York: Random House, 2000).
10. David Stern and Mark Jay Mirsky, *The Rabbinic Fantasies: Imaginative Narrative from Classical Hebrew Literature*, ed. David Stern and Mark Jay Mirsky (Philadelphia and New York: The Jewish Publication Society, 1990), 352, 358.
11. Jonathan Safran Foer, *Everything is Illuminated* (Boston: Houghton Mifflin, 2002), 198–199.
12. Nathan Englander, *For the Relief of Unbearable Urges* (New York: Knopf, 1999).
13. Myla Goldberg, *The Bee Season* (New York: Doubleday, 2000).
14. Sanford Pinsker, *Jewish-American Fiction, 1917–1987* (New York: Twayne, 1992).
15. Murray Baumgarten, *City Scriptures* (Cambridge, MA: Harvard University Press, 1982).
16. Rebecca Goldstein, *Mazel* (New York: Penguin Books, 1996).
17. Delmore Schwartz, *In Dreams Begin Responsibilities* (Norfolk: New Direction, 1938).
18. Ibid., 186.
19. Ibid., 187.
20. Meyer Liben, "Homage to Benny Leonard," in his *Justice Hunger: A Sort of Novel and Nine Stories* (New York: Dial, 1967), 211–70.

21. Ibid., 177.
22. Meyer Liben, "Homage to Benny Leonard," in his *Justice Hunger: A Sort of Novel and Nine Stories* (New York: Dial, 1967), 179.
23. Isaac Babel, *Collected Stories of Isaac Babel*, ed. and trans. Walter Morison, with an introduction by Lionel Trilling (New York: Meridian, 1956).
24. Philip Roth, *Goodbye, Columbus* (Boston: Houghton Mifflin, 1959).
25. Saul Bellow, *The Adventures of Augie March* (New York: Viking Press, 1953).
26. Bernard Malamud, *The Assistant* (New York: Farrar, Straus & Cudahy, 1957).
27. Rebecca Goldstein, *The Mind-Body Problem* (New York: Random House, 1983).
28. Ibid., 232.
29. Edward Alexander, *The Jewish Idea and its Enemies: Personalities, Issues, Events* (New Brunswick: Transaction Books, 1988), 1.
30. Rebecca Goldstein, *Mazel* (New York: Penguin Books, 1996).
31. Georg Simmel, *The Metropolis and Mental Life, in The Sociology of George Simmel*, trans., ed., and with an introduction by Kurt H. Wolff (New York: The Free Press, 1950), 409–24.
32. Rebecca Goldstein, *Mazel*, 206.
33. Ibid., 333.
34. Cynthia Ozick, "Toward a New Yiddish," in *Art and Ardor* (New York: Knopf, 1983), 151–77.
35. Cynthia Ozick, *Metaphor and Memory* (New York: Knopf, 1989), 276.
36. Ibid., 276, 279.
37. Ben Katchor, *Julius Knipl, Real Estate Photographer*; introduction by Michael Chabon (Boston: Little, Brown, 1996).
38. Philip Roth, *Operation Shylock* (New York: Simon & Schuster, 1993).
39. Isaac Bashevis Singer, "Gimpel the Fool," in his *Gimpel the Fool and Other Stories* (New York: Farrar, Straus & Giroux, 1957), 3–21.

21 Recent trends in new American Jewish music

MARK KLIGMAN

Sociologist and music critic Simon Frith states that the study of popular music assumes that sounds reflect or represent "a people." This homology is described as "some sort of structural relationship between material and cultural forms." A piece of music not only reflects but, in effect, produces popular values through its performance, and thus "gives a way of being in the world."[1] Popular music is a commercial industry striving to blend the artistry of music with business. The new Jewish music from the late 1960s through the 1990s is not *only* an artistic creation but also a positive and desirable expression of Jewish identity. "Jewish music" can be defined as a self-conscious effort to express a message, idea, or sound that is considered by its creators, performers, and listeners to be Jewish. This sphere of music, which has grown significantly over the past few decades, raises intriguing questions of expressions of Jewishness, continuity with the past, change, and the creation of a new American Jewish sensibility. It is estimated that over 2,000 recordings of Jewish music are currently available and that close to 250 records are released each year.[2] While Jewish music is not a recent phenomenon, the creation of new Jewish music is found throughout the Jewish community in a vast range of musical styles; it represents a vehicle for the new generation of American Jews to express music with some connection to Judaism while distinguishing itself from the immigrant generation. At a time when Jewish literacy is declining, self-expression of Jewishness is increasing by means of the Jewish music industry.[3] Interestingly, the phenomenon has concurrently spread to all segments of American Judaism, from Orthodox to Reform, religious to secular, and Yiddish to Zionist. In both religious and nonreligious contexts, this new music represents various responses to the past and has become an integral part of Jewish life in America that interconnects and shapes Jewish identity.

RELIGIOUS CONTEXTS

New Jewish music in religious contexts illustrates the functional role of music in religious Jewish life in America. For the Orthodox community, their new Jewish music replaces the role of popular American culture. New recordings, concerts, and programs have become an integral part of Orthodoxy. For Reform Jews, their new Jewish music is closely connected to making liturgy and prayer accessible and interesting. In large measure, new music in the Reform community was driven by the folk music of summer camps. The Conservative movement displays traces of the Orthodox and Reform communities. Each religious community has a different need for music to express, enhance, or engage the Jewish life of its members.

Orthodox community

One of the most interesting features of new popular music in the Orthodox community is the sheer volume of it, which represents at least half of all the music available. The Orthodox music industry, based predominantly in Brooklyn, has grown significantly over the past 25 years. This growth is attributed to the limited involvement and participation of right-wing members in secular culture. As a result, they have developed their own type of popular music, whose sources include the Bible, liturgy, and a genre of English songs, which delivers a powerful message of faith and devotion. This new music satisfies the need for religiously appropriate entertainment, as other forms of amusement such as television, film, or theater are discouraged. In this regard the right-wing Orthodox need for music is different than Modern Orthodox and non-Orthodox, who do not limit their listening to music with only "Jewish" content.

In the late 1950s and early 1960s, the pivotal contribution to Orthodox music was from recordings other than cantorial. This began in the early 1950s with Benzion Shenker's recording of Modzitz melodies and continued into the early 1960s with Cantor Duvid Werdyger's recording of Hassidic melodies, which featured the music of Gerrer, Skulener, and Bobover.[4] Recordings of other Hassidic groups followed, which presented the music that was traditionally sung in arrangements that were fitting for that style of folk music. In many cases, orchestral accompaniment and choral arrangements followed a more "classical" musical style.[5]

Shlomo Carlebach (1925–94), who effectively linked folk music and Jewish music, is credited as the father of new Jewish music. Innovatively drawing from the European tradition and combining it with a new style, Carlebach provided a novel form of music consisting of two or three repeated sections to communicate a Jewish message. The participatory nature of folk music, the energy of newly created music from Israel, and the religious fervor of the Hassidic *niggun* (melody) were effectively combined in his songs and performances. Commenting on his own singing, Carlebach said this:

> I'm never satisfied with my singing. I don't think I have a good voice. I think my voice is just good enough to inspire people to sing with me. If I would have a *gevald* [incredible] voice like, let's say, Moshe Koussevitzky, then nobody would want to sing with me, because then they'll think they don't want to miss my voice, but my voice is just good enough to make them sing.[6]

Carlebach's goal was to use music to educate and inspire Jews to renew their Jewish identity and discover the beauty of living a Jewish life. His music marks a transition point from writing music specifically for liturgical contexts to a new role for Jewish music specifically created for record albums and performances in intimate settings such as a *kumsitz* (religious gathering) or in broader settings such as nightclubs or concert halls. Following his initial recording in 1959, Carlebach was almost instantly reknowned throughout the Jewish world and went on to record over twenty-five albums and write close to 1,000 melodies.

In the 1960s and 1970s, the crucial feature of the new Jewish music was its detachment from the use of Eastern European musical modes, styles, and aesthetics. The 1970s ushered in a new influence in response to popular American music, whose lyrics and musical experimentations were becoming more intertwined with that era's drug culture. Orthodox Jewish artists endeavored to convey a strong message and maintain a positive influence in their music. During this period, Mordechai Ben David made the most significant musical impact by appropriating American popular musical styles and adapting a secular idiom to fit a Jewish message, particularly in his English songs. "*Yidn*," which was written in Yiddish to fit the song "Dzingis Kahn" by the German group Dzingis Kahn, displays Ben David's adaptation whereby new words are added to a well-known melody. Nevertheless, Ben David performs mainly for the right-wing Orthodox community. The majority of his original songs are in Hebrew with settings to liturgical texts; he also writes English songs that convey a message about religious life. Another popular singer, Avraham Fried, was inspired to write music with a good message after hearing a discourse by the Lubavitcher Rebbe in the early 1980s.[7] His first recording, *No Jew Will Be Left Behind*, incorporated the message of the Messiah and redemption and featured as the title song written in English. Fried, a Lubavitcher Hassid, felt that the majority of the music in the Orthodox world was not truly uplifting but instead dealt with pain and the Holocaust. Similar messages about redemption and the Messiah are found in many of Fried's English songs, which he viewed as "a chance to say how I'm feeling at that moment, in my own words, not based on a verse or taken out of psalms."[8] Songwriter Yossi Green, who has written over 320 songs appearing on forty recordings of the most successful Orthodox performers, stated the following about the lack of relevance of Eastern European music:

> Klezmer[9] music is more of a caricature of what Jewish music used to be.... An instrumentalist can show off his instrument, show off his ability to play. And that really has nothing to do with where Jewish music is today.... New Hassidic music [his name for new Orthodox music] has definitely replaced klezmer. If klezmer was the downtrodden, stepped on poor little *shetl* Jew's music then this is the music of today for the young, wealthier, more educated, forward thinking Jewish mind.... You listen to *"Tanyeh"* or *"Didoh Bei"*[10] and you'll tell me how beautiful these songs are. It is fresh, it is new. It is the young Jewish person saying, 'I'm here, it's the 90s, I'm proud of my Judaism, I'm learning a lot but I'm also having fun – it's allowed and it's okay, my kids are having fun, we're relaxing and enjoying ourselves, we're Jewish and we're proud of it.' Music today is about the new, a new spirit.[11]

This new spirit necessitated a new musical style. Both Yossi Green and Avraham Fried commented that the goal of a new album was to include one or more dance melodies that would become "dance floor" requests during a wedding with corresponding dance steps. Orthodox weddings today include many of these new melodies and dances, such as *"Dido Bei,"* which are known as simcha dancing. The use of non-Jewish melodies at American weddings represented a potential threat to religious life and necessitated the creation of music with original melodies to keep the Orthodox focused on Observant Jewish life during these occasions.

In terms of musical style, new Orthodox music is rooted in the past with modern innovations. Jewish tradition is combined with modernity but the connection today is much less obvious than it was in Carlebach's music. The music is stylized with pop, rock, easy listening, blues, country, and other musical influences. Orthodox musicians from the more religious segment of the Orthodox community freely adapt new styles. The Jewishness is found in the lyrics and the context in which it is found. The significant change from Hassidic music of the past is that new Orthodox music is "recorded music" or "performance music." Orthodox concerts are now held in venues such as Carnegie Hall, Radio City Music Hall, the Paramount Theater of Madison Square Garden, Nassau Coliseum, Westbury Music Fair, and the Metropolitan Opera House. Nevertheless, Orthodox popular music, which has experienced a rapid rise, is as much a part of Orthodox Jewish life as popular music is in American life. While it fills a social need, many wonder if Orthodox popular music has not become too commercial and no longer serves its role of spiritually uplifting its listeners.[12]

Reform community

Music in the Reform Community is a reaction to life in America, but the response it generates is different than that of the Orthodox community. For Reform Jews, the most significant Jewish experience in their lives is the synagogue, thus signaling the importance of its music. In the 1960s, musicians felt that synagogue music was too formal and out of date, so they opted instead for folk and popular styles. From the 1960s to the 1990s, in the synagogue American Reform popular music was heard more frequently than the pre-1960s repertoire. However, this resulted in a mixed reaction from Reform cantors, who are the professional body of clergy responsible for music and prayer in synagogues. Although not the sole context for Jewish expression, the synagogue is the main institutional body that Reform Jewish professionals are trained to serve. Presently, the litmus test of a good melody is often expressed in terms of its use in a synagogue service.

Prior to the 1960s, music in Reform synagogues consisted mostly of hymns sung by the congregation, compositions sung by the cantor, choir accompanied on the organ, and artistic settings of the liturgy by Binder, Freed, and Fromm, among others. The *Union Hymnal* used in the Reform synagogue contained 284 hymns, of which 280 were in English and four were in Hebrew. Cantor Jeff Klepper described the lack of a tradition in music for Reform youth:

> We were not the inheritors of a Jewish music tradition, as a group, maybe individually. But what was our Jewish music heritage? Well in *schul* it was Freed and Binder . . . it was nothing to come away with. That was artistic and professional music. . . . What we were doing [at camp in 1968] was a direct slap in the face at the places where we had been educated, places we had grown up, there was nothing for us in the synagogues in the late '60s, nothing. . . . If there were Jewish melodies in that music we didn't hear it.[13]

However, following Israel's Six Day War in 1967, there was a dramatic increase in the number of Hebrew songs sung by Reform congregations and a corresponding decrease in choral singing. According to Rabbi Daniel Freelander, Director of Programs for the Union of American Hebrew Congregations, the switch to Hebrew was dramatic. "Our people wanted to hear Hebrew and they wanted to sing Hebrew, so Hebrew becomes a real crucial piece in the songbooks of NFTY.... Yiddish goes out of fashion in '67."[14] In fact, the camp songbooks of the 1970s and onward demonstrate a considerable decrease in the amount of English repertoire songs, comprised of American folk tunes and Black spirituals. Over the course of the next two decades, the camp repertoire made its way into the synagogue liturgy, resulting in decreasing usage of music written for the *Union Prayer Book* and the *Union Hymnal.*

In the 1970s, the style of synagogue music reflected the influence of Reform youth who were motivated to participate in prayer through their camp experiences. The musical aesthetic of folk singers such as Pete Seeger, Bob Dylan, Tom Paxton, and James Taylor was much preferred because it was participatory and more current than European Jewish music. This led to folk-rock services such as Ray Smolover's *Edge of Freedom* (1967) and *Gates of Freedom* (1970) and Michael Isaacson's *Songs NFTY Sings* (1972). In the mid-1970s through the 1980s, those returning camp attendees called upon their Reform cantors, unfamiliar with the new camp music, to sing these new melodies. The reception of this musical change ranged from enthusiastic endorsement to disdain. Rabbi Freelander argues for the folk-rock style of music on the basis of its effect on the communal experience:

> I'm forced to contrast that "high art" [composed synagogue music of the nineteenth and twentieth century] with the "popular art" [folk-rock style music] for large communal song sessions we experience at the conventions of the UAHC, CAJE and now even the GA [the Jewish Federation's General Assembly]. They remind us baby boomers of our youth days singing together at summer camp, on the college campus or at the protest rally. Those were special and spiritual moments these adult communal singing sessions recreate for us. Our souls open up, and we sing familiar sounding melodies and words, and feel comfortably connected once again to our community and our God.[15]

Referring to this as "spiritual entertainment," composer Sam Adler says that supporters of communal singing were eager to blame low synagogue attendance on the music rather than on the decline in familiarity with and affinity to synagogue ritual life. Critical of this change in synagogue music, Adler sharply attacked the pseudo-Hassidic or Israeli tunes as "the trademark of the Jewish commercial sacred music norm."[16] Whereas the new folk-rock music does not make use of the Eastern European modal tradition, some elements such as niggun singing has become more commonplace but viewed as "pseudo-Jewish." For many cantors, the biggest loss was the lack of use of traditional *nusach* or chant and the decreasing desire for an aesthetic of excellence in artistic music. Through the synthesis of folk, classical, and traditional music, Reform liturgical music struggles with the past to innovate and make Judaism meaningful for the present.

Currently, the most influential performer and creator of new Reform liturgical music is Debbie Friedman. Finding Reform worship nonparticipatory and thus lacking in excitement, Friedman has committed herself to expressions of the liturgical text in order to make the congregant's worship experience accessible. Her first recording was a youth service she wrote for high school students entitled *Sing Unto God* (1972). Intended as a "new experience in worship that emphasizes through song the importance of community involvement in worship.... It enables those who are willing, to join together as a community in New songs of prayer."[17] The social action songs in the folk music of the 1960s and 1970s remains a model for her to create new Jewish songs that communicate a message of engagement with the Jewish tradition. Influenced by Peter, Paul, and Mary, as well as Joan Baez, Judy Collins, and Melissa Manchester, Friedman sought to make prayers and melodies accessible for Reform congregants. Like the new music in the Orthodox community, Friedman composes Hebrew songs to known liturgical or Biblical texts and English songs. In fact, her music has become an important part of Reform Jewish life. "*Mi Shebeirach*," derived from the traditional practice of praying to God for a sick person, may be her most often requested song in Reform congregations, as it combines Hebrew and English phrases and provides a unique view of the Jewish world with images of beauty and simplicity. Through her work at Reform camps, adult Jewish programs, and youth groups and her participation in Jewish educators' conferences, Friedman has made a lasting impact on new Jewish music. Her recordings are among the most widely sold in the Jewish market throughout the country, and her songs are commonly a part of song sessions for youth and adults at camps and conventions. While the style of Friedman's music is in the American folk tradition, perhaps it is the European "roots" that convey a powerful sentiment. Some have compared Friedman to Shlomo Carlebach, because of her approach in educating and engaging listeners into her positive Jewish world; others have stated that her music is not based on a Jewish musical tradition. Friedman gives this response:

Who is my music hurting? I don't want to compete with anybody. I'm not a great lover of organ music, but I am a great lover of nussach [sic]. How is writing in our own musical vernacular not an acceptable or legitimate expression of our culture? My music may be uniquely American, but it is rooted in a tradition that is Russian and Hungarian, and influenced by Israel.[18]

For Friedman, who is committed in the effort to make Judaism relevant to modern life, praying in a synagogue or singing on stage are both approached with the goal of connecting and uplifting the audience. Thus, the boundaries of song and pray are blurred. Reform new Jewish music makes liturgy accessible and projects a liberal and modern sensibility for Jewish life in America.

Conservative community

New Jewish music in the Conservative movement shares similarities with that in both the Orthodox and Reform movements. On one hand, new music recordings and concerts serve as a means of entertainment, much like in the Orthodox movement. On the other hand, even though Conservative Jews prefer worship that is relatively fixed and minimally changed, they are similar to Reform Jews in that the younger generation wants to carry on its camp experiences and incorporate new music within the liturgy, even though the synagogue is not committed to making any changes. Whereas an organizational network to disseminate music of Reform youth camps exists for Reform, Conservative Ramah camps solely provide a basis for youth to energize their Jewish awareness and subsequent commitment. Those campers who had experienced participatory prayer at Ramah camps sought to continue worshiping in this style with egalitarian services and the inclusion of communal song singing. This became the hallmark of the smaller and more intimate *chavurah minyanim*. New music is heard mostly on recordings and in concerts in Conservative settings functioning as a means of entertainment, like that of the Orthodox, rather than being used within the synagogue. While no particular groups create so-called Conservative music, various performers regularly concertize in predominantly Conservative settings.

Performer Craig Taubman, who grew up in the Conservative movement, performs in Reform synagogues and other venues. Taubman's songs, which are in Hebrew and English, are responses to events in his life such as the birth of a child and the death of a relative.[19] The style of his songs ranges from rock-and-roll and pop to adult contemporary music; a contemporary style and high production quality in his recordings are evident. He feels that music communicates a powerful and magical message and that some things are better left untranslated, since meaning is conveyed through music, as in *"Anim Zmirot"* and *"Shema B'ni"* from *Journey* (1991). Other well-known songs, such as *"Shir Chadash"* from *Encore* (1989), combine Biblical and rabbinic texts. Other English ballads, such as "Where Heaven and Earth Touch," articulate his thoughts and feelings concerning the liturgy and Biblical passages. Taubman does desire to see the bulk of his songs incorporated into synagogue services, as he considers his music as performance pieces and artistic statements. The exception is for the songs on recordings of his special services: *Yad B'Yad* (1986), *Friday Night Live* (1999), and *One Shabbat Morning* (2002). In many congregations throughout America, the music from *Friday Night Live* and *One Shabbat Morning* is the basis for a monthly service that typically draws a significant turnout. Another group, Safam, writes a variety of songs in a mix of styles through the synthesis of Jewish elements, such as cantorial and Hassidic music, stylized with a variety of rock, pop, Latin, and reggae rhythms. Performing since 1974, Safam considers that their songs are similar to those of Shlomo Carlebach, except for the use of electric guitars and rock-and-roll style rather than a folk style.[20] Other performers catering to Conservative settings include cantors such as Sol Zim, who has released over 20 recordings in 30 years. After completing recordings with his brother Paul, Sol's own recordings are in a variety of Jewish styles such as cantorial, Hassidic, and Yiddish.

Unlike Orthodox Jews, Conservative Jews do not have the same religious or social needs, and they seek out all types of entertainment. Although these new music settings are not as established as those of Reform new music, these performers provide a Jewish venue for Conservative Jews to hear Jewish music at religious and organizational functions.

NONRELIGIOUS CONTEXTS

Throughout the twentieth century, the number of American Jews who have chosen not to affiliate with a synagogue has risen. Secular Yiddish and Israeli culture became viable alternatives for those who wanted to be connected to Judaism through the cultural dimension of Jewish life without religious obligations. For others music (performed in concert halls) provided the venues for the expression of their Jewishness. Yiddish songs, Hebrew songs of Israel, Klezmer music, and art music satisfied the desire of those who wanted to be connected to Judaism but not through religion.

Concert hall

Early in the twentieth century, composers of the St. Petersburg Society for Jewish Folk Music sought to collect Jewish folk songs and incorporate their use in compositions. Taking their impetus from Russian nationalism, composers wrote music based on Jewish folk music and incorporated the modal tradition found in the music of the synagogue: *hazzanut* (cantorial stylization often including improvisation), Hassidic *nigunnim* (wordless songs), and Yiddish songs. Throughout the twentieth century, composers sought to express their Jewish identity in the concert hall.

During this period, Ernest Bloch (1880–1959) composed *Schelomo* (1915–16) and *Avodath ha-Kodesh*, "Sacred Service" (1930–33), consciously using original material written in the style of Jewish folk and modal music to express Jewishness. Bloch was reflective of his compositional procedures:

> In all those compositions of mine which have been termed Jewish, I have not approached the problem from without, i.e. by employing more or less authentic melodies, or more or less sacred oriental formulas, rhythms, or intervals! No! I have hearkened to an inner voice, deep, sacred, insistent, burning, an instinct rather than any cold, dry reasoning process, a voice which seemed to come from far beyond, beyond myself and my parents, a voice which surged up in me on reading certain passages in the Bible.... It was this Jewish heritage as a whole which stirred me, and music was the result. To what extent such music is Jewish, to what extent just Ernest Bloch – of that I know nothing. The future alone will decide.[21]

Another seminal composer was Leonard Bernstein (1918–90), whose larger symphonic works incorporate, in some capacity, Jewishness. *"Jeremiah," Symphony No. 1* (written in 1942) uses cantillation motifs, while *Symphony No. 3* (1963) as well as the *Dybbuk* ballet (1974) uses the text of the *Kaddish*. Some vocal works are based on liturgical and Biblical texts, such as *Hashkievenu* (1945) and *Chicester Psalms* (1965), based on six Psalm texts set in Hebrew. A recurring perfect fourth descent is detected in these works, which he claims are reminiscent of the ending phrase of the cantor on the High Holidays.[22] Some consider Bernstein's use of Jewish elements as a novelty since Jewishness is not part of the fabric of the composition. Nevertheless, ever since his overnight rise to fame, when he filled in for an ill Bruno Walter as conductor on November 14, 1943 to make his New York Philharmonic debut, Bernstein has become a household name and a quintessential American Jewish icon.

Similar to Bloch, composer David Diamond incorporates a free, modal, and expressive style in his compositions, which include *David Mourns for Absalom* for voice and piano, an orchestral work *Psalm* (1936), and other vocal works commissioned by Park Avenue Synagogue in New York. Diamond has written over 200 works, a dozen of which express Jewishness by using tonal and modal traditions. His most recent Jewish work, *Kaddish for Violoncello and Orchestra* (1987–89), was written for and premiered by Yo-Yo Ma on April 9, 1990 with the Seattle Symphony, and it has been compared with Ravel's *Kaddish*. Inspired by Ravel's music, Diamond stated "[It] to this day remains to me the ideal ... the most perfect, the most imaginative and the most moving new music."[23] Diamond sees the *Kaddish*, like his composition *Psalm*, as falling into the category of "ritual" pieces. He gives this explanation:

> The Hebrew Prayer for the Dead has traditional melodies; in *Kaddish* I created my own concept of them and of Hebrew cantillation. These are distinct from my totally abstract pieces, like the symphonies, and my theater works which whether intended for the stage or the concert hall have been inspired by writers like Shakespeare.[24]

Diamond sees his *Kaddish* as possessing the mood and feeling of exaltation, not mourning. He says "My *Kaddish* praises the Almighty."[25]

Composer Steve Reich's interest in cantillation grew following his attendance at an adult education program at a synagogue in New York City. He studied Jewish music in New York and Israel as well as the singing of different Eastern Sephardic communities, which resulted in his work, *Tehillim* (1981). Cantillation serves as the focus of Reich's view on Jewish music.

> For many people, Jewish music means "Fiddler on the Roof" or Hasidic folk songs.... I would go back to the homeland, to the origin, and see what is particular about my tradition, independently of how it was influenced, in the Ashkenazic experience, in Germany, France and England, or, in the Sephardic experience, in Spain.... The center of the tradition is the chanting of the Scriptures.[26]

Reich's compositional approach does not entail quotation of cantillation phrases but rather the incorporation of the structure of cantillation rather than the sound. Rather than imitate Hebrew cantillation to produce a "Jewish-sounding piece," Reich seeks "to try and understand the structure of Hebrew cantillation and apply that to the pitches and timbres one has grown up with so as to hopefully create something new."[27] Reich's compositional approach, which usually receives the label *minimalism*, is outlined in his 1974 publication *Writings about Music*, which holds "music as a gradual process" that should be perceptible. Serialism for Reich contains a process that is seldom audible, as hidden structures never appealed to him. He states, "while performing and listening to gradual musical processes one can participate in a particular liberating and impersonal kind of ritual. Focusing in on the musical process makes possible that shift of attention away from *he* and *she* and *you* and *me* outwards towards *it*."[28] For Reich, process is a "religious" experience, which unfolds through repetitive rhythms, as melodic and harmonic patterns change in a slow and subtle fashion. To date, Reich's fifty-plus works are organized by process. *Tehillim* effectively combines Reich's approach to gradual process with his desire to make use of the structure of cantillation. In a prefatory note in the musical score, Reich states that the instrumentation of *Tehillim* includes the use of tambourines without jingles, "perhaps similar to the small drum called *tof* in Hebrew Psalm 150 and several other places in Biblical text. Hand clapping, small pitched cymbals and rattles were also commonly used throughout the Middle East in the Biblical period. Beyond this, there is not musicological content to TEHILLIM [sic]." He states that he does not use Jewish themes or melodic material. He has chosen Psalms opposed to other Biblical texts since there is no oral tradition among Ashkenazic Jews for the singing of Psalms because the practice was lost. A particularly interesting feature of this work is the lack of use of short repeating patterns. There is no fixed meter or metric pattern, a common feature in his earlier works. Instead, the rhythm comes directly from the Hebrew text.

Jewishness is thus individually expressed not through novelty but through references to Jewish rituals that composers intend to be transcendent spirituality. Diamond and Reich self-consciously express Jewishness as a part of their overall oeuvre. Like the precedent set by Bloch and Bernstein, quotation of known musical phrases is avoided. Jewishness, then, is part of the motivation or impetus of their work. Both Diamond and Reich incorporate Jewish elements into the fabric of their works that are motivated by an inner spiritual desire. As Reich expresses, Jewishness is not merely "exotic" but a basis to evoke something beyond the human experience. Similarly, music critic Arthur Holde states that the Jewishness of Bloch's work is "the magic element beyond the tonal realm."[29] While identifiable and descriptive Jewish musical features of works in the concert hall decreased in the first half of the twentieth century, since the 1950s expressions of Jewishness have increased. More composers explore the Jewish heritage as a source of their new works (*Yerusha* by David Stock, 1986; *Kaddisch-Requiem* and *Prayer for Jerusalem* in 1971 by Richard Wernick). Several of the Bloch, Bernstein, Diamond and Reich compositions based on Jewishness are some of their best known works. Perhaps in these pieces each composer draws from their personal experience and seeks to communicate a universal ideal.

Klezmer revival bands

When compared with other revival efforts in America, the klezmer music revival of the 1970s is among the most successful,[30] primarily because of four revival bands: The Klezmorim, Kapelye, The Klezmer Conservatory Band, and the Andy Statman Klezmer Orchestra. For Frank London, leader of The Klezmatics and formerly a member of the Klezmer Conservatory Band, klezmer music was an interesting style to learn and absorb like any other music style. "I was already playing Salsa, Balkan, Haitian, and other musics. Why not Jewish?"[31] At the New England Conservatory where Klezmer Conservatory Band members studied, The Klezmatics began by playing a few tunes at concerts and went on to eventually record the songs. The Klezmatics are presently still among the most prominent klezmer bands, frequently performing at nightclubs and reaching a broad audience. Weaving popular and world music styles and adding new lyrics on a variety of social issues, The Klezmatics seek to move beyond the playing of nostalgic melodies to entertain their broad audience. London says this:

> [At first, we] were trying to play some music, make some money, and have some fun. Many of the musicians who were doing klezmer music weren't Jewish, so they weren't discovering their roots.... People ask, "why klezmer?" What many miss is that when I listen to this music, I get aesthetically interested. It cuts through all the *shlock*, all the *shmaltz*, all the things about Jewish music that never interested me, all the Israeli music, all the Yiddish theater music, about all that sentimentality. Why klezmer music? Because it's good, just on its own terms.[32]

What separates klezmer performers from other performers in the religious community is their approach to Jewish music through the music itself; klezmer musicians challenge themselves to sharpen their virtuosic skills and deepen their understanding of another musical system. Klezmer music became a way to access a lost world. While veteran klezmer musicians trained some revival musicians, the younger musicians sought to learn the style of the early twentieth century through the recordings of clarinetists Dave Tarras and Naftule Brandwein. This led to the reissuing of older recordings of the repertoire on 78 rpms, which became the staple repertoire of the revival bands. Andy Statman of the Andy Statman Klezmer Orchestra, a former student of Dave Tarras, describes his own music as being informed by klezmer. In the late 1980s, klezmer music took a turn as groups moved away from the revival approach of mainly performing the traditional repertoire to creating new music as well as combining it with classical, pop, jazz, and many other styles. The four leading klezmer bands by the end of the 1990s were these: The Klezmer Conservatory Band, The Klezmatics, Brave Old World, and Andy Statman. Many of the musicians from these groups are active as instructors in various venues. The largest educational venue is Klezkamp, which began in 1984. Hundreds of bands record and perform klezmer music and expand the influences of styles. A younger generation born since the 1970s has grown up with klezmer music and experiences this form of instrumental Eastern European music as a vital part of the Jewish experience. A music that was once "revived" has now, in the words of Mark Slobin, been "revitalized."

Alternative contexts

Other areas of Jewish music have a small but loyal following. Sephardic music serves as an exotic style to Jews of Ashkenazic decent, but it functions as a familiar style to those of Sephardic descent. The Ladino songs have created a devoted following because of active performers and groups such as Judy Frankel, Judith Cohen, Voice of the Turtle, and Alhambra, who incorporate a variety of distinct European and Middle Eastern styles in their music. A renewed interest in choral music can be attributed to The Zamir Chorale of Boston, who has influenced a resurgence of a cappella choirs in colleges throughout the country as well as the staging of a one-week choral festival in the Catskills. Another smaller musical community is the Jewish music corner of the New York avant-garde jazz style, whose growing popularity is pushing the boundaries of its local appeal. The recordings of the group Hassidic New Wave has drawn much interest, as evidenced by their performances at the Knitting Factory in Downtown New York. Using stylized Hassidic and klezmer music and placing it within the New York avant-garde jazz framework, Hassidic New Wave moves from pop, rock, jazz, blues, and new classical styles within a piece. Knitting Factory record producer, Seth Rosner, explains that groups such as Hassidic New Wave express Jewish music through their own filter and transform traditional melodies by utilizing their complete musical experience.[33] Through their eclectic tastes and nontraditional uses of a variety of music, these musicians push the limits of Jewish music.

American interest in Israeli music was evident early on in the twentieth century, when Yiddish waned as an active language for Jewish musical expression and Hebrew took its place. A significant repertoire of patriotic songs stemming from the 1948 war became a part of the American Jewish music repertoire. In the 1950s to 1970s, Israeli music was an important stable repertoire to day schools and summer camps and was eventually integrated into the liturgy in American worship. However, its influence was limited since an understanding of the lyrics required sufficient knowledge of Hebrew, which most American Jews did not possess. After the Six Day War in 1967, the influence of Israeli music was renewed. Consequently, a limited number of songs during the late 1970s and onward have been incorporated into the American "Israeli song canon."[34] By the late 1970s, American Jews were creating their own music, and they relied less on Israel for new music. By the 1990s, American Jews were not as warm to Israel or its music because of the ongoing political issues of religious pluralism. One arena that remains constant, however, is the Israeli dance circuit, which often features new music from Israel.

Artists such as Shlomo Artzi, Mati Caspi, Tzvika Pik, Yehudit Ravitz, and the group Poogy were well known to American Jews in the 1970s, and the performing troupes of the Hassidic Song Festival featured individual artists such as Shoshana Damari, Yaffa Yarkoni, Yehoram Gaon, Naomi Shemer, and Chava Alberstein. In the 1990s, artists that achieved acclaim in Israel attempted to expand beyond this area and increase their popularity. In some cases, artists such as Ofra Haza have moved out of Israel and relocated to the United States. Another Israeli artist, Chava Alberstein, recorded forty-five albums for CBS Israel, to include Hebrew, Yiddish, and children's songs. Dudu Fisher, who frequently performs a range of musical styles throughout the world, performed the role of Jean Valjean in *Les Miserables* in Tel Aviv as well as in London and Broadway. David Broza has released four albums in America with English titles since 1989 and was the opening act for Sting in 1995. Achinoam Nini, who was born in Israel and raised in New York, has several recordings with guitarist Gil Dor. The record *NOA* launched her career in 1994.

Well-known American recording artists have also explored aspects of Jewish music, from Kenny G's *Jazz Service* (1986), Itzhak Perlman's *In the Fiddler's House* (1995), Mandy Patinkin's *Mamaloshen* (1997), and Barbra Streisand's recording of Max Janowski's "*Avinu Malkeinu*" on *Higher Ground* (1997).

CONCLUSION

While synagogue attendance has dropped for all Jewish movements over the past thirty years, the increase in new Jewish music indicates that expressions of Jewishness are found in new places. New Jewish music becomes a vehicle to be Jewish and to express Jewishness in diverse, complex, and new ways. A recording becomes an entirely new opportunity for the listener to autonomously create one's own context. Like Judaism in America, these musical expressions adapt from the legacy of Jewish heritage and reinvent it for the present.

Viewing the critical and supportive reactions to new Jewish music, one sees that two features clearly emerge: its musical style and its context or use. Different musical styles are utilized, but the process and goal are the same: a young generation of American Jews is refashioning Judaism for today. For Orthodox musicians, Eastern European elements are used to a limited degree, but the Jewishness of the music is found in the intent to uplift a person spiritually. Reform musicians, who have previously rejected Eastern European elements, regard the success of their music to be the inclusion of congregants during worship, and the accessibility of prayer. Where Jewish musical content is virtually absent in Orthodox and Reform movements, in terms of a traditional musical style, the context defines it as Jewish (synagogue, wedding, or camp). For klezmer musicians, using a traditional melody and playing some form of Eastern European stylization makes the music "Jewish." For klezmer musicians and art music composers, use of Jewish elements is therefore more logical because the context – a nightclub or concert setting – is not a Jewish one. In the concert hall and nightclub, noted artists have been inspired to express their Jewishness in a personal style.

Frith states this:

> [M]usic gives us a real experience of what the ideal could be.... Communal values can only be grasped as musical aesthetics in action. "Authenticity" in this context is a quality not of the music as such (how it is actually made), but of the story it is heard to tell, the narrative of musical interaction in which the listeners place themselves.[35]

The creators of this music, who are products of the baby boom, accept, reject, and reshape their Eastern European heritage through music. Judaism is positively expressed in new Jewish music, thus showing ways of accommodating Jewish life and its ideas, in various forms, by a younger generation. The present looks toward the past in order to reinvent it in the future. Comfortably shifting synchronously, American Jews more easily synthesize history and blur cultural and musical boundaries. The simultaneity of new musical developments in different corners of the Jewish community points toward the powerful need of a younger generation to eagerly create its own destiny in America.

Notes

1. Simon Frith, *Performing Rites: On the Value of Popular Music* (Cambridge, MA: Harvard University Press, 1996), 269–72.
2. This estimate is based on the number of items that appear in the *Mostly Music Catalogue* (1996–97) and discussions with Izzy Taubenfeld of Sameach music (interview by author 27 July 1998) and Velvel Pasternak of Tara Music (interview by author 14 September 1998). See Mark Kligman, "Contemporary Jewish Music in America," *American Jewish Yearbook* 101 (2001), 88.
3. Jack Wertheimer, "Recent Trends in American Judaism," *American Jewish Yearbook* 89 (1989), 162.
4. Duvid Werdyger, *Songs of Hope, the Holocaust Diaries* (New York: CIS Publishers, 1993), 308–14.
5. Velvel Pasternak, interview by author, 14 September 1998.
6. Elli Wohlgelernter, "Simply Shlomo," *The Jerusalem Post Magazine* (1995), 9; also appears in *Brandwine* (1997), 79.
7. Avraham Fried, interview by author 6 July 1998; see also *Ben-David* (1995), 42.

8. Avraham Fried, interview by author 6 July 1998.

9. The term *klezmer* music refers to the music of Jewish life in Eastern Europe in a variety of life-cycle contexts such as a wedding. Mark Slobin sees the use of the term *klezmer* as an American phenomenon because the terms itself refers to the musicians who play the music; see "Klezmer Music: An American Ethnic Genre," *Yearbook for Traditional Music* 16 (1984), 34–41.

10. These are among the most popular songs composed by Yossi Green and performed by Avraham Fried.

11. Yossi Green, interview by author, 1 July 1998.

12. David Sears, "Who Took the 'Jewish' Out of Jewish Music?" *Jewish Observer* 29/10 (1997), 12–16.

13. Jeff Klepper, interview by author, 16 June 1998. See also the introduction to Jeff Klepper and Dan Freelander, *The Kol B'Seder Songbook* (Owings Mills: Tara Publications, 1996), 5–6.

14. Danny Freelander, interview by author, 27 March 1998. The introduction by Jeff Klepper and Dan Freelander, *The Kol B'Seder Songbook* (Owings Mills: Tara Publications, 1996), 5–6, describes the lack of involvement in synagogue music and the need to create participatory music.

15. Daniel H. Freelander, "The Role of Jewish Communal Singing," *Sh'ma A Journal of Jewish Responsibility* 21, 518 (4 October 1996), 6.

16. Sam Adler, "Sacred Music in a Secular Age," in *Sacred Sound and Social Change: Liturgical Music in Jewish and Christian Experience*, ed. Lawrence Hoffman and Janet Walton (Notre Dame and London: University of Notre Dame Press, 1992), 297.

17. This is taken from liner notes of the recording.

18. Susan Josephs, "Queen of Souls," *Baltimore Jewish Times* (19 January 1996), 48.

19. Craig Taubman, interview by author, 23 July 1998.

20. Robbie Solomon, interview by author, 8 July 1998.

21. Irene Heskes, *Passport to Jewish Music: Its History, Traditions, and Culture* (Wesport: Greenwood Press, 1994), 285.

22. Jack Gottlieb, "Symbols of Faith in the Music of Leonard Bernstein," *Musical Quarterly* 66/2 (1980), 287–95.

23. Victoria Kimberling, *David Diamond, a Bio-Bibliography* (Metuchen: Scarcrow Press, 1987), 7.

24. David Diamond, "A Conversation with David Diamond," interview by Adam Stern, *David Diamond* Delos recording DE 3103, CD booklet (1991–93), 7.

25. Ibid., 7.

26. Antonella Puca, "Steve Reich and Hebrew Cantillation," *Musical Quarterly* 81/4 (1997), 539.

27. Ibid., 541, 543.

28. Robert P. Morgan, ed., "Steve Reich," *Source Readings in Music History*, ed. Leo Treitler (New York: Norton, 1998), 117.

29. Arthur Holde, *Jews in Music: From the Age of Enlightenment to the Mid-Twentieth Century* (New York: Bloch Publishing, 1974), 44.

30. Kip Lornell and Anne K. Rasmussen, *Musics of Multicultural America: A Study of Twelve Musical Communities* (New York: Schirmer Books, 1997).

31. Frank London, "An Insider's View: How We Traveled from Obscurity to the Klezmer Establishment in Twenty Years," *Judaism* 47/1, 185 (1998), 40.

32. Ibid., 41, 43.

33. Seth Rosner, interview by author, 7 August 1998.

34. This is based on an investigation of Israeli songs that appear in Reform (*Shireinu: Our Songs*, 1997), Conservative (*Kol BeRamah*, 1996), Orthodox (*Shiron Hashulchan*, 1993), and Jewish communal (*United Jewish Appeal Book of Songs and Blessings*, 1993) songbooks, and sheet music publications (Pasternak, *The International Jewish Songbook*, 1994; *The Jewish Fake Book*, 1997).

35. Simon Frith, *Performing Rites: On the Value of Popular Music* (Cambridge, MA: Harvard University Press, 1996), 274–75.

22 The visual arts in the American Jewish experience

MATTHEW BAIGELL

Many have pondered if there is any such thing as Jewish art, while others have wondered if there is any such thing as Jewish American art. In fact, critics and historians in America have tried to describe the nature of Jewish art for decades. While Jewish artists have acknowledged that aspects of their cultural and religious experiences and backgrounds as Jews inspired them and their art, most have refused to admit that there is something called Jewish art. Even though many American artists were and are Jewish, virtually all of them have denied the label of *Jewish artist*. Thus, by the artists' very standards, neither Jewish art nor Jewish American art can be said to truly exist. Nevertheless, discernibly Jewish works have been called an art done by any Jew, an art with Jewish subject matter, as well as an art that applies only to liturgical objects. In addition, it has been considered to be overly intellectual, overly emotional, and given predominantly to abstract or figurative formulations. Some had contended that true Jewish art would ultimately make its appearance either once Jewish artists were properly supported or in a Jewish national state, in reference to Israel. However, the former never truly occurred and the latter would lead to an Israeli, but not a specifically Jewish, art. Nevertheless, one commonality of so-called Jewish art currently exists: Virtually all assessments of it encompass only ancient and modern works, sidestepping the multitude of intervening works that held any Jewish content and affected both its audience and creator in the process.

In America, the search for a definition has proven to be fruitless, if for no other reason than that most accounts revolve around a handful of male artists born just before and just after 1900 in Eastern Europe or as the children of immigrants in America. What these artists shared is the immigrant experience and first-hand memories of their early lives abroad or in Jewish neighborhoods in this country, usually in New York City. Such descriptions of the nature of Jewish art fail to account for differences between men and women, rural and urban upbringings, secular and religious childhoods, varying political interests, Ashkenazic and Sephardic cultural distinctions, and those who will and those who refuse to include any kind of Jewish subject matter in their work. To think that a formulation broad enough to encompass all these differences exists is to assume that there is a Jewish gene for a certain kind of art shared by all Jewish artists. It does not exist.

EARLY JEWISH AMERICAN ARCHITECTURE

The earliest evidence of Jewish art exists in the architectural styles developed during the Colonial American period, which reflected a pronounced European heritage and influence. Since there were no Jewish laws describing the shape that a house of worship must take, the first synagogues erected for Sephardic congregations were either adorned with architectural ornament considered appropriate to the Jewish religion or else followed contemporary architectural styles.[1] As early as 1695, a synagogue, or at least prayer rooms, existed in New York, and in 1730 the Mill Street Synagogue of Congregation Shearith Israel was dedicated there. In 1763, the oldest surviving synagogue, the Touro Synagogue of Congregation Jeshuat Israel, was erected in Newport, Rhode Island. Designed by Peter Harrison in the academic, Palladian style replete with columns, balustrades, and carved ornaments, it possesses one of the most beautiful Colonial interiors in the country. In the following decades, synagogues reflecting different architectural styles were built in cities where Jews had settled. Examples include the Georgian church-styled building for Congregation Beth Elohim in Charleston, South Carolina in 1794, the Egyptian Revival structure for Congregation Mikveh Israel in Philadephia, Pennsylvania in 1824, and a building in the Greek Revival style for Bene Israel in Cincinnati, Ohio in 1836. In 1841, David Lopez, the earliest known Jewish builder, supervised the construction of the "new" Beth Elohim in Charleston in the Greek Revival style.

In 1847, Leopold Eidlitz (1823–1908), the first Jewish architect to practice in America, assisted in the design of the Wooster Street Synagogue in New York. Neither he nor subsequent Jewish architects developed a particular style of design for synagogues. Through the middle years of the nineteenth century, synagogues were designed in medieval Romanesque and Gothic modes as well as in the Moorish and Byzantine styles with bulbous domes. Some synagogues even had twin towers in imitation of French Gothic cathedrals. By the 1850s, the interior arrangements of many new structures broke with tradition when the large central readers' platform in Ashkenazic synagogues was repositioned near the ark, as was customary in Sephardic synagogues. By 1854, synagogue construction had reached the West Coast with the building of Sherith Israel in San Francisco. The use of large, Moorish-styled synagogues with minarets and domes, considered appropriate for a religion that began in the Middle East, gained popularity in the years just after the Civil War. Notable examples include Temple B'nai Yeshurum built in Cincinnati in 1866 and Rodeph Sholem in Philadelphia in 1879. The first American-born Jewish architect, Arnold Brummer (1857–1925), designed Shearith Israel, erected in New York in 1897, in the Classical Revival style. By that time, synagogues were being designed by major Jewish architects, including Dankmar Adler (1844–1900), who designed Anshe Maariv in Chicago in 1891, and Albert Kahn, who provided plans for Beth El in Detroit in 1922.

In the years after World War II, an enormous number of synagogues were erected as Jews migrated to suburban areas around the country. Percival Goodman alone designed about fifty synagogues, including B'nai Israel, in Milburn, New Jersey, which included sculptural and other decorative adornments by important artists such as Herbert Ferber, Adolph Gottlieb, and Robert Motherwell. Responding to the needs of suburban congregations, these designers provided buildings with open plans that allowed for the quick conversions of the sanctuary into spaces for other kinds of activities. In effect, synagogues became community centers, complete with classrooms, meeting rooms, and gymnasiums. Congregation B'nai Amoona in St. Louis, designed by Eric Mendelsohn in 1946, was perhaps the first flexibly planned synagogue of the postwar period.

EARLY AMERICAN JEWISH PAINTINGS

The history of Jewish painting in the Colonial period is just as sparse as that of Jewish architecture. No Jewish portrait painters are known to have immigrated during this period until after the Revolutionary War, when Joshua (1767–1826) and John (1782–1823) Canter arrived from Denmark at the end of the eighteenth century and settled in Charleston; Theodore Sidney Moïse (1809–85) settled in New Orleans; Jacob Hart Lazarus (1822–91) immigrated to New York; and Solomon Nunes Carvalho (1815–97); all settled in America.[2] Carvalho was best known as a portraitist and photographer who accompanied a western exploration party and made daguerreotypes of Indians, buffalo, the plains, and mountains from Missouri to Utah in 1853. Other well-known figures included Toby Edward Rosenthal (1848–1907), from New Haven, and Robert Blum (1857–1903), from Cincinnati, who explored a range of styles from academic to Impressionist. Moses Jacob Ezekial (1844–1917), another popular portraitist and one of the last Neoclassical sculptors, carved scenes from the Hebrew Bible. However, neither he nor any other American painter or sculptor of this period portrayed scenes of Jewish life, as the Jewish community did not support them or their art. Like many others until the present time, these Jewish artists preferred to abandon their religious and cultural heritage in order to enter mainstream artistic life.

JEWISH AMERICAN ART AND ARTISTS
IN THE TWENTIETH CENTURY

Art that describes the Jewish experience in America really begins, therefore, around 1900 with the enormous influx of immigrants from Eastern Europe.[3] Institutions such as the Educational Alliance, set up to help acculturate the new arrivals, had begun art instruction in 1895, thereby providing subsequently famous artists with both their first substantial exposure to art as well as their first art lessons. Exhibitions held by these institutions, which often included scenes of immigrant life by both Jewish and non-Jewish artists, also helped bring art to the attention of the general populace. Unfortunately, virtually all of the works by Jewish artists shown at the earliest exhibitions have been lost. However, a set of illustrations published in 1902 by Jacob Epstein (1880–1959) for Hutchins Hapgood's book, *Spirit of the Ghetto*, provides us with a fleeting and sympathetic glance at the teeming streets of New York's Lower East Side. Epstein, who ultimately became one of England's most famous sculptors, included a scene of men praying in a synagogue as well as street scenes of people at work and at leisure. By 1910, several Jewish artists had already begun or completed their studies at mainstream schools, such as the National Academy of Design, while others had traveled to Europe, returning as important modernist artists. Photographer Alfred Stieglitz (1864–1946), born in Hoboken, New Jersey, emerged during these years as the most important impresario of modern art in America as a result of his Little Galleries of the Photo-Secession and his magazine *Camera Work*, published from 1903 to 1917. Stieglitz, however, avoided any contact with organized Jewry, except for some art and culture writers, including Waldo Frank and Paul Rosenfeld, as well as avant-garde artists such as Abraham Walkowitz (1878–1965) and Max Weber (1881–1961). Although these artists shared the same immigrant experience and occasionally depicted scenes of Jewish life, they nevertheless wanted to become part of the mainstream. Their proclivity was strongly reinforced, particularly by gallery owners, who felt that Jewish subject matter had little commercial value.

At the turn of the twentieth century, because of the prevailing anti-Semitism, Jewish artists did not want to call attention to themselves as Jews. Moreover, there were few Jewish artists known outside of the Jewish community that painted scenes of Jewish life. Abraham Walkowitz, a native of Siberia, recorded East Side street views, dressing his subjects in western styles of dress as opposed to old-fashioned Eastern European clothing.

Works of this sort symbolized the great desire of the immigrant population to become American as quickly as possible. In contrast, Max Weber, one of the most important American modernists of the first half of the twentieth century, created a gallery of Old World types that included bearded rabbis, men studying holy books in synagogues and yeshivas, Hasidic men dancing in a circle, and other occasional religious rituals. Neither contemporary Jewish life nor ancient Biblical narratives seemed to interest him at all. Of a painting called *The Talmudists* (1934), he wrote that he found "a living spiritual beauty" emanating from a group of Jewish patriarchs studying the Talmud.[4] His interest in this subject matter probably grew from the awareness of events that would overtaken the Jewish world in Eastern Europe during II as well as from his own nostalgia for the life he left behind when he and his family immigrated from Bialystok, now in Poland, to America.

By the 1910s and 1920s, Jewish artists had become part of the mainstream as well as an acknowledged part of the Jewish art world. Major exhibitions, such as the Forum Exhibition of Modern American Painting in 1916, included Jewish organizers and participants. The Jewish Art Center, lasting from 1925 until 1927, promoted the works of Jewish artists, and the group known as The Ten, which flourished between 1935 until about 1940, was composed of Jewish artists. After World War II, the primary institutional support for Jewish art and artists came from museums such as The Jewish Museum (New York), the Spertus Museum of Judaica (Chicago), the Skirball Cultural Center and Museum (Los Angeles), and the Judah L. Magnus Museum (Berkeley).

During the Great Depression of the 1930s, political and social causes provided major routes by which artists could abandon their parochial backgrounds. While some Jewish artists remained more conservative and were engaged in social humanitarianism, many others became entranced by left-wing politics and became Communists. Class consciousness replaced religious and cultural consciousness, or so many artists thought. For many Jewish artists, it can be argued that the religious messianic belief central to Judaism was transferred to the secular socialist belief in the perfection of society through political action. Such messianic or socialist values, and the attendant concerns for social justice, were all that remained of their Judaism. However, these beliefs helped propel them into the ranks of activist artists who hoped that their art would help change society for the better by possibly putting an end to anti-Semitism and allowing Jews to function as equal members of society.

During this era, Jewish artists flocked to Communist-controlled art organizations. The John Reed Club (1929–35), which had artist branches in many major cities, was formed to help support the Soviet Union, proletarianize artists, fight racial prejudice, and promote the welfare of artists. In 1936, the American Artists' Congress replaced the John Reed Club when the Popular Front was instituted to galvanize the world in the fight against Nazism. Artists and critics of all political beliefs were now welcome as long as they opposed German, Italian, and Japanese fascism. In 1937, the Yiddisher Kultur Farband (YKUF) was founded in Paris in the face of Nazi anti-Semitism, to promote Jewish cultural achievements. The varying points of view of these organizations may be summed up in the words of Max Weber, who became very active in the American Artists' Congress. "We workers in the field of the fine arts," he said, "owe to this and future generations a legacy of as perfectly balanced a vision as our talents will afford.... A truly modern art is yet to come, but not until the new life is here, and not before the imminent emancipation of mankind that we envisage." Even in the face of the imminent destruction of the Jewish community in Europe, artists such as Weber still hoped that political action might lead to a new and better world. They had little else to believe in.

Most artists created from within their inner resources rather than follow Communist Party directives. As a result, the histories of the most interesting artists of the 1930s are separate from the histories of the art organizations, even if they supported or exhibited with them. For example, Lithuanian-born Ben Shahn (1898–1969), concerned with innocent victims of official abuse, created one of the first examples of Social Realism, as left-wing art came to be called. However, the betrayal of socialist ideals by Stalin and the destruction of European Jewry caused many left-leaning artists to abandon Social Realism for "personal realism," fantasy, and abstraction. The initial version of Shahn's major work, the fresco for the Roosevelt, New Jersey community center completed in 1937–38, included images of Jews forced to leave Europe for safer shores. The final version acknowledged European anti-Semitism and the benefits accruing to workers by labor unions. The mural included figures of German soldiers posted in front of Jewish-owned stores, forbidding customers entry. Adjacent to these figures is a view of immigration rooms at Ellis Island from which Albert Einstein leads a group of people into America. In quick succession, the viewer sees people working at sweatshop sewing machines and doing piecework at home. A labor organizer addresses the workers, while education classes sponsored by the union are started. With the support of federal funds and union support, the community of Roosevelt, New Jersey is shown under construction. In effect, the mural records the dreams of immigrants across the centuries: America as the land of opportunity, a place for self-betterment and for making a better home for one's children. Shahn also completed a set of paintings in 1960 that were based on the deaths of Japanese fishermen caught under the fallout of a nuclear test in the Pacific. He made several paintings with Jewish themes, which often include Hebrew lettering as well as direct quotes from the Torah and the Prophets. Shahn's series on Job are deeply felt works that reflect on the hubris of people who think they have the answers. Like other artists who had an attraction–rejection dilemma with their cultural and religious heritage, Shahn came not only to acknowledge his legacy but to embrace it, and to come out of the closet, as it were, as a Jew, albeit in a sometimes coded visual language. Nevertheless, he avoided creating Holocaust scenes because of his desire to avoid "ethnic self-pity." While Shahn's other works appear to be about the Civil Rights movement, they actually represent the survival of both the ancient Jewish state as well as the modern state of Israel, if one reads the Commentaries on the Hebrew texts printed in the paintings.

Several other Jewish artists who ignored their Jewish heritage paradoxically created many works saturated with a sense of social justice and humanitarianism based on that very same heritage. Artists such as the Soyer brothers, Raphael (1899–1987), Moses (1899–1974), and Isaac (1907–81), revealed their large-hearted sympathies through ample subject matters such as daily life in New York City, as well as in the historic events of the Spanish Civil War. Others, such as Harry Gottlieb (1895–ca. 1990) traveled to coal-mining districts in Pennsylvania to record the daily hardships sustained by miners in those areas. During the 1930s, native New Yorker Philip Evergood (1901–75) spent time with the homeless and participated in strikes, believing that one could not paint those types of scenes without experiencing them. Similar to that of Shahn, his work reflected the agonies of the Depression without preaching a specific course of action. His mural, *The Story of Richmond Hill* (1936–37), tells the story of enlightened social planning by a private enterprise in the development of a suburban, garden community inhabited by formerly impoverished, urban residents. Following World War II, Evergood found topical and political themes less appealing, so he allowed a more poetic, fantastic vein to emerge in his work. These works depicted an America that was not based on myth, tradition, or a heroized past, but on what these artists experienced and saw each day during their own lifetimes.

During the 1930s and 1940s, two artists, among others, distinctly used Jewish themes in their works.[5] Ben-Zion, born in the Ukraine, probably made more paintings of Jewish subjects than any other artist in America, gathering his main material from the Bible, predominantly depicting the lives of Moses and Job, and from the Prophets. A former poet, Ben-Zion found that his paintings on the Holocaust became a more expressive vehicle for him than writing. In 1946, he was among the first to exhibit works in response to the Holocaust, such as the group of paintings, *De Profundis*, in which he presents portrait heads of bearded rabbis surrounded by barbed wire.

Unlike the youthful Ben Shahn, Ben-Zion affirmed his desire to combine his Judaism with his desire to live in the present:

> "Although identification of an artist must be first and foremost with humanity as a whole, nevertheless the really genuine one never dissociates himself from his creed. On the contrary, he thrives on the sources of his origin, and through his background reaches humanity which no matter how multiple and different its creeds and upbringing may be – at the roots is the same humanity. The true artist, then, while remaining in touch with his background rises above provincial, nationalistic, or religious bigotry."

The second artist, Hyman Bloom, from Lithuania, exhibited two works entitled *Synagogue* at the Museum of Modern Art in 1942 as well as a portrait of bearded rabbis holding Torahs. In the *Synagogue*, Bloom captured the moment in which the cantor is about to sing *kol nidre* at the start of the Yom Kippur service. The sanctuary, in which several Torahs are depicted, is filled with elders wearing prayer shawls and the cantor seems transported to another realm. It is as if Bloom created a work in which all of the displaced Jews of Europe with no place to worship were invited to join in witnessing the beginning of this particular service. Given its date, it remains among the most moving Jewish works created in America, an assertion of Jewish pride and resilience.

Around 1940, several European Jewish artists and American émigré artists arrived in America, some just a few steps ahead of the Germans. The most famous included Marc Chagall, who returned to Europe after the war, and Jacques Lipchitz, who eventually settled in New York and made sculptures with explicit Jewish content. Although they exhibited their work regularly, they seemed not to have had a significant enough impact on American artists to become part of American or Jewish American art history. There were nevertheless very interesting developments in Jewish American art during the 1940s, most notably among those artists associated with Abstract Expressionism. All of the artists mentioned so far had Orthodox religious training during their youth and maintained some connection to Judaism through their work, however tenuous at times. Artists such as Mark Rothko (1903–70), Barnett Newman (1905–70), and Seymour Lipton (1903–86), however, wanted to be "modern" artists, whose tradition traces back to figures such as Cezanne and the Impressionists. Even though Rothko had Orthodox schooling and Newman came from a strongly Zionist family, they largely cut themselves off from any sort of Jewish institutional or cultural sources. Their allegiance was not to the parochial communities from which they emerged, but to the international community of modern culture. Nevertheless, as their mature styles were formed, it was impossible for them to escape awareness of world events, especially as inhabitants of New York. In spite of themselves, their art, abstract and nonobjective, displayed identifiable Jewish elements as well as elements based on their experiences as Jews during one of the most difficult times in the history of Judaism.

Born in Dvinsk, Russia, now part of Latvia, Rothko was a member of The Ten along with Ben-Zion. He initially painted city scenes in a soft-edged realistic manner, until late in 1941 when it became apparent that Germany planned to annihilate Europe's Jewry. As a result, his style changed and he explored three main types of subject matter in an abstract but usually recognizable manner. One type of subject matter was usually based on Aeschylus' play, *Agamemnon*, which told the story of a dysfunctional family involved in cannibalism and murder. It might be suggested that Rothko used this Greek myth as a way to comment on the horrors of the Holocaust taking place then. Rothko's second set of subjects, the so-called archaeological–biological works, point to time lines dating back to the beginnings of living creatures and seem like cross-sections of excavations or of striations of the fossil record of extinct sea creatures. These works, created immediately after the full impact of the Holocaust became evident at the end of World War II, may be interpreted as a rejection of western civilization and the beginning of life again that might someday lead to a civilized future. Rothko's third set of subjects, dating from the mid-1940s, depicts pietalike forms of an emaciated horizontal figure supported by several vertical ones, suggesting Jewish burial activities. In some paintings, he includes shroudlike forms in which the body is wrapped as well as scratchy passages of pigment to suggest the traditional practice of initially placing the corpse on a straw mat. Since photographs of the piles of Jewish corpses from World War II had become well known to the general public, these paintings might be a commentary on the burial, or rather, the nonburial and the burning and desecration of Jewish corpses murdered by the Germans and their allies. In *Entombment I* (1946) the horizontal body is present, but a mysterious, transparent form hovers around the heads of the vertical figures, a form that does not appear in earlier versions. It is likely, then, that Rothko intended the transparent form to represent the souls of the 6 million Jews who were murdered and not properly buried according to Jewish practice, who will never be remembered in the annual observances of the dead, the saying of *kaddish*, because their families had also been murdered, and who will thus never find their place of rest. This painting is arguably the most original and most profoundly Jewish response by an American artist to the Holocaust in terms of cultural memory and religious observance.

Barnett Newman, a contemporary of Rothko, was also profoundly affected by current events such as the Holocaust and the use of atomic bombs. In the mid-1940s, Newman often wrote about the idea of terror he saw in

African, Oceanic, Pre-Columbian, and Northwest American Indian art. The degree to which the art contained elements of terror is moot, as this was Newman's perception. Similar to Rothko and his references to Greek mythology, Newman found his surrogates for the destruction of the Temple in Jerusalem in non-European art. After rejecting European art as too decorative, Newman wrote in 1948 that he wanted to build "cathedrals to the self," that is, to create art from his own being without the impediments of history, memory, or tradition. Similar to Rothko's archaeological–biological works, this suggested a rejection of western civilization. Newman then turned to the Kabbalah for inspiration, finding in the thoughts of Rabbi Isaac Luria (1534–72) of Safad a way to proceed with his art. Luria had posited the idea that God withdrew into himself to allow space for the creation of the world and then marked the moment of creation with a ray of light. In his signature paintings, Newman created a "zip" consisting of a single or a handful of vertical lines set in large fields of a single color, which represents the first ray of light. In this manner, Newman imitated God by creating something out of nothing in his visualization of that first moment before anything in our universe was formed. His work is an affirmation of individual strength and spirit in a world he wanted metaphorically to re-create. Nourished by his cultural rather than religious identification as a Jew, Newman created the zips as one person's single and solitary gesture, a raw assertion of self against a society and a God that did not merit his full respect. Perhaps not coincidentally, the first zip painting was completed during the time the United Nations began its debate on the partition of Palestine and the creation of the modern state of Israel. Newman's zips, then, might be understood as an act of resistance as well as celebrations of renewal and rebirth, an affirmation of life during a time of Jewish trauma and national revival.

In the years following World War II, some artists continued to mask and simultaneously reveal their Jewish background in their work. For example, Seymour Lipton created abstract sculptures that grew from his awareness of the brutality inherent in humans, in effect shifting blame for the present horrors of the time from the German Nazis to human nature. He even named some pieces with enormous gaping jaws *Moloch* after the Biblical figure to whom children were sacrificed by fire. These pieces, based on pre-Columbian forms, contained jagged, razor-toothed figures with spiky edges that were literally menacing to the sight. Another sculpture, *Exodus I* (1947, collection unknown), was made "as part of a tragic mood of history and reality.... It is possible that Israeli history and emergence entered. I don't know really ... [it is] a kind of wailing wall monument to human suffering." Lipton's hesitation in assigning Jewish meanings to this work reminds us of the desire to be considered a mainstream artist, the embarrassment about openly admitting one's Jewishness, and the fear many artists held, and still hold, concerning anti-Semitism. On one occasion, in 1967, Lipton said that he did not practice the formal credo of Judaism, but that he had some nostalgia for it in deference to his parents. Other artists, such as Jack Levine (b. 1915) made similar statements, claiming that his father's death "started me down the path of painting these Jewish sages [King David in 1940 and King Solomon in 1941 among others]. It was his religion, not mine." Nevertheless, Levine began to learn Hebrew and to create many paintings with Jewish subject matter during the course of traveling to Israel during the 1960s. William Gropper (1897–1977) said, "I'm not Jewish in a professional sense, but in a human sense." Perhaps from a generalized left-wing concern for universalizing rather than particularizing the horror of persecution, he felt that he responded to prejudice in the same way as any member of a mistreated minority group.

Responses to the Holocaust by younger artists were much slower in coming, but two military veterans did record their indignation in a far more aggressive manner than did their elder contemporaries.[6] Although Leon Golub (b. 1922) did not see the concentration camps when he was stationed abroad, his lithograph, *Charnel House* (1946), is a violent swirl of figures aflame, and his *Burnt Man* series of the early 1950s depicts mutilated and torn bodies, victims of the horrible devastation that took place in Dachau, Hiroshima, and Vietnam (in later works). Harold Paris (1925–79) did witness the concentration camp at Buchenwald. His experience resulted in a series of kaddish environments that culminated in *Koddesh-Koddashim* (1972), a sealed room based on the Holy of Holies in the Temple in Jerusalem. So overwhelming were the effects of what he had seen and read that he could not find the visual language to articulate his feelings. Instead, they were literally and figuratively bottled up in that sealed room. By the 1970s, many other artists began to create Holocaust-derived works. Inspired by Israeli victories in the 1967 and 1973 wars and the various liberation movements in America, artists finally felt comfortable in openly creating art based on Jewish experiences such as the Holocaust. Using documentary photographs or imaginative reconstructions, artists created works in a variety of media that portrayed life before the roundups, the deportations, camp life, and the deaths. Many felt that their works acted not only as witnesses to the event but also as memorials in the hope that such carnage would never happen again in humanity. Nancy Spero's pieces documented the heroic acts of European Jewish women as well as the tortures they endured. Howard Oransky painted portraits of survivors with shaved heads and tattooed arms in an attempt to help them reclaim their individuality. Marty Kalb recorded camp scenes as well as desecrated synagogues. By the end of the twentieth century, Holocaust scenes have become a major Jewish theme in art by those who survived the camps and as well as those born after the end of the war.

Since the last decades of the past century, there has been an incredible increase in the number of artists all over America who paint the Jewish experience. It would seem that the further the immigrant generations recede into history, the more insistent artists have become in their desire to remember the Jewish past and to record the Jewish present.

There are artists who produce time-honored subjects such as a grandmother lighting the Sabbath candles, families at the Sabbath or Passover meals, and Eastern European life in the *shtetl*. Other artists, working in both representational and abstract styles, are enlarging the boundaries of Jewish subject matter in ways that make the present time perhaps the most exciting in the entire history of the art of the Jewish experience in America.[7] They are artists of the Jewish experience by choice rather than because they come from parochially Jewish backgrounds grounded in East European or immigrant ghettos. Some artists are openly religious and observant, finding their subject matter in the Torah and the Talmud; others artists are openly mystical and search the Kabbalah for inspiration; still others are openly feminist and add a kind of subject matter never seen before. Many insist that their Jewish cultural and religious backgrounds have profoundly shaped their attitudes toward their art, regardless of its subject matter. Some artists openly hope that their art contributes to the notion of *tikkun olam*, "repair of the world," in returning the secular messianism of the 1930s derived from Karl Marx to its religious roots in the Prophets and in the Kabbalah. These artists want to be both Jewish and mainstream (American or international), and they refuse to hide the former in the latter or to let the former peek out through the latter.

The range of Jewish subjects and attitudes currently being explored is seen in the art of Ruth Weisberg. *The Shtetl, a Journey and a Memorial* (1971) depicts the tensions and fears in Eastern European ghettos just before the outbreak of war in 1939. In remembering, Weisberg feels that she helps redeem the memory of those murdered and at the same time gives meaning to her own life. "I might have been among them," she has said, "but I was born in Chicago in 1942. I am a branch, a resting place for their souls. This book [*The Shtetl*] is my life's journey in place of theirs." *The Scroll* (1986–87) combines narrative elements from the Bible, Biblical commentary, past and present Jewish history, and personal history in ways that make the Jewish past and present relevant to contemporary Jewish life. Portraying men and women in leadership roles, these scenes include the Exodus; American, Israeli, and prewar European children at play; a female rabbi officiating at her daughter's *bat mitzvah*; and a concentration camp scene. In 2002, Weisberg's illustrated

Haggadah, entitled *The Open Door*, stressed the role of women in preparing the *seder* meal as well as the participative aspects of those at the meal. Through her work, Weisberg accents the liturgical elements of Judaism as well as the communal.

Since the 1970s, the tenets of the Jewish feminist movement are also evident in the work of several other artists. Perhaps the most outspoken among them is Helène Aylon, born in New York, who in effect has taken on the entire patriarchy beginning with Moses. Although the product of strict Orthodox schooling, she decided to rescue "G-d from damaging patriarchal projections" after reading the Torah from a feminist point of view in the late 1980s. Since the 1990s, she has made a series of installations that radically challenge all prior masculinist assumptions found in the Torah that have been espoused by rabbis and male scholars. A good example is *The Liberation of G-d* (1996), an installation piece that includes fifty-four books (for the fifty-four chapters of the Bible) on glass shelves. As she explained,

> "I began the liberation of G-d searching the Five Books of Moses for sections where G-d has been spoken for. I look into passages where patriarchal attitudes have projected onto G-d as though man has the right to have dominion even over G-d.... I highlight [with a pink marker] onto the parchment that covers each page; between words in the empty spaces where a female presence has been omitted, where only the father's name is recorded as the parent who begot the offspring and I highlight over words of vengeance, deception, cruelty, and misogyny, words attributed to G-d."

Her critique is a challenge, not a dismissal, for she still acknowledges Orthodoxy as "the real Judaism." Her real question is this: Where in Judaism can an emancipated person, especially a woman, seriously committed to religious and spiritual values find a home? Native New Yorker Tobi Kahn addresses spiritual issues his own way. A yeshiva-trained, observant Jew, he aspires to blend spiritual aspects of Judaism with everyday life. Both through his art and his daily activities, he tries to celebrate the wonders and the holiness of the world. Thus the setting of a beautiful Sabbath table is as important to him as the creation of a beautiful abstract painting. He has also devoted considerable energy to making ritual objects for mitzvahs and commemorations, such as holders for *yahrzeit* candles and *tzedakah* boxes, no doubt agreeing with the mystic and philosopher Abraham Joshua Heschel, who felt that the purpose of ritual objects was not to inspire a love of God but to enhance the love of doing a mitzvah.

Several artists who feel culturally Jewish but choose not to exhibit the same degree of religiosity in their work portray the Jewish experience in different ways. Perhaps the most interesting is R. B. Kitaj, who was born in Cleveland, spent most of his adult years in England, and now resides in California. Self-educated in Jewish history and religion, he began exploring Jewish themes around 1960 by including figures such as political activist Rosa Luxembourg and writer–critic Walter Benjamin in his paintings as well as coded themes related to the central condition of his life, the Holocaust. Aside from the quality of his work, what makes him so interesting is that since there was so little Judaism in his childhood, he has little sense of the Jewish community at large. Thus, well-known Jewish political and intellectual figures, such as Franz Kafka, have become his community. His anchorage is not in a place or in a group but in the words contained in books. Self-awareness as a Jew has become his homeland. Books about Jewish figures who lacked or lack a sense of the Jewish community but have identified as Jewish are also his homeland. In recent years, he has begun to portray Biblical figures with whom he has gained more familiarity, so to speak, and is also exploring religious imagery. His is a kind of personal journey, which, similar to those of Aylon, Kahn, and Weisberg, would be unimaginable a century ago.

Other artists explore the Kabbalah, rather than the Torah or Prophets, for artistic inspiration and personal illumination. For example, Bruria Finkel has created sculptures based on her explorations of Merkavah Mysticism, the branch of Kabbalah ultimately descended from Ezekiel's vision of the throne-chariot of God. Beth Ames Swartz, who has created performance pieces honoring Biblical matriarchs, also combines an interest in Kabbalah with spiritual systems of other religions in an ongoing series of abstract paintings. Finally, Robert Kirschbaum finds relationships between geometry and certain elements of Kabbalistic thought in projecting images of the facade of the Temple in Jerusalem. Their general aim is to gain access in some way to the "mystical stream" in order to feel at one with the universe. Taken as a group, these and other like-minded artists might be in the process of creating a new and important movement in Jewish American art of the twenty-first century.

The trajectories of the Jewish experience in American art, then, have included artists from Eastern European backgrounds who could move easily between parochial and mainstream currents, artists who wanted to become "modern" at any cost, artists who ignored their backgrounds but came to terms with it during their mature years, and artists for whom being simulta-neously mainstream and Jewish is no longer a problem but rather a desired state. Exhibitions are regularly held in Jewish museums and synagogues, as well as commercial galleries, across the country. Artists are commissioned by synagogues to create stained-glass windows, mosaics, sculptures, and paintings. If advertisements in magazines and catalogues are an indication, the field of Judaica and the making of ritual objects has grown exponentially. The future is now entirely open for these artists to freely create American Jewish art.

Notes

1. Architectural material is taken from Rachel Wishnitzer, *Synagogue Architecture in the United States* (Philadelphia: The Jewish Publication Society, 1955) and Avram Kampf, *Contemporary Synagogue Art* (Philadelphia: The Jewish Publication Society, 1965).
2. Information of pre-twentieth-century painting and sculpture is taken mainly from Joseph Gutman, "Jewish Participation in the Visual Arts of Eighteenth and Nineteenth-Century America," *American Jewish Archives* 15 (April 1963), 21–57.
3. Additional information on art between 1900 and 1940 can be found in Norman Kleeblatt and Susan Chevlowe, *Painting a Place in America: Jewish Artists in New York, 1900–1945* (New York: The Jewish Museum, 1991).
4. The most complete essay on Weber's Jewish art is Matthew Baigell, "Max Weber's Jewish Paintings," *American Jewish History* 88 (September 2000), 341–60.
5. For the most accessible source on the Jewish art of Ben-Zion, Hyman Bloom, Mark Rothko, Barnett Newman, and Seymour Lipton, see Matthew Baigell, *Jewish Artists in New York: The Holocaust Years* (New Brunswick: Rutgers University Press, 2002). See also Ziva Amishai-Maisels, *Depiction and Interpretation: The Influence of the Holocaust on the Visual Arts* (New York: Pergamon Press, 1993).
6. Ziva Amishai-Maisels, *Depiction and Interpretation: The Influence of the Holocaust on the Visual Arts* (New York: Pergamon Press, 1993) and Matthew Baigell, *Jewish American Artists and the Holocaust* (New Brunswick: Rutgers University Press, 1997).
7. Since there is no survey of contemporary Jewish art, material on the artists considered here was gleaned from exhibition catalogues, newspaper clippings, personal interviews, and correspondence. Some of these artists will be featured in Baigell's forthcoming book, *American Artists, Jewish Views*.

23 American Judaism in the twenty-first century
BRUCE PHILLIPS

The three classic works on American Judaism in the twentieth century appeared just after midcentury, all echoing the theme of Jews "fitting in" America and reflecting the rapid upward social mobility of American Jews. In *American Judaism*, Nathan Glazer noted the trend toward religious identification among Jews as a way to fit in as an ethnic group by using a religious framework.[1] Even though America at midcentury was hostile to ethnicity, it was open to religiosity. In *Conservative Judaism*, Marshall Sklare observed that this most mainstream of the three movements differed from Orthodoxy in terms of decorum.[2] While the core beliefs and practices of Conservative Judaism mirrored Orthodoxy, the former emphasized decorum in worship that was congruent with American religious life. In *Jewish Identity on the Suburban Frontier*, Sklare found that the Jews in the Midwestern suburb of Lakeville were ambivalent about Jewish particularism.[3] The midcentury perspective tended to appreciate American Judaism in terms of assimilation. Adaptations to American life were most readily visible in religious behaviors. This perspective has continued to inform more recent studies such as Steven M. Cohen's *Jewish Identity and American Modernity*, which used religious observance to gauge assimilation.[4] Beginning in the 1980s, American sociologists of religion introduced two new perspectives that have informed the understanding of contemporary American Judaism. In *Habits of the Heart*, Robert Bellah introduced the notion of religious privatization and the sovereignty of the individual in making religious decisions.[5] While churches and seminaries may proscribe belief and practice, individuals decide for themselves what is most meaningful to them. Arnold Eisen and Steven M. Cohen took Bellah's research into the Jewish community and found that Jews, like other Americans, insisted on discovering religious meaning on their own without worrying about what was or was not "kosher."[6] The second new approach, often referred to as the "new paradigm," was to understand American religion as part of a "religious marketplace." Researchers using the new paradigm emphasized the role of "rational choice" in religious behavior. Most recently, this perspective has

Table 1. *Current religious identification of all adult Jews*

Current religious identification	% of adult Jews
Born Jewish; religion Judaism	62.0
Formally converted to Judaism	2.2
Jewish by religion without conversion	1.6
Secular Jew – "no religion"	13.1
Jew practicing an Eastern religion	3.5
Christian Jew	17.6
TOTAL	100.0

informed the analysis in *Jewish Choices* by Lazerwitz, Winter, Dashefsky, and Tabory.[7]

At the dawn of the twenty-first century, there are many trends at work within American Judaism and its major denominations. The goal of this discussion, based on the Year 2000 National Jewish Population Survey (NJPS), is to provide a sense of what Judaism will be like in the United States.[8] Therefore, this chapter is focused not on Jewish thought or issues of denominational doctrine, but on the religious beliefs and practices of persons who identify themselves as Jews in some way.

THE DECLINE OF JUDAISM AMONG AMERICAN JEWS

Perhaps the most important phenomenon emerging in the twenty-first century is the declining number of Jews whose religion is Judaism. Largely as a result of intermarriage, the once seamless overlap between Jewish ethnicity and Judaism has begun to unravel. Writing in the late 1960s, Marshall Sklare[9] observed that American Judaism was a special case of the "ethnic church" in which all members of the ethnic group (Jews) professed the same religion (Judaism) and all members of the religion shared the same ethnicity. This is no longer the case, as evidenced in Table 1, which presents the religious identification of all adult Jews. Two out of five Jewish adults did not identify Judaism as their religion. Instead they identified themselves either as secular (meaning that they had no religious identification) or as Christian Jews. Christian Jews are individuals who identify themselves as Jews by ethnicity but are at least nominally Christian. They are the offspring of mixed marriages and were not counted as part of the Jewish population in the report issued by the United Jewish Communities. I include them in this analysis because they are essential for an understanding of the contemporary American Jewish reality.

Table 2. *Current religious identification by Jewish parentage (all adult Jews)*

Current religious identification	Two Jewish parents (%)	One Jewish parent (%)	Jewish grandparent only (%)
Born Jewish, religion Judaism	87.0	23.3	4.5
Secular Jew	8.4	25.5	16.3
Jew practicing an Eastern religion	0.8	8.5	13.3
Christian Jew	3.8	42.7	65.9
TOTAL	100.0	100.0	100.0

Adults who were identified as Christian Jews in the NJPS 2000 were not converts to Christianity but rather the offspring of mixed marriages. Table 2 compares the religious identification of Jewish adults of three kinds of Jewish parentage: two Jewish parents, one Jewish (and one non-Jewish) parent, and no Jewish parents. Individuals with no Jewish parents had at least one Jewish grandparent and identified themselves as Jewish by ethnicity or ancestry. Adults of Jewish parentage overwhelmingly identified themselves as Jews by religion (86 percent). Jewish adults with a non-Jewish parent were twice as likely to identify themselves as a Christian by religion (41 percent)[10] than as a Jew by religion (22 percent). Adults with no Jewish parents identified themselves either as Christians or as practicing an Eastern religion.

The number of adherents to Judaism will decline as the twenty-first century progresses. This numerical decline can be anticipated from parents' answers to how their children are being raised. Fewer than half of all Jewish children are being raised as Jews. Table 3 shows how children are being raised according to the religious composition of the family. Endogamous couples almost universally raise their children as Jews, but mixed-married couples do not. Among the mixed-married couples, Jews married to secular non-Jews are the most likely to raise their children in Judaism, but less than two-thirds do so (61 percent). Mixed-married couples in which both the Jewish parent and the non-Jewish parent are completely secular predominantly raise their children in no religion at all (79 percent). A dual-religion couple is made up of a Jew by religion married to a Christian. Only one-quarter of the children in dual-religion couples are being raised as Jews, and almost one-third are being raised as Christians. Although the parents identify with two different religions, less than one-tenth of the children are being raised in two religions. Christian Jews overwhelmingly are raising their children as Christians.

On the basis of the Jewish parentage of the child, Table 4 projects adherence to Judaism into the future. Almost all (98 percent) of the children with two Jewish parents are being raised as Jews. If one of the two Jewish

Table 3. *How children are being raised according to the religious identification of the parents*

How child is being raised	Parents are inmarried (%)	Parents are mixed married					All (%)
		Jew by religion – secular non-Jew (%)	Both Jew and non-Jew are secular (%)	Jew by religion – Christian (%)	Christian Jew (%)	Jewish parent is single parent (%)	
In Judaism exclusively	95.7	60.5	6.4	25.9	1.4	52.1	43.0
In no religion	1.7	26.0	78.6	34.9	13.9	35.4	22.7
In two religions	0.2	9.5	–	9.0	1.3	2.0	2.3
As a Christian	2.4	3.9	15.0	30.2	83.4	10.5	32.0
TOTAL	100.0	100.0	100.0	100.0	100.0	100.0	100.0

Table 4. *Long-range impact of intermarriage
on children*

Jewish lineage of child	% raised as Jewish by religion
Fully Jewish*	97.7
Three-quarters Jewish**	67.2
Half-Jewish***	38.7
One-quarter Jewish****	4.1
Jewish ancestry only*****	1.7
Fully Jewish single parent	70.2
Half-Jewish single parent	28.3
Single parent of Jewish ancestry	9.3
All children	43.0

* Jewish parents and grandparents.
** Jewish parent of Jewish parentage married to Jew of partial parentage.
*** Jew of Jewish parentage married to non-Jew.
***** Jewish parent of partial parentage married to non-Jew.
***** Only a grandparent is Jewish.

parents is only "half-Jewish" (i.e., one of the two was raised in a mixed marriage), the percentage of the children raised as Jews drops to 67 percent. Just over one-third (39 percent) of the "half-Jewish" children (one Jewish and one non-Jewish parent) are being raised as Jews. Children who are one-quarter Jewish show the results of two generations of mixed marriage. When one Jewish parent is half-Jewish (raised in a mixed marriage) and the other is non-Jewish, only 4 percent of the children are raised as Jews. Among children raised in single-parent families, we do not know about the absent parent. However, the same pattern is apparent based on the Jewish lineage of the child's parent: Children of a fully Jewish single parent are three times as likely to be raised as Jews than children of a half-Jewish single parent. Even if the rate of mixed marriage remains steady, the number of adherents to Judaism will decline as the children of today become adults in the future. The number of Jews, however, may not decline if the children and grandchildren of mixed marriages continue to identify themselves ethnically as Jews. It is doubtful, however, that they will be participants in Jewish communal life.

Within the scope of this sea change in adherence to Judaism, there is one consistency that has persisted over the past decades: Children with mixed-married Jewish mothers are more likely to be raised as Jews than children with mixed-married Jewish fathers (62 percent vs. 31 percent; see Table 5). The gender gap is also evident among the children of Jewish single parents. Secular Jewish single-parent mothers are almost four times

Table 5. *Children raised Jewish by intermarriage of Jewish parent*

Gender and Jewish status of parents	The parent of the child is		
	Inmarried (%)	Mixed married (%)	Single parent (%)
Mother is Jewish by religion	98.4	61.8	82.8
Father is Jewish by religion	98.2	31.2	81.8
Mother is Jew by choice[11]	97.1	100.0	95.0
Father is Jew by choice	100.0	0.0	60.5
Mother is secular Jew	28.0	2.0	10.8
Father is secular Jew	27.7	3.1	3.1

as likely to raise Jewish children as are secular Jewish single-parent fathers (11 percent vs. 3 percent). Almost all the children of single-parent mothers who converted to Judaism are being raised as Jews (95 percent) as compared with less than two-thirds (61 percent) of the children whose single-parent fathers converted to Judaism.

DENOMINATIONAL CHANGE

One of the distinctly American aspects of American Judaism is denominationalism. Denominations are a reflection of an open society in which there are no officially recognized religions. This analysis uses an expanded definition of denomination that combines the four movements (Reform, Reconstruction, Conservative, and Orthodox) with the two additional categories of "no religion" and Christianity. These are not Jewish denominations per se, but they are necessary to capture the dynamic of Jewish denominational change as it is currently unfolding.

An enduring topic of interest within the American approach to the sociology of religion is denominational change or "religious switching." Religious switching has occurred when an individual's current religion or denomination is different from that of his or her family of origin.

The single most important Jewish denominational change is the movement out of Judaism, which in part is associated with intermarriage (Table 6). Among respondents with one Jewish parent, the shift is away from Judaism; 45 percent of respondents with one Jewish parent were raised in one of the four Jewish denominations, but only 15 percent currently identify with a Jewish denomination. The move was not into secularism but rather into Christianity or a dual Jewish–Christian identity. Among respondents with

Table 6. *Respondents' current and childhood denominations*
(Jewish parentage controlled for)

Denomination	Both parents Jewish (%)		One Jewish parent (%)		Grandparents or ancestry (%)	
	Current	Raised	Current	Raised	Current	Raised
Orthodox traditional Sephardic	8.3	18.5	1.0	2.0	0.5	1.7
Conservative	22.9	31.0	3.8	5.9	2.4	0.9
Reform	30.6	25.2	8.2	8.1	1.8	2.2
Reconstruction	1.9	0.4	0.3	0.1	–	–
Jewish by religion, but has no denominational identification	20.4	14.7	7.8	6.2	1.4	11.1
Secular (ethnic, atheist, etc.)	10.1		29.5		26.6	
Postdenominational Jew, Jewish Renewal, Jewish Spirituality, etc.	1.1	0.1	8.1	0.0	15.9	0.0
Jew + Eastern religion or Eastern religion only	0.4	3.2	1.2	13.2	0.6	14.5
Christian Jew	4.3	6.8	40.2	64.3	50.8	69.5
TOTAL	100.0	100.0	100.0	100.0	100.0	100.0

two Jewish parents, there has been a parallel but less dramatic movement away from denominations; 81 percent of respondents with two Jewish parents were raised in one of the four denominations, but only 68 percent currently identify with one of those denominations as adults. Within this move away from denominations, Reform was the only denomination that grew. Orthodox and Conservative Judaism decreased by 11 percent and 9 percent, respectively, while Reform increased by 5 percent. The greatest increase was among respondents who identify with no denomination; 16 percent of respondents with two Jewish parents were raised in no denomination, but 25 percent currently identify with no denomination as adults. Identification with a religion other than Judaism also increased among respondents with two Jewish parents; 4 percent were raised outside of Judaism, but 7 percent identify with a religion other than Judaism as adults.

The shift from Judaism into no denomination observed among respondants of Jewish parentage has a parallel among respondents of mixed parentage: a shift away from Christian identification into the "no religion" category. Three-quarters of the respondents raised in mixed marriages were raised as Christians (64 percent) or in an Eastern religion (13 percent). As adults, however, only 41 percent identified as Christians or with an Eastern religion. Only 6 percent reported being raised in no religion, but as adults, 38 percent identified themselves either as secular or as nondenominational Jews. They have moved to the neutral territory of no religion. A similar pattern is evident among respondents of Jewish ancestry only; 85 percent reported being raised as Christians or in an Eastern religion. As adults, only 52 percent identified themselves in this way. By contrast, only 11 percent were raised in no religion, but as adults, 28 percent identified as secular or nondenominational Jews. There has been much speculation in denominational circles regarding the rise in "postdenominational" Judaism and the Jewish Renewal movement. This is not born out by the NJPS 2000, at least among respondents of Jewish parentage. Instead, the respondents most likely to identify themselves as "postdenominational" Jews or with the Jewish Renewal movement were either of Jewish ancestry only (16 percent) or had only one Jewish parent (8 percent).

Nondenominational Jews

If twentieth-century Judaism was characterized by denominational tensions, the emerging divide in the twenty-first century will be between Jews who have a denomination and those who do not. Nondenominational Jews (whether they be secular or Jewish by religion without a denomination) do not join synagogues. As their numbers increase, the growth of new synagogues will slow. I ran a logistic regression to understand what differentiates Jews who have a denomination from those who have none. This regression identified the impact of each variable on denominational identification while controlling for the impact of all the other variables. The four strongest predictors were the following.

1. Denomination: Respondents who grew up in a denomination tend to stay in a denomination.
2. Marriage: Inmarried respondents are the most likely to have a denominational affiliation (83 percent), and mixed-married respondents are the least likely (25 percent). Single respondents fell in the middle (42 percent).
3. Generation: Third- and fourth-generation respondents are less likely to identify with a denomination than first- and second-generation respondents.

4. Education: The more Jewish education a respondent received, the more likely he or she was to identify with a denomination as an adult.

Two of the four factors have to do with socialization. Being raised in a denomination and having a Jewish education are both associated with denominational identification in adulthood. The relationship between intermarriage and denominational identification is not so easily explained, because cause and effect are harder to identify. One possibility is that Jews who are attached to Judaism (as measured by denominational identification) are more likely to seek out Jewish spouses. This might explain why denominational identification is higher among the inmarried than among the nonmarried couples. It might also be that so-called normative behavior such as inmarriage leads to more normative behaviors such as denominational identification.

There are two kinds of nondenominational Jews: those who were raised that way, and those who abandoned the denominational identification in which they were raised. To understand this second phenomenon, I ran a second logistic regression to identify those variables that best predict "denominational abandonment." Denominational abandonment means that the respondent was raised in a denomination but now identifies with no Jewish denomination. Thus, this analysis included only respondents who were raised in a Jewish denomination.

There were three important predictors of denominational abandonment. The first and most important predictor was marital status. Inmarried respondents were more likely to have remained denominationally identified than either mixed-married respondents or single respondents. The second strongest predictor of denominational abandonment was Jewish education. Respondents who had no Jewish education were the most likely to drop their original denominational identification, followed by respondents whose Jewish education ended with Bar Mitzvah. Respondents who continued beyond Bar Mitzvah in a supplementary or day school were the most likely to have retained a denominational identification. The coefficients in the logistic regression equation indicate that, although Jewish education is a predictor of inmarriage, Jewish education predicts denominational abandonment when intermarriage is controlled for. The highest rate of denominational abandonment was found among currently mixed-married respondents who had no Jewish education at all. The lowest rate was found among currently inmarried day school graduates. The third strongest predictor is Jewish parentage. Respondents with one Jewish parent were more likely to abandon denominational identification than respondents with two Jewish parents. Again, this factor works in tandem with the other two predictors. Within every level of Jewish education, respondents with two Jewish parents are less likely to have abandoned denominational identification than respondents with one Jewish parent. Similarly, Jewish parentage and endogamy each have an independent impact on denominational abandonment. Inmarried respondents with two Jewish parents were the most likely to continue identifying with a denomination as adults. Conversely, mixed-married respondents of mixed parentage were the most likely to have discontinued denominational identification as adults.

The strong association between marriage and denominational abandonment is partially unexpected. Not surprisingly, mixed-married respondents are more likely to have abandoned denominational identification than inmarried respondents, and this remains true regardless of age. Less obvious is why single respondents, regardless of age, would be more likely to abandon denominational identification than inmarried respondents. Which is the cause and which is the effect? One factor is previous marriage. Single respondents who were widowed or divorced from an inmarriage were less likely to have abandoned denominational identification than those who were previously married to a non-Jewish spouse. A second factor, as suggested herein, is self-selection. Perhaps Jews for whom religion is important are the most likely to marry endogamously. In other words, retaining some sort of Jewish denominational attachment into adulthood is a reflection of loyalty to Judaism. It could also be that endogamy reinforces Jewish attachments in the marriage. Conversely, Jewish denominational loyalty may weaken in a mixed marriage because it is a potential source of friction with the non-Jewish spouse.

Denominational retention

In addition to the abandonment of denominational identification, there are shifts taking place among the Jewish denominations. I examined denominational change in the previous paragraphs by comparing the percentage of Jews raised in a particular denomination with the percentage currently identified with it. Another way to understand denominational change is through the rate of "retention" in which the percentage of respondents who were raised in that denomination continue to identify with that denomination as adults. When retention rates are considered by age, Orthodoxy is seen to have experienced an important transition. For respondents aged sixty years and older, only 20 percent of those raised as Orthodox currently identify with this denomination. The retention rate increased to 35 percent of respondents between forty and fifty-nine years of age and to an impressive 72 percent of respondents younger than forty years of age. The proclivity to leave Orthodoxy is a phenomenon of the past. The retention rate among respondents raised Conservative is consistently about 50 percent across all age groups. In contrast, Reform has a consistently higher retention rate between 67 and

71 percent. The higher retention rate of Reform combined with the tendency of respondents raised as Conservative to switch to Reform explains the numerical decline of the former and the growth of the latter. In addition, the higher retention rate among younger Orthodox respondents dries up what was a major source of recruitment for the Conservative movement.

If we take these together, we can see that there are three trends of denominational change evident at the dawn of the twenty-first century: a move out of Judaism associated with intermarriage; a move to Reform on the part of Jews raised in the Conservative movement; and a strong loyalty to Orthodox Judaism among younger Jews.

SYNAGOGUE MEMBERSHIP

What will the synagogue of the twenty-first century look like, given the denominational trends described here? Overall, only one-quarter of all Jewish households currently pay dues to a synagogue. Orthodox households are the most likely to have a synagogue membership (77 percent), followed by Conservative households (53 percent) and Reform and Reconstructionist households (42 percent). Jewish households in which the respondent had no denominational identification were largely unaffiliated; only one out of ten nondenominational Jewish households claimed a synagogue membership.

Synagogue membership is strongly associated with family by way of intermarriage. Intermarriage marks the great divide between affiliated and unaffiliated households. Currently inmarried households have the highest rate of synagogue membership (62 percent), followed by households in which the respondent is currently divorced or widowed but was previously inmarried (42 percent). Currently mixed-married households have the lowest rate of synagogue membership (9 percent). Respondents divorced from a mixed marriage have a higher rate of synagogue membership than respondents currently married to non-Jews, but the rate is still relatively low (16 percent). Single, never-married households are also largely unaffiliated (16 percent).

After intermarriage, household structure is the next most important predictor of synagogue affiliation. Marriage and children are strongly associated with synagogue membership. Endogamous couples with children have the highest rate of synagogue membership (78 percent), followed by endogamous married couples without children (53 percent). In contrast, only 10 percent of mixed-married couples with children and 7 percent of mixed-married couples without children are synagogue members. Having a Jewish spouse is the strongest predictor of synagogue membership, followed by having children in the household. Among endogamous couples, those with children under the age of eighteen are 1.5 times as likely to belong to a synagogue as couples without children. A similar pattern can be seen among single parents. Single parents who were previously inmarried were twice as likely to belong to a synagogue as single parents who were previously married to a non-Jewish spouse (57 percent vs. 21 percent). Interestingly, single parents who were divorced from a mixed marriage were themselves twice as likely to belong to a synagogue than mixed-married couples with children (21 percent vs. 10 percent). This is consistent with other research, and it suggests both that single parents divorced from mixed marriages look to the Jewish community for support and that conflicts over the religious orientation of the family may have led to the divorce in the first place.

The synagogue population

Households that belong to a synagogue are most likely to belong to a Reform synagogue (39 percent). Although those households identified as Orthodox account for only 10 percent of all Jewish households, they make up 20 percent of all household memberships. This is because the synagogue affiliation rate is much higher among Orthodox Jews than among Reform and Conservative Jews.

The kinds of changes taking place within synagogues can be seen when the denominational roots of the respondent's family of origin is broken down by age and type of synagogue.[12] The majority of the oldest members of Reform synagogues (sixty years of age or older) were raised either Orthodox or Conservative, while only one-quarter were raised in the Reform movement. The youngest members (under forty years of age), in contrast, were overwhelmingly raised in the Reform movement. About half of the oldest members of Conservative synagogues were raised Conservative, but almost 70 percent of the youngest members were raised Conservative. Conservative Jews raised Orthodox are decreasingly present among younger ages groups; almost 40 percent of the oldest Conservative synagogue members were raised Orthodox, declining to 16 percent of the cohort under the age of forty to fifty-nine, and only 5 percent of the cohort under forty. In contrast, the Conservative movement seems to have some attraction to younger Reform Jews; 14 percent of the youngest cohort of Conservative synagogue members were raised in the Reform movement. In the long run, this may have a liberalizing effect on the Conservative movement with regard to such issues as patrilineal descent.

The age profile of Orthodox synagogue members is the most volatile of the three major movements. The oldest members of Orthodox synagogues were overwhelmingly raised Orthodox. In the cohort that roughly corresponds to the Baby Boom (forty to fifty-nine years of age), just over half of the membership were raised Orthodox, and one-quarter were raised in the Conservative movement. Marshall Sklare commented on the defection of the cream of the Conservative movement to Orthodoxy as a result of the intensive religious socialization they experienced in Conservative institutions such as Camp Ramah. Although many more Baby Boom Conservative Jews defected to Reform than to Orthodoxy, there was also a large defection into Orthodoxy in this cohort. As a result, "Camp Ramah" Jews are a significant segment of middle-aged members in Orthodox synagogues. The youngest members (under forty years of age) of Orthodox synagogues were raised Orthodox, and this is consistent with the high retention rate already discussed for younger Orthodox Jews. The youngest Orthodox Jews are also the most geographically concentrated; 80 percent of them live in the Northeast, as compared with 66 percent of the forty- to fifty-nine-year-olds and 46 percent of the oldest cohort (one-third of whom now live in Florida). This suggests that the rightward movement within Orthodoxy will either stabilize or continue, but it will not decrease. The youngest Orthodox synagogue members are concentrated in a region (the Northeast) that is losing its Jewish population. Thus, Orthodox Jews will constitute an increasingly larger proportion of the northeastern Jewish population and will have a growing influence.

The popular conception that American synagogues are too "family oriented" to be attractive to single persons turns out to be only partially correct. While it is true that single households are underrepresented among synagogue members, they constitute one-third or more of synagogue members in the three major dominations. Within the single population, previously married respondents are more prevalent than never-married respondents among synagogue members. Thus, while it is true that married couples are more likely to join synagogues than single Jews, the synagogue population is becoming more evenly divided between married couples and single Jews. Perhaps this is the result of greater sensitivity to singles on the part of synagogues in response to previous criticism.

The presence of mixed-married couples in the synagogue population varies according to the openness of each movement toward including them. Mixed-married couples are almost nonexistent in Orthodox synagogues. Only 7 percent of Conservative synagogue members are currently mixed married, and another 3 percent were previously mixed married. The proportion of mixed-married couples in the Reform synagogue population is double that in the Conservative movement, and one out of five Reform synagogue members is either currently or previously mixed married. This figure might seem low given the emphasis on outreach to mixed-married couples in the Reform movement and the preference that mixed-married couples have for the Reform movement. Nevertheless, two other trends must be kept in mind. First, even though mixed-married couples prefer the Reform movement (62 percent of affiliated mixed-married couples belong to a Reform synagogue), synagogue affiliation among the mixed-married population is low to begin with, so it is safe to assume that they do not attend synagogue services often. Second, mixed-married couples have a greater impact on Reform synagogues than on Conservative and Orthodox synagogues. Mixed-married couples have an even greater impact on the Reconstructionist synagogue, where they make up 44 percent of Reconstructionist synagogue members. However, there were not many Reconstructionist cases in the sample, so this high figure must be interpreted with some caution.

JEWISH OBSERVANCE

Joining a synagogue is a public expression of Judaism. Jewish observance is more private, usually taking place in the home. In his classic work, *Jewish Identity on the Suburban Frontier*, Sklare observed that the most widely practiced Jewish observances were infrequent and associated with children (i.e., family). His observation remains true fifty years later. Among the Jewish rituals and observances included in the NJPS 2000, those associated with family are the most widely practiced. Attending a Passover Seder or a Jewish mourning ritual were the most widely practiced Jewish observances, followed closely by lighting Hanukah candles and fasting on Yom Kippur at least part of the day. Although not a child-centered holiday in the sense described by Sklare, the High Holidays can be considered family events because the whole family attends synagogue together.

Surprisingly, Jews who are not Jewish by religion claim to practice Jewish observances. Among respondents who experienced a death in the family, for example, one-quarter of the Christian Jews and one-third of the secular Jews reported observing a Jewish mourning ritual. This was probably not so much self-initiated but rather the result of an invitation to a funeral or a shiva at the home of a Jewish relative. This may say less about this person's connection to Judaism than to his or her extended Jewish family.

An unexpectedly large proportion of secular and Christian Jews observed dietary Judaism in some way. One-quarter of the secular and Christian-Jewish respondents reported fasting for part of the day on Yom Kippur. Similarly, one out of ten of the secular respondents and one out of five Christian Jews said that they refrained from eating pork or observed kashrut through vegetarianism. These are essentially passive observances in the sense that the person refrains from eating. There is a difference between fasting part of Yom Kippur day at home or at work and fasting for part of Yom Kippur day in a synagogue.

Lighting Sabbath candles, by contrast, is an active and regularly recurring observance. Only one-quarter of respondents who are Jewish by religion reported usually or always lighting Sabbath candles. Only 5 percent of secular and Christian Jews reported lighting Sabbath candles on some sort of regular basis. This is a much smaller percentage than Jews by religion, but it is much higher than would be expected from persons who do not identify Judaism as their religion. One explanation for this phenomenon is socially desirable responses. Christian Jews in the sample were sufficiently identified as Jewish as to want to be interviewed, and they may have exaggerated their observance somewhat. It could also be that these Jewish observances have strong personal relevance to the respondent outside of a religious context; for example, a Catholic daughter whose Jewish mother lit candles on Friday night might continue the practice in her home.

Overall, Jews by religion and Jews by choice are more consistent about practicing Judaism than secular Jews or Christian Jews. More than 90 percent of them practiced at least one out of nine possible rituals.[13] Half of the secular Jews observed at least one of the nine rituals, and two out of five Christian Jews observed at least one of the nine rituals. Jews by religion and Jews by choice, however, practiced many more rituals (an average of four out of the nine) than did secular Jews and Christian Jews (an average of one).

I have argued that, for Christian Jews, Jewish observance has a primarily private meaning. Consistent with this interpretation, public association with other Jews is relatively rare among them. While 71 percent of Jews by religion and Jews by choice attended synagogue at least once during the year, only 12 percent of Christian Jews attended synagogue. The contrast between Jews who practice Judaism and those who do not is even more dramatic when synagogue membership is considered. Jews by choice are the most likely to belong to a synagogue (51 percent), followed by Jews by religion (43 percent). In contrast, almost none of the secular and Christian Jews paid dues to a synagogue (3 percent or less).

ATTITUDES AND IDENTITY

The Jewish observance of Christian Jews and secular Jews raises the question of personal meaning. Why do individuals who do not claim Judaism as their religion practice Jewish rituals? How do secular and Christian Jews understand themselves as Jews, and does this understanding explain why they maintain some degree (however small) of Jewish observance? The NJPS 2000 had a number of attitude statements that provide some sense of what being Jewish might mean to secular and Christian Jews. Writing in the 1970s, the Israeli sociologist Simon Herman introduced the notions of salience and valence to the study of Jewish identity. Salience means that being Jewish is important to the individual, while valence indicates either a positive or negative feeling about being Jewish. More than three-quarters of Jews by religion and Jews by choice indicated that they feel "very positive" about being Jewish, but more than one-half of secular and Christian Jews feel this way as well. In contrast, four out of five secular and Christian Jews indicated that being Jewish was not "very important" to them. They were also more likely than born Jews and Jews by choice to strongly agree that "being Jewish has very little to do with how I see myself." Christian and secular Jews were also much less likely than born Jews and Jews by choice to strongly agree with this statement: "Judaism guides important life decisions." As compared with born Jews and Jews by choice, secular and Christian Jews generally feel positive about being Jewish, but it has few if any consequences for them and is not particularly important to them. Secular Jews and Christian Jews accurately described themselves as not being Jewishly observant. Christian Jews and Jews by choice are much more likely than born Jews to describe themselves as "personally very religious" and to say religion is very important in their life.[14] This is consistent with numerous studies that have found American Jews to be less religious than other Americans. Both Christian Jews and Jews by choice (formerly Christian) are both more religious than born Jews.

Another set of attitudinal statements in the NJPS 2000 relates to Jewish peoplehood. Secular and Christian Jews indicate that they do not feel as strongly about belonging to the Jewish people as do born Jews and Jews by choice, but almost two-thirds somewhat agreed that they have "a strong sense of belonging to the Jewish people." Interestingly, Jews by choice were less likely to strongly agree with this statement (38 percent) than were born Jews. Secular and Christian Jews are less attached to Israel than born Jews, but they are slightly more attached than Jews by choice. Thus, attachment to Israel is a product both of Jewish religious identification and of Jewish descent. Born Jews are both of Jewish descent and of the Jewish religion. Secular and Christian Jews are Jewish by descent only, while Jews by choice are Jewish by religion only.[15] Jews by choice, in contrast, are less personally connected to Israel than secular or Christian Jews, but they are the most likely to "strongly agree" in the abstract that "Israel is the spiritual center of the Jewish people."

Respondents were asked about what is important in how they are Jewish. The question was worded like this: "Personally, how much does being Jewish involve. . . ." For all respondents, remembering the Holocaust was the most central aspect to being Jewish. The second most central aspect of being Jewish for all categories except Jews by choice was "connecting to your family's heritage." This was the least central aspect of being Jewish for Jews by choice because they have no Jewish family. Instead, "celebrating Jewish holidays" is the second most central aspect of being Jewish for Jews by choice. Countering anti-Semitism was the third most central aspect for all groups. The pattern discussed so far shows that born Jews have something in common with secular Jews and even Christian Jews: common ancestry. The Holocaust and anti-Semitism are negative aspects of that ancestry that put Jews in common danger, while connecting to the family's heritage is a positive aspect.

Celebrating Jewish holidays is not at all central for secular and Christian Jews because Judaism is not their religion. This supports the interpretation already put forth that Jewish observance for secular and Christian Jews represents a family connection more than a religious observance per se. For all the religious categories, "attending synagogue" is in last place, although it is more central for born Jews and Jews by choice than for secular and Christian Jews. Similarly, being part of the Jewish community and supporting Jewish organizations are relatively unimportant for all four categories, but born Jews by religion and Jews by choice place a greater emphasis on these than do secular and Christian Jews.

The order of importance for the various aspects of being Jewish is strikingly similar among all four religious categories of Jews (born Jewish, secular, Christian, and Jew by choice). Born Jews and Jews by choice give all the items relatively more importance than do secular and Christian Jews. The biggest difference between Jews by religion (whether born Jewish or not) and secular and Christian Jews is Jewish education for children. Jews by religion give this much more importance than do secular and Christian Jews, which is logical since neither of the latter two categories are Jewish by religion.

CONCLUSION

This analysis is but a preliminary reconnaissance of the NJPS 2000, but it has revealed four trends that will shape the contours of American Judaism. The first trend is the separation of Jews from Judaism. Largely as a result of intermarriage, the number of adherents to Judaism will decrease, and the number of synagogue members will decrease as a result. The adult children of intermarriage will, according to the NJPS 2000, continue to identify as Jews by ethnicity. Many of them will be at least nominally Christian, and the Reform and Reconstructionist movements may find themselves having to respond to a religious syncretism among these so-called Christian Jews. The second trend is the numerical decline of Conservative Judaism. At the current pace of change, the Conservative movement will continue to lose numbers while the Reform movement will grow. The greatest shift, however, is the trend into nondenominational Judaism and no religion at all. Both Orthodox and Reform congregations will increasingly see an adult membership that grew up in the respective movements if the youngest cohort of synagogue members is typical. The number of Orthodox Jews will either stabilize or grow, given the high retention rates in the youngest age cohort. Orthodox Jews will continue be concentrated in the Northeast, where they will make up an increasingly larger proportion of Jews in that region. One aspect of American Judaism that will not change is that the family will remain the most important connection to Judaism for American Jews. Among adherents of Judaism, family-oriented rituals will remain central to Jewish practice. For the growing population of secular Jews, the trend will be a sense of connection to the broad family of the Jewish people that leads them to identify ethnically as Jews. Some may even return to the faith that is at the origin of that peoplehood.

Notes

1. Nathan Glazer, *American Judaism* (Chicago: University of Chicago Press, 1957).
2. Marshall Sklare, *Conservative Judaism, An American Religious Movement* (New York: Schocken Books, 1955).
3. Marshall Sklare and Joseph Greenblum, *Jewish Identity on The Suburban Frontier* (New York: Basic Books, 1967).
4. Steven M. Cohen, *American Modernity and Jewish Identity* (New York and London: Tavistock Publications, 1983).
5. Robert N. Bellah et al., *Habits of the Heart, Individualism and Commitment in American Life* (Berkeley and Los Angeles: University of California Press, 1985).
6. Steven M. Cohen and Arnold M. Eisen, *The Jew Within, Self, Family, and Community in America* (Indianapolis: University of Indiana Press, 2000).
7. Bernard M. Lazerwitz, J. Alan Winter, Arnold Dashefsky, and Ephraim Tabory, *Jewish Choices, American Jewish Denominationalism* (Albany: State University of New York Press, 1998).
8. The data for the 2000–2001 National Jewish Population Survey was provided by the United Jewish Communities through the North American Jewish Data Bank.
9. Marshall Sklare, *America's Jews* (New York: Random House, 1971).
10. There were a small number of Jewish adults who identified themselves as both Jewish and Christian, and they are included in the Christian Jew category.
11. Here a Jew by choice means a formal conversion to Judaism. Individuals who said their religion was Judaism but had not formally converted were counted as non-Jews for this table.
12. Here were too few cases of Reconstruction synagogue members for this detailed of an analysis.
13. They lit Hannukah candles at least part of the week, lit Sabbath candles at least usually, fasted on Yom Kippur at last part of the day, kept kosher at least symbolically, attended a seder, observed a mourning ritual, or attended synagogue at least once during the year.
14. The attitudinal questions were asked only of Jews by choice, Jews by religion, and secular and Christian Jews who answered affirmatively that they considered

themselves Jewish. It is probable that secular and Christian Jews who answered these questions were more positive about being Jewish than their counterparts who did not consider themselves Jewish.

15. It should be noted that only about one-third of the Jews by choice had formally converted to Judaism.

Afterword

The Study of American Judaism: A Look Ahead

JONATHAN D. SARNA

As the appearance of this *Cambridge Companion* amply demonstrates, the study of American Judaism has, at long last, come into its own. For much of the past half-century, scholars of American Jewish life neglected "religion" and focused upon the Jewish "people." Ethnic studies and American studies supplied the field's dominant paradigms, while religious studies, largely the province of Christians, languished in the shadows. Those who did pursue the study of the Jewish religion were, for the most part, rabbis. Trained in Classical Judaism, they examined American Judaism through the prism of Jewish texts and history, rather than through comparisons with American Protestants and Catholics. The stunning freshness of Lou Silberman's pioneering essay in 1964 on "Judaism in the United States in the Early Nineteenth Century,"[1] which examined the Charleston Reform Movement (1824) against the background of the rise of Unitarianism in that city, is the exception that proves the rule.

Religion is an inherently comparative subject. Unless one is familiar with at least two religious traditions, scholars like Diana Eck remind us, one cannot claim to understand even one. The best of the articles in this volume do make reference to the larger scholarship on American religion. Indeed, Jonathan Woocher's work on "civil religion" and Rela Mintz Geffen's study of "rites of passage" both apply to the study of Judaism concepts initially developed by scholars working in far different arenas. It is precisely this kind of cross-fertilization that the study of American Judaism demands.

Here I want to suggest five new directions for students of American Judaism to pursue. While in some cases familiar to students of American religion, these approaches and subjects have not been closely examined within American Judaism, and are not much reflected in this volume. They represent an agenda for the future.

(1) *Studies of religious practice.* "We know next-to-nothing about religion as practiced and precious little about the everyday thinking and doing of lay men and women," historian David Hall writes in a path-breaking volume entitled *Lived Religion in America.*[2] While his volume focuses on Catholics

and Protestants, the situation with respect to American Jews is no better. How have American Jews distinguished Shabbat from the rest of the week? How have they celebrated such widely practiced holidays as Passover, the High Holidays, and Chanukah? How have they conducted themselves in synagogue? How have they marked their homes as Jewish homes? A thick descriptive literature (as opposed to the prevailing prescriptive literature) would serve as a useful first step in answering such questions, but as readers of Robert Orsi's classic studies of *The Madonna of 115th Street* (1985) and *Thank You, St. Jude* (1996) know, to properly understand "lived religion" one must also pay attention to history, cultural context, gender, class, and the interrelationship of religion and life. Several articles in this *Cambridge Companion*, as well as studies by Jewish social scientists like Samuel Heilman and Riv-Ellen Prell, have begun to address aspects of religious practice, but unanswered questions abound. Until we do know more about the day-to-day religious lives of America's Jews – their rituals, their customs, the traditions that they have maintained and transformed over time – our understanding of American Judaism must remain woefully incomplete.

(2) *Studies of the Jewish book in America.* Jews have long prided themselves on being "the people of the book," but the role of books in American Jewish religious life has scarcely been examined. We know something about Jewish Bible translations, the history of the prayer book, the spread of Jewish libraries, and the growth of Jewish publishing in America.[3] But we know exactly nothing about Jewish scribal arts – the creation of handwritten Torah scrolls and of other handwritten ritual objects critical to Jewish religious life – and next-to-nothing about the production and distribution of printed sacred works like the Hebrew Bible, the Talmud, the Code of Jewish Law, and the mystical Zohar. A remarkable website (www.hebrewbooks.org) has recently made available on-line some 1280 Hebrew-language "*seforim*" (religious books) such as sermons, rabbinic responsa, and sacred commentaries published in America since 1860. The subculture of Orthodox Jews who wrote, read, published and distributed these books, however, has scarcely been penetrated by scholars, nor do we properly understand what the mere existence of this literature reveals. Robert Singerman's magisterial bibliography of *Judaica Americana* published to 1900[4] discloses that hundreds of volumes of Jewish religious literature likewise appeared in English and German in America, some of it dating back even earlier than 1860. This literature spans a much broader theological spectrum than its Hebrew counterpart, and was composed by a different group of Jewish religious leaders. But it too lies virtually unexplored. Even the contemporary Jewish publishing phenomenon known as The ArtScroll Library (www.artscroll.com) – notwithstanding the remarkable range and distribution of its works – has largely

been ignored by students of American Judaism. Insights from scholars dealing with subjects like the "history of the book" and the development and
spread of "Christian publishing" suggest possible avenues for future research.
For now, though, even as Jewish books in America continue to proliferate,
the study of the Jewish book in America languishes from neglect.

(3) *Local and Regional studies.* Anyone who travels across the United
States knows that Judaism differs from region to region and from place to
place across the land. The practice of Judaism in the synagogue and in the
home, the relationship of Jews one to another and outwardly to their neighbors, the demands made upon rabbis, the public face of Judaism – all these
(and more) look and feel different depending upon whether one is in the
South, the West, the Midwest or the East, and likewise as one moves within
each particular region of the country. Factors such as geography, culture,
immigration patterns, the size, density, and make-up of the Jewish community, and the religious character of the general community help to explain
these differences. They distinguish Judaism in New Orleans from Judaism
in Atlanta or Miami, and account for the discernible religious differences
that transform the character of local Judaism as one moves southwestward
in Ohio from Cleveland to Columbus to Cincinnati or northwestward in
California from San Diego to Los Angeles to San Francisco. The literature on
American Judaism, taking its cue from the broader literature on American
religion,[5] rarely notices or explains such differences, positing instead a ho-
mogenized "American Judaism" drained of enlivening regional and local
flavorings. Community and synagogue histories, for the most part, are too
narrowly conceived to focus upon questions of distinctiveness. But in the
end, all religion, like all politics, *is* actually local. Understanding such local
and regional variations – customs, practices and preferences; social and class
composition; religious and cultural norms; everything, in short, that shapes
the character of local and regional religious life – would help us to paint a
richer, more nuanced, and more finely-grained portrait of American Judaism
than any we now possess.

(4) *Transnational studies.* Students of American Judaism, like their counterparts who study other ethnic and religious groups in America, easily
fall prey to the "fallacy of tunnel history." They pay all-too-little attention
to the world at large and are (to use the current buzzword) frustratingly
"internalist." This is particularly lamentable in the case of American Jews,
who have always maintained close, even intimate family ties to Jews throughout the diaspora and in Israel. Paradoxically, while Judaism itself is the
paradigmatic "transnational faith" – transcending borders and committed
to the idea that all Jews, wherever they may live, are interconnected – those
who study modern Judaism tend in their approaches and outlooks to be

much more provincial. The same problem besets the study of American Catholicism, which has been perceptively criticized by a recent scholar for divorcing the faith "from its international matrix, the original and enduring context that preserved its distinctiveness and ensured its survival as a minority faith in the United States."[6] A transnational understanding of American Judaism would explore more closely the involvement of European and, more recently, Israeli Jewish leaders in Jewish religious life in America – and vice versa. It would examine the ties linking American Jewry with the other major communities within the English-language Jewish diaspora: Canada, the Caribbean, England, South Africa, Australia, and New Zealand. It would reinterpret the role of rabbis and scholars who repeatedly crossed borders in search of learning, collegiality, and employment, and whose correspondence and publications likewise spanned the globe, shaping different Jewish communities' images of one another. In short, a transnational approach would remind us that American Judaism was never "an island entire of itself," and would help to restore American Judaism to its rightful place within a global universe.

(5) *Studies of Secular Judaism.* "The concept of religion," the great historian of American religion, Sydney E. Ahlstrom, wrote in 1972, "must be extended to include 'secular' movements and convictions, some of which opposed or sought to supplant the churches." "Agnosticism," he observed, "does not preclude religiosity and moral seriousness."[7] The study of American Judaism must likewise extend to include secular movements, particularly since they embraced, at their peak, tens of thousands of Jews and influenced far more. Socialists, Communists, Hebraists, Yiddishists, Zionists, Culturalists, Humanists, as well as self-proclaimed secularists, agnostics and atheists all insisted that Jewish life could thrive in America even in the absence of synagogue attendance, ritual practice, and traditional forms of Jewish education. Some of America's foremost Jews – Louis Brandeis and Abraham Cahan, for example – were devotedly secular. Unfortunately, secular forms of Judaism have not yet found their chronicler, so we know all too little about their history, their leading personalities, their many conflicting ideologies, their values, their folk practices, and their "sacred" texts.[8] What we do know is that Jewish secularism has played a significant role in the history of American Judaism – one that deserves to be better understood and appreciated.

If it does not reflect these proposed future directions for the field, *The Cambridge Companion to American Judaism* does summarize much of what we know today as we mark Judaism's 350th anniversary on American soil. Looking ahead to the 21st century, a new and exciting era of creative scholarship awaits, taking its cue from the variable, vital, frequently chaotic, and always kaleidoscope configurations of American Judaism itself.

Notes

1. Lou H. Silberman, *American Impact: Judaism in the United States in the Early Nineteenth Century.* The B. G. Rudolph Lectures in Judaic Studies (Syracuse: 1964), reprinted in A. Leland Jamison, *Tradition and Change in Jewish Experience* (Syracuse: Syracuse University, 1978), 106–140.

2. David D. Hall, *Lived Religion in America: Toward A History of Practice* (Princeton: Princeton University Press, 1997), vii.

3. Jonathan D. Sarna and Nahum M. Sarna, "Jewish Bible Scholarship and Translations in the United States," *The Bible and Bibles in America,* ed. Ernest S. Frerichs (Atlanta: Scholars Press, 1988), 83–116; Sharona R. Wachs, *American Jewish Liturgies* (Cincinnati: Hebrew Union College Press, 1997); Dana Evan Kaplan (ed.), *Platforms and Prayer Books* (Lanham, MD: Rowman and Littlefield, 2002); Robert Singerman, "Books Weeping for Someone to Visit and Admire Them: Jewish Library Culture in the United States, 1850–1910," *Studies in Bibliography and Booklore* 20 (1998), 99–144; Jonathan D. Sarna, *JPS: The Americanization of Jewish Culture 1888–1988* (Philadelphia: Jewish Publication Society, 1988); Jonathan D. Sarna, "Jewish Publishing," *A History of the Book in America,* vol 4, eds. Carl F. Kaestle and Janice Radway (forthcoming).

4. Robert Singerman, *Judaica Americana: A Bibliography of Publications to 1900* (2 vols. New York: Greenwood Press, 1990).

5. A new series of volumes entitled "Religion By Region," edited by Mark Silk for Altamira Press, promises to address regional differences in American religion.

6. Peter R. D'Agostino, *Rome in America: Transnational Catholic Ideology from the Risorgimento to Fascism* (Chapel Hill: University of North Carolina Press, 2004), 6.

7. Sydney E. Ahlstrom, *A Religious History of the American People* (New York: Yale University Press, 1972), xiv.

8. Saul L. Goodman (ed.), *The Faith of Secular Jews* (New York: Ktav, 1976) is the best English-language source.

Further Reading

Abrams, Elliott. *Faith or Fear: How Jews can Survive in a Christian America.* New York: The Free Press, 1997.

Abrams, Elliott, and David G. Dalin. *Secularism, Spirituality, and the Future of American Jewry.* Washington, DC: Ethics and Public Policy Center, 1999.

Alpert, Rebecca T., Sue Levi Elwell, and Shirley Idelson, eds. *Lesbian Rabbis: The First Generation.* New Brunswick: Rutgers University Press, 2001.

Alpert, Rebecca. *Like Bread on the Seder Plate.* New York: Columbia University Press, 1997.

Antler, Joyce. *The Journey Home: Jewish Women and the American Century.* New York: The Free Press, 1997.

Ariel, Yaakov. *Evangelizing the Chosen People.* Chapel Hill: University of North Carolina Press, 2000.

Bamberger, Bernard. *The Search for Jewish Theology.* New York: Behrman House, 1978.

Bauman, Mark K., and Berkley Kalin, eds. *The Quiet Voices: Southern Rabbis and Black Civil Rights, 1880s to 1990s.* Tuscaloosa: University of Alabama Press, 1997.

Baumgarten, Murray. City Scriptures: Modern Jewish Writing. Cambridge: Harvard University Press, 1982.

Berger, Alan L. *Judaism in the Modern World, The B. G. Rudolph Lectures in Judaic Studies.* New York: New York University Press, 1994.

Berkovits, Eliezer. *Faith After the Holocaust.* New York: KTAV Publishing House, 1973.

Berkovits, Eliezer. *God, Man and History.* New York: Jonathan David, 1959.

Berkovits, Eliezer. *Jewish Women in Time and Torah.* Hoboken: KTAV Publishing House, 1990.

Berlin, George L. *Defending the Faith: Nineteenth-Century Writings on Christianity and Jesus.* New York: State University of New York Press, 1989.

Bershtel, Sara, and Allen Graubard. *Saving Remnants: Feeling Jewish in America.* New York: The Free Press, 1992.

Blau, Joseph Leon. *Judaism in America: From Curiosity to Third Faith, Chicago History of American Religion.* Chicago: University of Chicago Press, 1976.

Blau, Joseph Leon. *Modern Varieties of Judaism, Lectures on the History of Religions/Sponsored by the American Council of Learned Societies.* New Series; No. 8. New York: Columbia University Press, 1966.

Bleich, J. David. *Contemporary Halakhic Problems, Library of Jewish Law and Ethics. Vol. 4.* New York: KTAV Publishing House, 1977.

Bleich, J. David. *Judaism and Healing: Halakhic Perspectives*. New York: KTAV Publishing House, 1981.

Borowitz, Eugene B. *A New Theology in the Making*. Philadelphia: Westminster Press, 1968.

Borowitz, Eugene B. *Liberal Judaism*. New York: Union of American Hebrew Congregations, 1984.

Borowitz, Eugene B. *Renewing the Covenant: A Theology for the Postmodern Jew*. Philadelphia: The Jewish Publication Society, 1991.

Brewer, Joan Scherer, Lynn Davidman, and Evelyn Gross Avery. *Sex and the Modern Jewish Woman: An Annotated Bibliography*. Fresh Meadows: Biblio Press, 1986.

Brown, Michael, and Bernard Lightman. *Creating the Jewish Future*. Walnut Creek: Altamira Press, 1999.

Cohen, Arthur A., and Paul Mendes-Flohr, eds. *Contemporary Jewish Religious Thought*. New York: The Free Press, 1987.

Cohen, Arthur. *The Natural and Supernatural Jew*. New York: McGraw-Hill, 1964.

Cohen, Arthur. *The Tremendum: A Theological Interpretation of the Holocaust*. New York: Crossroad, 1981.

Cohen, Steven. *American Modernity and Jewish Identity*. New York: Tavistock Publications, 1983.

Cohen, Steven. *Content or Continuity?* New York: American Jewish Committee, 1991.

Cohen, Steven M., and Arnold M. Eisen. *The Jew Within: Self, Family and Community in America*. Indianapolis: Indiana University Press, 2000.

Cohn-Sherbok, Dan. *Issues in Contemporary Judaism, Library of Philosophy and Religion*. Houndmills: Macmillan St. Martin's Press, 1991.

Cohn-Sherbok, Dan. *Modern Judaism*. Houndmills: Macmillan St. Martin's Press, 1996.

Cohn-Sherbok, Dan. *Problems in Contemporary Jewish Theology*. Lewiston: E. Mellen Press, 1991.

Cohon, Samuel S. *Jewish Theology*. Assen: Royal Vangorcum, 1971.

Cohon, Samuel S. *Judaism: A Way of Life*. New York: Union of American Hebrew Congregations, 1948.

Commentary Magazine, eds. *The Condition of Jewish Belief: A Symposium*. Northvale: Jason Aronson, 1994.

Cowan, Niel M., and Ruth Schwartz Cowan. *Our Parents' Lives: Jewish Assimilation and Everyday Life*. New Brunswick: Rutgers University Press, 1996.

Danzger, Herbert. *Returning to Tradition: The Contemporary Revival of Orthodox Judaism*. New Haven: Yale University Press, 1989.

Dawidowicz, Lucy S. *The Golden Tradition: Jewish Life and Thought in Eastern Europe*. Syracuse: Syracuse University Press, 1996.

Dershowitz, Alan M. *The Vanishing American Jew: In Search of Jewish Identity for the Next Century*. New York: Simon & Schuster, 1997.

Diamond, Etan. *And I Will Dwell in their Midst*. Chapel Hill: University of North Carolina Press, 2000.

Dinnerstein, Leonard. *Anti-Semitism in America*. New York: Oxford University Press, 1994.

Dorff, Elliot N. *A Living Tree: The Roots and Growth of Jewish Law*. Albany: State University of New York Press, 1988.

Dorff, Elliot N., and Louis E. Newman. *Contemporary Jewish Ethics and Morality.* Oxford: Oxford University Press, 1995.

Dorff, Elliot N., and Louis E. Newman. *Contemporary Jewish Theology: A Reader.* New York: Oxford University Press, 1999.

Eisen, Arnold M. *Galut: Modern Jewish Reflection on Homelessness and Homecoming, The Modern Jewish Experience.* Bloomington: Indiana University Press, 1986.

Eisen, Arnold M. *Rethinking Modern Judaism.* Chicago: University of Chicago Press, 1997.

Eisen, Arnold M. *Taking Hold of Torah: Jewish Commitment and Community in America.* Indianapolis: Indiana University Press, 1997.

Eisen, Arnold M. *The Chosen People in America: A Study in Jewish Religious Ideology.* Bloomington: Indiana University Press, 1983.

Elazar, Daniel J. *Community and Polity: The Organizational Dynamics of American Jewry.* Philadelphia: The Jewish Publication Society, 1995.

Elazar, Daniel J., and Rela Mintz Geffen. *The Conservative Movement in Judaism: Dilemmas and Opportunities.* Albany: State University of New York Press, 2000.

Ellenson, David Harry. *Tradition in Transition: Orthodoxy, Halakhah, and the Boundaries of Modern Jewish Identity, Studies in Judaism.* Lanham: University Press of America, 1989.

Fackenheim, Emil. *The Jewish Return into History.* New York: Schocken Books, 1978.

Farber, Roberta Rosenberg, and Chaim I. Waxman, eds. *Jews in America: A Contemporary Reader.* Hanover: Brandeis University Press/University Press of New England, 1999.

Feher, Shoshanah. *Passing Over Easter: Constructing the Boundaries of Messianic Judaism.* Walnut Creek: Altamira Press, 1998.

Feingold, Henry L., ed. *The Jewish People in America.* Vols. 1–5. Baltimore: The Johns Hopkins University Press, 1992.

Feldman, Egal. *Dual Destinies.* Urbana: University of Illinois Press, 1990.

Feldman, Jan. *Lubavitchers as Citizens: A Paradox of Liberal Democracy.* Ithaca: Cornell University Press, 2003.

Fishkoff, Sue. *The Rebbe's Army: Inside the World of Chabad-Lubavitch.* New York: Schocken Books, 2003.

Fishman, Sylvia Barack. *A Breadth of Life: Feminism in the American Jewish Community.* New York: The Free Press, 1993.

Fishman, Sylyia Barack. Double or Nothing? Jewish Families and Mixed Marriage. Hanover, New Hampshire and London: University of New England Press, 2004.

Fishman, Sylvia Barack. *Jewish Life and American Culture.* Albany: State University of New York Press, 2000.

Flanzbaum, Hilene, ed. *Jewish American Literature: A Norton Anthology.* New York: Norton, 2000.

Forster, Brenda, and Joseph Tabachnik. *Jews by Choice: A Study of Converts to Reform and Conservative Judaism.* Hoboken: KTAV Publishing House, 1991.

Freedman, Samuel G. *Jew vs. Jew: The Struggle for the Soul of American Jewry.* New York: Simon & Schuster, 2000.

Fried, Stephen. *The New Rabbi.* New York: Bantam Books, 2002.

Friesel, Evyatar. *Atlas of Modern Jewish History.* Rev. from the Hebrew ed. *Studies in Jewish History.* New York: Oxford University Press, 1990.

Frommer, Myrna Katz, and Harvey Frommer. *Growing Up Jewish In America: An Oral History*. Lincoln: University of Nebraska Press, 1995.

Frymer-Kensky, Tikva, ed. *Christianity in Jewish Terms*. Colorado: Westview Press, 2002.

Gal, Allon. *The Changing Concept of 'Mission' in American Reform Judaism*. American Jewish Archives, 1991.

Geffen, Rela M., ed. *Celebration and Renewal: Rites of Passage in Judaism*. Philadelphia: The Jewish Publication Society, 1993.

Gillman, Neil. *Conservative Judaism: The New Century*. West Orange: Behrman House, 1993.

Gillman, Neil. *Sacred Fragments: Recovering Theology for the Modern Jew*. Philadelphia: The Jewish Publication Society, 1992.

Glatzer, Nahum Norbert. *Modern Jewish Thought: A Source Reader*. New York: Schocken Books, 1977.

Glazer, Nathan. *American Judaism*. 2nd ed. Chicago and London: University of Chicago Press, 1972.

Goldman, Karla A. *Beyond the Synagogue Gallery: Finding a Place for Women in American Judaism*. Cambridge, MA: Harvard University Press, 2000.

Goldman, Shalom. *Hebrew and the Bible in America: The First Two Centuries*. Hanover: University Press of New England, 1993.

Goldsmith, Emanuel S., Mel Scult, and Robert M. Seltzer. *The American Judaism of Mordecai M. Kaplan, Reappraisals in Jewish Social and Intellectual History*. New York: New York University Press, 1990.

Goldstein, Sidney, and Alice Goldstein. *Jews on the Move: Implications for Jewish Identity*. Albany: State University of New York Press, 1996.

Goldy, Robert G. *The Emergence of Jewish Theology in America: The Modern Jewish Experience*. Bloomington: Indiana University Press, 1990.

Gordis, David M., and Dorit P. Gary, *American Jewry: Portrait and Prognosis*. West Orange: Behrman House, 1997.

Gordis, Robert, Josiah Derby, and National Academy for Adult Jewish Studies. *Conservative Judaism: An American Philosophy*. New York: Publications for the National Academy of Adult Jewish Studies of the Jewish Theological Seminary of America, Behrman House, 1945.

Gordis, Robert. *Love & Sex: A Modern Jewish Perspective*. New York: Farrar, Straus & Giroux, 1978.

Goren, Arthur A., *The Politics and Public Culture of American Jews*. Bloomington: Indiana University Press, 1999.

Green, Arthur. *Seek My Face, Speak My Name*. Northvale: Jason Aronson, 1992.

Greenberg, Simon, and the Jewish Theological Seminary of America. *The Ordination of Women as Rabbis: Studies and Responsa, Moreshet Series*. Vol. 14. New York: Jewish Theological Seminary of America, 1988.

Greenstein, Howard R. *Turning Point: Zionism and Reform Judaism*. Chico: Scholars Press, 1981.

Grossman, Lawrence. "Jewish Communal Affairs," in *American Jewish Year Book*. New York: American Jewish Committee, 1988–present.

Gurock, Jeffrey S. *The Men and Women of Yeshiva: Higher Education, Orthodoxy, and American Judaism*. New York: Columbia University Press, 1988.

Heilman, Samuel C., and Steven Martin Cohen. *Cosmopolitans & Parochials: Modern Orthodox Jews in America.* Chicago: University of Chicago Press, 1989.

Heilman, Samuel C. *Defenders of the Faith: Inside Ultra-Orthodox Jewry.* New York: Schocken Books, 1992.

Heilman, Samuel C. *Portrait of American Jews.* Seattle: University of Washington Press, 1995.

Heilman, Samuel C. *Synagogue Life: A Study in Symbolic Interaction.* New Brunswick: Transaction Publishers, 1998.

Heilman, Samuel C. *The People of the Book: Drama, Fellowship, and Religion.* Chicago: University of Chicago Press, 1983.

Helmreich, William B. *The World of the Yeshiva: An Intimate Portrait of Orthodox Jewry.* New York: The Free Press, 1982.

Herberg, Will. *Judaism and Modern Man: An Interpretation of Jewish Religion, Temple Books.* New York: World Publishing, 1951.

Herberg, Will. *Protestant, Catholic, Jew: An Essay in American Religious Sociology.* Chicago: University of Chicago Press, 1983.

Herman, Simon N. *Jewish Identity: A Social Psychological Perspective.* New York: Herzl Press, 1977.

Hertzberg, Arthur. *Being Jewish in America: The Modern Experience.* New York: Schocken Books, 1979.

Hertzberg, Arthur. *Jewish Polemics.* New York: Columbia University Press, 1992.

Hertzberg, Arthur. *The Jews in America: Four Centuries of an Uneasy Encounter.* New York: Columbia University Press, 1997.

Heschel, Abraham Joshua. *God in Search of Man.* New York: Farrar, Straus & Cudahy, 1955.

Heschel, Abraham Joshua. *Moral Grandeur and Spiritual Audacity.* New York: Farrar, Straus & Giroux, 1996.

Hirsch, Samson Raphael. *Horeb: A Philosophy of Jewish Laws and Observances.* 4th ed. London: Soncino Press, 1975.

Hoffman, Lawrence A. *The Journey Home: Discovering the Deep Spiritual Wisdom of the Jewish Tradition.* Boston: Beacon Press, 2002.

Horowitz, Bethamie. *Connections and Journeys: Assessing Critical Opportunities for Enhancing Jewish Identity.* New York: United Jewish Appeal–Federation of Jewish Philanthropies of New York, 2000.

Hyman, Paula E. *Gender and Assimilation in Modern Jewish History.* Seattle: University of Washington Press, 1995.

Jacobs, Louis. *A Jewish Theology.* New York: Behrman House, 1973.

Jacobs, Louis. *A Tree of Life: Diversity, Flexibility, and Creativity in Jewish Law.* New York: Oxford University Press, 1984.

Jacobs, Louis. *Religion and the Individual.* Cambridge, MA: Cambridge University Press, 1992.

Jacobs, Louis. *We Have Reason to Believe: Some Aspects of Jewish Theology Examined in the Light of Modern Thought.* 2nd ed. London: Valentine Mitchell, 1962.

Jick, Leon A. *The Americanization of the Synagogue, 1820–1870.* Hanover: University Press of New England, 1976.

Joselit, Jenna Weissman. *Reinventing Jewish Culture, 1880–1950: The Wonders of America.* New York: Hill and Wang, 1994.

Kamin, Ben. *Stones in the Soul: One Day in the Life of an American Rabbi*. New York: Macmillan, 1990.

Kaplan, Dana Evan. *American Reform Judaism: An Introduction*. New Brunswick: Rutgers University Press, 2003.

Kaplan, Dana Evan. *Contemporary Debates in American Reform Judaism: Conflicting Visions*. New York: Routledge, 2001.

Kaplan, Dana Evan. *Platforms and Prayerbooks: Theological and Liturgical Perspectives on Reform Judaism*. Lanham: Rowman & Littlefield, 2002.

Kaplan, Mordecai M. *Judaism as a Civilization: Toward a Reconstruction of Jewish Life*. New York: Macmillan, 1934.

Kaplan, Mordecai Menahem, and Mel Scult. *Communings of the Spirit: The Journals of Mordecai M. Kaplan, American Jewish Civilization Series*. Detroit: Wayne State University Press and The Reconstructionist Press, 2001.

Kaplan, Mordecai Menahem, Emanuel S. Goldsmith, and Mel Scult. *Dynamic Judaism: The Essential Writings of Mordecai M. Kaplan*. New York: Schocken Books: The Reconstructionist Press, 1985.

Karff, Samuel E. *Hebrew Union College – Jewish Institute of Religion at One Hundred Years*. Cincinnati: Hebrew Union College Press, 1976.

Karp, Abraham J. *Jewish Continuity in America: Creative Survival in a Free Society*. Tuscaloosa: University of Alabama Press, 1998.

Kaufman, David. *Shul with a Pool*. Hanover: Brandeis University Press, 1999.

Kaufman, Debra. *Rachel's Daughters*. New Brunswick: Rutgers University Press, 1993.

Kaufman, William E. *Contemporary Jewish Philosophies*. New York: Behrman House, 1976.

Kaufman, William E. *The Evolving God in Jewish Process Theology*. Lewiston: Edwin Mellen Press, 1997.

Kellner, Menachem M. *Must a Jew Believe Anything?* London: Littman Library of Jewish Civilization, 1999.

Kellner, Menachem M., ed. *The Pursuit of the Ideal: Jewish Writings of Steven Schwarzschild*. Albany: State University of New York Press, 1990.

Kepnes, Steven. *Interpreting Judaism in a Postmodern Age*. New York: New York University Press, 1996.

Kohler, Kaufmann. *Jewish Theology: Systematically and Historically Considered* [1918]. 2nd ed. New York: KTAV Publishing House, 1968.

Kolsky, Thomas A. *Jews Against Zionism*. Philadelphia: Temple University Press, 1990.

Kranzler, George G., and Irving Illus Hertzberg. *The Face of Faith: An American Hassidic Community, by George Kranzler. Photographs by Irving I. Herzberg*. Baltimore: Baltimore Hebrew College Press, 1972.

Kronish, Ronald, ed. *Towards the Twenty-First Century: Judaism and the Jewish People in Israel and America*. Hoboken: KTAV Publishing House, 1988.

Kurzweil, Z. E. *The Modern Impulse of Traditional Judaism*. Hoboken: KTAV Publishing House, 1985.

Lazerwitz, Bernard, M., J. Alan Winter, Arnold Dashefsky, and Ephraim Tabory. *Jewish Choices: American Jewish Denominationalism*. Albany: State University of New York Press, 1998.

Lederhendler, Eli. *New York Jews and the Decline of Urban Ethnicity, 1950–1970*. Syracuse: Syracuse University Press, 2001.

Lew, Alan, and Sherril Jaffe. *One God Clapping: The Spiritual Path of a Zen Rabbi.* Woodstock: Jewish Lights Publishing, 2001.

Libowitz, Richard. *Mordecai M. Kaplan and the Development of Reconstructionism. Studies in American Religion.* Vol. 9. Lewiston: Edwin Mellen Press, 1983.

Liebman, Charles S. *The Ambivalent American Jew: Politics, Religion, and Family in American Jewish Life.* Philadelphia: The Jewish Publication Society, 1976.

Liebman, Charles S., and Steven M. Cohen. *Two Worlds of Judaism: The Israeli and American Experiences.* New Haven: Yale University Press, 1990.

Linzer, Norman, Jerome A. Chanes, and David J. Schnall, eds. *A Portrait of the American Jewish Community.* Westport: Praeger, 1998.

Linzer, Norman. *The Jewish Family: Authority and Tradition in Modern Perspective.* New York: Human Sciences Press, 1984.

Marcus, Jacob Rader, and Abraham J. Peck, eds. *The American Rabbinate.* Hoboken: KTAV Publishing House, 1985.

Marcus, Jacob Rader. *The Jew in the American World: A Source Book.* Detroit: Wayne State University Press, 1996.

Maslin, Simeon J., ed. *Gates of Mitzvah: A Guide to the Jewish Life Cycle.* New York: Central Conference of American Rabbis, 1979.

Meyer, Michael A., *Response to Modernity: A History of the Reform Movement in Judaism, Studies in Jewish History.* New York: Oxford University Press, 1988.

Meyer, Michael A. and W. Gunther Plaut. *The Reform Judaism Reader.* New York: Union of American Hebrew Congregations Press, 2001.

Mittleman, Alan. *Between Kant and Kabbalah: An Introduction to Isaac Breuer's Philosophy of Judaism, Suny Series in Judaica.* Albany: State University of New York Press, 1990.

Mittleman, Alan, Jonathan Sarna, and Robert Licht, eds. *Jewish Polity and American Civil Society: Communal Agencies and Religious Movements in the American Public Square.* Lanham: Rowman & Littlefield, 2002.

Mittleman, Alan, Jonathan Sarna, and Robert Licht, eds. *Jews and the American Public Square: Debating Religion and Republic.* Lanham: Rowman & Littlefield, 2002.

Mittleman, Alan, ed., *Religion as a Public Good: Jews and Other Americans on Religion and the Public Square.* Lanham: Rowman & Littlefield, 2003.

Morgan, Michael L. *Beyond Auschwitz: Post-Holocaust Jewish Thought in America.* Oxford: Oxford University Press, 2001.

Moore, Deborah D. *To the Golden Cities.* New York: The Free Press, 1994.

Nadell, Pamela Susan, and Marc Lee Raphael, eds. *Conservative Judaism in America: A Biographical Dictionary and Sourcebook, Jewish Denominations in America.* New York: Greenwood Press, 1988.

Nadell, Pamela Susan, and Jonathan D. Sarna, eds. *Women and American Judaism.* Hanover: Brandeis University Press, 2001.

Nadell, Pamela Susan. *Women Who Would Be Rabbis: A History of Women's Ordination, 1889–1985.* Boston: Beacon Press, 1998.

Neusner, Jacob. *Introduction to American Judaism.* Minneapolis: Fortress Press, 1994.

Neusner, Jacob. *Judaism in Modern Times: An Introduction and Reader.* Cambridge, England: Blackwell, 1995.

Neusner, Jacob. *Understanding American Judaism: Toward the Description of a Modern Religion.* New York: KTAV Publishing House, 1975.

Neusner, Jacob. *Understanding Jewish Theology.* New York: KTAV Publishing House, 1973.

Noveck, Simon. *Great Jewish Personalities in Modern Times, The B'nai B'rith Great Books Series.* Vol. 2. New York: Farrar, Straus & Cudahy, 1960.

Olitzky, Kerry M., ed. *The American Synagogue.* Westport: Greenwood Press, 1996.

Olitzky, Kerry M., and Marc Lee Raphael. *An Encyclopedia of American Synagogue Ritual.* New York: Greenwood Publishing Group, 2000.

Olitzky, Kerry M., Lance J. Sussman, and Malcolm H. Stern, eds. *Reform Judaism in America.* Westport: Greenwood Press, 1993.

Patai, Raphael, and Emanuel S. Goldsmith. *Events and Movements in Modern Judaism.* 1st ed. New York: Paragon House, 1995.

Petsonk, Judy. *Taking Judaism Personally: Creating a Meaningful Spiritual Life.* New York: The Free Press, 1996.

Plaskow, Judith. *Standing Again at Sinai.* San Francisco: Harper & Row, 1990.

Prell, Riv-Ellen. *Fighting to Become Americans: Jews, Gender, and the Anxiety of Assimilation.* Boston: Beacon Press, 1999.

Raphael, Marc Lee. *Judaism in America.* New York: Columbia University Press, 2003.

Raphael, Marc Lee. *Profiles in American Judaism: The Reform, Conservative, Orthodox, and Reconstructionist Traditions in Historical Perspective.* San Francisco: Harper & Row, 1984.

Raphael, Marc Lee, ed. *What is American about the American Jewish Experience?* Williamsburg: The College of William and Mary, Department of Religion, 1993.

Rosenthal, Steven T. *Irreconcilable Differences?: The Waning of the American Jewish Love Affair with Israel.* Hanover: Brandeis University Press, 2003.

Rosner, Fred. *Modern Medicine and Jewish Ethics.* Hoboken: KTAV Publishing House, 1986.

Rubenstein, Richard. *After Auschwitz: Radical Theology and Contemporary Judaism.* Indianapolis: Bobbs-Merrill, 1966.

Sachar, Howard M. *A History of the Jews in America.* New York: Knopf, 1992.

Sachar, Howard M. *The Course of Modern Jewish History.* New rev. ed. New York: Vintage Books, 1990.

Sanders, Ronald. *Shores of Refuge: A Hundred Years of Jewish Emigration.* New York: Schocken Books, 1988.

Sarna, Jonathan D., *American Judaism: A History.* New Haven and London: Yale University Press, 2004.

Sarna, Jonathan D., and David G. Dalin. *Religion and State in the American Jewish Experience.* Notre Dame: University of Notre Dame Press, 1997.

Sarna, Jonathan D., ed. *The American Jewish Experience.* New York: Holmes & Meier, 1986.

Schechter, Solomon. *Aspects of Rabbinic Theology.* New York: Macmillan, 1909.

Schwarz, Sidney. *Finding A Spiritual Home.* San Francisco: Jossey-Bass, 2000.

Schweid, Eliezer, and Caroline McCracken-Flesher. *Judaism and Mysticism According to Gershom Scholem: A Critical Analysis and Programmatic Discussion, Scholars Press Reprints and Translations Series.* Atlanta: Scholars Press, 1985.

Scult, Mel. *Judaism Faces the Twentieth Century: A Biography of Mordechai M. Kaplan.* Detroit: Wayne State University Press, 1993.

Seltzer, Robert M. *Jewish People, Jewish Thought: The Jewish Experience in History.* New York: Macmillan, 1980.

Seltzer, Robert M., and Norman J. Cohen, eds. *The Americanization of the Jews.* New York: New York University Press, 1995.

Shapiro, Edward S. *A Time for Healing: American Jewry Since World War II.* Baltimore: Johns Hopkins University Press, 1992.

Sherman, Moshe D., ed. *Orthodox Judaism in America.* Westport: Greenwood Press, 1996.

Sherwin, Byron L. *Toward a Jewish Theology.* Lewiston: Edwin Mellen Press, 1991.

Showstack, Gerald L. *Suburban Communities: The Jewishness of American Reform Jews.* Atlanta: Scholars Press, 1988.

Siegel, Seymour. *Conservative Judaism and Jewish Law, Studies in Conservative Jewish Thought. Vol. 1.* New York: Rabbinical Assembly, distributed by KTAV Publishing House, 1977.

Siegel, Seymour, and Elliot Gertel. *God in the Teachings of Conservative Judaism, Emet Ve*Emunah. Vol. 3.* Hoboken: Rabbinical Assembly, distributed by KTAV Publishing House, 1985.

Sklare, Marshall. *Conservative Judaism: An American Religious Movement.* New augmented ed. New York: Schocken Books, 1972.

Sklare, Marshall, and Joseph Greenblum. *Jewish Identity on the Suburban Frontier.* Chicago: University of Chicago Press, 1979.

Sklare, Marshall. *Observing America's Jews.* Hanover: Brandeis University Press, 1993.

Slobin, Mark. *Chosen Voices: The Story of the American Cantorate.* Urbana and Chicago: University of Illinois Press, 1989.

Sokol, Moshe, ed. *Rabbinic Authority and Personal Autonomy.* Northvale: Jason Aronson, 1992.

Soloveitchik, Haym. "Rupture and Reconstruction: The Transformation of Contemporary Orthodoxy," *Tradition*, 64–130. Summer 1994.

Soloveitchik, Joseph Dov. *Halakhic Man.* 1st English ed. Philadelphia: The Jewish Publication Society, 1983.

Soloveitchik, Joseph Dov. *The Halakhic Mind: An Essay on Jewish Tradition and Modern Thought.* Ardmore: Seth Press, 1986.

Svonkin, Stuart. *Jews Against Prejudice.* New York: Columbia University Press, 1997.

Syme, Daniel B. *Why I Am a Reform Jew.* New York: Donald I. Fine, 1989.

Temkin, Sefton D. *Creating American Reform Judaism: The Life and Times of Isaac Mayer Wise.* London: The Littman Library of Jewish Civilization, 1998.

Urofsky, Melvin I. *A Voice That Spoke for Justice: The Life and Times of Stephen S. Wise.* Albany: State University of New York Press, 1982.

Waxman, Chaim I. *American Aliya: Portrait of an Innovative Migration Movement.* Detroit: Wayne State University Press, 1989.

Waxman, Chaim I. *America's Jews in Transition.* Philadelphia: Temple University Press, 1983.

Waxman, Chaim I. *Jewish Baby Boomers: A Communal Perspective,* Albany: State University of New York Press, 2001.

Waxman, Mordecai. *Tradition and Change: The Development of Conservative Judaism.* New York: Burning Bush Press, 1970.

Wertheimer, Jack. *A People Divided: Judaism in Contemporary America.* New York: Basic Books, 1993.

Wertheimer, Jack, ed. *Jews in the Center: Conservative Synagogues and Their Members.* New Brunswick: Rutgers University Press, 2000.

Wertheimer, Jack, ed. *The American Synagogue: A Sanctuary Transformed.* Hanover: Brandeis University Press, 1987.

Wertheimer, Jack, ed. *Tradition Renewed: A History of the Jewish Theological Seminary of America.* New York: Jewish Theological Seminary, 1997.

Wigoder, Geoffrey. *Jewish-Christian Relations since the Second World War, Sherman Studies of Judaism in Modern Times.* Manchester: Manchester University Press, 1988.

Winer, Mark L., Sanford Seltzer, and Steven J. Schwager. *Leaders of Reform Judaism.* New York: Union of American Hebrew Congregations Press, 1987.

Wirth-Nesher, Hana. What Is Jewish Literature? Philadelphia: Jewish Publication Society, 1994.

Wolf, Arnold Jacob, ed. *Rediscovering Judaism: Reflections on a New Jewish Theology.* Chicago: Quadrangle Books, 1965.

Woocher, Jonathan S. *Sacred Survival: The Civil Religion of American Jews.* Bloomington: Indiana University Press, 1986.

Wyschogrod, Michael. *The Body of Faith.* New York: HarperCollins, 1983.

Zucker, David J. *American Rabbis: Facts and Fiction.* Northvale: Jason Aronson, 1998.

Zuckerman, Phil. *Strife in the Sanctuary: Religious Schism in a Jewish Community.* Walnut Creek: Altamira Press, 1999.

Index

beginnings of, 97
characteristics of, 97
crisis in, 98
revitalization of, 190
Hassidic New Wave, 376
Hatch, Nathan, 300
Havurah movement, 68–69, 229, 279
religious personalization and,
105–107
women and, 69
Haynes, John, 330
Haza, Ofra, 377
hazan
changing role of, 32
in colonial America, 27
The Heartbreak Kid
as American Jewish tragedy, 260
Hebrew Free Loan Societies,
The Hebrew Hammer, 265
Hebrew Immigrant Aid Society (HIAS),
322
Hebrew Union College, 44, 53, 82, 121
"classical reform" and, 52
female rabbi at, 74
merging of, 88
Trefa Banquet at, 83
Heilman, Samuel, 68, 174
Hendricks, Uriah, 28, 29
Herberg, Will, 61, 64, 76, 102, 124
religious faith and, 126
thesis of, 103
herem
in colonial America, 26
Herman, Simon, 411
Hertzberg, Arthur, 5, 67, 76, 222, 322
Heschel, Rabbi Abraham Joshua, 16, 66,
124, 196
"authentic" thinking and, 126
revelation and, 126
ritual objects and, 393
Heschel, Susannah, 171
Higher Ground, 377
Hilberg, Raul, 193, 194
Hillel: The Foundation for Jewish Campus
Life, 150
Hirsch, Emil G., 45, 327
Hirsch, Samson Raphael, 85, 156
history
lachrymose conception of, 5
triumphs, tragedies and, 191
Zionist conceptions of, 191
Hitler, Adolf
American Jews' response to, 211
American neutrality to, 187

Hitler's Willing Executioners (Goldhagen),
201
Hochhuth, Rolf, 195
Hoffman, Allen, 358
classical Jewish learning, culture and,
358
modern experience and, 350
Holde, Arthur, 374
holidays
centrality of, 413
Hollywood
stereotypes in, 257
Holocaust. *See also* Auschwitz
abandonment of, 187
activism, apathy and, 66–67
American Judaism and, 190
Americanization of, 202
artists' response to, 391
assimilation and, 189
awareness of, 127
belief in, 204
centrality of, 278
civil, human rights awareness and, 198
commemoration of, 193
compensation claims and, 201
consciousness of, 193–196
as defining event, 5
downplaying of, 191
education of, 201
influence of, 203
interest in, 193, 196
Israeli narratives of, 191
Jewish identity and, 193, 202
Jewish interest in, 201
Jewish refugees, 187
mainstreaming of, 196–200, 203
media and, 200, 205
Orthodox Jews and, 57
philanthropy and, 202
in popular culture, 201
public discourse of, 193, 196
to rebirth, 197
redemption and, 197
Reform Judaism and, 88
religious context of, 67
second generation of, 198
survivors of, 71, 189, 194
term of, 194
theology of, 128
victimization and, 196
Zionism and, 211
Zionist conceptions of, 191
Holocaust: The Story of the Family Weiss,
199–200

Lightning Source UK Ltd.
Milton Keynes UK
UKOW042349200313

207940UK00001B/114/P